John Ray

Sams Teach Yourself
iOS® 9 Application Development

in **24** Hours

SAMS 800 East 96th Street, Indianapolis, Indiana, 46240 USA

Sams Teach Yourself iOS9® Application Development in 24 Hours

Copyright © 2016 by Pearson Education, Inc.

All rights reserved. Printed in the United States of America. This publication is protected by copyright, and permission must be obtained from the publisher prior to any prohibited reproduction, storage in a retrieval system, or transmission in any form or by any means, electronic, mechanical, photocopying, recording, or likewise. For information regarding permissions, request forms, and the appropriate contacts within the Pearson Education Global Rights & Permissions Department, please visit www.pearsoned.com/permissions/. No patent liability is assumed with respect to the use of the information contained herein. Although every precaution has been taken in the preparation of this book, the publisher and author assume no responsibility for errors or omissions. Nor is any liability assumed for damages resulting from the use of the information contained herein.

ISBN-13: 978-0-672-33767-3
ISBN-10: 0-672-33767-3

Library of Congress Control Number: 2015917495

First Printing February 2016

Trademarks

All terms mentioned in this book that are known to be trademarks or service marks have been appropriately capitalized. Sams Publishing cannot attest to the accuracy of this information. Use of a term in this book should not be regarded as affecting the validity of any trademark or service mark.

Warning and Disclaimer

Every effort has been made to make this book as complete and as accurate as possible, but no warranty or fitness is implied. The information provided is on an "as is" basis. The author and the publisher shall have neither liability nor responsibility to any person or entity with respect to any loss or damages arising from the information contained in this book.

Special Sales

For information about buying this title in bulk quantities, or for special sales opportunities (which may include electronic versions; custom cover designs; and content particular to your business, training goals, marketing focus, or branding interests), please contact our corporate sales department at corpsales@pearsoned.com or (800) 382-3419.

For government sales inquiries, please contact governmentsales@pearsoned.com.

For questions about sales outside the U.S., please contact international@pearsoned.com.

Editor-in-Chief
Greg Wiegand

Acquisitions Editor
Laura Norman

Development Editor
Keith Cline

Managing Editor
Kristy Hart

Senior Project Editor
Lori Lyons

Copy Editor
Keith Cline

Indexer
Publishing Works

Proofreader
Laura Hernandez

Technical Editor
Anne Groves

Editorial Assistant
Sandra Fugate

Cover Designer
Mark Shirar

Compositor
Nonie Ratcliff

Contents at a Glance

Note: Appendix A is a bonus online chapter. To access it, go to
www.informit.com/title/9780672337673 and click the Downloads tab.

Table of Contents

Note: Appendix A is a bonus online chapter. To access it, go to www.informit.com/title/9780672337673 and click the Downloads tab.

About the Author

John Ray currently serves as the Director of the Office of Research Information Systems at The Ohio State University. He has written numerous books for Macmillan/Sams/Que, including *Using TCP/IP: Special Edition, Teach Yourself Dreamweaver MX in 21 Days, Mac OS X Unleashed, My OS X – El Capitan Edition*, and *Sams Teach Yourself iOS 8 Development in 24 Hours.* As a Macintosh user since 1984, he strives to ensure that each project presents the Macintosh with the equality and depth it deserves. Even technical titles such as Using TCP/IP contain extensive information about the Macintosh and its applications and have garnered numerous positive reviews for their straightforward approach and accessibility to beginner and intermediate users.

You can visit his website at http://teachyourselfios.com or follow him on Twitter at @johnemeryray or #iOSIn24.

Dedication

This book is dedicated to the stray cat living in my garage.
It appears to like the cat food I bought.

Acknowledgments

Thank you to the group at Sams Publishing—Laura Norman, Keith Cline, Mark Renfrow—and my Tech Editor, Anne Groves, for helping me survive another year of OS and Xcode updates. The evolution of Swift (and the Xcode tools) has been incredibly rapid, and the ride for developers is definitely a bit bumpy. The Pearson team does a great job of keeping me organized, honest, and on target.

We Want to Hear from You!

As the reader of this book, *you* are our most important critic and commentator. We value your opinion and want to know what we're doing right, what we could do better, what areas you'd like to see us publish in, and any other words of wisdom you're willing to pass our way.

We welcome your comments. You can email or write to let us know what you did or didn't like about this book—as well as what we can do to make our books better.

Please note that we cannot help you with technical problems related to the topic of this book.

When you write, please be sure to include this book's title and author as well as your name and email address. We will carefully review your comments and share them with the author and editors who worked on the book.

Email: feedback@samspublishing.com

Mail: Sams Publishing
           ATTN: Reader Feedback
           800 East 96th Street
           Indianapolis, IN 46240 USA

Reader Services

Register your copy of *Sams Teach Yourself iOS 9 Application Development* at informit.com for convenient access to downloads, updates, and corrections as they become available. To start the registration process, go to informit.com/register and log in or create an account*. Enter the product ISBN, 9780672337673, and click Submit. Once the process is complete, you will find any available bonus content under Registered Products.

*Be sure to check the box that you would like to hear from us in order to receive exclusive discounts on future editions of this product.

Introduction

When you pick up an iOS device and use it, you feel connected. Whether it be an iPad, an iPhone, or an iPod, the interface acts as an extension to your fingers; it is smooth, comfortable, and invites exploration. Other competing devices offer similar features, and even sport gadgets such as wraparound screens and trackpads, but they cannot match the user experience that is iOS.

iOS and its associated development tools have changed rapidly over the past few years. iOS 7 brought us a new user interface that used depth and translucency to keep users connected to their content and aware of the context in which they are accessing it. iOS 8 surprised everyone with a brand new language for developing apps: Swift. Alongside the introduction of iOS 9, Swift became an open source language, solidifying it as the future of development on Apple platforms and beyond.

Swift marks a dramatic change in the history of iOS and OS X development. With Swift, Apple has effectively retired the Objective-C language—used on Apple and NeXT platforms for over 25 years. Swift offers a friendlier development platform with more modern language features and tools. While in development for more than 4 years at Apple, by the time this book reaches you, Swift will have existed as a public programming language for a little over a year.

Unfortunately, there are some caveats to writing about a young language. Swift is rapidly evolving, and changes with each release of Apple's development environment: Xcode. Code that is written in one version of Xcode sometimes breaks in the next. In the version of Swift shipping with iOS 9, for example, the language took syntax used for creating loops and changed its purpose entirely. Suddenly, code that was only a few months old stopped working.

Swift presents challenges, but I also think you'll find that programming in Swift is *fun* (yes, really) and intuitive.

When creating Swift and the iOS development platform, Apple considered the entire application lifecycle. From the interface design tools, to the code that makes it function, to the presentation to the user, everything is integrated and works together seamlessly. As a developer, does this mean that there are rules to follow? Absolutely. But, by following these rules, you can create applications that are interactive works of art for your users to love—not software they will load and forget.

Through the App Store, Apple has created the ultimate digital distribution system for iOS applications. Programmers of any age or affiliation can submit their applications to the App Store for just the cost of a modest yearly Developer Membership fee. Games, utilities, and full-feature applications have been built for everything from pre-K education to retirement living. No matter what the content, with a user base as large as the iPhone, iPod touch, and iPad, an audience exists.

My hope is that this book brings iOS development to a new generation of developers. *Sams Teach Yourself iOS 9 Application Development in 24 Hours* provides a clear and natural progression of skills development, from installing developer tools and registering your device with Apple, to debugging an application before submitting it to the App Store. It's everything you need to get started, in 24 one-hour lessons.

Who Can Become an iOS Developer?

If you have an interest in learning, time to invest in exploring and practicing with Apple's developer tools, and an Intel Macintosh computer running Yosemite, El Capitan, or later, you have everything you need to begin creating software for iOS. Starting with Xcode 7, Apple even lets you run your applications on your own devices (no developer membership required)!

Developing an app won't happen overnight, but with dedication and practice, you can be writing your first applications in a matter of days. The more time you spend working with the Apple developer tools, the more opportunities you'll discover for creating new and exciting projects.

You should approach iOS application development as creating software that *you* want to use, not what you think others want. If you're solely interested in getting rich quick, you're likely to be disappointed. (The App Store is a crowded marketplace—albeit one with a lot of room—and competition for top sales is fierce.) However, if you focus on building useful and unique apps, you're much more likely to find an appreciative audience.

Who Should Use This Book?

This book targets individuals who are new to development for iOS and have experience using the Macintosh platform. No previous experience with Swift, Cocoa, or the Apple developer tools is required. Of course, if you do have development experience, some of the tools and techniques may be easier to master, but the author does not assume that you've coded before.

That said, some things are expected of you, the reader. Specifically, you must be willing to invest in the learning process. If you just read each hour's lesson without working through the tutorials, you will likely miss some fundamental concepts. In addition, you need to spend time reading the Apple developer documentation and researching the topics presented in this book. A vast amount of information on iOS development is available, but only limited space is available in this book. Therefore, this book covers what you need to forge your own path forward.

What Is (and Isn't) in This Book?

The material in this book specifically targets iOS release 9.1 and later on Xcode 7.1 and later. Much of what you'll learn is common to all the iOS releases, but this book also covers several important areas that have only come about in recent iOS releases, such as gesture recognizers, embedded video playback with 3D Touch, AirPlay, Core Image, social networking, multitasking, universal (iPhone/iPad) applications, auto layout, size classes, and more!

Unfortunately, this is not a complete reference for the iOS application programming interfaces (APIs), nor do I explicitly cover AppleTV or Apple Watch development; some topics just require much more space than this book allows. That said, this book should provide ample exposure to the tools and techniques that any iOS developer needs to be successful. In addition, the Apple developer documentation is available directly within the free tools you install in Hour 1, "Preparing Your System and iDevice for Development." In many hours, you'll find a section titled "Further Exploration." This identifies additional related topics of interest. Again, a willingness to explore is an important quality in becoming a successful developer.

Each coding lesson is accompanied by project files that include everything you need to compile and test an example or, preferably, follow along and build the application yourself. Be sure to download the project files from this book's website at http://teachyourselfios.com. If you have issues with any projects, view the posts on this site to see whether a solution has been identified.

In addition to the support website, you can follow along on Twitter! Search for #iOSIn24 on Twitter to receive official updates and tweets from other readers. Use the hashtag #iOSIn24 in your tweets to join the conversation. To send me messages via Twitter, begin each tweet with @johnemeryray.

HOUR 1
Preparing Your System and iDevice for Development

What You'll Learn in This Hour:

▶ The iOS hardware limitations you face

▶ Where to get the tools you need to develop for iOS devices

▶ How to join the iOS Developer Program

▶ The need for (and use of) provisioning profiles

▶ What to expect during the first few hours of this book

The iOS device family opens up a whole realm of possibilities for developers: Multitouch interfaces, always-on Internet access, video, and a whole range of built-in sensors can be used to create everything from games to serious productivity applications. Believe it or not, as a new developer, you have an advantage. You are starting fresh, free from any preconceived notions of what is possible in a mobile application. Your next big idea may well become the next big thing on Apple's App Store.

This hour prepares you for your first development project. You're about to embark on the road to becoming an iOS developer, but you need to do a bit of prep work before you start coding.

Welcome to the iOS Platform

If you're reading this book, you probably already have an iOS device, and that means you already understand how to interact with its interface. Crisp graphics, amazing responsiveness, multitouch, and hundreds of thousands of apps—this just begins to scratch the surface. As a developer, however, you need to get accustomed to dealing with a platform that, to borrow a phrase from Apple, forces you to "think different."

IOS Devices

The iOS platform family currently consists of the iPhone, iPad, and iPod touch. The Apple Watch (watchOS) and Apple TV (tvOS) are similar platforms, but have unique user interfaces and require unique development approaches. As you work on the tutorials in this book, you'll notice in many figures that I focus on iPhone-centric (specifically 4.7-inch screen) projects. This isn't because I'm lacking love for larger devices; it's because it is difficult to capture iPad and the "plus" model iPhone interfaces in a screenshot because they are so large. The good news is that if you want to develop a project on the iPad, you develop it on the iPad. If you want to develop it for the iPhone 6s+, you develop it for the iPhone 6s+. In almost all cases, the coding process is identical. In the few cases where it isn't, I make sure that you understand what is different between the devices (and why). You'll also find that each tutorial is available in an iPad and iPhone version on this book's website (http://teachyourselfios.com), so you can follow along with a working application on whatever device you choose.

NOTE

Like Apple's developer tools and documentation, I do not differentiate between the iPhone and iPod touch in the lessons. For all intents and purposes, developing for these devices is identical, although some capabilities aren't available in earlier versions of the iPod touch (but the same can be said for earlier versions of the iPhone and iPad, as well).

Display and Graphics

The iOS devices offer a variety of different resolutions, but iOS provides a simple way of thinking about them. The traditional iPhone screen (before the iPhone 5 and 6), for example, is 320×480 points. Notice that I said *points*, not pixels. Before the release of the iPhone 4's Retina display, the iPhone was 320×480 pixels. Now, the actual resolution of an iOS device is abstracted behind a scaling factor. This means that although you may be working with the numbers like 320×480 for positioning elements on a "small" device, like an iPhone 4s, the actual device may have more pixels than that. The iPhone 4(s), 5(s), and 6, for example, have a scaling factor of 2. This means that the iPhone 4s is really a (320×2) × (480×2) or 640×960 pixel resolution device. The iPhone 5 changed things a bit by using a longer 320×568 point (640×1136 pixel) screen, and the iPhone 6 upped the ante with a 375×667 point (750×1334 pixel) screen (see Figure 1.1).

So, what about the gigantic iPhone 6+/6s+? It changes things even more, with a scaling factor of 3, meaning that each point on the screen represents 3 pixels. What size is the screen in points? 414×736 points. With a scaling factor of 3, that means it has 1242×2208 pixels, right? Not quite. The iPhone plus models have a resolution of 1080×1920—but an "internal" resolution of 1242×2208. In essence, you can treat it like it has the higher resolution, but it automatically scales things down to fit the 1080×1920 display.

With all of these pixels (even in the iPhone 5), it might seem like you will have tons of screen real estate. Keep in mind, however, that these pixels are displayed on a screen that is likely only an inch or two larger than your index finger.

The iPad family follows a similar pattern. The iPad 2 and first-generation iPad mini use screens with 768×1024 points and a scaling factor of 1. Retina display iPad Airs and Minis still have a 768×1024-point screen, but with a scaling factor of 2 and a resolution of 1536×2048 pixels. The iPad Pro sports a gigantic 1024×1366 point screen with a scaling factor of 2 (or 2048×2732 pixels).

We take a closer look at how scaling factors work when we position objects on the screen throughout this book. The important thing to know is that when you're building your applications, iOS automatically takes the scaling factor into play to display your apps and their interfaces at the highest possible resolution (with rarely any additional work on your part).

FIGURE 1.1
The flagship iPhone 6s screen is measured in points—375×667 (portrait), 667×375 (landscape)—but each point is made up of more than 4 pixels (2 horizontal, 2 vertical).

The screen limits aren't a bad thing. As you'll learn, the iOS development tools give you plenty of opportunities to create applications with just as much depth as your desktop software—albeit with a more structured and efficient interface design.

The graphics that you display on your screen can include complex animated 2D and 3D displays thanks to the OpenGL ES and Metal implementation available on all iOS devices. OpenGL is an industry standard for defining and manipulating graphic images that is widely used when creating games, and Metal is an Apple-specific application programming interface (API) for accessing the 3D hardware with as little overhead as possible. Each year's device revisions improve these capabilities with more advanced 3D chipsets and rendering abilities, but even the original iPhone has very respectable imaging abilities.

Accommodating Different Screens... Should I Be Worried?

When the iPhone 4 introduced the Retina display, Apple made it remarkably simple to deal with. Without writing any additional code, developers could add Retina-ready resources to their applications that would be loaded automatically as needed. This was possible because even though the resolution of the screen changed, the aspect ratio didn't; there were still the same number of horizontal and vertical points on the screen.

The iPhone 5 added a new wrinkle. The screen was now longer, meaning that, for the first time in the iPhone's lifetime, the number of points on the screen changed—from 320×480 to 320×568. Again, Apple updated its interface tools so that interfaces could smoothly scale to accommodate different screen sizes.

Fast-forward to 2013 and Apple shook things up yet again, by introducing iOS 7 with an entirely new user interface (UI). Applications suddenly had to take into account a very different appearance with controls and fonts sized differently from previous years.

In 2014, Apple gave us iOS devices in a range of different sizes that go way beyond what we had to work with on the iPhone 5 (and subsequent 5s), and in 2015, iPads gained the ability to resize applications on the fly and run them side by side.

Thankfully, as Apple has been making all of these changes, they've been working on the tools that enable your application to adapt to different screen sizes and layouts.

Later in this book, you'll learn how to use these adaptive tools—called the *Auto Layout system*—in conjunction with *size classes* to build applications that adapt to any screen size that you have today, and any that Apple may introduce tomorrow.

Application Resource Constraints

As with the HD displays on our desktops and laptops, we've grown accustomed to processors that can work faster than we can click. The iOS devices use a range of processors, from a ~400MHz ARM in the early iPhones to the multicore A9 in the current top-of-the-line iPhone and iPad devices. The "A" chips are a "system on a chip" that provide central processing unit (CPU), graphics processing unit (GPU), and other capabilities to the device, and this series is the first Apple-designed CPU series to be used in quite a while.

Because Apple has gone to great lengths to keep the iOS devices responsive, your device's capability to multitask is limited. Starting in iOS 4, Apple created a limited set of multitasking APIs for very specific situations. In recent releases, the restrictions on these APIs have been loosened, but your application can never assume that it will remain running if iOS deems it to be a resource hog. iOS preserves the user experience above all else.

Another constraint that you need to be mindful of is the available memory. In the original iPhone, 128MB of RAM is available for the entire system, including your application. There is no virtual memory (slower storage space used as RAM), so you must carefully manage the objects that your application creates. In the latest models of the iPhone, Apple has provided 2GB, while the iPad Pro includes a full 4GB. This is great for us, but keep in mind that there are no RAM upgrades for earlier models.

Connectivity

The iPhone and iPad can always be connected to the Internet via a cellular provider (such as AT&T, Verizon, and Sprint in the United States). This wide-area access is supplemented with built-in WiFi and Bluetooth. WiFi can provide desktop-like browsing speeds within the range of a wireless hot spot. Bluetooth, in contrast, can be used to connect a variety of peripheral devices to your device, including a keyboard.

As a developer, you can make use of the Internet connectivity to update the content in your application, display web pages, and create multiplayer games. The only drawback is that applications that rely heavily on 3G, 4G, or LTE data usage may have a smaller audience due to the costs associated with data plans, and the popularity of WiFi-only models. Design your apps for WiFi, but support conservative use of cellular data if you can.

Input and Feedback

iOS devices shine when it comes to input and feedback mechanisms and your ability to work with them. You can read the input values from the capacitive multitouch (up to 11 fingers on the iPad) screen, force touch (pressure) on 2015 models, sense motion and tilt via the accelerometer and gyroscope, determine where you are using the global positioning system (GPS) (cellular-enabled devices required), see which way you're facing with the digital compass, and understand how a device is being used with the proximity and light sensors. iOS can provide so much data to your application about how and where it is being used that the device itself truly becomes a controller of sorts—much like (but surpassing) devices such as the Nintendo Wii U and PlayStation DualShock 4 controllers.

iOS devices also support capturing pictures and video directly into your applications, opening a realm of possibilities for interacting with the real world. Already applications are available that identify objects you've taken pictures of and that find references to them online (such as the Amazon Mobile app) or perform real-time translation of printed text (Word Lens).

Finally, for each action your user takes when interacting with your application, you can provide feedback. This, obviously, can be visible feedback on the screen, or it can be high-quality audio and haptic feedback via vibration (iPhone only). As a developer, you can leverage all these capabilities (as you'll learn in this book).

That wraps up our quick tour of the iOS platform. Never before has a single device defined and provided so many capabilities for a developer. As long as you think through the resource limitations and plan accordingly, a wealth of development opportunities await you.

Becoming an iOS Developer

Being an iOS developer requires more than just sitting down and writing a program. You need a modern Intel Macintosh desktop or laptop running Mavericks or Yosemite and at least 8GB of free space on your hard drive. The more screen space you have on your development system, the easier it is to create an effective workspace. You can even take Xcode into full-screen mode, removing all distractions. That said, I've worked perfectly happily on a 13-inch MacBook Air, so an ultra-HD multimonitor setup certainly isn't necessary.

So assuming you already have a Mac running Yosemite or El Capitan, what else do you need? The good news is that there isn't *much* more, and it won't cost you a cent to write your first application and run it on your iOS device.

But I Don't Have a Mac, What Do I Do?

Despite the iOS development tools being available only for the Mac, I am often asked if there is a Windows option for development. The answer is no, and yes. There isn't a Windows native version of the tools, but you *could* develop applications using Adobe's Flash Professional (https://www.adobe.com/products/flash.html). I'm not a fan of Flash, so I recommend another approach: using a hosted version of the development tools that you can access from Windows. The company vmOSX (http://virtualmacosx.com) offers remote access to a hosted version of the Apple development tools, making it possible to develop on applications on your Windows, Linux, or even iOS devices.

The Apple Developer Program

Despite somewhat confusing messages on the Apple website, there really is no fee associated with downloading the iOS SDK (software development kit), writing iOS applications, and running them on Apple's iOS Simulator or on your personal device. The ability to run applications on your device without joining the Developer Program is new with Xcode 7, so if you're attempting to use an earlier version, you'll need to upgrade.

Limitations do apply to what you can do for free. If you want to have early access to beta versions of the iOS and SDK, you must join the Developer Program. If you want to distribute applications via the App Store or send them to colleagues for testing, you also need to pay the membership fee.

Perhaps you aren't yet sure whether a membership is right for you. Don't worry; you can join at any time. I recommend that you start with the free tools and upgrade if you want to take advantage of pre-release software or deploy a finished application to the App Store. The only thing you need for the free program is an Apple ID. If you don't have one already, you can register a new ID at https://appleid.apple.com.

NOTE

Although you can run apps on your device with Xcode 7, it isn't necessarily the easiest approach to development. Most everything we do in this book can be (and will be) run and tested using the iOS Simulator. Obviously, things such as motion sensor input and GPS readings can't be accurately presented in the Simulator, but these are special cases and aren't needed until later in this book.

If you choose to join the paid Apple Developer Program, there are two levels to consider: a standard program ($99) for those who will be creating applications that they want to distribute from the App Store, and an enterprise program ($299) for large (500+ employees) companies that want to develop and distribute applications in-house but not through the App Store. Most likely, the standard program is what you want.

The standard program is available for both companies and individuals. If you want to publish to the App Store with a business name, you are given the option of choosing a standard "individual" or "company" program during the registration.

Becoming a Paid Developer Member

To start, visit the Apple Developer Enrollment page (https://developer.apple.com/programs/enroll/), shown in Figure 1.2.

Scroll to the bottom of the page and click the Start Your Enrollment button, and then log in using your credentials. If you don't have an ID, or you want a new ID to use solely for development, you can create a new Apple ID from the login page as well.

The registration process then walks you through the process of agreeing to Apple's Developer terms, and collecting information about you or your company, development interests, and experience, as shown in Figure 1.3.

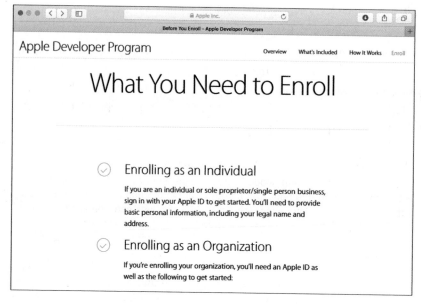

FIGURE 1.2
Visit the Developer Registration site to register or create a new Apple ID.

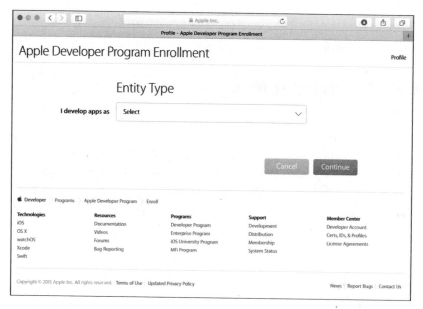

FIGURE 1.3
Walk through the registration process, providing information about you and your experience.

Click Continue to walk through the registration screens. At the end of the process, you are asked to complete the purchase of the program membership and enable automatic renewal, as shown in Figure 1.4.

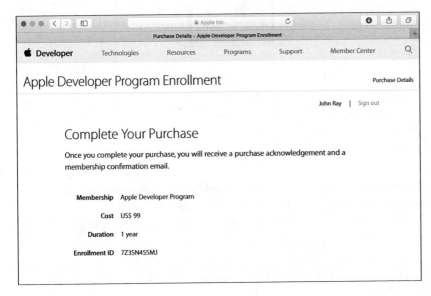

FIGURE 1.4
Complete your purchase (buttons not visible) and become a paid member of the Apple Developer Program.

The Developer Program membership does not take effect immediately. When the App Store first launched, it took months for new developers to join and be approved into the program. Today, however, it might take a few hours or a day. Just be patient.

Installing Xcode

Thanks to the Mac App Store, downloading Xcode (the iOS development suite) is as easy as point and click. Open the App Store from your Dock, search for Xcode, and download it for free, as shown in Figure 1.5. Sit back while your Mac downloads the large (~3GB compressed) application.

If you're interested in the cutting-edge beta releases of Xcode, you can download preview versions directly from the Developer Xcode site: https://developer.apple.com/xcode/.

When the download completes, you have either a disk image (if you downloaded a preview release from the iOS Developer site) or an application (if you downloaded from the Mac App Store). Open the disk image, if necessary, and copy the application to your Mac's Applications folder. You can have multiple copies of Xcode installed, so feel free to install both the beta from the dev center and the current stable release from the Mac App Store.

FIGURE 1.5
Download the release version of Xcode from the App Store.

Xcode is interesting in that it is both an application that provides a development environment *and* a wrapper around a collection of standalone tools (such as the iOS Simulator). These additional tools are launched from within Xcode. Xcode itself is started like any other application, by using the Finder or Launchpad (see Figure 1.6).

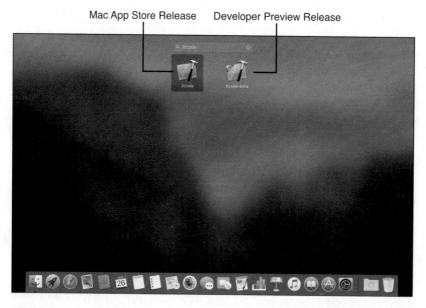

FIGURE 1.6
Your work will start with Xcode (which you can find in the Applications folder or Launchpad).

Once the Xcode application itself is installed, you might still need to install some additional software before you can use it. Launch Xcode from the Finder or Launchpad, and then wait for it to start. If it's your first time using the application, you'll likely be presented with a license agreement, and then Xcode will install updates and additional components to support iOS development (see Figure 1.7). If prompted, click Install to continue.

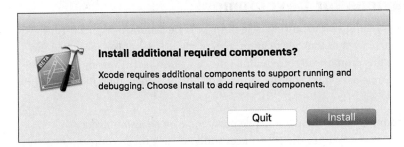

Install additional required components?

Xcode requires additional components to support running and debugging. Choose Install to add required components.

Quit   Install

FIGURE 1.7
Xcode requires the installation of additional components before you can use it.

When the installation completes, you can exit out of Xcode by choosing Quit from the Xcode menu. Your development environment is now ready to go. Although we do not get into real development for a few more hours, we will be configuring a few options in Xcode in the next section, so make sure you've properly installed the software before proceeding.

Running an iOS App

Even after you've obtained an Apple developer membership, joined a paid Developer Program, and downloaded and installed the iOS development tools, you still cannot run any applications that you write on your actual device. Why? Because you haven't created a development provisioning profile.

In many development guides, this step isn't covered until after development begins. In my mind, after you've written an application, you're going to want to run it on a real device immediately. Why? Because it's just cool to see your own code running on your own iPhone or iPad.

What's a Development Provisioning Profile?

Like it or not, Apple's current approach to iOS development is to make absolutely certain that the development process is controlled—and that groups can't just distribute software to anyone they want. The result is a rather confusing process that ties together information about you, any development team members, and your application into a *provisioning profile*.

A development provisioning profile identifies the developer who may install an application, an ID for the application being developed, and the "unique device identifiers" for each device that will run the application. This is only for the development process. When you are ready to distribute an application via the App Store or to a group of testers (or friends) via ad hoc means, you must create a separate "distribution" profile (paid developer memberships only). If you're just starting out, this isn't something you need right away.

Configuring Devices for Development

In the past, creating a provisioning profile for the sole purpose of development was a frustrating and time-consuming activity that took place in an area of the iOS developer site called the Provisioning Portal. Apple has dramatically streamlined the process in recent versions of Xcode, making provisioning as simple as adding your developer Apple ID to Xcode, then (literally), running your app.

To begin, start Xcode and immediately load the Xcode preferences by choosing Xcode, Preferences from the Xcode menu. Within the Preferences window, click the Accounts button. Click the + button in the lower-left corner, and choose Add Apple ID from the menu that appears. When prompted, enter your Apple ID, as shown in Figure 1.8, and then click the Add button. Close the Preferences window when finished.

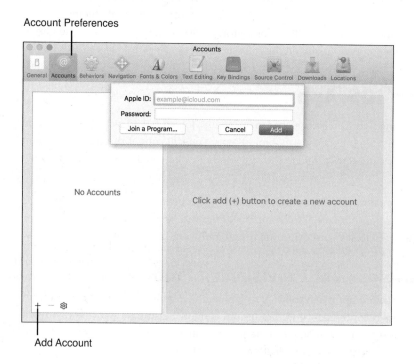

FIGURE 1.8
Adding an Apple ID to Xcode.

Next, make sure that your unlocked device is connected to your computer, and then choose Window, Devices from the menu bar. You should see your iOS device listed in the leftmost column of the window under the Devices heading, as shown in Figure 1.9. As long as your device is visible here, you should be ready to go! As soon as you attempt to run an application on your iDevice, Xode will automatically create all the provisioning profiles and certificates for you. If you don't see your device, make sure you're using an official Apple Lightning cable and the latest supported version of iOS.

FIGURE 1.9
Open the Xcode Devices window and find your device.

Behind the Scenes

In case you're wondering what actually happens when you run an app on a device, here's the not-so-short of it: Xcode adds a unique identity to the iOS developer portal that identifies you and is used to digitally sign any applications you generate; this is called the *signing identity*. It also registers your device with Apple so that it can run the software you create (and beta releases of iOS).

Xcode continues to communicate with Apple to create a development profile that will be named *iOS Team Provisioning Profile* and to create a unique App ID. This ID identifies a shared portion of the iOS device keychain to which your application will have access.

The keychain is a secure information store on iOS devices that you can use to save passwords and other critical information. Most apps don't share a keychain space (and therefore cannot share protected information). If you use the same App ID for multiple applications, however, those applications can share keychain data.

For the purposes of this book, there's no reason the tutorial apps can't share a single App ID, so letting Xcode generate an ID for us is just fine. Xcode will, in fact, create a "wildcard" App ID that will be applied to any application you create using the team provisioning profile.

Finally, Apple's servers use all of this information, along with the unique identifier of your connected iOS device, to provide Xcode with a completed provisioning profile. Xcode then transparently uploads the profile to your device the first time Xcode attempts to run an application on it.

NOTE

Only developers who have paid for a membership can access the member center and directly modify their provisioning profiles. Otherwise, you'll use Xcode to auto-magically configure things for you and deploy to your personal devices.

NOTE

In case you're wondering, Apple's Mac Developer Program creates and maintains similar profiles for deploying to the Mac App Store. The biggest difference is that unlike with iOS apps, you are free to run your Mac apps on any machine you want. In the Mac Developer Program, your certificates are used for deploying to the Mac App Store and for testing Apple-hosted services like Game Center and iCloud integration. In iOS development, you need the appropriate certificates installed to run your software *anywhere* outside of the iOS Simulator.

TIP

After you have a single development machine configured, you can easily configure other workstations by exporting your signing identities and provisioning profiles. To do this, open the Xcode preferences (Xcode, Preferences) and click the Accounts icon on the toolbar. Click the gear icon at the bottom of the Accounts list, and choose Export Accounts. This option (and the corresponding Import Accounts selection) exports (and subsequently imports) all your developer profiles/certificates in a single package.

Launching the App

It seems wrong to go through a whole hour about getting ready for iOS development without any payoff, right? For a real-world test of your efforts, let's actually try to run an application on your iOS device. If you haven't downloaded the project files to your computer, now is a good time to visit http://teachyourselfios.com and download the archives.

TIP

If you feel adventurous, a tutorial is available on http://teachyourselfios.com that will teach you about the basics of Xcode source control, including how you can connect to a live repository of the latest versions of all the book's sample projects.

Now let's run that app:

1. Within the Hour 1 Projects folder, choose between iPhone and iPad versions of the project, and then open the Welcome folder. Double-click Welcome.xcodeproj to open a simple application in Xcode. When the project opens, your display should look similar to Figure 1.10. If it isn't exactly the same, no biggie.

TIP

When you open a project using a more recent version of Xcode than what was used to create the project, you may be prompted to upgrade the project - convert the code to the latest Swift syntax. If this happens, go ahead and tell Xcode to make the necessary changes. Chances are, *nothing* will change. I get this message with each new beta of Xcode that comes out and have yet to see any required changes to the iOS 9 projects in this book.

FIGURE 1.10
The opened project should look a bit like this. Don't worry if it isn't exactly the same.

2. Make sure that your iOS device is plugged into your computer. Skip this if you don't happen to have an iOS device available.

3. Using the right side of the pop-up menu in the upper-left corner of the Xcode window (called the *Scheme menu*), choose your iOS device, as shown in Figure 1.11. This tells Xcode that when the project is built it should be installed on your device, not run in the Simulator. If you don't have a physical device handy, choose one of the Simulator options, depending on which version of the project you're using.

You'll usually only see options for running an application on either a variation of the iPhone Simulator *or* the iPad Simulator. In Figure 1.11, you see *all* the available Simulator options. This occurs when you are using an iPhone-targeted app (because they run on both iPhones and iPads) or when an app is a universal application (more on that later in the book). In this case, the screenshot was captured using the iPhone version of the project so that you could see all the options.

FIGURE 1.11
Choose where you want the app to run (on a device or in the Simulator).

4. Make sure your device is unlocked, and then click the Run button in the upper-left corner of the Xcode toolbar. After a few seconds, the application should be installed and launched. Figure 1.12 demonstrates what it looks like running on a 4.7-inch iPhone (an iPhone 6).

5. Click Stop on the Xcode toolbar to exit the application. You can now quit Xcode. We're done with it for the hour.

FIGURE 1.12
Congratulations! You've just installed your first homegrown iOS application.

When you clicked Run, the Welcome application was installed and started on your iOS device. It remains there until you remove it manually. Just touch and hold the Welcome icon until it starts wiggling, and then delete the application as you would any other. Applications installed with your development certificate stop working when the certificate expires (120 days after issuance).

TIP

The first time you run an application on your device using a new Apple ID (or if something is amiss with your developer account), Xcode may prompt you with a warning about provisioning your device.

If you see such a warning, simply click Fix, and (hopefully) all warnings and errors will go away.

Viewing the Provisioning Profiles

After you've run your first app on your iDevice, you can view the provisioning profile that has been installed on it. To see this elusive beast, open the Devices window (Window, Devices), and then right-click your device and choose Show Provisioning Profiles. A dialog will appear showing the iOS Team Provisioning Profile that was created automatically for you, as shown in Figure 1.13.

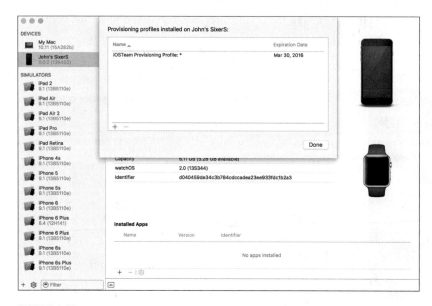

FIGURE 1.13
View the provisioning profiles that have been installed on your device.

But Wait... I Have More Than One iOS Device

We've discussed provisioning a single device for development. But what if you have multiple devices that you want to install onto? No problem. Just connect the additional devices and run your apps! They will be provisioned automatically.

If you have paid for a developer account and are not just using a free Apple ID account, Apple allows you to distribute your apps online for testing—no need to use Xcode for installation. In this scenario, you are limited to registering 100 unique devices to receive your application within the span of 1 year.

Developer Technology Overview

Over the course of the next few hours, you are introduced to the technologies that you can use to create iOS applications. The goal is to get you up to speed on the tools and technology, and then you can start actively developing. This means you're still a few hours away from writing your first app, but when you start coding, you'll have the necessary background skills and knowledge to successfully create a wide variety of applications.

The Apple Developer Tools

In this hour, you downloaded and worked with the Xcode application. This, coupled with the iOS Simulator, will be your home for the duration of the book. These two applications are so critical and feature packed that we spend a couple more hours (Hour 2, "Introduction to Xcode and the iOS Simulator," and Hour 5, "Exploring Interface Builder") covering their capabilities and use.

It's worth mentioning that almost every iPhone, iPad, iPod, and Macintosh application you run, whether created by a single developer at home or by a huge company, is built using the Apple developer tools. This means that you have everything you need to create software as powerful as any you've ever run.

Swift

Swift is the language that you'll be using to write your applications. It provides the structure for our applications and controls the logic and decision making that goes on when an application is running.

If you've never worked with a programming language before, don't worry. Hour 3, "Discovering Swift and the iOS Playground," covers everything you need to get started. Developing for iOS in Swift is a unique programming experience, even if you've used other programming languages in the past. The language is unobtrusive and structured in a way that makes it easy to follow. After your first few projects, Swift will fade into the background, letting you concentrate on the specifics of your application.

Cocoa Touch

Swift defines the structure for iOS applications, and Cocoa Touch defines the functional building blocks, called *classes*, that can make iOS devices perform certain actions. Cocoa Touch isn't a "thing," per se, but a collection of interface elements, data storage elements, and other handy tools that you can access from your applications.

As you'll learn in Hour 4, "Inside Cocoa Touch," you can access literally hundreds of different Cocoa Touch classes and do thousands of things with them. This book covers quite a few of the most useful classes and gives you the pointers necessary to explore even more on your own.

Model-View-Controller

The iOS platform and Macintosh use a development approach called *Model-View-Controller* (MVC) to structure applications. Understanding why MVC is used and the benefits it provides will help you make good decisions in structuring your most complex applications. Despite the complicated-sounding name, MVC is really just a way to keep your application projects arranged so that you can easily update and extend them in the future. You learn more about MVC in Hour 6, "Model-View-Controller Application Design."

Further Exploration

Xcode is the cornerstone of your iOS development experience. You will design, code, and test your apps in Xcode. You'll provision your devices and even submit apps to the App Store, all through Xcode. Noticing my emphasis yet? Xcode. Xcode. Xcode. Although we'll be spending time going through the Xcode features now, take a moment to watch Apple's introductory videos to get a sense for what you'll be seeing. To do this, open Xcode, and then choose Xcode Help from the Help menu.

The more you familiarize yourself with the tools, the quicker you'll be able to use them to build production-ready applications.

Summary

This hour introduced you to the iOS platform, its capabilities, and its limitations. You learned about the different iOS devices' graphic features, RAM sizes, and the various sensors that you can use in your applications to create uniquely "aware" experiences. We also discussed the Apple iOS developer tools, how to download and install them, and the differences between the various paid Developer Programs. To prepare you for actual on-phone development, you explored the (largely automated) process of creating and installing a development provisioning profile in Xcode and even ran an application on your device.

The hour wrapped up with a quick discussion about the development technologies that make up the first part of this book and form the basis for all the iOS development you'll be doing.

Q&A

Q. I thought that iOS devices ranged from a minimum of 16GB of RAM in the low-end iPad and iPhone to 128GB on the high-end models. Don't they?

A. The "memory" capabilities of devices that are advertised to the public are the storage sizes available for applications, songs, and so forth. It is separate from the RAM that can be used for executing programs. If Apple implements virtual memory in a future version of iOS, it is possible that the larger storage could be used for increasing available RAM.

Q. What platform should I target for development?

A. That depends on your goals. If you want to reach the largest audience, consider a universal application that works on the iPhone, iPad, and iPod touch. We explore this in a few projects later in this book. If you want to make use of the most-capable hardware, you can certainly target the unique capabilities of a specific device, but by doing so you might be limiting the size of your customer base.

Q. **Why isn't the iOS platform open?**

A. Great question. Apple has long sought to control the user experience so that it remains "positive" regardless of how users have set up their device, be it a Mac, an iPad, or an iPhone. By ensuring that applications can be tied to a developer and by enforcing an approval process, Apple attempts to limit the potential for a harmful application to cause damage to data or otherwise negatively impact the user. With nearly 1.5 million active applications on the App Store, I think Apple must be doing something right.

Workshop

Quiz

1. You will work with iOS device screens using which unit?

    a. Em

    b. Pixel

    c. Point

    d. Pica

2. What is the individual developer membership cost per year?

    a. $99

    b. $199

    c. $299

    d. Free

3. For apps to run on your device, which of the following must be installed?

    a. Provisioning profile

    b. Provisioning center

    c. Profile provision

    d. Provisioning ID

4. Paid access to a Developer Program is needed to download which Xcode releases?

    a. iOS

    b. OS X

    c. App Store

    d. Beta

5. Which version of the iPad introduced video capture capability?

  a. iPad 1

  b. iPad 2

  c. Retina iPad

  d. iPad Air

6. Which iPhone model introduced a Retina display?

  a. iPhone 4s

  b. iPhone 4

  c. iPhone 3GS

  d. iPhone 5

7. The scaling factor on a modern iPad is what?

  a. 1

  b. 2

  c. 3

  d. 4

8. The iPhone 5 changed what about iOS development?

  a. Screen height

  b. Screen width

  c. Pixel density

  d. Pixel shape

9. The provisioning profile created automatically for you by Xcode is named what?

  a. iOS Profile

  b. iOS Team Provisioning Profile

  c. App Provisioning Profile

  d. Testing iOS Profile

10. The smallest amount of RAM contained in an iOS device was what?

  a. 128MB

  b. 512MB

  c. 1024MB

  d. 2048MB

Answers

1. C. Points are used, rather than pixels, when working with iOS device screens.

2. A. You'll need to spend $99 to join the individual Developer Program to run apps on your iDevices and submit creations to the App Store.

3. A. A provisioning profile ties your device to your iOS developer account.

4. D. Paid developers can access and download Xcode beta releases before the general public.

5. B. The original iPad had no video capture capabilities. It wasn't until the iPad 2 that Apple's tablet could record video.

6. B. The iPhone 4 included the first Retina display in an iOS device.

7. B. All shipping iPads use a scaling factor of 2 for their displays.

8. A. The iPhone 5 threw app developers for a loop by introducing a new screen height.

9. B. Although running an app on your device can be as simple as plugging it in and clicking Run, behind the scenes Xcode will install the iOS Team Provisioning Profile to make everything work.

10. A. It's hard to believe, but the original iPhone shipped with only 128MB of RAM!

Activities

1. Review the online developer membership information and download and install the developer tools. This is an important activity that you should complete before starting the next hour's lesson (if you didn't do so while following along in this hour).

2. Review the resources available in the iOS dev center. Apple has published several introductory videos and tutorials that supplement what you'll learn in this book.

HOUR 2
Introduction to Xcode and the iOS Simulator

What You'll Learn in This Hour:

▶ How to create new projects in Xcode

▶ Code editing and navigation features

▶ Where to add classes and resources to a project

▶ How to modify project properties

▶ Compiling for iOS devices and the iOS Simulator

▶ How to interpret error messages

▶ Features and limitations of the iOS Simulator

▶ Adding new devices to the iOS Simulator

The core of your development work will be spent in two applications: Xcode and the iOS Simulator. These apps provide the core tools that you need to design, program, and test applications for the iPhone and iPad. And, unlike other platforms, they're entirely free.

This hour walks you through the basics you need to work with Xcode's code-editing tools and the iOS Simulator, and you get some hands-on practice working with each. We cover Xcode's interface-creation tools in Hour 5, "Exploring Interface Builder."

Using Xcode

When you think of coding—actually typing the statements that will make your iDevice meet Apple's "magical" mantra—think Xcode. Xcode is the IDE, or integrated development environment, that manages your application's resources and lets you edit the code and user interface (UI) that ties the different pieces together.

After you install Xcode, as described in Hour 1, "Preparing Your System and iDevice for Development," you should be able to find it in the Applications folder located at the root level of your hard drive or in Launchpad. We walk through the day-to-day use of Xcode's tools in this hour. If you haven't finished the installation, do so now.

Launch Xcode now. After a few moments, the Welcome to Xcode screen displays, as shown in Figure 2.1.

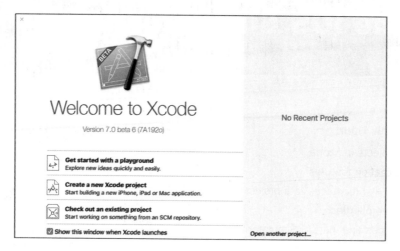

FIGURE 2.1
Create a new project (or open an existing one), right from the Xcode Welcome screen.

You can choose to disable this screen by unchecking the Show This Window When Xcode Launches check box. In Hour 4, "Inside Cocoa Touch," we take a detailed look at the documentation system included in Xcode, which is quite extensive. For now, click the close box (X) in the upper-left corner to exit the Welcome screen.

Creating and Managing Projects

Most of your development work will start with an Xcode project. A *project* is a collection of all the files associated with an application, along with the settings needed to "build" a working piece of software from the files. This includes images, source code, and a file that describes the appearance and objects that make up the interface.

Choosing a Project Type

To create a new project, choose File, New Project (Shift-Command-N) from the Xcode menu. Do this now. Xcode prompts you to choose a template for your application, as shown in Figure 2.2. The Xcode templates contain the files you need to quickly start a new development effort.

Although it is possible to build an application completely from scratch, the time saved by using a template is significant. We use several templates throughout this book, depending on what type of application we're building.

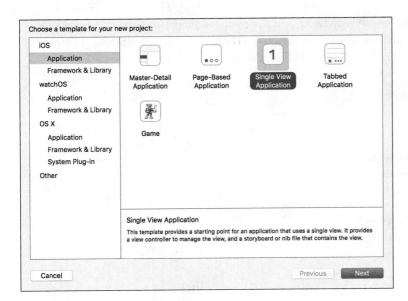

FIGURE 2.2
To create a new project, start by choosing an appropriate template.

Along the left side of the Template window are the categories of templates available. Our focus is on the iOS Application category, so be sure that it is selected.

On the right side of the display are the templates within the category, with a description of the currently highlighted template. For this tutorial, click the Single View Application template, and then click Next.

After choosing the template, you are prompted for a product name, organization name, and a company identifier. The product name is the name of your application, and the organization name can be anything you want, such as your name or your company name. The Company Identifier field is a bit different. This is typically the domain name of the organization or individual producing the app, but in reverse order. Together, the product name and the company identifier make up something called the *bundle identifier*, which uniquely identifies your application among all other iOS apps.

For example, in this hour, we create an app called HelloXcode. This becomes the product name. I own the domain teachyourselfios.com, so I enter **com.teachyourselfios** in the Company Identifier field. If you do not own a domain name, you'll need to enter *something*, because this is a required field.

Go ahead and enter **HelloXcode** as your product name, and then provide an organization name and a company identifier of your choice.

Set the Language to Swift (Apple's preferred programming language), and then choose which device (iPad or iPhone) you are using from the Device Family pop-up. The remaining check boxes should be unchecked. Your screen will look similar to mine, shown in Figure 2.3.

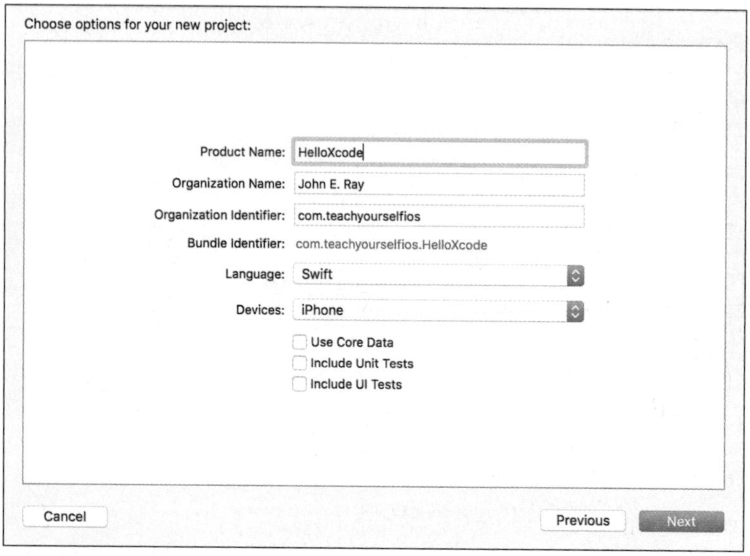

FIGURE 2.3
Choose a product name, organization name and identifier, and development platform for your app.

NOTE

Wondering what those check boxes are for? Core Data is an advanced means of storing application data that may be of interest as your project's needs grow. The UI and Unit Testing check boxes enable automated tests to be written to test the functionality of your app over time. These may be of interest to you as you begin to write larger and larger apps.

These topics are, unfortunately, beyond the scope of this book, but you can read more about Core Data and the testing tools using the Xcode documentation system discussed in the next hour.

When satisfied with your settings, click Next. Xcode prompts for a save location for the project. Navigate to an appropriate location on your drive, leave the Source Control option unchecked, and then click Create. Xcode makes a folder with the name of the project and places all the associated template files within that folder.

TIP

Within your project folder, you'll find a file with the extension .xcodeproj. This is the file you need to open to return to your project workspace after exiting Xcode.

Getting Your Bearings

After you've created or opened a project in Xcode, the interface displays a single window that will be used for everything from writing code to designing your application interfaces. If this is your first time in Xcode, the assortment of buttons and menus and icons can be more than a little intimidating. To help get a feel for what all of this is, let's start by defining the major functional areas of the interface, shown in Figure 2.4.

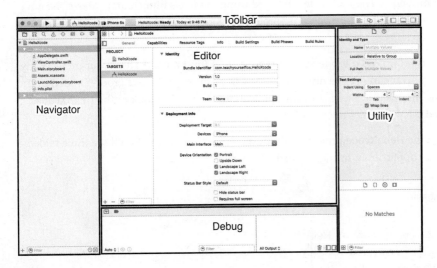

FIGURE 2.4
Finding your way around the Xcode interface can be intimidating at first.

Toolbar: Displays project status and provides easy access to common functions.

Navigator: Manages files, groups, and other information related to your project.

Editor: Edits project content (code, interfaces, and more).

Utility: Provides quick access to object inspectors, help, and project components.

Debug: If something goes wrong with your code during execution or you generate log output, this is where you'll find it.

NOTE

By default, the debug and utility areas are usually hidden. You can toggle the debug visibility using the second-to-last button on the toolbar and the utility area using the last. This cluster of three buttons comprises the view controls. The first button in the set is used to hide and show the navigator. You'll get accustomed to the features offered within each of these areas as we work through the book. For now, we focus on the navigator and editor areas.

If you ever find that your display seems completely different from what you're expecting, use the View menu on the Xcode menu bar to show the toolbar, navigator, or any other pieces that have gone missing.

Navigating Your Project

The navigator can operate in many different modes, from navigating your project files to search results and error messages. The modes are changed using the icons immediately above the navigator content area. The folder icon shows the project navigator and is where you'll spend most of your time.

The project navigator displays a top-level icon representing (and named after) your project; this is the project group. You can use the disclosure arrow in front of the project group to open and show the files and groups that make up your application. Let's take a look at the HelloXcode project we created a few minutes ago.

In Xcode, expand the HelloXcode project group in the project navigator. You'll see three folders associated with the application, as highlighted in Figure 2.5.

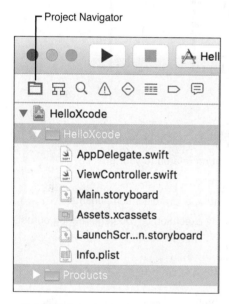

FIGURE 2.5
Use the project navigator to browse your project resources.

NOTE

The folders you see in Xcode are logical groupings. You won't necessarily find all these files in your project directory, nor will you find the same folder structure. The Xcode layout is designed to help you find what you're looking for easily, not to mirror a file system structure.

Within the project group are two subgroups:

▶ **Project Code:** Named after the project, this group contains the code for the class files and resources that you add to your project. As you'll learn in the next hour, classes group together application features that complement one another. Most of your development will be within a file located here.

▶ **Products:** Anything produced by Xcode is included here (typically, the executable application).

If you dig a bit further, you'll also notice a folder icon labeled Assets.xcassets. This is an asset catalog, which we cover in more detail in a few minutes.

TIP

If you find that you want additional logical groupings of files, you can define your own groups via File, New, Group. The organization of the project is up to you.

Finding Your Way with Filtering

At the bottom of the navigator area is a small toolbar that you can use to filter or adjust what is currently being displayed. In the project navigator, for example, you can enter text in the search field to only display project resources (groups or files) that match. You can also use the clock icon to the left of the field to limit the results to recently edited files. The square beside the clock is for showing file outside of source control. You can learn more about Source Control by reading the online appendix to this book.

Filtering options are contextual; they change based on what is currently being displayed in the navigator. Be sure to take advantage of Xcode's extensive tooltips to explore the interface as you encounter new areas and features.

Adding New Code Files to a Project

Even though the Apple iOS application templates give you a great starting point for your development, you'll find, especially in more advanced projects, that you need to add additional code files to supplement the base project. To add a new file to a project, first highlight the group you want to add the file to (usually the project code group). Next, choose File, New or click the + button located at the bottom-left corner of the navigator. In an interface similar to the project templates, Xcode prompts you, as shown in Figure 2.6, for the category and type of file that you want to add to the project. You are fully guided throughout this book, so don't worry if the options in the figure look alien at first.

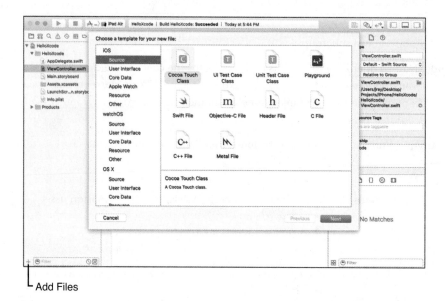

Add Files

FIGURE 2.6
Use Xcode to add new files to a project.

Can I Add Empty Files Manually?

Yes, you could drag your own files into one of the Xcode groups and copy them into the project. However, just as a project template gives you a head start on implementation, Xcode's file templates do the same thing. They often include an outline for the different features that you must implement to make the code functional.

Adding Resources to a Project

Many applications will require sound or image files that you'll integrate into your development. Obviously, Xcode can't help you "create" these files, so you'll have to add them by hand. To do this, just click and drag the file from its location into the project code group in Xcode. You are prompted to copy the files. Always make sure that the Copy check box is selected so that Xcode can put the files where they need to go within your project directory.

In the provided HelloXcode project folder that corresponds with what you're building this hour, you'll find a Resources folder containing the file Test.wav. Drag this file into your project code group within the Xcode navigator. Choose to copy if needed, as shown in Figure 2.7. Copying the files ensures that they are correctly placed within your project and accessible by your code.

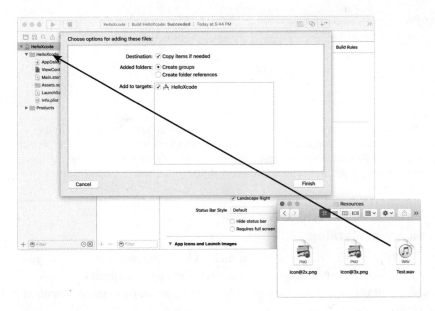

FIGURE 2.7
Drag the Test.wav file into the project code folder and choose to copy if needed.

TIP
If you drag a folder with multiple files into your project, Xcode, by default, automatically creates a group containing all the files.

Removing Files and Resources

If you've added something to Xcode that you decide you don't want, you can delete it easily. To remove a file or resource from your project, simply select it within the project navigator and press the Delete key. Xcode gives you the option to move the file to the Trash or just to delete the project's reference to the file (see Figure 2.8).

If you choose to delete references, the file itself will remain but will no longer be visible in the project.

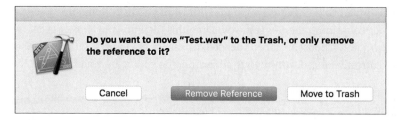

FIGURE 2.8
Deleting a file's reference leaves the actual file untouched.

NOTE

If Xcode can't find a file that it expects to be part of a project, that file is highlighted in red in the Xcode interface. This might happen if you accidentally use the Finder to delete a file from the project folder. It also occurs when Xcode knows that an application file will be created by a project but the application hasn't been generated yet. In this case, you can safely ignore the red .app file within the Products group.

Using the Xcode Asset Catalog

Starting in Xcode 5, Apple provided a new (and better) method for managing your files that you want to include in your projects: asset catalogs. Used mainly for images (but capable of holding other data as well), asset catalogs provide a central location for storing and managing all of your project's data files.

Asset catalogs offer two features "above and beyond" just dragging an image folder into Xcode. First, they provide a nice clean interface for defining Retina and non-Retina images and device-specific images. Second, images in an asset catalog can be "sliced," which is Apple's term for defining areas of an image that can be resized if the image is stretched. We put that feature to the test in Hour 7, "Working with Text, Keyboards, and Buttons."

NOTE

Asset catalogs don't just help *you*, the developer, they also give Apple a way of delivering only the images that a particular device needs to that device—no more iPad graphics stored on iPhone applications and vice versa. This feature was introduced in iOS 9 to help reduce application sizes.

Adding New Asset Catalogs   All projects created in Xcode include a default asset catalog named Assets.xcassets. If you open an older project, or have a need to create multiple asset catalogs, you can add a new asset catalog by choosing File, New, File from the menu bar and then selecting the Resource category and Asset Catalog from the New File dialog, as shown in Figure 2.9.

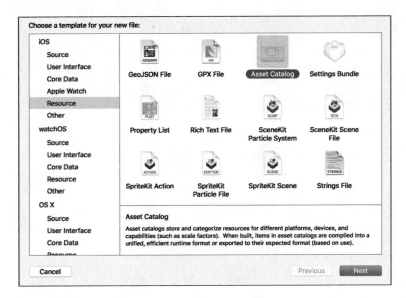

FIGURE 2.9
Create a new asset catalog, if needed. All *new* Xcode projects include an asset catalog by default.

Adding Files to an Asset Catalog   To view the contents of an asset catalog, select the asset catalog (usually Assets.xcassets) in the project navigator. Your screen will refresh to show a column of resource names on the left of the content area. Selecting an entry in the list displays it on the right. You'll notice there is one item already in the list by default: AppIcon. This is a special placeholder for your application icons.

For now, let's concentrate on how we add new content to the catalog. Our HelloXcode project relies on the file Background.png found in the Resources folder within this hour's Projects folder. We'll get our feet wet by adding this file to the asset catalog:

1. Open the Resources folder containing the Background.png file in the Finder.

2. Select the Assets.xcassets file in your HelloXcode project navigator.

3. Drag Background.png into the left column of the asset catalog, as shown in Figure 2.10.

You're done. No prompting to make copies, nothing. You've added your first image to an asset catalog.

For the projects throughout the book, this is the method we'll be using to add images to our projects. In the tutorials, I usually add multiple files by dragging the whole folder into the asset catalog; doing so adds a group to the catalog list, making organization a cinch.

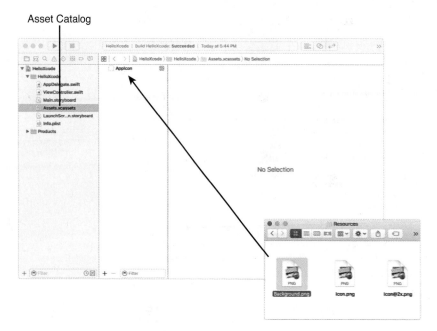

FIGURE 2.10
Drag from the Finder into the asset catalog list. The new item will be added.

TIP
If you're more into point-n-click versus click-n-drag, you can use the + and – buttons at the bottom of the asset catalog entry list to add (+) or remove (–) entries.

NOTE
When you're viewing an image in an asset catalog, you'll see a Show Slicing button in the lower-right corner. Slicing is a feature that enables you to define *slices* in your images that should be repeated to fill space when an image is resized. Although this is a rather strange sounding concept, you'll learn how it can prove very useful in creating small images that can dynamically expand to fill a large space. We explore this feature later in Hour 7.

Retina Assets

After you add an image to their asset catalog, you'll notice something interesting when you view it in the catalog: There are spots for three images, one labeled 1x, another 2x, and a final one named 3x (as shown in Figure 2.11). These represent non-Retina (1x), Retina (2x), and iPhone 6+/6s+ Retina (3x) graphics.

Retina Asset

Asset Catalog   Asset Entry   Non-Retina Asset   Retina Asset (iPhone 6+/6s+)

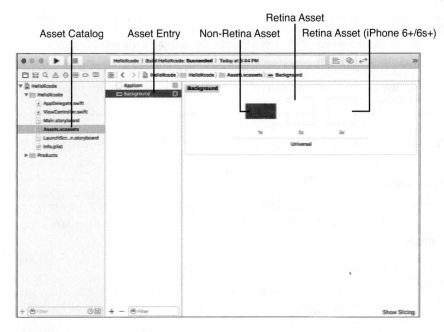

FIGURE 2.11
Asset catalogs track both Retina and non-Retina versions of images.

Most Retina graphics are twice the vertical and horizontal resolution of non-Retina images (hence 2x). The iPhone 6+/6s+ includes a display with three times the vertical and horizontal resolution of a non-Retina display (hence, 3x).

Although these image assets make up a total of three separate graphic files (1x, 2x, and 3x), they are presented under a single image name in the asset catalog. If you add an image into a catalog, and then want to add the corresponding Retina images, just drag an image into the 2x spot, and one into the 3x spot. The asset catalog does the rest.

Apple requires that all applications include Retina resources, so you'll want to consider that when creating application graphics. Non-iPhone 6+/6s+ Retina images are named with a @2x suffix. A Retina version of the Background.png image would be named Background@2x.png, for example. Versions to accommodate the iPhone 6+/6s+ screen use an @3x suffix (for example, Background@3x.png).

Although naming isn't important if you're using an asset catalog and adding images by dragging them into the available spots, using the Retina naming convention will automatically pair up the Retina and non-Retina images properly just by dragging them into the asset catalog.

TIP

When you reference an image in your code, you'll always refer to the non-Retina name (for example, what you see listed as the image name in the asset catalog). iOS automatically substitutes the correct Retina version of the image into your application as it runs. In other words, you don't need to do anything special to use the right image at the right time. Just add your images into the asset catalog, make sure that the 1x, 2x, and 3x images are defined, and then reference the image using the name shown in the left column of the catalog.

Enough about images. Let's move on to editing code.

Editing and Navigating Code

To edit code in Xcode, just use the project navigator to find the file you want to edit, and then click the filename. The editable contents of the file are shown in the editor area of the Xcode interface (see Figure 2.12).

FIGURE 2.12
Choose the group, then the file, and then edit.

The Xcode editor works just like any text editor, with a few nice additions. To get a feel for how it works, open the project code group within the HelloXcode project, and then click ViewController. swift to begin editing the source code. Notice that above the editor is a visual path to the file you are editing. Clicking any portion of the path reveals a pop-up menu for quickly jumping to other files in same location. To the left of the path are forward and back arrows that move back and forth between files that you've been editing, just like pages you visit in a web browser.

For this project, we use an interface element called a label to display the text Hello Xcode on your device's screen. This application, like most that you write, uses a method to show our greeting. A method is just a block of code that executes when some thing needs to happen. In this example, we use an existing method called `viewDidLoad` that runs as soon as the application starts and loads its interface.

Jumping Through Code with the Symbol Navigator

The easiest way to find a method or property within a source code file is to use the symbol navigator, opened by clicking the icon to the immediate right of the project navigator. This view, shown in Figure 2.13, enables you to expand your project classes to show all the methods and variables that are defined. Choosing an item from the list jumps to and highlights the relevant line in your source code.

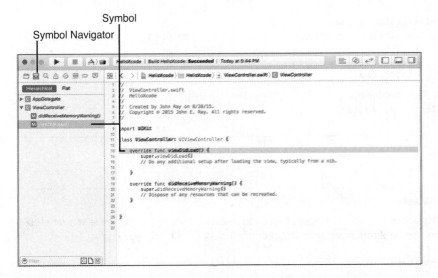

FIGURE 2.13
The symbol navigator is a quick way to jump between methods and properties.

Switch to the symbol navigator and expand the `ViewController` item. This is the only class we'll be using in this application. Next, find and select `viewDidLoad` from the list that is displayed. Xcode jumps to the line where the method begins. Let's start coding.

TIP
_____

When you are editing a file, the visual path above the editor ends in the symbol label where your cursor is currently located (if any). Clicking this label displays a list of the symbols defined in code you are working on, and choosing one jumps to that section of code.
_____

Using Code Completion

Using the Xcode editor, type the following text to implement the `viewDidLoad` method. Start a new line immediately following the line with the text **// Do any additional setup after loading the view, typically from a nib.** (a comment). You need to enter just the bolded code lines shown in Listing 2.1.

LISTING 2.1   Your First Code Exercise

```
override func viewDidLoad() {
    super.viewDidLoad()
    // Do any additional setup after loading the view, typically from a nib.

    var myMessage: UILabel
    var myUnusedVariable: String
    myMessage=UILabel(frame:CGRectMake(30.0,50.0,300.0,50.0,50.0))
    myMessage.font=UIFont.systemFontOfSize(48.0)
    myMessage.text="Hello Xcode"
    myMessage.textColor=UIColor(patternImage: UIImage(named: "Background")!)
    view.addSubview(myMessage)
    NSLog("Hello Xcode, Again")
}
```

CAUTION

Haste Makes Waste

If you decide to skip ahead and run this application, you'll quickly realize that the code you entered is *not going to work*. Some errors have been intentionally included here that you correct later this hour.

NOTE

It's not important to understand exactly what this code does. At this point, you just need to get experience in the Xcode editor. The "short and sweet" description of this fragment, however, is that it creates a label object reading "Hello Xcode" in the upper-left corner of the screen; sets the label's text, font, size, and color; and then adds it to the application's window. As a final step, once the "Hello Xcode" message is displayed onscreen, the application also logs a message ("Hello Xcode (again)") to the debugger area in Xcode.

As you type, you should notice something interesting happening. As soon as you get to a point in each line where Xcode thinks it knows what you intend to type, it displays an autocompleted version of the code, as demonstrated in Figure 2.14.

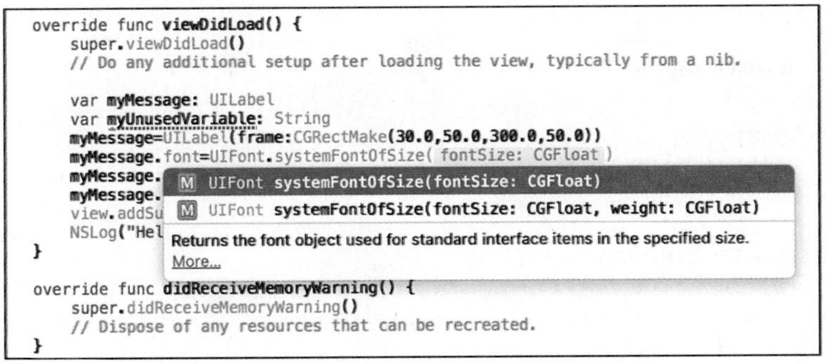

```
override func viewDidLoad() {
    super.viewDidLoad()
    // Do any additional setup after loading the view, typically from a nib.

    var myMessage: UILabel
    var myUnusedVariable: String
    myMessage=UILabel(frame:CGRectMake(30.0,50.0,300.0,50.0))
    myMessage.font=UIFont.systemFontOfSize( fontSize: CGFloat )
    myMessage.  ┌─────────────────────────────────────────────────────┐
    myMessage.  │ Ⓜ UIFont systemFontOfSize(fontSize: CGFloat)         │
    view.addSu  │ Ⓜ UIFont systemFontOfSize(fontSize: CGFloat, weight: CGFloat) │
    NSLog("Hel  │ Returns the font object used for standard interface items in the specified size. │
}               │ More...                                              │
                └─────────────────────────────────────────────────────┘
override func didReceiveMemoryWarning() {
    super.didReceiveMemoryWarning()
    // Dispose of any resources that can be recreated.
}
```

FIGURE 2.14
Xcode automatically completes the code as you type.

To accept an autocompletion suggestion, press Tab, and the code will be inserted, just as if you typed the whole thing. If there are multiple possible outcomes for the autocomplete line, you can arrow up and down to select the one you want and then press Tab. Xcode tries to complete method names, variables that you've defined, and anything else related to the project that it might recognize.

If you are completing a method name, chances are that you need to provide parameters as well. (In the case of `systemFontOfSize`, it is a floating-point value that describes the size of the text.) You can again use the arrow keys to move between the parameter fields and enter the values you want, or you can just press Tab to skip from parameter to parameter.

After you've made your changes, you can save the file by choosing File, Save.

NOTE

In addition to automatically completing your code, Xcode automatically inserts the complementary curly brace or parenthesis when you type the first character. In other words, if you type {, Xcode automatically adds a corresponding } for you. You can disable this behavior in the Xcode Text Editing preferences (Xcode, Preferences, Text Editing, Editing).

Searching Your Code with the Search Navigator

Searching for text anywhere in your project is trivial using the search navigator. To access this search feature, click the magnifying glass icon on the icon bar above the navigator. A search field is displayed at the top of the navigator area where you can enter whatever you want to find. Press Return to show the results, as shown in Figure 2.15. Click the button under the search term to change the scope of the search, which is initially set to In Project (searching all files within the project). Use the menu to the right of the Search Scope button to choose whether the search is case sensitive.

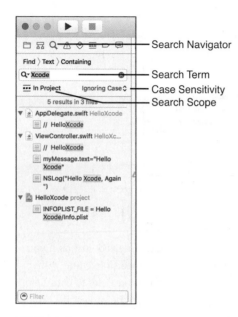

FIGURE 2.15
Use the search navigator to find text throughout your project.

The search results display below the search field, along with a snippet of the file containing the text you were looking for. Clicking a search result opens the corresponding file in the editor and jumps to the line containing your search string.

To make things even more interesting, you can use the filter field at the bottom of the search navigator to filter your search results by a secondary term. You can also click the Find label at the top of the search navigator to switch to a Replace mode—enabling you to perform project-wide find and replace.

TIP
___

If you're looking for a string within a file you are actively editing, choose Edit, Find (Command-F) to open a more traditional Find field at the top of the editor. This gives you quick access to find (or find/replace) within a given file, rather than across the entire project.

___

Adding Marks, To Do's, and Fix Me's

Sometimes navigating code by symbols or with a search isn't very efficient. To help denote important pieces of code in plain English, you can insert specially formatted comments in your code. These comments do not add any features to your application; instead, they create logical sections within your code. These sections are then displayed, with the rest of the code symbols, when you click the last item in the visual path above the editor.

There are three types of comment marks that you can use:

```
// MARK: - <label name>
// TODO: <text you want to remember>
// FIXME: <text you want to remember>
```

The first, MARK, inserts a horizontal line in the symbol menu and is useful for segmenting off different methods based on what they do or which developer is working on them.

The TODO and FIXME marks insert an arbitrary string into the menu, and, as their names suggest, can be helpful for remembering things you need to do or fix.

For example, to add a section called "Method for handling memory management" followed by a horizontal line, you could type the following:

```
// MARK: - Method for handling memory management
```

After a mark has been added to your code and saved, the symbol menu updates accordingly, as shown in Figure 2.16. Choosing a mark from the symbol menu jumps to that portion of the code.

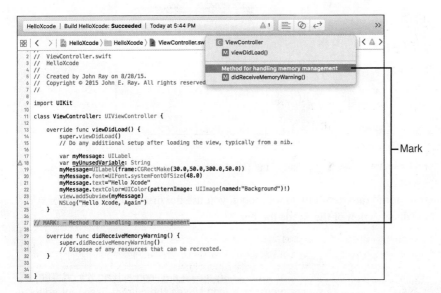

FIGURE 2.16
Marks can create logical divisions in your code.

Using the Assistant Editor

For those lucky enough to have large monitors, you can take advantage of Xcode's assistant editor mode. In the next hour, you learn about the different files you need to edit to create working programs. What you'll quickly realize is that most program functionality comes from editing an interface file (called a *storyboard*) or a Swift (.swift) file that contains the code to make the interface work. You'll also learn that when you make changes to one of these two files you often need to make changes to the other.

Xcode simplifies this back-and-forth editing with the assistant editor mode. The assistant editor (or called just *assistant* in Apple documentation) automatically looks at the file you have opened for editing and opens, right beside it (or under it, if you prefer), the related file that you also need to work on, as shown in Figure 2.17.

Standard Editor ⌐ ⌐ Assistant Editor

Close Assistant
Add Assistant

FIGURE 2.17
The assistant editor opens related files to the right of the file you are working on.

To switch between standard and assistant editor modes, you use the first and second buttons, respectively, in the Editor section of the Xcode toolbar.

NOTE

In the upper-right corner of the assistant editor's jump bar, notice a + icon and an X icon. The + icon adds *another* assistant editor to your screen; the X icon closes the current assistant editor.

Use the View, Assistant Editor menu to choose how the editor is added to the display and what will happen if multiple assistant editors are in use.

Activating Tabbed Editing

Tabbed editing is just like tabbed browsing in your favorite web browser. Using tabbed editing, you can have many files open simultaneously and switch between them by clicking tabs at the top of the editor area.

To create a new tab, choose File, New, Tab (Command-T). A new tab appears with the contents of the file you are currently editing. You can switch the contents of the tab to whatever you want by clicking a file in the project navigator. You can repeat this process to create as many tabs as you want, with whatever file contents you want, as shown in Figure 2.18.

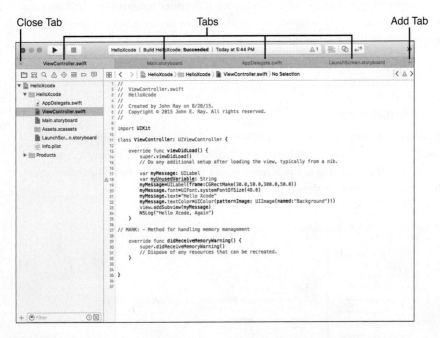

FIGURE 2.18
Keep multiple editors open simultaneously with tabs.

To close a tab, click the X that is displayed on the left side of the tab when hovering over it with your mouse. As with all files in Xcode, the files you edit in tabs are automatically saved when you close them; you do not have to explicitly use the Save command.

CAUTION

Goodbye Snapshots

Prior to Xcode 7, Apple included a feature called *Snapshots* in the Xcode editor. Snapshots made it possible to save copies of your code at any point in time, and compare (and revert to) different versions.

Unfortunately, this feature has been removed. To have access to the same functionality, you'll need to use Xcode's source control. Read the Appendix A online for an introduction to source control on Xcode. It's a shame to see snapshots go; they were a quick and easy way to use versioning without the overhead (and learning curve) of source control.

Building Applications

After you've completed your source code, it's time to build and run the application. The build process encompasses several different steps, including compiling and linking. Compiling translates the instructions you type into something that your iOS device understands. Linking combines your code with the necessary frameworks the application needs to run. During these steps, Xcode displays any errors that it might find.

Before building an application, you must first choose what it is being built to run on: the iOS Simulator or a physical iDevice.

Choosing the Build Scheme

To choose how your code will be built, use the Scheme pop-up menu at the upper left of the Xcode window. This pop-up menu is actually two separate menus in one, depending on which side you click. Click to the right side of the Scheme menu to display the possible devices that can be targeted in the build process, as shown in Figure 2.19.

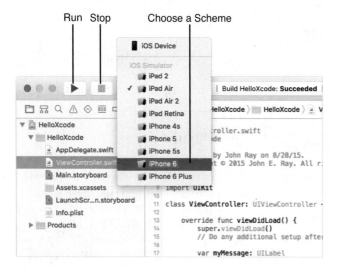

FIGURE 2.19
Change the scheme to target an iOS device or one of the variants of the iOS Simulator.

Choose between iOS Device (your physical iPhone or iPad) and the iOS Simulator devices. For most day-to-day development, you'll want to use the Simulator; it is faster than transferring an application to your device each time you make a simple change.

By default, the schemes that you use to run your application run it with a debugger. This helps identify problems in your application by allowing you to trace its execution. For applications you intend to submit to the App Store, you switch to a release configuration. You learn more about debugging in Hour 24, "Application Tracing, Monitoring, and Debugging."

Building, Analyzing, and Running the Application

To build and run the application, click the Run icon on the Xcode toolbar (Command-R) (visible in Figure 2.19). Depending on the speed of your computer, this run process might take a minute or two to complete. Once done, the application is transferred to your iOS device and started (if selected in the Scheme menu and connected) or started in the chosen iOS Simulator.

To just build without running the application (useful for checking for errors), choose Build (Command-B) from the Product menu. Better yet, you can choose Product, Analyze (Command-Shift-B) to locate build errors and identify potential issues with your application logic that wouldn't stop the code from building but might crash your program.

TIP

Quite a few intermediate files are generated during the build process. These take up space and aren't needed for the project itself. To clean out these files, choose Clean from the Product menu.

Figure 2.20 shows the HelloXcode application running in the iOS Simulator. Try clicking the run icon on the Xcode toolbar to build and start your version of the application now.

If you've been following along, your application should... *not work*. There are two problems with the code you were asked to type in earlier. Let's see what they are.

Correcting Errors and Warnings in the Issue Navigator

You can receive three general types of feedback from Xcode when you build and analyze an application: errors, warnings, and logic problems. Warnings are potential problems that may cause your application to misbehave and are indicated by a yellow caution sign. Errors, however, are complete showstoppers. You can't run your application if you have an error. The symbol for an error, appropriately enough, is a red stop sign. Logic problems, found by the Xcode analyze process, are shown as a blue badge. All of these bugs, across all of your files, are consolidated in the issue navigator, shown in Figure 2.21. The issue navigator displays automatically if problems are found during a build or analyze process. You may also open it directly by clicking the exclamation point icon on the toolbar above the navigator area.

FIGURE 2.20
The iOS Simulator is a quick and easy way to test your code.

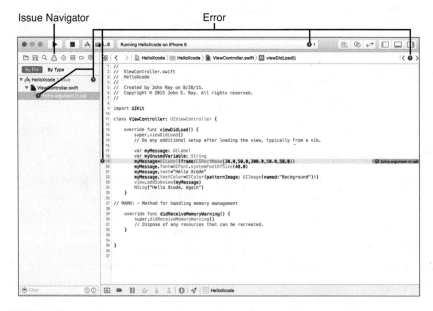

FIGURE 2.21
Use the issue navigator to find and correct problems in your code.

To jump to an error in your code, just click it in the issue navigator. The corresponding code is opened, and the error message is visible directly after the line that caused the problem.

TIP

If you are in the middle of editing a file that contains errors and you attempt to build, run, or analyze the code, you'll see the errors immediately displayed onscreen; there's no need to jump back and forth to the issue navigator. You can also quickly cycle through your errors using the forward and backward arrows found at the rightmost side of the window, directly above the editor. These controls are visible only if there are errors, however.

When you first try to build the HelloXcode, you will encounter an error: "Extra argument in call!" (shown in Figure 2.21). The reason for this is that the function `CGRectMake` takes four numbers and uses them to make a rectangle for the label—we've typed in five numbers. Delete the fifth number and preceding comma from the `CGRectMake` function. Almost immediately after you fix the error, the issue navigator updates to show a new warning, as shown in Figure 2.22.

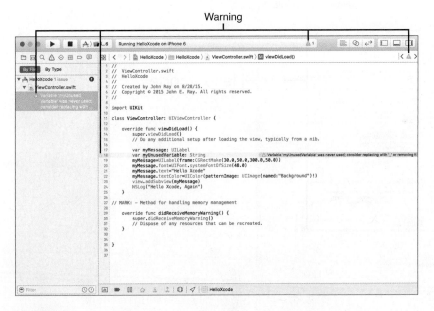

FIGURE 2.22
Some errors and warnings are detected only after you've solved another.

TIP

If you've surmised that the numbers used by CGRectMake are for positioning, you might want to try changing them to see how they control where text is displayed on your iDevice's screen. The first two values represent the distance over and down on the display that the label is positioned; the third and fourth values are the width and height of the label.

The second warning points out that we have a variable, myUnusedVariable, in the code. Remember, this is just a helpful warning, not necessarily a problem. If we choose to remove the variable, the message goes away; but even if we don't, the application will still run. Go ahead and delete the line that reads var myUnusedVariable: String in ViewController.swift. This fixes the warning, and the issue navigator is empty. We're ready to run.

Click the Run icon. HelloXcode should now start in the iOS Simulator. You'll also notice that the debugger area in Xcode appears and displays the message "Hello Xcode (again)", as shown in Figure 2.23. This is produced by the NSLog command and demonstrates where output not related to your iPhone application's onscreen display is shown.

HelloXcode Output

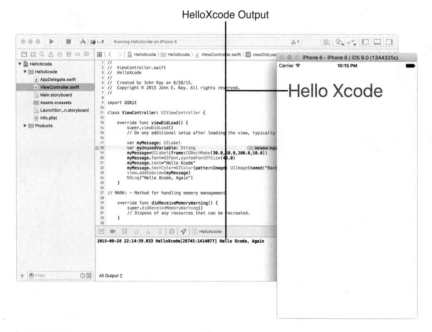

FIGURE 2.23
The HelloXcode application (finally) runs and displays output on both the iPhone screen and in the Xcode debugger area.

NOTE

The first time you run the iOS Simulator, you may receive a message asking whether developer mode should be enabled on your Mac. Enabling developer mode allows the Simulator to run seamlessly with Xcode and forego prompting you for a password each time it starts.

CAUTION

Fix Your Bugs to Find Your Bugs!

As you've discovered in this exercise, sometimes not all errors are detected and displayed in the issue navigator. After fixing a line or two, you might find that new, previously undetected errors appear. Conversely, you'll also sometimes see false errors that disappear when you correct other errors.

Managing Project Properties

Before finishing our brief tour of the Xcode interface, quickly turn your attention to something a bit different: the properties that describe a project itself. An application's icons, launch screen, supported device orientations, and so on need to be set somewhere, so where is that? The answer is the project plist file.

This file, found in a project's main code folder, is created automatically when you start a new project and is named Info.plist. Although you can edit the values directly in the plist file, Xcode provides an easier approach. Let's take a look at how it works.

Switch to the project navigator and click the top-level project icon for HelloXcode (the blue paper icon), and make sure that the application icon under Targets in the column to the right is highlighted. The editor area refreshes to display several tabs across the top, shown in Figure 2.24.

The first, General, allows you to set many of the project's general attributes (version, supported devices, and so on). The second, Capabilities, gives you on/off switches to activate certain iOS application features, such as iCloud, Game Center, and Backgrounding (running in the background). Changing the settings in these two tabs is actually altering settings in your project's plist.

The fourth tab (and the last mentioned for now), Info, provides direct access to the plist file itself. As you make changes in the first two tabs, you'll see them appear in the Info tab. Yes, I skipped the third tab (Resource Tags); it is for creating groups of application resources that can be downloaded as needed from Apple's servers (not something we're going to need anytime soon).

Project Group   Project Properties

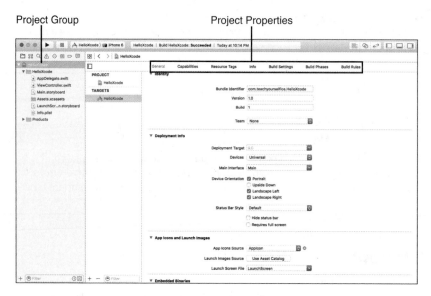

FIGURE 2.24
Project properties control a few important settings for your application.

Setting Supported Device Orientations

As I'm sure you're well aware, not all applications support all device orientations (portrait, landscape right, landscape left, upside down). To denote which device orientations your app will support, you can edit the Deployment Info section within the General area. Scroll down through the different sections until you see the Deployment Info section. Use the disclosure arrow to expand the section if needed.

Near the middle of the Deployment Info, you'll find settings for Supported Device Orientations. To set the orientations you plan to use, just click the corresponding check boxes beside Portrait, Upside Down, Landscape Left, and Landscape Right, as shown in Figure 2.25. To remove support for an orientation, uncheck the check box. Simple!

CAUTION

It's Not Quite That Simple

Unfortunately, just setting a device orientation doesn't magically make your application work correctly in that orientation. It just signals your intent to make it work. You'll still have to code for device rotation, which you learn about in Hour 16, "Building Responsive User Interfaces."

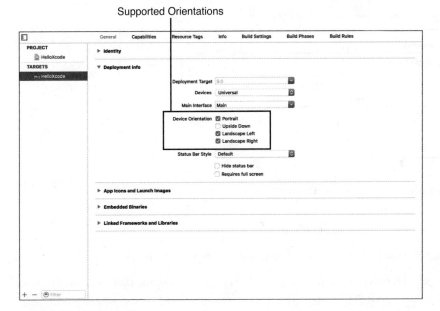

FIGURE 2.25
Choose the orientations your app will support.

Application Icons, Launch Images, and Launch Screens

Next up are app icons, launch images, and launch screens. App icons are the icon files used to represent your application on the iOS home screen. Launch images are essentially static "splash screens" that display as the application launches. An alternative to launch images is launch screens. Launch screens are iOS interface files that can be used to visually design a splash screen using graphics, text, and the Interface Builder tools, which you'll learn about in Hour 5.

These small but important resources for your application are found under the App Icons and Launch Images section within the General config, as shown in Figure 2.26.

Looking at these settings, I imagine most people are wondering what in the world they mean. Apple has changed how you configure icons and launch images almost every single year. To clear things, up, let's take a look at each.

Setting an Application Icon

First up are application icons. As you can see in Figure 2.26, the source for application icons is AppIcon; this refers to the asset catalog. In other words, the icons are just images that we drag into Assets.xcassets.

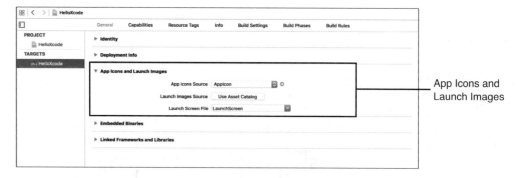

FIGURE 2.26
The source for app icons, launch images, and launch screens in Xcode. What?!

To set an icon, for example, follow these steps:

1. Open the asset catalog by clicking the Assets.xcassets item in the project navigator.

2. Select the AppIcon entry in the Asset Catalog list on the left. On the right, Xcode refreshes the display to show placeholder spots for the different icon files you can add to your project.

3. Drag from a properly sized PNG file in the Finder into the dotted lines around the placeholder (known as an *image well*), as shown in Figure 2.27. Xcode copies the icon into the asset catalog and names it properly.

By default, there are three types of icons you'll want to consider adding: Settings, Spotlight, and the App icon (spread across multiple versions of the OS).

The Settings icon is what is displayed in the iOS Settings application (if your application offers settings), the Spotlight icon is displayed in iOS Spotlight search results, and the App icon is what your users will see front and center on their iDevice screen. In this book, we are worrying only about App icons; once you know how to set those, everything else should be easy.

Now, you might be wondering what a "properly sized PNG file" is. Apple has been kind enough to provide the sizes of icons in *points* underneath each placeholder. On non-Retina displays, a point is a pixel, but Apple also requires Retina graphics, which have twice the width and height as non-Retina on most devices, but *three* times the width and height on the iPhone 6+/6s+. To determine the pixel size for an icon, look at the label under the placeholder in the asset catalog and note what the multiplier is (currently 1x, 2x, or 3x). You will multiply the point size by *that* number to get the number of pixels (height and width) for each icon. There are no "non-Retina" iPhones anymore, so all the image wells will always read 2x and 3x. On iPad projects, you'll see 1x under some of the image wells because Apple still supports non-Retina iPads.

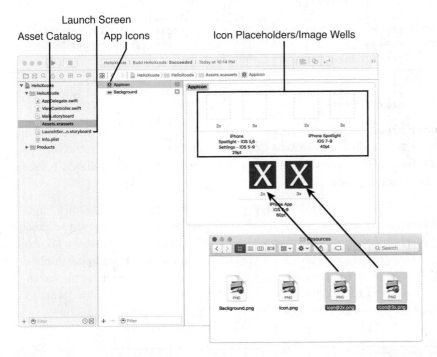

FIGURE 2.27
The asset catalog contains placeholders for all your application icons.

Why Oh Why Is This So Confusing?

For the time being, just know that Apple requires Retina image files for all applications. (You need to drag images that are 2x the point size into the 2x wells and 3x images into the 3x wells.) Apple may release devices with even higher resolutions in the future, which would cause the multiplier to go up (4x or 5x, for example).

The idea is that a *point* will represent roughly the same size *dot* on the screen on *any* iOS device. On a non-Retina display, a 10-by-10-pixel image would have the same size as a 20-by-20-pixel image on a Retina display, or a 30-by-30 pixel on an iPhone 6+ display.

Still not making sense? No worries. When it matters throughout this book, we'll let you know what to do.

You'll notice icon files in the archive you downloaded for this book. iPhone icon files are named Icon@2x.png and Icon@3x.png. iPad files are named Icon-iPad.png and Icon-iPad@2x.png.

TIP

The icons you create do not need to have rounded corners; iOS automatically styles them for you. To learn more about icon sizes and design standards for iOS, I recommend reading the *iOS Design Cheat Sheet*, by Ivo Mynttinen: http://iosdesign.ivomynttinen.com.

Setting a Launch Image/Screen

Next up are launch images (or launch screens). Referring back to Figure 2.26, notice that beside the Launch Images Source label is a Use Asset Catalog button. If you click this button (don't do it!), Xcode adds a LaunchImage entry into the asset catalog that you can fill with splash screens in *exactly* the same manner as you did the icons.

In new Xcode releases (version 6 and later), however, the preferred approach is to use a launch screen, because it can easily adapt to multiple devices without requiring different sizes of images to be added for every single supported device. By default, every new project includes a launch screen file named LaunchScreen.storyboard. Clicking this file in the project navigator displays the Interface Builder editor, demonstrated in Figure 2.28, where you can customize the screen using any of the iOS interface tools. The default launch screen is just white; so, you'll want to make it a bit more interesting for your apps.

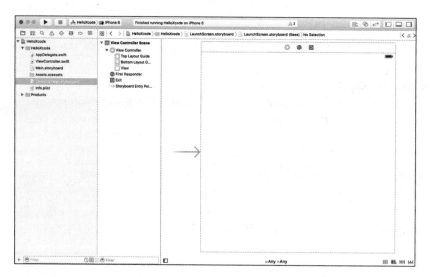

FIGURE 2.28
You'll create your launch screens using the Interface Builder tools.

Creating launch images is left as an exercise for you, the reader. I recommend revisiting the LaunchScreen.storyboard file after working through Hour 5.

CAUTION

Just for Looks

The property settings covered here are the ones that relate to how your app looks on an iDevice and in the Simulator. You'll also learn other settings throughout this book that govern how the application runs.

That's it for Xcode! There's plenty more that you'll find as you work with the software, but these should be the foundational skills you need to develop apps for iOS. Let's round out this hour by looking at the next best thing to your phone: the iOS Simulator.

NOTE

Note that although it isn't covered here, Xcode includes a wonderful documentation system. You learn more about this as you start to get your feet wet with the Cocoa framework in Hour 4.

Using the iOS Simulator

In Hour 1, you learned that you don't even need an iOS device to start developing for the platform. The reason for this is the iOS Simulator is included with Xcode. The Simulator does a great job of simulating the Apple iPhone and iPad, with the Safari, Photos, Contacts, Settings, Game Center, Calendar, Maps, News, Reminders, Health, Watch, and Wallet apps available for integration testing, as shown in Figure 2.29.

Targeting the Simulator for the early stages of your development can save you a great deal of time; you won't need to wait for apps to be installed on your physical device before seeing the effects of changes in your code. In addition, you don't need to buy and install a developer certificate to run code in the Simulator.

The Simulator, however, is not a perfect iDevice. It can't simulate complex multitouch events or provide real readings from some sensors (gyroscope, accelerometer, and so on). The closest it comes on these counts is the ability to rotate to test landscape interfaces and a simple "shake" motion simulation. That said, for most apps, it has enough features to be a valuable part of your development process.

CAUTION

A Fast Mac Doesn't Equal a Fast iPhone!

One thing that you absolutely *cannot* count on in the Simulator is that your simulated app performance will resemble your real app performance. The Simulator tends to run silky smooth, whereas real apps might have more limited resources and not behave as nicely. Be sure to occasionally test on a physical device so that you know your expectations are in line with reality.

FIGURE 2.29
The iOS Simulator includes a stripped-down version of Apple's standard iOS apps.

Launching Applications

To launch an application in the Simulator, open the project in Xcode, make sure that the scheme is set to the iOS device of your choosing (iPad Air, iPhone 6, iPhone 6+, and so on), and then click Run. After a few seconds, the Simulator launches, and the application loads. You can test this using the HelloSimulator project included in this hour's Projects folder.

Once up and running, the HelloSimulator app, shown here on the iPad Simulator, displays a simple line of text and a random image fetched from a website (see Figure 2.30).

When an application is running, you can interact with it using your mouse as if it were your fingertip. Click buttons, drag sliders, and so on. If you click into a field where input is expected, the onscreen keyboard displays. You can "type" using your physical keyboard or by clicking the onscreen keyboard's buttons. The iOS copy and paste services are also simulated by clicking and holding on text until the familiar loupe magnifier appears.

Click the Stop button on the Xcode toolbar to exit the app. Choosing Hardware, Home from the menu also exits the application, but Xcode itself may continue to think it's running and get "out of sync."

FIGURE 2.30
Click the Run button in Xcode to launch and run your application in the Simulator.

NOTE

Launching an application in the Simulator installs it in the Simulator, just like installing an app on a real device. When you exit the app, it is still present on the Simulator until you manually delete it.

To remove an installed application from the Simulator, click and hold the icon until it starts "wiggling," and then click the X that appears in the upper-left corner. In other words, remove apps from the Simulator in the same way you would remove them from a physical device.

To quickly reset the Simulator back to a clean slate, choose Reset Content and Settings from the iOS Simulator menu.

TIP

At any time, you can switch your simulated hardware to a different simulated device by making a selection from the Hardware, Device menu.

Generating Multitouch Events

Even though you have only a single mouse, you can simulate simple multitouch events, such as two-finger pulls and pinches, by holding down Option when your cursor is over the Simulator "screen." Two circles, representing fingertips, are drawn and can be controlled with the mouse. To simulate a touch event, click and drag while continuing to hold down Option. Figure 2.31 shows the "pinch" gesture.

FIGURE 2.31
Simulate simple multitouch with the Option key.

Try this using the HelloSimulator app. You should be able to use the Simulator's multitouch capabilities to shrink or expand the onscreen text and image.

TIP
_____
To move the simulated multitouch fingertips around in the Simulator (so that you can "pinch" near the top of bottom of the screen, for example), hold down Shift while dragging them. As long as you keep Shift pressed down, you can reposition the fingertips anywhere you want.
_____

Rotating the Simulated Device

To simulate a rotation on your virtual device, choose Rotate Right or Rotate Left from the Hardware menu (see Figure 2.32). You can use this to rotate the Simulator window through all four possible orientations and view the results onscreen.

Again, test this with HelloSimulator. The app will react to the rotation events, orient the text properly, and fetch a new image with each rotation.

FIGURE 2.32
Rotate the interface through the possible orientations.

Testing Other Conditions

You want to test against a few other esoteric conditions in the Simulator. Using the Hardware menu, you can access these additional features:

▶ **Device:** Chooses a different iOS device to emulate.

▶ **Shake Gesture:** Simulates a quick shake of the device.

▶ **Home:** Presses the Home button.

▶ **Lock:** Simulates the condition of a locked device. Because a user can lock an iPhone or iPad while an application is running, some developers choose to have their programs react uniquely to this situation.

▶ **Reboot:** Restarts the simulated iOS device

▶ **Touch ID Enrolled/Simulate Finger Touch:** Enables/disables a Touch ID device and simulates a valid or invalid touch on the Touch ID sensor.

▶ **Simulate Memory Warning:** Triggers an application's low-memory event. Useful for testing to make sure your application exits gracefully if resources run low.

▶ **Toggle In-Call Status Bar:** When a call is active and an application is started, an additional line appears at the top of the screen. (Touch to return to call.) This option simulates that line.

▶ **Simulate Hardware Keyboard:** Simulates a connected keyboard. (Just use your physical keyboard.)

▶ **TV Out:** Displays a window that will show the contents of the device's TV out signal. We do not use this feature in this book.

Test the rotation, shake, or low memory conditions on the HelloSimulator application. Figure 2.33 shows the application's reaction to a simulated shake gesture.

FIGURE 2.33
The iOS Simulator can test for application handling under several unique conditions.

CAUTION

Recover from iOS Application Crashes

If something goes wrong in your application and it crashes while running in the iOS Simulator, Xcode changes its view to show the debugger. To recover from this, use the Xcode toolbar's Stop button to exit the application; then hide the debugger and check your work. You learn how to use the debugger to find crashing bugs in Hour 24.

Adding Additional Simulated Devices

By default, Xcode displays only the current shipping Apple iOS devices as possible simulation options (visible in the Xcode Scheme menu, and the Devices menu in the Simulator). To add additional devices, choose Hardware, Device, Manage Devices from the Simulator's menu, as shown in Figure 2.34. Alternatively, if you're in Xcode, you can get there from the Window, Devices menu item.

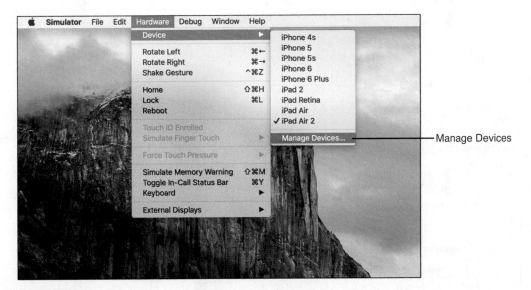

FIGURE 2.34
Choose Manage Devices from the Hardware, Device iOS Simulator menu.

The Devices window that appears, listing the available Simulator hardware (and iOS versions), demonstrated in Figure 2.35.

To remove devices, click to select them, then press delete. To add a new device, click the + button in the lower-left corner. Xcode displays the new Simulator dialog, visible in Figure 2.36.

Available Devices

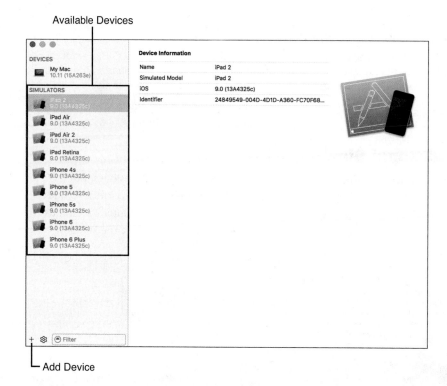

Add Device

FIGURE 2.35
The iOS Simulator device options are listed on the left.

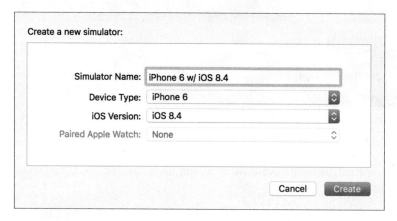

FIGURE 2.36
Configure the new Simulator.

Enter a name for the Simulator, choose a device type, and an iOS version, and then click Create. The new Simulator option will be immediately listed in both Xcode and the iOS Simulator.

Further Exploration

You're not quite at the stage yet where I can ask you to go off and read some code-related tutorials, but if you're interested, you might want to take some time to look into more of the features offered in Xcode. This introduction was limited to roughly a dozen pages, but entire volumes can be (and have been) written about this unique tool. Anything else you need is covered in the lessons in this book, but you should still review Apple's Xcode Overview. You can find this document by choosing Help, Xcode Overview from the menu while in the Xcode application.

Summary

This hour introduced you to the Xcode development environment and the core set of tools that you'll be using to create your applications. You learned how to create projects using Apple's iOS templates and how to supplement those templates with new files and resources. You also explored the editing and navigation capabilities of Xcode that you'll come to depend on every day. To illustrate the concepts, you wrote and built your first iOS application, and even corrected a few errors that were intentionally added to try to trip you up.

This hour finished with a walkthrough on the use of the iOS Simulator. This tool will save wear and tear on your device (and your patience) as it provides a quick and easy way to test code without having to install applications on a physical device.

Q&A

Q. What is Interface Builder, and how does it fit in?

A. IB is a very important component of Xcode that gets its own lesson in Hour 5. As the name implies, Interface Builder is mostly used for creating the UI for your applications.

Q. Do I have to worry about constantly saving if I'm switching between files and making lots of changes in Xcode?

A. If you switch between files in the Xcode Editor, you won't lose your changes. Xcode even saves your files for you if you close the application.

Q. I noticed that there are OS X templates that I can access when creating a project. Can I create an OS X application?

A. Yes, but.... All the coding skills you learn in this book can be transferred to OS X development. iOS devices, however, have a different user experience than the Mac, so you need to learn the Mac model for windowing, UI, and so on.

Q. Can I run commercial applications on the iOS Simulator?

A. You can only run apps that you have built within Xcode.

Workshop

Quiz

1. When creating new projects, you'll choose what programming language?

   a. Swift

   b. Objective-C

   c. Object Swift

   d. C#

2. What tool will you eventually use to create user interfaces?

   a. UI Builder

   b. iOS Simulator

   c. Interface Builder

   d. Swift User Tool

3. What type of coding problem will show up in Xcode, but still allow your application to run?

   a. Error

   b. Failure

   c. Warning

   d. Notice

4. If you want to add a notice to your code to fix an error, which of the following might you use?

   a. FIXME mark

   b. ERROR mark

   c. BUG mark

   d. METHOD mark

5. Which Xcode editor feature provides information about the methods you're using, as you type them?

   a. Genius Tool

   b. Reference Library

   c. Code Master

   d. Autocompletion

6. Errors in code are shown with what symbol?

   a. Stop sign

   b. Exclamation point

   c. An X

   d. A red underline

7. The file that contains many of the configuration details for your application is called what?

   a. Info.plist

   b. Config.xml

   c. Settings.cfg

   d. Xcode.ini

8. If my domain is johnray.poisontooth.com, what is my usual Xcode project organization identifier?

   a. johnray.poisontooth.com

   b. johnray.com.poisontooth

   c. com.poisontooth.johnray

   d. com.poisontooth

9. In which of the following can you find all of the errors in your code listed?

   a. Issue navigator

   b. Project navigator

   c. Debugger

   d. Symbol n navigator

10. What is the name of the entry in the asset catalog for your application's icon?

    a. ApplicationIcon

    b. AppIcon

    c. Icon

    d. PlistIcon

Answers

1. A. Swift is Apple's new language for iOS development and is used in all projects in this book.

2. C. Interface Builder is part of the Xcode suite of tools and is used to create your app's user interface.

3. C. Warnings display in Xcode, but don't prevent your code from executing.

4. A. The `FIXME` mark can be used to add a reference in your code to remind you to fix a bug or other issue.

5. D. Xcode's autocompletion function helps you write code without knowing the exact syntax of the methods you're using.

6. A. If you see a stop sign in your code, it indicates an error that must be corrected.

7. A. The Info.plist file stores many of the settings that determine how your application will work, such as supported orientations.

8. C. In most cases, you'd use the domain in reverse order, so com.poisontooth.johnray.

9. A. The issue navigator lets you view all errors and warnings in a single location.

10. B. The AppIcon entry is where you should add 1x, 2x, and 3x versions of your application's icon.

Activities

1. Begin creating projects and navigating the Xcode editor. Try out some of the common editor features that were not covered in this lesson, such as Find and Replace. Test the use of *marks* for creating helpful jump-to points within your source code.

2. Go to the Apple iOS dev center and download a sample application. Using the techniques described in this hour's lesson, build and test the application in the iOS Simulator or on your device.

HOUR 3
Discovering Swift and the iOS Playground

What You'll Learn in This Hour:

▶ How Swift will be used in your projects
▶ The basics of object-oriented programming
▶ Simple Swift syntax
▶ Common Swift data types
▶ How to test your code in the iOS Playground

This hour's lesson marks the midpoint in our exploration of the Apple iOS development platform. It gives us a chance to sit back, catch our breath, and get a better idea of what it means to "code" for iOS. Both OS X and iOS share a common development environment and a common development language: Swift.

Swift provides the syntax and structure for creating applications on Apple platforms. Swift is a new language developed internally in Apple that still has that "new language smell," but also a few disconcerting knocks under the hood. It can seem a bit daunting at first, but after a few hours of practice, you'll feel right at home. This hour takes you through the steps you need to know to be comfortable with Swift and starts you down the path to mastering this unique and powerful language.

Object-Oriented Programming and Swift

To better understand the scope of this hour, take a few minutes to search for Swift or object-oriented programming in your favorite online bookstore. You will find quite a few books—lengthy books—on these topics. In this book, roughly 30 pages cover what other books teach in hundreds of pages. Although it's not possible to fully cover Swift and object-oriented development in this single hour, we can make sure that you understand enough to develop fairly complex apps.

To provide you with the information you need to be successful in iOS development, this hour concentrates on fundamentals—the core concepts that are used repeatedly throughout the examples and tutorials in this book. The approach in this hour is to introduce you to a pro-gramming topic in general terms, and then look at how it will be performed when you sit down to write your application. Before we begin, let's look a bit closer at Swift and object-oriented programming.

What Is Object-Oriented Programming?

Most people have an idea of what programming is and have even written a simple program. Everything from setting your DVR to record a show to configuring a cooking cycle for your micro-wave is a type of programming. You use data (such as times) and instructions (like "record") to tell your devices to complete a specific task. This certainly is a long way from developing for iOS, but in a way the biggest difference is in the amount of data you can provide and manipulate and the number of different instructions available to you.

Imperative Development

There are two primary development paradigms: imperative programming and object-oriented programming. First, imperative programming (a subset of which is called *procedural program-ming*) implements a sequence of commands that should be performed. The application follows the sequence and carries out activities as directed. Although there might be branches in the sequence or movement back and forth between some of the steps, the flow is from a starting con-dition to an ending condition, with all the logic to make things *work* sitting in the middle.

The problem with imperative programming is that it lends itself to growing, without structure, into an amorphous blob. Applications gain features when developers tack on bits of code here and there. Often, instructions that implement a piece of functionality are repeated over and over wherever something needs to take place. Procedural programming refers to an imperative programming structure that attempts to avoid repetition by creating functions (or procedures) that can be reused. This works to some extent, but long-term still often results in code bloat. The benefit of this approach, however, is that it is quite easy to pick up and learn: You create a series of instructions, and the computer follows them.

The Object-Oriented Approach

The other development approach, and what we use in this book, is object-oriented programming (OOP). OOP uses the same types of instructions as imperative development but structures them in a way that makes your applications easy to maintain and promotes code reuse whenever possible. In OOP, you create objects that hold the data that describes something along with the instructions to manipulate that data. Perhaps an example is in order.

Consider a program that enables you to track reminders. With each reminder, you want to store information about the event that will be taking place—a name, a time to sound an alarm, a location, and any additional miscellaneous notes that you may want to store. In addition, you need to be able to reschedule a reminder's alarm time or completely cancel an alarm.

In the imperative approach, you have to write the steps necessary to track all the reminders, all the data in the reminders, check every reminder to see whether an alarm should sound, and so on. It's certainly possible, but just trying to wrap your mind around everything that the application needs to do could cause some serious headaches. An object-oriented approach brings some sanity to the situation.

In an object-oriented model, you could implement a reminder as a single object. The reminder object would know how to store the properties such as the name, location, and so on. It would implement just enough functionality to sound its own alarm and reschedule or cancel its alarm. Writing the code, in fact, would be very similar to writing an imperative program that only has to manage a single reminder. By encapsulating this functionality into an object, however, we can then create multiple copies of the object within an application and have them each fully capable of handling separate reminders. No fuss and no messy code!

Most of the tutorials in this book make use of one or two objects, so don't worry about being overwhelmed with OOP. You'll see enough to get accustomed to the idea, but we're not going to go overboard.

Another important facet of OOP is inheritance. Suppose that you want to create a special type of reminder for birthdays that includes a list of birthday presents that a person has requested. Instead of tacking this onto the reminder object, you could create an entirely new "birthday reminder" that inherits all the features and properties of a reminder and then adds in the list of presents and anything else specific to birthdays.

The Terminology of Object-Oriented Development

OOP brings with it a whole range of terminology that you need to get accustomed to seeing in this book (and in Apple's documentation). The more familiar you are with these terms, the easier it will be to look for solutions to problems and interact with other developers. Let's establish some basic vocabulary now:

- **Class:** The code, usually consisting of a single Swift file, which defines an object and what it can do.

- **Subclass:** A class that builds upon another class, adding additional features. Almost everything you use in iOS development will be a subclass of something else, inheriting all the properties and capabilities of its parent class.

- **Superclass/parent class:** The class that another class inherits from.

▶ **Singleton:** A class that is instantiated only once during the lifetime of a program. For example, a class to read your device's orientation is implemented as a singleton because there is only one sensor that returns this information.

▶ **Object/instance:** A class that has been invoked and is active in your code. Classes are the code that makes an object work, whereas an object is the actual class "in action." This is also known as an *instance* of a class.

▶ **Instantiation:** The process of creating an active object from a class.

▶ **Instance method:** A basic piece of functionality, implemented in a class. For the reminder class, this might be something like `setAlarm` to set the alarm for a given reminder. Methods are, by default, available within the class they are defined and within other classes defined in the same project.

▶ **Extensions:** Provide a means of extending a class without modifying the class code itself.

▶ **Type method:** Similar to an instance method, but applicable to all the objects created from a class. The reminder class, for example, might implement a type method called `countReminders` that provides a count of all the reminder objects that have been created. If you're familiar with other OO languages, you may recognize this as a *static method* or a *class method*.

▶ **Variable property:** A storage place for a piece of information specific to a class. The name of a reminder, for example, might be stored in a variable property. All variables have a specific "type" that describes the contents of what they will be holding. Variable properties only differ from normal variables in where they are defined and where they can be accessed.

▶ **Variable:** A storage location for a piece of information. Unlike variable properties, a "normal" variable is accessible only in the method where it is defined.

▶ **Constant:** A Swift constant is another type of variable, but one that cannot be modified after it has been declared.

▶ **Parameter:** A piece of information that is provided to a method when it is use. If you were to use a `setAlarm` method, you would presumably need to include the time to set. The time, in this case, would be a parameter.

▶ **Protocol:** Protocols declare methods that can be implemented by a class—usually to provide functionality needed for an object. A class that implements a protocol is said to conform to that protocol. This is similar to a Java interface.

▶ **Self:** A way to refer to an object within its own methods. When an instance method or variable property is used in an application, it should be used with a specific object. If you're writing code within a class and you want it to access one of its own methods or variable properties, you *can* `self` to refer to the object. In Swift, `self` is usually implied and only needs to be used explicitly in very specific circumstances.

It's important to know that when you develop for iOS you're going to be taking advantage of hundreds of classes that Apple has already written for you. Everything from creating onscreen buttons to manipulating dates and writing files is covered by prebuilt classes. You'll occasionally want to customize some of the functionality in those classes, but you'll be starting out with a toolbar already overflowing with functionality.

Confused? Don't worry! This book introduces these concepts slowly, and you'll quickly get a feel for how they apply to your projects as you work through several tutorials in the upcoming hours.

What Is Swift?

For years, Apple development has centered on a decades-old language called Objective-C. Objective-C, while appealing to some, was about as far from a "modern" language as you could get. Languages like Python and Ruby have sprung up and attracted legions of followers with their simple syntax and focus on results, rather then esoteric concepts like memory management. Swift is Apple's answer to the call for a modern iOS and OS X development language.

Released in 2014, Swift carries with it many of the niceties of Objective-C, but loses much of the baggage. The biggest issue with Swift is that it is still evolving, and developers (including yours truly) are still trying to figure out the best way to use it. It will be several years before this churn settles down—but, in the meantime, the core of Swift is fast, flexible, and easy to learn.

Swift statements are easier to read than other programming languages and can often be deciphered just by looking at them. For example, code that checks to see if two dates are equal might be written like this:

```
if myBirthday.isEqualToDate(yourBirthday) {
    // We're the same age!
}
```

It doesn't take a very large mental leap to see what is going on in the code snippet. Throughout the book, I will try to `explain` what each line of code is doing—but chances are you can pick up on the intention just by reading the lines.

CAUTION

Case Counts

Swift is case sensitive. If a program is failing, make sure that you aren't mixing case somewhere in the code.

Now that you have an idea of what OOP and Swift are, let's take a look at how you'll be using them over the course of this book.

Exploring the Swift File Structure

In the preceding hour, you learned how to use Xcode to create projects and navigate their files. As mentioned then, the vast majority of your time will be spent in the project group of Xcode, which is shown for the MyNewApp project in Figure 3.1. You'll be adding methods to class files that Xcode creates for you when you start a project or, occasionally, creating your own class files to implement entirely new functionality in your application.

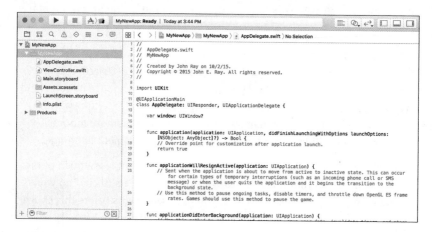

FIGURE 3.1
Most of your coding will occur within the files in your project group.

Okay, sounds simple enough, but where will the coding take place? If you create a new project look, you'll see quite a few different files staring back at you.

Class Files

In Swift, a class is implemented within a single file with the .swift extension. This file contains all of the variable/constant definitions, and all of the methods containing the application logic. Other classes in your project will automatically be able to access the methods in this file, if needed.

Let's review the structure of an entirely made-up class file in Listing 3.1.

LISTING 3.1 A Sample Swift Class File

```
1: import UIKit
2:
3: class myClass: myParent, myProtocol {
4:
5:     var myString: String = ""
6:     var myOtherString: String?
7:     var yetAnotherVariable: Float!
8:     let myAge: Int = 29
9:
10:     @IBOutlet weak var userOutput: UILabel!
11:     @IBOutlet var anotherUserOutput: UILabel!
12:
13:     class func myTypeMethod(aString: String) -> String {
14:         // Implement a Type method here
15:     }
16:
17:     func myInstanceMethod(myString: String, myURL: NSURL) -> NSDate? {
18:         // Implement the Instance method here
19:     }
20:
21:     override func myOverriddenInstanceMethod() {
22:         // Override the parent's method here
23:     }
24:
25:     @IBAction func myActionMethod(sender: AnyObject) {
26:         // React to an action in the user interface
27:     }
28:
29: }
```

CAUTION

Line Numbers Are for Reference Only!

In each hour, I present code samples like this one. Often, they include line numbers so that I can easily reference the code and explain how it works. Swift does not require line numbers, nor will the code work if you leave them in your application. If you see a line prefixed with a number and a colon (#:), don't type the line number prefix!

The import Declaration

```
1: import UIKit
```

First, in line 1, the interface file uses the import declaration to include any other files that our application will need to access. The string UIKit designates a system framework that gives us access to a vast majority of the classes.

Whenever we need to import something, I explain how and why in the text. The UIKit example is included by default when Xcode sets up your classes and covers most of what you need for this book's examples.

NOTE

Wait a sec, what's a declaration? *Declarations* are commands that are added to your files that introduce a new object or feature within the application. They don't implement the logic that makes your app work, but they are necessary for providing information on how your applications are structured so that Xcode knows how to deal with them.

The `class` Declaration

The class declaration, shown in line 3, tells Xcode what class the file is going to be implementing. In this case, the file should contain the code to implement `myClass`:

```
3: class myClass: myParent, myProtocol {
```

Notice that line 3 includes a few additional items as well: that is, `myParent, myProtocol`. The class name (`myClass`) is always followed by a colon (`:`) and a list of the classes that this class is inheriting from (that is, the *parent classes*) and any *protocols* it will be implementing. In this example, `myClass` is going to by inheriting from `myParent` and will be implementing the `myProtocol` protocol.

The `class` line ends with an opening curly brace `{`. All blocks of code are contained in curly braces. The rest of the class code will follow this brace and eventually by terminated with a closing brace `}` (line 29).

NOTE

Protocol? What's a protocol? Protocols are a feature of Swift that sound complicated but really aren't. Sometimes you will come across features that require you to write methods to support their use, such as providing a list of items to be displayed in a table. The methods that you need to write are grouped together under a common name; this is known as a *protocol*.

Some protocol methods are required, and others are optional; it just depends on the features you need. A class that implements a protocol is said to *conform* to that protocol.

Variable Property Declarations

Lines 5–6 declare three different variable properties. A variable property is just a variable that can be accessed from any method in the class, or from code within other classes.

```
5:     var myString: String = ""
6:     var myOtherString: String?
7:     var yetAnotherVariable: Float!
```

In this example, a variable named `myString` that contains a `String` is declared and initialized with an empty string (`""`). A second `String` (`myOtherString`) is also declared, but designated as "optional" with the `?` modifier. A third variable property, `yetAnotherVariable`, is declared as a floating-point number and set to be "implicitly unwrapped" by including the `!` modifier. We'll get to the point of these modifiers in a little bit. (They look confusing, but they have an important role to play.)

NOTE

To retrieve a variable property from an object, you write `<objectname>.<variable property>` to access it. That means that if there is a property `myProperty` in an object `myAmazingObject`, you type `myAmazingObject.myProperty`. This is known as *dot notation*.

What if you want to access the variable property from inside the class where it is defined? Simple. You just refer to it by name (for example, `myProperty`). If you want to be overly pendantic, you can also use `self` to refer to the current object, as in `self.<variable property>`.

This will all be obvious once you start coding.

Getters and Setters/Accessors and Mutators

Variables in Swift don't necessarily just store and retrieve static data. Your variables can declare their own methods that define the information that is returned or committed to memory. This is done by getters and setters (also called accessors and mutators). A "time" variable, for example, might not store the time at all, but instead declare a custom "getter" that retrieves the time from the system clock when it is accessed. We'll see this behavior a bit later in the book.

A Constant Declaration

Just below the variable properties is a constant declaration:

```
8:    let myAge: Int = 29
```

This creates a constant (`myAge`) and sets it to the integer value 29. Constants declared alongside variable properties (that is, outside of a method) are nearly identical to variable properties in how they are used—but with one important difference—they can't be changed or reassigned. In other words, I'm 29 forever.

`IBOutlet` Declarations

Lines 9–10 are, yet again, variable property declarations, but they include the keyword `IBOutlet` at the start. This indicates that they are going to be connected to objects defined within an application's user interface:

```
10:      @IBOutlet weak var userOutput: UILabel!
11:      @IBOutlet var anotherUserOutput: UILabel!
```

You learn more about IBOutlet in Hour 5, "Exploring Interface Builder."

TIP

The attribute weak that is provided with the variable declaration tells Xcode how to treat the object when it isn't in use. The weak attribute informs the system that the object it is referring to can be cleaned up from memory when it isn't being used anymore. It also avoids what is called a *circular reference*, where an object can't be removed from memory, because it points to another object that, in turn, points back to it. In general, try to declare your variables with the weak attribute.

Unfortunately, sometimes the system may be a bit overzealous in its desire to keep things clean for us, and we need to leave weak out of the picture—thus creating a strong reference. (Lines 5–7, 8, and 11 all declare strong references.) A strong reference means that the object will be kept in memory unless we explicitly tell the system to remove it or the object that contains it is removed from memory. It's pretty rare that we need to worry about these, but I'll point it out when it's a concern.

Declaring Methods

The final pieces of the class file are the method declarations. Lines 13, 17, 21, and 25 declare four methods that will be implemented in the class:

```
13:      class func myTypeMethod(aString: String) -> String {
14:          // Implement a Type method here
15:      }
16:
17:      func myInstanceMethod(myString: String, myURL: NSURL) -> NSDate? {
18:          // Implement the Instance method here
19:      }
20:
21:      override func myOverriddenInstanceMethod() {
22:          // Override the parent's method here
23:      }
24:
25:      @IBAction func myActionMethod(sender: AnyObject) {
26:          // React to an action in the user interface
27:      }
```

Method declarations follow a simple structure. They begin with the word func, but can include the prefix modifiers class and override. A method that begins with class func is a *Type* method (often also referred to as a *Class* method). A method starting with override func is one that is redefining a method already provided in a parent class. This indicates that rather than inheriting functionality from a higher class, we're going to write our own logic.

In the example file, line 13 defines a Type method named `myTypeMethod` that returns a `String` and accepts a `String` as a parameter. The input parameter is made available in a variable called `aString`.

Line 14 defines an instance method named `myInstanceMethod` that returns an *optional* `NSDate` object, taking a `String` and an `NSURL` as parameters. These are made available to the code in the method via the variables `myString` and `myURL`. I'll rant about what optional values are and how to deal with them later in the hour. For the moment, just understand that by saying this method has an optional return type, it may return an `NSDate` object, or nothing (`nil`).

Line 21 declares an instance method, `myOverriddenInstanceMethod`, that takes no parameters and returns no results. What makes this interesting is that it uses the keyword `override` to indicate that it will be replacing a method provided by the parent class (`myParent`). When you start defining methods in your classes, Xcode knows what methods are inherited, so the moment you go to define a method provided by a parent class, it will automatically add the `override` keyword for you.

The fourth instance method, `myActionMethod`, declared in line 25 differs from the others because it defines an *action*, as indicated by the `@IBAction` keyword. Methods that begin with `@IBAction` are called when the user touches a button, presses a switch, or otherwise interacts with your application's user interface (UI). These methods take a single parameter, usually denoted as `sender` that is set to whatever object the user interacted with. Just as with the `@IBOutlet` mentioned earlier, you'll be learning much more about `IBAction` in Hour 5.

TIP
_____
You will often see methods that accept or return objects of the type `AnyObject`. This is a special type in Swift that can reference *any* kind of object and proves useful if you don't know exactly what you'll be passing to a method or if you want to be able to return different types of objects from a single method.
_____

TIP
_____
You can add a text comment on any line within your class files by prefixing the line with two forward slash characters: `//`. If you want to create a comment that spans multiple lines, you can begin the comment with the characters `/*` and end with `*/`.
_____

Ending the Class File

To end the class file, you just need a closing brace: }. You can see this on line 29 of the example file:

```
29: }
```

Although this might seem like quite a bit to digest, it covers almost everything you'll see in a Swift class file.

Public Versus Private... Internal It Is!

If you've worked in other languages, you might be familiar with the concepts of *public* versus *private* classes, methods, and variables. This lets you limit what can be accessed within a given class. Swift provides three access levels: public, internal, and private. Internal access, the default, allows access to methods and variables within the application where they are defined. This is perfect for writing standalone applications. The other access levels are really only a concern when sharing code; so, it isn't something that will really impact most projects.

To learn more about Swift access control, visit https://developer.apple.com/library/ios/documentation/Swift/Conceptual/Swift_Programming_Language/AccessControl.html.

Structure for Free

Even though we've just spent quite a bit of time going through the structure of a Swift class file, you're rarely (if ever) going to need to type it all out by hand. Whenever you add a new class to your Xcode project, the structure of the file will be set up for you. What's more, much of the work of declaring variable properties and methods can be done visually. Of course, you still need to know how to write code manually, but Xcode goes a long way toward making sure that you don't have to sweat the details.

When Is a Class Not a Class?

Not every "object" that you use in Swift will actually *be* an object. Swift includes data structures called `structs` that you can think of as lightweight objects. A `CGRect`, for example, defines a rectangle on the screen and has a variety of variable properties used to describe it. You can use data structures just like objects, and rarely give it another thought.

The biggest difference, from the perspective of a developer using an object versus a struct, is that if you assign any one object to two variables, both variables will reference the same object. When you assign a structure to two variables, each variable gets a unique copy of that structure.

Swift Programming Basics

We've explored the notion of classes, methods, and instance variables, but you probably still don't have a real idea of how to go about making a program do something. So, this section reviews several key programming tasks that you'll be using to implement your methods:

▶ Declaring variables and constants

▶ Understanding built-in Swift data types

▶ Making sense of optional values

▶ Initializing objects

▶ Using an object's instance methods

▶ Making decisions with expressions

▶ Branching and looping

Declaring Variables and Constants

Earlier we documented what variable properties will look like in your Swift files, but we didn't really get into the process of how you declare them (or use them). Nor did we talk about variables *within* methods!

Whatever the purpose, you declare your variables using this syntax:

```
var <Variable Name>[: Variable Type] [Optional modifier] [ = Initialization]
```

Holy cow—that looks complicated! In practice, nearly everything but the `var` keyword and the variable name are optional. I make a point of always trying to provide the variable type, but if you don't, Swift will try to figure it out for you. The type is either a Swift data type or the name of a class that you want to instantiate and use.

Let's begin by taking a look at a few Swift data types and how they are declared and used.

Swift Data Types

Swift includes a number of data types that enable you to work with common types of information. Most basic logic that we implement in this book will take advantage of one of these data types:

▶ `Int:` Integers (whole numbers such as 1, 0, and –99).

▶ `Float:` Floating-point numbers (numbers with decimal points in them).

▶ `Double:` Highly precise floating-point numbers that can handle a large number of digits.

▶ `String:` Collections of characters (numbers, letters, and symbols). Throughout this book, you'll often use strings to collect user input and to create and format user output.

▶ `Bool:` A Boolean value (that is, `true` or `false`), often used to evaluate conditions within your code.

▶ `Arrays:` A collection of ordered values that are accessed via a numeric index.

▶ `Dictionaries:` A collection of key/value pairs. A given value is accessed by providing its key.

Integers and Floating-Point Numbers   Let's start with something easy: integers (`Int`) and floating-point numbers (`Float` or `Double`). To declare an integer variable that will hold a user's age, you might enter the following:

```
var userAge: Int
```

If you wanted, you could even initialize it with a value, all in the same line:

```
var userAge: Int = 30
```

After a variable is declared, it can be used for assignments and mathematical operations. The following code, for example, declares two variables, `userAge` and `userAgeInDays`, and uses the first (an age in years) to calculate the second (the age in days):

```
var userAge: Int = 30
var userAgeInDays: Int
userAgeInDays = userAge * 365
```

Notice that for the `userAgeInDays`, I declare it and then use it later. You're welcome to do this, or declare and initialize the variables on the exact same line.

Floating-point numbers work the same way—you declare them, then use them. A simple example to calculate the circumference of a circle (circumference = diameter * 3.141), for example, could be written like this:

```
var diameter: Float = 2.5
var circumference: Float = diameter * 3.141
```

Pretty easy, don't you think? Swift data types have much more to offer as well. Let's see what else they can do!

NOTE

As I said earlier, everything but the `var` keyword and the variable name is optional in a variable declaration. For example, the age calculation code could be written to leave out the variable type entirely:

```
var userAge = 30
var userAgeInDays = userAge * 365
```

Swift will automatically figure out what the variable is based on the initialization. Personally, I prefer including the variable type so that I can quickly see what each variable represents in my code.

Strings   Strings are one of the most often used Swift types in this book. You'll be using strings for user input and output, data manipulation, and so on. As with every other variable, the life of a string begins with a declaration and an initialization:

```
var myName: String = "John"
```

Here, a string (myName) is initialized to the value "John". Once initialized, the string can be manipulated using a number of techniques. String *concatenation* (adding two or more strings together) is performed with the addition (+) operator. To change myName to include my last name, I'd write the following:

```
myName = myName + " Ray"
```

You can even use a process called *string interpolation* to combine existing Strings, values returned by methods, and other Swift data types into a new String. Consider this line:

```
var sentence: String = "Your name is \(myName) and you are \(userAge) years old."
```

Here I've combined the myName string and userAge integer into a single string, assigned to a new variable named sentence. Any time Swift encounters the pattern \(<variable or method name>) in your code, it takes the result, turns it into a string, and substitutes it in place of the pattern. You can use this to quickly format strings based on other variables and methods.

In many languages, strings require special functions to check for equality. In Swift, the same comparison operators you'd use to compare two numbers also work for strings. We'll look at comparisons a bit later.

NOTE

String Theory

Strings are actually made up of an individual data type elements called (drum roll) *characters*. You won't need to break strings down to this lower type often, but it is handy to know that a string is actually a collection of smaller pieces of data.

Boolean Values   A Boolean value has only two states—represented by true or false in Swift. Booleans are most often used in comparisons, although some methods have Boolean parameters that you'll need to supply. As expected, Booleans are initialized using the same pattern you've seen for numbers and strings:

```
var myFlag: Bool = false
```

Arrays A useful category of data type is a collection. Collections enable your applications to store multiple pieces of information in a single object. An `Array` is an example of a collection data type that can hold multiple objects, accessed by a numeric index.

You might, for instance, want to create an array that contains all the user feedback strings you want to display in an application:

```
var userMessages: [String] = ["Good job!", "Bad Job", "Mediocre Job"]
```

Notice that the word `Array` doesn't even appear in the declaration and initialization? That's because all we need to do to declare an array is wrap the type we want to store (in this case, `String` values) in square brackets. If I wanted an array of integers, I'd use a type of `[Int]` and so on. The initialization values are provided as a comma-separated list enclosed in square brackets; if you use `[]` alone, the array is initialized as empty.

To access the strings in the `userMessages` array, you use an index value. This is the number that represents a position in the list, starting with `0`. To return the `"Bad job"` message, we use the number `1` (the second item in the list):

```
userMessages[1]
```

You can also use the index to assign values to an array, replacing what is currently stored:

```
userMessages[1] = "Try again!"
```

Swift lets you add new items to the end of the list using the array's `append` method. For example, to add a new message ("Meh") to the end of `userMessages`, I might write the following:

```
userMessages.append("Meh")
```

There are several other means of accessing and modifying arrays that we'll use over the course of the next 21 hours.

TIP

Don't Care About Order? Use a Set

Although we won't be using them in this book, I recommend taking a look at the Swift `Set` data type when you have a chance. Sets are like arrays, but where each value is unique and the order of the values doesn't matter. You can create sets and use built-in Swift functions to find their overlaps, differences, and so on.

You could use sets, for instance, to represent music libraries for different people, and then with a few built-in functions, see which music is shared between two people, which music is entirely unique to a person, and so on.

There's so much cool stuff in Swift and so little room left in this chapter. Arrgh!

Dictionaries   Like arrays, dictionaries are another collection data type, but with an important difference. Whereas the objects in an array are accessed by a numeric index, dictionaries store information as key/value pairs. The key is usually an arbitrary string, whereas the value can be anything you want, even objects. If the previous userMessages array were to be created as a Dictionary instead, it might look like this:

```
var userMessages: [String:String] =
    ["positive":"Good job!", "negative":"Bad Job", "indifferent":"Mediocre Job"]
```

Similar to declaring the strings, I declare the dictionary without ever using the word *dictionary*. Instead, I provide the type data types that will form the keys and values within square brackets—for example, [<key data type>:<value data type>]. For the userMessage dictionary, I'm using keys that are strings, and values that are strings. The initialization is similar to an array, but consists of the key, a colon (:), and then the value. Each key/value pair is separated by a comma. Empty dictionaries can be created with the initializer [:].

To access a value in the dictionary, I index into userMessages just like an array, but using the key rather than an integer. To access the "Bad Job" message (tied to the "negative" key), I could type the following:

```
userMessages["negative"]
```

Keys can also be used to modify or assign new values. Here the key "apathy" is assigned the value "Meh":

```
userMessages["apathy"] = "Meh"
```

Dictionaries are useful because they let you store and access data in abstract ways rather than in a strict numeric order.

TIP

Counting the Contents

Both dictionaries and arrays include a read-only variable property called count that returns the number of elements they've stored. The number of elements in the userMessages array (or dictionary), for example, can be accessed with the expression userMessages.count.

Enumerations   Another useful (and commonly encountered) data type is an enumeration. The first time I encountered this word, I imagined complex structures and all sorts of fun stuff. In reality, enumerations (enum) is easy to use *and* to understand.

Suppose, for instance, that you want to create a custom variable type to work with the colors of the rainbow. You might define an array of strings, or assign each color a number... or you could use an enumeration. Enumerations are just custom types that can only take on one of a predefined number of values. They are created using the following syntax. Note that enumation names usually start with a capital letter:

```
enum <enumeration name> {
    case <value 1>, <value 2> ...
}
```

Translated to the example of "colors of the rainbow," this looks like:

```
enum ColorsOfRainbow {
    case Red, Orange, Yellow, Green, Blue, Indigo, Violet
}
```

Once defined, you can declare variables of the type `<enumeration name>`:

```
var myRainbow: ColorsOfRainbow
```

Assign values to the variable by referencing `<enumeration name>.<value>`:

```
myRainbow = ColorsOfRainbow.Blue
```

When referencing values of enumerations, you can leave out the name of the enumeration and just use `.<value>` because Swift knows that what type of enumeration your variable is:

```
myRainbow = .Blue
```

I prefer leaving in the enumeration name, personally, because I believe it leads to more readable code. That's all there is to it! You'll encounter enumerations often in iOS development. They are often used to return the "state" of objects, such as the current orientation of your iOS device.

Object Data Types

Just about everything that you'll be working with in your iOS applications will be an object. Onscreen text, for example, will be instances of the class `UILabel`. Buttons that you display are objects of the class `UIButton`. You'll learn about several of the common object classes in the next hour's lesson. Apple has literally provided thousands of different classes that you can use to store and manipulate data.

Objects are declared and initialized just like Swift data types. For example, to declare and create a new instance of the `UILabel` class, you could use the following code:

```
var myLabel: UILabel = UILabel()
```

Here, the initializer is `UILabel()`. This returns a new, ready-to-use instance of the `UILabel` class. You can initialize all classes using this same syntax `<class name>()`, but most will require additional setup after initialization. To speed things along, many will provide *convenience* methods. Convenience methods speed the process of creating a new object by taking the basic parameters needed to create and configure the object, all at once.

NOTE

When you read through the Xcode documentation (discussed in the next hour), you'll see initialization methods denoted with the function name `init` for Swift. This is the internal method name in the class. It is automatically invoked by using the `<class name>()` syntax.

Convenience Methods   When we initialized the `UILabel` instance, we did create an object, but it doesn't yet have any of the additional information that makes it useful. Attributes such as what the label should say, or where it should be shown on the screen, have yet to be set. We would need to use several of the object's other methods to really turn it into something ready to be displayed.

These configuration steps are sometimes a necessary evil, but Apple's classes often provide a special initialization method called a *convenience method*. These methods can be invoked to set up an object with a basic configuration so that it can be used almost immediately.

For example, the `NSURL` class, which you use later to work with web addresses, defines a convenience method called `initWithString`. We can use it to create a brand-new `NSURL` object, complete with the URL, just by typing the following:

```
var iOSURL: NSURL = NSURL(string: "http://www.teachyourselfios.com/")!
```

This is where we (briefly) go off the tracks. Notice that nowhere in that line does `initWithString` appear. The `initWithString` method is the name of a convenience method in Objective-C. The method still goes by the same name when used in Swift, but it takes on a simplified form.

The general rule of thumb is that, in Swift, the `initWith` is removed from the name of convenience method. Whatever remains of the name becomes the first *named* parameter of the method. A named parameter, as you'll learn a bit later, is a parameter that requires you to spell out its name in the method call (in this case, `string`).

Because Xcode supports autocompletion, it is usually pretty easy to start typing in a method named and find it in the list that appears. Just keep in mind that what you see in the Xcode documentation doesn't necessarily apply to both Objective-C and Swift.

Type Conversion and Type Casting

In your adventures in Swift, you will encounter code that doesn't quite work the way you want. You'll find legacy `CGFloat` floating-point numbers that must be used in place of Swift `Float`. You'll find places where you need to turn `Floats` into `Ints`, and vice versa. You'll even encounter objects that have no idea what they are. To get around these little snags, you'll likely employ type conversion, or type casting.

Type Conversion   For most of the simple data types, you can convert between types by using the syntax: `<Type Name>(<Value to Convert>)`. For example, if a method calls for a `CGFloat` and you have a `Float` value (in the variable `myFloat`), you can convert it to the proper type with the following:

```
CGFloat(myFloat)
```

Swift does everything it can to silently bridge these older data types with the new built-in Swift types—and it is usually very successful. Unfortunately, sometimes this manual conversion will have to happen.

Another common circumstance is when a method returns an object of one type when it needs to be another. When this happens, you must type cast the result.

Downcasting (Type Casting)   Downcasting takes an object of a higher-level class and tells Xcode which specific subclass it should be. In general terms, this process is called *type casting*. You may encounter methods will return an object of the type `AnyObject` rather than a specific type – or have to work with collections of objects stored as the type `AnyObject`. For example, assume that we wanted to access the first element of an array (index 0!) defined to contain generic objects (`AnyObject`). We may know that the first element is of the type `MyObject`, so we could reference it like this:

```
var myVariable: MyObject = myArray[0] as MyObject
```

Because `myArray[0]` is an object of the type `AnyObject`, we must "tell" Xcode that it is really an `NSDate` by adding `as MyObject` to the end of the assignment. Using the syntax `as <class name>` after any object will attempt to downcast that object as being of whatever subclass you name.

After a variable is cast to an object of the correct type, we can interact with it directly as that type. This looks a bit unusual, I know, but it will come in handy later in the book. It's easier to understand when you see it in an actual application; so for the moment, just be aware that it is an available development tool.

Constants

Constants are declared and initialized just like variables, except they begin with the keyword `let`. For example, to create a constant named `lastName` that holds a `String` with my last name, I would write the following:

```
let lastName: String = "Ray"
```

The key difference between a constant and a variable is that constants, once assigned, cannot be changed or reassigned. This, however, isn't as limiting as you might think. When you assign an object to a constant, you can access and modify all the variable properties in that object, execute all its methods, and so on. It can still be used just like any other variable; you just can't reassign it later.

Constants are more efficient than variables and should be used in their place wherever possible. I think you'll be surprised to find that we use more constants in our applications than actual variables.

NOTE

Constants Are Good! You've Been Warned

If you create a variable and never modify the contents, Swift will produce a warning in your code. If you're used to just declaring variables wherever you want to store a value, Swift is going to put up a nice shiny yellow warning mark to point out that a constant would be a better choice.

Optional Values

Possibly the most confusing, infuriating thing about Swift is the notion of optional values. In theory, it's really quite simple. If you've developed in other languages, you've almost certainly written code that *thought* it was working with a value, only to find that the value had never been set or that a method that was supposed to return a value didn't. Making the assumption that we *know* what is in a variable is dangerous, but it's something that developers do every day.

In Swift, Apple decided that developers should acknowledge when they're using a value that might not contain what they expect. The result requires interesting additions to the development process:

1. Method, variable, and constant declarations should state when they *may not have, or may not return*, a value. These are known as *optional* values.

2. Why would a method programmed to return a result ever make that result optional? If the method has bad input, or otherwise can't complete the operation it is tasked with performing, it makes perfect sense to return "nothing"—represented in Swift using the keyword `nil`.

3. When attempting to access methods or variables that are optional, developers must `unwrap` the values. This means that the developer acknowledges that he or she knows what is in a variable (or returned by a method), and wants to access and use the results.

Now, you might think to yourself, "Hey, I know what I'm doing, I'm not going to write any code where I name a variable or method return type as optional. That would just be extra work!" You're right, it is extra work—but it's utterly unavoidable.

All the code that makes up the Cocoa Touch classes is being updated by Apple to denote which variable properties and methods return optional values—and there are *many* (and the list is growing). I could tell you stories about the number of times I've opened a project while writing this book, only to find that Apple has changed a class somewhere that breaks the code I've written. That's one of the difficulties of being an early technology adopter.

Okay, enough ranting. What does all of this actually mean in terms of coding?

Declaring Optionals   First, when declaring a variable, you can define it as optional by adding a ? after the type name:

```
var myOptionalString: NSString? = "John"
```

This also means that if the string isn't immediately initialized, it automatically contains the value `nil`.

NOTE

What the... It's an Optional Value, But It Has a Value (`nil`)?

Yes, this is as weird as it sounds. In Swift, `nil` represents literally *nothing*. When we need some value to represent no value at all, `nil` is used. We can't use something like an empty string (`" "`) or 0 because those *are* values. Get used to the idea of `nil`, because even though it is something, it is also nothing. (Cue *Seinfeld* music.)

For method definitions, you denote an optional return value by adding ? after the return type. In the sample class in Listing 3.1, I defined the method as having an optional return value of `NSDate` using this syntax in the declaration:

```
func myInstanceMethod(myString: String, myURL: NSURL) -> NSDate? {
```

NOTE

Constants can also be assigned as optional using the same syntax as variables. Although this might seem counterintuitive (don't you assign a value when you create a constant?), it makes sense when you consider that you might be assigning a constant to the return value of a method with an optional return type.

Unwrapping and Implicit Unwrapping   After you've either created (or encountered Swift variables and methods) that are optional, you need to know how to access them. Accessing optional values is called *unwrapping* in Swift. The easiest, most brute-force way is to use optional values is to *unwrap* them by adding an exclamation mark (!) to the end of their name.

In other words, each time I wanted to use the value in `myOptionalString`, I would reference it as follows:

```
myOptionalString!
```

The same goes for the `myInstanceMethod` method. To use it, I might write a line like this:

```
var myReturnedDate: NSDate = myInstanceMethod("A cool string", myURL: iOSURL)!
```

The addition of the `!` tells Xcode that we want to access the return value and that we don't care if it is `nil`. We can take this a step further by defining what is called an *implicitly unwrapped* optional. This is just an optional value that will *always* be unwrapped automatically when we use it.

To create an implicitly unwrapped variable, you add a `!` after the type name. For example, I could write the preceding line of code using an implicitly unwrapped variable, like this:

```
var myReturnedDate: NSDate! = myInstanceMethod("A cool string", myURL: iOSURL)
```

This declares `myReturnedDate` as an optional `NSDate` variable, but one that will be implicitly unwrapped. I can assign it the result of an optional method without unwrapping the return value of the method (because both are optional). However, when I go to use `myReturnedDate` elsewhere in my code, it will automatically be unwrapped for me—just as if I had put the `!` after it each time.

You really won't be doing this very often, but Xcode is going to do it *a lot* when it writes code for you. Why? Because every interface object that connects to your code will be referenced through an implicitly unwrapped variable. An interface object may be `nil` before it is loaded, so it has to be optional; but once your code is active, it should always have a value, and there's no point in hindering its use—thus, it is implicitly unwrapped for you.

Optional Binding   Another (gentler) way to deal with optional values is called *optional binding*. This is the assignment of an optional value to a constant. If the assignment succeeds, the optional value is accessible through the constant. If it fails, the optional value is `nil`.

Applying optional binding to the `myOptionalString` variable, I might write this simple logic to test to see whether an optional value should be used:

```
if let stringValue:String = myOptionalString {
    // myOptionalString has a non-nil value.
}
```

This is a good approach for working with optionals in production-ready code. It gives you an opportunity to react to situations where optionals are set to `nil` and errors may have arisen. If you unwrap an optional and try to work with it even if it is `nil`, you may crash your code.

For most of the examples in the book, I manually unwrap values with `!` because the code is simple and we know how the different components are going to interact. In apps bound for the App Store, I recommend using optional binding to trap for error conditions that you may not have anticipated.

Optional and Forced Downcasting   You've seen the syntax for downcasting, but consider what happens if the class you're downcasting cannot be cast to what you want. In this case, your app is likely going to crash. To deal with this scenario, you can create an *optional downcast*. With an optional downcast, if the downcast fails, the resulting variable will contain `nil`.

To define a downcast operation as optional, simply add a ? to the end of the as keyword, as follows:

```
var myVariable: myObjectType? = anotherVariable as? myObjectType
```

At the opposite end of the spectrum is a *forced downcast*. A forced downcast should be used when you *know* the downcast will work. It completes the downcast and also forces the resulting value to be unwrapped. To use a forced downcast, you append an ! to the as keyword:

```
var myVariable: myObjectType = anotherVariable as! myObjectType
```

Of course, using a forced downcast in a case where something can go wrong (either with the downcasting or the unwrapping of the resulting value) will result in an error.

TIP

Optionals: Don't Be Scared

Optionals exist to help protect you from making bad assumptions in your code. At times, you'll feel like every single method or variable property you use has been declared as optional—and you'll likely start to think that your hair is optional as well. The good news is that Xcode recognizes optional values throughout Cocoa Touch and will prompt you if you're missing the required ? or ! characters. In most cases, it will even correct simple optional unwrapping errors for you.

Don't feel like you need to start memorizing the tens of thousands of optional values in Cocoa Touch. Xcode knows, and it will let you know.

Using Methods

You've already seen how to declare and initialize objects, but this is only a tiny picture of the methods you'll be using in your apps. Let's start by reviewing the syntax of calling methods in Swift.

Method Syntax

To use a method, provide the name of the variable that is referencing your object followed by the name of the method, followed by a period, the name of the method, and empty parentheses () (empty if there are no parameters). If you're using a type (class) method, just provide the name of the class rather than a variable name:

```
<object variable or class name>.<method name>()
```

Things start to look a little more complicated when the method has parameters. A single parameter method call looks like this:

```
<object variable or class name>.<method name>([parameter:]<parameter value>)
```

Earlier I noted that convenience initialization methods will usually include at least one named parameter, such as `string` when initializing an `NSURL` object:

```
var iOSURL: NSURL = NSURL(string: "http://www.teachyourselfios.com/")!
```

This is important to note because the style of using an initial named parameter is only really used in convenience initialization methods. In other (general use) methods, the first parameter is just provided as a value.

TIP
_____

If you aren't sure whether the first parameter to a method is named or not, the Xcode documentation can help. If the first character after the parenthesis in a Swift method definition is an underscore (_), that parameter is _not_ named. You'll learn all about the documentation system in the next hour.

_____

For example, let's look at a method that takes multiple parameters:

```
var myFullName: String = "John Ray"
var myDescription: String =
    myFullName.stringByReplacingOccurrencesOfString("Ray",
        withString: "is awesome!")
```

This code fragment stores my name in the `myFullName` variable, and then uses the `stringByReplacingOccurrencesOfString:withString` method to change my last name from "Ray" to "is awesome!"

In this example, the first parameter to the `stringByReplacingOccurrencesOfString:with String` method has no name; I just put in the value (`"Ray"`). The second parameter _does_ have a name (`withString:`), which must be provided along with the value.

The syntax for multiple parameter method calls looks like this:

```
<object variable or class name>.<method name>([parameter:]<parameter value>,
    <parameter>:<parameter value>, <parameter>:<parameter value> ...)
```

NOTE
_____

It can be very difficult to break lines in Swift without literally breaking the code. I've found that you can break lines around assignment statements (`<blah> = <blah>`) as long as there are spaces around the `=`, as well as after a comma (`,`) in lists of parameters.

_____

NOTE

Throughout the lessons, methods are referred to by name. If the name includes a colon (:), this indicates a required named parameter. This is a convention that Apple has used in its documentation and that has been adopted for this book.

Making Sense of Named Parameters

If you've gotten to this point and you aren't sure what a *named parameter* is, I am not surprised. To work, methods take parameter values as input. A named parameter is just a string, followed by a colon, that provides context for what a given value is or does. For example, a method that looked like this doesn't really tell you much:

```
myString.stringByReplacingOccurrencesOfString(String1, String2)
```

Is `String1` replacing `String2`? Vice versa?

By making the second parameter a *named* parameter, it becomes obvious:

```
myString.stringByReplacingOccurrencesOfString(String1, withString:String2)
```

The named parameter, `withString:`, shows us that `String2` will be used to replace `String1`. This also shows why the first parameter is *rarely* named: because the name of the method itself implies that the first parameter is a string that is going to be replaced.

Chaining

Something that you'll see when looking at Swift code is that often the result of a method is used directly as a parameter within another method. In some cases, if the result of a method is an object, a developer may immediately use a method or variable property of that object without first assigning it to a variable. This is known as *chaining*.

Chaining results directly eliminates the need for temporary variables and can make code shorter and easier to maintain.

For example, consider this completely contrived code:

```
var myString: String = "JoHN ray"
myString = myString.lowercaseString
myString = myString.stringByReplacingOccurrencesOfString("john",
    withString: "will")
myString = myString.capitalizedString
```

Here I've created a string (`myString`) that holds my name with very very poor capitalization. I decide that I want to replace my first name (John) with my brother's name (Will). Because I cannot just search and replace on John because my capitalization is all messy and I don't want to try to remember how I wrote my name (this is *contrived* folks), I decide to first convert `myString` to lowercase by accessing the `lowercaseString` variable property. Once complete, I can just search for john and replace it with will without worrying about capitalization. Unfortunately, that means I still need a properly capitalized version of the string when I'm done. So, I access the `capitalizedString` variable property of my string when finished, and use its value for `myString`. (In case you're wondering, `capitalizedString` provides a copy of the string with all of the first letters capitalized.)

The code should make sense, even if my logic is a bit shaky. That said, each of the methods and variable properties I've used return a string. Instead of assigning things over and over, I can chain each of these actions together into a single line:

```
var myString: String = "JoHN ray".lowercaseString
    .stringByReplacingOccurrencesOfString("john",
        withString: "will").capitalizedString
```

Chaining can be a powerful way to structure your code, but when overused it may lead to lines that can be difficult to parse. Do what makes you comfortable; both approaches are equally valid and have the same outcome.

TIP

Although I tend to leave chained lines unbroken in my projects, you *can* break a chained line without causing an error if you break it immediately *before* one of the periods.

Optional Chaining

Time for optionals to rear their head one more time this hour. As you've just seen, chaining can be a great way to use values without lots of temporary variables and multiple lines of code. What happens, however, if one of the values (the results of a method, or a variable property) in the middle of the chain is optional? You can unwrap the values using ! and hope that they *do* exist, or you can take advantage of *optional chaining*. In optional chaining, you can write out your chain, placing a ? after optional values. This allows the full chain to be evaluated, even if a value is missing somewhere in the middle. For example, assume I wrote a line of code like this:

```
myObject.optionalMethod()!.variableProperty.method()
```

If the `optionalMethod()!` in the middle didn't return what I was expecting, I wouldn't be able to access `variableProperty` or the subsequent `method()`. To get around this, I can write the chain as follows:

```
myObject.optionalMethod()?.variableProperty.method()
```

Doing this allows the line to be executed and fail gracefully. If `optionalMethod()` does not return a usable object, the entire line returns `nil`, which can be trapped and dealt with as you learned earlier.

Multiple Return Values with Tuples

When using methods, most frequently you'll be dealing with a single return value—a string, an integer, or some other object. Methods can, however, return *several* values all at once.

For example, consider a method that takes an integer and returns a first and last name. The method might be defined as follows:

```
func getName(id: Int) -> (String, String) {
    // Get and return a first and last name
    return (firstName, lastName)
}
```

Notice that instead of defining a return type of just `-> String`, the return is defined as `-> (String,String)`. To call the method, I could use code like this:

```
var myFirstName: String
var myLastName: String
(myFirstName,myLastName)=getName(1)
```

You can return any number of variables (of whatever type you want), by defining multiple return types in your methods, and subsequently access them by listing your receiving variables in parenthesis. A list of values in parenthesis is actually its own data type (known as a *tuple*). You'll use tuples almost exclusively for receiving multiple values from methods.

There is an interesting variation on multiple return values where the return types are *named*—just liked named parameters that you use when calling a method. Methods returning named tuples are defined by adding `<name>:` directly preceding the return type:

```
func getName(id: Int) -> (first: String, last: String) {
    // Get and return a first and last name
    return (firstName, lastName)
}
```

So, how is this helpful? To answer that, it's easiest just to show you.

You can assign the results (a tuple) to a single variable:

```
var nameResult = getName(1)
```

Then, access the members of the tuple by their names (that is, `nameResult.first` and `nameResult.last`). Using this approach can lead to code that is easier to read, and doesn't require you to define multiple variables to receive each value in the tuple.

Closures

Although most of your coding will be within methods, you will also encounter *closures* when using the iOS frameworks. Sometimes referred to *as handler blocks* in the Xcode documentation, these are chunks of code that can be passed as values when calling a method. They provide instructions that the method should run when reacting to a certain event.

For example, imagine a `personInformation` object with a method called `setDisplayName` that would define a format for showing a person's name. Instead of just showing the name, however, `setDisplayName` might use a closure to let you define, programmatically, how the name should be shown:

```
personInformation.setDisplayName({(firstName: String, lastName: String) in
         // Implement code here to modify the first name and last name
         // and display it however you want.
    })
```

Interesting, isn't it? Closures are relatively new to iOS development and are used throughout this book. You'll first encounter closures when writing alerts. The closure will provide the instructions that are executed when a person acts on an alert.

Writing Method Documentation

You already know that you can add comments to your code using `//`, `/*`, and . You can take this a step further in Xcode 7+ by using Markdown syntax to document your method definitions. This can be useful projects where you are sharing code with other people because it defines a standard (and pretty) mechanism for describing what a method does, what parameters it takes, and so on.

NOTE

What Is Markdown?

Markdown is a popular plain-text method for describing simple text formatting. To emphasize words, for example, you place them between asterisks (for example, `*This is important*`), or to add a horizontal rule, you type `---`. A full description of Markdown is beyond the scope of this book, but you can read a nice introduction at http://daringfireball.net/projects/markdown/basics.

To add Markdown documentation to a method, you insert comment lines beginning with `///` immediately preceding the method definition in your Swift file. In addition, because Markdown just defines text styles, Xcode provides some additional keywords that you can type inside your Markdown comments:

▶ `Parameter <parameter name>:<description>`: Describes a parameter to the method. Multiple parameters can be defined.

▶ `Returns: <description of what will be returned>`: Describes the results the method produces.

▶ **Throws: <description of any errors the method may produce>**: Describes the errors the method produces (if any).

▶ **```swift:** Sstarts a block of code, typically to hold examples. Subsequent lines of code should just be indented with spaces to continue the code block.

Here is an example of method documentation for a method called nada:

```
/// # nada - The useless method
/// ---
/// This method really doesn't do anything at all useful.
/// It's in the application purely as an example.
/// - Parameter this:String describing this
/// - Parameter that:String describing that
/// - Returns: 1
/// - Throws: Tons of errors
/// ```swift
///         let one = nada("blah", "blah")
///         NSLog("\(one)")
func nada(this: NSString, that: NSString) -> Int {
    return (1)
}
```

To see the results of the method documentation, hold Option and click the method name in your code, as shown in Figure 3.2.

You'll also see the styled documentation appear in the Quick Help inspector—something you'll learn about in the next hour.

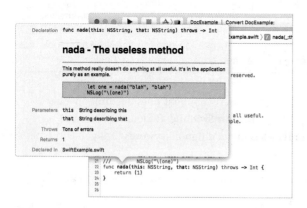

FIGURE 3.2
Use Markdown syntax to create method documentation.

Expressions and Decision Making

For an application to react to user input and process information, it must be capable of making decisions. Every decision in an app boils down to a true or false result based on evaluating a set of tests. These can be as simple as comparing two values, to something as complex as checking the results of a complicated mathematical calculation. The combination of tests used to make a decision is called an *expression*.

Using Expressions

If you recall your high school algebra, you'll be right at home with expressions. An expression can combine arithmetic, comparison, and logical operations.

A simple numeric comparison checking to see whether a variable `userAge` is greater than 30 could be written as follows:

```
userAge>30
```

When working with objects, we need to use variable properties within the object and values returned from methods to create expressions. If I have stored an NSDate object with my birthday in it (`myBirthday`), I could check to see whether the current day is my birthday with the expression:

```
myBirthday.isEqualToDate(NSDate())
```

Expressions are not limited to the evaluation of a single condition. We could easily combine the previous two expressions to find a person who is over 30 and is celebrating his or her birthday today:

```
userAge>30 && myBirthday.isEqualToDate(NSDate())
```

Common Expression Syntax

`()` groups expressions together, forcing evaluation of the innermost group first.

`==` Tests to see whether two values are equal (for example, `userAge == 30`).

`!=` Tests to see whether two values are not equal (for example, `userAge != 30`).

`&&` Implements a logical AND condition (for example, `userAge > 30 && userAge < 40`).

`||` Implements a logical OR condition (for example, `userAge > 30 || userAge < 10`).

`!` Negates the result of an expression, returning the opposite of the original result. (For example, `!(userAge == 30)` is the same as `userAge != 30`.)

It's good practice to put spaces on either side of the symbols you use for comparisons—especially when using `!=`. Recall that a `!` also indicates that a value should be unwrapped, so Xcode can be easily confused into thinking you want to unwrap something when really you're just testing for inequality.

As mentioned repeatedly, you're going to be spending lots of time working with complex objects and using the methods within the objects. You cannot make direct comparisons between objects as you can with simple data types. To successfully create expressions for the myriad objects you'll be using, you must review each object's methods and variable properties.

Making Decisions with `if-then-else` and `switch` Statements

Typically, depending on the outcome of the evaluated expression, different code statements are executed. The most common way of defining these different execution paths is with an `if-then-else` statement:

```
if <expression> {
    // do this, the expression is true.
} else {
    // the expression isn't true, do this instead!
}
```

For example, consider the comparison we used earlier to check a `myBirthday` `NSDate` variable to see whether it was equal to the current date. If we want to react to that comparison, we might write the following:

```
if myBirthday.isEqualToDate(NSDate()) {
    let myMessage: String = "Happy Birthday!"
} else {
    let myMessage: String = "Sorry, it's not your birthday."
}
```

Another approach to implementing different code paths when there are potentially many different outcomes to an expression is to use a `switch` statement. A `switch` statement checks a variable for a value and then executes different blocks of code depending on the value that is found:

```
switch (<some value>) {
    case <value option 1>:
        // The value matches this option
    case <value option 2>:
        // The value matches this option
    default:
        // None of the options match the number.
}
```

Applying this to a situation where we might want to check a user's age (stored in `userAge`) for some key milestones and then set an appropriate `userMessage` string if they are found, the result might look like this:

```
switch userAge {
    case 18:
        let userMessage: String = "Congratulations, you're an adult!"
    case 21:
        let userMessage: String = "Congratulations, you can drink champagne!"
```

```
case 50:
    let userMessage: String = "You're half a century old!"
default:
    let userMessage: String = "Sorry, there's nothing special about your age.";
}
```

Repetition with Loops

In some situations, you will need to repeat several instructions over and over in your code. Instead of typing the lines repeatedly, you can loop over them. A loop defines the start and end of several lines of code. As long as the loop is running, the program executes the lines from top to bottom and then restarts again from the top. The loops you'll use are of two types: `for` loops and condition-based `while`/`repeat-while` loops.

`for` Loops   In a `for` loop, the statements are repeated a (mostly) predetermined number of times. You might want to count to 1000 and output each number, or create a dozen copies of an object. These are perfect uses for a `for` loop.

The `for` loop you'll likely encounter most often consists of this syntax:

```
for <initialization>;<test condition>;<count update> {
    // Do this, over and over!
}
```

The three "unknowns" in the `for` statement syntax are a statement to initialize a counter variable to track the number of times the loop has executed, a condition to check to see whether the loop should continue, and finally, an increment for the counter. A loop that uses the integer variable `count` to loop 50 times could be written as follows:

```
for var count=0;count<50;count=count+1 {
    // Do this, 50 times!
}
```

The `for` loop starts by setting the `count` variable to `0`. The loop then starts and continues as long as the condition of `count<50` remains `true`. When the loop hits the bottom curly brace (`}`) and starts over, the increment operation is carried out and `count` is increased by `1`.

NOTE

Integers are usually incremented by using `++` at the end of the variable name. In other words, rather than using `count=count+1`, most often you'll encounter `count++`, which does the same thing. Decrementing works the same way, but with `--`.

```
for <variable> in <collection> {
    // Do this for each collection value, where <variable> contains the value
}
```

We can actually rewrite the loop that counts from 0 to 49 using this new syntax because the notation <number>...<number> creates a collection from a range of numbers:

```
for count in 0...49 {
    // Do this, 50 times!
}
```

NOTE

Don't Need a Count? Don't Use One

If you don't actually need to access the counter in a loop, you don't actually need to declare anything to hold it. Just substitution _ in place of the variable:

```
for _ in 0...49 {
    // Do this, 50 times!
}
```

The power of iterating over a collection becomes more apparent, however, when applied to a proper collection data type—such as the array of messages we created earlier in the hour:

```
var userMessages: [String] = ["Good job!", "Bad Job", "Mediocre Job"]
```

To loop over this array of messages, we can write a "for in" loop as follows:

```
for message in userMessages {
    // The message variable now holds an individual message
}
```

The same applies to dictionaries as well, but the syntax changes just a little bit. If userMessages is defined as a dictionary:

```
var userMessages: [String:String] = ["positive":"Good job!",
    "negative":"Bad Job", "indifferent":"Mediocre Job"]
```

We can loop over each key/value pair like this:

```
for (key, value) in userMessages {
    // The key and value variables hold an individual dictionary entry
}
```

while and **repeat-while** Loops

In a condition-based loop, the loop continues while an expression remains true. You'll encounter two variables of this loop type, while and repeat-while:

```
while <expression> {
    // Do this, over and over, while the expression is true!
}
```

and

```
repeat {
    // Do this, over and over, while the expression is true!
} while <expression>
```

The only difference between these two loops is when the expression is evaluated. In a standard `while` loop, the check is done at the beginning of the loop. In the `repeat-while` loop, however, the expression is evaluated at the end of every loop. In practice, this difference ensures that in a `repeat-while` loop, the code block is executed at least once; a `while` loop may not execute the block at all.

For example, suppose that you are asking users to input their names and you want to keep prompting them until they type John. You might format a `repeat-while` loop like this:

```
repeat {
    // Get the user's input in this part of the loop
} while userName != "John"
```

The assumption is that the name is stored in a string called `userName`. Because you wouldn't have requested the user's input when the loop first starts, you would use a `repeat-while` loop to put the test condition at the end.

Loops are a very useful part of programming and, along with the decision statements, will form the basis for structuring the code within your object methods. They allow code to branch and extend beyond a linear flow.

Error Handling

When we write code, we do everything we can to write code that doesn't include errors. That said, we can't always predict when errors are going to occur. Sometimes, bad input can result in an error. Other times, the state of the device might result in us trying to do something that produces an error. Rather than having an application that crashes when something unexpected happens, we can use Swift's new error handling to intercept and process the error.

do-catch Statements To add error handling to your code, you can add a `do-catch` block to code that might be producing an error. The `do-catch` statement executes code, watches for specific error conditions, and then allows you to react to them. The basic syntax is as follows:

```
do {
    try <code statement>
} catch <error type> {
    // Handle a specific error type
} catch <another error type> {
    // Handle another specific error type
```

```
} catch {
    // Handle other errors
}
```

Insert the code you want to execute after the `try` keyword, provide the specific errors you want to catch after the `catch` statement (this can be repeated as many times as needed), or use `catch` by itself to catch all errors.

You may be wondering how you know what, exactly, you're supposed to be catching. The answer is: You'll define those values yourself in your own methods, or find them in the documentation for other methods (or use `catch` by itself to handle any error condition).

So, how exactly do you "create" an error in your code? With the `throw` statement, of course!

throw **Statements**

If you've written a method and something goes wrong, you can either let it go and hope that the code that uses your method properly deals with it, or you can `throw` an error. Throwing errors gives other code the chance to evaluate what went wrong and deal with it accordingly.

To state that a method you've written will throw errors, you must first define the errors that your class will throw by adding an `ErrorType` variable before the `class` line in your Swift file:

```
enum <collection name>: ErrorType {
    case <error 1>
    case <error 2>
    . . .
}
```

NOTE

What's an Enum?

An enum is a special data type that can only contain certain values. You define these values ahead of time and can *only* set the variable to one of these values. In this case, we're defining variables that the class methods can throw.

For example, if I want to define a collection of errors named `MyErrors` with two possible error types (`badThing` and `awfulThing`), I'd use this code:

```
enum MyErrors: ErrorType {
    case badThing, awfulThing
}
```

Once defined, I can "throw" the badThing and awfulThing errors in my methods. To do this, I first identify the methods that *will* throw errors by adding the throws keyword before the return type in the method definition:

```
func nada(this: NSString, that: NSString) throws -> Int {
```

To actually throw an error, use the throw statement in your code in the format throw <error name>:

```
throw MyErrors.badThing
```

It should now be clear that to handle this error condition, the code calling your method would need to catch MyErrors.badthing.

guard Statements and Error Handling   Working hand in hand with the throw statement is the conditional guard statement. You aren't required to use guard for error handling, but it creates more readable code than just using if statements. So, what is this beast? It is simply an if-then statement where the code block is only executed if the expression being evaluated is false:

```
guard <expression> else {
    // Throw an error when the condition is false
}
```

Essentially the code says "make sure this is true," and if it isn't, *do this*. The code block that the guard statement executes must include a throw, return, break, or continue statement.

NOTE

Control Transfer Statements

continue, break, return, and throw are known as control transfer statements, because they transfer control to another part of the application. You already know how throw and return are used, but what about the others?

break is used to exit a loop or if-then block and continue executing at the statement immediately following the executing code block. continue exits the current loop within a looping statement and moves to the next iteration.

defer Statements   The final piece of error handling that we'll look at is the defer statement, which has this simple format:

```
defer {
    // Code to execute eventually
}
```

`defer` statements are executed when the code in which they are defined is finished. If you include it in an `if-then` block, it executed after the `if-then` is finished. If you include it in a method, it is executed when the method finishes. This happens regardless of *where* in your code blocks the statement is added.

Why is this good for anything? Because you may have code that needs to run (cleaning up memory, saving files, and so on) regardless of whatever else happens in your application. If an error occurs, `defer` ensures that code that still needs to run *will* run.

Whew. While error handling can sound like a chore, it leads to reliable and predictable code that can be shared and reused across applications.

Let's now close out Swift programming with a topic that causes quite a bit of confusion for beginning developers: memory management.

Memory Management and Automatic Reference Counting

In the first hour of this book, you learned a bit about the limitations of iOS devices as a platform. One of the biggies, unfortunately, is the amount of memory that your programs have available to them. Because of this, you must be extremely judicious in how you manage memory. If you're writing an app that browses an online recipe database, for example, you shouldn't allocate memory for every single recipe as soon as your application starts.

In the latest Xcode releases, Apple has implemented a new compiler called LLVM, along with a feature known as Automatic Reference Counting (ARC). ARC uses a powerful code analyzer to look at how your objects are allocated and used. When nothing is referencing an object, ARC ensures it is automatically removed from memory.

For most objects you declare and use in a method, you do not need to do anything; when the method is finished, there are no more references to the object, and it is automatically freed. The same goes for variable properties you've declared with the `weak` attribute. Of course, it's hyperbole to say that errors won't happen with ARC; we have to use strong references in a few places in this book to keep iOS from deciding that we have finished with an object before we actually do.

When using a variable property that has a strong reference, you should tell Xcode that you're finished using an object if you want it removed from memory. How do you do that? Easy: by setting its reference to `nil`.

For example, assume we've created a giant object called `myMemoryHog`:

```
var myMemoryHog: SomeHugeObject? = SomeHugeObject()
```

To tell Xcode when we're done using the object and let it free up the memory, we would type the following:

```
myMemoryHog = nil
```

Once the huge object isn't directly reference by any variables, it can be removed from memory, and all will be well with the world.

You've learned quite a bit in this hour's lesson, and there are plenty of places for even the most experienced developer to make mistakes. As with everything, practice makes perfect, which is why our final topic focuses on a tool that makes practicing Swift *fun*.

Introducing the iOS Playground

For a new developer, getting started with a language can be a pain. You've got to figure out how to create new projects, understand how a bunch of development tools work, and if you're lucky, after a few hours you might get "Hello World" to display on your screen.

When Apple introduced Swift, they realized that developers would need a way to get their feet wet (or hands dirty, if you prefer) without all the steps of creating new iOS applications. Heck, why would you want to try building an application if you aren't sure you're even going to be writing code that works? Therefore, the Playground was born. The Playground gives you an area to type in experimental code and see the result—*immediately*—without even pressing a Run button (unless you want to!).

Creating a New Playground

As a first step, you'll need to create a new Playground. We'll be using the Playground throughout the book, so understanding this process is a must.

To create a new Playground, choose File, New, Playground from the Xcode menu, as shown in Figure 3.3.

When prompted, provide a name for the playground and make sure that the platform is set to iOS, as demonstrated in Figure 3.4. The name can be anything you'd like. Unlike a project, a Playground creates a single file, so it's easy to rename later. Click Next to continue.

Finally, choose where the Playground will be saved, and then click Create. After a few seconds, the Playground window opens, as shown in Figure 3.5.

FIGURE 3.3
Create a new Playground from the Xcode File, New menu.

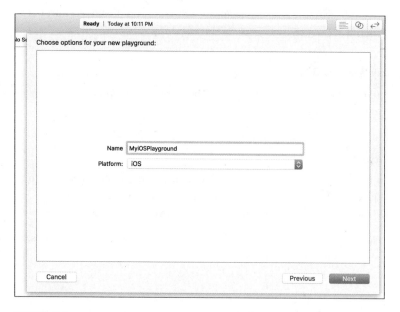

FIGURE 3.4
Name the playground and set the Platform to iOS.

FIGURE 3.5
The new playground opens, already populated with some sample code.

Using the Playground

When the Playground first opens, it already contains some sample code that imports the UIKit framework and defines a variable named str. You can safely delete the str line if you'd like, but I recommend that you leave the import statement at the top. This adds access to most of the objects and methods you'll need to actually do anything useful in the playground.

So, what do you do now? You *play*. Any code that you enter is immediately evaluated and the results appear in the margin on the right.

For example, remember the calculation of a person's age in days? Try typing this code into the playground:

```
var userAge: Int = 30
var userAgeInDays: Int
userAgeInDays = userAge * 365
```

As you type the lines, watch what happens in the margin on the right. For the first statement, declaring userAge, you'll see 30 appear in the margin because the variable contains the value 30. The second line won't generate any output because it doesn't contain anything yet. The third line, however, calculates and stores the age in days, which is displayed in the margin (10,950, if you're interested). You can see this in Figure 3.6.

TIP

Missing the Output? That's a Drag

If you don't see results in a margin on the right, it may be sized too small to see. Position your cursor near the right side of the window, and then click and drag to resize the margin and show the results.

Variable contents

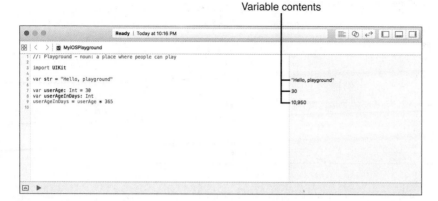

FIGURE 3.6
The contents of your variables are shown on the right.

Generating and Inspecting Output

The iOS Playground can be used to generate and display output as well as inspect variables. Later in the book, we'll use it to examine the contents of web pages retrieved by our code (and in a variety of other exercises). A simple way to generate output in Swift, however, is to use the `print(<String>)` function.

Add these lines to the end of the code in the Playground:

```
for count in 0...49 {
    print("Count is \(count)")
}
```

Shortly after typing the lines, you'll see a value in the margin quickly count to 50. This is a count of the number of times the `print` statement was executed. What you don't see, however, is the output that is generated.

To view the output, position your cursor over the line that reads "(50 times)." You'll notice two icons appear; the first (an outline of an eye) is the Quick Look icon and lets you inspect some variable contents more closely. (We'll do this in the next hour.) The second icon, a circle, adds the output in a block directly following the code, and lets you switch between viewing the current value and a history of the values that a variable has held.

Output History

Let's take a look at output history. Go ahead and click the circle by the `print` statement. The assistant editor displays the output from the `print` statement, as shown in Figure 3.7.

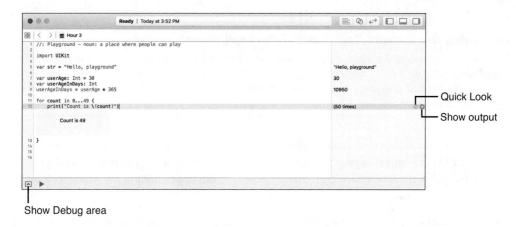

FIGURE 3.7
Add the output inline with the code.

Since the output of the `print` statement changes over time (as the loop executes), we can change the display to show the full history of its output. Right-click the output block and choose Value History. The output block changes to a scrolling list showing the full output from 0 to 49, shown in Figure 3.8.

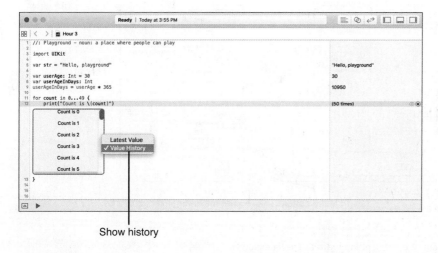

Show history

FIGURE 3.8
View the history of the output.

TIP

Not Seeing the Results You Expect? Perhaps There's a Bug

The Playground displays the same error and warning messages you learned about in the previous hour. If something isn't being displayed, look for the familiar yellow and red icons in your code listing. You can also click the Show Debug Area icon in the lower-left corner of the Playground to show any additional debugging output generated by the script.

If you want to take things even further, you can add a timeline to the Playground that makes it possible to view the output of your Playground script at any point during its execution. To view the timeline, show the Utility area by clicking the icon in the upper-right of the Xcode toolbar, or choose View, Utilities, Show Utilities from the menu.

With the Utilities area visible, make sure that the File Inspector icon (a piece of paper) is selected, and then check the Show Timeline check box. Use the timeline handle to choose the point in time to view. Set the maximum execution time using the -/+ buttons at the end of the timeline, as shown in Figure 3.9. This limits the time the script is given to finish.

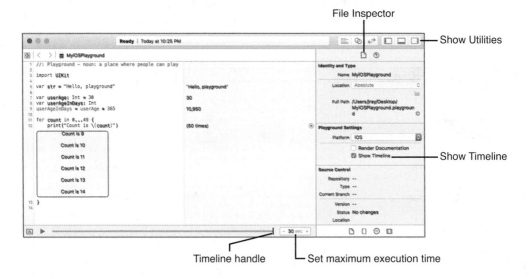

FIGURE 3.9
View the script output at a moment in time with the timeline.

Toggling Run Modes

The Playground, by default, is always evaluating what you've entered and producing results. For lengthy scripts, this can be time-consuming and result in sluggish behavior (and errors). To switch to a manual execution mode, click and hold the Play button at the bottom of the

Playground window and choose Manually Run, as shown in Figure 3.10. After you've made this selection, you need to click the Play icon to execute the Playground and view the results. You can switch back to Automatically Run at any time.

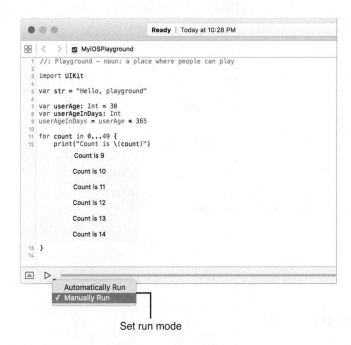

Set run mode

FIGURE 3.10
Switch between manual and automatic modes.

Playground Resources

Although not immediately apparent, the Playground is capable of interacting with resources just like a typical project. You can add images and other files to the Playground and reference them in your scripts. To do this, you must first show the Navigator area by clicking the third button from the right in the toolbar, or by choosing View, Navigators, Show Navigator from the menu. Once visible, make sure that the folder icon (project navigator) is clicked, as shown in Figure 3.11.

Using the techniques covered in Hour 2, "Introduction to Xcode and the iOS Simulator," you can add Swift source files to the Sources folder, or other files (images, sounds, and so on) to the Resources folder, and then reference them within your Playground script. We'll do this later in the book, so remember how to find these folders.

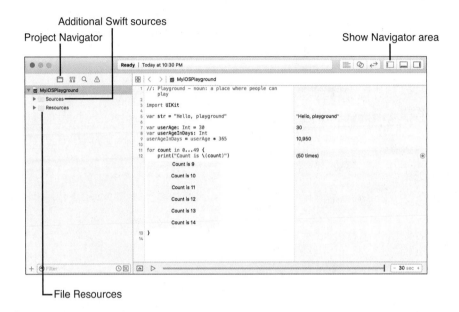

FIGURE 3.11
Use the project navigator to add resources to your Playground.

Further Exploration

Although you can be successful in learning iOS programming without spending hours and hours learning more Swift, you will find it easier to create complex applications if you become more comfortable with the language. Swift, as mentioned before, is not something that can be described in a single hour. It is a new language that is evolving to meet the specific needs of Apple's computing platform.

To learn more about Swift, check out *Sams Teach Yourself Swift in 24 Hours* (Sams, 2015).

Apple has also published a book (*The Swift Programming Language*) that covers the entirety of the Swift language, including Playground exercises. It is available directly with the iBook store on your Mac or iOS device. This isn't just recommended reading; it's a required download for any serious developer-to-be.

The beauty of the Playground is that you can do anything you want. Go back and try some of the Swift syntax discussed in this hour. Try comparing dates, test a few loops and `switch` statements... whatever you want.

We'll be using the Playground often to explore new code concepts, even making it do a few things that might surprise you. I recommend using it now to gain experience writing Swift.

Summary

In this hour, you learned about object-oriented programming and the Swift language. Swift will form the structure of your applications and give you tools to collect and react to user input and other changes. After reading this hour, you should understand how to make classes, declare objects, call methods, and use decision and looping statements to create code that implements more complex logic than a simple top-to-bottom workflow. You should also have an understanding of the iOS Playground and how it can be used to test code without needing to create a full iOS project.

Keep in mind that a typical book would spend multiple chapters on these topics, so our goal has been to give you a starting point that future hours will build on, not to define everything you'll ever need to know about Swift and OOP.

Q&A

Q. Is Swift on iOS the same as on OS X?

A. For the most part, yes. OS X includes thousands of additional application programming interfaces (APIs), however, and provides access to the underlying UNIX subsystem.

Q. Can an `if-then-else` statement be extended beyond evaluating and acting on a single expression?

A. Yes. The `if-then-else` statement can be extended by adding another `if` statement after the `else`:

```
if <expression> {
    // do this, the expression is true.
} else if <expression> {
    // the expression isn't true, do this instead.
} else {
    // Neither of the expressions are true, do this anyway!
}
```

You can continue expanding the statement with as many `else-if` statements as you need.

Q. Why is the Playground better than coding up a new project? Seems the same to me.

A. The biggest advantage of the iOS Playground is that it lets you see instant feedback from the code you enter. In addition, you don't even have to add output statements to inspect the contents of variables you declare; they appear automatically in the Playground margin.

Workshop

Quiz

1. ARC stands for what?

    a. Automatic Reference Counting

    b. Aggregated Recall Counts

    c. Automated Reference Cycling

    d. Apple Really Cares

2. The class files that you create for your applications will have which file extension?

    a. .swift

    b. .m

    c. .c

    d. .swf

3. Variables and methods that may return `nil` are known as what?

    a. Uncontrolled

    b. Controlled

    c. Optional

    d. Implicit

4. Declaring a variable with a `!` after the type definition makes it what?

    a. Unwrapped

    b. Optional

    c. Explicitly unwrapped

    d. Implicitly unwrapped

5. Stringing together method calls and variable properties is known as which of the following?

    a. Spanning

    b. Bridging

    c. Chaining

    d. Declaring

6. A variable that is defined outside of a method and that can be accessed from other classes is called what?

    a. Constant

    b. Instance variable

    c. Implicitly unwrapped variable

    d. Variable property

7. To declare a constant versus a variable, you replace the `var` keyword with which of the following?

    a. `set`

    b. `get`

    c. `let`

    d. `constant`

8. Variable types that can store multiple different values are known (in general) as what?

    a. Collections

    b. Sets

    c. Structs

    d. Aggregates

9. As of January 2016, Swift had been available to the public for how many years?

    a. 0-1

    b. 1-2

    c. 2-3

    d. 3-4

10. Swift classes are defined using how many files?

    a. 1

    b. 2

    c. 3

    d. 4

Answers

1. A. ARC stands for Automatic Reference Counting and is the process Apple's development tools use to determine whether an object can be freed from memory.

2. A. Class files developed in swift should include the .swift file extension.

3. C. A variable or method that returns `nil` (no value) is said to be optional.

4. D. Adding an exclamation point (`!`) after a variable's type definition sets that variable to be implicitly unwrapped.

5. C. Swift methods and variable properties can be strung together in a process called chaining.

6. D. Variable properties are declared outside of methods and can be accessed and used by other classes.

7. C. The `let` keyword is used to declare a constant.

8. A. Collections, including `Array`s and `Dictionary`s, are used to store multiple pieces of data.

9. B. As of January 2016, Swift will be roughly 18 months old – that's it!

10. B. A Swift class requires exactly one file for its implementation.

Activities

1. Start Xcode and create a new project using the iPhone or iPad Single View Application template. Review the contents of the classes in the project folder. With the information you've read in this hour, you should now be able to read and navigate the structure of these files.

2. Use iBooks on your iOS device or Mac to download Apple's free book *The Swift Programming Language*. This is an entirely free guide to the complete Swift language, straight from the source: Apple!

3. Use the iOS Playground to test your knowledge of Swift syntax and build simple procedural programs.

HOUR 4
Inside Cocoa Touch

What You'll Learn in This Hour:

▶ What Cocoa Touch is and what makes it unique

▶ The technology layers that make up the iOS platform

▶ A basic iOS application life cycle

▶ Classes and development techniques you'll be using throughout this book

▶ How to find help using the Apple developer documentation

When computers first started to appear in households almost 30 years ago, applications rarely shared common interface elements. It took an instruction manual just to figure out the key sequence to exit from a piece of software. Today, user interfaces (UIs) have been standardized so that moving from application to application doesn't require starting from scratch.

What has made this possible? Not faster processors or better graphics, but frameworks that enforce consistent implementation of the features provided by the devices they're running on. In this hour, we take a look at a few of the frameworks you'll be using in your iOS applications.

You've Used the Word *Framework* Several Times. What Exactly Is a Framework?

A framework is simply a collection of the files (code, interface files, images, and so on) that provide functionality to an application. To use Apple Maps, for example, you use Apple's MapKit framework. All of your apps include the Foundation, Core Graphics, and UIKit frameworks by default; otherwise they wouldn't be able to do anything! Later in the book, we'll build a few apps that require additional frameworks.

What Is Cocoa Touch?

In the preceding hour, you learned about the Swift language, the basic syntax, and what it looks like. Swift will form the functional skeleton of your applications. It will help you structure your applications, make logical decisions during the life cycle of your application, and enable you to control how and when events take place. What Swift doesn't provide, however, is a way to access what makes your iDevice the compelling touch-driven platform that it is.

Consider the following Hello World statement:

```
print("Hello world!")
```

This line of code is a completely valid Swift application that, when executed, generates output that reads "Hello World." You can compile this into an iOS project and execute it on your iPhone or iPad; but because iOS relies on Cocoa Touch for creating interfaces and handling user input and output, your users won't see a thing.

Cocoa Touch is the collection of software frameworks that is used to build iOS applications and the runtime that those applications are executed within. It includes hundreds of classes for managing everything from buttons and uniform resource locators (URLs) to manipulating photos and performing facial recognition.

Cocoa Touch is the highest of several "layers" of services in the iOS and isn't necessarily the only layer that you'll be developing in. That said, you don't need to worry too much about where Cocoa Touch begins and ends; the development will be the same, regardless. Later in this hour, you get an overview of iOS service layers.

Returning to the Hello World example, if we had defined a text label object named `iOSOutput` within a project, we could set it to read `"Hello World"` using Swift and the `UILabel text` variable property, just like this:

```
iOSOutput.text="Hello World"
```

Seems simple enough, as long as we know that the `UILabel` object *has* a `text` variable property, right?

Keeping Your Cool in the Face of Overwhelming Functionality

The questions that should be coming to most beginners right about now include these: I know there are many different features provided through iOS applications; how in the world will this book document all of them? How will I ever find what I need to use for my own applications?

These are great questions, and probably some of the biggest concerns that I've heard from those who want to program for the platform but have no idea where to start. The bad news is that we can't document everything. We can cover the fundamentals that you need to start building, but even in a multivolume set of *Teach Yourself* books, there is so much depth to what is provided by Cocoa Touch that it isn't feasible to create a comprehensive how-to reference.

The good news is that Cocoa Touch and the Apple developer tools encourage exploration. In Hour 6, "Model-View-Controller Application Design," you start building interfaces visually using

Xcode's Interface Builder (IB) tools. As you drag objects (buttons, text fields, and so on) to your interface, you create instances of Cocoa Touch classes. The more you "play," the quicker you will begin to recognize class names and variable properties and the role they play in development. Even better, Xcode developer documentation provides a complete reference to Cocoa Touch, enabling you to search across all available classes, methods, variable properties, and so on. We take a look at the documentation features later in this hour.

Young, Yet Mature

One of the most compelling advantages to programming using Cocoa Touch versus platforms such as Android is that although iOS and Swift are "young" platforms for Apple, the Cocoa frameworks are amazingly mature. Cocoa was borne out of the NeXTSTEP platform—the environment that was used by NeXT computers in the mid-1980s. In the early 1990s, NeXTSTEP evolved into the cross-platform OpenStep. Finally, in 1996, Apple purchased NeXT Computer, and over the next decade, the NeXTSTEP/OpenStep framework became the de facto standard for Macintosh development and was renamed Cocoa. You'll notice that there are still signs of Cocoa's origins in class names that begin with *NS*.

How Do Cocoa and Cocoa Touch Differ?

Cocoa and Cocoa Touch are not the same. Cocoa operates in a window-centric world with very different user events and far more capabilities due to running on machines with very fast processors and tons of RAM and storage.

The good news is that if you decide to transition from iOS developer to OS X developer, you'll follow many of the same development patterns on both platforms; it won't be like starting from scratch.

Exploring the iOS Technology Layers

Apple describes the technologies implemented within the iOS as a series of layers, with each layer being made up of different frameworks that can be used in your applications. As you might expect, the Cocoa Touch layer is at the top (see Figure 4.1).

Let's review some of the more interesting frameworks that make up each of the layers. If you want a comprehensive guide to all frameworks, just search for each layer by its name in the Apple Xcode documentation.

The Cocoa Touch Layer

The Cocoa Touch layer is made up of several frameworks that will provide the core functionality for your applications, including multitasking and advertising. UIKit could be described as the "rock star" of this layer, delivering much more than the UI in its name implies.

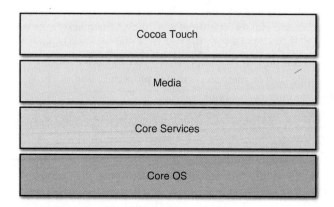

FIGURE 4.1
The technology layers that make up iOS.

UIKit

UIKit covers a wide range of functionality. It is responsible for application launching and termination, controlling the interface and multitouch events, and providing access to common views of data (including web pages and Word and Excel documents, among others).

UIKit is also responsible for many intra-iOS integration features. Accessing the Media Library, Photo Library, and accelerometer is also accomplished using the classes and methods within UIKit.

MapKit

The MapKit framework enables developers to add Apple's map views to any application, including annotation, location, and event-handling features.

GameKit

The GameKit framework adds network-interactivity to iOS applications. GameKit supplies mechanisms for creating and using peer-to-peer networks, including session discovery, mediation, and voice chat. These features can be added to any application or game (or not).

Message UI/Contacts UI/EventKit UI

Apple is sensitive to the need for integration between iOS applications. The Message UI, Contacts UI, and EventKit UI frameworks can be used to access mail, contacts, and calendar events from any application you develop.

Notification Center

Create widgets and display information in the iOS notification center by using the Notification Center framework.

iAd

The iAd framework supports the addition of ads to your applications. iAds are interactive advertising pieces that can be added to your software with a simple drag and drop. You do not need to manage iAds interactions in your application; Apple does this for you.

TextKit

TextKit provides rich text rendering for iOS applications seeking to implement word-processor-like layout and font controls. TextKit includes features for editing, displaying, and saving rich content.

The Media Layer

When Apple makes a computing device, you'd better believe that they put some thought into the media capabilities. The iDevice family can create complex graphics, play back audio and video, and even generate real-time 3D graphics. The Media layer's frameworks handle it all.

AV Foundation

The AV Foundation framework can be used to manage complex sound and video playback and editing. This should be used for implementing advanced features, such as movie recording, track management, and audio panning.

AVKit

The AVKit framework is used for simple video playback. It is also used to enable picture-in-picture playback under iOS 9 or later.

Core Audio

The Core Audio framework exposes methods for handling basic playback and recording of audio. It includes the AudioToolbox framework, which can be used for playing alert sounds or generating short vibrations, and the AudioUnit.framework for processing sounds.

Core Image

With the Core Image framework, developers can add advanced image and video processing capabilities to their applications without needing to understand the complex math behind them. Core Image, for example, provides facial-detection and image-filtering features that can easily be added to any application.

Core Graphics

Use the Core Graphics framework to add 2D drawing and compositing features to your applications. Although most of this book will use existing interface classes and images in its applications, you can use core graphics to programmatically manipulate the view.

Core Text

This provides precise positioning and control over text that is displayed on the screen. Core Text should be used in mobile text-processing applications and software that requires high-quality and fast presentation and manipulation of styled text.

Game Controller

Although not directly related to media, the Game Controller framework is also a member of the Media layer. This framework enables you to locate, connect, and configure game controllers that conform with Apple's Made-for-iPhone (MFi) program.

Image I/O

The Image I/O framework can be used to import and export both image data and image metadata for any file format supported by iOS.

Metal

Metal is Apple's new high-performance graphics framework. Unlike OpenGL, Metal provides much lower-level access to graphics hardware, enabling developers to push higher quality visuals in their apps.

OpenGL ES

OpenGL ES is a subset of the popular OpenGL framework for embedded systems (ES). OpenGL ES can be used to create 2D and 3D animation in your apps. Using OpenGL requires additional development experience beyond Swift but can generate amazing scenes for a handheld device—similar to what is possible on modern game consoles.

Photos

The Photos framework provides access to the Photos stored within an iOS library, including those on iCloud. Using this framework, you can create your own applications for managing and editing Photos in iOS.

Photos UI

Expand the capabilities of the Photos application by creating custom editing capabilities that can be used to extend the built-in iOS image editor.

SpriteKit

The SpriteKit framework provides a set of simple tools for animating graphics in 2D games. SpriteKit includes animation, collision detection, and object logic controls. If you've ever dreamed of making your own Mario-like world, SpriteKit is the place to start.

Quartz Core

The Quartz Core framework is used to create animations that will take advantage of the hardware capabilities of your device. This includes the feature set known as *Core Animation*.

The Core Services Layer

The Core Services layer is used to access lower-level operating system services, such as file access, iCloud storage, networking, and many common data object types. You'll make use of core services often by way of the Foundation framework.

Accounts

Because of their always-connected nature, iOS devices are often used to store account information for many different services. The Accounts framework simplifies the process of storing and authenticating users.

Address Book

The Address Book framework is used to directly access and manipulate address book information. This is used to update contact information and display it within your applications.

CFNetwork

The CFNetwork framework provides access to BSD sockets, HTTP and FTP requests, and Bonjour discovery.

Core Data

The Core Data framework can be used to create the data model of an iOS application. Core Data provides a relational data model based on SQLite and can be used to bind data to interface objects to eliminate the need for complex data manipulations in code.

Core Foundation

Core Foundation provides much of the same functionality of the Foundation framework, but it is a procedural framework and therefore requires a different development approach that is, arguably, less efficient than Swift's object-oriented model. You should probably avoid Core Foundation unless you absolutely need it.

Core Location

The Core Location framework can be used to obtain latitude and longitude information from the iPhone and iPad (3G/LTE) GPS (WiFi-based location service is available in non-3G/LTE devices, but is much less precise) along with a measurement of precision.

Core Motion

The Core Motion framework manages most motion-related events on the iOS platform, such as using the accelerometer or gyroscope.

EventKit

The EventKit framework is used to access calendar information stored on the iOS device. It also enables the developer to create new events within a calendar, including alarms.

Foundation

The Foundation framework provides an object-oriented wrapper around features in Core Foundation. Manipulation of strings, arrays, and dictionaries is handled through the Foundation framework, as are other fundamental application necessities, including managing application preferences, threads, and internationalization.

HealthKit

The HealthKit framework is used to store and access health-related data related to an iOS device user. If you are considering developing fitness-related apps, this framework is for you.

HomeKit

HomeKit provides a consistent interface to home automation hardware and tools. Using HomeKit, you can access automation functions across applications—additional hardware and software are necessary, however.

Newsstand

Use this framework to create periodical digital media, such as newspapers or magazines. The Newsstand framework supports automatic content updating, ensuring your customers see the most recent content without needing to manually update.

PassKit

The PassKit framework, coupled with web services, can provide electronic coupons, boarding passes, tickets, and other transaction information to the user.

Quick Look

The Quick Look framework implements file viewing within an application, even if the application does not "know" how to open a specific file type. This is intended for viewing files downloaded to the device.

Social

Rather than requiring developers to create Twitter and Facebook integration from scratch, Apple includes a framework for these popular social networking sites. Using this framework, you can write applications that access Twitter and Facebook without needing to manage account information or understand their proprietary network protocols.

StoreKit

The StoreKit framework enables developers to create in-application transactions for purchasing content without exiting the software. All interactions take place through the App Store, so no financial data is requested or transmitted through the StoreKit methods.

System Configuration

Use the System Configuration framework to determine the current state of a device's network configuration—what network it is connected to (if any) and what other devices are reachable.

The Core OS Layer

The Core OS layer, as you'd expect, is made up of the lowest-level services in the iOS. These features include threads, complex math, hardware accessories, and cryptography. You should only need to access these frameworks in rare circumstances.

Accelerate

The Accelerate framework simplifies complete calculations and large-number manipulation. This includes digital signal processing capabilities.

Core Bluetooth

The Core Bluetooth framework provides connectivity for low-energy Bluetooth devices. This is a unique class of Bluetooth peripheral that can communicate with extremely low power requirements.

External Accessory

The External Accessory framework is used to develop interfaces to accessories connected via the dock connector or Bluetooth.

Local Authentication

The Local Authentication framework provides the ability to authenticate users via passphrases or the Touch ID sensor.

Security

The Security framework provides functions for performing cryptographic functions (encrypting/ decrypting data). This includes interacting with the iOS keychain to add, delete, and modify items.

System

The System framework gives developers access to a subset of the typical tools they would find in an unrestricted UNIX development environment.

Tracing the iOS Application Life Cycle

To help you get a sense for where your "work" in developing an iOS application fits in, it helps to look at the application life cycle. Figure 4.2 shows Apple's simplified diagram of the life cycle.

Let's try to put some context around what you're looking at, starting on the left side of the diagram. As you've learned, UIKit is a component of the Cocoa Touch that provides much of the foundation of iOS applications: UI management, event management, and overall application execution management. When you create an application, UIKit handles the setup of the application object via the UIApplicationMain functions, neither of which you should need to touch.

Once the application is started, an event loop begins. This loop receives the events such as screen touches, and then hands them off to your own methods. The loop continues until the application is asked to move to the background (usually through the user pressing the Home button).

Your code comes into play on the right side of the diagram. Xcode automatically sets up your iOS projects to include an application delegate class. This class can implement the methods app lication:willFinishLaunchingWithOptions, application:didFinishLaunching WithOptions, and applicationDidEnterBackground (among others) so that your program can execute its own custom code when the application launches and when it is suspended by pressing the Home button.

Wait a Second! When Does My Application *Stop* Running?

To support this process, the application delegate provides the method applicationDid EnterBackground, which is called when the application enters the background. This method should be used by your code to store any information that the application needs, in case it is terminated while it is the background (either by iOS cleaning up resources or by the user manu- ally terminating it in the task manager). There are even more methods available for handling what happens when a suspended application becomes active again, but we won't concern ourselves with that until much later.

After an application finishes launching, the delegate object typically creates a view controller object and view and adds them to the iOS "window." You learn more about these concepts in the next hour, but for now, think of a view as what is being displayed on the device's screen and the view controller as an object that can be programmed to respond when it receives an event notification (such as touching a button) from the event loop.

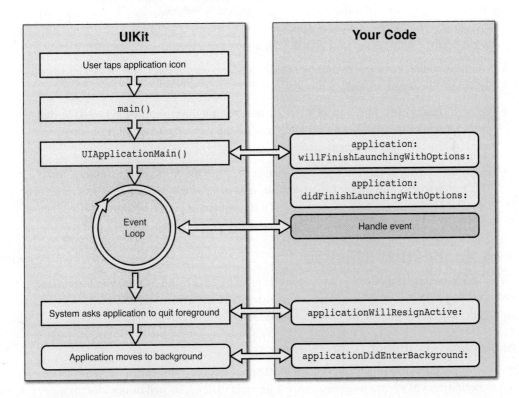

FIGURE 4.2
The (simplified) life cycle of a typical iOS application.

The majority of your work will take place within the view controller. You'll receive events from the Cocoa Touch interface and react to them by writing Swift code that manipulates other objects within the view. Of course, things can get a bit more complex than a single view and a single view controller, but the same basic approach can be applied in most cases.

Now that you have a better picture of the iOS service layers and application life cycle, let's take a look at some of the classes that you'll be seeing throughout this book.

Cocoa Fundamentals

Thousands of classes are available in the iOS software development kit (SDK), but most of your applications will be using a small set of classes to implement 90% of their features. To familiarize you with the classes and their purposes, let's review some of the names you're going to be seeing very, very often over the next few hours. Before we begin, keep these few key points in mind:

▶ Apple sets up much of the structure of your application for you in Xcode. Therefore, even though you need some of these classes, you won't have to lift a finger to use them. Just create a new Xcode project and they're added for you.

▶ You'll be adding instances of many of these objects to your projects just by dragging icons in Xcode's IB. Again, no coding needed!

▶ When a class is used, I tell you why it is needed, what it does, and how it is used in the project. I don't want you to have to jump around digging for references in the book, so focus on the concepts, not memorization.

▶ In the last section of this hour's lesson, you learn about the Apple documentation tool. This will help you find all the class, variable, and method information that you could ever hope for. If it's gritty details you want, you'll have them at your fingertips.

Core Application Classes

When you create a new application with even the most basic user interaction, you'll be taking advantage of a collection of common core classes. Many of these you won't be touching, but they still perform an important role. Let's review several of these classes now.

The Application Object (`UIApplication`)

Every iOS application implements a subclass of `UIApplication`. This class handles events, such as notification of when an application has finished loading, as well as application configuration, such as controlling the status bar and setting badges (the little red numbers that can appear on application icons). You won't need to create this yourself; just be aware it exists.

Window Objects (`UIWindow`)

The `UIWindow` class provides a container for the management and display of views. In iOS-speak, a view is more like a typical desktop application "window," whereas an instance of `UIWindow` is just a container that holds the view. You use only a single `UIWindow` instance in this book, and it is created automatically in the project templates that Xcode provides for us.

Views (`UIView`)

The `UIView` class defines a rectangular area and manages all the onscreen display within that region—what we will refer to as a view. Most of your applications will start by adding a view to an instance of `UIWindow`.

Views can be nested to form a hierarchy; they rarely exist as a single object. A top-level view, for example, may contain a button and field. These controls would be referred to as *subviews* and the containing view as the *superview*. Multiple levels of views can be nested, creating a complex hierarchy of subviews and superviews. You'll be creating almost all of your views visually in Xcode, so don't worry: Complex doesn't mean difficult.

Responders (`UIResponder`)

The `UIResponder` class provides a means for classes that inherit from it to respond to the touch events produced by iOS. `UIControl`, the superclass for nearly all onscreen controls, inherits from `UIView` and, subsequently, from `UIResponder`. An instance of `UIResponder` is just called a *responder*.

Because multiple objects could potentially respond to an event, iOS passes events up what is referred to as a *chain of responders*. The responder instance that can handle the event is called the first responder. When you're editing a field, for example, the field has first responder status because it is actively handling user input. When you leave the field, it "resigns" first responder status. For most of your iOS development work, you won't be directly managing responders in code.

Onscreen Controls (`UIControl`)

The `UIControl` class inherits from `UIView` and is used as the superclass for almost all onscreen controls, such as buttons, fields, and sliders. This class is responsible for handling the triggering of actions based on touch events, such as "pressing" a button.

As you'll learn in the next hour, a button defines a handful of events that you can respond to; IB enables you to tie those events to actions that you've coded. `UIControl` is responsible for implementing this behavior behind the scenes.

View Controllers (`UIViewController`)

You use the `UIViewController` class in almost all the application projects throughout this book to manage the contents of your views. You use a `UIViewController` subclass, for example, to determine what to do when a user taps a button. Make a sound? Display an image? However you choose to react, the code you use to carry out your action will be implemented as part of a view controller instance. You'll learn much more about view controllers over the next two hours.

Data Type Classes

An object can potentially hold data. In fact, most of the classes we'll be using contain a number of variable properties that store information about an object. There are, however, a set of Foundation classes that you use throughout this book for the sole purpose of storing and manipulating information.

There are two types of data types that you'll encounter: those that are bridged with Swift and those that aren't.

Bridged Data Types

iOS development has traditionally relied on Objective-C. In Objective-C, the primitive data types like Integers, Strings, and so on were tied to the C-language underpinnings and had very little functionality. In other words, to program useful applications, Apple needed to implement better versions of these common data types within custom classes.

With Swift, this is no longer necessary. Apple's implementation of Swift has robust primitive data types that don't rely on a 40-year-old language. This is both good and bad. It means that we can do a lot in Swift without worrying about creating instances of several data classes. Unfortunately, quite a bit of Cocoa still relies on using these legacy classes as arguments to methods, return data types, and so on; so, they still need to exist.

To make our developer lives easier, Apple has *bridged* the common Swift and Cocoa data types. This means that while we may work with data types we define in Swift, behind the scenes that are automatically translated to and from Cocoa objects. For the most part, this works well. Sometimes, however, we must still declare an instance of the original Cocoa data class, or use conversion functions or casting to covert between them.

The Cocoa classes and their Swift counterparts are as follows:

Strings (NSString/NSMutableString)

Arrays (NSArray/NSMutableArray)

Dictionaries (NSDictionary/NSMutableDictionary)

Integers/Floating-Point/Booleans (NSNumber/NSDecimalNumber)

When we work through projects over the next 20 hours, we'll make every effort to use the Swift primitive types—but sometimes you'll still see these Cocoa classes come into play.

Nonbridged Data Types

Data classes that aren't bridged aren't more difficult to work with, they just require a bit more setup in order to use them. Let's take a look at two Cocoa classes we'll be using later in the book that implement unique types of data.

Dates (`NSDate`) If you've ever tried to work with a date manually (interpreting a date string in a program, or even just doing date arithmetic by hand), you know it can be a great cause of headaches. How many days were there in September? Was this a leap year? And so on. The `NSDate` class provides a convenient way to work with dates as an object.

For example, assume you have a user-provided date (`userDate`) and you want to use it for a calculation, but only if it is earlier than the current date, in which case, you want to use *that* date. Typically, this would be a bunch of nasty comparisons and assignments. With `NSDate`, you would create a date object with the current date in it (provided automatically when the object is initialized):

```
let myDate: NSDate = NSDate()
```

And then grab the earlier of the two dates using the `earlierDate` method:

```
myDate.earlierDate(userDate)
```

Obviously, you can perform many other operations, but you can avoid much of the ugliness of data and time manipulation using `NSDate` objects.

URLs (`NSURL`) URLs are certainly a different type of data from what we're accustomed to thinking about, but on an Internet-connected device like the iPhone and iPad, you'll find that the ability to manipulate URLs comes in handy. The `NSURL` class enables you to manage URLs with ease. For example, suppose that you have the URL http://www.teachyourselfios.com/index.html and want to get just the machine name out of the string. You could create an `NSURL` object:

```
let myURL: NSURL = NSURL(string:"http://www.teachyourselfios.com/index.html")!
```

Then use the `host` variable property to automatically parse the URL and return the text "www. teachyourselfios.com":

```
myURL.host
```

No need to search through the string and figure out the different parts of the URL—Cocoa does it for us. As you can see, nonbridged data types can be useful, and there are dozens more that you can take advantage of during your development.

TRY IT YOURSELF ▼

Cocoa Data Types and the iOS Playground

The iOS Playground is a great place to try out the different data manipulation features offered by the various Cocoa Touch classes. You can see how these objects work without needing to create a full project or develop a user interface.

For example, open Xcode and Choose File, New from the Playground. When prompted, enter a name for the Playground (it doesn't matter), and make sure the platform is set to iOS.

Now, as the name suggests, you can play in the Playground!

For example, take the two lines that I just provided to demonstrate `NSURL` and add them into the Playground. (You can take out the sample `var` statement that is added by default.)

```
let myURL: NSURL = NSURL(string:"http://www.teachyourselfios.com/index.html")!
myURL.host
```

After entering the lines, you can immediately see the value of `myURL` and `myURL.host` to the right of the lines of code. Changes to make to the code are immediately reflected in the results.

The Playground can even display graphical objects. Add these additional lines to the bottom of the storyboard:

```
let myView: UIView = UIView(frame: CGRectMake(0, 0, 100, 100))
myView.backgroundColor = UIColor.redColor()
```

These lines create a new `UIView` that is 100 points wide and 100 points tall, then sets the background color to red. After the code is added, click the little Quick Look "eye" icon to the right of the code to see a visual representation of the UIView.

What's more, you can see the object change on a line-by-line basis. Try clicking the Quick Look icon beside the line that creates the UIView. You'll see a light gray rectangle (because no color has been defined). On the subsequent line, Quick Look will show the view as red. By using this feature, you can see exactly how changes you make to an object's configuration affect its appearance.

Interface Classes

Part of what makes iOS Devices so much fun to use are the onscreen touch interfaces that you can create. As we explore Xcode's IB in the next hour, you'll get your first hands-on experience with some of these interface classes. Something to keep in mind as you read through this section is that many UI objects can take on very different visual appearances based on how they are configured—so there is quite a bit of flexibility in your presentation.

Labels (`UILabel`)

You'll be adding labels to your applications both to present static text onscreen (as a typical label) and as a controllable block of text that can be changed as needed by your program (see Figure 4.3).

▫ ▫ ▫
▫ **Label (UILabel)** ▫
▫ ▫ ▫

FIGURE 4.3
Labels add text to your application views.

Buttons (`UIButton`)

Buttons are one of the simplest user input methods that you'll be using. Buttons can respond to a variety of touch events and give your users an easy way to make onscreen choices. Buttons are, by default, borderless, relying on their size, color, and location to make them an obvious control (see Figure 4.4).

FIGURE 4.4
Buttons provide a simple form of user input/interaction.

Switches (`UISwitch`)

A switch object can be used to collect "on" and "off" responses from a user. It is displayed as a simple toggle and is often used to activate or deactivate application features (see Figure 4.5).

FIGURE 4.5
A switch moves between on and off states.

Segmented Control (`UISegmentedControl`)

A segmented control creates an elongated touchable bar with multiple named selections (Category 1, Category 2, and so on). Touching a selection activates it and can trigger your application to perform an action, such as updating the screen to hide or show other controls (see Figure 4.6).

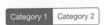

FIGURE 4.6
Segmented controls can be used to choose one item out of a set and react accordingly.

Sliders (`UISlider`)

A slider provides the user with a draggable bobble for the purpose of choosing a value from across a range. Sliders, for example, are used to control volume, screen brightness, and other inputs that should be presented in an "analog" fashion (see Figure 4.7).

FIGURE 4.7
Sliders offer a visual means of entering a value within a range.

Steppers (`UIStepper`)

Similar to a slider is a stepper (`UIStepper`). Like a slider, a stepper offers a means of inputting a number from a range of values visually (see Figure 4.8). Pushing a side of the control decrements or increments an internal variable property.

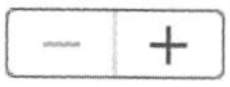

FIGURE 4.8
Use a stepper to increment or decrement values.

Text Fields (`UITextField`/`UITextView`)

Text fields are used to collect user input through the onscreen (or Bluetooth) keyboard. The `UITextField` is a single-line field, similar to what you'd see on a web page order form. The `UITextView` class, on the other hand, creates a larger multiline text entry block for more lengthy compositions (see Figure 4.9).

FIGURE 4.9
Collect user input through text fields.

Pickers (`UIDatePicker`/`UIPicker`)

A picker is an interesting interface element that vaguely resembles a slot machine display. By letting the user change each segment on the wheel, it can be used to enter a combination of several different values. Apple has implemented one complete picker for you: the `UIDatePicker` class. With this object, a user can quickly enter dates and times. You can also implement your own arbitrary pickers with the `UIPicker` class (see Figure 4.10).

Popovers (`UIPopoverPresentationController`)

Popovers are both a UI element and a means of displaying other UI elements. They allow you to display a view on top of any other view for the purpose of making a choice. The iPad's Safari browser, for example, uses a popover to present the user with a list of bookmarks to choose from, as shown in Figure 4.11.

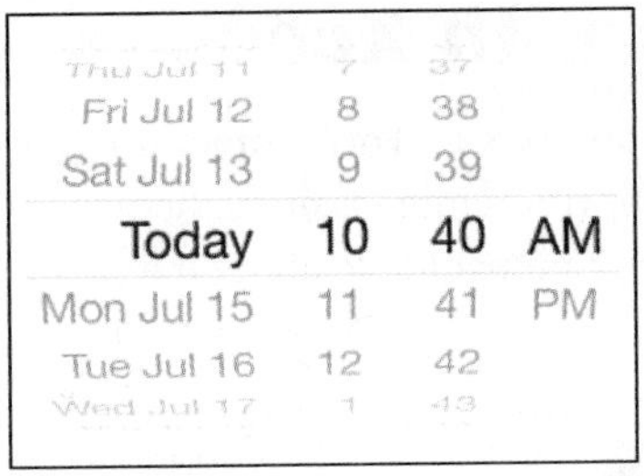

FIGURE 4.10
Pickers enable users to choose a combination of several options.

FIGURE 4.11
Popovers present information on top of other views.

Most often used on the iPad, Apple has made it possible to use popovers on iPhones as well. We'll use popovers often in the second half of this book.

These are only a sampling of the classes that you can use in your applications. We explore these and many others in the hours to come.

Exploring the iOS Frameworks with Xcode

So far in this hour, you've learned about dozens of frameworks and classes. Each framework could be made up of dozens of additional classes, and each class with hundreds of methods, and so on. In other words, there's a ridiculous amount of information available about the iOS frameworks.

One of the most efficient ways to learn more is to pick an object or framework you're interested in and then turn to the Xcode documentation system. Xcode provides an interface to the immense Apple development library in both a searchable browser-like interface (even with video tutorials!) and a context-sensitive Research Assistant. Let's take a look at both of these features now so that you can start using them immediately.

Xcode Documentation

Xcode is capable of connecting to the Internet and retrieving documentation on-the-fly, but it's much easier (and faster) to keep a copy of the documentation relevant to your development stored on your Mac. Let's start our look at the documentation system by making sure we have copies of the documents we want.

Setting Up Documentation Downloads

The Xcode documentation system is kept up-to-date by receiving feeds of document sets from Apple. Document sets are broad categories of documents that cover development for specific OS X versions, Xcode itself, and the iOS releases. To ensure that you have the latest and greatest iOS and Xcode docs stored locally, follow these steps:

1. Open the Xcode Preferences (Xcode, Preferences from the menu bar).

2. Click the Downloads icon on the preference window toolbar.

3. Make sure Check For and Install Updates Automatically is checked.

4. Click the download icon beside each documentation set that you want to retrieve, as shown in Figure 4.12.

5. Close the Xcode preferences when finished.

Documentation sets take up a surprising amount of room, so if you're space conscious, only download the sets you need. Now you're ready to read.

TIP

You can force a manual update of the documentation using the Check and Install Now button.

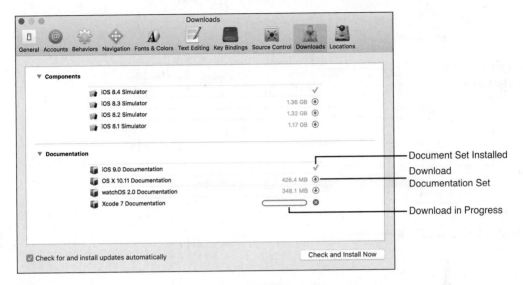

FIGURE 4.12
Download a copy of the documentation you need, and automatically keep it up-to-date.

Searching Documentation

To open the Xcode documentation application, choose Help, Documentation and API Reference from the menu bar. The help system will launch, with a very browser-like appearance. Begin typing a topic of interest into the search field, and, as you type, a list of results appear, as shown in Figure 4.13.

The results are divided into categories:

▶ **API Reference:** Documents that describe the technical details of a feature, such as the methods and variable properties a class makes available.

▶ **SDK Guides:** Tutorial-like documentation that takes a more high-level view of a feature and describes how it could/should be used.

▶ **Sample Code:** Xcode projects that you can download and use to see a feature demonstrated.

Clicking a result in the list will take you directly to the document you selected. Alternatively, you can click the Show All Results entry to see all possible matches for your search term.

TIP

You can fine-tune your search criteria by clicking the magnifying glass located *within* the search field. This displays a pop-up menu with selections for limiting your search to specific document sets.

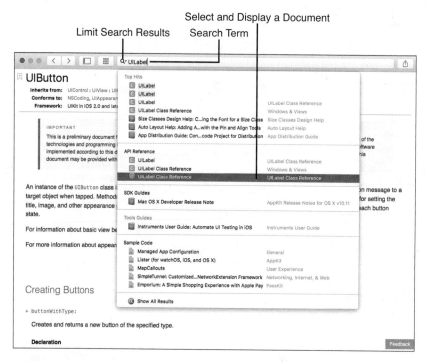

FIGURE 4.13
Search through the available documentation for topics you are interested in.

Browsing Documentation

In addition to searching for help, you can also browse all the available documents within your document sets, including online video and sample code. To do this, follow these steps:

1. Click the disclosure arrow in the toolbar if a sidebar isn't already available. A sidebar will appear in the window.

2. Click the documentation set icon (books on a shelf) to see all the available resources.

3. Drill down into the docs until you find what you're interested in, as demonstrated in Figure 4.14.

Navigating Documents

When you've arrived at a document that you're interested in, regardless of whether you searched or browsed to find it, you can read and navigate within the document using the blue links. You can also move forward and backward between documents using the arrow buttons located above the content.

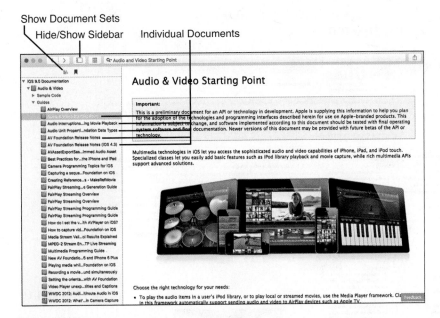

FIGURE 4.14
Explore all the available Xcode documentation resources.

If you're familiar with tabbed browsing, you can choose View, Show Tab Bar. Tabs are added by clicking the + icon at the far right of the tab bar. Command-clicking a link automatically opens it in a new tab, similar to Safari.

To speed up navigation within a document, you can click the table of contents icon in the toolbar to show a TOC (if available) for the document you are currently viewing, as demonstrated in Figure 4.15. Clicking an entry within the TOC jumps to the appropriate location within the document.

If you find a particularly interesting piece of information, you can bookmark it. To create a bookmark, you use the Share Sheet in the toolbar or simply click the Bookmark icon beside the content that interests you.

To access all your documentation bookmarks, make sure that the sidebar is visible, and then click the bookmark icon, as shown in Figure 4.16.

Back

Forward   Hide/Show TOC   Tabs   Add Tab

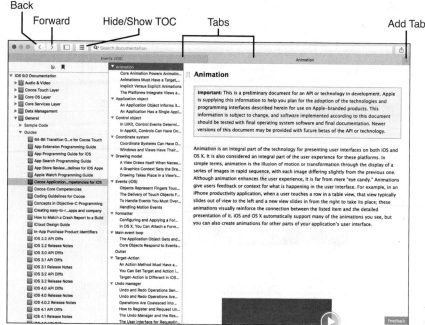

FIGURE 4.15
Display the TOC
for the current
document.

Bookmarks   Add Bookmark   Share

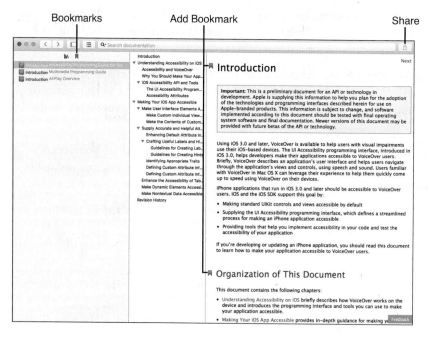

FIGURE 4.16
Keep track of
your favorite help
resources.

Quick Help

One of the easiest and fastest ways to get help while coding is through the Xcode Quick Help assistant. To open the assistant, hold down Option and click a symbol in Xcode (for example, a class name or method name) or choose Help, Quick Help. A small window opens with basic information about the symbol, as well as links to other documentation resources.

Using Quick Help

Consider the following line that initializes an NSDate object with a date in the far future (yes, such a feature does exist!):

```
let myDate: NSDate = NSDate.distantFuture() as NSDate
```

In this example, there is a class (NSDate) and a method (distantFuture()). To get information about the distantFuture method, hold down Option, and then click it within the code. The Quick Help popover appears, as shown in Figure 4.17. (Notice that the NSDate method returns an object with the type AnyObject—that's why we have to force it to be considered an NSDate with the as NSDate syntax.)

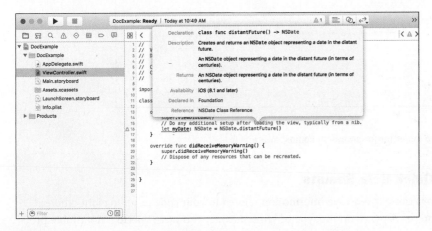

FIGURE 4.17
Quick Help brings reference information to your code editor.

Click any of the hyperlinks in Quick Help results to jump to a specific piece of documentation or code.

NOTE

You can tell when you're hovering over an item that you can click for Quick Help because it will be displayed with a blue dashed underline in the Xcode editor and your mouse cursor will change to show a question mark (?).

Activating the Quick Help Inspector

If you find Quick Help useful and wish you could access it even faster, you're in luck. The Quick Help Inspector can be used to display help information all the time. Xcode actually displays context-aware help for whatever you're typing, as you type it.

To display the Quick Help Inspector, open the utility area of the Xcode window using the third (rightmost) View button. Next, click the show Quick Help Inspector icon (a question mark in a circle), located at the top of the utility area, as shown in Figure 4.18. Quick Help automatically displays a reference for whatever code your text-entry cursor is located in.

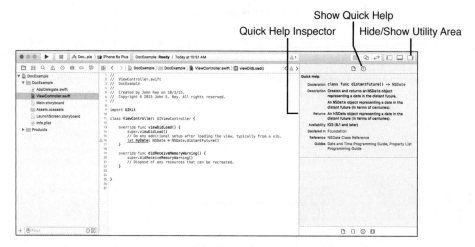

FIGURE 4.18
Open the Quick Help Inspector for always-on context-aware help.

Interpreting Quick Help Results

Quick Help displays context-sensitive information related to your code in up to eight different sections. What you see depends on the type of symbol (code) you have selected. A variable property, for example, doesn't have a return type, but a class method does:

▶ **Declaration:** The structure of a method or definition of a data type

▶ **Description:** A few sentences describing the feature that the class, method, or other symbol provides

▶ **Parameters:** The required or option information that can be provided to a method

▶ **Returns:** What information will be returned by a method when it completes

▶ **Availability:** The versions of the operating system where the feature is available

- ▸ **Declared In:** The file that defines the selected symbol

- ▸ **Reference:** The official reference documentation for the system

- ▸ **Related:** Other methods within the same class as your selected method

- ▸ **Guides:** Additional tutorial documentation that references the selected symbol

- ▸ **Sample Code:** Sample code files that include examples of class/method/variable use

Quick Help simplifies the process of finding the right method to use with an object. Instead of trying to memorize dozens of instance methods, you can learn the basics and let Quick Help act as an on-demand reference of all of an object's exposed methods.

NOTE

Help Yourself!

In the last hour, you learned how to use Markdown syntax-based comments to document your application methods. If you've done this, you'll see your pretty comments rendered in the Quick Help panel when you click a documented method.

Further Exploration

To say that Cocoa Touch is *big* is an understatement. Every year, Apple releases a major update of iOS and adds thousands of new classes and methods. I try to cover the highlights in this book, but there is much more to explore. To get a taste for the number of frameworks and classes available, I recommend starting with the *iOS Technology Overview* document, and work through the items under the each layer. This will show you what functionality is built in to the OS and let you focus on the topics that are important to your individual development efforts.

Summary

In this hour, you explored the layers that make up the iOS: Cocoa Touch, Media, Core Services, and Core OS. You learned the structure of a basic application: what objects it uses and how iOS manages the application life cycle. We also reviewed the common classes that you'll encounter as you begin to work with Cocoa, including data types and UI controls.

To give you the tools you need to find class and method references on your own, this hour introduced you to two features in Xcode. The first, the Xcode documentation window, offers a browser-like interface to the complete iOS documentation. The second, Quick Help, finds help for the class or method you are working with, automatically, as you type. Ultimately, it will be these tools that help you dive deeper into the Apple development environment.

Q&A

Q. Why are the operating system services layered? Doesn't that add complexity?

A. Using the upper-level frameworks reduces the complexity of your code. By providing multiple levels of abstraction, Apple has given developers the tools they need to easily use iOS features and the flexibility to highly customize their application's behavior by using lower-level services more closely tied to the OS.

Q. What do I do if I can't find an interface object I want?

A. Chances are, if you're writing a "normal" iOS application, Apple has provided a UI class to fill your need. If you find that you'd like to do things differently, you can always subclass an existing control and modify its behavior as you see fit—or create a completely new control.

Workshop

Quiz

1. All applications inherit from which of the following classes?

    a. `UISoftware`

    b. `UIRunLoop`

    c. `UIObject`

    d. `UIApplication`

2. The class file containing the methods required for starting, stopping, and pausing an application is usually which of the following?

    a. AppDelegate.swift

    b. App.swift

    c. Delegate.swift

    d. ApplicationDelegate.swift

3. To access Quick Help, hold down _____ while clicking a symbol you want to view.

    a. Control

    b. Option+Command

    c. Option

    d. Command

4. A _____ object provides a draggable interface for inputting a value from a range of numbers.

    a. `UISlider`

    b. `UITextView`

    c. `UIButton`

    d. `UIDraggable`

5. `Strings` and `Arrays` are examples of Swift data types that are _____ with their Cocoa class counterparts.

    a. spanned

    b. chained

    c. connected

    d. bridged

6. Which object contains provides a container for the presentation and management of `UIView` objects?

    a. `UIHolder`

    b. `UIWindow`

    c. `UIDesktop`

    d. `UISetup`

7. The NS you may encounter in some Cocoa Touch classes is a reference to which platform?

    a. NeXTStep

    b. OpenStep

    c. NixStep

    d. NeXTSoftware

8. The class responsible for managing the content of your views is generically known as a what?

    a. View Manager

    b. UI Manager

    c. View Controller

    d. Control Manager

9. Much of the technology in the Cocoa Touch classes can be traced back to its origins almost
   _____ years ago.

   a. 30

   b. 10

   c. 15

   d. 50

10. The combination of files and resources needed to implement a piece of functionality is
    known as a what?

    a. Target

    b. Class

    c. Library

    d. Framework

Answers

1. D. All applications you create will inherit from the `UIApplication` class.

2. A. To control what happens during the launch, termination, and backgrounding of an application, you will likely add code to the AppDelegate.swift file.

3. C. Hold down Option and click a symbol to view the Quick Help for that element.

4. A. The `UISlider` object creates a draggable interface element that is used to enter a
   value from a range of numbers.

5. D. Swift data types that are transparently translated to and from Cocoa classes are known
   as *bridged*. The `String` and `Array` data types are both bridged.

6. B. A `UIWindow` object acts as a container for the views displayed by your application.

7. A. The NS in some Cocoa Touch class names is a direct reference to the platforms origins
   in NeXTStep.

8. C. View controllers provide the glue between your interface and the logic implemented
   within your application.

9. A. The NeXTStep platform, which served as the basis for iOS and Cocoa Touch, is almost
   30 years old.

10. D. A framework is the combination of all the code and resources (images, sounds, and so
    on) required to implement a specific piece of functionality in an application.

Activities

1. Using the Apple Xcode Documentation utility, explore the NSDate class and methods. Identify the methods you'd use to set a date, create a date from a string, and perform common arithmetic functions on a date object.

2. Open Xcode and create a new, empty application. Expand the main code group and click the file named AppDelegate.swift. When the contents of the file appear, open Quick Help by holding Option and clicking inside the class name `UIApplication`. Review the results. Try clicking other symbols in the Xcode class file and see what happens.

HOUR 5
Exploring Interface Builder

What You'll Learn in This Hour:

- ▶ Where Xcode's Interface Builder fits in the development process
- ▶ The role of storyboards and scenes
- ▶ How to build a user interface using the Object Library
- ▶ Common attributes that can be used to customize interface elements
- ▶ Ways to make your interface accessible to the visually impaired
- ▶ How to link interfaces to code with outlets and actions

Over the past few hours, you've become familiar with the core iOS technologies, Xcode projects, and the iOS Simulator. Although these are certainly important skills for becoming a successful developer, there's nothing quite like laying out your first iOS application interface and watching it come to life in your hands.

This hour introduces you to Interface Builder: the remarkable user interface (UI) editor integrated into Xcode. Interface Builder provides a visual approach to application interface design that is fun, intuitive, and deceptively powerful.

Understanding Interface Builder

Let's get it out of the way up front: Yes, Interface Builder (or IB for short) does help you create interfaces for your applications, but it isn't just a drawing tool for graphical user interfaces (GUIs); it helps you symbolically build application functionality without writing code. This translates to fewer bugs, shorter development time, and easier-to-maintain projects.

If you read through Apple's developer documentation, you'll see IB referred to as an *editor* within Xcode. This is a bit of an oversimplification of a tool that previously existed as a stand-alone application in the Apple Developer Suite. An understanding of IB and its use is as fundamentally important to iOS development as Swift. Without IB, creating the most basic interactive applications would be an exercise in frustration.

This hour focuses on navigating IB and will be key to your success in the rest of the book. In Hour 6, "Model-View-Controller Application Design," you combine what you've learned about Xcode projects, the code editor, IB, and the iOS Simulator for the first time. So, stay alert and keep reading.

The IB Approach

Using Xcode and the Cocoa toolset, you can program iOS interfaces by hand—instantiating interface objects, defining where they appear on the screen, setting any attributes for the object, and finally, making them visible. For example, in Hour 2, "Introduction to Xcode and the iOS Simulator," you entered this listing into Xcode to make your iOS device display the text `Hello Xcode` on the screen:

```
var myMessage: UILabel
myMessage=UILabel(frame:CGRectMake(30.0,50.0,300.0,50.0))
myMessage.font=UIFont.systemFontOfSize(48.0)
myMessage.text="Hello Xcode"
myMessage.textColor=UIColor(patternImage: UIImage(named:"Background")!)
view.addSubview(myMessage)
```

Imagine how long it would take to build interfaces with text, buttons, images, and dozens of other controls, and think of all the code you would need to wade through just to make small changes.

Over the years, there have been many different approaches to graphical interface builders. One of the most common implementations is to enable the user to "draw" an interface but, behind the scenes, create all the code that generates that interface. Any tweaks require the code to be edited by hand (hardly an acceptable situation).

Another tactic is to maintain the interface definition symbolically but attach the code that implements functionality directly to interface elements. This, unfortunately, means that if you want to change your interface or swap functionality from one UI element to another, you have to move the code as well.

IB works differently. Instead of autogenerating interface code or tying source listings directly to interface elements, IB builds live objects that connect to your application code through simple links called *connections*. Want to change how a feature of your app is triggered? Just change the connection. As you'll learn a bit later this hour, changing how your application works with the objects you create in IB is, quite literally, a matter of connecting or reconnecting the dots as you see fit.

The Anatomy of an IB Storyboard

Your work in IB results in an XML file called a *storyboard*, containing a hierarchy of objects for each unique screen that your application is going to display. The objects could be interface elements—buttons, toggle switches, and so forth—but might also be other noninterface objects that you will need to use. The collection of objects for a specific display is called a *scene*. Storyboards can hold as many scenes as you need, and even link them together visually via *segues*.

For example, a simple recipe application might have one scene that consists of a list of recipes the user can choose from. A second scene may contain the details for making a selected recipe. The recipe list could be set to segue to the detail view with a fancy fade-out/fade-in effect when the name of a recipe is touched. All of this functionality can be described visually in an application's storyboard file.

Storyboards aren't just about cool visuals, however. They also help you create usable objects without having to allocate or initialize them manually. When a scene in a storyboard file is loaded by your application, the objects described in it are instantiated and can be accessed by your code.

NOTE

Instantiation, just as a quick refresher, is the process of creating an instance of an object that you can work with in your program. An instantiated object gains all the functionality described by its class. Buttons, for example, automatically highlight when clicked, content views scroll, and so on.

The Storyboard Document Outline

What do storyboard files look like in IB? Open the Hour 5 Projects folder and double-click the file Empty.storyboard to open IB and display a barebones storyboard file with a single scene. You will need to choose View, Show Toolbar from the menu bar to make the workspace look like a normal project. Once the file is open and the toolbar visible, we can get our bearings.

The contents of the file are shown visually in the IB editor area, and hierarchically by scene in the document outline area located in the column to the left of the editor area (see Figure 5.1).

TIP

If you do not see the document outline area in your Xcode workspace, choose Editor, Show Document Outline from the menu bar. You can also click the disclosure arrow button in the lower-left corner of the Xcode editor area.

Note that there is only a single scene in the file: View Controller Scene. Single-scene storyboards will be the starting place for much of your interface work in this book because they provide plenty of room for collecting user input and displaying output. We explore multiscene storyboards beginning in Hour 11, "Implementing Multiple Scenes and Popovers."

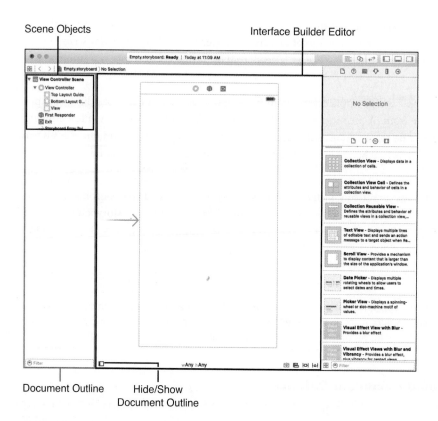

FIGURE 5.1
A storyboard scene's objects are represented by icons.

Click the arrow in front of View Controller Scene to show its hierarchy (and then expand the View Controller object within it, as well).

Six icons should be visible in the scene: View Controller, View (within View Controller), Top Layout Guide (within View Controller), Bottom Layout Guide (within View Controller), First Responder, and Exit. With the exception of View, these are special icons used to represent unique noninterface objects in our application; these will be present in most of the storyboard scenes that you work with:

▶ **View Controller:** The View Controller icon denotes the object that loads and interacts with a storyboard scene in your running application. This is the object that effectively instantiates all the other objects described within a scene. You'll learn more about the relationship between UIs and view controllers in Hour 6.

▶ **Top Layout Guide:** A guide line that marks the "top" of your content area (usually the bottom of the iOS status bar). You can use this guide to keep your UI objects below the portions of the display managed by iOS. This is part of the Auto Layout system that we discuss later this hour, and in depth in Hour 16, "Building Responsive User Interfaces."

▶ **Bottom Layout Guide:** A guide line that marks the "bottom" of your content area. This is usually the bottom of the view itself. Like the Top Layout Guide, this is used to help position your user interface. Again, this is an Auto Layout tool that we won't really need until much later in the book.

▶ **View:** The View icon is an instance of the object `UIView` and represents the visual layout that will be loaded by the view controller and displayed on the iOS device's screen. Views are hierarchical in nature. Therefore, as you add controls to your interface, they are contained within the view. You can even add views within views to cluster controls or create visual elements that can be shown or hidden as a group.

▶ **First Responder:** The First Responder icon stands for the object that the user is currently interacting with. When a user works with an iOS application, multiple objects could potentially respond to the various gestures or keystrokes that the user creates. The first responder is the object currently in control and interacting with the user. A text field that the user is typing into, for example, would be the first responder until the user moves to another field or control.

▶ **Exit:** The Exit icon serves a very specific purpose that will come into play only in multi-scene applications. When you are creating an app that moves the user between a series of screens, the Exit icon provides a visual means of jumping back to a previous screen. If you have built five scenes that link from one to another and you want to quickly return to the first scene from the fifth, you'll link from the fifth scene to the first scene's Exit icon. We test this out in Hour 11.

▶ **Storyboard Entry Point:** This icon is just an indicator that this scene is what your application is going to display when it launches. Storyboards can have many scenes, but they need to *start* somewhere. That somewhere is the entry point.

NOTE

The storyboard shown in this example is about as "vanilla" as you can get. In larger applications with multiple scenes, you may want to either name your view controller class to better describe *what* it is actually controlling or set a descriptive label, such as Recipe Listing.

Using unique view controller names/labels also benefits the naming of scenes. IB automatically sets scene names to the name of the view controller or its label (if one is set) plus the suffix *scene*. If you label your view controller as Recipe Listing, for example, the scene name changes to Recipe

Listing Scene. We'll worry about multiple scenes later in the book; for now, our projects will contain a generic class called View Controller that will be in charge of interacting with our single view controller scene.

As you build your UIs, the list of objects within your scenes will grow accordingly. Some UIs may consist of dozens of different objects, leading to rather busy and complex scenes, as demonstrated in Figure 5.2.

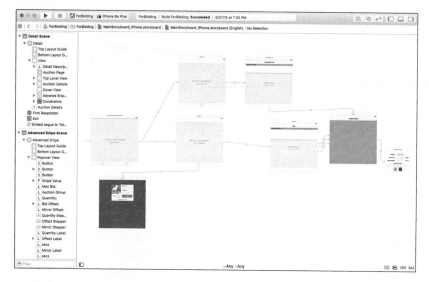

FIGURE 5.2
Storyboard scenes and their associated views can grow quite large and complex.

You can collapse or expand your hierarchy of views within the document outline area to help manage the information overload that you are bound to experience as your applications become more advanced.

NOTE

At its most basic level, a view (`UIView`) is a rectangular region that can contain content and respond to user events (touches and so forth). All the controls (buttons, fields, and so on) that you'll add to a view are, in fact, subclasses of `UIView`. This isn't necessarily something you need to be worried about, except that you'll be encountering documentation that refers to buttons and other interface elements referred to as *subviews* and the views that contain them as *superviews*.

Just keep in mind that pretty much everything you see onscreen can be considered a view and the terminology will seem a little less alien.

Working with the Document Outline Objects

The document outline area shows icons for objects in your application, but what good are they? Aside from presenting a nice list, do they provide any functionality?

Absolutely! Each icon gives you a visual means of referring to the objects they represent. You interact with the icons by dragging to and from them to create the connections that drive your application's features.

Consider an onscreen control, such as a button, that needs to trigger an action in your code. By dragging from the button to the View Controller icon, you can create a connection from the GUI element to a method that you want it to activate. You can even drag from certain objects directly to your code, quickly inserting a variable or method that will interact with that object.

Xcode provides developers with a great deal of flexibility when working with objects in IB. You can interact with the actual UI elements in the IB editor, or with the icons that represent them in the document outline area. In addition, any object that isn't directly visible in the UI (such as the first responder and view controller objects) can be found in an icon bar directly above the UI design in the editor. This is known as the scene dock, and is visible in Figure 5.3.

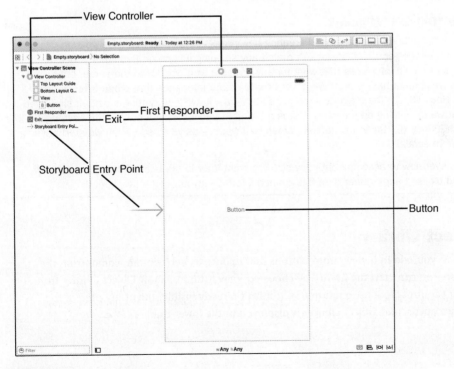

FIGURE 5.3
You will interact with objects either in the editor or in the document outline area.

NOTE

If the scene dock above your view does not show any icons and is displaying the text *View Controller* instead, just click it. The dock defaults to the name of a scene's view controller until it is selected.

We go through a hands-on example later this hour so that you can get a feel for how interacting with and connecting objects works. Before we do that, however, let's look at how you go about turning a blank view into an interface masterpiece.

Creating User Interfaces

In Figures 5.1 and 5.2, you've seen an empty view and a fully fleshed-out interface. Now, how do we get from one to the other? In this section, we explore how interfaces are created with IB. In other words, it's time for the fun stuff.

If you haven't already, open the Empty.storyboard file included in this hour's Projects folder. Make sure the document outline area is visible and that the view can be seen in the editor; you're ready to start designing an interface.

What's the "Default" iPhone?

When you're editing iPhone interfaces and creating new projects in Xcode, you'll be working, by default, with a "generic" screen that doesn't match any shipping iPhone or iPad. This is because Apple wants you to build interfaces that work for any device. I want you to do the same, but I want you to learn development basics first! We cover how to create interfaces that properly resize for any device in Hour 16. For the majority of projects in this book, we'll be setting a default simulated device so that we're working on a canvas that is a bit more familiar than a nonspecific rectangle. I'll use a 4.7-inch iPhone (6/6s) as my default screen for layouts—as you'll see when we start building applications from scratch.

Again, we *do* cover how to accommodate any size you want later in the book. Our focus now is on getting started building apps rather than fine-grained interface layout.

The Object Library

Everything that you add to a view, from buttons and images to web content, comes from the Object Library. You can view the library by choosing View, Utilities, Show Object Library from the menu bar (Control-Option-Command-3). If it isn't already visible, the utility area of the Xcode interface opens, and Object Library is displayed in the lower right.

CAUTION

Libraries, Libraries, Everywhere!

Xcode has more than one library. The Object Library contains the UI elements you'll be adding in IB, but there are also File Template, Code Snippet, and Media libraries that can be activated by clicking the icons immediately above the Library area.

If you find yourself staring at a library that doesn't seem to show what you're expecting, click the icon of a square surrounded by a circle above the library or reselect the Object Library from the View, Utilities menu to make sure that you're in the right place.

When you click and hover over an element in the library, a popover is displayed with a description of how the object can be used in the interface, as shown in Figure 5.4. This provides a convenient way of exploring your UI options without having to open the Xcode documentation.

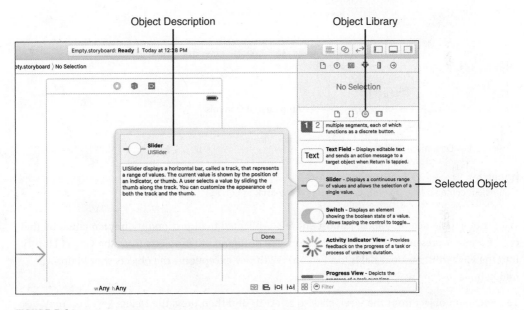

FIGURE 5.4
The library contains a palette of objects that can be added to your views.

Using view button (four squares) at the bottom-left of the library, you can switch between list and icon views of the available objects. If you know the name of an object but can't locate it in the list, use the filter field below the library to quickly find it.

Adding Objects to a View

To add an object to a view, just click and drag from the library to the view. For example, find the label object (`UILabel`) in the Object Library and drag it into the center of the view in the editor.

The label should appear in your view and read Label. Double-click the label and type **Hello**.
The text will update, as shown in Figure 5.5, just as you would expect.

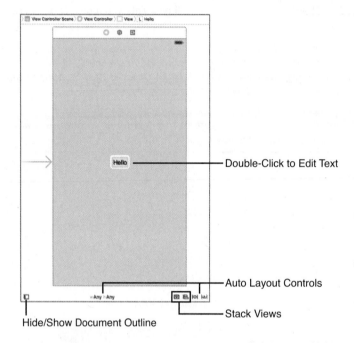

FIGURE 5.5
If an object contains text, in many cases, just double-click to edit it.

With that simple action, you've almost entirely replicated the functionality implemented by the
code fragment presented earlier in the lesson. Try dragging other objects from the Object Library
into the view (buttons, text fields, and so on). With few exceptions, the objects should appear
and behave just the way you'd expect.

To remove an object from the view, click to select it, and then press the Delete key. You may also
use the options under the Edit menu to copy and paste between views or duplicate an element
several times within a view.

NOTE

Notice the tools along the bottom of the editing area? These are largely related to view positioning
and Auto Layout (more on that shortly), with one exception:

The button in the lower left hides and shows the document outline, giving you more space to work.
You'll want to make use of this button *a lot*, especially if you're working on a laptop.

The middle set of menus (typically labeled "w Any" and "h Any") are used when designing interfaces to fit a variety of devices, while the buttons on the right are used to insert stack views and reveal menus for managing Auto Layout Alignment, Pinning, and Constraint issues.

Working with the IB Editing Tools

Instead of having you rely on your visual acuity to position objects in a view, Apple has included some useful tools for fine-tuning your interface design. If you've ever used a drawing program like OmniGraffle or Adobe Illustrator, you'll find many of these familiar.

Guides

As you drag objects in a view, you'll notice guides (shown in Figure 5.6) appearing to help with the positioning. These blue, dotted lines are displayed to align objects along the margins of the view, to the centers of other objects in the view, and to the baseline of the fonts used in the labels and object titles.

As an added bonus, guides automatically appear to indicate the approximate spacing requirements of Apple's interface guidelines. If you're not sure why it's showing you a particular margin guide, it's likely that your object is in a position that IB considers "appropriate" for something of that type and size.

TIP

You can manually add your own guides by choosing Editor, Guides, Add Horizontal Guide or by choosing Editor, Guides, Add Vertical Guide. You can position manually added guides anywhere in your view by dragging them; they will appear orange in color. When you drag an object close to the guide, the guide highlights in blue to show when they are aligned.

TIP

To fine-tune an object's position within a view, select it, and then use the arrow keys to position it left, right, up, or down, 1 point at a time. You can also zoom in and out of a view by pinching on a Magic Trackpad, or Control-clicking (or right-clicking) in the Interface Builder editor view and choosing an appropriate zoom level from the menu that appears.

Selection Handles

In addition to the guides, most objects include selection handles to stretch an object horizontally, vertically, or both. Using the small boxes that appear alongside an object when it is selected, just click and drag to change its size, as demonstrated using a text field in Figure 5.7.

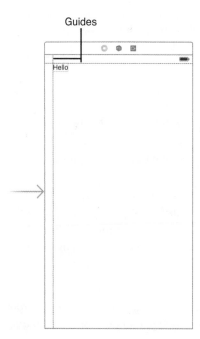

Guides

FIGURE 5.6
Guides help position your objects within a view.

Note that some objects constrain how you can resize them; this preserves a level of consistency within iOS application interfaces.

TIP
In busy interfaces, it can be difficult to figure out what object you've selected just by the appearance of selection handles. If you'd prefer Xcode also darken the selected object, choose Editor, Canvas, Show Selection Highlights.

Arrangement and Alignment

When you're working with UI objects in Interface Builder, you'll likely start to feel like you're working in a drawing program. Two commands common in object-based drawing applications are Arrange (where you can position objects in front of or behind one another) and Align (where you can make misplaced objects line up). You'll find both of these options also exist in Interface Builder.

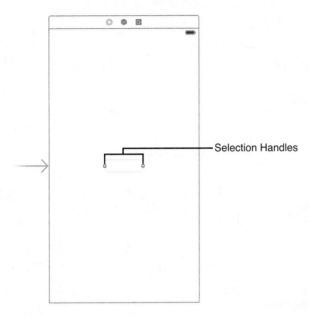

FIGURE 5.7
Use the selection handles around the perimeter of an object to change its size.

To arrange objects, you can choose from the Editor, Arrange menu. Use the Arrange selections (Send to Back, Send Forward, and so on) to move UI elements behind or in front of other elements.

To quickly align several objects within a view, select them by clicking and dragging a selection rectangle around them or by holding down the Shift key and then choosing Editor, Align and an appropriate alignment type from the menu.

For example, try dragging several buttons into your view, placing them in a variety of different positions. To align them based on their horizontal center (a line that runs vertically through each button's center), select the buttons, and then choose Editor, Align, Horizontal Centers. Figure 5.8 shows the before and after results.

The Size Inspector

Another tool that you may want to use for controlling your design is the Size Inspector. IB has a number of inspectors for examining the attributes of an object. As the name implies, the Size Inspector provides information about sizes, but also position and alignment. To open the Size Inspector, first select the object (or objects) that you want to work with, and then click the ruler icon at the top of the utility area in Xcode. Alternatively, choose View, Utilities, Show Size Inspector or press Option-Command-5 (see Figure 5.9).

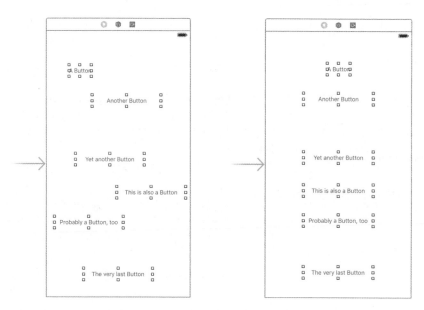

FIGURE 5.8
Use the Align menu to quickly align a group of items to an edge or center.

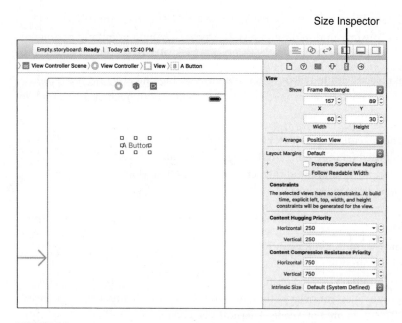

FIGURE 5.9
The Size Inspector enables you to adjust the size and position of one or more objects.

Using the fields at the top of the inspector, you can view or change the size and position of the object by changing the coordinates in the Height/Width and X/Y fields.

NOTE

At the top of Size Inspector's View settings, you'll often see a drop-down menu where you can choose between Frame Rectangle and Alignment Rectangle. These two settings will usually be similar, but there is a slight difference. The frame values represent the exact area a "raw" object occupies onscreen, whereas the alignment values take into account spacing around the object for drop shadows and the like.

The Arrange drop-down menu gives you quick layout arrangements for the selected object (or objects). Using this menu, you can center the object, align it with other objects, or size it to take up the width or height of the view that holds it. You can do all of this with the main Interface Builder tools as well; this menu is just another place to make quick tweaks to your layout.

Below the Arrange menu are options for controlling layout margins. Layout margins are the amount of space around an object in your design. By default, layout margins are 8 points on the top, bottom, left, and right of each object. You can explicitly set layout margins to include more (or less) space around an object. These margins, however, are only used when using Auto Layout. Bear with me, I'm about to tell you what Auto Layout is.

Notice that the Size Inspector includes a section at the bottom labeled Constraints. Constraints are part of the Auto Layout system that we will be using to create resizable user interfaces in Hour 16. Because you're likely to run into a few references to Auto Layout before we get there, let's take a few minutes to get an idea of what this beast is.

TIP

Hold down the Option key after selecting an object in IB. As you move your mouse around, you'll see the distance between the selected object and other objects that you point to.

The Auto Layout System

While the guides, Size Inspector, and other tools are helpful for laying out interfaces—even interfaces that can adapt to view changes—iOS applications can take advantage of a new powerful tool for managing layouts: the Auto Layout system. Auto Layouts are enabled by default on new projects and make it possible to write applications that adapt to a number of different screen sizes and orientations without needing to modify a single line of code. Do you want to write software to take advantage of all the available iOS device screen sizes? How about layouts that rearrange themselves when you move from portrait to landscape orientations? You'll want Auto Layouts!

Understanding Constraints

Auto Layout works by building a series of *constraints* for your onscreen objects. The constraints define distances between objects and how flexible these relationships are.

For example, open the Constraints.storyboard file included in the Projects folder. This storyboard contains a view with a single label positioned in the upper center. Expand the View Controller scene in the document outline so that you can see all the objects it contains. Notice that at the same level in the hierarchy as the label, a Constraints object is showing up, as shown in Figure 5.10.

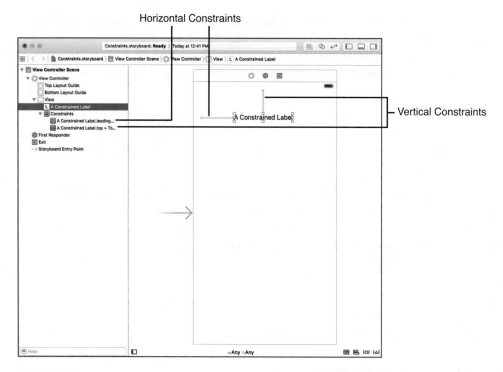

FIGURE 5.10
The Constraints object represents the positioning relationships within a view.

Within the Constraints object are two constraints: horizontal space and vertical space constraints. The horizontal constraint states that the left or right side of the label will be a certain number of points from the left or right edge of the view. These are known as *leading* and *trailing* constraints, respectively. A vertical constraint is the distance from the top or bottom of the view to the top or bottom of the label. Intuitively, these are called the *top* and *bottom* constraints.

Constraints, however, are more than just entries that tie an object to the view it is within. They can be flexible, ensuring that an object maintains *at least* or *at most* a certain distance from another object, or even that two objects, when resized, maintain the same distance between one another.

Constraints that set a specific size or distance between objects are called *pinning*. The flexibility (or inflexibility of a constraint) is managed by configuring a *relationship*.

Content Hugging and Content Compression Resistance

Now that you're viewing an object with constraints, the Size Inspector updates to show a bit more information than we saw earlier. Click the label in the Constraints storyboard file and make sure that the Size Inspector is visible (Option-Command-5), as shown in Figure 5.11.

The constraints affecting the label itself are shown near the bottom of the Size Inspector information, but there are additional settings now visible for Content Hugging (how friendly!) and Content Compression.

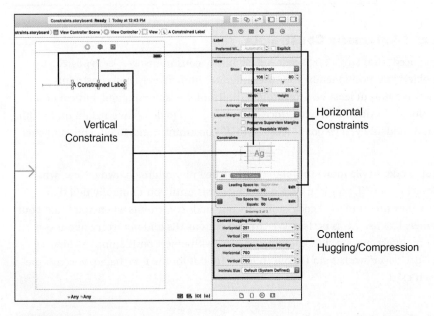

FIGURE 5.11
The Size Inspector shows information about how Auto Layout will affect an object.

These settings control how closely the sides of an object "hug" the content in the object and how much the content can be compressed or clipped. An object that can expand horizontally but not vertically would set horizontal hugging as a low priority and vertical hugging as a very high priority. Similarly, if the content of the object (say a label) should not be compressed or clipped at all, the content compression resistance settings for both horizontal and vertical compression could be set to a very high priority.

NOTE

Another Auto Layout option you'll encounter in the Size Inspector is an Intrinsic Size setting. The intrinsic size is just the size of the object as determined by your layout. If you're creating custom views, IB will have no idea how large the view actually is, so you'll need to use the Intrinsic Size drop-down to set a "placeholder" size. This is a relatively advanced topic and not something you're likely to encounter in day-to-day development.

I Miss the Old Autosizing Features! Boo Hoo

If you prefer to forego the new Auto Layout tools in Xcode, you can revert your storyboard to the "old" layout approach by first selecting the File Inspector (Option-Command-1) while viewing your storyboard. Next, *uncheck* the Use Autolayout check box within the Interface Builder Document section of settings. Everything will operate exactly as it did prior to Xcode 4.5.

Hour 16 focuses on the new Auto Layout tools, however, so I suggest leaving Auto Layout active.

Auto Layout and Automatic Constraints

When Apple introduced Auto Layout in Xcode 4.5, suddenly constraints were *everywhere*. Any label, button, or object you positioned in your user interface immediately had constraints appear. Each object requires at least two constraints (horizontal positioning and vertical positioning) to determine its location in the interface and (often) two to determine height and width. Add 10 objects, and suddenly you've got at least 20 to 40 constraints (and 40 blue lines all over your view).

In later releases of Xcode, Apple made this blue crosshatched nightmare go away. Now, when you position objects in your UI, you won't see any constraints until you manually add them. That doesn't mean they aren't there; Xcode automatically adds constraints when you build your project. For beginners like us, this is perfect. We can lay out our UIs and not worry about constraints until we absolutely need to do something "clever" with object positioning. As already mentioned, we'll "get clever" with Auto Layout in Hour 16, but for the time being, you can pretend it doesn't even exist.

Customizing the Interface Appearance

How your interface appears to the end user isn't just a combination of control sizes, positions, and constraints. For many kinds of objects, literally dozens of different attributes can be adjusted. Although you could certainly configure things such as colors and fonts in your code, it's easier to just use the tools included in IB.

Using the Attributes Inspector

The most common place you'll tweak the way your interface objects appear is through the Attributes Inspector, available by clicking the slider icon at the top of the utility area. You can also choose View, Utilities, Show Attributes Inspector (Option-Command-4) if the utility area isn't currently visible. Let's run through a quick example to see how this works.

Turn back to the Empty.storyboard file with the label you've added (or just use the Constraints. storyboard label). Select the label, and then open the Attributes Inspector, shown in Figure 5.12.

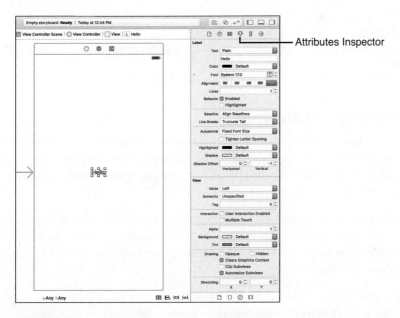

— Attributes Inspector

FIGURE 5.12
To change how an object looks and behaves, select it, and then open the Attributes Inspector.

The top portion of the Attributes Inspector contains attributes for the specific object. In the case of the text object, this includes settings such as font, size, color, and alignment (everything you'd expect to find for editing text).

In the bottom portion of the inspector are additional inherited attributes. Remember that onscreen elements are a subclass of a view. Therefore, all the standard view attributes are also available for the object and for your tinkering enjoyment. In many cases, you'll want to leave these alone, but settings such as background and transparency can come in handy.

TIP

Don't get hung up on trying to memorize every attribute for every control now. I cover interesting and important attributes when they are needed throughout the book.

Feel free to explore the many different options available in the Attributes Inspector to see what can be configured for different types of objects. There is a surprising amount of flexibility to be found within the tool.

NOTE

The attributes you change in IB are simply properties of the object's class. To help identify what an attribute does, use the documentation tool in Xcode to look up the object's class and review the descriptions of its properties.

Setting Accessibility Attributes

For many years, the "appearance" of an interface meant just how it looks visually. Today, the technology is available for an interface to vocally describe itself to the visually impaired. iOS includes Apple's screen-reader technology: Voiceover. Voiceover combines speech synthesis with a customized interface to aid users in navigating applications.

Using Voiceover, users can touch interface elements and hear a short description of what they do and how they can be used. Although you gain much of this functionality "for free" (the iOS Voiceover software will read button labels, for example), you can provide additional assistance by configuring the accessibility attributes in IB.

To access the Accessibility settings, you need to open the Identity Inspector by clicking the window icon at the top of the utility area. You can also choose View, Utilities, Show Identity Inspector or press Option-Command-3. The Accessibility options have their own section within the Identity Inspector, as shown in Figure 5.13.

You can configure four sets of attributes within this area:

▶ **Accessibility:** If enabled, the object is considered accessible. If you create any custom controls that must be seen to be used, this setting should be disabled.

▶ **Label:** A simple word or two that serves as the label for an item. A text field that collects the user's name might use "your name," for example.

▶ **Hint:** A short description, if needed, on how to use the control. This is needed only if the label doesn't provide enough information on its own.

▶ **Identifier:** Similar to the Label attribute, the Identifier should contain a more detailed description of the control (for example, "A text field for your first and last name").

▶ **Traits:** This set of check boxes is used to describe the features of the object—what it does and what its current state is.

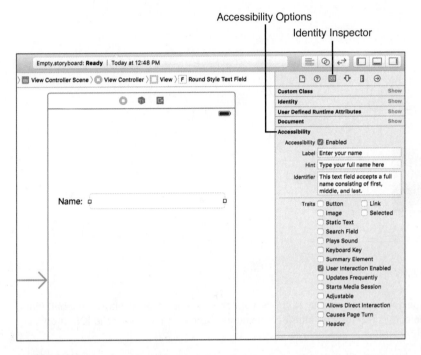

FIGURE 5.13
Use the Accessibility section in the Identity Inspector to configure how Voiceover interacts with your application.

TIP
_____

For an application to be available to the largest possible audience, take advantage of accessibility tools whenever possible. Even objects such as the text labels you've used in this lesson should have their traits configured to indicate that they are static text. This helps potential users know that they can't interact with them.

_____

Enabling the iOS Accessibility Inspector

If you are building accessible interfaces, you may want to enable the Accessibility Inspector in the iOS Simulator. To do this, start the Simulator and click the Home button to return to the home screen. Start the Settings application and navigate to General, Accessibility, and then use the switch to turn the Accessibility Inspector on, as shown in Figure 5.14.

FIGURE 5.14
Toggle the iOS Accessibility Inspector on.

The Accessibility Inspector adds an overlay to the Simulator workspace that displays the label, hints, and traits that you've configured for your interface elements. Note that navigating the iOS interface is *very* different when operating in accessibility mode.

Using the X button in the upper-left corner of the inspector, you can toggle it on and off. When off, the inspector collapses to a small bar, and the iPhone Simulator will behave normally. Clicking the X button again turns it back on. To disable the Accessibility Inspector altogether, just revisit the Accessibility setting in the Settings application.

Previewing the Interface

If you've worked with earlier versions of Xcode, you know that you could easily simulate your UI. This feature disappeared in Xcode 4, but has made a happy return in the latest Xcode releases (even if it is a bit difficult to find).

To use the preview feature, you must use the Xcode assistant editor feature that we reviewed in Hour 2. For example, open the PreviewUI.storyboard file included in this hour's Projects directory. This storyboard contains a simple user interface: a label, a field, and a button. Choose View, Show Toolbar from the menu bar so that all the typical window controls are showing. (On a normal project, the toolbar would already be visible.)

To preview the view as it will look on a device, first activate the assistant editor. Next, click the bar above the assistant editor pane where it reads Automatic. A drop-down menu appears, with Preview as the last option, as shown in Figure 5.15.

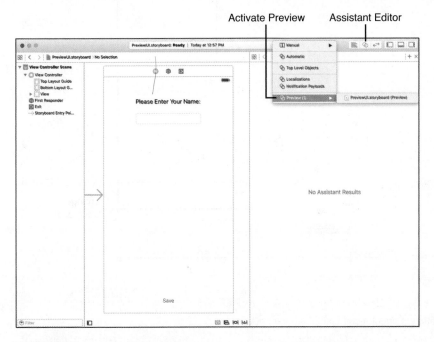

FIGURE 5.15
Select Preview (or choose from the options in its submenu) to activate a preview in the assistant editor.

Select Preview, and the assistant editor refreshes to show a live preview of what your UI will look like on a device. Use the button at the bottom of the preview to toggle between portrait and landscape orientations. In Figure 5.16, I'm previewing the UI on a 4.7-inch iPhone in landscape mode.

To add additional devices to the preview, click the + menu and choose the iOS device you'd like. If you're creating a project that runs on earlier versions of iOS, you can even choose to preview a device running a different OS version.

The preview is added to the right of the existing preview. You can even add multiples of the same device so that you can see a landscape and portrait view at the same time. To remove a preview, click to select it, and then press the Delete key.

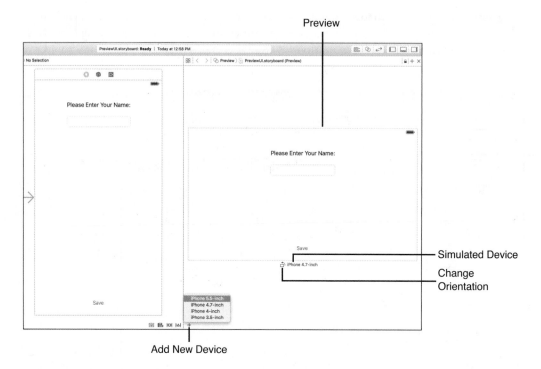

FIGURE 5.16
Preview the UI in different orientations and on different devices.

This will come in very handy when we explore Auto Layout more in Hour 16. In addition, if you want to test your application UIs, you can always run your apps in the iOS Simulator, even when they aren't entirely written. Apple's development tools make it possible to see results as you build, instead of having to wait until every single feature is in place.

Connecting to Code

You know how to make an interface, but how do you make it *do* something? Throughout this hour, I've been alluding to the idea that connecting an interface to the code you write is just a matter of "connecting the dots." In this last part of the hour, we do just that: take an interface and connect it to the code that makes it into a functional application.

Opening the Project

To get started, we use the project Disconnected contained within this hour's Projects folder. Open the folder and double-click the Disconnected.xcodeproj file. This opens the project in Xcode, as shown in Figure 5.17.

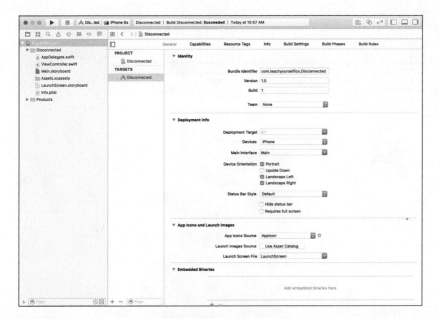

FIGURE 5.17
To begin, open the project in Xcode.

After the project is loaded, expand the project code group (Disconnected) and click the Main.storyboard file. This storyboard file contains the scene and view that this application displays as its interface. Xcode refreshes and displays the scene in IB, as shown in Figure 5.18.

Implementation Overview

The interface contains four interactive elements: a button bar (called a segmented control), a push button, an output label, and a web view (an integrated web browser component). Together, these controls interface with application code to enable a user to pick a flower color, touch the Get Flower button, and then display the chosen color in a text label along with a matching flower photo fetched from the website http://www.floraphotographs.com. Figure 5.19 shows the final result.

NOTE

A Blurry Visual Treat

You may notice one additional (noninteractive) element in this project: a visual effects view. This view lives behind the color controls and labels and blurs out the background behind it. It's used to very easily create the soft blurred backgrounds prevalent in iOS.

Storyboard File

Project Code Group

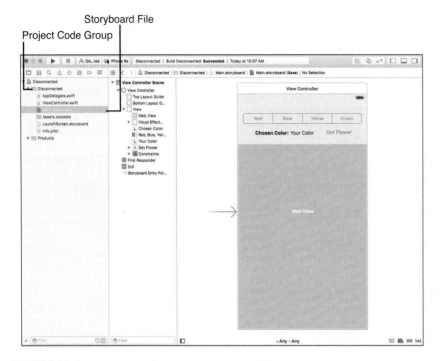

FIGURE 5.18
IB displays the scene and corresponding view for the application.

FIGURE 5.19
The finished application enables a user to choose a color and have a flower image returned that matches that color.

Unfortunately, right now the application does nothing. The interface isn't connected to any application code, so it is hardly more than a pretty picture. To make it work, we create connections to outlets and actions that have been defined in the application's code.

Outlets and Actions

An outlet is nothing more than a variable property by which an object can be referenced. For example, if you had created a field in IB intending that it would be used to collect a user's name, you might want to create an outlet for it in your code called userName. Using this outlet and a corresponding variable property, you could then access or change the contents of the field.

An action, however, is a method within your code that is called when an event takes place. Certain objects, such as buttons and switches, can trigger actions when a user interacts with them through an event, such as touching the screen. If you define actions in your code, IB can make them available to the onscreen objects.

Joining an element in IB to an outlet or action creates what is generically termed a connection. For the Disconnected app to function, we need to create connections to these outlets and actions:

- ▶ **colorChoice:** An outlet created for the button bar to access the color the user has selected

- ▶ **getFlower:** An action that retrieves a flower from the Web, displays it, and updates the label with the chosen color

- ▶ **chosenColor:** An outlet for the label that will be updated by getFlower to show the name of the chosen color

- ▶ **flowerView:** An outlet for the web view that will be updated by getFlower to show the image

Let's make the connections now.

Creating Connections to Outlets

To create a connection from an interface item to an outlet, Control-drag from a scene's View Controller icon (in the document outline area or the icon bar below the view) to either the visual representation of the object in the view or its icon in the document outline area.

Try this with the button bar (segmented control). Pressing Control, click and drag from the view controller in the document outline area to the onscreen image of the bar. A line appears as you drag, enabling you to easily point to the object that you want to use for the connect, as shown in Figure 5.20.

When you release the mouse button, the available connections are shown in a pop-up menu (see Figure 5.21). In this case, you want to pick colorChoice.

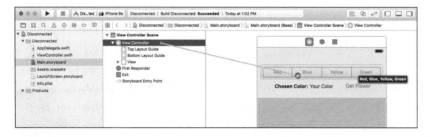

FIGURE 5.20
Control-drag from the view controller to the button bar.

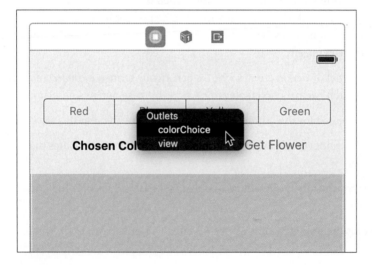

FIGURE 5.21
Choose from the outlets available for the targeted object.

NOTE

IB knows what type of object is allowed to connect to a given outlet, so it displays only the outlets appropriate for the connection you're trying to make.

Repeat this process for the label with the text "Your Color", connecting it to the chosenColor outlet, and with the web view, connecting to flowerView.

Connecting to Actions

Connecting to actions is a bit different. An object's events trigger actions (methods) in your code. So, the connection direction reverses; you connect from the object invoking an event to the view controller of its scene. Although it is possible to Control-drag and create a connection in the same manner you did with outlets, this isn't recommended because you don't get to specify which event triggers it. Do users have to touch the button? Release their fingers from a button?

Actions can be triggered by *many* different events, so you need to make sure that you're picking exactly the right one, instead of leaving it up to IB. To do this, select the object that will be connecting to the action and open the Connections Inspector by clicking the arrow icon at the top of the Xcode utility area. You can also show the inspector by choosing View, Utilities, Show Connections Inspector (or by pressing Option-Command-6).

The Connections Inspector, in Figure 5.22, shows a list of the events that the object, in this case a button, supports. Beside each event is an open circle. To connect an event to an action in your code, click and drag from one of these circles to the scene's View Controller icon in the document outline area.

Connections Inspector

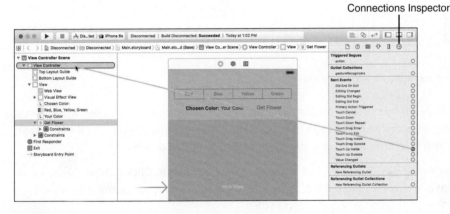

FIGURE 5.22
Use the Connections Inspector to view existing connections and to make new ones.

NOTE

I often refer to creating connections to a scene's view controller or placing interface elements in a scene's view. This is because IB storyboards can contain multiple different scenes, each with its own view controller and view. In the first few lessons, there is only a single scene, and therefore, a single view controller. That said, you should still be getting used to the idea of multiple View Controller icons appearing in the document outline area and having to correctly choose the one that corresponds to the scene you are editing.

For example, to connect the Get Flower button to the `getFlower` method, select the button, and then open the Connections Inspector (Option-Command-6). Drag from the circle beside the Touch Up Inside event to the scene's view controller and release, as demonstrated in Figure 5.22. When prompted, choose the `getFlower` action, shown in Figure 5.23.

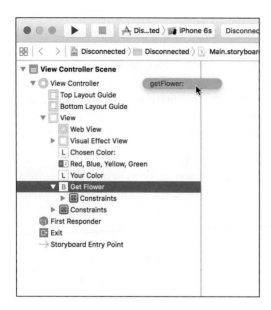

FIGURE 5.23
Choose the action you want the interface element to invoke.

After a connection has been made, the inspector updates to show the event and the action that it calls, demonstrated in Figure 5.24. If you click other already connected objects, you'll notice that the Connections Inspector shows their connections to outlets and to actions.

Well done! You've just linked an interface to the code that supports it. Click Run on the Xcode toolbar to build and run your application in the iOS Simulator or on your personal iDevice.

Connections Without Code

Although most of your connections in IB will be between objects and outlets and actions you've defined in your code, certain objects implement built-in actions that don't require you to write a single line of code.

The web view, for example, implements actions, including `goForward` and `goBack`. Using these actions, you could add basic navigation functionality to a web view by dragging from a button's Touch Up Inside event directly to the web view object (rather than the view controller). As described previously, you are prompted for the action to connect to, but this time, it isn't an action you had to code yourself.

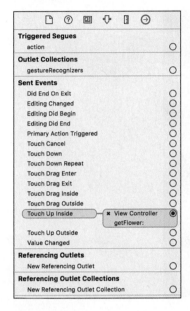

FIGURE 5.24
The Connections Inspector updates to show the actions and outlets that an object references.

Editing Connections with the Quick Inspector

One of the errors that I commonly make when connecting my interfaces is creating a connection that I didn't intend. A bit of overzealous dragging, and suddenly your interface is wired up incorrectly and won't work. To review the connections that are in place, you select an object and use the Connections Inspector discussed previously, or you can open the Quick Inspector by right-clicking any object in the IB editor or document outline area. This opens a floating window that contains all the outlets and actions either referenced or received by the object, as shown in Figure 5.25.

Besides viewing the connections that are in place, you can remove a connection by clicking the X next to a connected object (see Figure 5.24 and 5.25). You can even create new connections using the same "click-and-drag from the circle to an object" approach that you performed with the Connections Inspector. Click the X in the upper-left corner of the window to close the Quick Inspector.

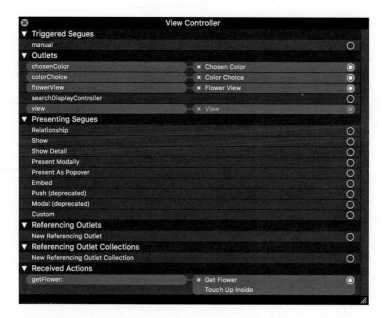

FIGURE 5.25
Right-click to quickly inspect any object connections.

NOTE

Although clicking an object, such as a button, shows you all the connections related to that object, it doesn't show you *everything* you've connected in the IB editor. Because almost all the connections you create will go to and from a scene's view controller, choosing it and then opening the inspector will give you a more complete picture of what connections you've made.

Writing Code with IB

You just created connections from UI objects to the corresponding outlets and actions that have already been defined in code. In the next hour's lesson, you write a full application, including defining outlets and actions and connecting them to a storyboard scene. What's interesting about this process, besides it bringing all the earlier lessons together, is that IB editor writes and inserts the necessary Swift code to define outlets and actions.

Although it is impossible for Xcode to write your application for you, it does create the instance variables and properties for your app's interface objects, as well as "stubs" of the methods your interface will trigger. All you need to do is drag and drop the IB objects into your source code files. Using this feature is completely optional, but it does help save time and avoid syntax errors.

TIP

A method stub (or *skeleton*) is nothing more than a method that has been declared but executes no instructions. You can add stubs to your code where you know what you'll be writing in the future but aren't yet ready to commit it to code. This is useful in the initial design stages of an application because it helps you keep track of the work you have left to do.

Stub methods are also helpful if you have code that needs to use a method that you haven't written. By inserting and referencing stubs for your unwritten methods, your application will compile and run—enabling the code that *is* complete to be tested at any stage of the development process.

Object Identity

As we finish up our introduction to IB, I'd be remiss if I didn't introduce one more feature: the Identity Inspector. You've already accessed this tool to view the accessibility attributes for interface objects, but there is another reason why we need to use the inspector in the future: setting class identities and labels.

As you drag objects into the interface, you're creating instances of classes that already exist (buttons, labels, and so on). Throughout this book, however, we build custom subclasses that we also need to be able to reference with IB's objects. In these cases, we need to help IB by identifying the subclass it should use.

For example, suppose we created a subclass of the standard button class (UIButton) that we named ourFancyButtonClass. We might drag a button into a scene to represent our fancy button, but when the storyboard file loads, it would just create the same old UIButton.

To fix the problem, we select the button we've added to the view, open the Identity Inspector by clicking the window icon at the top of the Xcode utility area or by choosing View, Utilities, Show Identity Inspector (Option-Command-3), and then use the drop-down menu/field to enter the class that we really want instantiated at runtime (see Figure 5.26).

This is something we cover on an as-needed basis; so if it seems confusing, don't worry. We come back to it later in the book.

NOTE

I see that Module Name field you're ignoring! When setting a custom class name, you can also set the name of the module that defines the class. Modules provide a way to organize large numbers of classes into functional groups, but aren't something you'll need for the projects in this book.

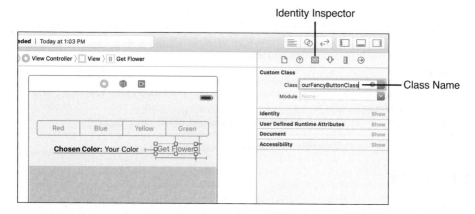

FIGURE 5.26
If you're using a custom class, you need to manually set the identity of your objects in the Identity Inspector.

Further Exploration

The IB editor gives you the opportunity to experiment with many of the different GUI objects you've seen in iOS applications and read about in the previous hours. In the next hour, the Xcode code editor is used in conjunction with IB for your first full project, developed from start to finish.

To learn even more about what you can do with IB, I suggest reading through the following five Apple publications:

▶ *Interface Builder Help:* Accessed by right-clicking the background in the IB editor, the IB help is more than a simple help document. Apple's IB Help walks you through the intricacies of IB using video tutorials and covers some advanced topics that will be important as your development experience increases.

▶ *Auto Layout Guide:* This document presents a good introduction to the Auto Layout system and is an excellent read for anyone wanting to get a jump start on adaptive interface layout techniques.

▶ *Xcode Overview: Build a User Interface:* Part of the larger "Xcode Overview" document, this section offers a nice tutorial on Interface Builder principals.

▶ *iOS Human Interface Guidelines:* The Apple iOS HIG document provides a clear set of rules for building usable interfaces on the iOS device family. This document describes when you should use controls and how they should be displayed, helping you create more polished, professional-quality applications.

▶ *Accessibility Programming Guide for iOS:* If you're serious about creating accessible apps, this is a mandatory read. The *Accessibility Programming Guide* describes the accessibility features in this hour's lesson as well as ways to improve accessibility programmatically and methods of testing accessibility beyond the tips given in this hour.

As a general note, from here on, you do quite a bit of coding in each lesson. So, now is a great time to review the previous hours if you have any questions.

Summary

In this hour, you explored the Xcode IB editor and the tools it provides for building rich graphical interfaces for your iOS applications. You learned how to navigate IB storyboards and access the GUI elements from the Object Library. Using the various inspector tools within IB, you reviewed how GUI elements can be placed within a scene using constraints, how the look and feel of onscreen controls can be customized, and how interfaces can be made accessible to the visually impaired.

More than just a pretty picture, an IB-created interface uses simple outlets and actions to connect to functionality in your code. You used IB's connection tools to turn a nonfunctioning interface into a complete application. By maintaining a separation between the code you write and what is displayed to the user, you can revise your interface to look however you want, without breaking your application. In Hour 6, you examine how to create outlets and actions from scratch in Xcode (and thus gain a full toolset to get started developing).

Q&A

Q. Why do I keep seeing things referred to as NIB/XIB files?

A. The origins of IB trace back to the NeXT Computer, which made use of NIB files to store individual views. These files, in fact, still bore the same name when Mac OS X was released. In recent years, however, Apple renamed the files to have the .xib extension, which has subsequently been mostly replaced by storyboards and scenes. You'll still see a XIB file used for your startup screen in your project (see Hour 2 for details), but, in general, anything that refers to a XIB or NIB file applies to storyboards as well.

Q. Some of the objects in the IB Object Library can't be added to my view. What gives?

A. Not all the items in the Object Library are interface objects. Some represent objects that provide functionality to your application. These can be added to the scene in the document outline area or on the icon bar located below a scene's layout in the IB editor.

Q. **I've seen controls in applications that aren't available here. Where are they?**

A. Keep in mind that the iOS objects are heavily customizable and frequently used as a start-ing point for developers to make their own UI classes or subclasses. The end result can vary tremendously from the stock UI appearance.

Workshop

Quiz

1. The default storyboard file is named what?

    a. Main

    b. iPhone

    c. Universal

    d. Default

2. Which inspector enables you to update the appearance of an interface object?

    a. Identity

    b. Appearance

    c. Visual

    d. Attributes

3. To change the height or width of an object, you could use which inspector?

    a. Attributes

    b. Constraints

    c. Volumetric

    d. Size

4. What system gives us a way to describe interfaces that resize and change depending on device screen size and orientation?

    a. Auto Adapt

    b. Attributes

    c. Auto Layout

    d. Content Autosizing

5. To set a custom class on an object, we would turn to which inspector?

    a. Class

    b. Identity

    c. Object

    d. Location

6. Invoking the Quick Inspector on which object is a good way to see most of your scene's connections?

    a. View

    b. View Controller

    c. First Responder

    d. Class

7. Through what is an interface object referenced in code?

    a. Plug

    b. Action

    c. Connection

    d. Outlet

8. Interactive interface elements often connect to code via which of the following?

    a. Classes

    b. Actions

    c. Connections

    d. Outlets

9. To test the accessibility of iOS interfaces, you can activate which of the following tools in the iOS Simulator?

    a. Accessibility Viewer

    b. Accessibility Chain

    c. Accessibility Inspector

    d. Accessibility Wizard

10. What library enables you to find and add interface objects to a scene?

   a. Object

   b. Media

   c. Interface

   d. Tool

Answers

1. A. The default storyboard name is simply Main.storyboard.

2. D. Use the Attributes inspector to change visual properties for any object in your interface layout.

3. D. You can use the Size Inspector to fine-tune the height and width of most interface elements.

4. C. Auto Layout is the name of Apple's system for describing size/orientation-independent interfaces.

5. B. The Identity Inspector enables you to set an object to a custom class.

6. B. Select the View Controller object and open the Quick Inspector to view most of the connections within a scene.

7. D. Outlets connect interface objects to a variable property in code.

8. B. Actions provide a connection point between an interface element and an underlying method in code.

9. C. Use the Accessibility Inspector to view the accessibility properties set on interface elements within the iOS Simulator.

10. A. You'll use the Object Library to find, select, and place interface elements in Interface Builder.

Activities

1. Practice using the interface layout tools on the Empty.storyboard file. Add each available interface object to your view, and then review the Attributes Inspector for that object. If an attribute doesn't make sense, remember that you can review documentation for the class to identify the role of each of its properties.

2. Revise the Disconnected project with an accessible interface. Review the finished design using the Accessibility Inspector in the iOS Simulator.

Model-View-Controller Application Design

What You'll Learn in This Hour:

▶ What the Model-View-Controller design pattern means

▶ Ways in which Xcode implements MVC

▶ Design of a basic view

▶ Implementation of a corresponding view controller

You've come a long way in the past few hours: You've provisioned your iDevice for development, learned the basics of the Swift language, explored Cocoa Touch, and gotten a feel for Xcode, the Playground, and the Interface Builder (IB) editor. Although you've already used a few prebuilt projects, you have yet to build one from scratch. That's about to change.

In this hour, you learn about the MVC application design pattern and create an iOS application from start to finish.

Understanding the MVC Design Pattern

When you start programming, you'll quickly come to the conclusion that there is more than one "correct" way to do just about everything. Part of the joy of programming is that it is a creative process in which you can be as clever as your imagination allows. This doesn't mean, however, that adding structure to the development process is a bad idea. Having a defined and documented structure means that other developers can work with your code, projects large and small are easy to navigate, and you can reuse your best work in multiple applications.

The application design approach that you'll be using in iOS is known as *Model-View-Controller* (MVC), and it can help you create clean, efficient applications.

NOTE

In Hour 3, "Discovering Swift and the iOS Playground," you learned about object-oriented (OO) programming and the reusability that it can provide. OO programs, however, can still be poorly structured—and therefore the need to define an overall application architecture that can guide the OO implementation.

Making Spaghetti

Before we get into MVC, let's first talk about the development practice that we want to avoid, and why. When creating an application that interacts with a user, several things must be taken into account. First, the user interface (UI). You must present *something* that the user interacts with: buttons, fields, and so on. Second, handling and reacting to the user input. And third, the application must store the information necessary to correctly react to the user (often in the form of a database).

One approach to incorporating all these pieces is to combine them into a single class. The code that displays the interface is mixed with the code that implements the logic and the code that handles data. This can be a straightforward development methodology, but it limits the developer in several ways:

▶ When code is mixed together, it is difficult for multiple developers to work together because no clear division exists between any of the functional units.

▶ The interface, application logic, and data are unlikely to be reusable in other applications because the combination of the three is too specific to the current project to be useful elsewhere.

▶ In short, mixing code, logic, and data leads to a mess. This is known as *spaghetti code* and is the exact opposite of what we want for our iOS applications. MVC to the rescue!

Structured Application Design with MVC

MVC defines a clean separation between the critical components of our apps. Consistent with its name, MVC defines three parts of an application:

▶ A model provides the underlying data and methods that offer information to the rest of the application. The model does not define how the application will look or how it will act.

▶ One or more views make up the UI. A view consists of the different onscreen widgets (buttons, fields, switches, and so forth) that a user can interact with.

▶ The logical isolation created between the functional parts of an application, illustrated in Figure 6.1, means the code becomes more easily maintainable, reusable, and extendable—the exact opposite of spaghetti code.

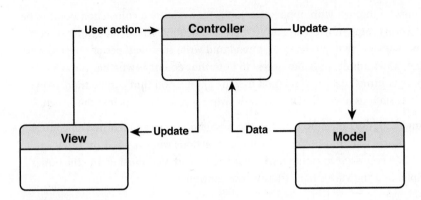

FIGURE 6.1
MVC design isolates the functional components of an app.

Unfortunately, MVC comes as an afterthought in many application development environments. When suggesting MVC design, I am often asked, "How do I do that?" This isn't indicative of a misunderstanding of what MVC is or how it works, but a lack of a clear means of implementing it.

In Xcode, MVC design is natural. As you create new projects and start coding, you are guided into using MVC design patterns automatically. It actually becomes more difficult to program poorly than it does to build a well-structured app.

How Xcode Implements MVC

Over the past few hours, you've learned about Xcode and the IB editor and have gotten a sense for how you will use them to write code and design interfaces. In Hour 5, "Exploring Interface Builder," you even connected storyboard scene objects to the corresponding code in an application. Although we didn't go into the nitty-gritty details at the time, what you were doing was binding a view to a controller.

Views

Views, although possible to create programmatically, are most often designed visually with IB. Views can consist of many different interface elements, the most common of which we covered in Hour 4, "Inside Cocoa Touch." When loaded at runtime, views create any number of objects that can implement a basic level of interactivity on their own (such as a text field opening a keyboard when touched). Even so, a view is entirely independent of any application logic. This clear separation is one of the core principles of the MVC design approach.

For the objects in a view to interact with application logic, they require a connection point to be defined. These connections come in two varieties: outlets and actions. An outlet defines a path between the code and the view that can be used to read and write specific types of information. A toggle-switch outlet, for example, provides access to data that describes whether the switch is on or off. An action, in contrast, defines a method in your application that can be triggered via an event within a view, such as a touch of a button or swiping your finger across the screen.

So, how do outlets and actions connect to code? In the preceding hour, you learned to Control-drag in IB to create a connection, but IB "knew" what connections were valid. It certainly can't guess where in your code you want to create a connection; instead, you must define the outlets and actions that implement the view's logic (that is, the controller).

CAUTION

The Relationship Between Views, Scenes, and Storyboards

At this point, it might seem logical to assume that a storyboard's scene and a view are the same thing. This isn't quite true. A scene is used to visually describe a view; it also references a corresponding controller for the view.

Put another way, a scene is where you go to edit a view and assign a controller to it. Storyboards are the files that contain the scenes you will use in a project.

View Controllers

A controller, known in Xcode as a *view controller*, handles the interactions with a view and establishes the connection points for outlets and actions. To accomplish this, two special directives, @ IBAction and @IBOutlet, are added to your project's code. @IBAction and @IBOutlet are markers that IB recognizes; they serve no other purpose within Swift. You add these directives to the Swift files of your view controller either manually or using a special feature of IB to generate the code automatically.

NOTE

View controllers can hold application logic, but I don't mean to imply that *all* your code should be within a view controller. Although this is largely the convention for the tutorials in this book, as you create your own apps, you can certainly define additional classes to abstract your application logic as you see fit.

Using @IBOutlet

An IBOutlet is used to enable your code to talk to objects within views. For example, consider a text label (UILabel) that you've added to a view. If you want to create a variable property for the label under the name `myLabel` within your view controller, you could declare it following the start of the class, like this:

```
var myLabel: UILabel!
```

Note that the exclamation point isn't there because we're super excited about having a label. This denotes that the `myLabel` variable is an "implicitly unwrapped optional" `UILabel`. While this sounds horrible, it simply means that at some point in time (like when the application is first starting), `myLabel` may not hold anything, but when we want to use it (that is, "unwrap" it), we don't need to do anything special; we just use it like any other variable.

`myLabel` gives your application a place to store and reference the text label, but it still doesn't provide a way to connect it to the label in the interface. To do this, you include the `@IBOutlet` keyword as part of the variable declaration:

```
@IBOutlet weak var myLabel: UILabel!
```

Once `@IBOutlet` is added, IB enables you to visually connect the view's label object to the `myLabel` variable property. Your code can then use the variable to fully interact with the onscreen label object—changing the label's text, calling its methods, and so on.

That's it. That line takes care of variable property and outlet—and is the pattern we will follow throughout the book.

Properties Versus Variables

In Hour 3, you learned about variables in Swift, but you're about to start using them *a lot*, so a refresher is in order.

If you're coming from Objective-C, you have a very clear understanding of the difference between properties and variables. Forget all that now. I'll wait.

In Swift, properties and variables aren't separate entities; they're the same thing. When I refer to a *variable property*, it is simply a variable that is being defined for the entire class (that is, it comes right after the `class` directive) or within a data structure. Officially, Apple calls this a *stored variable property*. If I refer to something as a *variable*, it's being defined within a method/function. Again, Apple's verbose nomenclature wants us to call it a *stored variable*, but I think "variable" alone will do just fine.

There's one additional "gotcha" that you need to understand, especially when working with other people's code; it's possible to define variables in your methods that have the same name as a variable property in the method's class.

For example, let's assume that I have a variable property named `myCommonVariableName` and a variable in a method also named `myCommonVariableName`. I want to reference both of these within the method, so what do I do? To differentiate between these two variables, you add the keyword `self` to the name of the *variable property*, as follows:

```
self.myCommonVariableName
```

If you don't do this, Swift will just assume you're referring to the variable defined within the method.

The good news is that this never needs to happen, just use unique variable and variable property names.

If all of this sounds like gibberish to you, don't worry. It'll become clear as you work on a few examples.

Using @IBAction

An IBAction is used to "advertise" a method in your code that should be called when a certain event takes place. For instance, if a button is pushed or a field updated, you will probably want your application to take action and react appropriately. When you've written a method that implements your event-driven logic, you can declare it with @IBAction in the Swift file, which subsequently exposes it to the IB editor. For example:

```
@IBAction func doCalculation(sender: AnyObject) {
    // Do something here!
}
```

Notice that the method includes a sender parameter with the type of AnyObject. This is a generic type that can be used when you don't know (or need to know) the type of object you'll be working with. By using AnyObject, you can write code that doesn't tie itself to a specific class, making it easier to adapt to different situations.

When creating a method that will be used as an action (like our doCalculation example), you can identify and interact with the object that invoked the action through the sender variable (or whatever you decide to call it in your code). This will prove handy if you decide to design a method that handles multiple different events, such as button presses from several different buttons.

Methods Versus Functions

It's a bit difficult for me to talk about "methods" while providing sample code that includes a "func" (function) keyword. Like *variable properties* and *variables*, this is just another case of semantics. All methods are functions, plain and simple. Methods, however, are functions defined within a class. It's possible to have functions that have nothing to do with any class, thus the distinction.

I will use the word *method* for any function we're defining inside a class, and that's nearly all the functions you'll be reading about in this book.

Data Models

Let me get this out of the way upfront: For many of the exercises in this book, a separate data model is not needed; the data requirements are handled within the controller. This is one of the trade-offs of small projects like the one you'll be working through in a few minutes. Although it would be ideal to represent a complete MVC application architecture, sometimes it just isn't possible in the space and time available. In your own projects, you must decide whether to implement a standalone model. In the case of small utility apps, you may find that you rarely need to consider a data model beyond the logic you code into the controller.

As you grow more experienced with the iOS development and start building data-rich applications, you'll want to begin exploring Core Data. Core Data abstracts the interactions between your application and an underlying datastore. It also includes an Xcode data modeling tool, like IB, that helps you design your application, but instead of visually laying out interfaces, you can use it to visually map a data structure, as shown in Figure 6.2.

For our beginning tutorials, using Core Data would be like using a sledgehammer to drive a thumbtack. Right now, let's get started building your first app with a view and a view controller.

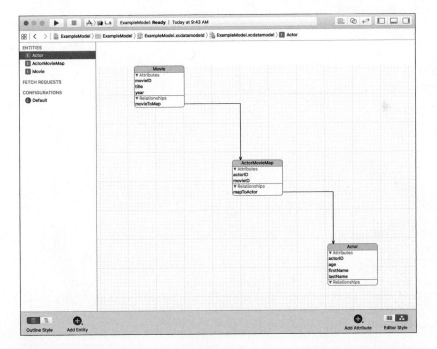

FIGURE 6.2
After you become more familiar with iOS development, you might want to explore the Core Data tools for managing your data model.

Using the Single View Application Template

The easiest way to see how Xcode manages to separate logic from display is to build an application that follows this approach. Apple has included a useful application template in Xcode that quickly sets up a project with a storyboard, an empty view, and an associated view controller. This Single View Application template will be the starting point for many of your projects, so for the rest of this hour you will learn how to use it.

Implementation Overview

The project we'll build is simple: Instead of just writing the typical Hello World app, we want to be a bit more flexible. The program presents the user with a field (`UITextField`) for typing and a button (`UIButton`). When the user types into the field and presses the button, the display updates an onscreen label (`UILabel`) so that the word *Hello* is shown, followed by the user's input. The completed HelloNoun, as I've chosen to call this project, is shown in Figure 6.3.

FIGURE 6.3
The app accepts input and updates the display based on what the user types.

Although this won't be a masterpiece of development, it does contain almost all the different elements we discuss in this hour: a view, a controller, outlets, and actions. Because this is the first full development cycle that we've worked through, we'll pay close attention to how all the pieces come together and why things work the way they do.

Setting Up the Project

First we want to create the project, which we'll call **HelloNoun**, in Xcode:

1. Launch Xcode from the Applications folder or Launchpad.

2. Choose File, New, Project.

3. You are prompted to choose a project type and a template. On the left side of the New Project window, make sure that Application is selected under the iOS project type. Select the Single View Application option from the icons on the right, and then click Next.

4. Type **HelloNoun** in the Product Name field. Use your full name for the organization name. For the Organization Identifier, enter a domain to represent yourself, in reverse order. (I'm using com.teachyourselfios; refer to the "Creating and Managing Projects" section in Hour 2, "Introduction to Xcode and the iOS Simulator," for more information.) Be sure that Swift is selected and Devices is set to either iPhone or iPad. Use Core Data, Include Unit Tests, and Include UI Tests should remain unchecked, as shown in Figure 6.4. Click Next.

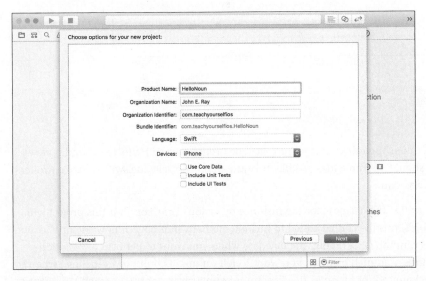

FIGURE 6.4
Choose the name and target device for your application.

5. Choose a save location when prompted and uncheck Create Git Repository. Do not add the new project to an existing project or workspace, if asked. Click Create to generate the project.

This creates a simple application structure consisting of an application delegate, a window, a view (defined in a storyboard scene), and a view controller. After a few seconds, your project window will open (see Figure 6.5).

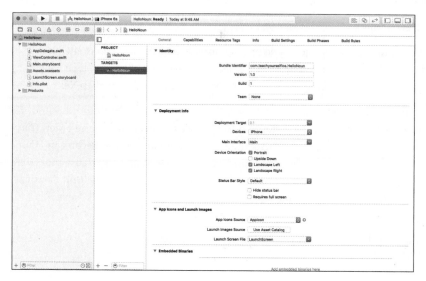

FIGURE 6.5
The workspace for your new project.

Class Files

If it isn't already visible, open the top-level project code group (named HelloNoun) and review the contents. You should see three files (visible in Figure 6.5): AppDelegate.swift, ViewController.swift, and Main.storyboard.

The AppDelegate.swift is the delegate for the instance of UIApplication that this project will create. In other words, this file can be edited to include methods that govern how the application behaves when it is running. You modify the delegate when you want to perform application-wide setup operations at launch or when you want to tell an application how to behave when it moves into the background (or becomes the foreground application again), or when you want to choose what to do when an application is forced to quit. For this project, you do not need to edit anything in the application delegate; but keep in mind the role that it plays in the overall application life cycle.

The second file, ViewController.swift, implements the class that contains the logic for controlling our view: a view controller (UIViewController). This file is mostly empty to begin, with just a basic structure in place to ensure that we can build and run the project from the outset. In fact, feel free to click the Run button at the top of the Xcode window. The application will compile and launch, but there won't be anything to do.

To impart some functionality to this app, we need to work on the two areas discussed previously: the view and the view controller.

The Storyboard File

In addition to the class files, the project contains a storyboard file that will store the interface design. Click the Main.storyboard file to open it in the IB editor, and then expand the objects in the document outline. Shown in Figure 6.6, Main.storyboard contains icons for the First Responder (an instance of UIResponder), the View Controller (our ViewController class), and our application's View (an instance of UIView). There are also icons for the Top and Bottom "layout guides"; these are tools you'll learn about later to help lay out and align your UI. The view controller and first responder are also visible in the bar above the view in the editor. Remember from Hour 5 that if you don't see the icons in the bar, just click it and they'll appear.

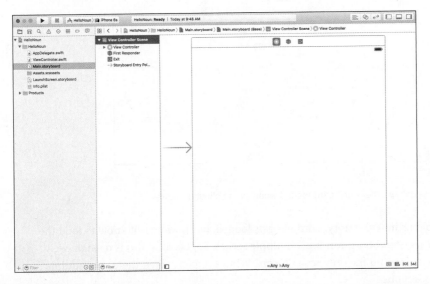

FIGURE 6.6
When the storyboard file is loaded, the application's view controller and initial view are instantiated.

As you learned earlier, when a storyboard file is loaded by an app, the objects within it are instantiated, meaning they become real, active parts of the application. In the case of Hello Noun (and any other application based on the Single View Application template), when the application launches, a window is created, Main.storyboard is loaded, along with an instance of the ViewController class and its view, which is added to the window.

Reasonable persons are probably scratching their heads right now wondering a few things. For example, how does Main.storyboard get loaded at all? Where is the code to tell the application to do this?

The Main.storyboard file is defined in the Info.plist file as the value for the key `Main story-board file base name`. You can see this yourself by the plist file in your main project code group to show the contents. Alternatively, just click the top-level project icon, make sure the HelloNoun target is selected, and view the Main Interface field in the Deployment Info section (see Figure 6.7).

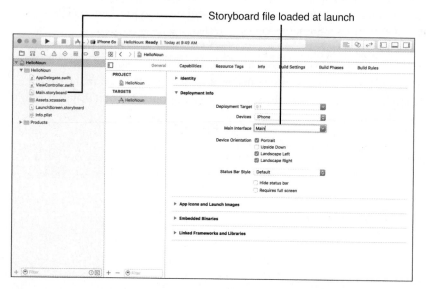

FIGURE 6.7
The project's plist file defines the storyboard loaded when the application starts.

Okay, so that explains how the storyboard file gets loaded, but how does it know to load the scene? If you recall, a storyboard can have multiple scenes. So, because this is a single-view application, is it just loading the only scene it can? What happens when there are multiple scenes? All good questions.

In typical Apple style, the initial scene (and corresponding view controller/view) is chosen rather subtly in the IB editor itself. Refer back to Figure 6.6. See the gray arrow in the editor area that points to the left side of the view? That arrow is draggable and, when there are multiple different scenes, you can drag it to point to the view corresponding to any scene. This action automatically configures the project to launch that scene's view controller and view when the application launches. In addition to showing an arrow in the editor area, you'll also notice a Storyboard Entry Point element contained within the initial scene in the document outline.

In summary, the application is configured to load Main.storyboard, which looks for the initial scene and then creates an instance of that scene's view controller class (`ViewController`, as defined in the ViewController.swift file). The view controller loads its view, which is added automatically to the main window. If that still doesn't make sense, don't fret; I guide you through this every step of the way.

Setting the Initial Scene

It's possible to delete the storyboard entry point, leaving you with a storyboard that won't know where to begin. If this happens, select the View Controller that should manage your initial scene, then open the Attributes Inspector (Command-Option-4). Within the View Controller section, click Is Initial View Controller, and the entry point will reappear in your project.

NOTE

I've mentioned "window" a few times in this discussion. In iOS development, your application has a window that covers the screen and is created when it loads. Views are then displayed within this window. The window is referenced through the variable property `window` in the application delegate class. Because your initial view is automatically displayed in the window when the application starts, you'll rarely need to interact with it directly.

Planning the Variables and Connections

The first step of building our project is to decide on all the things our view controller needs to make it work. What objects are we going to use? What outlets and variable properties do we need to connect to our objects, and what actions will our interface trigger?

For this simple project, we must interact with three different objects:

► A text field (`UITextField`)

► A label (`UILabel`)

► A button (`UIButton`)

The first two provide input (the field) and output (the label) for the user. The third (the button) triggers an action in our code to set the contents of the label to the contents of the text field.

Setting Up the Outlets and Actions

Based on what we now know, we could edit viewController.swift to define the variable properties we need to manipulate the interface elements.

We'll name the field (`UITextField`) that collects user input, `userInput`, and the label (`UILabel`) that provides output will be `userOutput`. Recall that we must define these with the `@IBOutlet` keyword so that we can make the connection between the interface and code. We must also make sure these variable properties are "implicitly unwrapped optionals"; that is, an exclamation mark (!) is added to the end of the declaration.

This boils down to two lines, which we could place right after the `class` line in ViewController. swift:

```
@IBOutlet weak var userInput: UITextField!
@IBOutlet weak var userOutput: UILabel!
```

To finish defining the connections, we also need to include the method definition for the action performed when the button is pressed. We will name this `setOutput`:

```
@IBAction func setOutput(sender: AnyObject) {
}
```

All of this, put into context, results in a ViewController.swift file that resembles Listing 6.1 (with bold lines showing what was added):

LISTING 6.1   ViewController.swift with Connections Defined

```
import UIKit
class ViewController: UIViewController {

    @IBOutlet weak var userInput: UITextField!
    @IBOutlet weak var userOutput: UILabel!

    @IBAction func setOutput(sender: AnyObject) {
    }

    override func viewDidLoad() {
        super.viewDidLoad()
        // Do any additional setup after loading the view, typically from a nib.
    }

    override func didReceiveMemoryWarning() {
        super.didReceiveMemoryWarning()
        // Dispose of any resources that can be recreated.
    }
}
```

That's all we'd need to do. We could then connect our interface to code, just as we did in the last hour, and implement a bit of logic in the `setOutput` method within ViewController.swift.

CAUTION

Stop! Don't Type a Thing

Notice that I've been saying we *could* and we *would* rather than directing you to start typing? That's because now that you understand how the code *could* be set up by hand, I'll show you how Xcode can automate the process for you.

Some developers prefer to set up outlets, actions, and such manually. You're welcome to do this, but you're about to learn that Xcode can generate the same code for you, with almost no typing.

NOTE

If you're skimming through the HelloNoun code files, you may notice that there are additional green comments (lines that start with the characters //). Many of these are left out of the code listings in the book to save space.

A Simplified Approach

Although you still haven't typed any code, what I'm hoping you've learned over the past few minutes is that a successful project begins with the planning and setup of your variable properties, and the use of @IBOutlet and @IBAction to define which interface objects will be connected to your code.

You've seen that this can be performed manually, but what if Xcode could do all the work for you? What if the IB editor, through the very process of making the connections that you learned about in Hour 5, could add variable property definitions, create outlets, *and* insert the empty (skeleton) methods for the actions into your swift file? It can!

While the core basis of binding views to view controllers still relies on the code you've just seen, you can use Xcode to automatically write it for you *as you build your interface*. You will still want to identify the variable properties, outlets, and actions to create before starting the interface, and you'll still sometimes need to do a bit of additional code setup beforehand, but allowing Xcode to generate code automatically dramatically speeds up the initial stages of development.

Now, without further ado, let's build our application.

Designing the Interface

You've seen that IB makes designing a user interface (UI) as much fun as playing around in your favorite graphics application. That said, our emphasis is on the fundamentals of the development process and the objects we have at our disposal. Where it isn't critical, we move quickly through the interface creation.

Setting Simulated Interface Attributes

Interface Builder defaults to a "generic" interface view in the editor area—it doesn't quite look like an iPhone or iPad. While we'll be looking at how to design within this view later in the book, for now I want you to be working with something that looks familiar.

To that end, the first thing we'll do is switch the simulated screen to the size of the device you own (or one you'd like to own!). Follow these steps to set a specific size screen:

1. Open Main.storyboard by selecting it within the Xcode project navigator.

2. The IB editor opens the file, displaying the view controller scene objects in the document outline, and a visual representation of the scene's view in the editor.

3. Select the View Controller Scene line in the document outline.

4. Open the Utility area and switch to the Attributes Inspector. You can do this by clicking the button at the far right of the Xcode toolbar, then the third icon from the right of the toolbar that appears underneath that (or save yourself some time and press Option-Command-4).

5. Set the Size drop-down to the iOS device screen size that you'd like. I'll be using iPhone 4.7-inch in most examples because it is the largest size I can easily fit in a screenshot. If you're developing for the iPad, that's great, but you're going to need a big screen.

6. By default, Xcode uses a portrait orientation for its layouts. If you'd like to switch this, you can use the Orientation drop-down to choose between landscape and portrait screen orientations.

7. After setting the size, the view in the editor should look a bit more like the iOS devices we know and love. Figure 6.8 shows these settings, and their result.

NOTE

If you choose to skip this step, don't worry, you can still develop and run your applications. However, you'll need to use the "resizable iPhone" and "resizeable iPad" devices in the iOS Simulator (see Hour 2); otherwise, your interface may be cut off or look unusual. By setting a simulated size, we can ignore all the fancy resizable interface cruft for now (and just learn how to develop). After all, isn't that why we're here?

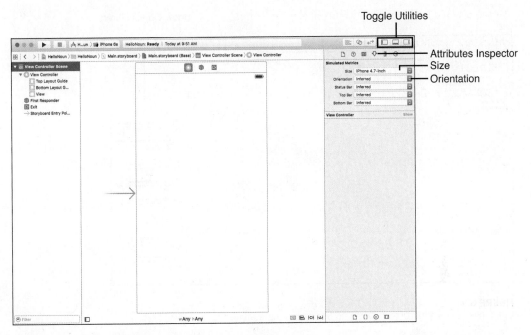

FIGURE 6.8
Begin by setting the simulated interface to something familiar.

Adding the Objects

The interface for the HelloNoun application is quite simple: It must provide a space for output, a field for input, and a button to set the output to the same thing as the input. Assuming the storyboard is still open from the preceding section, you just need to follow these steps:

1. With the storyboard open, make sure that the Object Library is visible on the right by choosing View, Utilities, Show Object Library (Control-Option-Command-3). Verify that the Objects button (a circle with a square in the center) is selected within the library; this displays all the components that we can drag into the view. Your workspace should now resemble Figure 6.9.

2. Add two labels to the view by clicking and dragging the label (UILabel) object from the Object Library into the view.

3. The first label is just static text that says Hello. Double-click the default text that reads Label to edit it and change the content to read **Hello**. Position the second label underneath it; this will act as the output area.

Show Object Library

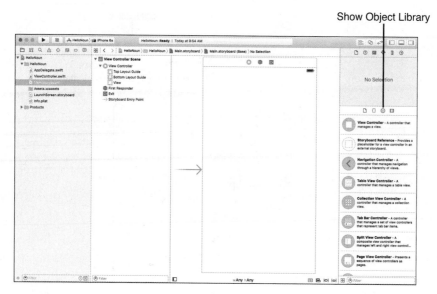

FIGURE 6.9
Open the view and the Object Library to begin creating the interface.

For this example, I changed the text of the second label to read **<Noun Goes Here!>**. This will serve as a default value until the user provides a new string. You might need to expand the text labels by clicking and dragging their handles to create enough room for them to display.

I also chose to set my labels to align their text to the center. If you want to do the same, select the label within the view by clicking it and then press Option-Command-4 or click the Attributes Inspector icon (a slider) at the top of the Xcode utility area. This opens the Attributes Inspector for the label.

Use the alignment buttons to change the default text alignment for the labels. You may also explore the other attributes to see the effect on the text, such as size, shadow, color, and so on. Your view should contain two labels and resemble Figure 6.10.

4. When you're happy with the results, it's time to add the elements that the user will be interacting with: the text field and button. Find the Text Field object (`UITextField`) within the Object Library and click and drag to position it under your two labels. Using the handles on the field, stretch it so that it matches the length of your output label.

5. Open the Attributes Inspector again (Option-Command-4) and set the text size to match the labels you added earlier, if desired. Notice that the field itself doesn't get any bigger. This is because the default field type on iOS has a set height. To change the height, you

can click one of the square Border Style buttons in the Attributes Inspector. The field then allows you to resize its height freely.

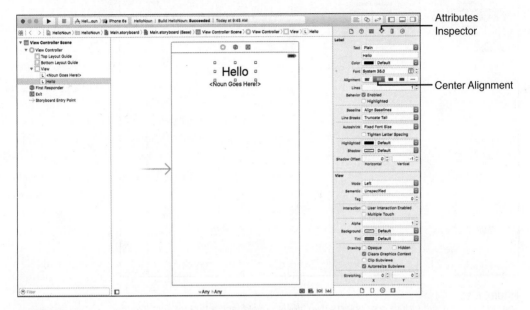

FIGURE 6.10
Use the Attributes Inspector to set the labels' text alignment to center and to increase the font size.

6. Finally, click and drag a button (UIButton) from the Object Library into the view, positioning it right below the text field. Double-click in the center of the button to add a title, such as Set Label. Resize the button to fit the label, if needed. You may also want to again use the Attributes Inspector to increase the font size. Figure 6.11 shows my version of the finished view.

Creating and Connecting the Outlets and Actions

Our work in IB is almost complete. The last remaining step is to connect the view to the view controller. If we had defined manually the outlets and actions as described earlier, this would be a matter of dragging from the code to the object icons. As it turns out, even though we're going to be creating the outlet and action code on-the-fly, it's still just a matter of click and drag.

To do this, we need to be able to drag from the IB editor to the area of the code where we want to add an outlet or an action. In other words, we need to be able to see the ViewController.swift file at the same time we see the view that we are connecting. This is a great time to use the assistant editor feature of Xcode.

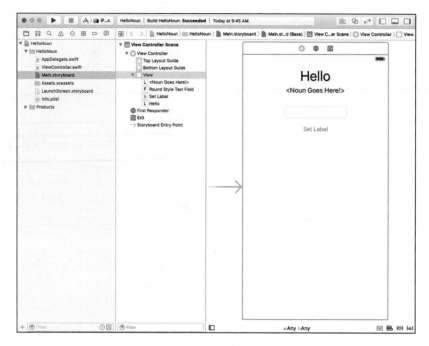

FIGURE 6.11
Your interface should include four objects (two labels, a field, and a button), just like this.

With your completed interface visible in the IB editor, click the Assistant Editor button (the button with overlapping circles at the top right of the Xcode toolbar). The ViewController.swift file automatically opens to the right of the interface because Xcode knows that this class file corresponds to the view controller you've been designing.

If Xcode opens the wrong file instead (sometimes it can be finicky), just click the name of the file directly above the editing area, and you'll see a menu where you can select the other files in the project.

At this point, you might be noticing a problem: If you're on a small MacBook, or editing an iPad version of the project, you're running out of screen space. To conserve space, you can hide the navigator area and utility area using the View menu, or by clicking the Hide/Show Navigator and Hide/Show Utility toolbar buttons. Find these buttons at the far right of the toolbar; they resemble boxes with vertical lines in them.

You can also use the Hide/Show Document Outline button (a rectangle with a line inside of it) found in the lower-left corner of IB editor to toggle the outline off. Your screen should now resemble Figure 6.12.

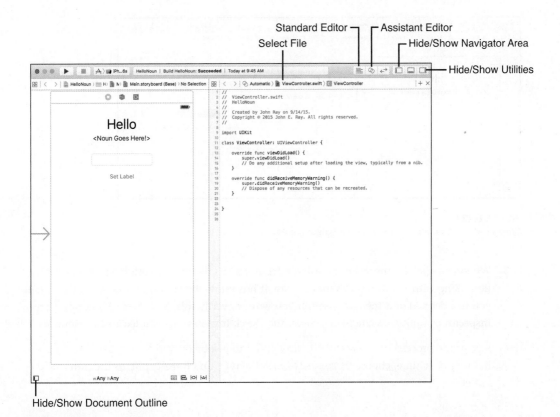

FIGURE 6.12
Turn on the assistant editor and make room in your workspace.

Adding the Outlets

We'll start by connecting the label we created for user output. Recall that we want this to be represented by a variable property called `userOutput`:

1. Control-drag from the label that you've established for output (titled <Noun Goes Here!> in the example) or its icon in the document outline. Drag all the way into the code editor for ViewController.swift, releasing the mouse button when your cursor is just under the `class` line. As you drag, you see a visual indication of what Xcode is planning to insert when you release the button, as shown in Figure 6.13.

2. When you release the mouse button, you are prompted to define an outlet. Be sure that the Connection menu is set to Outlet, Storage is Weak, and the type is set to `UILabel` (because that's what the object is). Finally, specify the name you want to use for the variable property (`userOutput`), and then click Connect, as shown in Figure 6.14.

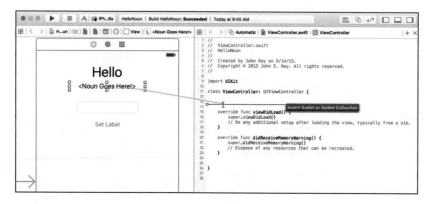

FIGURE 6.13
Choose where your connection code will be generated.

3. When you click Connect, Xcode automatically inserts the proper variable property defini-tion along with @IBOutlet. What's more, it has made the connection between the outlet you just defined and the code itself. If you want to verify this, just check the Connections Inspector or right-click the field to open the Quick Inspector, as you learned in Hour 5.

4. Repeat the process for the text field, dragging it to just below the @IBOutlet line that was inserted. This time, choose UITextField as the type and userInput as the name of the outlet.

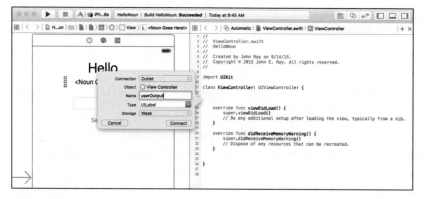

FIGURE 6.14
Configure the specifics of the outlet you're creating.

CAUTION

Watch Where You Drag

Placing your first connection is easy, but you must target the right part of the code in subsequent drags. It is important that you drag subsequent interface objects that you want to define in your code to an area below the @IBOutlet lines that Xcode adds.

With those few steps, you've created and inserted the proper code to support the input and output view objects, and the connections to the view controller are now established. To finish the view, however, you still must define a setOutput action and connect the button to it.

TIP

Xcode Naming and Outlets

As you connect your objects to outlets, you'll notice something interesting happening in the document outline. When you connect the "<noun goes here>" label to "userOutput", you'll see the corresponding object in the document outline change to "User Output." Xcode is automatically parsing your variable names and changing how it displays the objects in the outline so you can easily see how they are connected.

Adding the Action

Adding the action and making the connection between the button and the action follows the same pattern as the two outlets you just added. The only difference is that actions are usually defined after properties in an interface file, so you'll just be dragging to a slightly different location:

1. Control-drag from the button in the view to just below the two @IBOutlet directives that you automatically added earlier. Again, as you drag, you'll see Xcode provide visual feedback about where it is going to insert code. Release the mouse button when you've targeted the line where you want the action code to be inserted.

2. As with the outlets, you are prompted to configure the connection, as demonstrated in Figure 6.15. This time, be sure to choose Action as the connection type; otherwise, Xcode tries to insert another outlet. Set the Name to setOutput (the method name we chose earlier). Be sure that the Event pop-up menu is set to Touch Up Inside to configure the event that will trigger the action. Leave the rest of the fields set to their defaults and click Connect.

You've just added the variable properties, outlets, and actions, and connected them all to your code.

Go ahead and reconfigure your Xcode workspace to use the standard editor and make sure that the project navigator is visible before continuing. If you want to double-check your work, review the contents of the ViewController.swift and make sure it matches Listing 6.1 from earlier in this hour.

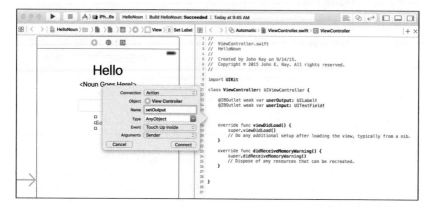

FIGURE 6.15
Configure the action that will be inserted into the code.

Xcode Helps You Write Code, But Is It the *Right* Code?

You've just worked through the process of having Xcode write the code to support your user interface objects for you. This can be a big time saver and can eliminate much of the unpleasant upfront work required when setting up a project. That said, it isn't perfect—not by a long shot.

The code that Xcode inserts is just as if you wrote it yourself. It can be changed, edited, moved around, and broken. If you attempt to add multiple outlets for the same object, Xcode lets you. Multiple actions for the same object and event? No problem. In short, Xcode writes the code you need, but it is up to you to make sure that it is writing the *right* code and making the *right* connections.

I strongly recommend making sure you that understand how to manually create outlets, actions, and variable properties by hand before moving past this hour. You'll need that knowledge, plus you'll need to know how to manually make connections between objects in the interface and preexisting outlets and actions in order to fix any errors that occur because Xcode didn't quite generate the connections and code you were expecting.

Implementing the Application Logic

With the view complete and the connection to the view controller in place, the only task left is to fill in the logic. Let's turn our attention back toward the ViewController.swift file and the implementation of `setOutput`.

The purpose of the setOutput method is to set the output label to the contents of the field that the user edited. How do we get/set these values? Simple. Both UILabel and UITextField classes have a variable property called text that contains their contents. By reading and writing to/from these variables, we can set userInput to userOutput in one easy step.

Open ViewController.swift and find the empty setOutput method. Insert the bolded line to make it read as shown in Listing 6.2.

LISTING 6.2   Completed setOutput Method

```
@IBAction func setOutput(sender: AnyObject) {
    userOutput.text=userInput.text
}
```

It all boils down to a single line. This single assignment statement does everything we need. Well done! You've written your first iOS application.

Building the Application

The app is ready to build and test. If you want to deploy to your iOS device, be sure it is connected and ready to go. Select your physical device or the iOS Simulator from Scheme menu on the Xcode toolbar, and then click Run.

After a few seconds, the application starts on your iDevice or within the Simulator window, as shown in Figure 6.16.

FIGURE 6.16
Your finished application makes use of a view to handle the UI and a view controller to implement the functional logic.

CAUTION

Quitting Applications

After you're done running an application, use the Stop button on the Xcode toolbar to exit it. If you use the Home button in the iOS Simulator, the application will move to the background and Xcode may get a bit confused. If this happens, you can double-click the iOS Simulator's Home button to access the task manager and manually stop the application (just like a real iOS device).

Further Exploration

Before moving on to subsequent hours, you may want to learn more about how Apple has implemented the MVC design versus other development environments that you may have used. An excellent document titled *About the Basic Programming Concepts for Cocoa and Cocoa Touch* provides an in-depth discussion of MVC as applied to Cocoa (read the section called "Model-View-Controller"). You can find and read this introduction by searching for the title in the Xcode documentation system, which you read about in Hour 4.

You might also want to take a breather and use the finished HelloNoun application for experimentation. We discussed only a few of the different IB attributes that can be set for labels, but dozens more can customize the way that fields and buttons display. The flexibility of the view creation in IB goes well beyond what can fit in one book, so exploration is necessary to take full advantage of the tools. This is an excellent opportunity to play around with the tools and see the results, before we move into more complex (and easy-to-break) applications.

Summary

In this hour, you learned about the MVC design pattern and how it separates the display (view), logic (controller), and data (model) components of an application. You also explored how Apple implements this design within Xcode through the use of Core Data, views, and view controllers. This approach will guide your applications through much of this book and in your own real-world application design, so learning the basics now will pay off later.

To reinforce the lesson, we worked through a simple application using the Single View Application template. This included first identifying the outlets and actions that would be needed and then using Xcode to create them. Although not the most complex app you'll write, it included the elements of a fully interactive user experience: input, output, and (very simple) logic.

Q&A

Q. I don't like the idea of code being written without seeing it. Should I create actions and outlets myself?

A. That is entirely up to the developer. The code-generation features in Xcode are several years old at this point, and quite stable. As long as you understand how to set up a project manually, I suggest that you use the Xcode tools to do the work but review the code it creates immediately afterward.

Q. I noticed some circles displayed beside code lines in the interface and implementation files. What are those?

A. These are yet another way to connect your interface to code. If you manually define the outlets and actions, circles appear beside potential connection points in your code. You can then drag from the circles to the interface objects to make connections. What's more, clicking these circles after connections are in place will highlight the endpoint of the connection.

Workshop

Quiz

1. What event do you use to detect a button tap?

    a. Touch True

    b. Touch Down Inside

    c. Touch Up Inside

    d. Touch Detect True

2. What Swift object type do you use to represent any object?

    a. `nil`

    b. `AnyObject`

    c. `AllObject`

    d. `PlaceholderObject`

3. Which Apple project template creates a simple view/view controller application?

    a. Single View Application

    b. Standard

    c. One View

    d. Basic

4. What project-level component contains the scenes and views for your application?

    a. View controller

    b. NIB file

    c. UI guide

    d. Storyboard

5. Which project file contains the functions for managing how an application acts at startup and when it transitions between the foreground and background?

    a. View controller

    b. Main

    c. AppDelegate

    d. Storyboard

6. What keyword is used to denote a connection point between a variable property and an interface builder object?

    a. `@IBOutlet`

    b. `@IBAction`

    c. `@IBTouchpoint`

    d. `@IBConnect`

7. Which variable property enables developers to read the contents of a text field?

    a. `text`

    b. `textcontent`

    c. `content`

    d. `fieldcontent`

8. How many files are needed to implement a class in Swift?

    a. 1

    b. 2

    c. 3

    d. 4

9. When editing a user interface, the assistant editor should open what?

    a. Storyboard scenes

    b. View controller class

    c. App delegate

    d. Xcode Help

10. A variable that is defined for an entire class is known as a what?

    a. Property

    b. Variable

    c. Variable property

    d. Stored property

Answers

1. C. The Touch Up Inside event is most commonly used to trigger actions based on a button press.

2. B. Variables of type `AnyObject` can hold any object of any type. This can be useful when functions need to accept a wide range of objects as a their input.

3. A. The Single View Application template is the starting point for many of our apps in this book. It provides a storyboard with a single scene/view and a corresponding view controller (everything a basic app needs).

4. D. Storyboards contain the scenes and views you will use in a project.

5. C. The AppDelegate file contains the functions that manage the startup and subsequent lifecycle of an iOS application.

6. A. Use `@IBOutlet` to set a connection point between a variable property and an interface builder object.

7. A. The `text` variable property can be used to access the information a user has entered into a text field.

8. A. Swift only requires a single file to implement a class. Objective-C, the previous iOS development language, required two.

9. B. When you are editing a user interface, the assistant editor should automatically open the corresponding view controller class.

10. C. A variable property is like any other variable, but is defined at the class level and is accessible in any of the class methods.

Activities

1. Explore the attributes of the interface objects that you added to the tutorial project in Interface Builder. Try setting different fonts, colors, and layouts. Use these tools to customize the view beyond the simple layout created this hour.

2. Rebuild HelloNoun using outlets, actions, and variable properties that you define and manage manually. Make your connections using the same techniques discussed in the Hour 5 tutorial. This is good practice for getting familiar with what goes on behind the scenes.

3. Review the Apple Xcode documentation for the Core Data features of Cocoa. Although you won't be using this technology in this book's tutorials, it is an important tool that you'll ultimately want to become more familiar with for advanced data-driven applications.

Working with Text, Keyboards, and Buttons

What You'll Learn in This Hour:

▶ How to use text fields
▶ Input and output in scrollable text views
▶ How to enable data detectors
▶ A way to spruce up the standard iOS buttons

In the preceding hour, you explored views and view controllers and created a simple application that accepted user input and generated output when a button was pushed. This hour expands on these basic building blocks. In this hour, we create an application that uses multiple different input and output techniques. You learn how to implement and use editable text fields, text views, and graphical buttons, and how to configure the onscreen keyboard.

This is quite a bit of material to cover in an hour, but the concepts are very similar, and you'll quickly get the hang of these new elements.

Basic User Input and Output

iOS gives us many different ways of displaying information to a user and collecting feedback. There are so many ways, in fact, that we're going to be spending the next several hours working through the tools that the iOS software development kit (SDK) provides for interacting with your users, starting with the basics.

Buttons

One of the most common interactions you'll have with your users is detecting and reacting to the touch of a button (UIButton). Buttons, as you may recall, are elements of a view that respond to an event that the user triggers in the interface, usually a Touch Up Inside event to indicate that the user's finger was on a button and then released it. Once an event is detected, it can trigger an action (@IBAction) within a corresponding view controller.

Buttons are used for everything from providing preset answers to questions to triggering motions within a game. Although the default iOS button style is minimalist, buttons can take on many different forms through the use of images. Figure 7.1 shows an example of a fancy button with gradients.

FIGURE 7.1
Buttons can be simple, fancy (like this one), or set to any arbitrary image.

Text Fields and Views

Another common input mechanism is a text field. Text fields (`UITextField`) give users space to enter any information they want into a single line in the application; these are similar to the form fields in a web form. When users enter data into a field, you can constrain their input to numbers or text by using different iOS keyboards, something we do later this hour. You can also enable editing of styles within the text, such as underlining and bold. Text fields, like buttons, can respond to events but are often implemented as passive interface elements, meaning that their contents (provided through the `text` variable property) can be read at any time by the view controller.

Similar to the text field is the text view (`UITextView`). The difference is a text view can present a scrollable and editable block of text for the user to either read or modify. These should be used in cases where more than a few words of input are required. Figure 7.2 shows examples of a text field and text view.

Labels

The final interface feature that we're going to be using here and throughout this book is the label (`UILabel`). Labels are used to display strings within a view by setting their `text` variable property.

The text within a label can be controlled via a wide range of label attributes, such as font and text size, alignment, and color. As you'll see, labels are useful both for static text in a view and for presenting dynamic output that you generate in your code.

Now that you have basic insight into the input and output tools we'll be using in this hour, let's go ahead and get started with our project: a simple substitution-style story generator.

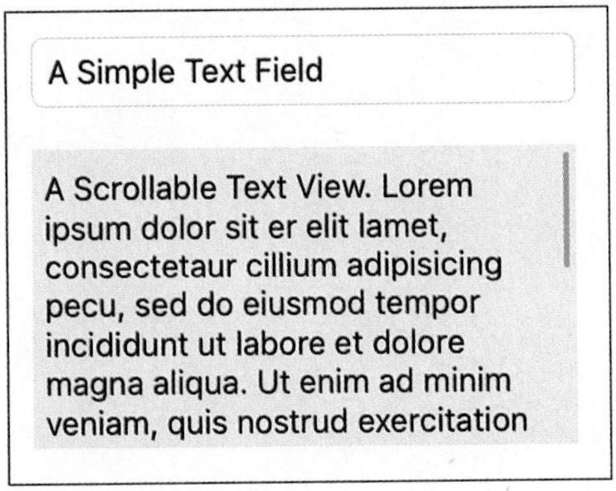

> A Simple Text Field

> A Scrollable Text View. Lorem ipsum dolor sit er elit lamet, consectetaur cillium adipisicing pecu, sed do eiusmod tempor incididunt ut labore et dolore magna aliqua. Ut enim ad minim veniam, quis nostrud exercitation

FIGURE 7.2
Text fields and text views provide a means for entering text using a device's virtual keyboard.

Using Text Fields, Text Views, and Buttons

Although not everyone will agree with my sentiment, I enjoy entering text on my iPhone and iPad. The virtual keyboard is responsive and simple to navigate. What's more, the input process can be altered to constrain the user's input to only numbers, only letters, or other variations. (This varies depending on device.) You can have iOS automatically correct simple misspellings, allow text styling, or capitalize letters—all without a line of code. This project reviews many aspects of the text input process.

Implementation Overview

In this project, we create a Mad Libs-style story creator. Users enter a noun (place), verb, and number through three text fields (UITextField). They may also enter or modify a template that contains the outline of the story to be generated. Because the template can be several lines long, we use a text view (UITextView) to present this information. A button press (UIButton) triggers an action that generates the story and outputs the finished text in another text view, demonstrated in Figure 7.3.

Although not directly part of the input or output process, we also investigate how to implement the now-expected "touch the background to make the keyboard disappear" interface standard, along with a few other important points. In other words, pay attention!

We'll name this tutorial project **FieldButtonFun**. You may certainly use something more creative if you want.

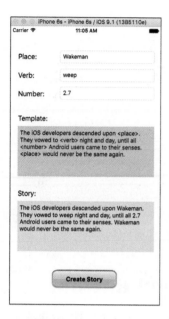

FIGURE 7.3
The tutorial app in this hour uses two types of text input objects.

Setting Up the Project

This project uses the same Single View Application template as the preceding hour. If it isn't already running, launch Xcode, and then complete these steps:

1. Choose File, New, Project.

2. Select the iOS application project type.

3. Find and select the Single View Application option in the Template list, and then click Next to continue.

4. Enter the project name, **FieldButtonFun**. Be sure that your device is chosen, Swift is set as the language, and that Use Core Data, Include Unit Tests, and Include UI Tests remain unchecked. Then click Next.

5. Choose your save location, and then click Create to set up the new project.

As before, we focus on the view, which has been created in Main.storyboard, and the view controller class `ViewController`.

Planning the Variables and Connections

This project contains a total of six input areas that must connect to our code via outlets. Three text fields are used to collect the place, verb, and number values. We'll access these through variable properties named `thePlace`, `theVerb`, and `theNumber`, respectively. The project also requires two text views: one to hold the editable story template, `theTemplate`; and the other to contain the output, `theStory`.

NOTE

Yes, we'll use a text view for output as well as for input. Text views provide a built-in scrolling behavior and can be set to read-only, making them convenient for both collecting and displaying information.

Finally, a single button is used to trigger an action method, `createStory`, which creates and displays the story text.

TIP

If UI elements are used only to trigger actions, they do not need outlets. If your application needs to manipulate an object, however—such as setting its label, color, size, position, and so on—it needs an outlet and a corresponding variable property defined.

Now that you understand the objects we'll add and how we'll refer to them, let's turn our attention to building the user interface (UI) and creating our connections to code.

Preparing Button Templates with Slicing

In the preceding hour's lesson, you created a button (`UIButton`) and connected it to the implementation of an action (`@IBAction`) within a view controller. Nothing to it, right? Working with buttons is relatively straightforward, but what you may have noticed is that, by default, the buttons you create in the Interface Builder (IB) are, well, not very button-like. To create visually appealing graphical buttons that don't require a new image for each button, we can prepare a button template using a technique called *slicing*.

The Xcode slicing tool is used to define areas of an image that can be resized when the image is stretched. You can choose to create both vertical and horizontal slices to accommodate both vertical and horizontal stretching. We can use this to create graphically rich buttons that take on any size and look great.

Adding the Images

Slices are added using a tool within the Xcode asset catalog. So, our first task is to add some images.

Inside this hour's Projects directory is an Images folder with two Apple-created button templates: whiteButton.png and blueButton.png. Within the Xcode project navigator, click the Assets.xcassets assets catalog icon. Next, drag the Images folder from the OS X Finder into the left column of the asset catalog in Xcode. Your display should resemble Figure 7.4.

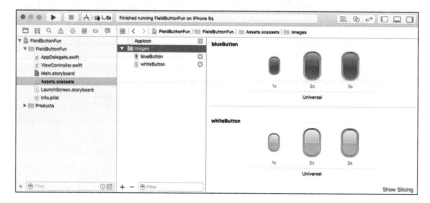

FIGURE 7.4
To use custom buttons, drag the project images folder into the Assets.xcassets folder in Xcode.

TIP

@2x and @3x

The whiteButton.png and blueButton.png files are accompanied by their Retina equivalents—with @2x (two times the vertical and horizontal pixels) and @3x (three times the vertical and horizontal pixels) suffixes. Recall that the iPhone 6+/6s+ supports a high enough pixel density display that it uses "@3x" resources.

When you drag the Images folder into the asset catalog, Xcode automatically pairs all of these images up under the headings "whiteButton" and "blueButton." As far as the system is concerned, you can interact with all of the images using just those two names, and the right graphic for the right display will automatically be selected.

Creating Slices

Slicing may sound complicated, but it is easy to understand, and even easier to perform. When creating a slice, you visually specify a horizontal or vertical (or both) stripe of pixels within an image. This is the "slice," and it will be repeated to fill in space if the image needs to grow. You'll also (optionally) get to choose a portion (also a stripe of pixels) that is replaced by the slice when the image resizes.

To create your slices, first make sure that you've opened the asset catalog by selecting the Assets.xcassets icon in the project navigator, and then follow these steps:

1. Expand the Images folder within the asset catalog.

2. Select one of the button images to slice; I'm starting with `whiteButton`.

3. Click the Show Slicing button in the lower-right corner of the asset catalog content area, as shown in Figure 7.5.

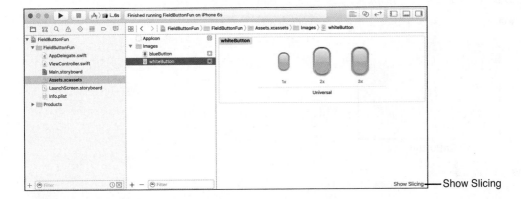

FIGURE 7.5
Use the Show Slicing button to start the slicing process.

4. The screen refreshes to show an enlarged copy of the graphic (both non-Retina (1x) and Retina (2x and 3x), if available). Click the Start Slicing button on the non-Retina image to begin.

5. Xcode prompts for the type of slicing. Use the buttons, as demonstrated in Figure 7.6, to choose between Horizontal, Horizontal & Vertical, or just Vertical slicing. For our button, we want both horizontal and vertical.

6. The slicing editor displays three dragging lines in the horizontal/vertical directions. The horizontal lines determine the vertical slicing, and the vertical lines determine the horizontal slicing.

   The first and second lines (going left to right/top to bottom) determine the slice that can grow. The second and third lines define the area that will be replaced by copies of the slicing when the image resizes, as shown in Figure 7.7. The second and third lines can be positioned right next to one another if you simply want the stripe to stretch without replacing any other parts of the image.

7. For the button template, we want the pretty, curvy corners to always stay the same, so they aren't resized. The portion we want to grow is a stripe about 12 pixels in (horizontally and vertically), and can just be a single pixel wide. Drag the first vertical line about 12 pixels in.

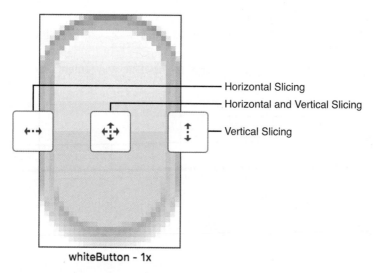

whiteButton - 1x

FIGURE 7.6
Choose the type of slicing you want to perform.

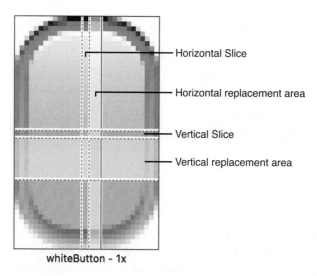

whiteButton - 1x

FIGURE 7.7
Use the lines to choose your slices.

8. Drag the second vertical line so that it creates a 1-pixel-wide stripe (that is, about 13 pixels in).

9. Drag the third vertical line so that it is right next to the second line; there's no reason to replace any portion of the image with the repeated stripe. You've just completed the horizontal slice.

10. Repeat steps 7–9 for the horizontal lines, creating the vertical slice. Your finished slicing layout should look almost identical to Figure 7.8.

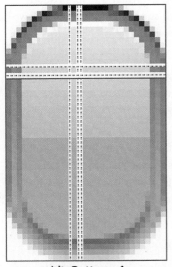

whiteButton - 1x

FIGURE 7.8
The finished slicing.

TIP

To fine-tune your slices, open the Attributes Inspector while slicing. This shows the position of the slice in pixels and enables you to manually enter X and Y values.

After you've finished the slicing for the non-Retina white button, do the same for the Retina versions. You'll need to position your slices about 24 pixels in on the 2x images, and 36 pixels in on the 3x (versus 12 on the 1x non-Retina). Repeat the process for the blue button assets.

When you finish, you've created images that can be resized to create attractive buttons regardless of how large the button needs to be. When it comes time to use the images in a few minutes, you'll treat them like any other image; the slicing is applied automatically when they are resized.

TIP
Slicing works great for buttons, but can be used for *any* image that you may want to resize. Just set the slicing for the graphics and when you stretch them, they'll resize using your slicing preferences.

Designing the Interface

In the preceding hour, you learned that the Main.storyboard is loaded when the application launches and that it instantiates the default view controller, which subsequently loads its view from the storyboard file. Locate Main.storyboard in the project's code folder, and click to select it and open the IB editor.

When IB has started, be sure that the document outline area is visible (Editor, Show Document Outline) and hide the navigator area (Command-0) if you need room.

Setting Simulated Interface Attributes

Just like the last hour, the first thing I recommend doing after settling down in Interface Builder is setting a simulated screen size. While not strictly necessary, this makes it easier to visualize the final product without getting bogged down in screen layout details. This is the last hour where I'm going to explicitly provide these steps, so you may want to memorize them.

To that end, the first thing we'll do is switch the simulated screen to the size of the device you want to target. Follow these steps to set a specific size screen:

1. With the Main.storyboard selected and the IB editor visible, select the View Controller Scene line in the document outline.

2. Open the Utility area and switch to the Attributes Inspector (Option-Command-4).

3. Set the Size drop-down to the iOS device screen size that you'd like. I use iPhone 4.7-inch so that the interface fits in the space I have for screenshots.

4. (Optional) Use the Orientation drop-down to choose between landscape and portrait screen orientations. *Portrait* is the default, (and the layout I use for my designs).

Adding Text Fields

Now, let's create the user interface. Open the Object Library (View, Utilities, Show Object Library) and drag the top of it *up* within the Utility area to make more of the library visible at once.

Begin creating the UI by adding three text fields to the top of the view. To add a field, locate the Text Field object (`UITextField`) in the library and drag it into the view. Repeat this two more times for the other two fields.

Stack the fields on top of one another, leaving enough room so that the user can easily tap a field without hitting all of them. To help the user differentiate between the three fields, add labels to the view. Click and drag the label (`UILabel`) object from the library into the view. Align three labels directly across from the three fields. Double-click the label within the view to set its text. I labeled my fields Place, Verb, and Number, from top to bottom, as shown in Figure 7.9.

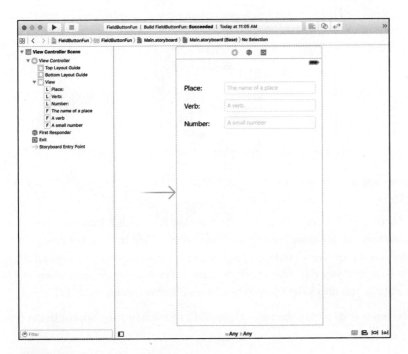

FIGURE 7.9
Add text fields and labels to differentiate between them.

Editing Text Field Attributes

The fields that you've created are technically fine as is, but you can adjust their appearance and behavior to create a better user experience. To view the field attributes, click a field, and then press Option-Command-4 (View, Utilities, Show Attributes Inspector) to open the Attributes Inspector (see Figure 7.10).

For example, you can use the Placeholder field to enter text that appears in the background of the field until the user begins editing. This can be a helpful tip or an additional explanation of what the user should be entering.

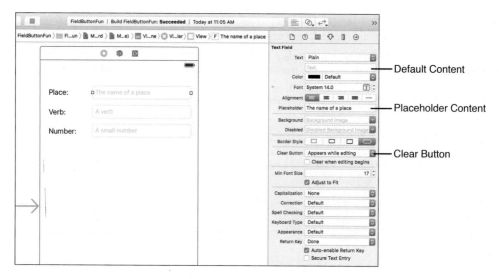

FIGURE 7.10
Editing a field's attributes can help create a better UI.

You may also choose to activate the Clear button. The Clear button is a small X icon added to a field that the user can touch to quickly erase the contents. To add the Clear button, just choose one of the visibility options from the Clear button pop-up menu; the functionality is added for free to your application. Note that you may also choose to automatically clear the field when the user taps it to start editing. Just check the Clear When Editing Begins check box.

Add these features to the three fields within the view. Figure 7.11 shows how they appear in the application.

TIP

Placeholder text also helps identify which field is which within the IB editor area. It can make creating your connections much easier down the road.

In addition to these changes, attributes can adjust the text alignment, font and size, and other visual options. Part of the fun of working in the IB editor is that you can explore the tools and make tweaks (and undo them) without having to edit your code.

Attributed Versus Plain Text

In many of controls that allow the display of text, you'll find the Text drop-down menu that can toggle between Plain or Attributed options. In general, you want to leave this on Plain, but by setting it to Attributed, you can gain much finer control over the layout of the text, as shown in Figure 7.12.

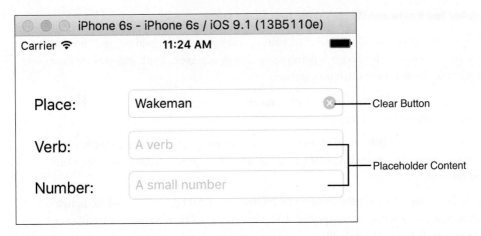

FIGURE 7.11
Placeholder text can provide helpful cues to the user, and the Clear button makes it simple to remove a value from a field.

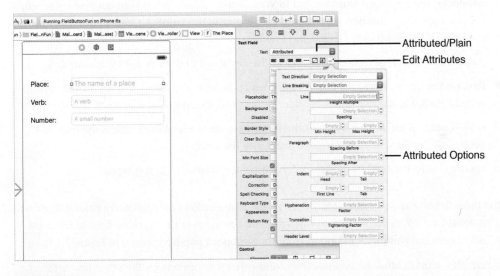

FIGURE 7.12
Attributed text fields and other UI elements offer more detailed control over presentation.

Using this feature, you can provide more richly styled text output and even enable user editing of the text style by simply checking the Allows Editing Attributes check box.

Customizing the Keyboard Display with Text Input Traits

Probably the most important attributes that you can set for an input field are the "text input traits," or simply, how the keyboard is going to be shown onscreen. Eight different traits appear at the bottom of the text field attributes section:

▶ **Capitalize:** Controls whether iOS automatically capitalizes words, sentences, or all the characters entered into a field.

▶ **Correction:** If explicitly set to on or off, the input field corrects (on) or ignores (off) common spelling errors as you type. If left to the defaults, it inherits the behavior of the iOS settings.

▶ **Spell Checking:** If explicitly set to on or off, the input field displays a red underline on words that are potentially misspelled. Touching the word then displays a list of possible corrections. If left to the defaults, the field inherits the behavior of the iOS system settings.

▶ **Keyboard Type:** Sets a predefined keyboard for providing input. By default, the input keyboard lets you type letters, numbers, and symbols. A total of 10 different keyboards are available, ranging from Number Pad to Web Search. If the option Number Pad is chosen, for example, only numbers can be entered. Similarly, the Email Address option constrains the input to strings that look like email addresses.

▶ **Appearance:** Changes the appearance of the keyboard to dark or light variations.

▶ **Return Key:** If the keyboard has a Return key, it is set to this label. Values include Done, Search, Next, Go, and so on.

▶ **Auto-Enable Return Key:** Disables the Return key on the keyboard unless the user has entered at least a single character of input into the field.

▶ **Secure:** Treats the field as a password, hiding each character as it is typed.

Of the three fields that we've added to the view, the Number field can definitely benefit from setting an input trait. With the Attributes Inspector still open, select the Number field in the view, and then choose the Number Pad option from the Keyboard pop-up menu (see Figure 7.13).

You may also want to alter the capitalization and correction options on the other two fields and set the Return key to Done. Again, all this functionality is gained "for free." So, you can return to edit the interface and experiment all you want later on. For now, let's call these fields "done" and move on to the text areas.

Copy and Paste

Your text entry areas automatically gain copy and paste without your having to add anything to your code. For advanced applications, you can override the protocol methods defined in `UIResponderStandardEditActions` to customize the copy, paste, and selection process.

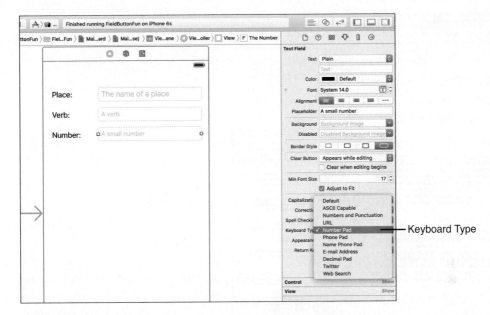

FIGURE 7.13
Choosing a keyboard type will help constrain a user's input.

Adding Text Views

Now that you know the ins and outs of text fields, let's move on to the two text views (`UITextView`) present in this project. Text views, for the most part, can be used just like text fields. You can access their contents the same way, and they support many of the same attributes as text fields, including text input traits.

To add a text view, find the Text View object (`UITextView`) and drag it into the view. Doing so adds a block to the view, complete with Greeked text (*Lorem ipsum...*) that represents the input area. Using the resizing handles on the sizes of the block, you can shrink or expand the object to best fit the view. Because this project calls for two text views, drag two into the view and size them to fit underneath the existing three text fields.

As with the text fields, the views themselves don't convey much information about their purpose to the user. To clarify their use, add two text labels above each of the views: **Template** for the first, and **Story** for the second. Your view should now resemble Figure 7.14.

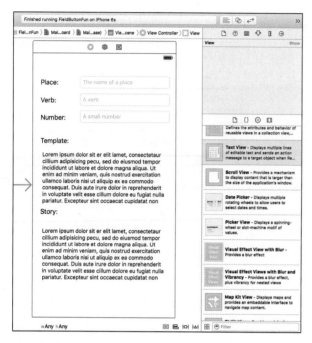

FIGURE 7.14
Add labels to clarify your text views.

CAUTION

Size Doesn't Matter (For Now)

The size of your iPhone design doesn't matter at this stage. In Hour 16, "Building Responsive User Interfaces," you learn how a single layout can work on the multiple screen sizes as well as multiple versions of iOS. Right now, be aware that when you position controls, they probably won't adjust correctly to work on other devices or earlier versions of iOS. In addition, your layout might not exactly match my screenshots. That's okay. I don't want you to get caught up in the details of UI design while you're still learning to program!

Editing Text View Attributes

Text view attributes provide many of the same visual controls as text fields, including plain and attributed modes. Select a view, and then open the Attributes Inspector (Option-Command-4) to see the available options, as shown in Figure 7.15.

To start, we need to update the default content to remove the initial Greeked text and provide our own input. For the top field, which will act as the template, select the content within the Text attribute of the Attributes Inspector (this is directly below the Plain/Attributed drop-down menu), and then clear it. Enter the following text, which will be available within the application as the default:

The iOS developers descended upon <place>. They vowed to <verb> night and day, until all <number> Android users came to their senses. <place> would never be the same again.

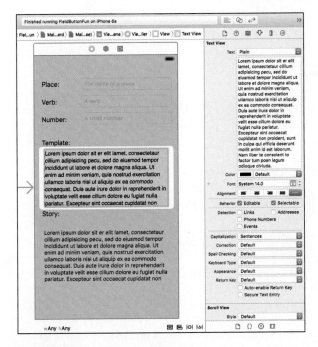

FIGURE 7.15
Edit the attributes of each text view to prepare them for input and output.

When we implement the logic behind this interface, the placeholders (`<place>`, `<verb>`, `<number>`) are replaced with the user's input.

Next, select the "story" text view, and then again use the Attributes Inspector to clear the contents entirely. Because the contents of this text view are generated automatically, we can leave it empty. This view is a read-only view, as well, so uncheck the Editable attribute.

In this example, to help provide some additional contrast between these two areas, I set the background color of the template to a light red and the story to a light green. To do this in your copy, simply select the text view to stylize, and then click the Attributes Inspector's View Background attribute to open a color chooser. Figure 7.16 shows our final text views.

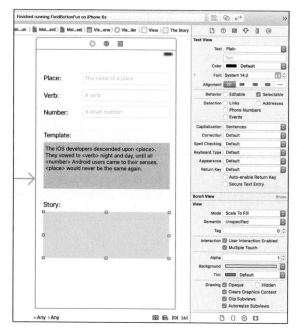

FIGURE 7.16
When completed, the text views should differ in color, editability, and content.

Using Data Detectors

Data detectors automatically analyze the content within onscreen controls and provide helpful links based on what they find. Phone numbers, for example, can be touched to dial the phone; detected web addresses can be set to launch Safari when tapped by the user. All of this occurs without your application having to do a thing. No need to parse out strings that look like URLs or phone numbers. In fact, all you need to do is click a button.

To enable data detectors on a text view, select the view and return to the Attributes Inspector. Within the Text View Attributes area, click the check boxes under Detection: Phone Numbers to identify any sequence of numbers that looks like a phone number, Addresses for mailing addresses, Events for text that references a day/time, and Links to provide a clickable link for web and email addresses.

CAUTION

Practice Moderation!

Data detectors are a great convenience for users, but *can* be overused. If you enable data detectors in your projects, be sure they make sense. For example, if you are calculating numbers and outputting them to the user, chances are you don't want the digits to be recognized as telephone numbers.

Setting Scrolling Options

When editing the text view attributes, you'll notice that a range of options exist that are specifically related to its ability to scroll, as shown in Figure 7.17.

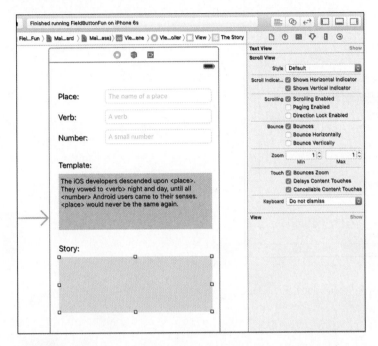

FIGURE 7.17
Scrolling regions have a number of attributes that can change their behavior.

Using these features, you can set the color of the scroll indicator (black or white), choose whether both horizontal and vertical scrolling are enabled, and even choose whether the scrolling area should have the rubber band "bounce" effect when it reaches the ends of the scrollable content.

Adding Styled Buttons

We need a single button in this project, so drag an instance of a button (UIButton) from the Object Library to the bottom of the view. Title the button **Create Story**. Figure 7.18 shows the final view and document outline, with a default button.

Although you're certainly welcome to use the standard buttons, our goal is do to something a bit more "flashy." Before we get to the details, let's see what we can configure using the Xcode button attributes.

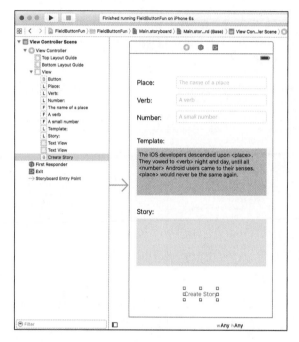

FIGURE 7.18
The default button style is little more than a label.

Editing Button Attributes

To edit a button's appearance, your first stop is, once again, the Attributes Inspector (Option-Command-4). Using the Attributes Inspector, you can dramatically change the appearance of the button. Use the Type drop-down menu, shown in Figure 7.19, to choose common button types:

▶ **System:** The default iOS button style.

▶ **Detail Disclosure:** An arrow button used to indicate additional information is available.

▶ **Info Light:** An *i* icon, typically used to display additional information about an application or item. The light version is intended for dark backgrounds.

▶ **Info Dark:** The dark (light background) version of the Info Light button.

▶ **Add Contact:** A + button, often used to indicate the addition of a contact to the address book.

▶ **Custom:** A button that has no default appearance. Usually used with button images.

In addition to choosing a button type, you can make the button change depending on the current state of user interaction, a concept known as *changing state*. For instance, when a button is displayed before being touched, it is considered to be in its *default* state. When a user touches a button, it changes to show that it has been touched; this is the *highlighted* state. Use the State Config menu to select the button state you want to set up, and then use the various button attributes (images, colors, fonts, and so on) that should be applied in that state.

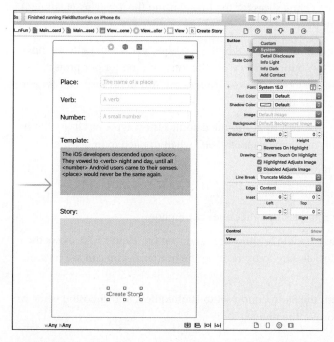

FIGURE 7.19
The Attributes Inspector gives several options for common button types and even a custom option.

Other options include the ability to create shadowed text (Shadow Offset), show a tinted color when the button is highlighted, or display a "glow" around a user's finger when he or she touches a button (Shows Touch on Highlight).

Setting Custom Button Images

Even with all the settings available to configure your buttons, to create truly custom controls, you need to make custom images, including versions for the highlighted on state and the default off state. These can be any shape or size, but the PNG format is recommended because of its compression and transparency features.

After you've added these to the project through Xcode, you can select the image from the Image or Background drop-down menus in the Attributes Inspector. Using the Image menu sets an image that appears inside the button alongside the button title. This option enables you to decorate a button with an icon.

Using the Background menu sets an image that is stretched to fill the entire background of the button. The option lets you create a custom image as the entire button, but you must size your button exactly to match the image (*or* define slices for the image using the Xcode asset catalog). Do you get where we're heading with this?

Assuming you followed the steps for defining button templates earlier, you should already have images that can resize to create "pretty" buttons. To create the fancy button for our project, select the `UIButton` you've added to the layout, make sure that the Attributes Inspector is open (Option-Command-4), and then complete these steps:

1. Set the button type to Custom. You can try using the default system type, but it applies its own highlighting effect that (in my opinion) looks "off" when applied to images.

2. Set the State Config drop-down to Default.

3. Use the Text Color drop-down to choose Black Color.

4. Use the Background drop-down to pick the `whiteButton` image.

5. Your layout should immediately update to show the fancy button. Figure 7.20 shows the button appearance and settings. Be sure to try resizing the button so you can see how the slicing comes into play.

6. Repeat steps 3–5, this time with the State Config set to Highlighted, and choosing white as the text color and `blueButton` for the image.

Because of the Xcode slicing tools, everything "just works." Your button looks great, regardless of the size, and you don't have to write a single line of code to completely customize what it looks like!

Creating and Connecting the Outlets and Actions

With the interface finished, we now have a total of six text input/output areas that we need to access through our view controller code. In addition, we must create an action for the button that will trigger the generation of our story using the template and field contents.

In summary, a total of six outlets and one action require creation and connection:

▶ **Place field** (`UITextField`): `thePlace`

▶ **Verb field** (`UITextField`): `theVerb`

▶ **Number field** (`UITextField`): `theNumber`

▶ **Template Text view (`UITextView`):** `theTemplate`

▶ **Story Text view (`UITextView`):** `theStory`

▶ **Action triggered from Create Story button:** `createStory`

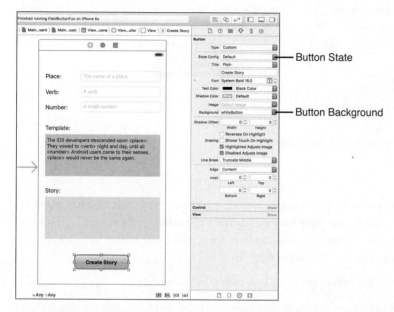

FIGURE 7.20
The "pretty" button appears, thanks to your earlier slicing.

Making sure that the Main.storyboard file is open in the IB editor, use the editor toolbar buttons to switch to the assistant mode. You should now see your UI design and the ViewController.swift file where you will be making your connections side by side.

Adding the Outlets

Start by Control-dragging from the Place text field to the line following the `class` line in the ViewController.swift file. When prompted, be sure to configure the connection as an outlet and the name as `thePlace`, leaving the other values set to their defaults (type `UITextfield`, storage weak), as shown in Figure 7.21.

Repeat the process for the Verb and Number fields, connecting them to `theVerb` and `theNumber` outlets, this time dragging to just below the `@IBOutlet` directive created when you added the first outlet. Connect the text views to `theTemplate` and `theStory` outlets. The process is identical (but the type is `UITextView`).

That does it for the outlets. Now let's create our action.

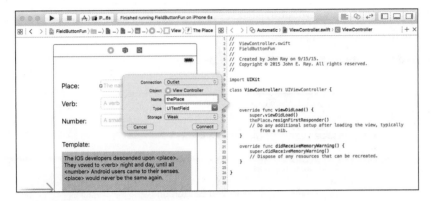

FIGURE 7.21
Create and connect outlets for each input/output element.

Adding the Action

In this project, we add an action for a method we will call `createStory`. This action is triggered when the user clicks the Create Story button. To create the action and generate an empty method that we can implement later, Control-drag from the Create Story button to below the last `@IBOutlet` directive in the ViewController.swift file.

Name the action `createStory`, when prompted, as shown in Figure 7.22.

The connections to our interface are complete. The resulting ViewController.swift file should have a block of code at the top resembling the following:

```
import UIKit

class ViewController: UIViewController {

    @IBOutlet weak var thePlace: UITextField!
    @IBOutlet weak var theVerb: UITextField!
    @IBOutlet weak var theNumber: UITextField!
    @IBOutlet weak var theTemplate: UITextView!
    @IBOutlet weak var theStory: UITextView!

    @IBAction func createStory(sender: AnyObject) {

    }
...
```

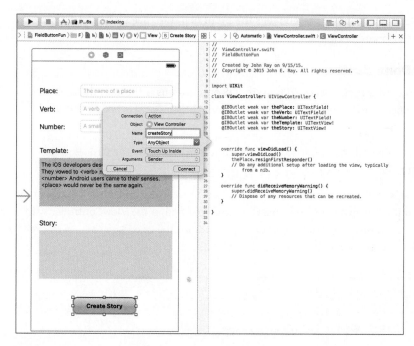

FIGURE 7.22
Create the action that will ultimately be used to generate our story.

Implementing Keyboard Hiding

Before completing the application by implementing the view controller logic to construct the story, we need to look at a "problem" that is inherent to applications with character entry: keyboards that won't go away! To see what we mean, start the application again either on your device or in the iOS Simulator.

With your app up and running, click in a field. The keyboard appears. Now what? Click in another field; the keyboard changes to match the text input traits you set up, but it remains onscreen. Touch the word *Done*. Nothing happens. And even if it did, what about the number pad that doesn't include a Done button? If you try to use this app, you'll also find a keyboard that sticks around and that covers up the Create Story button, making it impossible to fully utilize the UI. So, what's the problem?

Hour 4, "Inside Cocoa Touch," described *responders* as objects that process input. The first responder is the first object that has a shot at handling user input. In the case of a text field or text view, when it gains first-responder status, the keyboard is shown and remains onscreen until the field gives up or resigns first-responder status. What does this look like in code? For the field `thePlace`, we could resign first-responder status and get rid of the keyboard with this line of code:

```
thePlace.resignFirstResponder()
```

Calling the `resignFirstResponder` method tells the input object to give up its claim to the input; as a result, the keyboard disappears.

Hiding with the Done Button

The most common trigger for hiding the keyboard in iOS applications is through the `Did End on Exit` event of the field. This event occurs when the Done (or similar) keyboard button is pressed.

We'll implement a new method called `hideKeyboard` that is activated by the `Did End on Exit` events from our fields.

Turn your attention back to the Main.storyboard file and open the assistant editor. Control-drag from the Place field to the line just below the `createStory` method in the ViewController.swift file. When prompted, configure a new action, `hideKeyboard`, for the `Did End on Exit` event. Leave all the other defaults the same, as shown in Figure 7.23.

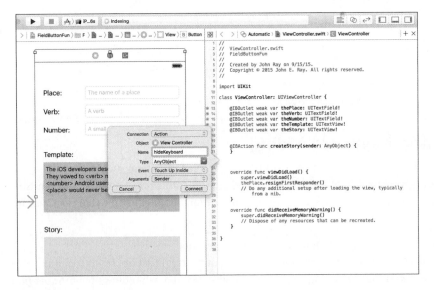

FIGURE 7.23
Add a new action method for hiding the keyboard.

Now you must connect the Verb field to the newly defined `hideKeyboard` action. There are many different ways to make connections to existing actions, but only a few enable us to target specific events. We'll use the technique you learned about in the tutorials in Hour 5, "Exploring Interface Builder": the Connections Inspector.

First switch back to the standard editor and make sure that the document outline is visible (Editor, Show Document Outline). Select the Verb field, and open the Connections Inspector by pressing Option-Command-6 (or choosing View, Utilities, Connections Inspector). Drag from the circle beside Did End on Exit to the View Controller icon in the document outline area. Release your mouse button and choose `hideKeyboard` when prompted, as shown in Figure 7.24.

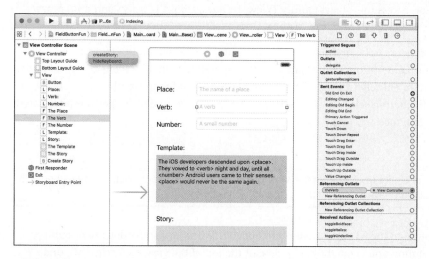

FIGURE 7.24
Connect the Verb field to the `hideKeyboard` action.

Unfortunately, now we run into a problem. The number input doesn't have a Done button, and the text view doesn't support the `Did End on Exit` event, so how do we hide the keyboard for these variations?

NOTE

Check Out Your Events!

As you add objects to your storyboard, take a few minutes to select them and check out the events that they can send and receive using the Connections Inspector. You'll find that there are hundreds of ways of integrating functionality into your apps by using events supported by the operating system. Text views, for example, can be controlled by your own UI elements (such as buttons) by receiving events for cut, paste, select all, and event stylizing (bold, italic, and so on) text.

Hiding with a Background Touch

A popular iOS interface convention is that if a keyboard is open and you touch the background (outside of a field), the keyboard disappears. This is the approach we need to take for the number-input text field and the text view—and functionality that we need to add to all the other fields to keep things consistent.

Wondering how we detect an event outside of a field? Nothing special: All we do is create a big invisible button that sits behind all the other controls, and then attach it to the `hideKeyboard` action method.

Within the IB editor, access the Object Library (View, Utilities, Object Library) and drag a new button (`UIButton`) from the library into the view.

Because this button needs to be invisible, make sure that it is selected, and then open the Attributes Inspector (Option-Command-4) and set the type to Custom and delete the button title. This makes the button entirely transparent. Use the selection handles to size the button to fill the entire view. With the button selected, choose Editor, Arrange, Send to Back to position the button in the back of the interface.

TIP

You can also drag an object to the top of the view hierarchy in the document outline to position it in the back. The objects are layered from the top (back) to the bottom (front).

To connect the button to the `hideKeyboard` method, it's easiest to use the document outline. Select the custom button you created (it should be at the top of the view hierarchy list), and then Control-drag from the button to the View Controller line. When prompted, choose the `hideKeyboard` method.

Nicely done. You're now ready to implement the `hideKeyboard` so that the Place and Verb fields can hide the keyboard when Done is touched, or the background can be touched to hide the keyboard in any situation.

Adding the Keyboard-Hiding Code

Because the user could be making changes in four potential places (`thePlace`, `theVerb`, `theNumber`, `theTemplate`), we must either identify the field the user is editing *or* simply resign first-responder status on all of them. As it turns out, if you resign first-responder status on a field that isn't the first responder, it doesn't matter. That makes implementing the `hideKeyboard` method as simple as sending the `resignFirstResponder` message to each of the variable properties representing our editable UI elements.

Scroll through the ViewController.swift file to find the `hideKeyboard` method stub that Xcode inserted for us when we created the `action`. Edit the method so that it reads as shown in Listing 7.1.

LISTING 7.1   **Hiding the Keyboard**

```
@IBAction func hideKeyboard(sender: AnyObject) {
    thePlace.resignFirstResponder()
    theVerb.resignFirstResponder()
```

```
theNumber.resignFirstResponder()
theTemplate.resignFirstResponder()
}
```

TIP

You might be asking yourself whether the `sender` variable isn't the field that is generating the event. Couldn't we just resign the responder status of the sender? Yes, absolutely. This would work just fine, but we need the `hideKeyboard` method to work when `sender` isn't necessarily the field (for example, when the background button triggers the method).

Save your work, and then try running the application again. This time, when you click outside of a field or the text view or use the Done button, the keyboard disappears.

TIP

If you're interested in taking the keyboard configuration even further, Xcode lets you choose what happens to an onscreen keyboard as a user scrolls within a view, such as the text views used in this tutorial. To access the keyboard options for a scrolling view, select the view, and then open the Attributes Inspector and look for the Keyboard setting within the Scroll View section.

Implementing the Application Logic

To finish off `FieldButtonFun`, we need to fill in the `createStory` method within the view controller (ViewController.swift). This method searches the template text for the `<place>`, `<verb>`, and `<number>` placeholders, and then replaces them with the user's input, storing the results in the text view. We'll make use of the `String` method `stringByReplacingOccurrencesOf` `String:withString` to do the heavy lifting. This method performs a search and replace on a given string and returns the results in a new string.

For example, if the `String` variable `myString` contains "Hello town", and you want to replace *town* with *world*, returning the result in a `String` variable called `myNewString`, you might use the following:

```
var myNewString=myString.stringByReplacingOccurrencesOfString("town",
    withString:"world")
```

Try It in the Playground

You can test many of the examples of application logic in this book in Xcode Playground feature (see Hour 3, "Discovering Swift and the iOS Playground," for details). To test string replacement, open a new (or existing) Playground (File, New, Playground), and add this code:

```
import UIKit

var myString="Hello town"
var myNewString=myString.stringByReplacingOccurrencesOfString("town",
    withString:"world")
```

You'll see the contents of the strings and the results of the replacement appear on the right side of the Playground as you type!

Watch for other Playground examples throughout the book, where I'll demonstrate that the code we discuss actually works, and I'm not just making things up.

In the case of our application, our strings are the text variable properties of the text fields and text views (thePlace.text, theVerb.text, theNumber.text, theTemplate.text, and theStory.text). Note that in the text *fields* the text variable property is optional and we must unwrap by adding ! to the end.

Add the final method implementation, shown in Listing 7.2, to ViewController.swift within the createStory method stub that Xcode generated for us.

LISTING 7.2   Implementing the createStory Method

```
1: @IBAction func createStory(sender: AnyObject) {
2:     theStory.text=theTemplate.text
3:     theStory.text=theStory.text.stringByReplacingOccurrencesOfString("<place>",
4:         withString: thePlace.text!)
5:     theStory.text=theStory.text.stringByReplacingOccurrencesOfString("<verb>",
6:         withString: theVerb.text!)
7:     theStory.text=theStory.text.stringByReplacingOccurrencesOfString("<number>",
8:         withString: theNumber.text!)
9: }
```

Line 2 begins by copying the text from the template field (theTemplate) into the output text view (theStory). Lines 3–4 replace the <place> placeholder in theStory text view with the contents of the thePlace field, storing the results back in theStory. Lines 5–6 then update the story text view again by replacing the <verb> placeholder with the appropriate user input. This is repeated once more in lines 7–8 for the <number> placeholder. The end result is a completed story, output in the theStory text view.

Our application is finally complete.

Building the Application

To view and test the FieldButtonFun, click the Run icon in the Xcode toolbar. Your finished app should look similar to Figure 7.25, fancy button and all!

FIGURE 7.25
The finished application includes scrolling views, text editing, and a pretty button. What more could we want?

This project provided a starting point for looking through the different properties and attributes that can alter how objects look and behave within an iOS interface. The takeaway message: Don't assume anything about an object until you've reviewed how it can be configured.

CAUTION

Plain Is Pretty, Pretty Is Pretty

In this tutorial, we built a button that looks nothing like the default iOS buttons. Be careful, though, when creating "graphically rich" UIs for iOS apps. Apple has embraced a simple and subtle approach to its UIs, so you might want to follow its lead. Create your UI to best fit with the application experience you want for your users.

Further Exploration

Throughout the next few hours, you'll explore a large number of UI objects, so your next steps should be to concentrate on the features you've learned in this hour—specifically, the object variable properties, methods, and events that they respond to.

For text fields and text views, the base object mostly provides for customization of appearance. However, you may also implement a delegate (`UITextFieldDelegate`, `UITextViewDelegate`) that responds to changes in editing status, such as starting or ending editing. You'll learn more about implementing delegates in Hour 10, "Getting the User's Attention," but you can start looking ahead to the additional functionality that can be provided in your applications through the use of a delegate.

In addition, keep in mind that although there are plenty of variable properties to explore for these objects, there are additional variable properties and methods that are inherited from their superclasses. All UI elements, for example, inherit from `UIControl`, `UIView`, and `UIResponder`, which bring additional features to the table, such as manipulating size and location of the object's onscreen display, as well as for customizing the copy and paste process (through the `UIResponderStandardEditActions` protocol). By accessing these lower-level methods, you can customize the object beyond what might be immediately obvious.

Apple Tutorials

Apple has provided a sample project that includes examples of almost all the available iOS UI controls:

UICatalog (accessible via the Xcode documentation): This project also includes a wide variety of graphic samples, such as the button images used in this hour's tutorial. It's an excellent starting point for experimenting with the iOS UI elements.

Summary

This hour described the use of common input features and a few important output options. You learned that text fields and text views both enable the user to enter arbitrary input constrained by a variety of different virtual keyboards. Unlike text fields, however, text views can handle multiline input as well as scrolling, making them the choice for working with large amounts of text. We also covered the use of buttons and button states, including how buttons can be manipulated through code.

We continue to use the same techniques you used in this hour throughout the rest of the book, so don't be surprised when you see these elements again.

Q&A

Q. Why can't I use a `UILabel` in place of a `UITextView` for multiline output?

A. You certainly can. The text view, however, provides scrolling functionality "for free," whereas the label displays only the amount of text that fits within its bounds.

Q. Why doesn't Apple just handle hiding text input keyboards for us?

A. Although I can imagine some circumstances where it would be nice if this were an automatic action, it isn't difficult to implement a method to hide the keyboard. This gives you total control over the application interface—something you'll grow to appreciate.

Q. Are text views (`UITextView`) the only way to implement scrolling content?

A. No. You'll learn about implementing general scrolling behavior in Hour 9, "Using Advanced Interface Objects and Views."

Workshop

Quiz

1. What tool will you use to create resizable images?

    a. Cutting tool

    b. Slicing tool

    c. Resize Navigator

    d. Interface Builder

2. What method do you use to get rid of the onscreen keyboard?

    a. `resignFirstResponder`

    b. `clearResponder`

    c. `resignKeyboard`

    d. `resignActiveStatus`

3. What object have we used for both input and output?

    a. Text views

    b. Text fields

    c. Labels

    d. Text areas

4. What feature can be applied to fields to identify common elements, such as web addresses, that a user may type?

   a. Element detectors

   b. Smart data guides

   c. Data element lookup

   d. Data detectors

5. Disabling this keyboard feature prevents iOS from changing input as you type?

   a. Rewrite rules

   b. Spelling

   c. Correction

   d. Auto Fix

6. To make an invisible button, we set its type to what?

   a. Custom

   b. System

   c. Clear

   d. Info

7. Before images can be made resizable, what must they be added to?

   a. Image library

   b. Asset catalog

   c. Asset library

   d. Image catalog

8. Outlets and sections for interface objects are added after which Swift keyword?

   a. `class`

   b. `interface`

   c. `implementation`

   d. `begin`

9. Text fields that allow styled text input and output are of this type.

   a. Rich

   b. Classed

   c. Styled

   d. Attributed

10. A common UI element used to display static text and application-generated output is what?

    a. `UITextView`

    b. `UIKit`

    c. `UILabel`

    d. `UIOutput`

Answers

1. B. To define images that can be resized, you'll use the Xcode slicing tool, found within your asset catalog.

2. A. To clear the onscreen keyboard, you must send the `resignFirstResponder` message to the object that currently controls the keyboard (such as a text field).

3. A. Text views (`UITextView`) can be implemented as scrollable output areas or multiline input fields (just like we did in this hour's project).

4. D. Data detectors can be activated on input fields to detect a range of elements including phone numbers, addresses, dates, and more.

5. C. Disabling the Correction feature of the iOS keyboard prevents the dreaded "autocorrect" text fixes from being applied.

6. A. Invisible buttons are best created using the Custom UIButton type.

7. B. The asset catalog is used to store and organize images and also contains the slicing tools.

8. A. Outlets, actions, and their associated variable properties are added after the `class` keyword in a Swift file.

9. D. Fields that contain styled text are known as "attributed" in Xcode's Interface Builder.

10. C. The common `UILabel` object is frequently used for adding static text through Interface Builder and presenting dynamically generated content when an application runs.

Activities

1. Expand the story creator with additional placeholders, word types, and styled text editing. Use the same string manipulation functions described in this lesson to add the new functionality.

2. Modify the story creator to use a graphical button of your design. Use either an entirely graphical button or the stretchable image approach described in this hour's tutorial. If you're feeling truly adventurous, experiment with the text field's events to make the story update as the fields change (without even pressing the Create Story button).

HOUR 8
Handling Images, Animation, Sliders, and Steppers

What You'll Learn in This Hour:

▶ The use of sliders and steppers for user input

▶ Configuring and manipulating slider and stepper input ranges

▶ How to add image views to your projects

▶ Ways of creating and controlling simple animations

▶ How to change the appearance of the iOS status bar

The text input and output that you learned about in the preceding hour is certainly important, but iOS is known for its attractive graphics and "touchable" user interface (UI). This hour expands our interface toolkit to include images, animation, and the very touchable slider and stepper controls.

We'll implement an application to combine these new features with some simple logic to manipulate input data in a unique way. These new capabilities will help you build more interesting and interactive applications—and of course, there's more to come.

User Input and Output

Although application logic is always the most important part of an application, the way the interface works plays a big part in how well it will be received. For Apple and the iDevices, providing a fun, smooth, and beautiful user experience has been key to their success; it's up to you to bring this experience into your own development. The iOS interface options give you the tools to express your application's functionality in fun and unique ways.

This hour introduces four very visual interface features: sliders and steppers for input, image views for output, and visual effects views for that cool iOS frosted-glass blur appearance.

Sliders

The first new interface component that we use this hour is a slider (`UISlider`). Sliders are a convenient touch control used to visually set a point within a range of values. Huh? What?

Suppose that you want your user to be able to speed something up or slow it down. Asking users to input timing values is unreasonable. Instead, you can present a slider, as shown in Figure 8.1, where they can touch and drag an indicator (called a *thumb*) back and forth on a line. Behind the scenes, a `value` variable property is being set that your application can access and use to set the speed. There is no need for users to understand the behind-the-scenes details or do anything more than drag with their fingers.

0   100

FIGURE 8.1
Use a slider to collect a value from a range of numbers without requiring users to type.

Sliders, like buttons, can react to events or can be read passively like a text field. If you want the user's changes to a slider to immediately have an effect on your application, you must have it trigger an action.

Steppers

Similar to a slider is a stepper (`UIStepper`). Like a slider, a stepper offers a means of inputting a number from a range of values visually. How it accomplishes this, however, differs a bit. A stepper, shown in Figure 8.2, offers–/+ buttons in a single control. Pushing a side of the control decrements or increments an internal `value` variable property.

FIGURE 8.2
The stepper performs a similar function to the slider control.

You can use steppers as alternatives to traditional text input fields for values, such as setting a timer or controlling the speed of an onscreen object. Because they do not provide an onscreen representation of their current internal value, you must make sure that when a stepper is used to update a portion of your interface that you indicate a change has been made.

Steppers provide the same range of events as sliders, making it possible to easily react to changes or read the internal `value` variable at any time.

Image Views

Image views (`UIImageView`) do precisely what you'd think: They display images. You can add them to your application views, using them to present information to the user. You can even use an instance of `UIImageView` to create a simple frame-based animation with controls for starting, stopping, and even setting the speed at which the animation is shown.

With Retina display devices, your image views can even take advantage of the high-resolution display for crystal-clear images. Even better, you need no special coding. Instead of checking for a specific device, you can just add multiple images to your project, and the image view will load the right one at the right time. We do not go through all the steps to make this happen each time we use an image in this book, but later in this hour's lesson, you will learn how you can add this capability to your projects.

Visual Effect Views

When Apple introduced iOS 7, they created a new visual design for applications: flat colors, but with depth added through translucency and layering. Most often, you'll see this as a frosted-glass overlay that appears on top of images – like when you swipe up from the bottom of the screen to reveal the iOS control center.

You can easily add this effect to your applications using a special view of the type `UIVisualEffectView` that automatically applies an effect called the `UIBlurEffect`. This is simply a view that you can drag into your designs that blurs the views (such as image views) that fall beneath it.

Although we will just use a visual effect view to apply a blur to our applications, they can actually contain other views (controls, images, and so on) and apply a secondary effect called "vibrancy" that makes objects translucent - but also brighter and more noticeable. Vibrancy has a "love it or hate it" effect on developers and designers, so don't assume that just because it's available that you need to use it.

Creating and Managing Image Animations, Sliders, and Steppers

There's something about interface components that make users take notice. They're visually interesting, attract and keep attention, and, on a touch screen, are fun to play with. In this hour's project, we take advantage of all of our new UI elements (and some old friends) to create a user-controlled animation.

Implementation Overview

As mentioned earlier, image views can be used to display image file resources and show simple animations, whereas sliders provide a visual way to choose a value from a range. We'll combine these in an application we're calling ImageHop.

In ImageHop, we create a looping animation using a series of images and an image view instance (UIImageView). We allow the user to set the speed of the animation using a slider (UISlider). What will we use as an animation? A field of hopping bunnies. What will the user control? Hops per second for the "lead" bunny, of course. The "hops" value will be set by the slider and displayed in a label (UILabel). A stepper provides another way of changing the speed in precise increments. The user can also stop or start the animation using a button (UIButton).

While it won't require any code, we'll also introduce the use of a visual effect view to blur a portion of the background. This is very popular in iOS applications and adds a nice effect to the interface.

Figure 8.3 shows the completed application with the bunnies at rest.

FIGURE 8.3
ImageHop uses image views, an effects view, a slider, and a stepper to create and control a simple animation.

We should discuss two pieces of this project before getting too far into the implementation:

▶ First, image view animations are created using a series of images. I've provided a 20-frame animation with this project, but you're welcome to use your own images if you prefer.

▶ Second, although steppers and sliders enable users to visually enter a value from a range, there isn't much control over how that is accomplished. For example, the minimum value must be smaller than the maximum, and you can't control which dragging direction of the slider (or which side of the stepper) increases or decreases the result value. These limitations aren't showstoppers; they just mean that you might have to do a bit of math (or experimentation) to get the behavior you want.

Setting Up the Project

Begin this project in the same way as the last:

1. Launch Xcode, and then choose File, New, Project.

2. Select the iOS Application project type, and then find and select the Single View Application option in the Template list on the right.

3. Click Next to continue.

4. Enter the project name **ImageHop**.

5. Be sure that the appropriate device is selected, along with the Swift programming language, and then click Next.

6. Choose a save location and click Create to generate the new project.

Adding the Animation Resources

This project makes use of 20 frames of animation stored as PNG files. The frames are included in the Images folder within the ImageHop project folder.

Because we know upfront that we need these images, we can add them to the project immediately. Open the project group in the project navigator area of Xcode. Click the main Assets. xcassets file to open the project's image assets. Now, drag the Images folder from the Finder into the column on the left inside the asset catalog. You'll see a new Images folder appear within the assets library; this folder contains all the animation images we need for the project.

We can now access the image files easily within our code and the Interface Builder (IB) editor.

Planning the Variables and Connections

In this application, we need to provide outlets and actions for several objects.

A total of nine outlets are required. First we need five image views (UIImageView), which will contain the five copies of our bunny animation. These are referenced through the variable properties bunnyView1, bunnyView2, bunnyView3, bunnyView4, and bunnyView5. The slider control (UISlider) sets the speed and is connected via speedSlider, and the speed value itself is output in a label named `hopsPerSecond` (`UILabel`). A stepper control (`UIStepper`) gives another means of setting the speed and can be accessed with `speedStepper`.

Finally, a button (`UIButton`) toggles the animation on and off and is connected to an outlet `toggleButton`.

NOTE

Why do we need an outlet for the button? Shouldn't it just be triggering an action to toggle the animation? Yes, the button could be implemented without an outlet, but by including an outlet for it, we have a convenient way of setting the button's title in the code. We can use this to change the button to read Stop when the image is animating or Start when the animation has stopped.

We need three actions. `setSpeed` is the method called when the slider value has changed and the animation speed needs to be reset. `incrementSpeed` serves a similar purpose and is called when the stepper control is used. And `toggleAnimation` is used to start and stop the animation sequence.

Now let's create the UI.

Designing the Interface

With all the outlets and actions we just discussed, it might seem like creating the UI for ImageHop will be a nightmare. In reality, it's quite simple because the five animation sequences are really just copies of a single image view (`UIImageView`). Once we add one, we can copy it four times almost instantly.

To get started, I recommend opening the Main.storyboard file, selecting the view controller for your scene, and then using the Attributes Inspector to set the simulated screen size to something manageable (the 4.7-inch iPhone, for me). This will make it easier to layout an interface for the animations.

Adding an Image View

In this exercise, our view creation begins with the most important object of the project: the image view (`UIImageView`). With the Main.storyboard file open, access the Object Library, and drag an image view into the application's view.

Because the view has no images assigned, it is represented by a light-gray rectangle. Use the selection handles on the rectangle to size it to fit in the upper center of the interface (see Figure 8.4).

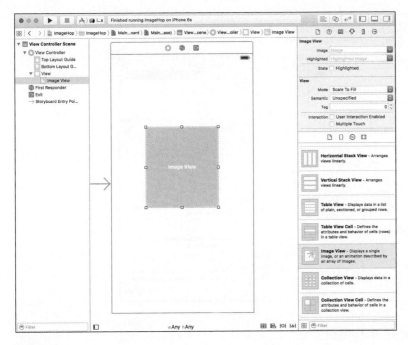

FIGURE 8.4
Set the image view to fill the upper center of the interface.

Setting the Default Image

There are very few settings for configuring the functionality of an image view. We are interested in the image property: the image that is going to be displayed. Select the image view and press Option-Command-4 to open the Attributes Inspector (see Figure 8.5).

Using the Image drop-down menu, choose one of the image resources available. This is the default image that is shown before the animation runs, so using the first frame (frame-1) is a good choice.

The image view updates in IB to show the image resource that you've chosen.

NOTE

What about the animation? Isn't this just a frame? Yes, if we don't do anything else, the image view shows a single static image. To display an animation, we need to create an array with all the frames and supply it programmatically to the image view object. We do this in a few minutes, so just hang in there.

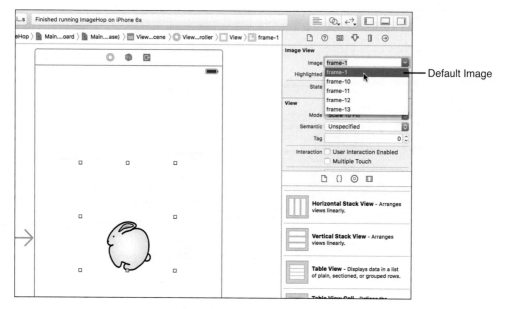

FIGURE 8.5
Set the image that will be shown in the view.

Making Copies

After you've added the image view, create four additional copies by selecting it in your UI and choosing Edit, Duplicate (Command-D) from the menu. Scale and position the copies around the first image view. Don't worry if there is some overlap between the image views; this does not affect the application at all. For my implementation, I also used the Attributes Inspector (Option-Command-4) to set an alpha of .75 and .50 on some of the image views to make them partially transparent.

You've just created your field of bunnies. Your display should now resemble Figure 8.6.

You Said You'd Tell Us About Loading Hi-Res Images for the Retina Display. How Do We Do It?

That's the best part! There's really nothing to do that you don't already know. To accommodate the higher scaling factor of the standard Retina display (iPhone and iPad) and iPhone 6+/6s+ Retina display, you just create image resources that are two and three times the horizontal and vertical resolution, respectively. Name the images with the same filename as your original low-res images, but with the suffix @2x (Retina) and @3x (iPhone 6+/6s+ Retina). (For example, Image.png becomes Image@2x.png and Image@3x.png.) Finally, just drag them into your image assets like any other resource.

Within your projects, just reference the low-res image, and the appropriate hi-res image is loaded automatically, as needed.

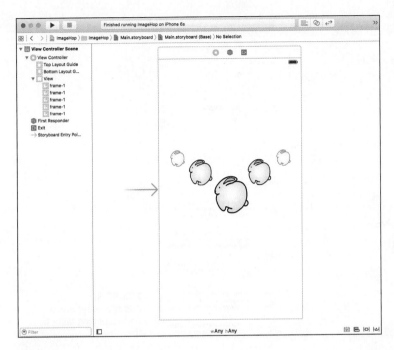

FIGURE 8.6
Create your own field of bunnies.

Adding a Slider

The next piece that our interface needs is the slider that will control the speed. Open the Object Library and drag the slider (`UISlider`) into the view, under the image views. Using the selection handles on the slider, click and drag to size it to take up width of the view, using the alignment guides to leave an appropriate space on the left and right.

Because a slider has no visual indication of its purpose, it's a good idea to always label sliders so that your users will understand what they do. Drag a label object (`UILabel`) from the library into your view (just above the slider). Double-click the text and set it to read **Speed:**. Position it so that it is center-aligned with the slider, as shown in Figure 8.7.

Setting the Slider Range Attributes   Sliders make their current settings available through a value variable property that we'll be accessing in the view controller. To change the range of values that can be returned, we need to edit the slider attributes. Click to select the slider in the view, and then open the Attributes Inspector (Option-Command-4), as shown in Figure 8.8.

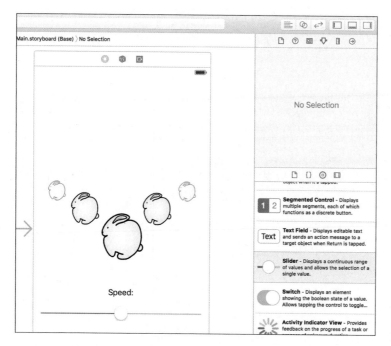

FIGURE 8.7
Add the slider and a corresponding label to the view.

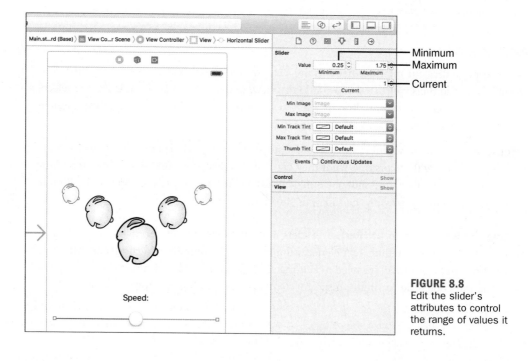

FIGURE 8.8
Edit the slider's attributes to control the range of values it returns.

You should change the Minimum, Maximum, and Initial fields to contain the smallest, largest, and starting values for the slider. For this project, use **.25**, **1.75**, and **1.0**, respectively.

Where Did These Min, Max, and Current Values Come From?

This is a great question, and one that doesn't have a clearly defined answer. In this application, the slider represents the speed of the animation, which, as previously discussed, is set through the `animationDuration` variable property of the image view as the number of seconds it takes to show a full cycle of an animation. Unfortunately, this means the faster animations use smaller numbers and slower animations use larger numbers, which is the exact opposite of traditional user interfaces, where "slow" is on the left and "fast" is on the right. Because of this, we need to reverse the scale. In other words, we want the big number (1.75) to appear when the slider is on the left side and the small number (.25) on the right.

To reverse the scale, we take the combined total of the minimum and maximum (1.75 + 0.25) and subtract the value returned by the slider from that total. For example, when the slider returns 1.75 at the top of the scale, we calculate a duration of 2–1.75, or 0.25. At the bottom of the scale, the calculation will be 2–0.25, or 1.75.

Our current (initial) value is 1.0, which falls directly in the middle of the scale.

Make sure that the Continuous check box is *not* checked. This option, when enabled, has the control to generate a series of events as the user drags back and forth on the slider. When it isn't enabled, events are generated only when users lifts their finger from the screen. For our application, this makes the most sense and is certainly the least resource-intensive option.

You can also configure the slider with images at the minimum and maximum sliders of the control. Use the Min Image and Max Image drop-downs to select a project image resource if you want to use this feature. (We do not use it in this project.)

Adding a Stepper

With the slider in place, our next UI element is the stepper. Using the Object Library, drag a stepper button (`UIStepper`) into the view. Position the stepper directly below, and centered on, the slider, as shown in Figure 8.9.

Setting the Stepper Range Attributes

Once the stepper is added, you must configure its range attributes just as you did the slider. Ultimately, we want to use the value of the stepper to change the speed in exactly the same way as with the slider, so the closer the two elements mirror one another, the better.

To set the range allowed on the stepper, select it in the view, and then open the Attributes Inspector (Option-Command-4). Again, provide **.25**, **1.75**, and **1.0** for the Minimum, Maximum, and Current (initial) values for the stepper. Set the step value to **.25**. This is the amount added to or subtracted from the current value when the stepper is pressed.

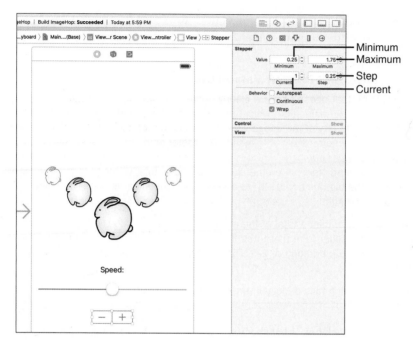

FIGURE 8.9
Add the stepper element to your view.

Use the Behavior check box to turn off Autorepeating, meaning that the user will not be able to press and hold to continue incrementing or decrementing the stepper's value. You should also uncheck the Continuous check box so that only distinct events are generated when the user finishes interacting with the control. Finally, turn on the Wrap behavior. Wrap, when on, automatically sets the stepper's value to the minimum value when the maximum is exceeded (or vice versa), effectively wrapping around the range of values it can represent. If Wrap is off, the stepper stops at the minimum or maximum value and does not change. Figure 8.9 shows the final stepper configuration in the Attributes Inspector.

Finishing the Interface

The remaining components of the ImageHop application are interface features that you've used before, so we've saved them for last. We finish things up by adding a button to start and stop the animation, a readout of the speed of the lead animated rabbit in maximum hops per second, and a pretty background for the bunnies to hop on.

Adding the Speed Output Labels

Drag two labels (`UILabel`) to the top of the view. The first label should be set to read **Maximum Hops Per Second:** and be located in the upper left of the view. Add the second label, which is used as output of the actual speed value, to the right of the first label.

Change the output label to read **1.00 hps**. (The speed that the animation will be starting out at.) Using the Attributes Inspector (Option-Command-4), set the text of the label to align right; this keeps the text from jumping around as the user changes the speed.

Adding the Hop Button

The last functional part of the ImageHop interface is the button (`UIButton`) that starts and stops the animation. Drag a new button from the Object Library to the view and positioning it at the bottom center of the UI. Double-click the button to edit the title and set it to **Hop!**.

Setting a Background Graphic and Visual Effect View

For fun, we can spruce up the application a bit by toning down the blinding-white screen that the iOS views use by default. To do this, we'll set a background for the application, and then add a blur visual effect over the background so that our ImageHop controls remain visible.

To add a background image, drag another instance of `UIImageView` to the view. Resize it to cover the entire scene - stretch all the way to the top and bottom of the view. Use Editor, Arrange, Send to Back to place the background image view behind the animation image views and the "hops per second" labels.

With the background image view selected, use the Attributes Inspector to set the Image value to the background image resource that you added earlier in this hour. Your interface should now resemble Figure 8.10.

You'll notice the controls are difficult to read. We can solve this by placing a visual effect view in front of the background image, but behind the controls. This special view will blur whatever images are behind it, giving a nice and soft background for the controls to appear over. Find the Visual Effect View with Blur object in the Object Library and drag it into your view. Size it to fit over the bottom portion of the view, acting as a backdrop to your controls. Use the Editor, Arrange, Send Backward menu item to move the visual effect view so that it is behind your buttons, labels, and sliders, but in front of the background image. (You can also drag it in the document outline so that it is listed just below the background image – this has the same effect).

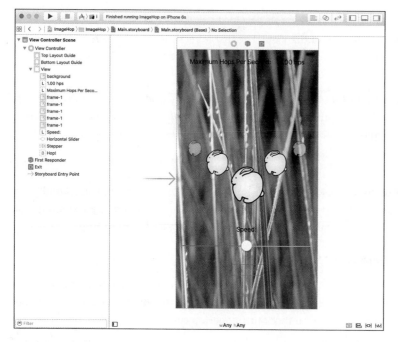

FIGURE 8.10
Set a background image for the application.

NOTE

Visual Effect View with Blur and Vibrancy

When adding your visual effect view, you'll notice that there are two listed in the Object Library. One includes Vibrancy, the other doesn't. Although we aren't using Vibrancy, it's worth noting that this is identical to the Visual Effect View with Blur. The only difference is checking (or unchecking) a check box beside Vibrancy in the Attributes Inspector. Why these are two separate objects in the library boggles my mind.

Finally, to make sure the blurred background is light enough to read our labels, select the visual effect view, and open the Attributes Inspector (Option-Command-4). Use the Blur Style drop-down menu to choose Extra Light, as shown in Figure 8.11.

As a final change, you'll need to make the "hops per second" labels at the top of the view easier to read. Select the labels and use the Attributes Inspector to set their color to white. This change is visible in Figure 8.11.

With that change, it's time to create the outlets and actions and begin coding.

Visual Effect View   Blur Style

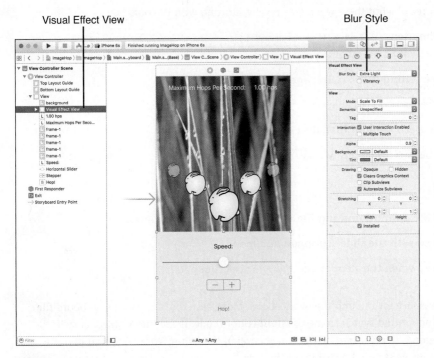

FIGURE 8.11
The final ImageHop application interface, with visual effect view added and configured.

NOTE

Gray with a Blurry Lining

Sadly, visual effect views are not rendered in the Interface Builder editor. They just look gray. You won't see the nice blurring effect until you run the application.

TIP

Transparent Blur

I find that setting the visual effect view to *just* slightly transparent (an alpha of 0.9, for example) leads to a very neat effect. You can see some detail of the image behind the view, but it is surrounded by a blurry haze. I highly recommend trying it.

Creating and Connecting the Outlets and Actions

Whew! That's the most complicated application interface we've had to deal with yet. Reviewing what we've done, we have a total of nine outlets that need to be created, along with three actions.

In case you don't recall what these were, let's review, starting with the outlets:

- ► **Bunny animations (UIImageView):** bunnyView1, bunnyView2, bunnyView3, bunnyView4, and bunnyView5

- ► **Slider speed setting (UISlider):** speedSlider

- ► **Stepper speed setting (UIStepper):** speedStepper

- ► **Maximum speed readout (UILabel):** hopsPerSecond

- ► **Hop/Stop button (UIButton):** toggleButton

And the actions:

- ► **Start/stop the animation using the Hop/Stop button:** toggleAnimation

- ► **Set the speed with the slider changes:** setSpeed

- ► **Set the speed when the stepper changes:** incrementSpeed

Prepare your workspace for making the connections. Make sure that the Main.storyboard file is open in the IB editor and switch to the assistant editor mode. If the ViewController.swift file isn't picked by default, select it from the bar at the top of the editor. Your UI design and the ViewController.swift file should be visible side by side.

Adding the Outlets

Start by Control-dragging from the main ImageView instance (the large bunny) to the line following the class directive in the ViewController.swift file. When prompted, be sure to configure the connection as an outlet and the name as **bunnyView1**, leaving the other values set to their defaults (type UIImageView, storage Weak), as shown in Figure 8.12.

Repeat the process for the remaining images views that we want to animate, targeting each successive connection below the last line that was added. It doesn't matter which bunny is bunnyView2, bunnyView3, bunnyView4, or bunnyView5, just as long as they're all connected.

After connecting the image views, proceed with the rest of the connections. Control-drag from the slider (UISlider) to the line under the last @IBOutlet declaration and add a new outlet named speedSlider. Do the same for the stepper (UIStepper), adding an outlet named speedStepper. Finish off by connecting the hops per second output UILabel (1.00 hps initially) to hopsPerSecond and the Hop! UIButton to toggleButton.

Our outlets are finished. Let's take care of our actions.

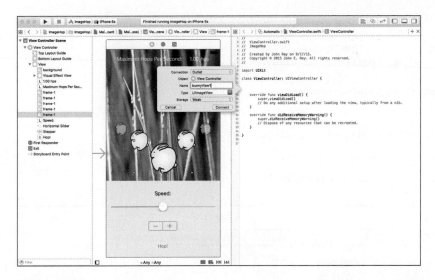

FIGURE 8.12
Begin by connecting the main bunny `UIImageView` instance.

Adding the Actions

This project requires three distinct actions. The first, `toggleAnimation`, is triggered when the user presses the Hop! button, and it starts the animation sequence. Add a definition for this action by Control-dragging from the button in your interface to a line below the outlet declarations. When prompted, set the connection type to Action and provide `toggleAnimation` as the name, leaving all other values as the defaults, as shown in Figure 8.13.

Next, Control-drag from the slider to a line below the just-added `IBAction` line. Create an action named `setSpeed` that is triggered from the `UISlider`'s Value Changed event.

Finally, create the third action, this one triggered from the stepper, naming it **incrementSpeed** and again using the Value Changed event.

To check your work, the code at the top of your ViewController.swift file should now resemble Listing 8.1.

LISTING 8.1 The ViewController.swift Outlets and Actions

```swift
class ViewController: UIViewController {

    @IBOutlet weak var bunnyView1: UIImageView!
    @IBOutlet weak var bunnyView2: UIImageView!
    @IBOutlet weak var bunnyView3: UIImageView!
    @IBOutlet weak var bunnyView4: UIImageView!
    @IBOutlet weak var bunnyView5: UIImageView!
```

```
@IBOutlet weak var speedSlider: UISlider!
@IBOutlet weak var speedStepper: UIStepper!
@IBOutlet weak var hopsPerSecond: UILabel!
@IBOutlet weak var toggleButton: UIButton!

@IBAction func toggleAnimation(sender: AnyObject) {
}

@IBAction func setSpeed(sender: AnyObject?) {
}

@IBAction func incrementSpeed(sender: AnyObject) {
}
```

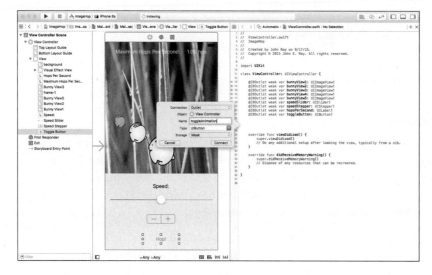

FIGURE 8.13
Create the action for toggling the animation on and off.

We're ready to start coding the implementation of our magical hopping bunny animation. Surprisingly, the code needed to make this work is really quite minimal.

Implementing the Application Logic

The view controller needs to manage a total of four different things to make our application work as we envision.

First, we need to load the image animations for each of the ImageViews (bunnyView1, bunnyView2, and so on); we managed to set a static frame of the image in IB, but that isn't enough to make them animate. Next, we must implement toggleAnimation so that we can start and stop the onscreen animation from the Hop! button. Finally, the `setSpeed` and `incrementSpeed` methods must be written to control the maximum speed of the animations.

Implementing Animated Image Views

Animating images requires us to build an array of image objects (`UIImage`) and pass them to an image view object. Where should we do this? As with setting button templates in the last hour's project, the `ViewDidLoad` method of our view controller provides a convenient location for doing additional setup for the view, so that's what we'll use.

LISTING 8.2 Loading the Animation

```
 1: override func viewDidLoad() {
 2:     super.viewDidLoad()
 3:     // Do any additional setup after loading the view, typically from a nib.
 4:     let hopAnimation: [UIImage] = [
 5:         UIImage(named: "frame-1")!,
 6:         UIImage(named: "frame-2")!,
 7:         UIImage(named: "frame-3")!,
 8:         UIImage(named: "frame-4")!,
 9:         UIImage(named: "frame-5")!,
10:         UIImage(named: "frame-6")!,
11:         UIImage(named: "frame-7")!,
12:         UIImage(named: "frame-8")!,
13:         UIImage(named: "frame-9")!,
14:         UIImage(named: "frame-10")!,
15:         UIImage(named: "frame-11")!,
16:         UIImage(named: "frame-12")!,
17:         UIImage(named: "frame-13")!,
18:         UIImage(named: "frame-14")!,
19:         UIImage(named: "frame-15")!,
20:         UIImage(named: "frame-16")!,
21:         UIImage(named: "frame-17")!,
22:         UIImage(named: "frame-18")!,
23:         UIImage(named: "frame-19")!,
24:         UIImage(named: "frame-20")!
25:     ]
26:     bunnyView1.animationImages=hopAnimation
27:     bunnyView2.animationImages=hopAnimation
28:     bunnyView3.animationImages=hopAnimation
29:     bunnyView4.animationImages=hopAnimation
30:     bunnyView5.animationImages=hopAnimation
31:     bunnyView1.animationDuration=1.0
32:     bunnyView2.animationDuration=1.0
33:     bunnyView3.animationDuration=1.0
34:     bunnyView4.animationDuration=1.0
35:     bunnyView5.animationDuration=1.0
36: }
```

To configure the image views for animation, first an array constant of `UIImage` objects is declared in line 4. This array is named `hopAnimation` and is populated in lines 5–24. To build the array, all we need to do is provide a comma-separated list of objects (in this case, `UIImage` objects). To create these objects, we use the `UIImage` convenience initialization method `initNamed` that takes a single string parameter, `named`, and returns a `UIImage` object of the image with that name.

Each use of the `UIImage` initialization method requires the an exclamation point (!) suffix to unwrap it. This is because the initialization, if given a bad image name, will return nothing. The ! tells Xcode that we know what we're doing and we want to unwrap (use) the value returned regardless. Note that lines 10–19 have been removed to save space; if you don't add them, the animation will be missing a few frames.

How Convenient!

If you're wondering what a "convenience initialization method" is (and didn't want to refer back to the introduction to Swift), wonder no more. This awkwardly termed construct is just a method that returns a new instance of a class. It does this quickly, and with a minimum amount of hassle. That is, it is *convenient*.

What makes convenience initialization methods a bit different is that they will often *require* an "external" named parameter (such as `named` for creating an `UIImage` object) as the first argument.

Most methods in Swift don't require you to prove a name for the first parameter, but these do. Go figure!

Once an array is populated with image objects, you can use it to set up the animation of an image view. To do this, set the `animationImages` variable property of the image view to the array. Lines 26–30 accomplish this for `bunnyView1` through `bunnyView5` in our sample project.

Another `UIImageView` variable property that we want to set right away is the `animationDuration`. This is the number of seconds it takes for a single cycle of the animation to be played. If the duration is not set, the playback rate is 30 frames per second. To start, our animations are set to play all the frames in 1 second, so lines 31–35 set the `animationDuration` to `1.0` for each `bunnyView` `UIImageView`.

We've now configured all five of our image views to be animated, but even if we build and run the project, nothing is going to happen. That's because we haven't added controls for actually *starting* the animation.

Starting and Stopping the Animation

You've just learned how the `animationDuration` variable property can change the animation speed, but we need three more variables/methods to actually display the animation and accomplish everything we want:

▶ **isAnimating:** This variable property is `true` if the image view is currently animating its contents.

▶ **startAnimating:** This method starts the animation.

▶ **stopAnimating:** This method stops the animation if it is running.

When the user touches the Hop! button, the `toggleAnimation` method is called. This method should use the `isAnimating` variable property of one of our image views (bunnyView1, for example) to check to see whether an animation is running. If it isn't, the animation should start; otherwise, it should stop. To make sure that the user interface makes sense, you should also alter the button itself (`toggleButton`) to show the title Sit Still! if the animation is running and Hop! when it isn't.

Add the code in Listing 8.3 to the `toggleAnimation` method in your view controller swift file.

LISTING 8.3   Starting and Stopping the Animation in `toggleAnimation`

```
 1: @IBAction func toggleAnimation(sender: AnyObject) {
 2:        if (bunnyView1.isAnimating()) {
 3:            bunnyView1.stopAnimating()
 4:            bunnyView2.stopAnimating()
 5:            bunnyView3.stopAnimating()
 6:            bunnyView4.stopAnimating()
 7:            bunnyView5.stopAnimating()
 8:            toggleButton.setTitle("Hop!", forState: UIControlState.Normal)
 9:        } else {
10:            bunnyView1.startAnimating()
11:            bunnyView2.startAnimating()
12:            bunnyView3.startAnimating()
13:            bunnyView4.startAnimating()
14:            bunnyView5.startAnimating()
15:            toggleButton.setTitle("Sit Still!", forState: UIControlState.Normal)
16:        }
17: }
```

Lines 2 and 9 provide the two different conditions that we need to work with. Lines 3–8 are executed if the animation is running, and lines 10–15 are executed if it isn't. In lines 3–7 and lines 10–14, the `stopAnimating` and `startAnimating` methods are called for the image views to stop and start the animation, respectively.

Lines 8 and 15 use the `UIButton` instance method `setTitle:forState` to set the button title to the string `"Hop!"` or `"Sit Still!"`. These titles are set for the button state of `UIControlState.Normal`. The normal state for a button is its default state, prior to any user event taking place.

At this point, if you're *really* anxious, you can run the application and start and stop the animation. That said, we've only got a few more lines of code required to set the animation speed, so let's move on.

Setting the Animation Speed

The slider triggers the `setSpeed` action after the user adjusts the slider control. This action must translate into several changes in the actual application: First, the speed of the animation (`animationDuration`) should change. Second, the animation should be started if it isn't already running. Third, the button (`toggleButton`) title should be updated to show the animation is running. And finally, the speed should be displayed in the `hopsPerSecond` label.

Add the code in Listing 8.4 to the `setSpeed` method stub, and then let's review how it works.

LISTING 8.4   The Completed `setSpeed` Method

```
 1: @IBAction func setSpeed(sender: AnyObject?) {
 2:     bunnyView1.animationDuration=NSTimeInterval(2.0-speedSlider.value)
 3:     bunnyView2.animationDuration =
 4:         bunnyView1.animationDuration+NSTimeInterval(arc4random_uniform(10))/10
 5:     bunnyView3.animationDuration =
 6:         bunnyView1.animationDuration+NSTimeInterval(arc4random_uniform(10))/10
 7:     bunnyView4.animationDuration =
 8:         bunnyView1.animationDuration+NSTimeInterval(arc4random_uniform(10))/10
 9:     bunnyView5.animationDuration =
10:         bunnyView1.animationDuration+NSTimeInterval(arc4random_uniform(10))/10
11:
12:     bunnyView1.startAnimating()
13:     bunnyView2.startAnimating()
14:     bunnyView3.startAnimating()
15:     bunnyView4.startAnimating()
16:     bunnyView5.startAnimating()
17:
18:     toggleButton.setTitle("Sit Still!", forState: UIControlState.Normal)
19:
20:     let hopRateString=String(format: "%1.2f hps", 1/(2-self.speedSlider.value))
21:     hopsPerSecond.text=hopRateString
22: }
```

In line 2, the `bunnyView1 animationDuration` variable property is set to 2 minus the value of the slider (`speedSlider.value`); this sets the speed of our "lead" bunny animation. This, if you recall, is necessary to reverse the scale so that faster is on the right and slower is on the left.

Lines 3–10 set the remaining image animations to the same speed as the lead animation (`bunnyView1.animationDuration`) plus a fraction of a second. How do we get this fraction of a second? Through the magic of this randomization function:

`NSTimeInterval(arc4random_uniform(10))/10`. The function `arc4random_uniform(10)/10` returns a random number between 0 and 10. We divide this by 10 to give us a fraction (1/10, 2/10, and so on). We must use the function `NSTimeInterval()` with `arc4random_uniform()` because the `animationDuration` variable property expects a value of the type NSTimeInterval and `arc4random_uniform` returns just a floating-point number. Behind the scenes, NSTimeInterval is just a double-precision floating-point value, so why doesn't Xcode convert this for us automatically? I'm not sure, but if you *don't* use `NSTimeInterval()`, you'll get an error noting that a conversation is necessary. Perhaps in the future, this won't be required.

Lines 12–16 use the `startAnimating` method to start the animations running. Note that it is safe to use this method if the animation is already started, so we don't really need to check the state of the image view. Line 18 sets the button title to the string "`Sit Still!`" to reflect the animated state.

Line 20 creates a `hopRateString` constant. The string is initialized with a format of "`%1.2f`", based on the calculation of `1/(2-animationSpeed.value)`.

Let's break that down a bit further: Remember that the speed of the animation is measured in seconds. The fastest speed we can set is 0.25 (a quarter of a second), meaning that the animation plays four times in 1 second (or four hops per second). To calculate this in the application, we simply divide 1 by the chosen animation duration, or `1/(2-animationSpeed.value)`. Because this doesn't necessarily return a whole number, we use the `stringWithFormat` method to create a string that holds a nicely formatted version of the result. The `format` parameter string "`%1.2f hps`" is shorthand for saying the number being formatted as a string is a floating-point value (`f`) and that there should always be one digit on the left of the decimal and two digits on the right (`1.2`). The `hps` portion of the format is just the hops per second unit that we want to append to the end of the string. For example, if the equation returns a value of .5 (half a hop a second), the string stored in `hopRateString` is set to "`0.50 hps`".

In line 21, the output label (`UILabel`) in the interface is set to the `hopRateString`.

With that, the slider speed control is in place. Just one more method to implement: `incrementSpeed`, triggered by the `UIStepper` (`speedStepper`) interface object.

Try It Yourself: Testing the Math in Xcode Playground

It's easy for me to type instructions in a book and say, "This is how it all works out." (I've had the luxury of testing my code to see how it behaves.) The math in this section is no exception. Although this is not critical to understanding Cocoa or iOS development, it can be helpful to understand what is actually going on behind the scenes.

To that end, we can try out some of our numeric manipulations in the Xcode Playground. Create a new iOS Playground, and then add the following code:

```
import UIKit

let sliderMax=10
let sliderMin=1
let sliderValue=1
```

Earlier I said that to reverse the scale of the slider (have smaller values on the left), we simply add up the maximum and minimum slider values, and then subtract the current value of the slider. The constants and equation let us test this right in the Playground (no sliders even required). In this initial setup, the maximum is 10, minimum is 1, and the current value is 1 (what would be the lowest value on the slider scale)—which means that we *really* want the value 10 (the highest value on the scale).

As you can see immediately in the Playground, `realValue` does, indeed, equal 10! Try changing the `sliderValue` to **10**; the `realValue` immediately changes to 1. You can test this logic out for any of the slider values you might be interested in.

Next add this code after the slider test:

```
let initialDuration=2.0
let randomizedDuration=NSTimeInterval(arc4random_uniform(10))/10.0
var finalDuration=initialDuration+randomizedDuration
```

This code fragment simulates the randomized duration that we use to make the bunnies move independently. The `initialDuration` represents the animation duration of the "lead" animation (the main bunny). The `randomizedDuraction` variable a randomized number between 0 and 10, divided by 10 (that is, 0.1, 0.5, 0.6, and so on). The `finalDuration` (used for the other bunnies) is just the addition of these two values.

The code here executes as soon as you type it into the Playground, which means you can't really see the randomization at work. To execute it again, click the Play button in the lower-right corner of the Playground, wait for it to change to a square (stop), and then click it again. After a few seconds, the numbers will update.

Incrementing the Animation Speed

This hour's lesson has been pretty intensive, and, if you're like me, your fingers are probably getting tired of clicking and typing. The bad news is that we aren't quite done; we still need to implement the `incrementSpeed` method. The good news? It takes two lines to complete.

Given all the work required to set the speed with the slider, how is this possible? Quite simple. Because we configured the stepper to generate the same range of values as the slider, we set the slider's value variable property to the value of the stepper. When that is done, we can manually call the `setSpeed` method and everything will (almost) just work.

Update the incrementSpeed method stub in your view controller to read as shown in Listing 8.5.

LISTING 8.5   Implementing the incrementSpeed Method

```
@IBAction func incrementSpeed(sender: AnyObject) {
    speedSlider.value=Float(speedStepper.value)
    setSpeed(nil)
}
```

The first line, as expected, sets the value variable property of the slider to the value of the stepper. What isn't expected, however, is that we must use a function, this time Float(), to convert the value of the stepper (a Double) to a float. Again, this is something I'd expect to happen automatically, but at present, it doesn't.

The assignment in the first line *will* trigger the slider to update visually in your interface, but it *won't* trigger its Value Changed event and call the setSpeed method. We do that manually by calling the setSpeed method we implemented in Listing 8.4.

Unfortunately, that's not quite the end of the story. Notice that nil is passed as a parameter when we call setSpeed. This is because setSpeed, as an action method, was created with a sender parameter that is automatically set to the object that triggered the action. The method can then examine the sender and react accordingly.

In the case of setSpeed, we never used the sender variable in the implementation, so sending the nil value will satisfy the method's requirement for a parameter, but one minor adjustment still needs to be made. So, revisit the setSpeed method from Listing 8.4, and make the sender value optional by adding a question mark at the end of the parameter declaration, as follows:

```
@IBAction func setSpeed(sender: AnyObject?)
```

This change enables us to use nil ("nothing") as the parameter value when we call the method. As long as a variable is declared as optional, it can hold a value, or nothing (nil).

One More Thing: Fixing That Unreadable Status Bar

If you build your application, it will run and behave just as we planned. Unfortunately, you'll have an iOS status bar that doesn't quite fit with your background. Instead of a dark status bar lost on a background of lush beautiful grass, wouldn't it be great to have a light status bar that you can actually read? Unfortunately, there isn't an IB setting to make this happen, but fixing it is simple. Add the code in Listing 8.6 to your ViewController.swift file.

LISTING 8.6   Setting the Status Bar Appearance in `preferredStatusBarStyle`

```
override func preferredStatusBarStyle() -> UIStatusBarStyle {
    return UIStatusBarStyle.LightContent
}
```

This method, added to your view controller, tells iOS what kind of status bar it should display. You can choose from `UIStatusBarStyle.Default` (a dark status bar) or `UIStatusBarStyle.LightContent` (a light status bar).

Well done. With the inclusion of the status bar fix, you've just completed the app.

Building the Application

To try your hand at controlling an out-of-control bunny rabbit, click Run on the Xcode toolbar. After a few seconds, the finished ImageHop application will start, as shown in Figure 8.14.

Although ImageHop isn't an application that you're likely to keep on your device (for long), it did provide you with new tools for your iOS application toolkit. The `UIImageView` class can easily add dynamic images to your programs, and `UISlider` and `UIStepper` offer uniquely touchable input solutions.

FIGURE 8.14
Bouncing bunnies! What more could we ask for?

Further Exploration

Although many hours in this book focus on adding features to the UI, it is important to start thinking about the application logic that will bring your UI to life. As we experienced with our sample application, sometimes creativity is required to make things work the way we want.

Review the properties and methods for UISlider and UIStepper classes and consider how you might use these elements in your own apps. Can you think of any situations where the stepper values couldn't be used directly in your software? How might you apply application logic to map slider values to usable input? Programming is very much about problem solving; you'll rarely write something that doesn't have at least a few "gotchas" that need solved.

In addition to UISlider and UIStepper, you may want to review the documentation for UIImage. Although we focused on UIImageView for displaying our image animation, the images themselves were objects of type UIImage. Image objects will come in handy for future interfaces that integrate graphics into the user controls themselves.

For fun, check out the UIVisualEffectView class to learn more about how you can apply iOS's distinctive visual appearance to your own applications. Users expect apps to be pretty, and this easy-to-use class can bring complex blur and vibrancy effects to any interface.

Finally, for a complete picture of how your applications will almost automatically take advantage of the higher-resolution Retina display, be sure to read the section "Supporting High-Resolution Screens in Views" within the *Drawing and Printing Guide for iOS*.

Apple Tutorials

UIImageView, UIImage, UISlider–UICatalog (accessible via the Xcode developer documentation): Once again, this project is a great place for exploring any and everything (including images, image views, and sliders) related to the iOS interface capabilities.

Summary

Users of highly visual devices demand highly visual interfaces. In this hour's lesson, you learned about the use of three visual elements that you can begin adding to your applications: image views, visual effects views, sliders, and steppers. Image views provide a quick means of displaying images that you've added to your project—even using a sequence of images to create animation. Visual effects views can be used to add subtle translucency to your application interfaces. On the UI control side, sliders can be used to collect user input from a continuous range of values. Steppers also provide user input over a range of numbers, but in a more controlled, incremental fashion. These new input/output methods start our exploration of iOS interfaces that go beyond simple text and buttons.

Although not complex, the information you learned in this hour will help pave the way for mega-rich, touch-centric user interfaces.

Q&A

Q. Is the `UIImageView` the only means of displaying animated movies?

A. No. iOS includes a wide range of options for playing back and even recording video files. The `UIImageView` class is not meant to be used as a video playback mechanism.

Q. Is there a vertical version of the slider control (`UISlider`)?

A. Not really. Only the horizontal slider is currently available in the iOS UI library. If you want to use a vertical slider control, you can use the horizontal slider, but apply a transformation (basically "spin" it in code). For example, if your slider is named `mySlider`, you could add the following to `viewDidLoad` to turn it into a vertical slider:

```
let transformSlider : CGAffineTransform =
    CGAffineTransformMakeRotation(-(CGFloat(M_PI_2)))
speedSlider.transform = transformSlider
```

Workshop

Quiz

1. What method would you use to set the text on a `UIButton`?

    a. `setText:forState`

    b. `setTitle:forState`

    c. `setButton:forState`

    d. `setButtonTItle:forState`

2. Which of the following is a series of images that you can use to create an animation with this object?

    a. `UIImageView`

    b. `UIImageAnimation`

    c. `UIImageMovie`

    d. `UIImage`

3. What type of UI control is used to increment and decrement values by way of two connected buttons?

    a. Segmented control

    b. Slider

    c. Switch

    d. Stepper

4. You can choose how long it takes for an animation to run by using which `UIImageView` variable property?

    a. `playDuration`

    b. `animationLength`

    c. `animationDuration`

    d. `timeInSeconds`

5. To pass `nil` to the parameter of a method, that parameter must be defined as which of the following?

    a. Unwrapped

    b. Optional

    c. Implied

    d. Unneeded

6. Which `UIImageView` method is used to start an animation sequence?

    a. `beginAnimation`

    b. `startAnimation`

    c. `beginAnimating`

    d. `startAnimating`

7. To check the status of an animation, you could turn to which variable property?

    a. `isAnimating`

    b. `isAnimationRunning`

    c. `animationStatus`

    d. `animateStatus`

8. The Continuous check box for a slider generates a continuous stream of *what* as the slider is moved?

    a. Events

    b. Methods

    c. Functions

    d. Outlets

9. Which function is used to turn a numeric value into a `double` floating-point value?

    a. `Double()`

    b. `Float()`

    c. `DoubleFloat()`

    d. `CGFloat()`

10. The iPhone 6 and 6+ use these suffixes to denote their respective image scaling factor:

    a. @1x, @2x

    b. @1x, @3x

    c. @3x, @4x

    d. @2x, @3x

Answers

1. B. Use the `setTitle:forState` method to set the title of a `UIButton`.

2. A. Use a `UIImageView` object to animate a series of still `UIImage` objects.

3. D. A stepper moves through values using connected +/–buttons.

4. C. The `animationDuration` variable property of a `UIImageView` can be used to configure the length (in seconds) of the animation.

5. B. When a method's parameter is defined as "optional" using the question mark (?) character, you can pass `nil` to that parameter.

6. D. To begin an animation, the `startAnimating` method is used.

7. A. To check whether an animation is running, you can query the `isAnimating` variable property to see if it is `true` or `false`.

8. A. A slider that is set to Continuous will generate a series of *events* as the user drags it from side to side.

9. A. If a Swift method or variable property expects a `Double` floating-point value, the `Double()` function can be used to convert other values to a double precision floating point number.

10. D. The @2x and @3x suffixes are used to denote the scaling factors of the iPhone 6 and iPhone 6+ displays, respectively.

Activities

1. Increase the range of speed options for the ImageHop animation example. Be sure to set the default value for the slider thumb to rest in the middle and update the stepper accordingly.

2. Provide an alternative means of editing the speed by enabling the user to manually enter a number in addition to using the slider. The placeholder text of the field should default to the current slider value.

HOUR 9
Using Advanced Interface Objects and Views

What You'll Learn This Hour:

▶ How to use segmented controls (a.k.a. button bars)

▶ Ways of inputting Boolean values via switches

▶ How to include web content within your application

▶ The use of scrolling views to overcome screen-size limitations

▶ Creating orderly, organized content with stack views

After the past few lessons, you now have a good understanding of the basic iOS interface elements, but we've only just scratched the surface. Additional user input features are available to help a user quickly choose between several predefined options. After all, there's no point in typing when a touch is enough. This hour's lesson picks up where the last left off, providing you with hands-on experience with a new set of user input options that go beyond fields, buttons, and sliders.

In addition, we look at three new views you can use to present data to the user: web, scrolling, and stack views. These features make it possible to create applications that can extend beyond the hardware boundaries of your device's screen, automatically create rows and columns of content, and include information from remote web servers.

User Input and Output (Continued)

When I set out to write this book, I originally dedicated a couple of hours to the iOS interface *widgets* (fields, buttons, and so on). After we got started, however, it became apparent that for learning to develop on iOS, the interface was not something to gloss over. The interface options are what makes the device so enjoyable to use and what gives you, the developer, a truly rich canvas to work with. You'll still need to come up with ideas for what your application will do, but the interface can be the deciding factor in whether your vision "clicks" with its intended audience.

In the past two hours, you learned about fields, sliders, steppers, labels, and images as input and output options. In this lesson, you explore two new input options for handling discrete values, along with three new view types that extend the information you can display to web pages and beyond.

Switches

In most traditional desktop applications, the choice between something being *active* or *inactive* is made by checking or unchecking a check box or by choosing between radio buttons. In iOS, Apple has chosen to abandon these options in favor of switches and segmented controls. Switches (UISwitch) present a simple on/off user interface (UI) element that resembles a traditional physical toggle switch, as shown in Figure 9.1. Switches have few configurable options and should be used for handling Boolean values.

FIGURE 9.1
Use switches to provide on/off input options to your user.

NOTE

Check boxes and radio buttons, although not part of the iOS UI Library, can be created with the UIButton class using the button states and custom button images. Apple provides the flexibility to customize to your heart's content—but sticking with controls your users will find familiar will often provide superior usability.

To work with the switch, we'll make use of its Value Changed event to detect a toggle of the switch and then read its current value via the on variable property.

The value returned when checking a switch is a Boolean, meaning that we can compare it to true or false to determine its state, or evaluate the result directly in a conditional statement.

For example, to check whether a switch mySwitch is turned on, we can use code similar to this:

```
if (mySwitch.on) { <switch is on> } else { <switch is off> }
```

Segmented Controls

When user input needs to extend beyond just a Boolean value, you can use a segmented control (UISegmentedControl). Segmented controls present a linear line of buttons (sometimes referred to as a *button bar*), within which a single button can be active within the bar, as shown in Figure 9.2.

FIGURE 9.2
Segmented controls combine multiple buttons into a single control.

Segmented controls, when used according to Apple guidelines, result in a change in what the user sees onscreen. They are often used to choose between categories of information or to switch between the display of application screens, such as configuration and results screens. For just choosing from a list of values where no immediate visual change takes place, the Picker object should be used instead. We look at this feature in Hour 12, "Making Choices with Toolbars and Pickers."

NOTE

Apple recommends using segmented controls to update the information visible in a view. If the change, however, means altering *everything* onscreen, you are probably better off switching between multiple independent views using a toolbar or tab bar. We start looking at the multiview approach in Hour 11, "Implementing Multiple Scenes and Popovers."

Handling interactions with a segmented control is very similar to handling them with the toggle switch. We'll watch for the Value Changed event and determine the currently selected button through the selectedSegmentIndex, which returns the number of the button chosen (starting with 0, from left to right).

We can combine the index with the object's instance method titleForSegmentAtIndex to work directly with the titles assigned to each segment. To retrieve the name of the currently selected button in a segmented control called mySegment, we could use the following code fragment:

```
mySegment.titleForSegmentAtIndex(mySegment.selectedSegmentIndex)
```

We use this technique later in the lesson.

Web Views

In the previous applications that you've built, you've used the typical iOS view: an instance of `UIView` to hold your controls, content, and images. This is the view you will use most often in your apps, but it isn't the only view supported in iOS. A web view, or `UIWebView`, provides advanced features that open up a whole new range of possibilities in your apps.

TIP

In Hour 7, "Working with Text, Keyboards, and Buttons," you used another view type, `UITextView`, which provides basic text input and output, and which straddles the line between an input mechanism and what we'll typically refer to as a *view*.

Think of a web view as a borderless Safari window that you can add to your applications and control programmatically. You can present HTML, load web pages, and offer pinching and zooming gestures, all "for free," using this class.

Supported Content Types

You can also use web views to display a wide range of files, without needing to know anything about the file formats:

- ▶ HTML, images, and CSS
- ▶ Word documents (.doc/.docx)
- ▶ Excel spreadsheets (.xls/.xlsx)
- ▶ Keynote presentations (.key)
- ▶ Numbers spreadsheets (.numbers)
- ▶ Pages documents (.pages)
- ▶ PDF files (.pdf)
- ▶ PowerPoint presentations (.ppt/.pptx)

You can add these files as resources to your project and display them within a web view, access them on remote servers, or read them from an iDevice's file storage (which you learn about in Hour 15, "Reading and Writing Application Data").

NEED SAFARI? USE SAFARI!

Beginning in iOS 9, you can display a "mini" version of Safari (complete with all your cookies and form-fill information) within your applications. This is useful when you want to enable users to access a website without having to build your own browser or exit your application and start Safari. You'll learn more about this capability in Hour 20, "Interacting with Other iOS Services."

Loading Remote Content with NSURL, NSURLRequest, and loadRequest

Web views implement a method called `loadRequest` that you can use to load an arbitrary URL; unfortunately, however, you can't just pass it a string and expect it to work.

To load content into a web view, you'll often use `NSURL` and `NSURLRequest`. These two classes enable you to manipulate URLs and prepare them to be used as a request for a remote resource. You first create an instance of an `NSURL` object, most often from a string using the `NSURL` convenience initialization method. For example, to create an `NSURL` that stores the address for Apple's website, you could use the following:

```
var appleURL: NSURL
appleURL=NSURL(string: "https://www.apple.com")!
```

Notice the exclamation mark at the end of that line? The `!` indicates that we're "unwrapping" (accessing) the value that precedes it (that is, the object returned by the `NSURL` initialization method). Why is this necessary? If you use the Xcode documentation for `NSURL`, you'll see that it may return `nil`. In other words, it may return the `NSURL` object we want, or, if something is wrong with the string, it may return nothing at all! Xcode wants us (very much) to understand and acknowledge this, so it forces us to explicitly "unwrap" the value by adding the `!`. If you fail to add the exclamation mark, you'll get an error, and Xcode will offer to add it for you.

Once the `NSURL` object is created, you need to create an `NSURLRequest` object that can be passed to a web view and loaded. To return an `NSURLRequest` from an `NSURL` object, we can use the `NSURLRequest` convenience initialization method that, given an `NSURL`, returns the corresponding request object:

```
NSURLRequest(URL:appleURL)
```

Finally, this value is passed to the `loadRequest` method of the web view, which then takes over and handles loading the process. Putting all the pieces together, loading Apple's website into a preexisting web view called `appleView` looks like this:

```
var appleURL: NSURL
appleURL=NSURL(string: "https://www.apple.com")!
appleView.loadRequest(NSURLRequest(URL:appleURL))
```

We implement web views in this hour's first project, so you'll soon have a chance to put this to use.

More Convenience, Less Consistency

Recall that convenience initialization methods usually require an "external" named parameter (such as `string` for creating an `NSURL` object, or `URL` for an `NSURLRequest`) as the first argument:

```
NSURL(string: "https://www.apple.com")
NSURLRequest(URL:appleURL)
```

It can be a bit disconcerting to see these methods with their named parameters popping up around other single-parameter methods without this required syntax.

TIP

Another way that you get content into your application is by loading HTML directly into a web view. For example, if you generate HTML content in a string called `myHTML`, you can use the `loadHTMLString:baseURL` method of a web view to load the HTML content and display it. Assuming a web view called `htmlView`, you might write this as follows:

```
htmlView.loadHTMLString(myHTML, baseURL: nil)
```

▼ TRY IT YOURSELF

Testing Web Views in the Xcode Playground

As mentioned previously in this book, one of the best things about Xcode is the use of "Playgrounds" to test your code. You've just seen how to create and load a web view, so why not test it out yourself? To do that, create a new iOS Playground, and then add the following code:

```
import UIKit
import XCPlayground

var appleView: UIWebView=UIWebView(frame:CGRectMake(0, 0, 400, 400))

var appleURL: NSURL
appleURL=NSURL(string: "https://www.apple.com")!
appleView.loadRequest(NSURLRequest(URL:appleURL))

XCPlaygroundPage.currentPage.liveView = appleView
```

Look closely and notice that a few lines in the Playground code aren't in the example we just covered. The `import XCPlayground` line adds an important capability to the playground—the ability to work with views that change over time and load in the background. That's exactly what a `UIWebView` does, so we need to include this framework in the Playground. To load a request in a `UIWebView`, an instance of `UIWebView` class must exist. Normally, we would drag that into an interface visually, but here we use the `UIWebView` convenience initialization method to create one that is 401×401 points. The new web view object is stored in `appleView`, giving us everything we need to setup the URL, create a request, and load it—just like the sample code.

The final line in this example displays the view (here, `appleView`) with the Playground timeline.

After you've added the code, open the assistant editor using the toolbar, or by choosing View, Assistant Editor, Show Assistant Editor from the menu bar. After a few seconds, you'll see the web view appear. Using the timeline scrubber at the bottom, you can even scrub back in time and see how the page loaded.

In many instances, you can view objects you create in the Playground just by clicking the QuickLook (eye) icon that appears to the right of the line. In this case, however, the web view can be seen only in the Assistant editor, and only if we use the `XCPlayground` framework.

Scrolling Views

You've certainly used applications that display more information than what fits on a single screen; in these cases, what happens? Chances are, the application allows you to scroll to access additional content. Often, this is managed through a scrolling view, or `UIScrollView`. Scrolling views, as their name suggests, provide scrolling features and can display more than a single screen's worth of information.

Unfortunately, Apple has gone about halfway toward making scrolling views something that you can add to your projects using the Interface Builder (IB) tools. You can add the view, but until you add a line of code to your application, it won't scroll.

Stack Views

As you build-content rich applications, you'll eventually reach a state where you just want to add objects to your screen and have them displayed in a nice orderly fashion—without dealing with spacing issues and complex calculations. Stack views (`UIStackView`) do exactly that. Stack views can be oriented either horizontally or vertically, and simply stack up the content that you add to them.

Want a row of 5 icons spaced 10 points apart? Add the icons to a horizontal stack view and set the spacing to 10. Want a grid of icons? Add several horizontal stack views of icons to a vertical stack view. Combining these views with the Auto Layout system (Hour 16, "Building Responsive User Interfaces"), you'll be able to create layouts featuring lots of objects that adapt to different sized devices, and don't require tons of code.

We close out this hour's lesson with a quick example (a *single line* of code) that embeds multiple `UIStackView` instances in a `UIScrollView` to create a scrolling grid of icons.

Using Switches, Segmented Controls, and Web Views

As you've probably noticed by now, we prefer to work on examples that *do* something. It's one thing to show a few lines of code in a chapter and say "this will do <blah>," but it's another to take a collection of features and combine them in a way that results in a working application. In some cases, the former approach is unavoidable, but this isn't one of them. Our first hands-on example makes use of web views, a segmented control, and a toggle switch.

Implementation Overview

In this project, we create an application that displays flower photographs and flower information fetched from the website TeachYourselfiOS.info. The application enables a user to touch a flower color within a segmented control (`UISegmentedControl`), resulting in a flower of that color being fetched and displayed from the site in a web view (`UIWebView`). The user can then use a toggle switch (`UISwitch`) to show and hide a second web view that contains details about the flower being displayed. Finally, a standard button (`UIButton`) enables the user to fetch another flower photo of the currently selected color from the site. The result should look very much like Figure 9.3.

FIGURE 9.3
The finished application will make use of a segmented control, a switch, and two web views.

Setting Up the Project

This project will, once again, use the Single View Application template we're starting to love. If it isn't already running, launch Xcode, and then create a new project using the same settings as in the previous hours. Call this project **FlowerWeb**.

You should now be accustomed to what happens next. Xcode sets up the project and creates the default view in Main.storyboard and a view controller class named `ViewController`. We'll start as we always do: planning the variables, outlets, and actions we need in the view controller.

Planning the Variables and Connections

To create the web-based image viewer, we need three outlets and two actions. The segmented control will be connecting to variable property called `colorChoice` because we'll use it to choose which color is displayed. The web view that contains the flower will be connected to `flowerView`, and the associated details web view to `flowerDetailView`.

For the actions, the application must do two things: get and display a flower image, which we'll define as the action method `getFlower`; and toggle the flower details on and off, something we'll handle with a `toggleFlowerDetail` action method.

Why Don't We Need an Outlet for the Switch?

We don't need to include an outlet for the switch because we are connecting its Value Changed event to the `toggleFlowerDetail` method. When the method is called, the sender parameter sent to the method references the switch, so we can just use `sender` to determine whether the switch is on or off.

If we have more than one control using `toggleFlowerDetail`, it is helpful to define outlets to differentiate between them; in this case, however, sender suffices. This is our first use of sender, so pay attention. It can help save you the trouble of creating properties/instance variables in cases such as this.

Designing the Interface

By now, this process should seem a bit familiar. We've defined the outlets and actions, so it's time to build the UI. Prepare your Xcode workspace for developing the UI: Choose the Main. storyboard file to open the IB editor, and then close the project navigator, if necessary, to make room on your display.

As with the previous projects, I recommend selecting the view controller for your scene and then using the Attributes Inspector to set the simulated screen size to something familiar, like the 4.7-inch iPhone. Once your workspace is configured, we can get down to the design.

We begin by adding the segmented control.

Adding a Segmented Control

To add a segmented control to the user interface, open the Object Library (View, Utilities, Object Library), find the segmented control (`UISegmentedControl`) object, and drag it into the view. Position the control near the top of the view in the center. Because this control is ultimately used to choose colors, click and drag a label (`UILabel`) into the view, as well, position it above the segmented control, and change it to read **Choose a Flower Color:**. Your view should now resemble Figure 9.4.

FIGURE 9.4
The default segmented control has two buttons: First and Second.

By default, the segmented control has two segments, titled First and Second. You can double-click these titles and edit them directly in the view, but that doesn't quite get us what we need.

For this project, we need a control that has four segments, each labeled with a color: Red, Blue, Yellow, and Green. These are the colors that we can request from the TeachYourselfiOS.info website for displaying. Obviously, we need to add a few more segments to the control before all the choices can be represented.

Adding and Configuring Segments

The number of segments displayed in the segmented control is configurable in the Attributes Inspector for the object. Select the control that you've added to the view, and then press Option-Command-4 to open the Attributes Inspector, shown in Figure 9.5.

Using the Segments field, increase the number from 2 to 4. You should immediately see the new segments displayed. Notice that directly below where you set the number of segments in the inspector is a drop-down with entries for each segment you've added. You can choose a segment in this drop-down and then specify its title in the Title field. You can even add image resources and have them displayed within each segment.

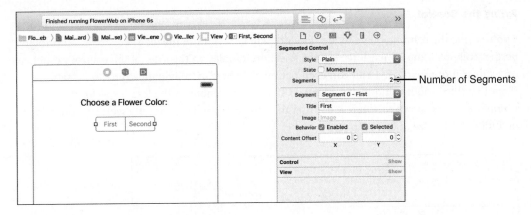

FIGURE 9.5
Use the Attributes Inspector for the segmented control to increase the number of segments displayed.

NOTE

Note that the first segment is segment 0, the next is segment 1, and so on. It's important to keep this in mind when you're checking to see which segment is selected. The first segment is *not* segment 1, as you might assume.

Update the four segments in the control so that the colors Red, Blue, Yellow, and Green are represented. The segmented control should now have titles for all the colors and a corresponding label to help the user understand its purpose.

NOTE

iPad developers who want to take advantage of their extended screen space might try adding a few more segments to the segmented control. The colors violet and magenta can be added and will be automatically recognized by the TeachYourselfiOS.info site.

Segmented Control Appearance: iOS 6 Versus iOS 7+

In iOS 7 and later, a segmented control is a segmented control; consistency is king.

If you're developing for iOS 6, however, segmented controls have more appearance customizations. In addition to the usual color options and controls available in the Attributes Inspector, you have three choices for presenting the segmented control. Use the Style drop-down menu to choose between Plain, Bordered, and Bar.

Sizing the Control

Chances are, the control you've set up doesn't quite look right in the view. To size the control to aesthetically pleasing dimensions, use the selection handles on the sides of the control to stretch and shrink it appropriately. You can even optimize the size of individual segments by setting them to a fixed width using the Segmented Control Size options in the Size Inspector (Option-Command-5), as shown in Figure 9.6, or set the Auto-Size mode so that the segments are scaled according to the size of their content.

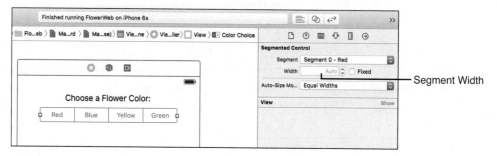

FIGURE 9.6
You can use the Size Inspector to size each segment individually, if desired.

Adding a Switch

The next UI element we'll add is the switch (`UISwitch`). In our application, the switch has one role: to toggle a web view that displays details about the flower (`flowerDetailView`) on and off. Add the switch to the view by dragging the switch object from the Object Library into the view. Position it along the right side of the screen, just under the segmented control.

As with the segmented control, providing some basic user instruction through an onscreen label can be helpful. Drag a label (`UILabel`) into the view and position it to the left of the switch. Change the text to read Show **Photo Details:**. Your view should now resemble Figure 9.7, but your switch will likely show up as *on*.

Setting the Default State   I know you're getting used to many of the different configuration options for the controls we use, but in this case, the switch has only a few options: whether the default state is on or off and what custom tints (if any) should be applied in the on state and to the "thumb" (the little round thing) of the switch.

The switch that you added to the view is set to on. We want to change it so that it is off by default. To change the default state, select the object and open the Attributes Inspector (Option-Command-4). Using the State pop-up menu (see Figure 9.7), change the default state to off.

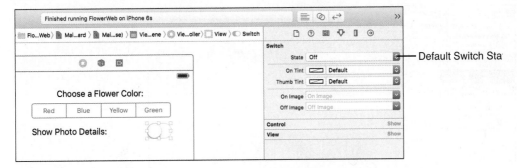

FIGURE 9.7
Add a switch to toggle flower details on and off.

Adding the Web Views

The application that we're building relies on two different web views. One displays the flower image itself; the other view (which can be toggled on and off) shows details about the image. The details view will be overlaid on top of the image itself, so let's start by adding the main view, `flowerView`.

To add a web view (`UIWebView`) to your application, locate it in the Object Library and drag it into your view. The web view will display a resizable rectangle that you can drag and position anywhere you want. Because this is the view that the flower image is shown in, position it to fall about halfway down the screen, and then resize it so that it is the same width as the device screen and so that it covers the lower portion of the view entirely.

Repeat this to add a second web view for the flower details (`flowerDetailView`). This time, size the view so that it is about half an inch high and locate it at the very bottom of the screen, over top of the flower view, as shown in Figure 9.8. Remember that you can drag items in the document outline to change their ordering. The closer an element is to the top of the list, the further "back" it is.

Setting the Web View Attributes   Web views, surprisingly, have few attributes that you can configure, but what is available can be very important. To access the web view attributes, select one of the views you added, and then press Open-Command-4 to open the Attributes Inspector (see Figure 9.9).

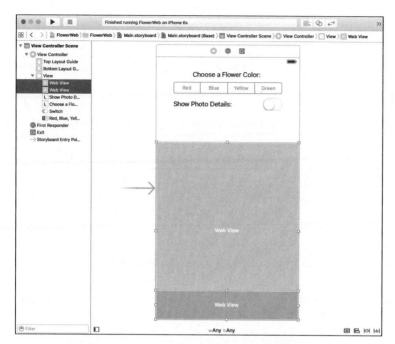

FIGURE 9.8
Add two web views
(`UIWebView`) to your
screen, and then position
them as shown here.

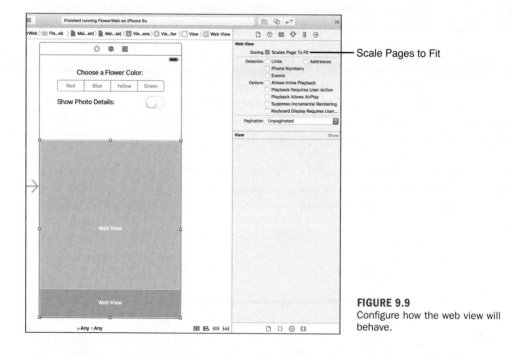

FIGURE 9.9
Configure how the web view will
behave.

You can select from three types of settings: Scaling, Detection (Phone Numbers, Addresses, Events, Links), and a generic Options. If you select Scales Page to Fit under Scaling, large pages are scaled to fit in the size of the area you've defined. If you use Detection options, the iOS data detectors go to work and underline items that it has decided are phone numbers, addresses, dates, or additional web links. The Options settings apply to media playback—whether you can use AirPlay, how media plays in your web view (inline or not)—as well as to how web pages render (most do it incrementally) and whether pages are allowed to display a keyboard automatically.

For the main flower view, we absolutely want the images to be scaled to fit within the view. Select the web view, and then use the Attributes Inspector to choose the Scales Page to Fit option.

For the second view, we do *not* want scaling to be set, so select the web view where the application will be showing the flower details and use the Attributes Inspector to ensure that no scaling takes place. You might also want to change the view attributes for the detail view to have an alpha value of around 0.65. This creates a nice translucency effect when the details are displayed on top of the photograph.

CAUTION

Understand the Effects of Scaling

Scaling doesn't necessarily do what you might expect for "small" web pages. If you display a page with only the text `Hello World` on it in a scaled web view, you might expect the text to be shown to fill the web view. Instead, the text will be *tiny*. The web view assumes that the text is part of a larger page and scales it down rather than making it appear bigger.

If you happen to have control of the web page itself, you can add a `"viewport"` meta tag to tell Safari how wide (in pixels) the full page is, as follows:

```
<meta name="viewport" content="width=320"/>
```

With the tough stuff out of the way, we just have one more finishing touch to put on the interface, and then we're ready to code.

Finishing the Interface

The only functional piece currently missing from our interface is a button (`UIButton`) that we can use to manually trigger the `getFlower` method anytime we want. Without the button, we have to switch between colors using the segmented control if we want to see a new flower image. This button does nothing more than trigger an action (`getFlower`), something you've done repeatedly in the past few hours, so this should be quite easy for you by now.

Drag a button into the view, positioning it in the center of the screen above the web views. Edit the button title to read Get New Photo. We're done. You know what that means: time to wire the interface to the code.

TIP

Although your interface may be functionally complete, you might want to select the view itself and set a background color. Keep your interfaces clean and friendly.

Creating and Connecting the Outlets and Actions

We have quite a few interface elements to connect for this project. Our segmented control, switch, button, and web views all need the proper connections to the view controller. Here's what we'll use.

Starting with the outlets:

▶ **Segmented control for choosing colors (UISegmentedControl):** colorChoice

▶ **Main flower web view (UIWebView):** flowerView

▶ **Flower detail web view (UIWebView):** flowerDetailView

And then the actions:

▶ **Fetch a new flower using the Get New Flower button:** getFlower

▶ **Turn the flower detail view on and off with the UISwitch:** toggleFlowerDetail

Okay, the same old story: Prepare your workspace by making sure that the Main.storyboard file is selected and then opening the assistant editor. Hide the project navigator and document outline if you need space.

I assume you're getting pretty familiar with this process, so we'll move quickly through the connections here and in later hours. After all, it's just click, drag, and connect.

Adding the Outlets

Begin by Control-dragging from the segmented color button control to the line following the class line in the ViewController.swift file. When prompted, configure the connection as an outlet and its name as colorChoice, leaving the other values set to the defaults. This gives us an easy way to get the currently selected color in our code.

Continue building the rest of the outlets, connecting the main (large) web view to the outlet flowerView by Control-dragging to just below the first @IBOutlet line in ViewController.swift. Finish the outlets by connecting the second web view to flowerDetailView with the same approach, as shown in Figure 9.10.

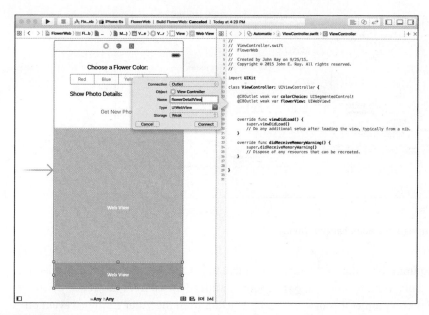

FIGURE 9.10
Connect the web views to appropriately named outlets.

Adding the Actions

Our UI triggers two action methods. The switch hides and shows details about the flower through the method `toggleFlowerDetail`, and the standard button loads a new image for us with `getFlower`. Straightforward, right? It is, but sometimes you need to think beyond the obvious actions users can take and consider what they will *expect* to happen when they use the interface.

In this application, users are presented with a simple interface. They should immediately recognize that they can choose a color and push a button to get a flower of that color. But shouldn't the application be smart enough to load a new flower as soon as the user switches the color? Why should the user have to switch the color and then press another button? By connecting the `UISegmentedControl`'s Value Changed event to the same `getFlower` method we trigger from the button, we gain this functionality without writing a single additional line of code.

Start by connecting the switch (`UISwitch`) to a new action named `toggleFlowerDetail` by Control-dragging to just below the last `@IBOutlet` directive in the ViewController.swift file. Make sure that the action is triggered from the event Value Changed, as shown in Figure 9.11.

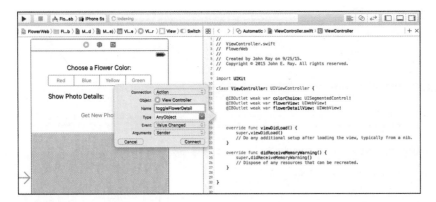

FIGURE 9.11
Connect the switch using the Value Changed event.

Next, Control-drag from the button (`UIButton`) to a line under the `@IBAction` you just defined. When prompted, configure a new action, `getFlower`, that is triggered from the Touch Up Inside event. Finally, we need to target this new `getFlower` action from the Value Changed event on the segmented control (`UISegmentedControl`) so that the user can load a new flower just by touching a color.

Switch to the standard editor and make sure that the document outline is visible (Editor, Show Document Outline). Select the segmented control, and open the Connections Inspector by pressing Option-Command-6 (View, Utilities, Connections Inspector). Drag from the circle beside Value Changed to the View Controller line in the document outline, as demonstrated in Figure 9.12. Release your mouse button and choose `getFlower` when prompted.

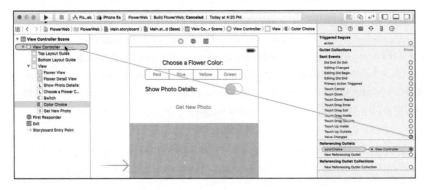

FIGURE 9.12
Connect the Value Changed event of the segmented control to the `getFlower` method.

NOTE

Okay, I admit it. In this example, we took a roundabout way of connecting the segmented control to the `getFlower` method. We could have also Control-dragged from the segmented control onto the `IBAction getFlower` line in the assistant editor and instantly had our connection.

The problem with the "easy" approach, however, is that you aren't given the opportunity of choosing which event triggers the action. It just so happens that in this case, Xcode would choose `Value Changed` for you.

The interface and its connections are finished. The block of code at the top of your ViewController.swift file should look much like this:

```
import UIKit

class ViewController: UIViewController {

    @IBOutlet weak var colorChoice: UISegmentedControl!
    @IBOutlet weak var flowerView: UIWebView!
    @IBOutlet weak var flowerDetailView: UIWebView!

    @IBAction func getFlower(sender: AnyObject) {
    }

    @IBAction func toggleFlowerDetail(sender: AnyObject) {
    }
```

Implementing the Application Logic

Our view controller needs to implement two pieces of functionality via two action methods. The first, `toggleFlowerDetail`, shows and hides the `flowerDetailView` web view, depending on whether the switch has been flipped on (show) or off (hide). The second method, `getFlower`, loads a flower image into the `flowerView` web view and details on that photograph into the `flowerDetailView` web view. We start with the easier of the two, `toggleFlowerDetail`.

Hiding and Showing the Detail Web View

A useful feature of any object that inherits from `UIView` is that you can easily hide (or show) it within your iOS application interfaces. Because almost everything you see onscreen inherits from this class, this means that you can hide and show labels, buttons, fields, images, and yes, other views. To hide an object, you just set its Boolean variable property `hidden` to `true`. So, to hide the `flowerDetailView`, we write the following:

```
flowerDetailView.hidden=true
```

To show it again, we just reverse the process, setting the `hidden` property to `false`:

`flowerDetailView.hidden=false`

To implement the logic for the `toggleFlowerDetail` method, we need to figure out what value the switch is currently set to. As mentioned earlier in the lesson, we can check the state of a toggle switch through the `on` variable property: `true` if the switch is set to on, `false` if it is off.

Because we don't have an outlet specifically set aside for the switch, we'll use the `sender` variable to access it in our method. When the `toggleFlowerDetail` action method is called, this variable is set to reference the object that invoked the action (in other words, the switch). Unfortunately, the `sender` is defined as being of the type `AnyObject`, so we'll get an error if we try to access the `on` variable property because Xcode doesn't know that it's a switch. We could just redefine the method so that the incoming parameter is a `UISwitch` (rather than `AnyObject`), but why take the easy way out? Instead, we can use a form of *typecasting* called *downcasting* to force `sender` to be recognized as a `UISwitch` by using the syntax `<variable> as! <object>`.

In other words, to access `sender` as an object of type `UISwitch`, we use the format `sender as! UISwitch`. The exclamation point forces the downcasting and is required by Xcode when a downcast operation may fail. Because we know that the method is always going to be called by a switch, we can safely force the downcast.

To access the `on` variable property, wrap the type cast object in parentheses like this:

`(sender as! UISwitch).on`

So, to check to see whether the switch is on, we can write the following:

`if (sender as! UISwitch).on { <switch is on> } else { <switch is off> }`

Now, here's where we can get clever. (You are feeling clever, right?) We want to hide and show the `flowerDetailView` using a Boolean value and we *get* a Boolean value from `(sender as! UISwitch).on`. This maps to two conditions:

▶ When `(sender as! UISwitch).on` is `true`, the view should *not* be hidden (`flowerDetailView.hidden = false`).

▶ When `(sender as! UISwitch).on` is `false`, the view *should* be hidden (`flowerDetailView.hidden = true`).

In other words, the state of the switch is the exact opposite of what we need to assign to the `hidden` variable property of the view. In Swift, to get the opposite of a Boolean value, we just put an exclamation mark in front (`!`). So, all we need to do to hide or show `flowerDetailView` is to set the `hidden` variable property to `!(sender as! UISwitch).on`. That's it. *A single line of code.*

Implement `toggleFlowerDetail` in the `FlowerWeb` method stub that Xcode provided for you. The full method should look a lot like Listing 9.1.

LISTING 9.1   Implementing the `toggleFlowerDetail` Method

```
@IBAction func toggleFlowerDetail(sender: AnyObject) {
    flowerDetailView.hidden = !(sender as! UISwitch).on
}
```

Loading and Displaying the Flower Image and Details

To fetch our flower images, we use a feature provided by the TeachYourselfiOS.info website specifically for this purpose. We follow four steps to interact with the website:

1. We get the chosen color from the segmented control.

2. We generate a random number called a "session ID" so that TeachYourselfiOS.info can track our request.

3. We request the URL `https://teachyourselfios.info/?hour=9&color=<color>&session=<sessionID>`, where `<color>` is the chosen color and `<session ID>` is the random number. This URL returns a flower photo.

4. We request the URL `https://teachyourselfios.info/?hour=9&session=<sessionID>&type=detail`, where `<session ID>` is the same random number. This URL returns the details for the previously requested flower photo.

CAUTION

Gee, Apple, Thanks for Keeping Me Secure!

In iOS 9, Apple has implemented something called App Transport Security (ATS). This sounds like a good thing, yes? It is, and it isn't. ATS forces your web requests to use https rather than http. This is fine for web services that provide secure access to secure data, but in many cases, the information doesn't need to be secure, nor does the web service provide encrypted communications over HTTPS. To get around this, you can enter exceptions into your application's Info.plist file, but there is no way to change the default behavior. For more information on this helpful feature, be sure to search for "App Transport Security" in the iOS documentation.

Let's go ahead and see what this looks like in code and then discuss details behind the implementation. Add the `getFlower` implementation, as shown in Listing 9.2.

LISTING 9.2   Adding the getFlower Implementation

```
1: @IBAction func getFlower(sender: AnyObject?) {
2:       var imageURL: NSURL
3:       var detailURL: NSURL
4:       var imageURLString: String
5:       var detailURLString: String
6:       var color: String
7:       let sessionID: Int=random()%50000
8:
9:       color=colorChoice.titleForSegmentAtIndex(colorChoice.selectedSegmentIndex)!
10:
11:      imageURLString =
12:      "https://teachyourselfios.info/?hour=9&color=\(color)&session=\(sessionID)"
13:      detailURLString =
14:       "https://teachyourselfios.info/?hour=9&session=\(sessionID)&type=detail"
15:
16:      imageURL=NSURL(string: imageURLString)!
17:      detailURL=NSURL(string: detailURLString)!
18:
19:      flowerView.loadRequest(NSURLRequest(URL: imageURL))
20:      flowerDetailView.loadRequest(NSURLRequest(URL: detailURL))
21: }
```

This is the most complicated code that you've written so far, but let's break it down into the individual pieces, so it's not difficult to understand.

In line 1, I've added a ? after AnyObject because I want to be able to call this method without providing a value for sender. We'll get back to the reason behind this a bit later.

Lines 2–6 declare the variables that we need to prepare our requests to the website. The first variables, imageURL and detailURL, are instances of NSURL that contain the URLs that are loaded into the flowerView and flowerDetailView web views. To create the NSURL objects, we need two strings, imageURLString and detailURLString, which we format with the special URLs that we presented earlier, including the color and sessionID values.

Line 7 declares a constant sessionID as an integer and assigns it a random number between 0 and 49999. I've used the let (instead of var) keyword to denote that this is a constant rather than a variable—but a variable would work just as well.

In line 9, we retrieve the title of the selected segment in our instance of the segmented control: colorChoice. To do this, we use the object's instance method titleForSegmentAtIndex along with the object's selectedSegmentIndex variable property. The result, colorChoice.titleForSegmentAtIndex(colorChoice.selectedSegmentIndex)!, is stored in the string color and is ready to be used in the web request. Notice the exclamation mark at the end of that line? The `!` indicates that we're explicitly unwrapping the value returned by `titleForSegmentAtIndex`. This is required because the definition of the method indicates it could return a string; or, if a title was never set, it could return `nil`. Obviously we've set titles for everything, so this should be a nonissue for us. However, because `titleForSegmentAtIndex` was written to return optional strings, we have to acknowledge this fact and explicitly tell Xcode we want to use (unwrap) the value by adding the `!` to the end.

Lines 11–14 prepare `imageURLString` and `detailURLString` with the URLs that we will be requesting. The color and session ID are substituted into the string definitions using "string interpolation." That is, we add in the variables we want substituted into the string (`color` and `sessionID`) by placing their names in parentheses and adding a backslash to the start: `\(color)` and `\(sessionID)`.

Lines 16–17 create the `imageURL` and `detailURL` `NSURL` objects using the `NSURL` convenience initialization method and the two strings `imageURLString` and `detailURLString`. Like the `selectedSegmentIndex` in line 9, we have to explicitly unwrap the value returned by `NSURL` by adding an `!` to the end, because `NSURL` documentation states that it may return *no* value if the string you give it is bad. Because we know we're giving it a good URL, we can add the `!` to the end and move on.

Lines 19–20 use the `loadRequest` method of the `flowerView` and `flowerDetailView` web views to load the `NSURL`s `imageURL` and `detailURL`, respectively. When these lines are executed, the display updates the contents of the two views.

NOTE
_____
Remember that `UIWebView`'s `loadRequest` method doesn't handle `NSURL` objects directly; it expects an `NSURLRequest` object instead. To work around this, we create and return `NSURLRequest` objects using the `NSURLRequest` convenient initialization method.
_____

Fixing Up the Interface When the App Loads

Now that the `getFlower` method is implemented, you can run the application and everything should work—except that when the application starts, the two web views are empty and the detail view is visible, even though the toggle switch is set to off.

To fix this, we can start loading an image as soon as the app is up and running and set `flowerDetailView.hidden` to `true`. To do this, update the view controller's `viewDidLoad` method as follows in Listing 9.3.

LISTING 9.3   Updating the `viewDidLoad` Method to Set the Initial Display

```
override func viewDidLoad() {
    super.viewDidLoad()
    flowerDetailView.hidden=true
    getFlower(nil)
}
```

As expected, `flowerDetailView.hidden=true` hides the detail view. Using `getFlower(nil)`, we can call the `getFlower` method from within our instance of the view control and start the process of loading a flower in the web view. The method `getFlower` expects a parameter, so we pass it `nil`, just as we did in the last hour's lesson. This is also the reason why we added the `?` to the `getFlower` method definition, making the `sender`'s value optional. If it weren't optional, we would need to pass it some kind of object; otherwise, the application wouldn't compile. Because it *is* optional, sending `nil` works just fine. Keep in mind that we don't actually use `sender` for anything in the `getFlower` method, so we don't really care what value it has.

Adding Apple's Blur

In Hour 8, "Handling Images, Animation, Sliders, and Steppers," we added a blurred effect to the background of our sample application. This hour's project also presents an opportunity for blurring. Because this is just a visual effect, and not the focus of the chapter, however, it's entirely optional.

If you'd like to try adding a blur to the detail view of your version of FlowerWeb, do the following:

1. Using the Object Library, find and drag a copy of the Visual Effect View with Blur to the interface design. This special object blurs the views behind it (you can adjust the type of blur in the Attributes Inspector.)

2. Position the view so that it is the same size as the `flowerDetailView`, but underneath it—the Editor, Arrange menu can be handy for this. Alternatively, you could place `flowerDetailView` within the effects view.

3. Edit the detail view so that it is not opaque, and its background color is "clear color" (letting the blur show through).

4. Use the assistant editor to add an outlet for the blurView (`blurView`) to your code.

5. Add one line of code to ViewController.swift at the bottom of `viewDidLoad` to hide the blurred view initially:

   ```
   blurView.hidden = true
   ```

6. Add a second line to the end of `toggleFlowerDetail` that will toggle the blurred view on and off, just like the detail view:

   ```
   blurView.hidden = !(sender as! UISwitch).on
   ```

That's it. You can play around with this effects view to see what different blurring effects can be created, as well as with the Visual Effects View with Blur and Vibrancy object. Just remember: Too much of a good thing can be (literally) painful on the eyes.

I've included this additional code in the FlowerWeb sample.

Building the Application

Test out the final version of the FlowerWeb application by clicking Run in Xcode.

Notice that you can zoom in and out of the web view and use your fingers to scroll around. These are all features that you get without any implementation cost when using the `UIWebView` class.

Congratulations. Another app under your belt.

Using Scrolling and Stack Views

After working through the projects in the past few hours, iPhone users might begin to notice something: We're running out of space in our interfaces. Things are starting to get cluttered.

One possible solution, as you learned earlier in this hour, is to use the `hidden` variable property of UI objects to hide and show them in your applications. Unfortunately, when you're juggling a few dozen controls, this is pretty impractical. Another approach is to use multiple different views, something that you start learning about in Hour 11.

There is, however, a third way that we can fit more into a single view: by making it scroll. Using an instance of the `UIScrollView` class, you can add controls and interface elements to a canvas that stretches beyond the physical boundaries of your device's screen. Unfortunately, although Apple provides access to this object in the IB editor, making it work is a bit less obvious than one might hope.

To keep things nice and neat within a scrolling view, we can throw another object into the mix: the stack view (`UIStackView`). These, like scroll views, are container objects; they hold other things and are little use on their own. Stack views enable you to add objects to a view and "stack them up" (either vertically or horizontally) without having to worry about detailed placement.

Before closing out this hour, I want to show you how to start using simple scrolling and stack views views in a mini-project.

Implementation Overview

When I say *simple*, I mean it. This project consists of a scroll view (`UIScrollView`) with that contains several stack views—all added in the IB editor, as shown in Figure 9.13.

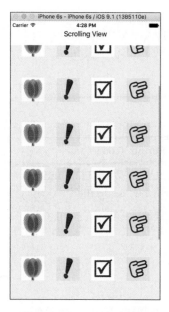

FIGURE 9.13
We're going to make a view. It will scroll.

To enable scrolling in the view, we need to set a variable property called contentSize, which describes how large the content is that needs to be scrolled. That's it.

Setting Up the Project

Begin by creating another Single View Application. Name the new project **Scroller**. For this example, we're going to be adding the scroll view (UIScrollView) as a subview to the existing view in Main.storyboard. This is a perfectly acceptable approach, but as you get more experienced with the tools, you might want to just replace the default view entirely. Within the scroll view, we'll add several stack views (UIStackView) to help arrange the content we want to scroll—in this case, icons.

Adding the Icon Resources

Let's get the icons that we'll be scrolling added into the project. Open the project group in the project navigator area of Xcode. Click the main Assets.xcassets file to open the project's image assets. Drag the Icons folder from the Finder into the column on the left inside the asset catalog. A new Icons folder appears within the assets library; time to move on.

Planning the Variables and Connections

We need to do just one thing programmatically in this project, and that's set a variable property on the `scrollView` object. To access the scroll view, we'll connect it, via an outlet, to a new variable property, which we'll call **theScroller**.

Designing the Interface

There isn't much to this project, just a scrolling view, some stack views, and content (a few images). Because you already know how to find objects in the Object Library and add them to a view, this should be trivial. Start by opening the Main.storyboard file for the project and making sure the document outline is visible (Editor, Show Document Outline).

Next, do the same thing you've done in previous projects: Set a simulated size for the view controller by selecting the View Controller line in the document outline and then opening the Attributes Inspector (Option-Command-4). Set the Size drop-down to the iOS device screen size that you want (iPhone 4.7-inch for me).

Adding a Scroll View

Using the Object Library (View Utilities, Show Object Library), drag an instance of a scroll view (`UIScrollView`) into your view. Position the view to fill the scene to the bottom, left, and right edges. Place a label above it that reads **Scrolling View** (just in case you forget what we're building). Figure 9.14 shows what your scene should look like at this point.

TIP
_____

The text view (`UITextView`) you used in Hour 7 is a specialized instance of a scrolling view. The same scrolling attributes that you can set for the text view can be applied for the scroll view, so you might want to refer to that earlier hour for more configuration possibilities. Or just press Option-Command-4 to bring up the Attributes Inspector and explore.

_____

Now that your scroll view is added to your design, you need to populate it with something.

SCROLLING THROUGH PAGES
_____

Scrolling views support the notion of pagination—displaying contents one page at a time rather than showing a single, pageless, stream of text. To turn on pagination, select your scrolling view and check the Paging Enabled property within the Scrolling section of the Attributes Inspector.

_____

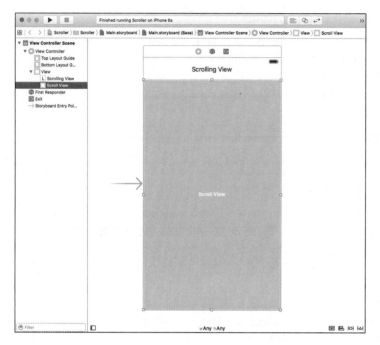

FIGURE 9.14
Add a scrolling view and label to the scene.

Adding Stack Views

The content for our application will be a series of images placed into a horizontal stack view, then several copies of that stack view placed in a vertical stack view. Start by adding four image views into the scrolling area; place them roughly one beside the other and size them to be "icon sized." You can use the Size Inspector or just eyeball it; we're not going for precision here. I used a width and height of 50 points in my example.

TIP

Another way to get objects into a scrolling view is to lay them out in your main view however you'd like, select them, and then choose Editor, Embed In, Scroll View from the menu bar. This adds a scrolling view to your interface that contains all the selected objects.

Once the image views are added, use the Attributes Inspector to set the image for each. Choose from one of the icon images that were imported at the start of the project (Icon1, Icon2, Icon3, Icon4, Icon5, or Icon6). Which icon you choose isn't important. Your design—consisting of just a scroll view, a label, and some icons—should resemble Figure 9.15.

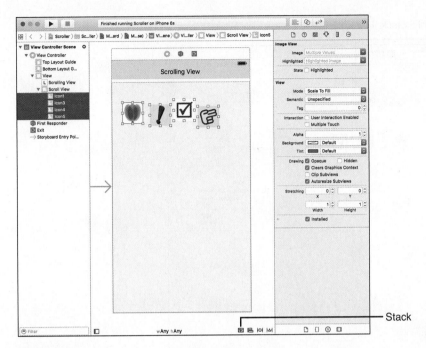

FIGURE 9.15
Add four icons (of your choosing) to the design.

Now, select all four of the image views in the design and click the Stack icon at the bottom of the Interface Builder editor (visible in Figure 9.15). The icons should snap into a horizontal row. If they turn into a vertical column, don't worry, that's an easy fix, as you'll see next.

Make sure that the stack view is selected in the Document Outline; you should see the four image views contained within it. Open the Attributes Inspector (Command-Option-4), and verify that Axis is set to Horizontal. This controls whether it is a horizontal or vertical stack. Next, set the spacing attribute to a visually pleasing number. I've used 30. You'll see the icons space themselves out in the design view, as shown in Figure 9.16.

The Alignment and Distribution menus control what happens if the items in the stack view are different sizes or are part of an Auto Layout controlled design; you'll learn about Auto Layout in Hour 16.

You now have the first row of your icon grid created. The next step is to make copies of the rows and place them in a vertical stack view. Go ahead and copy and paste the horizontal stack view around 10 times.

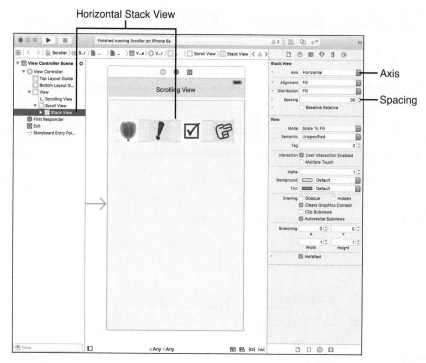

FIGURE 9.16
Add the 4 icons to a horizontal stack view.

Once you're done, select all 10 of the horizontal stack views, and then click the Stack icon in the editor once again. They should immediately stack up in a vertical stack view. Select the vertical stack view and use the Attributes Inspector to set the vertical spacing to around 50 points, as shown in Figure 9.17. If for some reason the stack wasn't created vertically, you can also use the Axis drop-down to switch it to Vertical.

Notice that not all the horizontal stacks are visible anymore? When we set the vertical spacing, it pushed some of them down below the visible area of the scroll view. The point of all of this was to make sure that some of the icons are off the screen, meaning we'll have to scroll to see them. (We've also learned about stack views, so that's a good thing too.)

Now we just need to make the whole thing scroll with a tiny bit of code. Don't worry, you'll be done before you even know you've started!

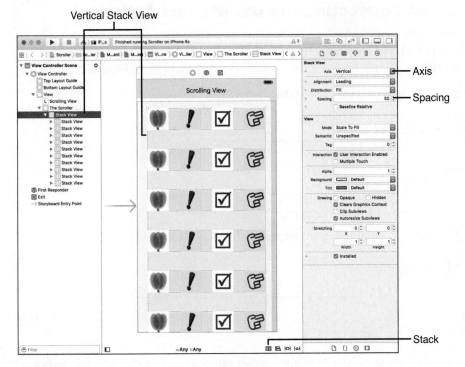

FIGURE 9.17
The final layout, with one vertical stack view, ten horizontal stack views, and one scrolling view.

STACK VIEWS AND THE OBJECT LIBRARY

If you look, you'll find the horizontal and vertical stack views living in the Object Library. In this example, we selected objects we wanted added to one of these views, and then used the Stack button in Interface Builder to add them to a stack view. You could also drag a stack view from the Object Library and then drag your objects into that view.

SETTING A FREEFORM SIZE

When laying out scrolling views (or any view that may hold more content than you can see on the simulated iOS device screen), you may want to switch to the Simulated Size for the scene (or the scene's view controller) to Freeform. Once in freeform mode, you can select the scene's main view and set the size to anything you want—making it easy to work with offscreen content.

Creating and Connecting the Outlets and Actions

This project needs only a single outlet and no actions. To create the outlet, switch to the assistant editor and disable the project navigator if you need to make a bit of extra room. Control-drag from the scroll view to the line following the `class` line in the ViewController.swift file.

When prompted, create a new outlet called **theScroller**, as shown in Figure 9.18.

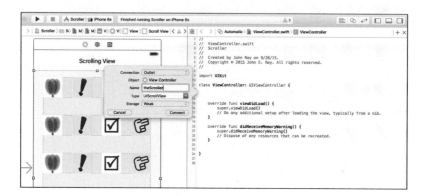

FIGURE 9.18
Create the connection to the `theScroller` outlet.

That finishes up our work in the IB editor; just a teensy bit of implementation remains. Switch back to the standard editor, enable the project navigator, and then select the ViewController. swift file to finish the implementation.

Implementing the Application Logic

For fun, try to run the application as it stands. It compiles and launches, but it doesn't scroll (at least not correctly). The reason for this is because iOS needs to know the horizontal and vertical sizes of the region it is going to scroll. Until the scrolling view knows that it *can* scroll, it doesn't.

Adding Scrolling Behavior

To add scrolling to our scroll view, we need to set the `contentSize` attribute to a `CGSize` value. `CGSize` is just a simple data structure that contains a height and a width, and we can easily make one using the `CGSizeMake(<width>,<height>)` function.

For example, to tell our scroll view (`theScroller`) that it can scroll up to 300 points horizontally and 1,000 points vertically, we could enter the following:

```
theScroller.contentSize=CGSizeMake(300.0,1000.0)
```

Guess what? That isn't just what we *could* do, it's what we *will* do. If you're developing on the iPhone, edit the ViewController.swift file and update the method `viewDidLoad` shown in Listing 9.4.

LISTING 9.4   Enabling Scrolling in Your Scroll View

```
override func viewDidLoad() {
    super.viewDidLoad()
    theScroller.contentSize=CGSizeMake(300.0,1000.0)
}
```

If you are working on the iPad, you need to adjust the size to be a bit larger because the screen is larger. Provide the arguments `900.0` and `2000.0` to the `CGSizeMake` function, instead of `300.0` and `1000.0`.

The single line we added to the method line sets the `contentSize` and enables the scrolling, ta da!

Where Did You Get the Width and Height Values?

The width we used in this example is the width of the scroll view itself (or smaller). Why? Because we don't have any reason to scroll horizontally. The height is just the vertical size of the view that would hold all of the icons (if we could see them). In other words, these change depending on the size that the scrolling view must be to fit all your content. Use whatever works best for your application. Feel free to play around; it won't hurt anything to experiment!

CAUTION

Wrong Makes Right

Depending on how much attention to pay to developer forums, you'll find that some who proselytize the notion that Auto Layout (a system you'll learn about in Hour 16, "Building Responsive User Interfaces") will automatically calculate the sizes of your scrolling views and will make them scroll automatically. Adding additional code is unnecessary.

Unfortunately, Auto Layout is still rapidly evolving, and *many* developers have spent sleepless nights trying to make it work for scrolling views. As of iOS 9, it's *still* not perfect. If we have to add two or three lines of code to ensure that it works right, no matter what, that seems like the *smart* thing to do.

Building the Application

The moment of truth has arrived. Does the single line of code make magic? Choose Run from the Xcode toolbar, and then try scrolling around the view you created. Everything should work like a charm.

TIP

Okay, so it's not *technically* a single line of code for the entire implementation, but it is a single line that makes the scrolling view work.

Yes, this was a quick-and-dirty project, but there seems to be a lack of information on getting started with `UIScrollView` and `UIStackView` objects. So, I thought it was important to run through a short tutorial. I hope this gives you new ideas about what you can do to create more feature-rich iOS interfaces.

CAUTION

The Warning Signs Are There. Ignore Them

When building this application, you'll notice a few warnings appearing in Xcode. These are related to the Auto Layout system and don't affect the functionality of the application. You can revisit this project (if you'd like) after Hour 16 and quickly correct them.

Further Exploration

As well as useful, the segmented control (`UISegmentedControl`) and switch (`UISwitch`) classes are pretty easy to get the hang of. The best place to focus your attention for additional exploration is on the feature set provided by the `UIWebView` and `UIScrollView` classes.

As described at the start of this hour, `UIWebView` can handle a large variety of content beyond what might be inferred by the "web" portion of its name. By learning more about `NSURL`, such as the `initFileURLWithPath:isDirectory` method, you'll be able to load files directly from your project resources. You can also take advantage of the web view's built-in actions, such as `goForward` and `goBack`, to add navigation functionality without a single line of code. One might even use a collection of HTML files to create a self-contained website within an application. In short, web views extend the traditional interface of your applications by bringing in HTML markup, JavaScript, and CSS—creating a potent combination.

The `UIScrollView` class, in contrast, gives us an important capability that is widely used in iOS applications: touch scrolling. We briefly demonstrated this at the end of the hour, but you can enable additional features, such as pinching and zooming, by implementing the `UIScrollViewDelegate` protocol. We take our first look at building a class that conforms to a protocol in the next hour, so keep this in mind as you get more comfortable with the concepts.

Finally, the `UIStackView` class can be used for creating orderly user interfaces that size nicely on any device. Coupled with Auto Layout (Hour 16), you can use stack views to create rows and columns of content that resize to fit iPhone and iPad displays without all the complexities of trying to calculate interface sizes yourself.

Apple Tutorials

Segmented Controls, Switches, and Web Views – UICatalog (accessible via the Xcode developer documentation): Mentioned in Hour 8, UICatalog shows nearly all the iOS interface concepts in clearly defined examples.

Scrolling – ScrollViewSuite (accessible via the Xcode developer documentation): The ScrollViewSuite provides examples of just about everything you could ever want to do in a scroll view.

Summary

In this hour, you learned how to use two controls that enable applications to respond to user input beyond just a simple button press or a text field. The switch and segmented control, while limited in the options they can present, give a user a touch-friendly way of making decisions within your applications.

You also explored how to use web views to bring web content directly into your projects and how to tweak it so that it integrates into the overall iOS user experience. This powerful class will quickly become one of your most trusted tools for displaying content.

Because we've reached a point in our development where interface layouts are getting a bit cramped, we closed out the hour with a quick introduction to two "container" views: scroll and stack views. You learned how that, despite appearances, you can easily add these unique views (and their associated capabilities) to apps.

Q&A

Q. Can stack views (`UIStackView`) resize with my windows?

A. Yes! You'll need the Auto Layout features of Hour 16 to accomplish this, but yes, it's absolutely possible. You will "pin" the sides of a stack view to the sides of your application view. The stack view will then resize and space its contents out evenly over your view.

Q. You mentioned the `UIWebView` includes actions. What does that mean, and how do I use them?

A. This means that the object you drag into your view is already capable of responding to actions (such as navigation actions) on its own—no code required. To use these, you connect from the UI event that should trigger the action to your instance of the web view and then choose the appropriate action from the pop-up window that appears.

Workshop

Quiz

1. What common iOS view feature can you add to a project through the Visual Effect view?

   a. Blurring

   b. Flashing

   c. Transparency

   d. Voiceover functionality

2. Which operator, when placed at the start of a Boolean value, results in the opposite of that value?

   a. ?

   b. *

   c. &

   d. !

3. What type of object does a web view expect as a parameter when loading a remote URL?

   a. `NSURL`

   b. `NSURLRequest`

   c. `NSRequestURL`

   d. LoadRequest

4. What variable property can be set to `true` on a view to make it not visible?

   a. `invisible`

   b. `noshow`

   c. `nodisplay`

   d. `hidden`

5. If we want to use a method and not supply a value to one of its parameters, that parameter must be set as which of the following?

   a. Transient

   b. Unwrapped

   c. Empty

   d. Optional

6. If an instance method returns an optional value, we can only use it after doing what?

    a. Opening it

    b. Unwrapping it

    c. Displaying it

    d. Querying it

7. This view accepts objects and presents them in a horizontal or vertical column?

    a. Freeform view

    b. Grid view

    c. Stack view

    d. Fixed view

8. The `selectedSegmentIndex` variable property of a segmented control assigns the first segment what value?

    a. `0`

    b. `1`

    c. `-1`

    d. `nil`

9. To typecast an object to another type, you use the syntax `<myObject>` _____ `<cast object type>`. What keyword is missing in the middle?

    a. `with`

    b. `from`

    c. `as`

    d. `using`

10. A method that quickly creates and returns an object is called what?

    a. An initialization method

    b. A quick start method

    c. A convenience initialization method

    d. A swift initialization method

Answers

1. A. Visual effects, such as the frosted glass/blurring effect in iOS, are easily added via the `UIVisualEffectView`.

2. D. To get the opposite of a Boolean value, simply prefix it with the `!` character.

3. B. The `NSURLRequest` object is needed prior to making a remote web request.

4. D. Set the `hidden` variable property to `true` to quickly hide most visual elements in iOS.

5. D. Method parameters must be defined as Optional if you want to invoke them without a value.

6. B. Methods that return an optional value must be unwrapped before use.

7. A. The stack view gives us a container view that organizes content into horizontal or vertical columns.

8. A. The first segment in a segmented control is considered the `0` segment.

9. C. To typecast one object to another, use the keyword `as` (for example, `<myObject> as <another Object type>`).

10. C. Methods that quickly create and return a new object are known as convenience initialization methods.

Activities

1. Create your own "mini" web browser by combining a text field, buttons, and a segmented control with a web view. Use the text field for URL entry, buttons for navigation, and hard-code some shortcuts for your favorite sites into the segmented control. To make the best use of space, you may want to overlay the controls on the web view and then add a switch that hides or shows the controls when toggled.

2. Change the FlowerWeb application to take on a more "Apple-y" appearance. Extend the main `UIWebView` to cover the entire screen, but blur the area behind the main controls.

Getting the User's Attention

What You'll Learn in This Hour:

▶ Different types of user notifications

▶ How to create alert controllers

▶ Methods for collecting input from alerts

▶ How to use action sheet alert styles

▶ How to implement short sounds and vibrations

iOS presents developers with many opportunities for creating unique user interfaces, but certain elements must be consistent across all applications. When users need to be notified of an application event or make a critical decision, it is important to present them with interface elements that immediately make sense. In this hour, we look at several different ways an application can notify a user that *something* has happened. It's up to you to determine what that something is, but these are the tools you need to keep users of your apps "in the know."

Alerting the User

Applications on iOS are user centered, which means they typically don't perform utility functions in the background or operate without an interface. They enable users to work with data, play games, communicate, or carry out dozens of other activities. Despite the variation in activities, when an application needs to show a warning, provide feedback, or ask the user to make a decision, it does so in a common way. Cocoa Touch leverages a variety of objects and methods to gain your attention, including alert controllers and System Sound Services. Unlike many of the other objects we've worked with, these require us to build them in code. So don't start digging through the Interface Builder (IB) Object Library just yet.

NOTE

Did you notice that I said applications *typically* don't operate in the background? That's because, with iOS 4 or later, some do. Applications running in the background have a unique set of capabilities, including additional types of alerts and notifications. You learn more about these in Hour 22, "Building Background-Ready Applications."

Alert Controllers

Alert controllers (UIAlertController) unify a few long-standing methods of getting user input. The UIAlertController is used for creating a view and view controller that can display either a simple alert, or a multiple-choice list. These alert styles are known as alerts and action sheets, respectively, and were previously handled by the UIAlertView and UIActionSheet classes (in iOS 7 and earlier).

The actions (buttons) that users can access within an alert controller are unique objects of the type UIAlertAction and are added to an alert controller using the addAction method. UITextField objects can also be added using the UIAlertController method addTextFieldWithConfigurationHandler.

Welcome to Closures. What's a Closure?

This chapter marks the first time that we'll work with closures. Each time you see reference to a *handler* in a method, it's likely that that handler is expected to be defined as a *closure*. A closure is a block of code that can be treated like an object (even passed as an argument to other objects).

In most of our uses, a closure will look like a function, but with two differences: First, it has no name; and second, it is defined within a method call. For example, suppose that you have an object named myObject and it has a method defineHandler that is supposed to be defined as a closure. It might be added to your code like this:

```
myObject.defineHandler ({(variable: AnyObject) in
    // Do something useful here with variable.
    })
```

The method call itself starts out like any other; but instead of a parameter, we provide a curly brace, then a list of parameters inside parentheses (just as if we were defining a function), and finally the word in and the code that should be executed whenever the handler is called. The closure ends with a closing curly brace, and then a closing parenthesis for the method. If you look closely, it's as if we listed a bunch of parameters, but those parameters were instead a chunk of code inside curly braces { } (that is, the closure).

What parameters are supposed to be listed at the start of the closure? For a method that expects you to define a handler, you can just look at that method in the Xcode application programming interface (API) documentation to see how many parameters the closure is expected to accept.

Alerts

Sometimes users need to be informed of changes when an application is running. More than just a change in the current view is required when an internal error event occurs (such as low-memory condition or a dropped network connection), for example, or upon completion of a long-running activity. In these cases, you want to display what we'll call an *alert*.

A `UIAlertController` with the `Alert` style is used to present a translucent floating modal window with a message, a few option buttons, and text entry fields, as shown in Figure 10.1.

FIGURE 10.1
An alert example, generated in Safari.

What *Modal* Means

Modal user interface (UI) elements require the user to interact with them (usually, to push a button) before the user can do anything else. They are typically layered on top of other windows and block all other interface actions while visible.

Implementing an alert takes little effort: You declare a `UIAlertController` object, initialize it, and present it. Consider the code fragment in Listing 10.1.

LISTING 10.1   Implementing an **Alert-Styled** `UIAlertController`

```
1:   let alertController = UIAlertController(title: "Email Address",
2:       message: "Please enter your email address:",
3:       preferredStyle: UIAlertControllerStyle.Alert)
```

```
 4:
 5:   let defaultAction = UIAlertAction(title: "Ok",
 6:       style: UIAlertActionStyle.Default,
 7:       handler: nil)
 8:
 9:   let destructiveAction = UIAlertAction(title: "Erase My Device",
10:       style: UIAlertActionStyle.Destructive,
11:       handler: nil)
12:
13:alertController.addTextFieldWithConfigurationHandler({ (textField:UITextField!)in
14:       textField.placeholder="Email Address"
15:       textField.keyboardType=UIKeyboardType.EmailAddress
16:   })
17:
18:   alertController.addAction(defaultAction)
19:   alertController.addAction(destructiveAction)
20:
21:   presentViewController(alertController, animated: true, completion: nil)
```

In lines 1–3, I declare a constant `alertController` to hold an instance of
`UIAlertController`. The initialization method of the alert view provides three parameters we
can customize:

> ▶ `title`: The title that is displayed at the top of the alert

> ▶ `message`: Sets the string that will appear in the content area of the dialog box

> ▶ `preferredStyle`: Defines whether the alert is a dialog box
>   (`UIAlertControllerStyle.Alert`) or an action sheet in appearance
>   (`UIAlertControllerStyle.ActionSheet`)

Lines 5–7 configure the first of two buttons that will be added to the alert. A constant,
`defaultAction`, of the type `UIAlertAction` is created using an alert action convenience
initialization method. This method uses a `title` parameter to set the title on the button, a
`handler` (code to be executed when the button is touched—we'll get to that in a minute or two),
and a `style`, which can be one of three values:

> ▶ `UIAlertActionStyle.Default`: The default button style—any general "actions" should
>   use this style. You might see this used for an Ok button.

> ▶ `UIAlertActionStyle.Cancel`: An action that will cancel the current operation (usually
>   labeled Cancel).

▶ **UIAlertActionStyle.Destructive:** This button uses red text in its label and is displayed when there is the potential to lose data by completing the action (such as erasing a form, for example).

This first button displays the label Ok, does nothing when it is touched (handler: nil), and uses the default alert action style.

Lines 9–11 configure a second button, destroyAction, using the destructive style, another nil handler, and the label Erase My Device.

Lines 13–16 add a text field to the controller with the addTextFieldWithConfiguration Handler. This method accepts a closure as its parameter, which, in turn, accepts a single textField variable. The textfield is automatically initialized for us, we just need to adjust its attributes as we see fit (lines 14–15). Any UITextField variable properties can be set in this closure.

Lines 18–19 use the UIViewController method addAction to add the defaultAction and destroyAction buttons to the alert controller.

Finally, in line 21, the alertController object that we've lovingly crafted is displayed to the user using the UIViewController method presentViewController.

So, what exactly does this alert *do* if we were to try to use it? Absolutely nothing. It will display, show the text field and buttons that we configured, and then just go away as soon as we touch a button. That's exactly what we get if we set the handler parameter to nil when defining the alert's actions.

Assuming the goal is to actually *react* to the alert, we'll need to do a teensy bit more work.

Responding to an Action   When I constructed the alert example in Listing 10.1, I defined two actions, both with a handler of nil. I also took the time to write a sidebar explaining (well, trying to explain) how handlers are often defined as blocks of code called closures. Putting two and two together, how do you think we'll be able to react to the user touching one of the buttons? That's right, you've got it: by defining a handler closure for each action! (That was your guess, yes?)

By using closures with actions, we can define what happens when the user touches any of the UIAlertAction buttons that are added to a UIAlertController. Each action is independent, so we don't have to worry about figuring out which button was pressed and then write a big method to handle everything.

If the alert view is displaying text fields, we can access the fields through the alert controller's textFields variable property (an array of AnyObject), where textFields[0] is the first text field added to the controller, textFields[1] is the second, and so on.

For example, if I were to revise the `defaultAction` that I created in lines 5–7 of Listing 10.1 so that it would retrieve the contents of the alert's Email Address field, the code would look at bit like the fragment in Listing 10.2.

LISTING 10.2   Defining Handlers Within Alert Actions

```
1: let defaultAction = UIAlertAction(title: "Ok",
2:     style: UIAlertActionStyle.Default,
3:     handler: {(alertAction: UIAlertAction) in
4:         // The user touched 'Ok'
5:         let emailAddress: String = alertController.textFields![0].text!
6: })
```

Line 3 starts the handler and its closure. This is the code that will be executed when the user invokes the action by touching the Ok button. Line 5 sets a constant `emailAddress` to the text variable property of the first text field within the `alertController`'s `textFields` array. Note that we have to unwrap `textFields`, *and* its `text` variable property.

While the syntax may look ugly, it should be pretty clear what it does. (If it isn't, don't worry; we'll try it out ourselves in a few moments.)

Action Sheets

Alerts are used to display messages that indicate a change in state or a condition within an application that a user should acknowledge, but are other instances where a different solution would be better. For example, if an application provides the option to share information with a friend, the user might be prompted for the method of sharing (such as sending an email, uploading a file, and so on). In this case, the iOS-way of alerting the user to making this decision is by way of an *action sheet*.

You can see this behavior when touching and holding a story in the News app, as shown in Figure 10.2.

In previous editions of this book, I stated that implementing action sheets were *very* similar to alerts. That statement is now false. In fact, implementing action sheets is now *identical* to alerts— with the exception of not being able to use text fields within an action sheet.

For example, take a look at Listing 10.3.

LISTING 10.3   Implementing a UIActionSheet Class

```
1: let alertController = UIAlertController(title: "Do Something",
2:     message: "Please choose an action:",
3:     preferredStyle: UIAlertControllerStyle.ActionSheet)
4:
5: let defaultAction = UIAlertAction(title: "Send Memo",
```

```
 6:        style: UIAlertActionStyle.Default,
 7:        handler: {(alertAction: UIAlertAction!) in
 8:             // The user touched Send Memo
 9: })
10:
11: let destructiveAction = UIAlertAction(title: "Erase My Device",
12:        style: UIAlertActionStyle.Destructive,
13:        handler: {(alertAction: UIAlertAction!) in
14:             // The user wants us to erase the device. Oh well!
15: })
16:
17: let cancelAction = UIAlertAction(title: "Cancel",
18:        style: UIAlertActionStyle.Cancel,
19:        handler: nil)
20:
21: alertController.addAction(defaultAction)
22: alertController.addAction(destructiveAction)
23: alertController.addAction(cancelAction)
24:
25: presentViewController(alertController, animated: true, completion: nil)
```

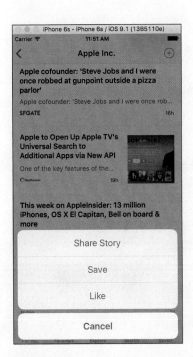

FIGURE 10.2
Action sheets ask you to choose between several options.

Lines 1–3 declare and instantiate an instance of `UIAlertController` called `alertContoller`. The setup of the controller is the same as with an alert, but we set the `preferredStyle` to `UIAlertControllerStyle.ActionSheet`.

Lines 5–9, 10–15, and 17–19 define three actions (buttons) that will be displayed by the controller. Remember, the `handler` for each action is where we can add code to react when the user touches the button. If the handler is set to `nil` (as in the case of the `cancel` action), touching the button simply dismisses the action sheet.

Lines 21–23 add the three actions to the alert controller, and line 25 presents the controller onscreen.

TIP
_____

Action sheet and alert styles are identical in how they are initialized, modified, and ultimately, acted upon. On some devices, however, an action sheet can be associated with an onscreen control—like a toolbar icon. This changes the onscreen appearance slightly, but doesn't affect how you create and populate the alert controller.

▼ TRY IT YOURSELF

Frustration in the Playground

The Playground is a great place to test things, but Apple, it seems, is still installing the Playground equipment. It would be great to test alerts in the playground, but in the current state, it only *barely* works. The problem with the Playground is that you don't have a view controller to play with. If you want one, you've got to programmatically create it—and by the time you've done that, you've pretty much written the application.

The Playground includes a module that gives us a kinda-sorta view controller that can display system-generated views like the alert view.

For example, create a new iOS Playground, then input the following code. This is exactly the same as the previous listing, with the addition of two new lines (bolded):

```
import UIKit
import XCPlayground

let alertController = UIAlertController(title: "Do Something",
    message: "Please choose an action:",
    preferredStyle: UIAlertControllerStyle.ActionSheet)

let defaultAction = UIAlertAction(title: "Send Memo",
    style: UIAlertActionStyle.Default,
    handler: {(alertAction: UIAlertAction!) in
        // The user touched Send Memo
})
```

```
let destructiveAction = UIAlertAction(title: "Erase My Device",
    style: UIAlertActionStyle.Destructive,
    handler: {(alertAction: UIAlertAction!) in
        // The user wants us to erase the device. Oh well!
})

let cancelAction = UIAlertAction(title: "Cancel",
    style: UIAlertActionStyle.Cancel,
    handler: nil)

alertController.addAction(defaultAction)
alertController.addAction(destructiveAction)
alertController.addAction(cancelAction)

XCPlaygroundPage.currentPage.liveView = alertController.view
```

The `import XCPlayground` line adds the module necessary to deal with dynamic views, like an alert. The last line's method `XCPlaygroundPage.currentPage.liveView` acts as our view controller. We use it to load the `view` variable property from the `alertController` and display it. It isn't displayed in a little pop-up window; however, it is shown in the assistant editor. Choose View, Assistant Editor, Show Assistant Editor. After a few seconds, you should see a somewhat cruddy visualization of the alert. Interestingly enough, once you've added the `XCPlaygroundPage.currentPage.liveView` line, you can access `alertController.view` (just add it on another line by itself, for example) by clicking the little "eye" or circle icons in the right-hand margin. This enables you to see the view directly in the main Playground editor (but only in code lines *after* `XCPlaygroundPage.currentPage.liveView`).

I fully expect the Playground will eventually handle things like this with ease, and it is certainly possible that I haven't yet found the magic recipe for displaying the alert view yet. Play around and see what you can make the Playground do. However, give it a bit of slack; the Playground equipment needs a bit more breaking in before we spend a lot of time there.

System Sound Services

Visual notifications are great for providing feedback to a user and getting critical input. Other senses, however, can prove just as useful for getting a user's attention. Sound, for example, plays an important role on nearly every computer system (regardless of platform or purpose). Sounds tell us when an error has occurred or an action has been completed. Sounds free a user's visual focus and still provide feedback about what an application is doing.

Vibrations take alerts one step further. When a device has the ability to vibrate, it can communicate with users even if they can't see or hear it. For the iPhone, vibration means that an app can notify users of events even when stowed in a pocket or resting on a nearby table. The best news of all? Both sounds and vibrations are handled through the same simple code, meaning that you can implement them relatively easily within your applications.

To enable sound playback and vibration, we take advantage of System Sound Services. System Sound Services provides an interface for playing back sounds that are 30 seconds or less in length. It supports a limited number of file formats (specifically CAF, AIF, and WAV files using PCM or IMA/ADPCM data). The functions provide no manipulation of the sound, nor control of the volume, so you do not want to use System Sound Services to create the soundtrack for your latest and greatest iOS game. In Hour 19, "Working with Rich Media," we explore additional media playback features of iOS.

iOS supports three different notifications using this API:

▶ **Sound:** A simple sound file is played back immediately. If the device is muted, the user hears nothing.

▶ **Alert:** Again, a sound file is played, but if the device is muted and set to vibrate, the user is alerted through vibration.

▶ **Vibrate:** The device is vibrated, regardless of any other settings.

Accessing Sound Services

To use System Sound Services from a project, you must add the AudioToolbox framework and any sound files you want to play. Because AudioToolbox is an Apple-provided framework and supports being imported as a module, we can prepare an application to use it by adding a single line to our code:

```
import AudioToolbox
```

Unlike most of the other development functionality discussed in this book, the System Sound Services functionality is not implemented as a class. Instead, you use more traditional C-style function calls to trigger playback.

To play audio, the two functions you use are `AudioServicesCreateSystemSoundID` and `AudioServicesPlaySystemSound`. You also need to declare a variable of the type `SystemSoundID`. This represents the sound file that we are working with. To get an idea of how it all comes together, look at Listing 10.4.

LISTING 10.4   Loading and Playing a Sound

```
1: var soundID: SystemSoundID = 0
2: let soundFile:String=NSBundle.mainBundle().pathForResource("mysound",ofType:"wav")!
3: let soundURL: NSURL = NSURL(fileURLWithPath: soundFile)
4: AudioServicesCreateSystemSoundID(soundURL, &soundID)
5: AudioServicesPlaySystemSound(soundID)
```

This might seem a bit alien after all the objects we've been using. Let's take a look at the functional pieces.

Line 1 starts things off by declaring a variable, soundID, that will be an iOS-generated integer that references the sound file we want to play. Next, in line 2, we declare and assign a string (soundFile) to the path of the sound file mysound.wav. This works by first using the NSBundle class method mainBundle to return an NSBundle object that corresponds to the directory containing the current application's executable binary. The NSBundle object's pathForResource:ofType method is then used to identify the specific sound file by name and extension.

Once we have the path as a String, we create an NSURL object from it in line 3. This is required for the AudioServicesCreateSystemSoundID function in line 4, which takes the location of the sound file as an NSURL object, along with a pointer to the soundID variable. The & denotes that we're sending a "pointer" to soundID rather than the value of soundID. The AudioServicesCreateSystemSoundID function's purpose is to update soundID with whatever magical integer references our sound on iOS.

After soundID has been properly set up, all that remains is playing it. Passing the soundID variable to the AudioServicesPlaySystemSound function, as shown in line 5, makes it happen.

Alert Sounds and Vibrations

The difference between an *alert sound* and a *system sound* is that an alert sound, if muted, automatically triggers a phone vibration. The setup and use of an alert sound is identical to a system sound. In fact, playing an alert is just a matter of substituting the function AudioServicesPlayAlertSound in place of AudioServicesPlaySystemSound.

Vibrations alone are even easier. To vibrate a compatible device (currently iPhones), you just provide the constant kSystemSoundID_Vibrate to AudioServicesPlaySystemSound:

```
AudioServicesPlaySystemSound(kSystemSoundID_Vibrate)
```

TIP
_____

The need to use UInt32() to convert the kSystemSoundID_Vibrate constant into something that AudioServicesPlaySystemSound can work with seems to be an oversight on Apple's part. I hope that in the future we can just use kSystemSoundID_Vibrate directly.

Now that you understand the different alert styles we have to work with, it's time to implement them for real. We'll test several variations of alerts, action sheets, and sounds in this hour's tutorial.

TIP

Attempting to vibrate a device without vibration capabilities (like an iPad) will fail silently. You can safely leave vibration code in your app regardless of the device you are targeting.

Exploring User Alert Methods

Because all the logic for implementing alerts, action sheets, or System Sound Services is contained in small, easy-to-understand chunks of code, this hour's project differs a bit from what you've seen in other hours. We treat this hour's project like a sandbox. We set it up, and then spend a good amount of time talking about the code that needs to be written to make it work, and we test it along the way.

You'll generate alerts, alerts with multiple buttons, alerts with fields, action sheet alerts, sounds, and even vibrate your device (if it's an iPhone, that is).

Implementation Overview

Unlike other projects where our UI design was intimately tied to the code, this tutorial's interface is rather inconsequential. We're simply interested in creating buttons to trigger actions that demonstrate the different alert methods and providing a single output area so we can see how the user responded. Everything to generate alerts, action sheets, sounds, and vibrations is handled entirely in code, so the sooner we get the framework set up for the project, the sooner we can get to the implementation logic.

Setting Up the Project

To practice using these alert classes and methods, we need to create a new project with buttons for activating the different styles of notifications. Open Xcode and create a new project based on the Single View Application template. Name the project **GettingAttention**.

Several resources that we need in this project aren't there by default, notably the sounds that we will be playing with System Sound Services. Let's add these important resources now.

Adding the Sound Resources

With your project open in Xcode, return to the Finder and navigate to the Sounds folder within this hour's project folder. Drag the folder into your Xcode project folder, choosing to copy the files and create groups when prompted.

You should now see the files listed in your project group, as shown in Figure 10.3.

Assets? Not Just Yet

Early in the book, I mentioned that as of iOS 9 you can use asset catalogs to hold any type of application resources you'd like—not just images. So, why not these sound files? The answer is that System Sound Services are not easily coerced into using asset catalogs. The AV tools we'll look at in Hour 19 *are*.

The big plus to using asset catalogs is that when your application resources are stored in an asset catalog, only the resources needed for your application to run on a specific device are delivered to that device. For system sounds and alerts, this really doesn't make much sense; they're needed on *all* devices. Don't assume that using an asset catalog is any better or worse than storing your resources outside of the catalog, in the main application.

Planning the Variables and Connections

The last step before we can create our GettingAttention application is to figure out what outlets and actions we need to fully test everything that we want. As mentioned earlier, this is a bare-bones app, nothing flashy. The only outlet we need is for a single label (`UILabel`) that provides some feedback to what the user has done. This will be named `userOutput`.

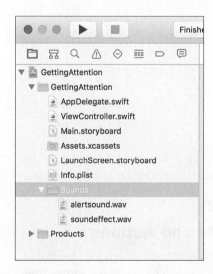

FIGURE 10.3
Add the sound files to your project.

In addition to the outlet, we need a total of seven different actions, all to be triggered by different buttons in the user interface: `doAlert`, `doMultiButtonAlert`, `doAlertInput`, `doActionSheet`, `doSound`, `doAlertSound`, and finally, `doVibration`.

That'll do it. Everything else is handled in code. Let's create the interface and make our connections.

Designing the Interface

Open the Main.storyboard file in Interface Builder (IB), select the view controller, then use the Attributes Inspector to set the simulated size to the device that you're using. This is, of course, optional, but it helps keep us focused on creating a quick and dirty UI rather than elegant design.

We need to add seven buttons and a text label to the empty view. You should be getting quite familiar with this process by now.

Add a button to the view by opening the Object Library (View Utilities, Show Object Library) and dragging a button (IUButton) to the View window. Add six more buttons using the library or by copying and pasting the first button.

Change the button labels to correspond to the different notification types that we'll be using. Specifically, name the buttons (top to bottom) as follows:

▶ **Alert Me!**

▶ **Alert with Buttons!**

▶ **I Need Input!**

▶ **Lights, Camera, Action Sheet**

▶ **Play Sound**

▶ **Play Alert Sound**

▶ **Vibrate Device**

Drag a label (UILabel) from the library to the bottom of the view. Remove the default label text and set the text to align center. The interface should resemble Figure 10.4. I've chosen to cluster my buttons based on their function. You can arrange yours however you want.

Creating and Connecting the Outlets and Actions

The interface itself is finished, but we still need to make the connection between the objects and our code. It's probably self-explanatory, but the connections you will be building are listed here.

First the outlet:

▶ **User Output Label (UILabel):** userOutput

And then the actions:

▶ **Alert Me! (UIButton):** doAlert

▶ **Alert with Buttons! (UIButton):** doMultiButtonAlert

- ▶ **I Need Input! (UIButton):** doAlertInput

- ▶ **Lights, Camera, Action Sheet (UIButton):** doActionSheet

- ▶ **Play Sound (UIButton):** doSound

- ▶ **Play Alert Sound (UIButton):** doAlertSound

- ▶ **Vibrate Device (UIButton):** doVibration

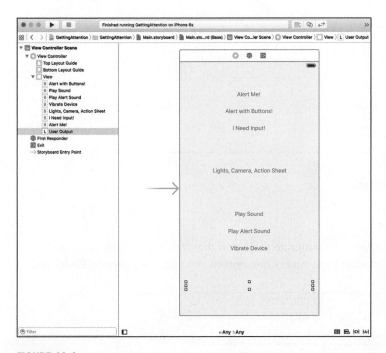

FIGURE 10.4
Create an interface with seven buttons and a label at the bottom.

With the Main.storyboard file selected, click the assistant editor button, and then hide the project navigator and document outline (Editor, Hide Document Outline) to make room for your connections. The ViewController.swift file should be visible to the right of your interface.

Adding the Outlet

Control-drag from our single lonely label to just below the class line in ViewController.swift. When prompted, choose to create a new outlet named **userOutput**, as shown in Figure 10.5.

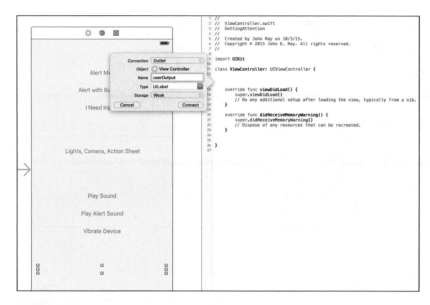

FIGURE 10.5
Connect the label to `userOutput`.

Adding the Actions

Now, Control-drag from the Alert Me! button to just below the `@IBOutlet` declaration in the ViewController.swift file, connecting to a new action named `doAlert`, as shown in Figure 10.6.

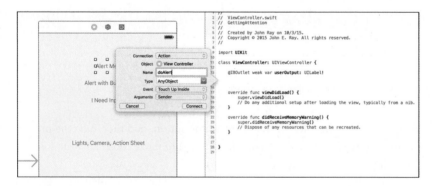

FIGURE 10.6
Connect each of the buttons to its corresponding action.

Repeat this for the other six buttons. Alert with Buttons! connects to `doMultiButtonAlert`; I Need Input! should connect to the `doAlertInput` method; Lights, Camera, Action Sheet to doActionSheet; Play Sound to doSound; Play Alert Sound to doAlertSound; and Vibrate Device to doVibration.

The framework for our test of notifications is finished, and we're ready to jump into code. Switch back to the standard editor and display the project navigator (Command-1). Open the ViewController.swift file; we start by implementing a simple alert-style dialog box.

Implementing Alerts

The simplest case of an alert that a user can encounter (and that a developer can develop) is an alert that is displayed and dismissed without changing the flow of the application at all. In other words, the alert is simply that: an alert. When the user presses the button to dismiss it, nothing else changes.

Edit ViewController.swift and enter the code shown in Listing 10.5 for the doAlert implementation.

LISTING 10.5   Implementing the doAlert Method

```
 1:  @IBAction func doAlert(sender: AnyObject) {
 2:      let alertController = UIAlertController(title: "Alert Me Button Selected",
 3:          message: "I need your attention NOW!",
 4:          preferredStyle: UIAlertControllerStyle.Alert)
 5:
 6:      let defaultAction = UIAlertAction(title: "Ok",
 7:          style: UIAlertActionStyle.Cancel,
 8:          handler: nil)
 9:
10:      alertController.addAction(defaultAction)
11:      presentViewController(alertController, animated: true, completion: nil)
12:  }
```

If you were paying attention at the start of this hour's lesson, this method should look familiar.

In lines 2–4, we declare and configure our instance of UIAlertController in a variable called alertController. The alert is initialized with a title (Alert Me Button Selected), a message (I need your attention NOW!), and a preferred style of Alert.

There is a single action, defaultAction, defined in lines 6–8. This creates a button with the title Ok, styled with UIAlertActionStyle.Cancel and a nil handler. Why the Cancel style? Because the purpose of the button is to just get rid of the alert; there is no handler to react to the action. You could also use the default style, but "cancel" just makes more sense to me.

Line 10 adds defaultAction to alertController, and line 11 displays it onscreen.

You can now run the project and test the first button, Alert Me!, Figure 10.7 shows the outcome of your first alert implementation.

FIGURE 10.7
In its simplest form, an alert view displays a message and button to dismiss it.

TIP

An alert doesn't have to be a single-use object. If you're going to be using an alert repeatedly, create a variable property for the alert controller, set it up when your view is loaded, and show it as needed.

Creating Multibutton Alerts

An alert with a single button is easy to implement because you do not have to program any additional logic. The user taps the button, the alert is dismissed, and execution continues as normal. In most cases, however, your application will display multiple button choices and react appropriately to whatever option the user chooses.

How difficult is this? Not at all. Each action that is added to an alert can include a handler closure to carry out specific tasks. Create actions, set handlers, add the actions to the alert controller—all done. To test this, write an updated multibutton version of the doAlert method within the doMultiButtonAlert method stub created earlier.

Listing 10.6 shows my implementation.

TIP

At most, an alert view can display five buttons (including the button designated as the cancel button) simultaneously. Attempting to add more may result in some unusual onscreen effects, such as display of clipped/partial buttons.

LISTING 10.6   Implementing the doMultipleButtonAlert Method

```
 1: @IBAction func doMultiButtonAlert(sender: AnyObject) {
 2:     let alertController = UIAlertController(title: "Alert with Buttons Selected",
 3:         message: "Options are good for people!",
 4:         preferredStyle: UIAlertControllerStyle.Alert)
 5:
 6:     let nowAction = UIAlertAction(title: "Do Something Now",
 7:         style: UIAlertActionStyle.Default,
 8:         handler: {(alertAction: UIAlertAction) in
 9:             self.userOutput.text="Pressed Now"
10:     })
11:
12:     let laterAction = UIAlertAction(title: "Do Something Later",
13:         style: UIAlertActionStyle.Default,
14:         handler: {(alertAction: UIAlertAction) in
15:             self.userOutput.text="Pressed Later"
16:     })
17:
18:     let cancelAction = UIAlertAction(title: "Never Do It",
19:         style: UIAlertActionStyle.Cancel,
20:         handler: {(alertAction: UIAlertAction) in
21:             self.userOutput.text="Pressed Never"
22:     })
23:
24:     alertController.addAction(nowAction)
25:     alertController.addAction(laterAction)
26:     alertController.addAction(cancelAction)
27:
28:     presentViewController(alertController, animated: true, completion: nil)
29: }
```

In this new implementation, three actions (buttons) are configured in lines 6–10, 12–16, and 18–22. Unlike the previous method, these actions all include a handler closure that sets the user-Output label to a message corresponding to the button pressed.

Notice that in each closure (lines 9, 15, and 21), I prefix the `userOutput` object with `self`. Closures act like independent isolated pieces of code and can't access variables and methods defined within your class without specifying `self`. If you happen to leave this off, Xcode will warn you of the error and offer to fix it for you.

Lines 24–26 add the actions to the alert controller, while line 28 displays it.

Give the application another test run. Pressing Alert with Buttons! should now open the alert view displayed in Figure 10.8.

FIGURE 10.8
The alert view now includes a total of three buttons.

Try touching one of the alert buttons. The alert view is dismissed, but, more important, the text in the `userOutput` label is set to a message identifying the button.

CAUTION

Always Active

Don't assume that application processing stops when the alert window is on the screen. Your code continues to execute after you show the alert.

Using Fields in Alerts

Although buttons can be used to generate user input from an alert, you might have noticed that some applications actually present text fields within an alert box. The App Store, for example, prompts for your Apple ID password before it starts downloading a new app.

To add fields to your alert dialogs, you use the alert controller's addTextFieldWithConfigurationHandler. The text field is added and can be configured using any of the variable properties supported by the UITextField class.

As an example, let's create an email entry alert that collects an email address, then displays it when the alert's button is touched. Update the doAlertInput method stub with the implementation shown in Listing 10.7.

LISTING 10.7 The doAlertInput Implementation

```
 1: @IBAction func doAlertInput(sender: AnyObject) {
 2:     let alertController = UIAlertController(title: "Email Address",
 3:         message: "Please enter your email address below:",
 4:         preferredStyle: UIAlertControllerStyle.Alert)
 5:
 6:alertController.addTextFieldWithConfigurationHandler({(textField: UITextField) in
 7:         textField.placeholder="Email Address"
 8:         textField.keyboardType=UIKeyboardType.EmailAddress
 9:     })
10:
11:     let defaultAction = UIAlertAction(title: "Ok",
12:         style: UIAlertActionStyle.Default,
13:         handler: {(alertAction: UIAlertAction) in
14:             let emailAddress: String = alertController.textFields![0].text!
15:             self.userOutput.text="Entered '\(emailAddress)'"
16:     })
17:
18:     alertController.addAction(defaultAction)
19:     presentViewController(alertController, animated: true, completion: nil)
20: }
```

The text field is added in lines 6–9. Note that the UITextField variable properties placeholder and keyboardType are used to configure the appearance of the field. You might also consider using the secureTextEntry Boolean variable to make the field appear as a password entry.

Lines 11–16 create an action, defaultAction, with a handler that updates the userOutput text to show the email address the user entered. As described earlier this hour, the text field is accessed from the `alertController` object's `textFields` array. This array is created for us automatically each time we add a text field to an alert.

Line 18 adds the `defaultAction` to the alert controller. Line 19 displays the alert controller.

Run the application and touch the I Need Input! button. You should see the alert, as demonstrated in Figure 10.9. Enter an email address and touch Ok; the address is retrieved from the alert and displayed in the output label.

FIGURE 10.9
The alert view now displays a plain-text entry field.

Implementing Action Sheets

Now that you've implemented several types of alerts, action sheets will pose no difficulty at all. The setup and handling of an action sheet is more straightforward than an alert view because action sheets can do one thing and only one thing: show a list of actions (buttons).

TIP

Action sheets can take up to seven buttons on a 3.5-inch iPhone (including "cancel" and the "destructive" button) while maintaining a standard layout. If you exceed seven, however, the display automatically changes into a scrolling list. This gives you room to add as many options as you need.

To create our action sheet, we'll implement the method stub doActionSheet created within the ViewController.swift file. Recall that this method is triggered by pushing the Lights, Camera, Action Sheet button. It displays the title Available Actions and has a cancel button named Cancel, a destructive button named Destroy, and two other buttons named Negotiate and Compromise.

Add the code in Listing 10.8 to the doActionSheet method.

LISTING 10.8   Implementing the doActionSheet Method

```
 1: @IBAction func doActionSheet(sender: AnyObject) {
 2:     let alertController = UIAlertController(title: "Available Actions",
 3:         message: "Choose something from this list",
 4:         preferredStyle: UIAlertControllerStyle.ActionSheet)
 5:
 6:     let negotiateAction = UIAlertAction(title: "Negotiate",
 7:         style: UIAlertActionStyle.Default,
 8:         handler: {(alertAction: UIAlertAction) in
 9:             self.userOutput.text="Pressed Negotiate"
10:     })
11:
12:     let compromiseAction = UIAlertAction(title: "Compromise",
13:         style: UIAlertActionStyle.Default,
14:         handler: {(alertAction: UIAlertAction) in
15:             self.userOutput.text="Pressed Compromise"
16:     })
17:
18:     let destroyAction = UIAlertAction(title: "Destroy",
19:         style: UIAlertActionStyle.Destructive,
20:         handler: {(alertAction: UIAlertAction) in
21:             self.userOutput.text="Pressed Destroy"
22:     })
23:
24:     let cancelAction = UIAlertAction(title: "Cancel",
25:         style: UIAlertActionStyle.Cancel,
26:         handler: {(alertAction: UIAlertAction) in
27:             self.userOutput.text="Pressed Cancel"
28:     })
29:
30:     alertController.addAction(negotiateAction)
31:     alertController.addAction(compromiseAction)
32:     alertController.addAction(destroyAction)
33:     alertController.addAction(cancelAction)
34:
35:
36:     if (alertController.popoverPresentationController != nil) {
37:         alertController.popoverPresentationController!.sourceView =
```

```
38:               sender as! UIButton
39:         alertController.popoverPresentationController!.sourceRect =
40:             (sender as! UIButton).bounds
41:     }
42:
43:     presentViewController(alertController, animated: true, completion: nil)
44: }
```

Lines 2–4 instantiate a new instance of `UIAlertController`—the same are our other methods—but this time, using the preferred style of `UIAlertControllerStyle.ActionSheet`.

The rest of the code should look exactly like what you've already seen this hour—with one major exception (lines 36–41). To understand why these lines are necessary, we have to know a bit about the action sheets and the iPad.

On the iPad, action sheets should not be displayed directly on top of a view. The Apple UI guidelines say that they must be displayed within a popover. A *popover* is a unique UI element that appears when an onscreen item is touched and usually disappears when you touch somewhere on the background. Popovers also incorporate a small arrow that points toward the UI element that invoked them. You learn more about popovers in the next hour's lesson.

When we create an action sheet on an iPad, iOS automatically configures a popover controller for us and stores it in the alert controller's variable property `popoverPresentation Controller`. For the popover controller to *work*, however, we need to set two variable properties of the popover controller: `sourceView` (the view that the popover is originating from) and `sourceRect` (a rectangle defining the area that the popover should point to). Aren't these the same thing? Yep. Apple's documentation even states we need one or the other. But unless both are set, the popover doesn't work. Lines 37–38 set the `sourceView` to the button that was touched, whereas lines 39–40 set the `sourceRect` to the bounds of the same button.

On devices that *aren't* an iPad, the `popoverPresentationController` is set to `nil`, so these configuration lines aren't executed. The result? When running on the iPad, the action sheet appears in a popover. When running on an iPhone, the action sheet is shown in exactly the same manner we'd expect.

Run the application and touch the Lights, Camera, Action Sheet button to see the results. Figure 10.10 demonstrates the display.

NOTE

In a Popover? No Canceling!

When iOS is displaying an action sheet within a popover, it automatically removes the `Cancel`-styled action from the sheet. On devices that support popovers, the interface convention for "canceling" a popover is to touch outside of the popover display—in other words, no separate action is needed.

FIGURE 10.10
Action sheets can include cancel and destructive buttons, as well as buttons for other options.

Implementing Alert Sounds and Vibrations

Recall that to use System Sound Services from a project, you need the AudioToolbox framework and any sound files you want to play. Because we already included the sound resources, we just need to add the framework. To import the AudioToolbox framework and make our code aware of its existence, add an `import` line to ViewController.swift. Insert this line immediately following the existing `import` directive:

```
import AudioToolbox
```

We're now ready to play sounds and vibrate the device. Very little changes from the example code that we covered earlier this hour.

Playing System Sounds

The first thing that we want to implement is the `doSound` method for playing system sounds. These are short sounds that, when muted, will *not* result in an accompanying vibration. The Sounds folder that you added to the project during the setup contains a file soundeffect.wav that we will use to implement system sound playback.

Edit the ViewController.swift implementation file and complete `doSound`, as shown in Listing 10.9.

LISTING 10.9   Implementing the doSound Method

```
1: @IBAction func doSound(sender: AnyObject) {
2:     var soundID: SystemSoundID = 0
3:     let soundFile: String = NSBundle.mainBundle().pathForResource("soundeffect",
4:         ofType: "wav")!
5:     let soundURL: NSURL = NSURL(fileURLWithPath: soundFile)
6:     AudioServicesCreateSystemSoundID(soundURL, &soundID)
7:     AudioServicesPlaySystemSound(soundID)
8: }
```

Line 2 declares soundID, a variable that refers to the sound file.

In lines 3–4, we declare and assign a string (soundFile) to the path of the sound file sound-effect.wav. Line 5 turns that string into an NSURL named soundURL.

In line 6, we use the AudioServicesCreateSystemSoundID function to create a SystemSoundID that represents the sound file.

Line 7 uses the AudioServicesPlaySystemSound function to play the sound.

Run and test the application. Pressing the Play Sound button should now play back the sound effect WAV file.

Playing Alert Sounds with Vibrations

As mentioned earlier this hour, the difference between an alert sound and a system sound is that an alert sound, if muted, automatically triggers a vibration. The setup and use of an alert sound is identical to a system sound. In fact, to implement the doAlertSound method stub in GettingAttentionViewController.swift, use the same code as the doSound method in Listing 10.13, substituting the sound file alertsound.wav and using the function AudioServicesPlayAlertSound rather than AudioServicesPlaySystemSound:

```
AudioServicesPlayAlertSound(soundID)
```

After implementing the new method, run and test the application. Pressing the Play Alert Sound button plays the sound, and muting an iPhone causes the device to vibrate when the button is pressed.

Vibrating the Device

For our grand finale, we implement the final method in our GettingAttention application: do-Vibration. As you've already learned, the same System Sound Services that enabled us to play sounds and alert sounds also create vibrations. The magic we need here is the kSystemSoundID_Vibrate constant. When this value is substituted for the SystemSoundID and AudioServicesPlaySystemSound is called, the device vibrates. It's as simple as that! Implement the doVibration method, as shown in Listing 10.10.

LISTING 10.10   Implementing the doVibration Method

```
@IBAction func doVibration(sender: AnyObject) {
    AudioServicesPlaySystemSound(kSystemSoundID_Vibrate)
}
```

That's all there is to it. You've now explored seven different ways of getting a user's attention. These are techniques that you can use in any application to make sure that your user is alerted to changes that may require interaction and can respond if needed.

Further Exploration

Your next step in making use of the notification methods discussed in this hour is to use them. These simple, but important, UI elements will help facilitate many of your critical user interactions. One topic that is beyond the scope of this book is the ability for a developer to push notifications to an iDevice.

Even without push notifications, you might want to add numeric badges to your applications. These badges are visible when the application isn't running and can display any integer you want—most often, a count of items identified as "new" within the application (such as new news items, messages, events, and so on). To create application badges, look at the UIApplication variable property applicationIconBadgeNumber. Setting this to anything other than 0 will create and display the badge.

Another area that you might like to explore is how to work with rich media (Hour 19). The audio playback functions discussed in this hour are intended for alert-type sounds only. If you're looking for more complete multimedia features, you need to tap into the AVFoundation framework, which gives you complete control over recording and playback features of iOS.

Finally, this hour covered notifications that occur when your application is running. For information about generating notifications when your app is stopped, check out Hour 22.

Summary

In this hour, you learned about two types of modal dialogs that can be used to communicate information to an application user and to enable the user to provide input at critical points in time. Alerts and action sheets have different appearances and uses but very similar implementations. Unlike many of the UI components we've used in this book, you cannot instantiate these with a simple drag and drop in IB.

We also explored two nonvisual means of communicating with a user: sounds and vibrations. Using the System Sound Services (by way of the AudioToolbox framework), you can easily add short sound effects and vibrate your iDevice. Again, you have to implement these in code, but in fewer than five lines, you can have your applications making noises and buzzing in your users' hands.

Q&A

Q. Can sounds be used in conjunction with alert views?

A. Yes. Because alerts are often displayed without warning, there is no guarantee that the user is looking at the screen. Using an alert sound provides the best chance for getting the user's attention, either through an audible noise or an automatic vibration if the user's sound is muted.

Q. Why don't popovers work on the iPhone?

A. As of iOS 8 and later, they do! That said, alert sheets, however, are still expected to be displayed in a certain way on both iPhone and iPad platforms. In other words, in this case, Apple has determined a UI standard that will automatically be enforced. It doesn't mean that popovers are impossible on an iPhone; it just means that in this particular case (action sheets), they'll only work on the iPad.

Workshop

Quiz

1. Both alerts and action sheets require the use of which of the following?

    a. `UISheetController`

    b. `UIDialogController`

    c. `UIActionController`

    d. `UIAlertController`

2. Buttons in an alert or an action sheet correspond to which of the following?

    a. `UIButtonAction`

    b. `UIAlertAction`

    c. `UIAlertObject`

    d. `UIAlertButton`

3. To create a vibration, you can use which of the following?

    a. The `NSVibrateDevice` class

    b. A specially recorded sound file

    c. The `kSystemSoundID_Vibrate` constant

    d. The `SystemSoundVibrate()` method

4. Handlers are often provided in what form?

    a. Structure

    b. Block

    c. Closet

    d. Closure

5. What type of button is styled with red in an alert or action sheet?

    a. Cancel

    b. Default

    c. Destructive

    d. Erasure

6. After you've created an alert controller and configured it, you can display it with what method?

    a. `presentViewController`

    b. `showViewController`

    c. `displayViewController`

    d. `useViewController`

7. System Sound Services don't play audio files directly. Instead, they require the use of what?

    a. A sound ID

    b. A sound path

    c. A waveform

    d. A sound descriptor

8. Alert controllers can display what to types of styles?

    a. Alerts, warnings

    b. Cautions, action sheets

    c. Alerts, action sheets

    d. Inputs, cautions

9. On some devices (just the iPad at the time of this writing), action sheets should be displayed with a what?

   a. `popoverController`

   b. `popoverPresentationController`

   c. `presentationController`

   d. `presentationPopoverController`

10. If you don't want an alert action to do anything but dismiss the alert, what should you set the handler to?

    a. `AnyObject`

    b. `null`

    c. `nill`

    d. `nil`

Answers

1. D. Alert controllers (`UIAlertController`) are required when creating alerts and action sheets.

2. B. Define `UIAlertActions` to add functionality (and buttons!) to your alerts.

3. C. You can use the vibration constant (`kSystemSoundID_Vibrate`) along with System Sound Services to quickly "play" a vibration.

4. D. Handlers are often implemented using a closure.

5. C. Destructive buttons are highlighted in red and should be used with any action that may result in data loss.

6. A. Use the `presentViewController` method to display alert controllers after they've been configured.

7. A. You must create a sound ID from an `NSURL` before you can play a sound resource.

8. C. Alerts and action sheets are the two visual styles currently available in the alert controller (`UIAlertController`).

9. B. When displaying an action sheet on the iPad, a `popoverPresentationController` is automatically created and should be used to display the sheet.

10. D. Use `nil` to set a handler that does nothing but dismiss the alert controller.

Activities

1. Practice adding text fields to a few alert controllers. Use a two-field alert to create a user-name and password dialog box.

2. Return to one or more of your earlier projects and add audio cues to the interface actions. Make switches click, buttons bing, and so on. Keep your sounds short, clear, and complementary to the actions that the users are performing.

Implementing Multiple Scenes and Popovers

What You'll Learn in This Hour:

▶ How to create multiple scenes in the storyboard

▶ The use of segues to transition between scenes

▶ Ways to transfer data between scenes

▶ How to present and use popovers

This hour marks a major milestone in your iOS app development capabilities. In the preceding hour's lesson, you learned about alert views and action sheets. These were the first user interface (UI) elements we've explored that act as (somewhat) independent views that a user interacts with. You've also seen how to hide and show views, making it possible to customize your user interface. All of these, however, took place within a single scene. That means that no matter how much was going on onscreen, we used a single view controller and a single initial view to deal with it. In this hour, we break through those limits and introduce the ability to create applications with multiple scenes—in other words, multiple view controllers and multiple views.

In this lesson, you learn how to create new scenes and the new view controller classes you need to back them up. You also learn how to visually define your transitions between scenes and trigger them automatically, or programmatically. In addition, you will explore the use of popovers to present information within a pseudo "window" on the display.

Before we begin, I want to add a disclaimer: In this hour, you learn several different ways to accomplish the same thing. Apple changes iOS often, and despite their somewhat elegant software development kit (SDK), you will encounter inconsistencies. The takeaway is that you should do what you feel comfortable with. There are plenty of "clever" solutions to problems that result in code that, although correct, is never going to make sense to anyone but the person who wrote it.

Introducing Multiscene Storyboards

We've been able to build apps that do quite a few things using a single view, but many don't lend themselves to a single-view approach. It's rare to download an app that doesn't have configuration screens, help screens, or other displays of information that go beyond the initial view that is loaded at runtime.

To use features like these in your apps, you need to create multiple scenes in your storyboard file. Recall that a scene is defined by the presence of a view controller and a view. You've been building entire applications in one view with one view controller for the past six hours. Imagine how much functionality you could introduce with unlimited scenes (views and view controllers). With the iOS project storyboard, that's exactly what you can do.

Not only that, but you can literally "draw" the connections between different scenes. Want to display an information screen if the user touches a Help button? Just drag from your button to a new scene. It "just works." Figure 11.1 shows a multiscene application design with segues.

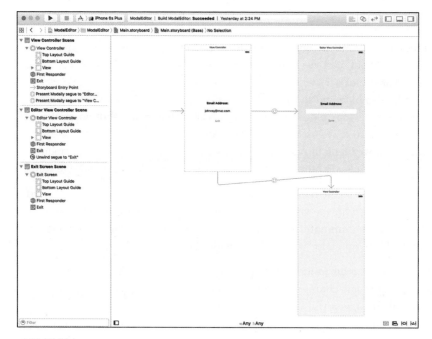

FIGURE 11.1
A multiscene application design.

The Terminology

Before we head into multiscene development, we should introduce/review a few pieces of terminology, several of which you've learned previously but may not have really had to think about until now:

▶ **View controller:** A class that manages the user's interactions with his iDevice. In many of the tutorials in this book, single-view controllers are used for most of the application logic, but other types exist (and are used in the coming hours).

▶ **View:** The visual layout that a user sees onscreen. You've been building views in view controllers for quite awhile now.

▶ **Scene:** A unique combination of view controller and view. Imagine you're building an image-editing application. You may choose to develop scenes for selecting files to edit, another scene for implementing the editor, another for applying filters, and so on.

▶ **Segue:** A segue is a transition between scenes, often with a visual transition effect applied. There are multiple types of segues available depending on the type of view controller you're using.

▶ **Exit:** The Exit icon appears in each scene in your storyboard. The exit can be used to transition *back to* a previous scene. If you display four scenes in sequence, for example, and want to move from the fourth back to the first, you would use the first scene's exit.

▶ **Unwind:** The process of moving back to an earlier scene by way of the exit. This is considered an "unwind" segue.

▶ **Modal views:** A modal view is one that is displayed over top of an original view when user interactions are required. You will mostly be using modal views (by way of the modal segue type) in this book.

▶ **Relationship:** A "segue" of sorts for certain types of view controllers, such as the tab bar controller. Relationships are created between buttons on a master tab bar that display independent scenes when touched. You learn about these in Hour 13, "Advanced Storyboards Using Navigation and Tab Bar Controllers."

▶ **Storyboard:** The file that contains the scene, segue, and relationship definitions for your project.

You must create new class files to support the requirement for multiple view controllers; so, if you need a quick refresher on adding new files to Xcode, refer to Hour 2, "Introduction to Xcode and the iOS Simulator." Other than that, the only prerequisite is the ability to Control-drag, something you should be very good at by now.

A Different Perspective

I've just described what the different pieces are that you need to know to create a multiscene application, but this doesn't necessarily help you conceptualize what Apple's "storyboarding" concept is going for.

Think of it this way: A storyboard provides an area where you can sketch out, visually, your application's visual design and workflow. Each scene is a different screen that your user will encounter. Each segue is a transition between scenes. If you're the type of person who thinks visually, you'll find that, with a little practice, you can go from a paper sketch of an application's operation and design to a working prototype in the Xcode storyboard very, very quickly.

Preparing a Multiscene Project

To create an application with multiple scenes and segues, you must first know how to add new view controller and view pairings to your project. For each of these, you also need supporting class files where you can code up the logic for your additional scenes. To give you a better idea of how this works, let's use a typical Single View Application template as a starting point.

As you're well aware, the Single View Application template has a single view controller and a single view (in other words, a single scene). This doesn't mean, however, that we're stuck with that configuration. You can expand a single view application to support as many scenes as you want; it just provides us with a convenient starting point.

Adding Additional Scenes to a Storyboard

To add a new scene to a storyboard, open the storyboard file (Main.storyboard) in the Interface Builder (IB) editor. Next, make sure that the Object Library (Control-Option-Command-3) is open and type **view controller** in the Search field to show the view controller objects that are available, as shown in Figure 11.2.

Next, drag the view controller into an empty portion of IB editor area. The view controller will add itself, with a corresponding view, to your storyboard, and just like that, you'll have a new scene, as shown in Figure 11.3. You can drag the new view around in the storyboard editor to position it somewhere convenient. By default, the new view controller's simulated size will *not* be set. Once you connect it to another view via a segue, however, it automatically inherits that view's simulated size.

NOTE

If you find it difficult to grab and drag the new view around in the editor, use the object dock above it. It provides a convenient handle for moving the object around.

Add a View Controller

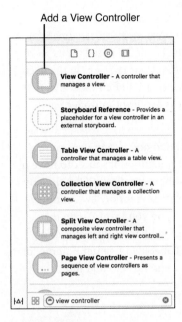

FIGURE 11.2
Find the view controller objects in the Object Library.

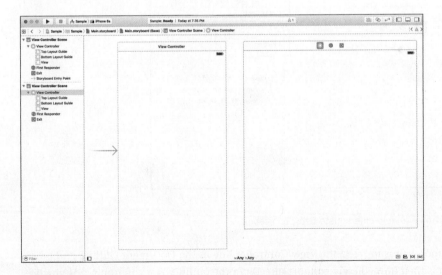

FIGURE 11.3
Adding a new view controller/view creates a new scene.

Naming Scenes

After adding a new scene, you'll notice there's a bit of a problem brewing in the document out-line area (Editor, Show Document Outline). By default, each scene is named based on its view controller class. We've been using a view controller class called `ViewController`, so the docu-ment outline shows the default scene as View Controller Scene. Once we add a new scene, it doesn't have a view controller class assigned yet, so it also appears as View Controller Scene. Add another, and that scene also appears as View Controller Scene (and so on).

To deal with the ambiguity, you have two options: First, you can add and assign view control-ler classes to the new scenes. We're going to do this anyway, but sometimes it's nicer to have a plain English name for a scene that can be anything we want without it reflecting the underly-ing code. ("John's Awesome Image Editor Scene" makes a horrible name for a view controller class.) The second option is to label a scene using any arbitrary string you want. To do this, select its view controller in the document outline, and then open the Identity Inspector and expand the Document section, as shown in Figure 11.4. Use the Label field to enter a name for the scene. Xcode automatically tacks *Scene* onto the end, so there's no need to add that.

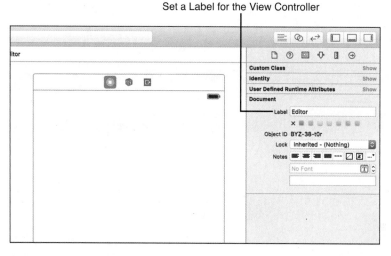

FIGURE 11.4
Label the view controller to help differentiate between scenes.

An even faster approach is to select the View Controller line in the Document Outline and press Return; the item is then immediately editable directly in the outline. You can apply this practice to the view controller to set the scene name, or to any objects within the scene to set easy-to-understand labels.

Adding Supporting View Controller Subclasses

After establishing the new scenes in your storyboard, you need to couple them to actual code. In the Single View Application template, the initial view's view controller is already configured to be an instance of the `ViewController` class—implemented by editing the ViewController.swift file. We need to create similar files to support any new scenes we add.

NOTE
_____

If you're just adding a scene that displays static content (such as a Help or About page), you don't need to add a custom subclass. You can use the default class assigned to the scene, `UIViewController`, but you won't be able to add any interactivity.
_____

To add a new subclass of `UIViewController` to your project, make sure that the project navigator is visible (Command-1), and then click the + icon at the bottom-left corner of the window and select File. When prompted, choose iOS, the Source category, then Cocoa Touch Class, and click Next. Now, select a subclass of `UIViewController`, as shown in Figure 11.5. You'll also be asked to name your class. Name it something that differentiates it from other view controllers in your project. EditorViewController is better than ViewControllerTwo, for example. Make sure that Language is set to Swift, and then click Next.

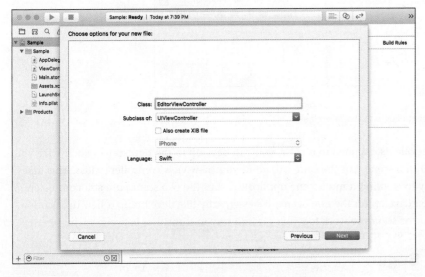

FIGURE 11.5
Choose the `UIViewController` subclass.

Finally, you're prompted for where to save your new class. Use the group pop-up menu at the bottom of the dialog to choose your main project code group, and then click Create. Your new class is added to the project and ready for coding, but it still isn't connected to the scene you defined.

To associate a scene's view controller with the `UIViewController` subclass, shift your attention back to the IB editor. Within the document outline, select the view controller line for the new scene, and then open the Identity Inspector (Option-Command-3). In the Custom Class section, use the drop-down menu to select the name of the class you just created (such as `EditorViewController`), as shown in Figure 11.6.

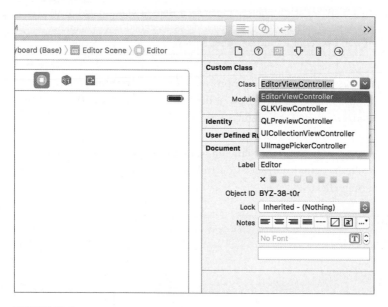

FIGURE 11.6
Associate the view controller with the new class.

After the view controller is assigned to a class, you can develop in the new scene exactly like you developed in the initial scene, but the code will go in your new view controller's class. This takes us most of the way to creating a multiscene application, but the two scenes are still completely independent. If you develop for the new scene, it's essentially like developing a new application; there is no way for the scenes to work together and no way to transition between them.

Creating a Segue

Creating a segue between scenes uses the same Control-drag mechanism that you have (hopefully) become very fond of over the first half of this book. For example, consider a two-scene storyboard where you want to add a button to the initial scene that, when clicked, will transition to the second scene. To create this segue, you Control-drag from the button to the second scene's view controller (targeting either the visual representation of the scene itself, or the view controller line in the document outline), as shown in Figure 11.7.

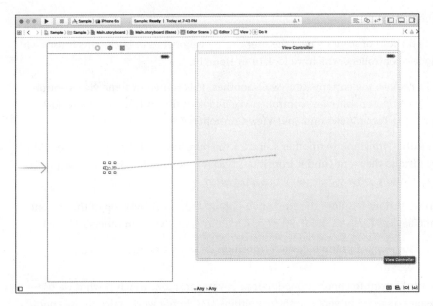

FIGURE 11.7
Control-drag from the object to the new scene's view controller.

When you release your mouse button, a Storyboard Segues box appears, as shown in Figure 11.8. Here you can choose the type of segue that you're creating, most likely Present Modally or Popover Presentation.

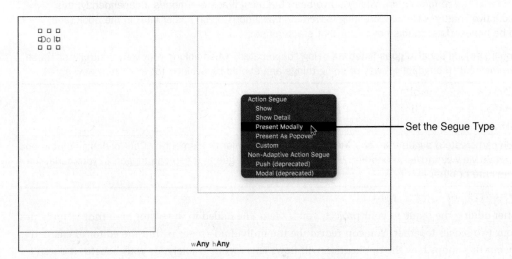

FIGURE 11.8
Choose the segue type to create.

A total of five options appear:

▶ **Show:** Create a chain of scenes where the user can move forward or back. This is used with navigation view controllers, which we look at in Hour 13.

▶ **Show Detail:** Replace the current scene with another. This is used in some view controllers, such as the popular split-view controller. We'll look at this in Hour 14, "Navigating Information Using Table Views and Split View Controllers."

▶ **Present Modally:** Transition to another scene for the purposes of completing a task. When finished, we dismiss the scene, and it transitions back to the original view. This or the Popover Presentation is the segue you'll use most often.

▶ **Popover Presentation:** Displays the scene in a pop-up "window" over top of the current view on some devices (such as the iPad) or as a sliding modal view on others (iPhone).

▶ **Custom:** Used for programming a custom transition between scenes.

For most projects, you'll want to choose a modal or popover transition, which is what we use here. The other segues are used in very specific conditions and do not work unless those conditions are met. If that piques your interest, good; you'll see more of these over the next few hours.

NOTE

Adaptive Segues

The segues listed here are known as *adaptive segues*. That means that they'll adapt to whatever platform they're running on. While you've been targeting iPads or iPhones independently, this "adaptive" nature will make creating universal applications much easier later in the book (and, to be honest, later in this hour—but that's a surprise).

You'll see additional segues listed as being "deprecated" when linking your view controllers. These are the "old" (nonadaptive) way of doing things and should be avoided for your shiny new apps.

TIP

You can create a segue that isn't attached to any particular UI element by Control-dragging from one scene's view controller to another. Doing so creates a segue that you can trigger, in your code, from a gesture or other event.

After adding the segue to your project, you'll see a line added to the editor area that visually ties your two scenes together. You can rearrange the individual scenes within the editor to create a layout that maps how the application will flow. This layout is solely for your benefit; it doesn't change how the application will operate.

You'll also notice a representation of it in your document outline. The scene that is initiating a segue will show a new line "<Segue name> to <destination>" in the outline. Selecting the segue line gives us the opportunity to configure an identifier (seen in Figure 11.9) and several other settings.

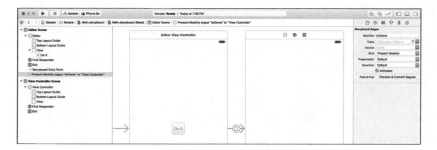

FIGURE 11.9
Set an identifier or change the type of segue being used.

The identifier is an arbitrary string that you can use to trigger a segue manually or identify which segue is underway programmatically (if you have multiple segues configured). Even if you don't plan to use multiple segues, it's a good idea to name this something meaningful (toEditor, toGameView, and so on).

The Segue drop-down appears on any segue you've added and enables you to switch between segue types at will. Depending on the type of segue you've chosen, you'll have a few additional options to set. Let's start with the most common type: modal segues.

Configuring Modal Segues

Modal segues offer many different settings for controlling the appearance of the destination view controller as it is displayed on the screen. When viewing a modally presented segue in the Attributes Inspector, you'll see two drop-downs—presentation and transition, visible in Figure 11.10. These options can dramatically alter how your scenes appear to the user.

As mentioned earlier, segues adapt to the device the application is running on. At present, most of the presentation settings will only result in a display difference on the iPad. The iPad has more screen real estate than an iPhone, so it can do things a little differently. You have four presentation style options:

▶ **Full Screen:** Sizes the view so that it covers the full screen.

▶ **Current Context:** Uses the same style display as the scene that is displaying it.

▶ **Page Sheet:** Sizes the scene so that it is presented in the portrait format.

▶ **Form Sheet:** Sizes the scene smaller than the screen (regardless of orientation), showing the original scene behind it. This, for all intents and purposes, is the equivalent of a
window.

FIGURE 11.10
Configure each segue you add.

The transition type is a visual animation that is played as iOS moves from one scene to another.
You have four options here (as shown in Figure 11.10):

▶ **Cover Vertical:** The new scene slides up over the old scene.

▶ **Flip Horizontal:** The view flips around horizontally, revealing the new scene on
the "back."

▶ **Cross Dissolve:** The old scene fades out while the new scene fades in.

▶ **Partial Curl:** The old scene curls up like a piece of paper, revealing the new scene
underneath.

CAUTION

Choose Your Styles Carefully!

Not all styles are compatible with all transitions. A page curl, for example, can't take place on a form sheet that doesn't completely fill the screen. Attempting to use an incompatible combination will result in a crash. So if you've chosen a bad pair, you'll find out pretty quickly (or you could review the documentation for the transition/style you plan to use).

The default transition—cover vertical—presents the new view by sliding it up over the initial view. This is perfectly acceptable, but I encourage you to try the other transitions for some nifty interactive effects. The partial curl, for example, can be moved with a finger to reveal more content, as demonstrated in Figure 11.11.

FIGURE 11.11
Modally presented segues offer a wide range of appearance options.

Configuring the Popover Segue

Popovers are variation on modal segues that display content on top of an existing view, with a small indicator that points to an onscreen object, such as a button, to provide context. Popovers are everywhere in the iPad interface, from Mail to Safari, as demonstrated in Figure 11.12.

FIGURE 11.12
Popovers are everywhere in the iPad UI.

Using a popover enables you to display new information to your users without leaving the screen you are on, and to hide the information when the user is done with it. There are few desktop counterparts to popovers, but they are roughly analogous to tool palettes, inspector panels, and configuration dialogs. In other words, they provide UIs for interacting with content on the screen, but without eating up permanent space in your UI.

What makes a popover different from a modally presented view is that it also requires an additional controller object, a popover controller (`UIPopoverPresentationController`). The controller determines the source view of the popover and where it points. When the user is done with the popover, touching outside of its visible rectangle automatically closes the view.

Preparing Popovers

To create a popover, follow the *exact* same steps as when creating a modally presented segue. Control-drag from the element you want to display a popover to the view controller providing the popover content. When prompted for the type of storyboard segue, as shown in Figure 11.13, choose Popover Presentation.

What makes the popover presentation attractive for *any* project is that when you create a popover segue and deploy it to the iPhone, it will be presented as a modally presented segue. The adaptive nature of iOS segues mean that the proper interface conventions are followed regardless of the platform. When will this come in handy? When you begin creating applications that run on both iPhones and iPads—which (hint hint) might be sooner than you think.

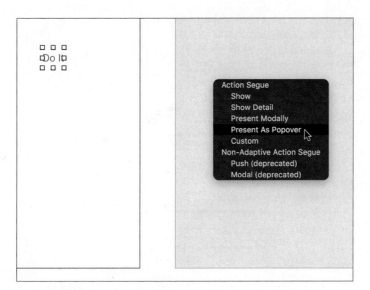

FIGURE 11.13
Set the segue type to Popover Presentation.

Setting the Popover Size

The default view associated with a new iPad scene is the same size as the main application interface. When you are displaying a popover, however, the scene needs to be *much* smaller. Apple
allows popovers up to 600 points wide, but recommends that they be kept to 320 points or less.
To set the size of the popover, select the view *within* the popover view controller, and open the
Size Inspector (Option-Command-5). Use the Width and Height fields to enter a size for the popover. After you set the size of the view, the scene's visual representation in the IB editor changes
to the appropriate size, as shown in Figure 11.14. This makes building the content view much
easier.

CAUTION

Can't Set Your Popover Size?

If you find yourself looking at a dimmed-out size setting for the popover view, you probably haven't
yet created the popover segue. It isn't until Xcode "knows" that you're adding a popover scene that
it unlocks the size settings.

Configuring the Presentation Directions and Passthrough Views

After setting the popover's size, you want to configure a few attributes on the segue itself. Select
the popover segue within the initiating scene, and then open the Attributes Inspector (Option-
Command-4), as shown in Figure 11.15.

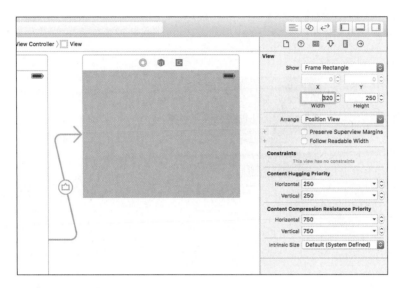

FIGURE 11.14
Edit the height and width of the popover view.

Within the Storyboard Segue settings, start by setting an identifier for the popover segue. Providing an identifier makes it possible to invoke the popover programmatically, something we look into shortly. Next, choose the directions that the popover's arrow will appear *from*; this determines where iOS will present the popover on the screen.

For example, if you only allow a presentation direction of *left*, the popover displays to the right of whatever object is invoking it.

When a popover is displayed, touching outside of it makes it disappear. If you want to exclude certain UI elements from dismissing the popover, just drag from the Passthrough field to those objects in your view.

NOTE

By default, a popover's "anchor" is set when you Control-drag from a UI object to a view controller. The anchor is the object that the popover's arrow will point to.

As with the modal segue covered earlier, you can create "generic" popover segues that aren't anchored. Control-drag from the originating view controller to the popover content view controller and choose a popover segue when prompted. We discuss how to display one of these generic popover segues from any button in a few minutes.

That's all you need to do to create a working popover in IB. Unlike a modal view, a popover is automatically dismissed when you touch outside of it, so you don't even need a single line of code to create a working interactive popover.

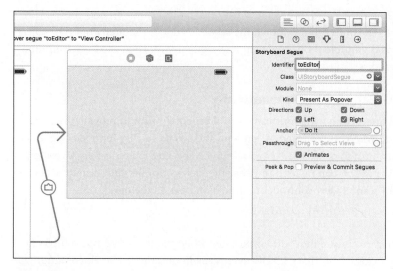

FIGURE 11.15
Configure the popover's behavior by editing the segue's attributes.

After setting the identifier, style, transition, and presentation for a segue, you're ready to use it. Without you writing any code, an application that has followed these steps can now present two fully interactive views and transition between them. What it cannot do, however, is interact with them programmatically. In addition, once you transition from one view to another, you cannot transition back. For that, you need some code. Let's take a look at how you can create and trigger modal segues programmatically, and then the different ways of transitioning back—all of which require *some* coding.

Presenting Modal Segues Manually

Although it is easy to create segues with a single Control-drag, in several situations you have to interact with them in programmatically. If you create a segue between view controllers that you want to trigger manually, for example, you need to know how to initiate it in code. When users are done with the task in another scene, they also need a mechanism to dismiss the modal scene and transition back to the original scene. Let's handle these scenarios now.

Starting the Segue

First, to transition to a scene using a segue that you've defined in your storyboard, but don't want to be triggered automatically, you use the `UIViewController` instance method `perform SegueWithIdentifier:sender`. For example, within your initial view controller, you can initiate a segue with the identifier `"toMyGame"` using the following line:

```
performSegueWithIdentifier("toMyGame", sender: self)
```

That's it. As soon as the line is executed, the segue starts and the transition occurs. The `sender` parameter should be set to the object that initiated the segue. (It doesn't matter what that object is.) It is made available as a variable property during the segue if your code needs to determine what object started the process.

Dismissing a Modal Scene Programmatically

After users have finished interacting with your view, you'll probably want to provide them with a means of getting back to where they started. At present, there is no facility in modal segues to allow for this, so you must turn to code. The `UIViewController` method `dismiss ViewCon trollerAnimated:completion` can be used in either the view controller that displayed the modal scene or the modal scene's view controller to transition back to the original scene:

```
dismissViewControllerAnimated(true, completion: nil)
```

The completion is an optional closure that will be executed when the transition has completed. You can learn more about closures in Hour 3, "Discovering Swift and the Xcode Playground," and you should have used a few in the previous hour's lesson. After you've dismissed a scene presented modally, control is returned to the original scene and the user can interact with it as she normally would.

What if you've performed several segues and want to jump back to where you started rather than just going back one? For that, you need to make use of exits and unwind segues.

Using Exits (and the Unwind Segue)

Apple has adopted the term *unwinding* to mean "moving backward in a storyboard." Storyboards show the path a user takes *forward* through an application, but (until now) haven't really shown a means of moving backward. In the preceding section, you learned how to move back to an earlier view controller using `dismissViewControllerAnimated:completion`. This will likely be the most common method you use for unwinding, but it's hardly a flexible solution for jumping back to an arbitrary point in your storyboard.

If you've displayed 10 modal view controllers, one after the other, and you want to jump from the tenth back to the second, do you really need to dismiss each view controller from number 10 back to number 2? Not if you make use of exits and the unwind segue.

Preparing a View Controller for an Exit

To use an exit, you must first decide what view controller should allow exits. This is the view controller for the scene that you want to exit *to* not *from*. Although this seems a bit counterintuitive to me, just remember that you implement the exit as your destination.

After you've made that determination, add a new `IBAction` method, shown in Listing 11.1, in the view controller's swift file.

LISTING 11.1   Setting an Exit Point

```
@IBAction func exitToHere(sender: UIStoryboardSegue) {
    // No code needed!
}
```

There are two unique things to recognize about this method. First, the name of the method can be *anything* you want, it just needs to have a single `UIStoryboardSegue` parameter. Second, you don't *have* to add any implementation code to the method. It can remain entirely empty.

Once the method is in place, you can use the Exit icon in your scene.

Connecting to an Exit (Unwind Segue)

To connect to an exit, you follow almost the same process as creating a segue. First, you need something that will trigger the exit (like a button). Control-drag from that object to the Exit icon in the scene you want to exit to, as demonstrated in Figure 11.16.

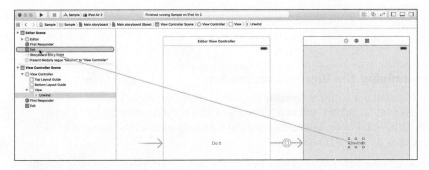

FIGURE 11.16
Connect to the exit.

When you release your mouse button, you'll be asked to pick from a list of the available exit/unwind methods; choose the exit/unwind method you implemented. You'll notice that a new unwind segue is added to the scene you are transitioning *from*, as shown in Figure 11.17.

Once the segue is in place, activating the segue will jump from the activating view controller to the controller with the exit. You can work with the exit/unwind segues exactly like any other segue—including setting an identifier, creating a manual segue (by dragging from a view controller rather than a GUI element), and executing the unwind segue programmatically.

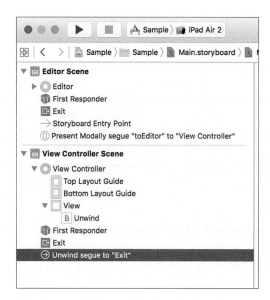

FIGURE 11.17
Dragging to the Exit icon creates an unwind segue.

Dynamically Determining the Unwind Destination

Unwinding segues can be quite a bit more complex than we can present here. You can, for example, implement custom view controllers that, within a hierarchy of views, dynamically decide whether they will become the destination of an unwind segue via the method `canPerformUnwindSegue Action:fromViewController:withSender`.

By overriding this method, your view controller can look at the view controller that wants to initiate an unwind, then return `true` or `false` to accept the unwind request. If it returns `false`, the initiating view controller can keep looking.

Programming a Segue from Scratch

Xcode storyboarding has made multiscene applications much easier to create than they were in the past, but that doesn't mean they're the right choice for all your applications. If you'd rather go the route of programmatically presenting a scene without defining a segue at all, you certainly can. Let's review the process.

Setting a Storyboard Identifier

After creating your storyboard scenes, but before coding anything, you must provide a storyboard identifier for the view controller you want to display programmatically. This is done by selecting the view controller instance and opening the Identity Inspector (Option-Command-3) in the IB editor. Within the Identity section of the inspector, use the Storyboard ID field to enter a simple string to identify the view controller within your application's storyboard. Figure 11.18 shows a view controller being configured with the storyboard ID myEditor.

Set the Storyboard ID for the View Controller

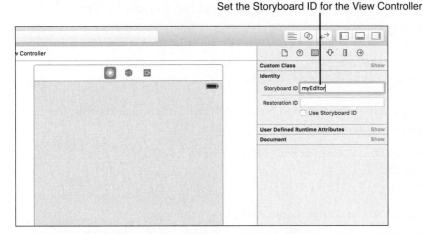

FIGURE 11.18
Create a storyboard identifier for the view controller.

Instantiating the View Controller and View

To display a scene within a storyboard, your application will need to create a UIStoryboard object using the method storyboardWithName that references your storyboard file. This can be used to load view controllers and their associated views (that is, scenes).

For example, to create an object mainStoryboard that references the project's Main.storyboard file, you could use the following:

```
let mainStorybord: UIStoryboard = UIStoryboard(name: "Main", bundle: nil)
```

Next, you configure the storyboard object to instantiate the view controller that you want to transition to using the instantiateViewControllerWithIdentifier method. Assume you've created a UIViewController subclass named EditorViewController and set the view controller storyboard identifier to "myEditor". You can instantiate a new instance of EditorViewController as follows:

```
let editorVC: EditorViewController =
    mainStorybord.instantiateViewControllerWithIdentifier("myEditor") as
    EditorViewController
```

The EditorViewController instance, editorVC, is now ready to be displayed. Before that happens, however, you may want to adjust how it will appear onscreen.

Configuring the Segue Style

Earlier I covered the different transition styles and presentation types that are available for displaying modal scenes. When displaying a view controller manually, you can apply the same effects programmatically by setting the `modalTransitionStyle` and `modalPresentationStyle` view controller variable properties, respectively. For example, to configure the `editorVC` view controller instance, I might use this:

```
editorVC.modalTransitionStyle=UIModalTransitionStyle.CoverVertical
editorVC.modalPresentationStyle=UIModalPresentationStyle.FormSheet
```

You can choose from the same transitions and presentation styles as mentioned earlier this hour, but you need to use these constants to identify your selections:

▶ **Transition styles:** `UIModalTransitionStyle.CoverVertical`, `UIModalTransitionStyle.FlipHorizontal`, `UIModalTransitionStyle.CrossDissolve`, or `UIModalTransitionStyle.PartialCurl`

▶ **Presentation styles:** `UIModalPresentationStyle.FormSheet`, `UIModalPresentationStyle.PageSheet`, `UIModalPresentationStyle.FullScreen`, `UIModalPresentationStyle.CurrentContext`, `UIModalPresentationStyle.OverFullScreen`, `UIModalPresentationStyle.OverCurrentContext`, or `UIModalPresentationStyle.Popover`

Notice that one of the presentation styles is `UIModalPresentationStyle.Popover`? If you set the `modalPresentationStyle` to this value, you've effectively configured a popover segue. There are a few additional attributes you can use to choose how the popover is displayed; we'll get to those in a few minutes.

Displaying the View Controller

The final step in programmatically displaying a view is to, well, display it. To do this, use the `UIViewController` method `presentViewController:animated:completion` from within your application's initial view controller:

```
presentViewController(editorVC, animated: true, completion: nil)
```

The view controller and its associated scene are displayed on the screen using the transition and presentation styles you've selected. From here out, you can work with the scene as if it were one you displayed via a segue. You dismiss it using the same `dismissViewControllerAnimated: completion` method:

```
dismissViewControllerAnimated(true, completion: nil)
```

NOTE

In this example, we're programmatically creating a segue to a scene. The methods we use to do this, however, refer to view controllers. Keep in mind that a scene is just a view controller and its associated view. Because we're instantiating a view controller (with an associated view) from the project's storyboard, we're effectively instantiating a "scene." We then configure the presentation of the view controller/view and display it (the same as a segue).

Although the terminology shifts when working in code, the end result is the same.

Popover Peculiarities

In the previous section, you learned how to create a modal segue (and even configure it as a popover) programmatically—but there are still some peculiarities that you must address when working with popovers. When creating one in Interface Builder, for example, you defined the direction of the popover "arrow" and what object it should point to. To do the same in code, you need to access the `UIPopoverPresentationController`—a special object that defines characteristics about the popover's appearance. When you manually set options for the arrow direction and so on for a popover segue in Interface Builder, you're actually configuring a `UIPopoverPresentationController` that is automatically created for you.

Let's get back to the example of an "editor" view controller that we want to present modally. Previously we covered the steps to display it as a modal view, but if we want to configure it as popover, we might start with this code:

```
let editorVC: EditorViewController =
    mainStorybord.instantiateViewControllerWithIdentifier("myEditor") as
        EditorViewController
editorVC.modalPresentationStyle=UIModalPresentationStyle.Popover
```

Once we've setup the view controller (`editorVC`) and set the presentation style to a popover, we can access a `UIPopoverPresentationController` that iOS automatically creates for us via the variable property - `popoverPresentationController`:

```
let presentationController:UIPopoverPresentationController =
    editorVC.popoverPresentationController!
```

With access to the presentation controller, we can now control several aspects of the popover display and dismissal process.

Setting the Popover Arrow

To finish the popover presentation, we must determine a few things about our display. First, what object is the popover going to presented from? Any object that you add to a view is a subclass of `UIView`, which has a `bounds` variable property. Popovers are easily configured to appear from the rectangle determined by an object's `bounds`; as long as you have a reference to the object displaying the popover, you're set. If you're triggering the popover from a UI action, the bounds property of the object that triggered the action, for example, is retrieved with this: `(sender as! UIView).bounds`.

Although Apple's documentation states that we only need a rectangle *or* a `UIView` (pretty much any onscreen object) to configure the source for a `UIPopoverPresentationController`, in practice it does *not* work. In the initial releases of iOS 9, this is exacerbated by the fact that Apple's own tools for visually creating popovers do *not* properly set both a `sourceRect` and a `sourceView`. Something we'll deal with later this hour.

Assuming the object you're presenting is stored in the `sender` variable of an IBAction, you might use the following:

```
presentationController.sourceRect = (sender as! UIView).bounds
presentationController.sourceView = sender as? UIView
```

NOTE

You could certainly cast the sender as the object it really is (such as a `UIButton`—we did this in the last hour), but this implementation gives us the flexibility to have *any* UI object trigger an action and grab its `frame` value.

In addition, the downcasts presented here are forced and optional (`as!` and `as?`) because of the definition of the `sourceRect` and `sourceView` variable properties. If you don't include ! or ?, Xcode will kindly point this out for you.

Then, we have determined the popover's presentation direction. Do this by choosing from these constants:

- ▶ **UIPopoverArrowDirection.Any:** The popover can be presented in any direction, giving iOS the greatest flexibility in determining how the popover is displayed.

- ▶ **UIPopoverArrowDirection.Up:** The arrow is only displayed pointing up, meaning that the popover appears below the object.

- ▶ **UIPopoverArrowDirection.Down:** The arrow is displayed pointing down, and the popover appears above the object.

- ▶ **UIPopoverArrowDirection.Left:** The arrow is displayed pointing left, and the popover appears to the right of the object.

- ▶ **UIPopoverArrowDirection.Right:** The arrow is displayed pointing right, and the popover appears to the left the object.

Apple recommends that whenever possible you should use the `UIPopoverArrowDirection.Any` constant. You can set the popover direction by assigning the constant (or multiple constants separated by a pipe (|)) to the `UIPopoverPresentationController` variable attribute `permittedArrowDirections`. For example, to present the `editorVC` popover with an arrow that points either up or down, you might use the following:

```
presentationController.permittedArrowDirections =
    UIPopoverArrowDirection.Up | UIPopoverArrowDirection.Down
```

A final display parameter that you need if creating and presenting a popover manually is to set the content size of the popover. This is *not* set on the presentation controller; it is set by assigning the `preferredContentSize` variable property on the popover's view controller. To set a popover size of 320 points wide and 400 points tall, you could type the following:

```
preferredContentSize = CGSizeMake(320.0, 400.0)
```

With the size set, the arrow directions configured, and the source location chosen, you can proceed to present the view with the `presentViewController` method (just like a "plain" modal segue).

There's still *one more thing* that we need to chat about with regards to popover presentation. When a popover is presented, a user can dismiss it by touching outside of it. This isn't tied to an IBAction, so how can we get ahold of the event of the user dismissing a popover? The answer is through implementing the `UIPopoverPresentationControllerDelegate` protocol.

Implementing the `UIPopoverPresentationControllerDelegate` Protocol

When I first started developing on Apple platforms, I found the terminology painful. It seemed that no matter how easy a concept was to understand, it was surrounded with language that made it appear harder than it was. A protocol, in my opinion, is one of these things.

Protocols define a collection of methods that perform a task. To provide advanced functionality, some classes, such as `UIPopoverPresentationController`, may require you to implement methods defined in a related protocol to add certain functionality. Doing this is called *conforming* to the protocol. Some protocol methods are required and others are optional; it just depends on the features you need.

To deal with the user dismissal of a popover, the class that is responding to the dismissal (usually just a view controller) should conform to the `UIPopoverPresentationControllerDelegate` protocol.

To declare that a class, such as a view controller, will be conforming to the `UIPopoverPresentationControllerDelegate` protocol, you just modify the `class` line in the swift file as follows:

```
class ViewController: UIViewController,
    UIPopoverPresentationControllerDelegate {
```

Next, you must set the `delegate` of the popover presentation controller to the object implementing the protocol. If this is the same object that is creating the popover, and you already have a copy of the presentation controller in `presentationController`, you can just use `self`, as follows:

`presentationController.delegate=self`

Now, when the popover is dismissed, the method `popoverPresentationControllerDid-DismissPopover` will be called from popover's view controller. All that remains is to implement that method, as demonstrated in in Listing 11.2.

LISTING 11.2 Handling a Popover Dismissal

```
func popoverPresentationControllerDidDismissPopover(
     popoverPresentationController: UIPopoverPresentationController) {
         // Handle any actions you want executed here.
}
```

As you can see, it isn't difficult to work with popovers programmatically, but a bit more setup is required.

Passing Data Between Scenes

You know how to create and display scenes, but there is one very critical piece of the puzzle missing: the ability to share information between the different scenes in your application. Right now, they act as entirely independent applications, which is perfectly fine if that is your intention; however, chances are, you want an integrated user experience. Let's make that happen.

The most straightforward way for any class to exchange information with any other is through its variable properties and methods. The only trouble with this is that we need to be able to get an instance of one scene's view controller from another, and, at present, when using a segue we create visually, this process isn't entirely obvious.

TIP

If you create and display a scene entirely programmatically, as demonstrated in the preceding section, you already have an instance of the new scene's view controller in your initial view controller. You can set/access variable properties on the new view controller (`editorVC.myImportantVariableProperty=<value>`) before displaying it and after it is dismissed.

The *prepareForSegue:sender* Method

One way to get references to the view controllers in a segue is by overriding `UIViewController prepareForSegue:sender` method. This method is automatically called on the initiating view controller when a segue is about to take place away from it. It returns an instance of `UIStoryboardSegue` and the object that initiated the segue. The `UIStoryboard` object contains the variable properties `sourceViewController` and `destinationViewController`, representing the view controller starting the segue (the source) and the view controller about to be displayed (the destination).

Listing 11.3 shows a simple implementation of this approach. In this example, I'm transitioning from my initial view controller (an instance of `ViewController`) to a new view controller, which is an instance of a hypothetical `EditorViewController` class.

LISTING 11.3   Using `prepareForSegue:sender` to Grab the View Controllers

```
override func prepareForSegue(segue: UIStoryboardSegue, sender: AnyObject?) {
    let startingViewController:ViewController =
        segue.sourceViewController as! ViewController
    let destinationViewController:EditorViewController =
        segue.destinationViewController as! EditorViewController
}
```

In this implementation, I declare two constants (`startingViewController` and `destinationViewController`) to reference the source and destination controllers. Then, I assign them to typecast versions of the source and destination variable properties returned by the `UIStoryboardSegue`. I have to typecast the view controllers so that Xcode knows what type of object they are; otherwise, I wouldn't be able to access their variables and methods. Of course, the source view controller is also just `self`, so this is a bit of a contrived example.

Once we have a reference to the destination view controller, however, we can set and access variable properties on it, even changing the presentation and transition styles before it is displayed. If it is assigned to a variable property, it can be accessed anywhere within the source view controller.

What if we want the destination view controller to send information back to the source? In this case, only the source can communicate with the destination, because that's where the `prepareForSegue:sender` method is implemented. One option is to create a variable property on the destination controller that stores a reference to the source controller. Another approach, however, is to use built-in variable properties of `UIViewController` that make working with modally presented scenes easy, easy, easy.

It's Not Just for Getting the Controllers!

The `prepareForSegue:sender` isn't just for getting the view controllers involved in a segue; it can also be used to make decisions during a segue. Because a scene can define multiple different segues, you might need to know which segue is happening and react accordingly. To do this, use the `UIStoryboardSegue` variable property `identifier` to get the identifier string you set for the segue:

```
if segue.identifier=="myAwesomeSegue" {
    // Do something unique for this segue.
}
```

The Easy Way

The `prepareForSegue:sender` gives us a generic way to work with any segue that is taking place in an application, but it doesn't always represent the easiest way to get a handle on the view controllers involved. For modal segues, the `UIViewController` class gives us variable properties that make it easy to reference the source and destination view controllers: `presentingViewController` and `presentedViewController`.

In other words, we can reference the original (source) view controller within a view controller that has just been displayed by accessing `presentingViewController`. Similarly, we can get a reference to the destination view controller from the original controller with `presentedViewController`. It's as easy as that.

For example, assume that the original view controller is an instance of the class `ViewController`, and the destination view controller is an instance of `EditorViewController`.

From the `EditorViewController`, you can access variable properties in the original view controller with the following syntax:

```
(presentingViewController as! ViewController).<variable property>
```

And within the original view controller, you can manipulate variable properties in the destination view controller with this:

```
(presentedViewController as! EditorViewController).<variable property>
```

The parentheses with the class name is necessary to typecast `presentingViewController`/ `presentedViewController` to the right object types. Without this notation, Xcode wouldn't know what types of view controllers these were, and we wouldn't be able to access their variable properties.

With this data-passing knowledge under our belts, we can go ahead and build our first multi-scene application—and there's even a surprise—you're going to make it work on both iPhone and iPad devices.

Using Segues

We've reached your favorite (I hope) part of the hour's lesson: proving that the things we've learned about actually work. This tutorial demonstrates the use of a second view as an editor for information in the first view. The project shows a screen with an email address and an

Edit button. When edit is clicked, a new scene is shown where the address can be changed. Dismissing the editor view updates the address in the original scene. The project is named **ModalEditor**.

Implementation Overview

To build the project, we start with a Single View Application *iPhone* template, and then add an additional view and supporting view controller class to the project. The first view contains a label that displays the current email address in use, along with an Edit button. The button initiates a segue to second controller, which shows the current address in an editable field, along with a Dismiss button. The Dismiss button updates the email label in the first view and dismisses the modal view. Although we could dismiss the view with a line of code, we'll make use of the Exit icon and unwind segue so that you can get your hands dirty with this new iOS feature.

Setting Up the Project

Begin by creating a new single-view iPhone application named **ModalEditor**. Remember that we're going to need to create additional views and view controller classes for the project, so the setup is very important. Don't skip ahead until you're sure you've done the preliminary work.

Adding the Editor View Controller Class

The view that is displayed to enable editing of the email address will be controlled by a class called `EditorViewController` that we add to our project. To do so, follow these steps:

1. After you've created the project, click the + button at the bottom-left corner of the project navigator, and then click File.

2. When prompted, choose the iOS Source category and the Cocoa Touch Class icon, and then click Next.

3. On the subsequent screen, name the new class **EditorViewController**, and pick the `UIViewController` subclass, as shown in Figure 11.19. Remember, you should be building this for the iPhone, so leave the device drop-down alone.

4. Click Next to continue.

5. On the final setup screen, pick the folder that contains your code files as the save location, choose your main project code group from the Group pop-up menu, and then click Create.

The new class will be added to your project. You now need to create an instance of it in the Main.storyboard file.

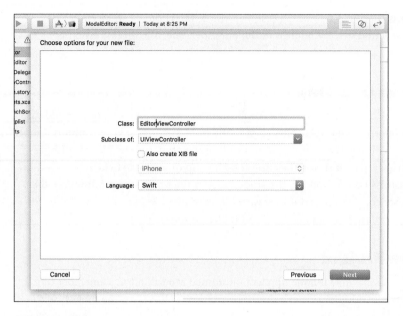

FIGURE 11.19
Create a new subclass of `UIViewController`.

Adding the New Scene and Associating the View Controller

Open the Main.storyboard file in the IB editor. Display the Object Library (Control-Option-Command-3) and drag a new instance of a view controller into an empty area of the IB editor. Your display should now resemble Figure 11.20. I've set a simulated size for my new scene's view controller (makes screenshots easier), but you don't need to do that just yet.

To associate the new view controller with the `EditorViewController` class you added to the project, select the View Controller icon in the second scene within the document outline, and then open the Identity Inspector (Option-Command-3). Use the Custom Class drop-down menu to select `EditorViewController`, as shown in Figure 11.21.

After making the association, you'll notice that the document outline area updates to show one scene named View Controller Scene and another named Editor View Controller Scene. How about we change those into something a bit more friendly?

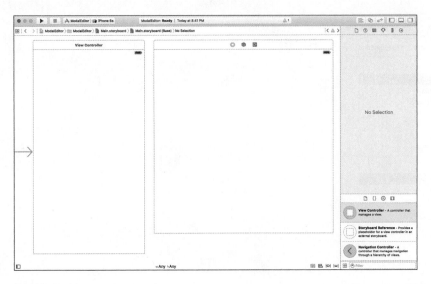

FIGURE 11.20
Add a new view controller to the project.

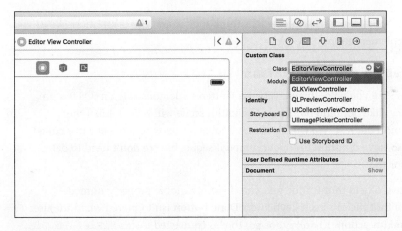

FIGURE 11.21
Associate the view controller in Interface Builder with the `EditorViewController` class.

Select the view controller line for the first scene and make sure the Identity Inspector is still onscreen. Within the Document section, set the label for the first view controller to **Initial**. Repeat this for the second scene, changing its view controller label to **Editor**. The document outline will now display Initial Scene and Editor Scene, as shown in Figure 11.22. If nothing else, this is easier to type.

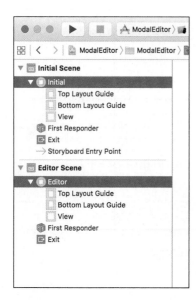

FIGURE 11.22
Set view controller labels to create friendly scene names.

Now the structure for the application is in place, let's think a bit about the connections we're going to need in the implementation.

Planning the Variables and Connections

This application, as I'm sure you've gathered, is being written to demonstrate an iOS feature, not to do anything fancy (like hopping bunnies). The initial scene will have a label that contains that current email address. We will create a variable property to reference this called `emailLabel`. It will also have a button to trigger a modal segue, but we don't need to define any outlets or actions for that.

The editor scene will have a field that will be referenced via a variable property named `emailField`. To ensure that the onscreen keyboard's Done button isn't ignored when the user finishes typing, we'll add an action, `hideKeyboard`, that is connected to `emailField`'s `Did End on Exit` event.

Clicking a button in the scene will update the email label in the initial scene, by way of an action called `updateEditor`. This button will also serve double duty and trigger an unwind segue by connecting to the Exit icon in the initial scene.

A label, a field, and a button—those are the only objects that we need to connect to code in this project.

Preparing the View Controller for an Exit

To use the storyboard Exit feature, we must add an action in the view controller that we want to exit/unwind *to*. In this case, it's the `ViewController` class. We'll name this action `exitToHere` and we'll have to create it manually, rather than with drag and drop.

Enter the method shown in Listing 11.4 in ViewController.swift.

LISTING 11.4   Add a Method as a Placeholder for the Unwind Segue

```
@IBAction func exitToHere(sender: UIStoryboardSegue) {
    // No code needed!
}
```

Note that the method doesn't really need to do anything; it just needs to be there! Everything is now in place to make all our connections in IB.

Designing the Interface

To create the interfaces for the initial and editor scenes, open the Main.storyboard file and focus on creating the initial scene. Begin by selecting the initial scene's View Controller line and using the Attributes Inspector (Option-Command-4) to set it to a reasonable simulated iPhone size. This isn't absolutely necessary (especially for this project), but it can make your IB area a bit less cluttered.

We're going to do something a bit different when building our interface this hour, so don't just look at the figure without reading the next few steps. The basic gist of it is this: Instead of just adding our labels and buttons and things into the view and calling it a day, we're going to position them all within a new view, and then set that view to remain centered in the scene's existing view.

Using the Object Library, drag a new view (`UIView`) into the existing view of your initial scene. Size it to be around 2 inches tall and stretch it to the margins on the sides of the display. Next, drag two labels and a button so that they nest inside that view.

Set one of the labels to read **Email Address:** and position it near the top center of the containing view. Beneath it, place the second label, with its content set to your personal email address. Stretch the second label so that its edges come close to the margins of the containing view (just in case we encounter a long email address). Finally, place the Edit button underneath the two labels. Use the Attributes Inspector (Option-Command-4) to set the style for the text to anything you want.

Now, the tricky part. We want to set *constraints* for the objects in our interface. Constraints are instructions that tell our onscreen objects how to position themselves properly no matter what the screen size. This process is covered in Hour 16, "Building Responsive User Interfaces," but today you'll get your first taste:

1. In many cases, Xcode can automatically add constraints for us, if we position our onscreen objects appropriately. In this project, all but one of the constraints will be automatically generated. To begin, select *only* the view that you added (the one that contains the labels and button), and then drag it until you see the horizontal and vertical centering guides (blue dotted lines) appear. This means we've centered the view and Xcode's autogenerated constraints will keep it centered.

2. Next, with the view still selected, click the Pin icon at the bottom of the Interface Builder editor and click the check box beside Height, and then click Add Constraints, as shown in Figure 11.23. This adds a constraint that tells iOS to keep the height of that view the same, no matter what. Without a height constraint, Xcode's automatically added constraints will stretch the view when it is displayed on larger screens. This removes an ambiguity of what we want, and lets us proceed to the final step—adding the rest of the constraints (automatically).

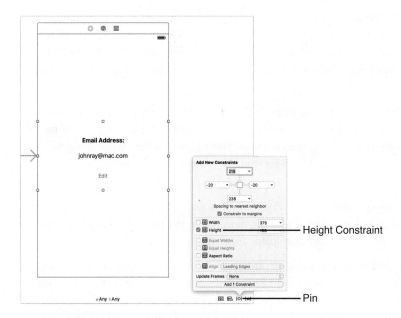

FIGURE 11.23
Set a Height constraint for the view.

3. Finally, choose Editor, Resolve Auto Layout Issues, Add Missing Constraints. (Make sure that you use the Add Missing Constraints under the All Views in View Controller heading in the menu—it appears twice.)

What you've done with these steps is tell the labels and button to stay exactly where they are, within the view that holds them. That view has been configured to stay in the center of the scene, no matter what. The reason for all this effort will be clear in a few minutes.

Figure 11.24 shows my implementation of the initial scene.

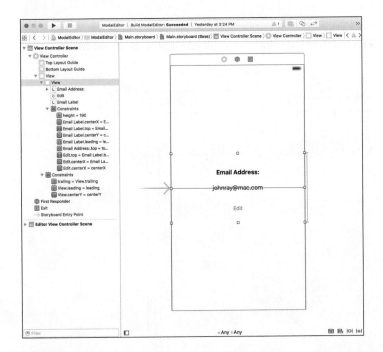

FIGURE 11.24
Create the initial scene.

Next, turn your attention to the editor scene. This scene will look very similar to the first scene, but with an empty text field (UITextField) replacing the label that held the email address. The field should be configured to use the E-mail Address keyboard and have Done set as the Return key.

This scene also contains a button, but rather than saying Edit, it should read Save. Again, you should add these elements to a new UIView that is added to the editor scene's existing view. Once you've completed the layout, follow the exact same steps as before to add some basic constraints:

1. Select *only* the view that you added (the one that contains the label, text field, and button), and then drag it until you see the horizontal and vertical centering guides (blue dotted lines) appear.

2. Click the Pin icon at the bottom of the Interface Builder editor and click the check box beside Height, and then click Add Constraints.

3. Finally, choose Editor, Resolve Auto Layout Issues, Add Missing Constraints. (Again, this option appears in the menu twice. Make sure you select it from the All Views in View Controller heading.)

My final implementation, with a background color set for the editor view, is shown in Figure 11.25.

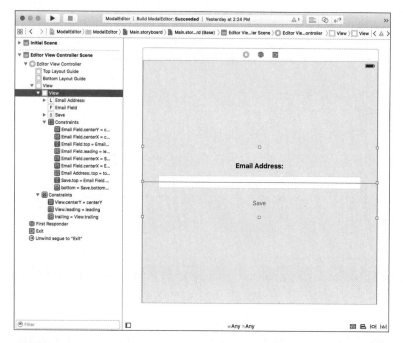

FIGURE 11.25
Create the editor scene.

With both scenes built, it's time to start making the connections that will pull everything together. Let's start by defining the segue.

Creating the Modal Segue

To create the segue from the initial view to the editor view, Control-drag from the Edit button to the onscreen representation of the editor in Interface Builder, or to the editor scene's view controller line in the document outline (now labeled Editor), as shown in Figure 11.26.

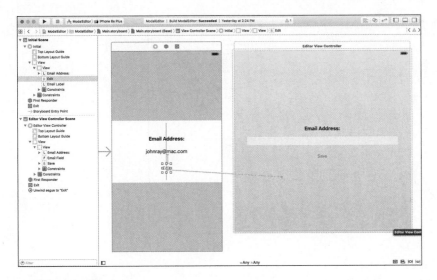

FIGURE 11.26
Create the modal segue.

When prompted for the storyboard segue type, choose Present Modally. You will see a line "Present modally segue to Editor View Controller" appear in the initial scene within the document outline. Select this line and open the Attributes Inspector (Option-Command-4) to configure the segue.

Although it is purely optional for a simple project like this, provide an identifier for the segue, such as `toEditor`. Next, choose the transition style, such as Partial Curl. You can also set a presentation style, but because this is (currently) running on the iPhone, you're not going to see much difference. Figure 11.27 shows the settings for my modal segue.

Unwinding Back to the Initial Scene

The storyboard has a segue configured to go from the initial scene to the editor scene, but has no way to get back. For this, we'll add an unwind segue by Control-dragging from the Save button in the editor scene to the Exit icon in the Initial Scene. (You can target the Exit icon in either the document outline or in the dock underneath the scene layout.)

Create the connection now. When you finish dragging, you'll be prompted to choose the method to execute when the exit finishes. There is only one option, `exitToHere`, so choose that, as shown in Figure 11.28.

Notice that a new unwind segue is added to your editor scene: Unwind segue to Exit. Your application now has what it needs to transition between scenes, but we still need to make the appropriate connections from the scene's view objects (the label, field, and button) to outlets/actions in their view controllers.

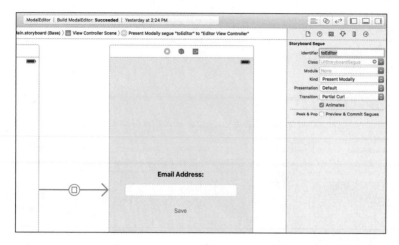

FIGURE 11.27
Configure the modal segue.

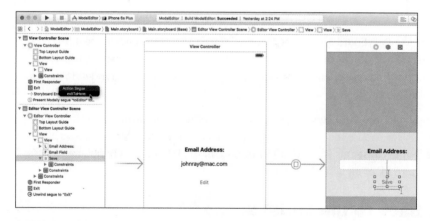

FIGURE 11.28
Choose the method to unwind to.

Creating and Connecting the Outlets and Actions

I know what you're thinking: "I've done this a million times, I've only got three items to connect, what's the big deal?" Although I have every faith you'll make the appropriate connections, remember that you're dealing with two distinct view controllers now.

Your outlets for `ViewController` should be in ViewController.swift, and your outlets and actions for `EditorViewController` will be placed in the EditorViewController.swift file. If you're not seeing what you should be seeing in the assistant editor, use the drop-down menus that appear to choose the file you should be editing.

Adding the Outlets

Begin by selecting the label in the initial scene that contains your email address, and then switch to the assistant editor. Control-drag from the label to just below the `class` line in ViewController.swift. When prompted, create a new outlet for a variable property named **emailLabel**. One down, one to go.

Move to the editor scene and select the `UITextField`. The assistant editor should update to show the EditorViewController.swift file on the right. Control-drag from the field to EditorViewController.swift, targeting a spot just below the `class` line. Name this outlet **emailField**, as shown in Figure 11.29.

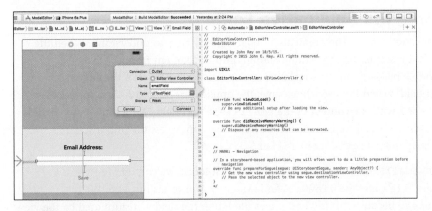

FIGURE 11.29
Connect the UI objects to their outlets.

Adding the Actions

There are two actions to add. With the assistant editor still active, Control-drag from the Save button in the editor scene to below the IBOutlet definition in EditorViewController.swift. When prompted, add a new action named **updateEditor**.

Next, select the field in the editor scene and display the Connections Inspector (Option-Command-6). Drag from the circle beside the Did End on Exit sent event to just under the previous action you added, shown in Figure 11.30. Name the new action **hideKeyboard**.

You're done with the interface and connections. Let's finish the implementation logic.

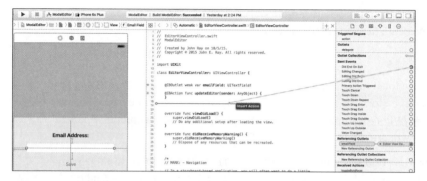

FIGURE 11.30
Connect the event `Did End On Exit` to an action `hideKeyboard`.

Implementing the Application Logic

You're in the home stretch now. The application logic is pretty easy to understand. When the user displays the editor scene, the application should grab the content from the existing `emailLabel` variable property on the source view controller and place it in the editor's `emailField` text field. When the user clicks Save, the application should reverse the process, updating `emailLabel` with the content of the `emailField` text field. We initiate both of these changes from the `EditorViewController` class where we can access the initial scene's view controller through `presentingViewController`.

To set the value of `emailField` when the editor scene first loads, we can add the `EditorViewController` method `viewWillAppear`, as shown in Listing 11.5. We need to put it in `viewWillAppear` because this method is executed after the field is instantiated by the view controller (that is, it is turned into a real object) but before it shown on the screen.

LISTING 11.5   Populating the Field with the Current Email Address

```
override func viewWillAppear(animated: Bool) {
    emailField.text =
        (presentingViewController as! ViewController).emailLabel.text
    super.viewWillAppear(animated)
}
```

This implementation sets the text variable property of `emailField` in the editor view controller to the `text` variable property of the `emailLabel` in the initial view controller. I can access the initial scene's view controller through the current view's `presentingViewController`, although I have to typecast it as a `ViewController` object; otherwise, it wouldn't know about the variable properties (`emailLabel`) that the `ViewController` class makes available.

Next, we need to implement the `updateEditor` method to do exactly the reverse of this. Update the `updateEditor` method with the full implementation, shown in Listing 11.6.

LISTING 11.6   Setting the Initial Scene's Label to the Editor Scene's Field

```
@IBAction func updateEditor(sender: AnyObject) {
    (presentingViewController as! ViewController).emailLabel.text =
        emailField.text
}
```

As you can see, this is exactly the reverse of what we did to set the default value for the field (see Listing 11.5).

Hiding the Keyboard

Finally, edit EditorViewController.swift to include the implementation of `hideKeyboard`. Update the method to ask the `emailField` to resign its first responder status, thus hiding the keyboard, as shown in Listing 11.7.

LISTING 11.7   Hiding the Keyboard When Its Done Key Is Pressed

```
@IBAction func hideKeyboard(sender: AnyObject) {
        emailField.resignFirstResponder()
}
```

That's it. There was more setup involved in this project than there was code.

About That Exit/Unwind Segue

You don't need to ask. The exit/unwind segue that we used in this project was overkill. Exits are most useful when you're unwinding across several view controllers. There's no reason you can't use it here, but there's also no reason why we couldn't have just skipped adding the `exitToHere` method, skipped adding the unwind segue, and instead added this line of code to `updateEditor`:

```
self.dismissViewControllerAnimated(true, completion: nil)
```

That said, now you know how to use an exit, and isn't that the most important thing?

Building the Application

Run the application and give it a thorough workout (as much as you can do in an application that has two buttons and a field). The end result, which took us three actual lines of functional code, is an application that switches between scenes and exchanges data between them, as shown in Figure 11.31.

FIGURE 11.31
The "final" application switch scenes and moves data between them.

Popovers, Universal Applications, and iPhones

If you were reading earlier editions of the book, you would now have reached the point where we began a whole new project for the purpose of demonstrating the similarities between popover and modal segues. Because of segues and storyboards, this is no longer necessary.

Remember how I asked (nicely) for you to build the ModalEditor as an iPhone application? Well, not only are we going to change it into an iPad application, but we're also going to make it use a popover segue.

Configuring the Popover Segue

When you add a segue to a project, it can be reconfigured at any time by selecting the segue line in the document outline or the visual representation within your storyboard. Let's change the modal segue in the project we just built so that it is a popover segue instead.

Open the Main.storyboard file and select the "Present modally segue to Editor View Controller" segue between the Initial and Editor scenes.

Next, open the Attributes Inspector (Option+Command+4) and use the Segue drop-down to choose Present as Popover. Configure the directions to Up, Left, and Right; these are the directions the arrow on the popover can point. Your setup should look similar to Figure 11.32.

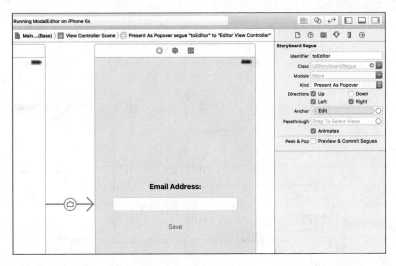

FIGURE 11.32
Configure the popover to point in whichever directions you'd like.

Now, as you've learned, popovers have a size that can either be set programmatically or by manually changing the size of one of the views in your storyboard. When you set up the views earlier, you added constraints that will automatically center our content in the views, no matter their size. For that reason, we can just programmatically set a size for the editor view within the EditorViewController.swift file. Update the viewDidLoad method to set the preferredContentSize for the editor, as shown in Listing 11.8.

LISTING 11.8   Set a Size for the Editor Popover

```
override func viewDidLoad() {
    super.viewDidLoad()
    // Do any additional setup after loading the view.
    preferredContentSize = CGSizeMake(340,160)
}
```

Before going any further, take a few moments to run the application on the iPhone simulator. Touch the Edit button and see what happens? If everything is going according to plan, you'll see a simple modal transition—but no popover! That's because popovers are adaptive, and Apple would prefer they weren't displayed on an iPhone. They will, however, display as a popover on the iPad. Unfortunately, if you try to run the application on the iPad simulator right now, it will just run the iPhone version, enlarged. To see the application display properly on the iPad, we need to make it a universal application.

Toggling to a Universal Application

Don't blink or you'll miss what we're about to do (that is, turn our iPhone app into a universal iPhone/iPad application). To do this, select the top-level project group in the project navigator (the blue document icon). Make sure that the ModalEditor target is highlighted and that General is selected at the top of the editor area.

Scroll down to the Deployment Info section, and use the Devices drop-down menu to switch from iPhone to Universal, as shown in Figure 11.33.

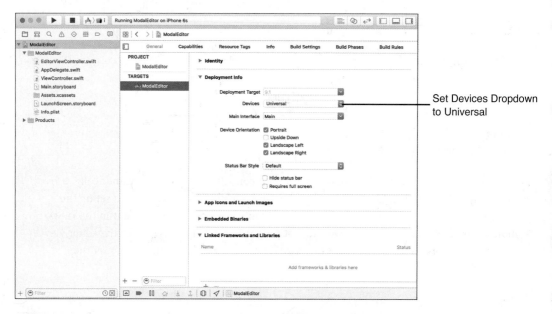

FIGURE 11.33
Set the Devices to Universal.

And here's the kicker: You're done! Try running the application on the iPad simulator. It will now run and display a popover, as shown in Figure 11.34. Try running it on an iPhone and display the popover; it shows as a modal view.

CAUTION

Popover Look Like Poo? Read On!

See how pretty my popover looks in Figure 11.34? If yours doesn't look like this (the popover arrow is pointing in the wrong place), you may be experiencing a known bug in iOS 9.x. When you create a popover using Interface Builder for an iOS 9.0 or 9.1 app, it just doesn't work. Ever. Apple does not properly set the origin for the popover.

To fix the issue, add these two lines of code to end of the viewDidLoad method in the view controller being displayed *within* the popover (here, EditorViewController.swift). This code properly sets the sourceRect of the popover, and makes everything look all nice and pretty:

```
let popoverController:UIPopoverPresentationController =
    self.popoverPresentationController!
popoverController.sourceRect = popoverController.sourceView!.bounds
```

FIGURE 11.34
The iPad simulator now shows a popover.

The two features of iOS and Xcode that make what we've done here possible (in terms of making the application universal) are size classes (which let us use a single storyboard for both iPhones and iPads) and Auto Layout constraints. You'll learn more about both of these features later in the book, but this should give you an idea of just how easy it can be to deal with all your iOS platforms in a single application.

▼ TRY IT YOURSELF

Where's My iPhone Popover, Already?!

As you've seen during our tutorial this hour, you can use a popover segue on an iPhone, but it adapts to the Apple's typical iPhone conventions and doesn't actually *display* as a popover. That's all fine and well, but with all these huge new iPhones, what if you really *do* want a popover displayed? You can do it, but it takes a bit of overriding the default segue behavior. This quick exercise takes you through the steps of making a popover segue on an iPhone behave *identically* to an iPad.

Begin by making a copy of your final popover-enabled ModalEditor project and opening the copy in Xcode.

To make iOS display a popover on the iPhone, we must tell the popover to stop being adaptive. This is accomplished by having the view controller that will invoke the popover (`ViewController`) adopt the `UIPopoverPresentationControllerDelegate` protocol. We'll also add one method from that protocol that disables adaptive popovers, and, finally, we'll set the popover controller's delegate to the `ViewController`.

To conform to the `UIPopoverPresentationControllerDelegate`, add the protocol name to the end of the `class` line in ViewController.swift:

```
class ViewController: UIViewController,
    UIPopoverPresentationControllerDelegate {
```

Next, add the `adaptivePresentationStyleForPresentationController` method to ViewController.swift. This method, shown in Listing 11.9, will return the constant `UIModalPresentationStyle.None` stating that the segue shouldn't try to adapt to any other style.

LISTING 11.9   Disable the Adaptive Segue

```
func adaptivePresentationStyleForPresentationController(controller:
    UIPresentationController) -> UIModalPresentationStyle {
        return UIModalPresentationStyle.None
}
```

Last but not least, the `prepareForSegue` method must be added to grab the `popoverPresentationController` and set its `delegate` variable property to the `ViewController` class (just `self`, since we're writing this code *in* the ViewController.swift).

LISTING 11.10   Set the Popover Presentation Controller Delegate

```
override func prepareForSegue(segue: UIStoryboardSegue, sender: AnyObject?) {
    let destinationViewController:EditorViewController =
        segue.destinationViewController as! EditorViewController
    destinationViewController.popoverPresentationController!.delegate=self
}
```

Now run the application on the iPhone Simulator and try pressing the Edit button. Your display should look pretty close to Figure 11.35.

FIGURE 11.35
Popovers on iPhones, be still my heart!

Note that this isn't really a practical application of iPhone popover capability (the keyboard will cover part of the popover), but this same technique can be used in other applications to make popovers appear in your apps (regardless of the device they're running on).

Further Exploration

Let me be clear: Storyboards and segues are new and evolving. In fact, many developers are still using the previous version of Apple's interface technology (NIB files) in their projects. The trick with turning our application instantly into a universal app has only been possible since the release of iOS 8, because of fundamental changes to storyboards. The point is this: What works today may work entirely differently tomorrow. The chapter you just finished reading is 20 pages shorter than the previous edition because of this.

To learn more, read the *View Controller Programming Guide for iOS*; it will give you a good background on views, view controllers, and how they can be manipulated in code. It's a very long guide, so you may want to jump around through the sections that interest you the most. The *View Controller Catalog for iOS* is another great reference and walks you through the different view controller types (such as the modal controllers and popovers you've used this hour).

Apple Tutorials

The Apple tutorial project Storyboards demonstrates several storyboarding techniques and is good practice for beginners. You'll learn a bit more about storyboards in the next few hours, but if you want more experience before moving on, this tutorial is worth a look.

Summary

This hour's lesson was, yes, I know, longer than an hour. The topics that it introduced—multiple scenes and segues—are very important aspects of iOS development that can take your apps from being simple single-view utility-style programs to full-featured software. You learned how to visually and programmatically create modal segues, handle interactions between scenes, and unwind to previous scenes via the storyboard exit. We also explored the popover UI element and how it can be created and displayed from a segue or via code.

Something to keep in the back of your mind while you develop is that while visually created segues are great, and handle many different situations, they might not always be the best approach. Programmatically switching between views gives us a flexibility that we don't have with preset segues in IB. If you find yourself struggling to make something work in IB, consider doing it through code.

Q&A

Q. Why doesn't iOS just provide windows?

A. Can you imagine managing windows with just your fingers? The iOS interface is designed to be touched. It is not meant to model a typical desktop application environment, which was built around the mouse.

Q. Should I use nonadaptive popovers on the iPhone?

A. If the popover fits the UI, absolutely! Apple's latest iPhones have lots of screen real estate, and popovers work just fine. However, if your popover is going to take up the whole iPhone screen, it really doesn't really add any usability by being a popover, does it?

Workshop

Quiz

1. Segues that change depending on the device you are running on are called what?

    a. Adaptive

    b. Conforming

    c. Device agnostic

    d. Modal

2. Popovers are a type of what kind of segue?

    a. Unwind

    b. Modal

    c. Presentation

    d. Navigation

3. In a typical multiscene application, unique scenes will have unique _____.

    a. Purposes

    b. Labels

    c. Colors

    d. View controllers

4. A form sheet is an example of a modal segue's what?

    a. Style mode

    b. Presentation type

    c. Presentation style

    d. Transition type

5. What method is used to display a scene programmatically?

    a. `presentViewController`

    b. `showViewController`

    c. `displayViewController`

    d. `useViewController`

6. To remove a view from being displayed, you could use which method?

    a. `hideViewControllerAnimated`

    b. `clearViewControllerAnimated`

    c. `removeViewControllerAnimated`

    d. `dismissViewControllerAnimated`

7. The process of moving back to an earlier scene is called what?

    a. Winding

    b. Unwinding

    c. Exiting

    d. Switching

8. Which variable property, set within a view controller, determines the size of the view when presented as a popover?

    a. `setContentSize`

    b. `forcedContentSize`

    c. `preferredContentSize`

    d. `desiredContentSize`

9. Which method is executed prior to a segue, giving developers an opportunity to configure or modify the segue's behavior?

    a. `prepareForSegue`

    b. `segueStart`

    c. `segueBegin`

    d. `prepareToSegue`

10. To access the parent view controller from the current view controller, you could use which variable property?

    a. `startViewController`

    b. `oldViewController`

    c. `presentingViewController`

    d. `topViewController`

Answers

1. A. Adaptive segues enable you to create one segue and use it across all your devices.

2. B. Popovers are a special type of modal segue that include a `UIPopoverPresentationController`.

3. D. Unique scenes usually have unique view controller classes to handle their display and operation.

4. C. A form sheet is an example of a presentation style.

5. A. The `presentViewController` method is used to display a scene's view controller programmatically.

6. D. Use the `dismissViewControllerAnimated` method to remove a view from the device's display.

7. B. The process of moving back to an earlier scene by way of an exit segue is called unwinding.

8. C. Setting the `preferredContentSize` for view controller will determine its size when displayed in a popover.

9. A. The `prepareForSegue` method is called as a segue begins, giving developers a chance to intercept and configure segue parameters before the display changes.

10. C. Use the `presentingViewController` method to access the controller that displayed another.

Activities

1. Return to a project in an earlier hour and implement a "configuration" interface by way of a segue.

2. Update the tutorials in this lesson to programmatically create and display a scene.

HOUR 12
Making Choices with Toolbars and Pickers

What You'll Learn in This Hour:

▶ The use of toolbars and pickers in iOS application interfaces
▶ How to implement the date picker object
▶ Ways to customize the display of a picker view
▶ The relationship between pickers, toolbars, and popovers

In this hour, we continue multiview application development in our tutorials, but our primary focus is on two new user interface elements: toolbars and pickers. Toolbars present a set of common functions in a static bar at the top or bottom of the screen. A picker is a unique user interface (UI) element that both presents information to users *and* collects their input.

Whereas toolbars are similar to any other graphical UI (GUI) element, pickers aren't implemented through a single method; they require several. This means that our tutorial code is becoming a bit more complex, but nothing you can't handle. We need to work fast to fit this in an hour, so we better get started now.

Understanding the Role of Toolbars

Toolbars (UIToolbar) are, comparatively speaking, one of the simpler UI elements that you have at your disposal. A toolbar is implemented as a slightly translucent bar, either at the top or bottom of the display (see Figure 12.1), with buttons (UIBarButtonItem) that correspond to actions that can be performed in the current view. The buttons provide a single selector action, which works nearly identically to the typical Touch Up Inside event that you've used with UIButtons numerous times.

Toolbar

Bar Button Items

FIGURE 12.1
Toolbars are a prevalent part of iOS application interfaces.

Toolbars and Pickers: Why Now?

Before we get too far, I need to explain the method to my (apparent) madness. In the preceding hour, you learned about storyboard segues, multiple views, and popovers. Now we're rolling back to a discussion of UI elements—and it probably feels a bit "off."

The reason for the shift back to the UI is that the two elements we will be working with in this hour are rarely mentioned without also mentioning popovers. In fact, on the iPad, it is against the Apple iOS user interface guidelines to implement pickers outside of popovers; as a result, we need to use Popover segues to present them.

Toolbars can be used independently but are often used to present popovers—so much so that the `UIPopoverPresentationController` class includes a variable property, `barButtonItem`, that is dedicated to displaying popovers from a toolbar button. This variable, when set to a toolbar button, automatically configures where the popover will appear.

Toolbars, as their name implies, are used for providing a set of choices to the user to perform functions on the content within the main view. They aren't intended for changing between completely different application interfaces; for that, you want to implement a tab bar, and that's in the next hour's lesson. Toolbars can be created almost entirely visually and are the de facto standard for triggering the display of a popover on the iPad. To add a toolbar to a view, open the Object Library and search for "toolbar." Drag the toolbar object to the top or bottom of your view; iPhone applications usually leave the toolbar on the bottom.

You might imagine that toolbars would be implemented similarly to a segmented control, but the controls on the toolbar are entirely independent objects. An instance of a `UIToolbar` is nothing more than a gray bar across your screen. For a toolbar to do something, it needs a button.

Bar Button Items

If I were naming a button that gets added to a toolbar, I'd call it a toolbar button. Apple named it a bar button item (`UIBarButtonItem`). Regardless of its name, bar button items are the interactive elements that make a toolbar do something besides look like a stripe on your iOS device's screen. The iOS Library provides three bar button objects, as shown in Figure 12.2. Although these may appear to be independent objects, they're really a single thing: an instance of a bar button item. Bar button items can be customized with over a dozen common system button types or set to any arbitrary text or image.

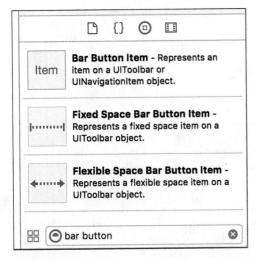

FIGURE 12.2
Three configurations of a single object.

To add a bar button to a toolbar, drag a bar button item into the toolbar in your view. The bar button items will appear as children of the toolbar within the document outline area. Double-clicking the name on a button enables editing, just like a standard `UIButton`. You can also use the handle on the side of the button to increase its size. What you can't do, however, is drag the button around in the bar.

To position buttons, you need to insert special bar button items into the toolbar: flexible and fixed spaces. Flexible spaces expand to fill all possible available space between the buttons on either side of it (or the sides of the toolbar). For example, to position a button in the center, you add flexible spaces on either side of it. To position two buttons on either side of the toolbar, a single flexible space between them gets the job done. Fixed spaces are exactly what they sound like: a fixed width that can be inserted before or after existing buttons.

Bar Button Attributes

To configure the appearance of any bar button item, select it and open the Attributes Inspector (Option-Command-4), shown in Figure 12.3. You have three styles to choose from: Plain (just text), Bordered (the same as Plain, except in versions of iOS 6 and earlier), and Done (bold text). In addition, you can set several "identifiers." These are common button icons/labels that help your toolbar buttons match Apple's iOS application standards—including flexible and fixed space identifiers that will make your bar button item behave as either of these two special button types.

FIGURE 12.3
Configure the bar button items.

If none of the standard button styles work for you, you can set an image to use as a button. The image should be a PNG between 20×20 and 25×25 points. Solid colors are automatically restyled into the toolbar tint, so don't worry about trying to color-match your bar item text.

Exploring Pickers

Because we're dedicating a good portion of an hour to pickers (`UIPickerView`), you can probably surmise that they're not quite the same as the other UI objects that we've been using. Pickers are a unique feature of iOS. They present a series of multivalue options in a clever spinning interface—often compared to a slot machine. Rather than fruit or numbers, the segments, known as components, display rows of values that the user can choose from. The closest desktop equivalent is a set of pop-up menus. Figure 12.4 displays the standard date picker (UIDatePicker).

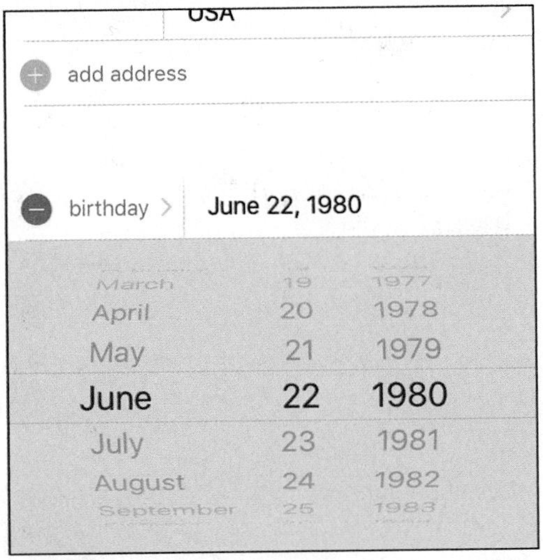

FIGURE 12.4
The picker offers a unique interface for choosing a sequence of different, but usually related, values.

Pickers should be used when a user needs to make a selection between multiple (usually related) values. They are often used for setting dates and times but can be customized to handle just about any selection option that you can come up with.

NOTE

In Hour 9, "Using Advanced Interface Objects and Views," you learned about the segmented control, which presents the user with multiple options in a single UI element. The segmented control, however, returns a single user selection to your application. A picker can return several values from multiple user selections—all within a single interface.

Apple recognized that pickers are a great option for choosing dates and times, so it has made them available in two different forms: date pickers, which are easy to implement and dedicated to handling dates and times; and custom picker views, which you can configure to display as many components as rows as you want—using whatever data you want.

Date Pickers

The date picker (UIDatePicker), shown in Figure 12.5, is very similar to the other objects that we've been using over the past few hours. To use it, we add it to a view, connect an action to its

`Value Changed` event, and then read the returned value. Instead of returning a string or integer, the date picker returns an `NSDate` object. The `NSDate` class is used to store and manipulate what Apple describes as a "single point in time" (in other words, a date and time).

FIGURE 12.5
Configure the appearance of the date picker in the Attributes Inspector.

To access the `NSDate` represented by a `UIDatePicker` instance, you use its `date` variable property. Pretty straightforward, don't you think? In our example project, we implement a date picker and then retrieve the result, perform some date arithmetic, and display the results in a custom format.

Date Picker Attributes

Like many GUI objects, the date picker can be customized using the Attributes Inspector. For example, the picker can be configured to display in one of four different modes:

- ▶ **Date and Time:** Shows options for choosing both a date and a time
- ▶ **Time:** Shows only times
- ▶ **Date:** Shows only dates
- ▶ **Count Down Timer:** Displays a clock-like interface for choosing a duration

You can set the locale for the picker, which determines the ordering of the different components. In addition, you can configure the interval between dates and times, set the default date/time that is displayed, and set date/time constraints to help focus the user's choices.

TIP
The Date attribute is automatically set to the Current (the current date and time) when you add the control to the view. You can also set the Date drop-down to Custom and choose your own date and time for the preset value.

Picker Views

Picker views (UIPickerView) are similar in appearance to date pickers but have an almost entirely different implementation. In a picker view, the only thing that is defined for you is the overall behavior and general appearance of the control; the number of components and the content of each component are entirely up to you. Figure 12.6 demonstrates a picker view that includes two components with images and text displayed in their rows.

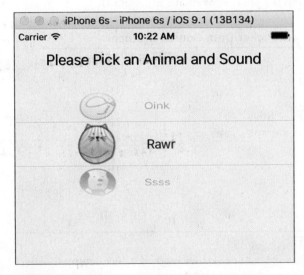

FIGURE 12.6
Picker views can be configured to display anything you want.

A custom picker is added to your application using the IB editor; just drag a picker view from the Object Library into your view. Unfortunately, a custom picker view's appearance is not configured in the Attributes Inspector. Instead, you need to write code that conforms to two protocols—one that will provide the technical layout of the picker (the data source), and another that provides the information it will contain (the delegate). You can use the Connections Inspector to connect the delegate and data source outlets to a class in IB, or you can set these in code. Let's review a simple implementation of these protocols before writing a real project.

The Picker View Data Source Protocol

The picker view data source protocol (UIPickerViewDataSource) includes methods that describe how much information the picker will be displaying:

▶ **numberOfComponentsInPickerView:** Returns the number of components (spinning segments) needed in the picker.

▶ **pickerView:numberOfRowsInComponent:** Given a specific component, this method is required to return the number of rows (different input values) in the component.

There's not much to it. As long as we create these two methods and return a meaningful number from each, we'll successfully conform to the picker view data source protocol. For example, if I want to create a custom picker that shows a total of two columns, with one selection value in the first, and two in the second, I can implement the protocol as shown in Listing 12.1.

LISTING 12.1 Implementing a Custom Picker Data Source Protocol

```
 1: func numberOfComponentsInPickerView(pickerView: UIPickerView) -> Int {
 2:     return 2
 3: }
 4:
 5: func pickerView(pickerView: UIPickerView,
 6:         numberOfRowsInComponent component: Int) -> Int {
 7:     if component==0 {
 8:         return 1
 9:     } else {
10:         return 2
11:     }
12: }
```

Lines 1–3 implement the numberOfComponentsInPickerView method, which returns 2—so the picker will have two components (that is, two little spinny wheels).

Lines 5–12 handle the pickerView:numberOfRowsInComponent method. When the component specified by iOS is 0 (this is the first component in the picker), the method returns 1 (line 8), meaning that there will be one label displayed in the wheel. When the component is 1 (the second component in the picker), the method returns 2 (line 10)—so there will be two possible options displayed to the user.

Obviously, a picker with components that have one or two possible values isn't very useful—and part of the fun of using a picker is giving the user a UI element that he can flick around. This does, however, make it possible to demonstrate a custom picker without having to fill 10 pages with code.

Once the data source protocol is implemented, we still have one protocol (the picker view delegate protocol) between us and a working picker view.

The Picker View Delegate Protocol

The delegate protocol (UIPickerViewDelegate) takes care of the real work in creating and using a picker. It is responsible for passing the appropriate data to the picker for display and for determining when the user has made a choice. We can use a few protocol methods to make the delegate work the way we want, but again, only two are required:

▶ **pickerView:titleForRow:forComponent:** Given a component and row number, this method must return the title for the row—that is, the string that should be displayed to the user.

▶ **pickerView:didSelectRow:inComponent:** This delegate method will be called when the user makes a selection in the picker view. It is passed a row number that corresponds to a user's choice, as well as the component that the user was last touching.

NOTE

If you check the documentation for the UIPickerViewDelegate protocol, you'll notice that really *all* the delegate methods are optional—but unless we implement at least these two, the picker view isn't going to be able to display anything or respond to a user's selection.

To continue our example of a two-component picker (the first component with one value, the second with two), let's implement the pickerView:titleForRow:forComponent method so that the picker shows Good in the first component, and Night and Day as the values in the second. Listing 12.2 demonstrates a simple picker view delegate protocol implementation.

LISTING 12.2   Implementing a Custom Picker Delegate Protocol

```
 1:  func pickerView(pickerView: UIPickerView,
 2:      titleForRow row: Int, forComponent component: Int) -> String? {
 3:
 4:          if component == 0 {
 5:              return "Good"
 6:          } else {
 7:              if row == 0 {
 8:                  return "Day"
 9:              } else {
10:                  return "Night"
11:              }
12:          }
13:  }
14:
```

```
15:   func pickerView(pickerView: UIPickerView, didSelectRow row: Int,
16:       inComponent component: Int) {
17:         if component == 0 {
18:             // User selected an item in the first component.
19:         } else {
20:             // The user selected an item in the second component
21:             if row == 0 {
22:                 // The user selected the string "Day"
23:             } else {
24:                 // The user selected the string "Night"
25:             }
26:         }
27:   }
```

Lines 1–13 provide the custom picker view with the label it should display for the component and row passed to the method. The first component (component 0) will only ever say Good, so line 4 checks to see whether the component parameter is 0, and, if it is, returns the string "Good".

Lines 6–12 handle the second component. Because it can show two values, the code needs to check the incoming row parameter to see which one we need to provide a label for. If the row is 0 (line 7), the code returns the string "Day" (line 8). If the row is 1, "Night" is returned (line 10).

Lines 15–27 implement the pickerView:didSelectRow:inComponent method. This is an exact mirror of the code that provides the values to be displayed in the picker, but instead of returning strings, the purpose of this method is to react to the user's choice in the picker. I've added comments where you'd normally add your logic.

As you can see, coding the picker's protocols isn't something terribly complicated—it takes a few methods, but there are only a couple lines of code.

Advanced Picker Delegate Methods

You can include several additional methods in your implementation of a picker view's delegate protocol that will further customize the appearance of the picker. We use the following three in this hour's project:

▶ pickerView:rowHeightForComponent: Given a component, this method returns the height of the row in points.

▶ pickerView:widthForComponent: For a given component, this method should return the width of the component in points.

▶ pickerView:viewForRow:viewForComponent:ReusingView: For a given component and row, return a custom view that will be displayed in the picker.

The first two methods are self-explanatory; if you want to change the height or width of a component or row in the picker, implement these methods to return the proper size in points. The third method is more involved (and for good reason): It enables a developer to completely change the appearance of what is displayed in a picker.

The `pickerView:viewForRow:viewForComponent:ReusingView` method takes a row and component and returns a view that contains custom content, such as images. This method overrides the `pickerView:titleForRow:forComponent`. In other words, if you use `pickerView:viewForRow:viewForComponent:ReusingView` for anything in your custom picker, you have to use it for everything.

As a quick (impractical and hypothetical) example, suppose that we want to present the Good / Day / Night picker as the row text in the first component and two asset library graphics (night, day) for the rows in the second. We would first get rid of the `pickerView:titleForRow:for Component` method and then implement `pickerView:view ForRow:viewForComponent:ReusingView`. Listing 12.3 shows one possible implementation.

LISTING 12.3   Presenting the Picker with Custom Views

```
 1: func pickerView(pickerView: UIPickerView, viewForRow row: Int,
 2:     forComponent component: Int, reusingView view: UIView?) -> UIView {
 3:
 4:         if component == 0 {
 5:             // return a label
 6:             let goodLabel: UILabel = UILabel(frame: CGRectMake(0,0,75,32))
 7:             goodLabel.backgroundColor = UIColor.clearColor()
 8:             goodLabel.text = "Good"
 9:             return goodLabel
10:         } else {
11:             if row == 0 {
12:                 // return day image view
13:                 return UIImageView(image: UIImage(named: "day"))
14:             } else {
15:                 // return night image view
16:                 return UIImageView(image: UIImage(named: "night"))
17:             }
18:         }
19: }
```

The custom view logic begins on line 4, where it checks to see what component it is being "asked" about. If it is the first component (0), it should display Good in the UI. Because this method is required to return a UIView, returning "Good" isn't a viable option. We can, however, initialize and configure a UILabel. Line 6 declares and initializes a label with a rectangle 75 points wide and 32 points high. Line 7 changes the background color to transparent (clearColor), and line 8 sets the text of the UILabel object to "Good".

The fully configured label is returned in line 9.

In the event that the method is queried for the second component (1), lines 10–18 are executed. Here, the row parameter is checked to determine whether it is being asked for the day (row 0) or night (row 1). For row 0, Lines 13 allocates a UIImageView object with an asset library image resource named day. Similarly, lines 20–21 create a UIImageView from the night image resource that is returned if the row parameter is 1.

It's tutorial time. We first ease into pickers with a quick date picker example and then move on to implementing a custom picker view and its associated protocols.

Using the Date Picker

In the first tutorial, we implement a date picker that is displayed from a bar button item centered in a toolbar. On the iPhone, the picker should be shown via a modal segue. On the iPad, however, the picker must appear in a popover, as required by Apple's human interface guidelines. Using the adaptive popover segue that you learned about in the last hour, we can write one piece of code and it will handle everything! (Yes, we're going to slyly build another universal application.)

After the user chooses a date, the modal view/popover disappears, and a message is displayed that shows the calculated number of days between the current date and the date selected in the picker, as demonstrated in Figure 12.7.

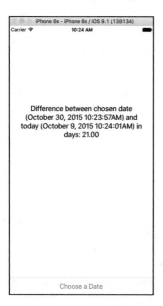

FIGURE 12.7
Display a date picker and use the chosen date in a calculation.

Implementation Overview

We build this project, named DateCalc, using the Single View Application template and following much of the same pattern as we did in the preceding hour's lesson. Our initial scene contains an output label for the date calculation, along with a toolbar and button. Touching the button triggers a popover presentation segue to another scene. This second scene contains the date picker and a button to dismiss the view.

We'll use the `presentingViewController` variable property that we learned about in the last lesson to access the initial view controller from the modal/popover view. All in all, the code will be quite straightforward with most of the difficult work being the date calculation itself.

Setting Up the Project

Create a new single-view application named **DateCalc**. Unlike previous projects, you should set the Devices drop-down to Universal.

The initial scene/view controller that is created with the template will contain the date calculation logic, but we need to add another scene and view controller that will be used to display the date picker interface.

NOTE

Universal Practice

The logic and UI layout for this hour's projects is simple enough that "going universal" will save us some time, and give us a little bit more practice with tools you will learn about later in Hour 16, "Building Responsive User Interfaces," and Hour 23, "Building Universal Applications." You can do quite a bit more to customize the interfaces of universal applications, so don't think that setting a drop-down is all it takes!

Adding the Date Chooser View Controller Class

To handle the display and selection of a date using the date picker, we add a class called `Date-ChooserViewController` to our project. Click the + button at the bottom-left corner of the project navigator and choose File.... When prompted, choose the iOS Source category and the Cocoa Touch class, and then click Next. When asked to name the class, enter **DateChooserViewController** and choose a subclass of `UIViewController`. Make sure that the language is set to Swift. On the last setup screen, choose your main project code group from the Group pop-up menu, and then click Create.

Next, create an instance of the `DateChooserViewController` in the Main.storyboard file.

Adding the Date Chooser Scene and Associating the View Controller

Open the Main.storyboard in the IB editor. Unlike other hours where we change the simulated size, we'll work with the default little generic squares—because this will be a universal application. If you'd prefer to set a simulated size, you can, but it isn't necessary.

Display the Object Library (Control-Option-Command-3) and drag a view controller into an empty area of the IB editor (or into the document outline area). Your project should now show two scenes.

Associate the new view controller with the `DateChooserViewController` class by first selecting the View Controller icon in the second scene within the document outline. Use the Identity Inspector (Option-Command-3) to set the Custom Class drop-down menu to `DateChooserViewController`.

Select the view controller object for the first scene and make sure the Identity Inspector is still onscreen. Within the Document section of the Identity Inspector, set the label for the first view to Initial. Repeat for the second scene, setting its view controller label to Date Chooser. The document outline will now display Initial Scene and Date Chooser Scene, as shown in Figure 12.8.

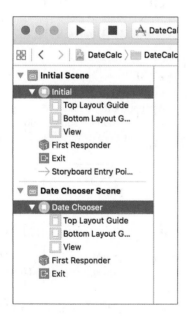

FIGURE 12.8
Set up your initial and date chooser scenes.

Planning the Variables and Connections

Not too many outlets and actions are required in today's projects. Let's start with the initial scene, handled by the `ViewController` class. We have a label that is used for output, represented by a variable property we'll call `outputLabel`. In addition, the `ViewController` class will have a method for calculating the difference between the current date and chosen date (`calculateDateDifference`).

For the date chooser scene, implemented in the `DateChooserViewController` class, there are two actions: `setDateTime`, called when the user selects a date in the date picker; and `dismissDateChooser`, used to exit the date chooser scene when a button in the view is touched.

Designing the Interface

To design the interface, follow these steps:

1. Open the Main.storyboard file and scroll so that you can see the initial scene in the editor.

2. Using the Object Library (Control-Command-Option-3), drag a toolbar into the bottom of the view.

3. By default, the toolbar contains a single button named item. Double-click the item title and change it to read **Choose a Date**.

4. Drag two Flexible Space Button Bar Items from the Object Library and position one on each side of the Choose a Date button. This forces the button into the center of the toolbar.

5. Add a label to the upper-center of the view.

6. Use the Attributes Inspector (Option-Command-4) to increase the default text size for the label (if desired), center it, and set it to accommodate at least five lines of text.

7. Change the default text to read **No Date Selected**.

Because this is a universal application, it must be modified to support differing screen sizes. To do this, we'll add constraints, just as we did in Hour 11, "Implementing Multiple Scenes and Popovers." Constraints define how interface objects behave under different situations.

1. Select the toolbar to begin. Make sure that it is snapped to the sides and the very bottom of the view.

2. Next, select the label and drag it to make sure that it is aligned with the horizontal centering guide. It should be positioned a bit above the center of the view. (You can also use the Editor, Align menu to get things centered.)

3. By using the guides when positioning, Xcode can add all the constraints we need auto-matically. Choose Editor, Resolve Auto Layout Issues, Add Missing Constraints. (This option appears in the menu twice. Make sure that you select it from the All Views in View Controller heading.)

Figure 12.9 shows my final view, with constraints.

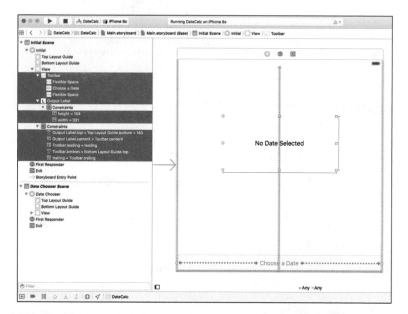

FIGURE 12.9
The initial scene.

Now, focus on the date chooser scene. For my design, I began by selecting the view and setting its background color to a light beige. This, of course, is unnecessary, but it does provide an additional visual cue to the user that the interface has changed. Drag a date picker into the top third of the view.

Above the date picker, drag a label and change its text to read **Please Pick a Date**. As a final step, drag a button to the bottom center of the view. This is used to dismiss the date chooser scene. Label the button **Done**.

As with the initial scene, the date picker scene must also have constraints added. Here's how to add them:

1. Select the label and drag it to make sure that it is aligned near the top and is horizontally centered. (You can also use the Editor, Align menu to center.).

2. Next up, the picker itself. This object must snap to the sides of the view, and be centered and positioned just below the label.

3. Finally, the Done button. This should be centered horizontally and snapped to the bottom view margin.

4. Choose Editor, Resolve Auto Layout Issues, Add Missing Constraints. (This option appears in the menu twice. Make sure that you select it from the All Views in View Controller heading.)

Figure 12.10 shows my finished date chooser interface.

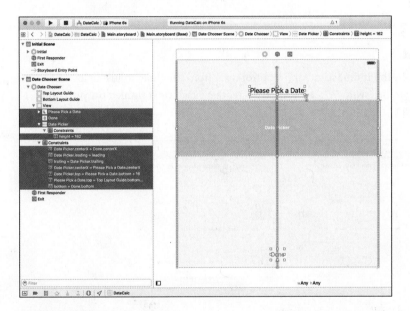

FIGURE 12.10
The date chooser scene.

Creating the Segue

Control-drag from the Choose bar button item in the initial scene to the view controller in the date chooser scene; you can do this either directly in the document outline area or using the visual representations of the scenes in the IB editor. When prompted for the storyboard segue type, choose Popover Presentation. A line labeled Popover presentation segue to Date Chooser appears in the initial scene within the document outline.

Creating and Connecting the Outlets and Actions

Between our two scenes, we have three connections to make: an outlet in the initial scene, and two actions in the date chooser scene. Let's review those now:

- ▶ **outputLabel (UILabel):** The label that will display the results of the date calculation in the initial scene.

- ▶ **dismissDateChooser:** An action method triggered by the Done button in the date chooser scene.

- ▶ **setDateTime:** An action method invoked when the date picker changes its value.

Switch to the assistant editor, and begin by wiring up the initial view's outlet.

Adding the Outlet

Select the output label in the initial scene and Control-drag from the label to just below the class line in ViewController.swift. When prompted, create a new outlet named **outputLabel**, as shown in Figure 12.11.

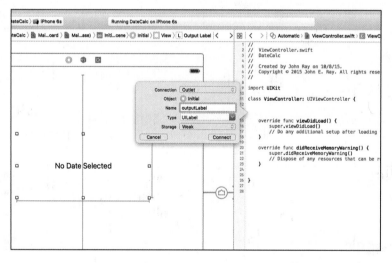

FIGURE 12.11
Connect to the output label.

Adding the Actions

Beyond the single outlet, every other connection in this project is an action.

Move to the second (date chooser) scene and Control-drag from the date picker to the Date-ChooserViewController.swift file, targeting below the class line. When prompted, create a new action named `setDateTime` that is triggered on the `Value Changed` event. Next, control-drag from the Done button to DateChooserViewController.swift. Create a new action called `dismissDateChooser` that will be triggered from the button.

Implementing the Date Calculation Logic

With the interface complete, the most difficult work that we have in front of us with the date picker implementation is writing the `calculateDateDifference` logic. To do what we've set out to (show the difference between today's date and the date in the picker), we must complete several tasks:

- ▶ Get today's date
- ▶ Display a date and time
- ▶ Calculate the difference between two dates

Before writing the code, let's look at the different methods and data types that we need.

Getting the Date

To get the current date and store it in an `NSDate` object, all that we need to do is to initialize a new `NSDate`. When initialized, it automatically stores the current date. This means that a single line takes care of our first hurdle:

```
let todaysDate: NSDate = NSDate()
```

Displaying a Date and Time

Unfortunately, displaying a date and time is a bit more tricky than getting the current date. Because we're going to be displaying the output in a label, we already know how it is going to be shown on the screen, so the question is really, how do we format a string with an `NSDate` object?

Interestingly enough, there's a class to handle this for us. We'll create and initialize an `NSDateFormatter` object. Next, we set object's `setdateFormat` variable property to create a custom format using a pattern string. Finally, we apply that format to our date using another method of `NSDateFormatter`, `stringFromDate`—which, given an `NSDate`, returns a string in the format that we defined.

For example, if we assume that we've already stored an `NSDate` in a variable `todaysDate`, we can output in a format like Month, Day, Year Hour:Minute:Second(AM or PM) with these lines:

```
let dateFormat: NSDateFormatter = NSDateFormatter()
dateFormat.dateFormat = "MMMM d, yyyy hh:mm:ssa"
let todaysDateString: String = dateFormat.stringFromDate(todaysDate)
```

First, `dateFormat` is initialized in a new object of the type `NSDateFormatter`. Then the string `"MMMM d, YYYY hh:mm:ssa"` is used to set the format internally in the object. Finally, a new string is returned and stored in `todaysDateString` by using the `dateFormat` object's instance method `stringFromDate`.

Where in the World Did That Date Format String Come From?

The strings that you can use to define date formats are defined by a Unicode standard that you can find here: http://unicode.org/reports/tr35/tr35-6.html#Date_Format_Patterns.

For this example, the patterns are interpreted as follows:

MMMM: The full name of the month

d: The day of the month, with no leading zero

YYYY: The full four-digit year

hh: A two-digit hour (with leading zero if needed)

mm: Two digits representing the minute

ss: Two digits representing the second

a: AM or PM

Determining the Difference Between Two Dates

The last thing that we need to understand is how to compute the difference between two dates. Instead of needing any complicated math, we can just use the `timeIntervalSinceDate` instance method in an `NSDate` object. This method returns the difference between two dates, in seconds. For example, if we have two `NSDate` objects, `todaysDate` and `futureDate`, we could calculate the time in seconds between them with this:

```
let difference: NSTimeInterval = todaysDate.timeIntervalSinceDate(futureDate)
```

NOTE

Notice that we store the result in a variable of type `NSTimeInterval`. This isn't an object. Internally, it is just a double-precision floating-point number. Apple abstracts this from us by using a new type of `NSTimeInterval` so that we know exactly what to expect out of a date difference calculation, but we can work with it just like any other floating-point number.

Note that if the `timeIntervalSinceDate:` method is given a date *before* the object that is invoking the method (that is, if `futureDate` was *before* `todaysDate` in the example), the difference returned is negative; otherwise, it is positive. To get rid of the negative sign, we use the function `fabs(<float>)` that, given a floating-point number, returns its absolute value.

Implementing the Date Calculation and Display

To calculate the difference and dates, we implement a method in ViewController.swift called `calculateDateDifference` that receives a single parameter (`chosenDate`). After writing the method for the calculation, we add code to the date chooser view controller to call the calculation when the date picker is used.

Add the `calculateDateDifference` implementation from Listing 12.4 to your ViewController. swift file now.

LISTING 12.4   Calculating the Difference Between Two Dates

```
 1: func calculateDateDifference(chosenDate: NSDate) {
 2:     let todaysDate: NSDate = NSDate()
 3:     let difference: NSTimeInterval =
 4:         todaysDate.timeIntervalSinceDate(chosenDate) / 86400
 5:
 6:     let dateFormat: NSDateFormatter = NSDateFormatter()
 7:     dateFormat.dateFormat = "MMMM d, yyyy hh:mm:ssa"
 8:
 9:     let todaysDateString: String = dateFormat.stringFromDate(todaysDate)
10:     let chosenDateString: String = dateFormat.stringFromDate(chosenDate)
11:
12:     let differenceOutput: String = NSString(format:
13:         "Difference between chosen date (%@) and today (%@) in days: %1.2f",
14:         chosenDateString, todaysDateString, fabs(difference)) as String
15:
16:     outputLabel.text=differenceOutput
17: }
```

Much of this should look pretty familiar based on the preceding examples, but let's review the logic. Lines 2 and 3–4 do most of the work we set out to accomplish.

In line 2, we initialize `todaysDate` as a new `NSDate` object. This automatically stores the current date and time in the object. In lines 3–4, we use `timeIntervalSinceDate` to calculate the time, in seconds, between `todaysDate` and `chosenDate` (the date selected by the Date Picker object).

The result is divided by 86400 and stored in the `difference` constant. Why 86400? This is the number of seconds in a day, so we will be able to display the number of days between dates, rather than seconds.

In lines 6–10, we create a new date formatter object (`NSDateFormatter`) and use it to format `todaysDate` and `chosenDate`, storing the results in `todaysDateString` and `chosenDateString`.

Lines 12–14 format the final output string by creating a new string (`differenceOutput`) and initializing it with `stringWithFormat`. The format string provided includes the message to be displayed to the user as well as the placeholders `%@` and `%1.2f`—representing a string and a floating-point number with a leading zero and two decimal places. These placeholders are replaced with the `todaysDateString`, `chosenDateString`, and the absolute value of the difference between the dates, `fabs(difference)`. I chose to use `stringWithFormat` to create the output, rather than string interpolation, because you can't format numbers directly with string interpolation.

In line 16, the label we added to the view, `differenceResult`, is updated to display `differenceOutput`.

Updating the Date Output

To finish the calculation object, we need to add code to call the `calculateDateDifference` method so that the display is updated when the user picks a date. There are actually two places we need to call the calculation: when the user picks a new date and when date chooser is first displayed. In the second case, the user hasn't picked a date and the current date is displayed in the picker.

Start with the most important use case: handling a user's action by calculating the date difference when the `setDateTime` method is called. Recall that this is triggered when the date picker value changes. Update the method stub in DateChooserViewController.swift with the code in Listing 12.5.

LISTING 12.5   Calculating the Date Difference

```
@IBAction func setDateTime(sender: AnyObject) {
    (presentingViewController as! ViewController).calculateDateDifference(
        (sender as! UIDatePicker).date)
}
```

The `presentingViewController` variable property is used to access the `calculateDateDifference` method in ViewController.swift. We pass it the `date` returned from the date picker, and we're done. Unfortunately, if the user exits the picker without explicitly making a choice, there won't be a date calculation displayed.

If the user exits the picker, we can assume that the *current* date is what the user wanted. To handle this implicit selection, add the `viewDidAppear` method in DateChooserViewController.swift, as shown in Listing 12.6.

LISTING 12.6   **Performing a Default Calculation When the Date Chooser Is First Displayed**

```
override func viewDidAppear(animated: Bool) {
    super.viewDidAppear(animated)
    (presentingViewController as! ViewController).calculateDateDifference(NSDate())
}
```

This is identical to the `setDateTime` method, but we pass it a new `date` object with the current date rather than querying the picker. This ensures that a calculated value is displayed, even if the user immediately dismisses the modal scene or popover.

Believe it or not, we're just about finished with the application. Our remaining task is dealing with some loose ends regarding the popover presentation segue—specifically, dismissing it, and sizing the popover itself for large screen devices.

TRY IT YOURSELF ▼

Time for a Playdate

If you have any questions about manipulating dates and times, the playground is a great place to test out `NSDate` and `NSDateFormatter` methods. With that introductory sentence out of the way, take a few moments to sit in awe of that heading I just wrote... "Time for a Playdate"... It incorporates, Time, Date, and part of **Playground**. I'm so very pleased with myself right now.

The reason we're here, however, is to try out some of the `NSDate` and `NSDateFormatter` logic so you can get an idea of a few of the nice features provided by these classes.

Create a new iOS playground, then input the following code:

```
import UIKit

let currentDate: NSDate = NSDate()

let dateFormat: NSDateFormatter = NSDateFormatter()
dateFormat.dateFormat = "MM/dd/yy hh:mm a"
```

As we've seen in the Date Picker application, this creates a new object `currentDate` that contains the current date and time, and an `NSDateFormatter` object in `dateFormat`. Unlike the application we've built, however, the formatter can be used to create a new date from a String!

For example, add this line to the end of the code block:

```
let myDate: NSDate = dateFormat.dateFromString("12/25/1970 10:00 AM")!
```

In the margin on the right, you'll see that `myDate` is now an `NSDate` object, that contains a date and time based on the string I provided.

If you wanted to know which of the two dates we have (`myDate` or `currentDate`) is earlier or later, you can use the `NSDate` instance methods `earlierDate` and `laterDate`. These, given another date, return the date that is earlier or later, respectively. Add these lines to see the logic in action:

```
currentDate.earlierDate(myDate)
currentDate.laterDate(myDate)
```

The first of the two lines returns the contents of `myDate`, since it is earlier, while the second returns the date in `currentDate`. You could also write this as:

```
myDate.earlierDate(currentDate)
myDate.laterDate(currentDate)
```

The method doesn't care which of the two objects is being tested it always returns the correct result.

To see the number of seconds between the two dates, add in this line:

```
currentDate.timeIntervalSinceDate(myDate)
```

For even more fun, you can divide this result by 60 to see the result in minutes, 3600 for hours, 86400 for days, and so on:

```
currentDate.timeIntervalSinceDate(myDate) / 60
currentDate.timeIntervalSinceDate(myDate) / 3600
currentDate.timeIntervalSinceDate(myDate) / 86400
currentDate.timeIntervalSinceDate(myDate) / 31536000
```

I highly recommend playing around with the methods in these two classes to see what they can do. Date/Time manipulation is a traditionally difficult thing to code, but with the Cocoa classes Apple provides, you can work calendar magic without breaking a sweat.

Implementing the Scene Segue Logic

We want to dismiss the modal/popover view when the user presses the Done button in the date chooser scene. You've already made the connection to `dismissDateChooser`; you just need to add a call to `dismissViewControllerAnimated:completion`. Listing 12.7 shows the appropriate one-line implementation of `dismissDateChooser` in DateChooserViewController.swift.

LISTING 12.7   Dismissing the Modal Scene

```
@IBAction func dismissDateChooser(sender: AnyObject) {
    dismissViewControllerAnimated(true, completion: nil)
}
```

NOTE

In the preceding hour, we used an exit/unwind segue to move back to the initial scene; it was meant as a learning exercise. In this implementation, we just use the `dismissViewController Animated:completion` method, because it is easier and quicker for a two-scene project.

The application should now work exactly as we intend, but the popover probably will be a bit larger that needed on the iPad. To limit the size of the popover to something manageable, we need to set the `preferredContentSize` variable property of the view controller that manages the popover's content—that is, `DateChooserViewController`. Update `viewDidLoad` in DateChooserViewController.swift, as shown in Listing 12.8.

LISTING 12.8   Set a Preferred Size for the Popover

```
override func viewDidLoad() {
    super.viewDidLoad()
    preferredContentSize = CGSizeMake(340,380)
}
```

This code sets a preferred size for the content of 340 points wide by 380 points tall. You may want to play around with the sizes after you run the app. These looked good to me based on my interface design.

Building the Application

The date picker application is complete. Run and test the app to get an idea for how the different pieces come together. Something to look for during your testing is the behavior of the application with the date choose is shown in a popover (that is, when you run it on an iPad). When an application displays a popover, the initial scene remains visible while the popover is displayed. In this example, the result is that the user can actually see live feedback in the initial scene as he picks new dates in the popover.

You've just made a toolbar, implemented a date picker, learned how to perform some basic date arithmetic, and even formatted dates for output using date formatting strings. What could be better? Creating your own custom picker with your own data, of course.

Using a Custom Picker

In the second project of this hour's lesson, you create a custom picker that presents two components: one with an image (an animal) and another with a text string (an animal sound). As with the previous project, the picker is displayed via a popover presentation segue—which results in a modal view on the iPhone and a popover on larger screened devices (usually just the iPad), as shown in Figure 12.12.

FIGURE 12.12
Create a working custom picker.

When users choose an animal or sound from the custom picker view, their selection is displayed in an output label.

Implementation Overview

While the implementation of the custom picker requires that we have a class that conforms to the picker's delegate and data source protocols, many of the core processes in this application are identical to the last. An initial scene contains an output label and a toolbar with a single button. Touching the button triggers a segue to the custom chooser's scene. From there, the user can manipulate the custom picker and return to the initial scene by touching a Done button. iPad users can also touch outside of the popover.

The variable names will change a bit to better reflect their role in this application, but logic and implementation are nearly identical to the last. Because of this similarity, we will work quickly and provide detailed instructions only where the projects differ.

Setting Up the Project

Create a new project named **CustomPicker** based on the Single View Application template. Again, make sure you set the Devices drop-down to Universal—because we'll be adding constraints to make it run nicely on all our devices.

Adding the Image Resources

For the custom picker to show animal pictures, we need to add a few images to the project. Because we know upfront that we need these images, we can add them to the project immediately. Open the project group in the project navigator area of Xcode. Click the main Assets.xcassets file to open the project's image assets. Now, drag the Images folder from the Hour's Projects folder in the Finder into the left-hand column inside the asset catalog.

Open the Images group that appears in the catalog and verify that you have seven image assets in your project: bear.png, cat.png, dog.png, goose.png, mouse.png, pig.png, and snake.png.

Adding the Animal Chooser View Controller Class

Like the DateChooserViewController class presented a scene with a date picker, the AnimalChooserViewController class will handle the display and selection of an animal and a sound. Click the + button at the bottom-left corner of the project navigator and choose File. Create a new Cocoa Touch class: a UIViewController subclass named AnimalChooserViewController using the Swift language. Save the new class files in your project's main code group.

Adding the Animal Chooser Scene and Associating the View Controller

Open the Main.storyboard and display the Object Library (Control-Option-Command-3). Drag a view controller into an empty area of the IB editor or the document outline area.

Select the new scene's view controller icon, and then use the Identity Inspector (Option-Command-3) to set the Custom Class drop-down menu to AnimalChooserViewController. Use the Identity Inspector's Document section to set the label for the first view to Initial and the second scene to Animal Chooser. These changes should be reflected immediately in the document outline.

Planning the Variables and Connections

The outlets and actions in this project mirror the last, with one exception. In the previous tutorial, we needed a method to be executed when the date picker changed its value. In this tutorial, we implement protocols for the custom picker that include a method that is called automatically when the picker is used.

The ViewController class's initial scene has a label for output (outputLabel). The class also shows the selected animal/sound using a method we'll call from the second scene: displayAnimal:withSound:fromComponent.

The animal chooser scene is implemented in the AnimalChooserViewController class. It features one action (dismissAnimalChooser) used to exit the animal chooser scene, and six methods to handle the custom picker data source and delegate protocols. Finally, there are three variable properties (`animalNames`, `animalSounds`, and `animalImages`) referencing `Array` objects. These contain the animal names that we are displaying, the sounds to display in the custom chooser components, and the image resource names that correspond to the animals.

Adding Custom Picker Component Constants

When creating custom pickers, we must implement a variety of protocol methods that refer to the various components (the spinny wheels) by number. To simplify a customer picker implementation, you can define constants for the components so that you can refer to them symbolically.

In this tutorial, we refer to component 0 as the animal component and component 1 as the sound component. By defining a few constants at the start of our code, we can easily refer to them by name. Edit AnimalChooserViewController.swift and add these lines so that they follow the `class` line:

```
let kComponentCount: Int = 2
let kAnimalComponent: Int = 0
let kSoundComponent: Int = 1
```

The first constant, `kComponentCount`, is just the number of components that we want to display in the picker, whereas the other two constants, `kAnimalComponent` and `kSoundComponent`, can be used to refer to the different components in the picker without resorting to using their actual numbers.

What's Wrong with Referring to Something by Its Number?

Absolutely nothing. The reason that it is helpful to use constants, however, is that if your design changes and you decide to change the order of the components or add another component, you can just change the numbering within the constants rather than each place they're used in the code.

Designing the Interface

Open the Main.storyboard file and scroll so that you can see the initial scene in the editor. Using the Object Library (Control-Command-Option-3), drag a toolbar into the bottom of the view. Change the default bar button item to read **Choose an Animal and Sound**. Use two Flexible Space Button Bar Items from the Object Library to center the button.

Next, add a label with the default text **Nothing Selected** just above the center of the view. Use the Attributes Inspector to center the text, increase the font size, and set the label to display at least five lines of text.

As with the previous project, you'll also need to add constraints so that the project displays properly on iPhone and iPad devices. Refer to the earlier instructions if you want additional details on what these changes do:

1. Select the toolbar and drag it so that it snaps to the right and left sides of the view and the very bottom.

2. Select the label and align it to horizontal center of the view with the Editor, Align menu, or by dragging the object until a guide appears.

3. Choose Editor, Resolve Auto Layout Issues, Add Missing Constraints. (This option appears in the menu twice. Make sure that you select it from the All Views in View Controller heading.)

Figure 12.13 demonstrates my initial view layout.

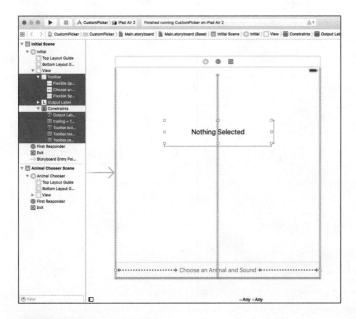

FIGURE 12.13
The initial scene.

Configure the animal chooser scene as you did the date chooser scene, setting a background label that reads **Please Pick an Animal and Sound**, but this time drag a picker view object into the scene. Add a button to the bottom of the view and label it **Done**. This, as before, is used to dismiss the animal chooser scene.

Same deal as before with the constraints:

1. Select the label and align it to horizontal center of the view with the Editor, Align menu, or by dragging the object until a guide appears.

2. Select the custom picker itself. Position it just below the label, and make sure that each side snaps to the side of the view.

3. Next, the Done button. This should be centered horizontally and snapped to the bottom view margin.

4. To add the constraints that keep everything in place, choose Editor, Resolve Auto Layout Issues, Add Missing Constraints. Make sure that you select it from the All Views in View Controller heading.

Figure 12.14 shows my finished animal chooser interface.

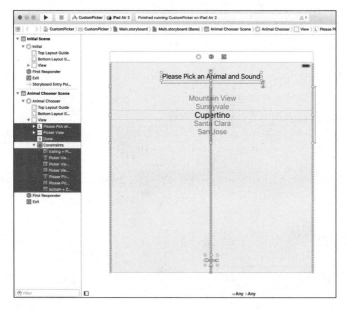

FIGURE 12.14
The animal chooser scene.

Setting the Picker View Data Source and Delegate

In this project, we have the `AnimalChooserViewController` class serve double-duty and act as the picker view's data source and delegate. In other words, the `AnimalChooserViewController` class is responsible for implementing all the methods needed to make a custom picker view work.

To set the data source and delegate for the picker view, select it in the animal chooser scene or the document outline area, and then open the Connections Inspector (Option-Command-6). Drag from the `dataSource` outlet to the `Animal Chooser View Controller` line in the document outline. Do the same for the `delegate` outlet. Once finished, the Connections Inspector should resemble Figure 12.15.

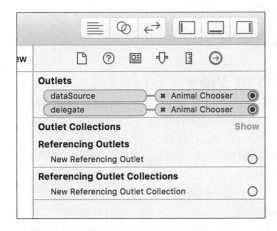

FIGURE 12.15
Connect the picker view's `delegate` and `dataSource` outlets to the animal chooser view controller object.

Creating the Segue

Control-drag from the Choose an Animal button in the initial scene to the view controller in the animal chooser. Create a modal segue for the iPhone or popover for the iPad. A line labeled "Popover presentation segue to Animal Chooser View Controller" will show when the segue has been created.

Creating and Connecting the Outlets and Actions

A total of just two connections are required (an outlet in the initial scene, and a single action in the animal chooser scene):

▶ `outputLabel` (`UILabel`): The label in the initial scene that will display the results of the user's interactions with the picker view.

▶ `dismissAnimalChooser`: An action method triggered by the Done button in the animal chooser scene.

Switch to the assistant editor and make the connections.

Adding the Outlet

Select the output label in the initial scene and Control-drag from the label to just below the `class` line in ViewController.swift. When prompted, create a new outlet named `outputLabel`.

Adding the Action

Move to the second scene and Control-drag from the Done button to AnimalChooserViewController.swift, targeting just below the constants you added earlier. Create a new action called `dismissAnimalChooser` that will be triggered from the button.

Implementing the Custom Picker View

Early in this hour, we presented a possible implementation of a very (very) limited custom picker view. Even though it didn't represent a real-world application, it is close to what we will need to do to finish this example and create a custom picker that displays images and text, side by side, in two components. We'll slow things down again and complete this hour's lesson with a full explanation of the creation of the custom picker view.

Loading the Picker Data

To present the picker, we need to supply it with data. We've loaded the image resources, but to provide the images to the picker, we need to be able to reference them by name. In addition, we need to be able to "translate" between the image of an animal and its real name. That is, if a user picks an image of a pig, we want the application to say Pig, not pig.png. To do this, we have an array of animal images (`animalImages`) and an array of animal names (`animalNames`) that share the same index. For example, if the user picks an image that corresponds to the third element of `animalImages`, we can get the name from the third element of `animalNames`. We also need the data for the list of animal sounds presented in the second picker view component. For that, we use a third array: `animalSounds`.

Declare these three arrays as variable properties in AnimalChooserViewController.swift by updating the code at the top of the file to include these new `Array` declarations after the existing constants:

```
var animalNames: [String] = []
var animalSounds: [String] = []
var animalImages: [UIImageView] = []
```

Now, we need to initialize the data in each array. For the names and sounds arrays, we will just be storing strings. In the images array, however, we will be storing initialized `UIImageViews`. Update the `viewDidLoad` method in AnimalChooserViewController.swift, as shown in Listing 12.9.

LISTING 12.9 Loading the Data Required for the Picker View

```
 1: override func viewDidLoad() {
 2:     super.viewDidLoad()
 3:
 4:     animalNames=["Mouse","Goose","Cat","Dog","Snake","Bear","Pig"]
 5:     animalSounds=["Oink","Rawr","Ssss","Roof","Meow","Honk","Squeak"]
 6:     animalImages=[
 7:         UIImageView(image: UIImage(named: "mouse.png")),
 8:         UIImageView(image: UIImage(named: "goose.png")),
 9:         UIImageView(image: UIImage(named: "cat.png")),
10:         UIImageView(image: UIImage(named: "dog.png")),
11:         UIImageView(image: UIImage(named: "snake.png")),
12:         UIImageView(image: UIImage(named: "bear.png")),
13:         UIImageView(image: UIImage(named: "pig.png")),
14:     ]
15: }
```

Line 4 initializes the `animalNames` array with seven animal names.

Line 5 initializes the `animalSounds` array with seven animal sounds.

Lines 6–14 populate the `animalImages` array with seven `UIImageView` instances loaded from the images that were imported at the start of the project.

Implementing the Picker View Data Source Protocol

The next step is to begin implementing the protocols that the custom picker requires. The first, the data source protocol, provides information to the picker about the number of components it will be displaying and the number of elements within each of those components.

Declare that we will be conforming to the `UIPickerViewDataSource` by editing AnimalChooserViewController.swift and modifying the `class` line to read as follows:

```
class AnimalChooserViewController: UIViewController,
    UIPickerViewDataSource {
```

Next, implement the `numberOfComponentsInPickerView` method in AnimalChooserViewController.swift. This method returns the number of components the picker will display. Because we defined a constant for this (`kComponentCount`), all we need to do is return the constant, as shown in Listing 12.10.

LISTING 12.10 Returning the Number of Components

```
func numberOfComponentsInPickerView(pickerView: UIPickerView) -> Int {
    return kComponentCount
}
```

The other data source method required is the `pickerView:numberOfRowsInComponent`, which, given a component number, returns the number of elements that will be shown in that component. We can use the `kAnimalComponent` and `kSoundComponent` to simplify identifying which component is which, and the `Array` method `count` to get the number of elements in an array. Using this, we can implement `pickerView:numberOfRowsInComponent` using the approach in Listing 12.11.

LISTING 12.11   **Returning the Number of Elements per Component**

```
1: func pickerView(pickerView: UIPickerView,
2:     numberOfRowsInComponent component: Int) -> Int {
3:     if component==kAnimalComponent {
4:         return animalNames.count;
5:     } else {
6:         return animalSounds.count;
7:     }
8: }
```

Line 3 checks whether the component being queried is the animal component. If it is, line 4 returns a count of the number of animals in the `animalNames` array. (The image array would work as well.)

If the component being checked isn't the animal component, we can assume it is the sound component (line 5) and return the count of elements in the `animalSounds` array (line 6).

That's all the data source needs to do. The remainder of the picker view work is handled by the picker view delegate protocol: `UIPickerViewDelegate`.

Implementing the Picker View Delegate Protocol

The picker view delegate protocol handles customizing the display of the picker and reacting to a user's choice within the custom picker. Update AnimalChooserViewController.swift to state our intention to conform to the delegate protocol:

```
class AnimalChooserViewController: UIViewController,
    UIPickerViewDataSource, UIPickerViewDelegate {
```

Several delegate methods are needed to produce the picker we want, but the most important is `pickerView:viewForRow:forComponent:reusingView`. This method takes an incoming component and row and returns a custom view that will be displayed in the picker.

For our implementation, we want the animal images to be returned for the first component, and a label with the animal sounds returned for the second. Add the method, as written in Listing 12.12, to your project.

LISTING 12.12   Providing a Custom View for Each Possible Picker Element

```
 1: func pickerView(pickerView: UIPickerView, viewForRow row: Int,
 2:     forComponent component: Int, reusingView view: UIView?) -> UIView {
 3:
 4:     if component==kAnimalComponent {
 5:         let chosenImageView: UIImageView = animalImages[row]
 6:         let workaroundImageView: UIImageView =
 7:             UIImageView(frame: chosenImageView.frame)
 8:         workaroundImageView.backgroundColor =
 9:             UIColor(patternImage: chosenImageView.image!)
10:         return workaroundImageView
11:     } else {
12:         let soundLabel: UILabel = UILabel(frame: CGRectMake(0,0,100,32))
13:         soundLabel.backgroundColor = UIColor.clearColor()
14:         soundLabel.text = animalSounds[row]
15:         return soundLabel
16:     }
17: }
```

In lines 4–10, we check to see whether the component requested is the animal component, and if it is, we use the row parameter to return the appropriate UIImageView stored in the animalImages array. *Wait. No we don't.* Returning the result of line 5 is all we *should* have to do to implement a custom picker view using an image, but it is broken in iOS 7+ (yes, really). If you try to use this approach, your images will flicker in and out of view in the picker.

To get around the iOS problem, my approach is to take the image view we created in viewDidLoad and allocate an initialize a new UIImageView with the same size (lines 6-7). Next, I set the backgroundColor variable property to the image referenced by the original image view (lines 8-9), and then return this new image view in line 10. There is *absolutely no reason* why this should work and the original method fail, but it does.

After digesting that little nugget of crazy, we can move on to the rest of the code.

If the component parameter isn't referring to the animal component, we need to return a UILabel with the appropriate referenced row from the animalSounds array. This is handled in lines 11–16.

In line 12, we declare a UILabel named soundLabel and initialize it with a frame. Remember from earlier hours that views define a rectangular area for the content that is displayed on the screen. To create the label, we need to define the rectangle of its frame. The CGRectMake function takes starting x,y values and a width and height. In this example, we've defined a rectangle that starts at 0,0 and is 100 points wide and 32 points tall.

Line 13 sets the background color attribute of the label to be transparent (UIColor.clearColor() returns a color object configured as transparent). If we leave this line out, the rectangle will not blend in with the background of the picker view.

Line 14 sets the text of the label to the string of the specified row in animalSounds.

Finally, line 15 returns the UILabel—ready for display.

Changing the Component and Row Sizes

If you were to run the application now, you'd see the custom picker, but it would look a bit squished. To adjust the size of components in the picker view, we can implement two more delegate methods: pickerView:rowHeightForComponent and pickerView:widthFor Component.

For this application example, some trial and error led me to determine that the animal component should be 75 points wide, while the sound component looks best at around 150 points.

Both components should use a constant row height of 55 points.

Translating this into code, implement both of these methods in AnimalChooserViewController. swift, as shown in Listing 12.13.

LISTING 12.13   Setting a Custom Height and Width for the Picker Components and Rows

```
func pickerView(pickerView: UIPickerView,
        rowHeightForComponent component: Int) -> CGFloat {
    return 55.0
}
func pickerView(pickerView: UIPickerView,
        widthForComponent component: Int) -> CGFloat {
    if component==kAnimalComponent {
        return 75.0;
    } else {
        return 150.0;
    }
}
```

Reacting to a Selection in the Picker View

In the date picker example, you connected the picker to an action method and used the Value Changed event to capture when they modified the picker. Custom pickers do not work this way. To grab a user's selection from a custom picker, you must implement yet another delegate method: pickerView:didSelectRow:inComponent. This method provides the component and row where a selection was made.

Notice anything strange about that method? It gives us the component and row the user selected but doesn't provide the status of the other components. To get the value of other components, we have to use the picker instance method `selectedRowInComponent` along with the component we're interested in checking.

In this project, when the user makes a selection, we call the method `displayAnimal:with Sound:fromComponent` to display the selection in the initial scene's output label. We haven't yet implemented this, so let's do so now.

The implementation of the method in ViewController.swift should take the incoming parameter strings and display them in the output label. Nothing fancy required. My implementation is provided in Listing 12.14.

LISTING 12.14   Creating a Method to Display the User's Selection

```
func displayAnimal(chosenAnimal: String, withSound chosenSound:String,
        fromComponent chosenComponent: String) {
    outputLabel.text =
    "You changed \(chosenComponent) (\(chosenAnimal) and the sound \(chosenSound))"
}
```

The output label is set to the contents of the `chosenComponent`, `chosenAnimal`, and `chosenSound` strings. Unlike the previous project, we don't need to deal with any number formatting, so we can use simple string interpolation to create the result.

Now that we have a mechanism for displaying the user's choice, we need to handle their selection. Implement `pickerView:didSelectRow:inComponent` in the AnimalChooserViewController.swift file, as shown in Listing 12.15.

LISTING 12.15   Reacting to a User's Selection

```
 1: func pickerView(pickerView: UIPickerView, didSelectRow row: Int,
 2:        inComponent component: Int) {
 3:
 4:    let initialView: ViewController = presentingViewController as! ViewController
 5:
 6:    if component==kAnimalComponent {
 7:    let chosenSound: Int = pickerView.selectedRowInComponent(kSoundComponent)
 8:        initialView.displayAnimal(animalNames[row],
 9:            withSound: animalSounds[chosenSound], fromComponent: "the Animal")
10:    } else {
11:    let chosenAnimal: Int = pickerView.selectedRowInComponent(kAnimalComponent)
12:        initialView.displayAnimal(animalNames[chosenAnimal],
13:            withSound: animalSounds[row], fromComponent: "the Sound")
14:    }
15: }
```

The first thing that the method does is grab a handle to the initial scene's view controller in line 4. We need this so we can display the user's selection within that scene.

Line 6 checks to see whether the selected component is the animal component. If it is, we still need to grab the currently selected sound (line 7). Lines 8–9 call the `displayAnimal:withSound: fromComponent` method we just wrote, passing it the animal name, using the incoming `row` to select the right value from the array, the currently selected sound, and a string (the `Animal`) to describe the component the user manipulated.

In the event that the user chose a sound, lines 10–14 are executed instead. In this case, we need to look up the currently selected animal (line 11), and then, once again, pass all the relevant values to the display method to get them onscreen for the user.

Handling an Implicit Selection

As was the case with the date picker, the user can display the custom picker and then dismiss it without choosing anything. In this case, we should assume that the user wanted to choose the default animal and sound. To make sure this is accounted for, as soon as the animal chooser scene is displayed, we can update the output label in the initial scene with the default animal name, sound, and a message that nothing has been selected from a component ("nothing yet...").

As with the date picker, we can do this by adding the `viewDidAppear` method in AnimalChooserViewController.swift. Implement the method as shown in Listing 12.16.

LISTING 12.16 Setting a Default Selection

```
override func viewDidAppear(animated: Bool) {
        super.viewDidAppear(animated)
        let initialView: ViewController =
        presentingViewController as! ViewController
        initialView.displayAnimal(animalNames[0],
            withSound: animalSounds[0], fromComponent: "nothing yet...")
}
```

The implementation is simple. It grabs the initial view controller, and then it uses it to call the display method, passing the first element of the animal names and sounds arrays (because those are the elements displayed first in the picker). For the component, it passes a string to indicate that the user hasn't chosen anything from a component... yet.

Implementing the Scene Segue Logic

As with the previous tutorial, we still have two things wrap up. First, we must implement the `dismissAnimalChooser` method in AnimalChooserViewController.swift (see Listing 12.17) to get rid of the scene when the user touches Done.

LISTING 12.17   Dismissing the Modal Scene

```
@IBAction func dismissAnimalChooser(sender: AnyObject) {
    dismissViewControllerAnimated(true, completion: nil)
}
```

Second, we need to set a reasonable size for the popover to use when it actually is displayed as a popover (on the iPad, for example). To do this, we'll set the preferredContentSize in the AnimalChooserViewController.swift file, as shown in Listing 12.18.

LISTING 12.18   Update AnimalChooserViewController's viewDidLoad Method

```
override func viewDidLoad() {
    super.viewDidLoad()
    animalNames=["Mouse","Goose","Cat","Dog","Snake","Bear","Pig"]
    animalSounds=["Oink","Rawr","Ssss","Roof","Meow","Honk","Squeak"]
    animalImages=[
        UIImageView(image: UIImage(named: "mouse.png")),
        UIImageView(image: UIImage(named: "goose.png")),
        UIImageView(image: UIImage(named: "cat.png")),
        UIImageView(image: UIImage(named: "dog.png")),
        UIImageView(image: UIImage(named: "snake.png")),
        UIImageView(image: UIImage(named: "bear.png")),
        UIImageView(image: UIImage(named: "pig.png")),
    ]
    preferredContentSize = CGSizeMake(340,380)
}
```

That finishes the handling of the popover/modal view segue and all the logic needed to make sure that it works as intended.

Building the Application

Run the application and test your new custom picker view. The behavior of the animal chooser view controller should be nearly identical to the date picker despite the differences in implementation. When the application displays the picket in a popover, it updates the output label as soon as a selection is made. When running modally (on the iPhone), it does this as well, but the view is obscured by the modal scene.

Popover Awareness

In the past two hours, we've built applications that run using modal views on smaller devices, and popovers on larger screens. You even learned (in Hour 11) how to force a modal view to display as a popover on an iPhone. This flexibility in iOS is great, but I've (inconveniently) ignored one fact:

Popovers don't necessarily need to have the same content as modal views. In all of our examples, we've included a Done button to close the modal view/popover when we're finished. A popover, however, allows the user to touch outside of the popover to close it—making a Done button redundant.

If you'd like to add the ability for your view controller (the `AnimalChooserViewController` class, for example) to modify its content prior to display, you can do this by checking to see if it is running in a popover. My solution for doing this is to check in the `viewWillAppear` method to see if the popover's arrow direction has been defined. From here, I could hide the done button (I'd need to assign an outlet for it first), or programmatically modify other attributes of the view:

```
override func viewWillAppear(animated: Bool) {
    super.viewWillAppear(animated)
    if (popoverPresentationController?.arrowDirection
        != UIPopoverArrowDirection.Unknown) {
        // This view controller is running in a popover
        NSLog("I'm running in a Popover")
    }
}
```

Further Exploration

As you learned in this lesson, `UIDatePicker` and `UIPickerView` objects are reasonably easy to use and quite flexible in what they can do. There are a few interesting aspects of using these controls that we haven't looked at that you may want to explore on your own. First, both classes implement a means of programmatically selecting a value and animating the picker components so that they "spin" to reach the values you're selecting: `setDate:animated` and `select-Row:inComponent:animated`. If you've used applications that implement pickers, chances are, you've seen this in action.

Another popular approach to implementing pickers is to create components that appear to spin continuously (instead of reaching a start or stopping point). You may be surprised to learn that this is really just a programming trick. The most common way to implement this functionality is to use a picker view that simply repeats the same component rows over and over (thousands of times). This requires you to write the necessary logic in the delegate and data source protocol methods, but the overall effect is that the component rotates continuously.

Although these are certainly areas for exploration to expand your knowledge of pickers, you may also want to take a closer look at the documentation for toolbars (`UIToolbar`) and the `NSDate` class. Toolbars provide a clean way to create an unobtrusive user interface and save a great deal of space versus adding buttons everywhere in your views. The ability to manipulate dates can be a powerful capability in your applications.

Apple Tutorials

UIDatePicker, UIPickerView – UICatalog (accessible via the Xcode developer documentation): This great example code package includes samples of both the simple `UIDatePicker` and a full `UIPickerView` implementation.

Dates, Times, and Calendars – Date and Time Programming Guide (accessible via the Xcode developer documentation): This guide provides information on just about everything you could ever want to do with dates and times.

Summary

In this hour's lesson, you explored three UI elements—`UIToolbar`, `UIDatePicker`, and `UIPickerView`—that each present the user with a variety of options. Toolbars present a static list of buttons or icons at the top or bottom of the screen. Pickers present a "slot-machine" type of view where the user can spin components in the interface to create custom combinations of options.

Although toolbars and date pickers work like other UI elements you've experienced over the past few hours, the custom picker view is rather different. It requires us to write methods that conform to the `UIPickerViewDelegate` and `UIPickerViewDataSource` protocols.

In writing the sample picker applications, you also had a chance to make use of `NSDate` methods for calculating the interval between dates, as well as `NSDateFormatter` for creating user-friendly strings from an instance of `NSDate`. Although not the topic of this lesson, these are powerful tools for working with dates and times and interacting with your users.

Q&A

Q. Why didn't you cover the timer mode of the UIDatePicker?

A. The timer mode doesn't actually implement a timer; it's just a view that can display timer information. To implement a timer, you actually need to track the time and update the view accordingly—not something we can easily cover in the span of an hour.

Q. Where did you get the method names and parameters for the UIPickerView protocols?

A. The protocol methods that we implemented were taken directly from the Apple Xcode documentation for `UIPickerViewDelegate` and `UIPickerViewDataSource`. If you check the documentation, you can just copy and paste from the method definitions into your code—or just start typing and let Xcode autocomplete the definitions for you.

Q. **Should I try just returning a normal `UIImageView` for a custom picker, or assume I need a workaround?**

A. Absolutely give it a try. The documentation shows that the original method should work. It just didn't work as intended at the time of this writing.

Workshop

Quiz

1. What class handles storing and manipulating dates and times?

   a. `NSTime`

   b. `NSDateTime`

   c. `NSDate`

   d. `NSCron`

2. You can control the size of a popover by setting what variable property within its view controller?

   a. `setContentSize`

   b. `forcedContentSize`

   c. `preferredContentSize`

   d. `desiredContentSize`

3. Toolbar buttons are called by what name in iOS?

   a. Bar button items

   b. Bar buttons

   c. Buttons

   d. Toolbar items

4. What class is used for formatting dates and times for output?

   a. `NSTimeFormatter`

   b. `NSDateTimeFormatter`

   c. `NSCronFormatter`

   d. `NSDateFormatter`

5. When using toolbars, what popover presentation controller variable property can be used to set the origin of the popover's arrow?

    a. `barButtonItem`

    b. `buttonItem`

    c. `barItem`

    d. `toolbarButtonItem`

6. Which protocol is responsible for generating a picker view and reacting to picker selection?

    a. `UIPickerViewDataSource`

    b. `UIPickerViewDelegate`

    c. `pickerViewDelegate`

    d. `UICustomPickerViewDelegate`

7. To create a custom picker that only uses text (versus custom views), we could use which of the following methods?

    a. `pickerView:viewForRow:forComponent`

    b. `pickerView:textForRow:forComponent`

    c. `pickerView:titleForRow:forComponent`

    d. `pickerView:labelForRow:forComponent`

8. By default, a date picker added to your project shows what?

    a. Nothing

    b. A date one year in advance

    c. The date and time the component was added to your project

    d. The current date and time

9. On the iPad, Apple requires that popovers _____.

    a. Be sized to fit the screen

    b. Appear in a popover

    c. Not be used to select dates

    d. Always use custom views

10. Picker components are referred to by an integer value where the first component is what?

    a. 0

    b. 1

    c. −1

    d. nil

Answers

1. C. The `NSDate` class is used to store and manipulate dates and times.

2. C. Setting the `preferredContentSize` for view controller will determine its size when displayed in a popover.

3. A. Toolbar buttons are referred to in iOS as bar button items.

4. D. The `NSDateFormatter` class is used to format dates and times for output.

5. A. You can use the `barButtonItem` property of a popover presentation controller to present the popover from a toolbar button.

6. B. The `UIPickerViewDelegate` protocol is responsible for generating custom picker views and reacting to a user's touch.

7. C. Simple text-only custom pickers can generate the picker components using the `picker View:titleForRow:forComponent` method.

8. D. By default, a date picker will show the current date and time—no programming required.

9. B. Apple requires that pickers displayed on an iPad always appear within a popover.

10. A. The first component in a picker is referred to by the integer 0.

Activities

1. Modify the projects in this chapter so that the secondary view controllers check to see whether they are running within a popover. Remove the Done button if they are.

2. Update the dateCalc project so that it allows the selection of two dates via two pickers. You can do this using two pickers in a single scene, or you can branch to two distinct scenes.

3. Update the CustomPicker project so that the user is rewarded for matching an animal to its sound. This was the original tutorial, but it had to be shortened for space. Here's a hint: The animal sounds are presented in the reverse order of the animals.

Advanced Storyboards Using Navigation and Tab Bar Controllers

What You'll Learn in This Hour:

▶ The purpose of navigation and tab bar controllers
▶ How to create navigation controller-based scenes with the storyboard
▶ How to build tab bar applications using the iOS tab bar template
▶ A way to share data between scenes using the navigation and tab bar controllers

Over the past few hours, you've become familiar with creating multiscene applications using modal scene segues and popovers. These are useful and common user interface (UI) features, but many iOS applications take a more "structured" approach to scene layout. Two of the most popular application layout methods involve the use of navigation controllers and tab bar controllers. Navigation controllers enable a user to drill down from one screen to another, exposing more detail as they go. You'll see this everywhere in iOS—from the settings app to bookmarks in Safari. The second approach, implementing a tab bar controller, is used for developing apps with multiple functional features, where each tab presents a different scene where the user can interact with a new set of controls.

In this hour, you learn about these two controllers and how they can provide a whole new world of interface options for your applications.

Advanced View Controllers

It is rare when an iOS (or any OS) update comes out that makes development simpler. Each release brings new features and new levels of complexity. Because of recent changes to Xcode and iOS, however, two common types of iOS view controllers have become much easier to integrate with your projects: navigation and tab bar controllers.

Previously relying on quite a bit of coding prowess, these advanced view controllers required multiple chapters just to cover basic implementation, and far more code than could be reasonably covered in a *24 Hours* book. Now, it's literally a matter of drag and drop.

Before we get started with looking at these new features, let's take a moment to review where we are in the book, and, specifically, what we've learned over the past few hours.

Multiscene Development

You've reached the second half of this book. Nicely done! You should now have a good sense of how to populate a scene and process a user's input.

We also started (in the past two hours) building apps with multiple scenes. This includes creating new view controller subclasses to handle each scene, adding segues, and, if necessary, writing code to manually trigger a segue. The key to being successful in creating multiscene applications is being able to easily exchange information between the different scenes so you can build a cohesive user experience. The more scenes you have, the more planning you need upfront to make sure that everything works the way you want it to.

In the preceding hour's lesson, you created a `delegate` attribute on one custom view controller subclass and used it to refer to the initial view controller object. Another approach is to create a brand-new class that does nothing but manage the information that needs to be shared across scenes. The two types of view controllers that we use in this hour include a "parent" view controller that manages multiple scenes that are presented to the user. This parent controller provides an excellent opportunity for creating variable properties to facilitate exchanging information between scenes—since it is present regardless of which scene is visible. We put this to the test in our sample projects a bit later.

CAUTION
_____

Segues Where You Don't Want Them

If you need to directly reference one scene's view controller from another, you always can use an outlet to connect them. Just Control-drag from one view controller into the other view controller's .swift file and add a variable property to reference it.

That said, if you attempt to add an outlet and then connect the view controller, Xcode prompts you to create a segue instead. Remember that if you want to create a connection and Xcode starts prompting you to make a segue, you can use the Connections Inspector to precisely target an outlet; no segue will get in the way.

_____

This hour is mostly visual—giving your typing fingers a break before kicking back in in the next hour. The Xcode storyboard feature makes what we're about to do possible in a *24 Hours* book and enables you to concentrate on coding application logic instead of worrying about getting the right scenes to display when you need them.

To Code or Not to Code, That Is the Question

Wherever it seems practical in this book, I provide instructions on how to perform actions through code. In the case of storyboard segues, the same code applies to any segue, so what you've learned over the past two hours to programmatically trigger a segue applies here as well.

Of course, there is still lower-level code than storyboard segues. In Hour 11, "Implementing Multiple Scenes and Popovers," for example, you learned how a popover can be created entirely in code and presented to a user. It wasn't difficult, but it also wasn't nearly as clean as presenting a popover via segue. It did, however, teach you how to instantiate and present view controllers programmatically.

In the case of navigation and tab bar controllers, the low-level code can get complex quickly, and, frankly, the utility of including it in the book is quite debatable; there isn't enough space to provide both working code examples and working storyboard examples. You may still need code for some advanced projects, but Apple has made it possible to create fully functional apps that don't require you to know all the inner details of implementing complex view controllers by hand.

To me, being able to pick up the book and create applications that work after only a few hours of reading is more important than a pedantic discussion of every iOS nuance, especially if you know where to look for more information. I write what I would want to read. If you have a different view, please let me know; I'm always striving to make the book more useful to the reader.

Exploring Navigation Controllers

The navigation controller (`UINavigationController`) class presents a series of scenes that represent hierarchical information. In other words, one scene presents a high-level view of a topic, a second scene drills down further, a third scene even further, and so on. For example, the iPhone version of the Contacts application presents a list of contact groups. Touching a group opens a list of contacts within that group. Touching an individual contact displays details on that person, as shown in Figure 13.1. At any point in time, a user can back out of a level of detail and return to the previous level or jump all the way to the starting point (called the root).

Managing this transition between scenes is the navigation controller. It creates a "stack" of view controllers. The root view controller is at the bottom. As a user navigates deeper into the scenes, each successive view controller is pushed on the stack, with the current scene's view controller at the very top. To return to a previous level, the navigation controller pops the topmost controller off the stack and returns to the one below it.

TIP

The terminology of *push* and *pop* is used to describe navigation controllers throughout the iOS documentation. Be sure that you understand this concept before using it in your application.

FIGURE 13.1
Navigation controllers are prevalent in iOS.

Navigation Bars, Items, and Bar Button Items

In addition to managing the stack of view controllers, the navigation controller manages a navigation bar (`UINavigationBar`). Appearing similar to the toolbar you used in the preceding hour, a navigation bar is populated from an instance of a navigation item (`UINavigationItem`) that is added to each scene that falls under the navigation controller.

By default, the navigation item for a scene contains a title for that scene and a Back button. The Back button is added as a bar button item (`UIBarButtonItem`) within the navigation item (yes, just like the bar buttons you used in the last hour). You can even drag additional bar button items into the navigation item to add your own custom buttons to the navigation bar that is displayed for that scene.

I fully expect that if you've made it through that description you're getting a bit worried about having to manually handle all those different objects (and that's why doing this in code is not trivial!). Don't fear: Interface Builder makes it painless, and once you see how each scene is constructed, you'll have no problem working with all of these objects in your apps.

Using Navigation Controllers in Storyboard

Adding a navigation controller to a storyboard is very similar to adding a view controller, something you've done several times over the past two hours. It looks a bit different, but the process is the same. Let's assume you're starting with a Single View Application template.

First, you want to establish the code files for one or more view controller subclasses to handle the user's interactions within a given navigation controller scene. This is the same as any other scene. If you don't recall how to add new subclasses to your project, review Hours 11 and 12 to see how the modal scenes tutorials work.

Open your storyboard file in the IB editor. If you want your entire application to fall under the navigation controller, select the view controller in the default view and delete it. (You want to remove the corresponding ViewController.swift file, as well.) This removes the default scene. Next, you drag an instance of the navigation controller object from the Object Library into the document outline or the editor. This adds what appears to be two scenes to your project, as shown in Figure 13.2.

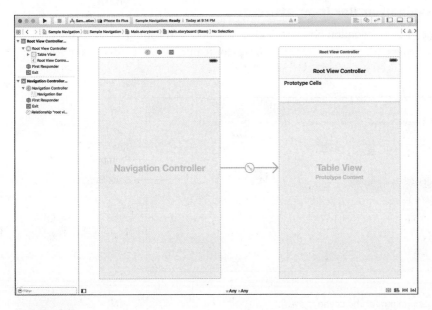

FIGURE 13.2
Add a navigation controller to your project.

The scene labeled Navigation Controller Scene represents the navigation controller. It is just a placeholder for the object that is going to control all the scenes that fall underneath it. Although you won't want to change much about the controller, you can use the Attributes Inspector to customize its appearance slightly (choosing a color scheme/tint, if desired).

The navigation controller is connected via a "relationship" to a scene titled with Root View Controller. By default, IB sets a table view controller as the root view controller. This can be removed, and the relationship to any custom view controller you'd like, created. We'll be doing that in one of today's tutorials.

The scenes under a navigation controller are exactly like any other scene; they just happen to have the navigation bar at the top and can use a segue to transition to further scenes. Development within the content area of the scenes is the same as developing in any other view.

TIP

I use the Single View Application template because it gives me an application with an associated storyboard file, and it gives me an initial view that I could, if needed, display before seguing into another view controller. If I don't want the initial scene, I delete it, and I delete the default ViewController.swift files. In my opinion, this is the fastest way to get a clean project and a consistent starting point.

Setting the Navigation Bar Item Attributes

To change the title in the navigation bar, just double-click and start editing, or select the navigation item in the scene and open the Attributes Inspector (Option-Command-4), as shown in Figure 13.3.

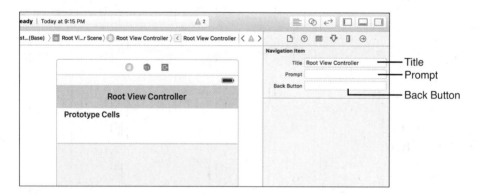

FIGURE 13.3
Customize the navigation item for the scene.

You can change three attributes:

▶ **Title:** The title string that is shown at the top of the view

▶ **Prompt:** A line of text that provides instruction to the user (if needed) and is shown above the title

▶ **Back Button:** The text that appears in the Back button of the next scene

Now wait a minute. You can edit the text of the button that appears in a scene you don't even have yet? Yes. By default, when you transition from one navigation controller scene to another, the "title" of the previous scene shows up as the title of the Back button in the next scene. Sometimes, however, the title may be long, or not necessarily appropriate. In these cases, you can set the Back button attribute to whatever string you want, and if the user drills down to the next scene, that text will be displayed in the button that takes you back to the scene.

The Back button text does one additional thing. Because iOS can no longer use its default behavior to create a Back button, it creates a new custom bar button item within the navigation item that contains the title you wanted. You can customize this bar button item even more, changing its color and appearance using the Attributes Inspector.

So far, there is only a single scene under the navigation controller, so the Back button would never be displayed. Let's see how you can chain together multiple scenes to create the "drill-down" hierarchy that navigation controllers are known for.

NOTE
Remember, you can drag additional bar button items into a scene's navigation item to add toolbar-like controls to the scene.

Adding Additional Navigation Scenes with Show Segues

To add an additional scene to the navigation hierarchy, we follow the same process as adding a new modally presented scene to an application. Begin by creating a new scene that you want to be managed by the navigation view controller. Next, just Control-drag from the object that you want to trigger the segue to the new scene's view controller. When prompted, choose the Show segue. You'll see a new segue line added to the originating scene, as well as a change to the scene you just connected. The new scene shows the navigation bar, but will require that you add your own navigation item to customize the title and back button. (This is a change from earlier versions of Xcode that added the navigation item for you.)

What's important to realize here is that you can keep doing this. You can add additional segues and even branch from multiple segues to follow different paths, as shown in Figure 13.4. Xcode keeps track of everything for you.

Keep in mind that these are just views, like any other, so you are welcome to add modal segues or popovers in your storyboard as well. One advantage that this hour's controllers have over other segues is that transitioning to and from views is handled automatically. You don't need to add any code to use the Back button or the swipe gesture within a navigation controller hierarchy, nor (as you learn shortly) any code to switch between scenes in a tab bar controller application.

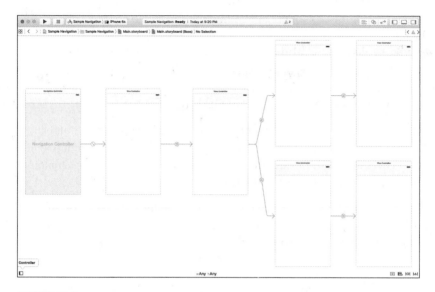

FIGURE 13.4
Create as many segues as you need, even branches.

Sharing Data Between Navigation Scenes

As I hinted early on, the navigation controller and tab bar controller classes, because they manage a series of views, give us a perfect place to share data. We can access these classes using the `parentViewController` variable property from any of the scenes we create—just like you used `presentingViewController` from a modal scene to access the view controller of the scene that presented it.

We can (and will) create a subclass of `UINavigationController` that does nothing but include variable properties we want to share between scenes, assign that as the identity class of the navigation controller that is managing all of our scenes, and then access those variables via `parentViewController` in any of the other views.

Understanding Tab Bar Controllers

The second type of view controller that we work with in this hour is the tab bar controller (`UITabBarController`). Tab bar controllers, like navigation controllers, are prominently featured in a wide range of iOS applications. As the name implies, a tab bar controller presents a series of "tabs" at the bottom of the screen, represented as icons and text. By touching these, you can switch between scenes. Each scene represents a different function in the application or a unique way of viewing the application's information.

The Health application on the iPhone, for example, presents different ways of viewing your health information by using a tab bar controller, as shown in Figure 13.5.

FIGURE 13.5
A tab bar controller switches between unique scenes.

Like a navigation controller, the tab bar controller handles everything for you. When you touch a button to transition between scenes, it just works. You don't need to worry about programmatically handling tab bar events or manually switching between view controllers. The similarity doesn't end there.

Tab Bars and Tab Bar Items

The implementation of a tab bar within the storyboard is also very similar to a navigation controller. It contains a `UITabBar` that resembles a toolbar, but in appearance only. Any scene that is presented with the tab bar controller inherits this navigation bar within its scene.

The scenes presented by a tab bar controller must contain a tab bar item (`UITabBarItem`) that has a title, an image, and, if desired, a badge (a little red circle with value in it).

TIP

If you're wondering why a tab might need a badge, imagine that you have a long-running calculation in one of the tab scenes in your application. If the user switches off of the tab, the calculation continues. You can have the scene's view controller update the badge in the tab, even when the user is viewing another tab's scene.

This gives an immediate visual indication that there is something to look at without the user needing to switch back and forth.

Using Tab Bar Controllers in Storyboard

Adding a tab bar controller to the storyboard is just as easy as adding a navigation controller. Let's walk through the steps of how to add the controller, configure the tab bar buttons, and add additional tab scenes to the storyboard.

CAUTION

We Don't Need No Stinkin' (Tabbed) Templates

Before you start building tab-based applications, I want to point out that Apple includes an iOS application template called the Tabbed Application. This template creates an application with two sample tabs already added and two view controller subclasses set up and associated with each tab. It also makes absolutely no sense (to me) to use.

This template may get you up and running a few seconds faster than adding a tab bar controller to a storyboard, but for production projects, it has a fatal flaw: Apple has associated two view controllers with the two default tabs in the application and named them `FirstViewController` and `SecondViewController`. There's nothing wrong with this for learning exercises, but in a real application, you want to name these in a way that reflects their actual use (`MovieListViewController`, `TheaterListViewController`, and so on). You could certainly rename all of their references in Xcode, but by the time you did that, it would have been faster to just add and associate your own tab bar controller and view controller subclasses.

To add a tab bar controller to an application, I recommend again starting with a Single View Application template. If you don't want the initial scene to segue into the tab bar controller, you just delete the initial scene by removing its view controller and then delete the corresponding `ViewController.swift` file. Once your storyboard is in the state you want, drag an instance of the tab bar controller object from the Object Library into the document outline or the editor. This adds a controller and two sample tab bar scenes to the view, as shown in Figure 13.6.

The tab bar controller scene represents the `UITabBarController` object that coordinates all the scene transitions. Within it is a tab bar object that can be customized slightly with IB, changing the color.

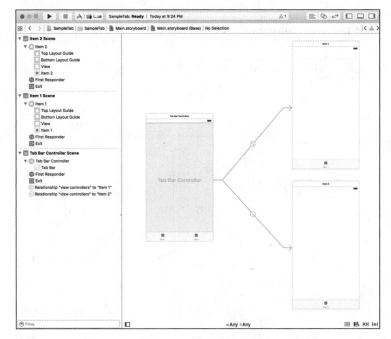

FIGURE 13.6
Adding a tab bar controller adds two default scenes to the application.

From the tab bar controller are two "relationship" connections to the two scenes that the tab bar will display. The scenes can be differentiated by the name of the tab bar button that is added to them (Item 1 and Item 2, by default).

TIP

Even though all the tab bar item buttons are shown in the tab bar controller scene, they are actually part of the each individual scene. To change the tab bar buttons, you must edit the tab bar item added to a scene. The controller scene is left alone.

Setting the Tab Bar Item Attributes

To edit the tab bar item (`UITabBarItem`) that is displayed for any scene, open that scene's view controller and select the tab bar item within the document outline area, and then open the Attributes Inspector (Option-Command-4), as shown in Figure 13.7.

Using the Tab Bar Item section, you can set a value to be displayed in the tab bar item badge. Typically, you want to set this via tab bar item's `badgeValue` variable property (a `String`) in code. You can also use the Identifier pop-up menu to choose from over a dozen predefined tab bar icons and labels. If you choose to use a predefined icon/label, you cannot customize it further, because Apple wants these to remain constant throughout iOS.

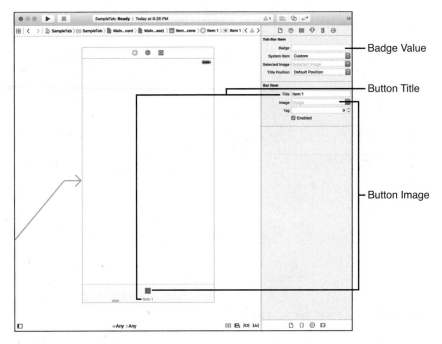

FIGURE 13.7
Customize each scene's tab bar item.

To set your own image and title, use the Bar Item settings. The Title field sets the label for the tab bar item, and the Image drop-down associates an image resource from your project for the item.

TIP

Tab bar images are "approximately" 30×30 points (60×60 pixels for 2× Retina displays, 90×90 pixels for the iPhone 6+ 3× display) or smaller and are automatically styled by iOS to appear in a monochromatic color scheme (regardless of what colors you choose). Simple line drawings with a transparent background turn out the best when creating your tab bar interface art.

That's everything you need to configure a scene for a tab bar controller. But what if you want to add additional scenes to the tab bar? We tackle that now, and, as you'll see, it's even easier than adding a scene to a navigation controller.

Adding Additional Tab Bar Scenes

Unlike other segues that we've used, a tab bar has a clearly defined item (the tab bar item) that triggers a change in scene. The scene transition isn't even called a segue; it is a relationship between the tab bar controller and a scene. To create a new scene, tab bar item, and the relationship between the controller and scene, start by adding a new view controller to the storyboard.

Drag a new view controller instance into the document outline or editor. Next, Control-drag from the tab bar controller to the new scene's view controller in document outline. When prompted, choose Relationship Segue, View Controllers, as shown in Figure 13.8.

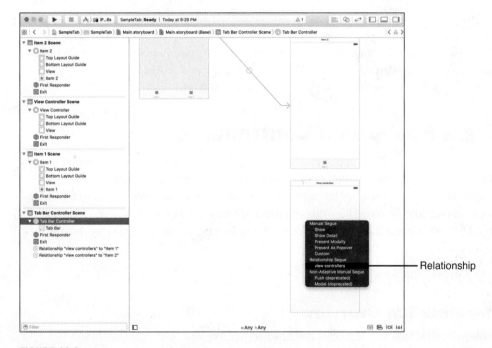

FIGURE 13.8
Create a relationship between controllers.

Creating the relationship does everything we need; it automatically adds a tab bar item to the new scene, ready to be configured. We can keep doing this to create as many tabs and scenes as we need in the tab bar.

NOTE

Let me repeat something I said earlier: The scenes that you're adding to the tab bar controller are the same as any other scene. You associate a view controller subclass using the Identity Inspector and then interact with the scene the same as you would any other.

To set the tab bar item's `badgeValue`, for example, you can just create an outlet in your view controller to reference the tab bar item. It's exactly the same as if you had added a button or a label to a view and wanted to modify it programmatically.

Sharing Data Between Tab Bar Scenes

Like the navigation controller, a tab bar controller presents us with an easy opportunity to share information. Create a tab bar controller (`UITabBarController`) subclass that is assigned as the identity of the tab bar controller. Add variable properties to the subclass that represent the data we want to share, and then access those variables through the `parentViewController` variable property in each scene.

Now that you've seen how to add these new view controllers to your project, let's actually create a few examples that demonstrate these principles in action. As promised, these will be light on the typing, so don't expect a masterpiece. The beauty is that once you know see how easy it is to use these controllers, the possibilities for your applications will open up tremendously.

Using a Navigation Controller

In the first project, we create an application that presents a series of three scenes through a navigation controller. Within each scene, we show a "next" button that increments a counter and then transitions to the next scene. The counter will be stored as a variable property in a custom subclass of the navigation controller. This will provide both an example of building a navigation-based UI and of using the navigation controller to manage a variable property that all the scenes can access.

Figure 13.9 shows what we want to accomplish.

Implementation Overview

The implementation follows the process described earlier. We start with a Single View Application template, remove the initial scene and view controller, and then add a navigation controller and two custom classes: one a subclass of a navigation controller that will enable each scene in the application to share information, the other a subclass of a view controller that will handle user interactions in the scenes.

We remove the default table view controller that is used with the navigation controller and add three scenes, designating one as the root view scene for the controller. A "next" button is included in each scene's view with an action method to increment a counter—as well as a segue from that button to the next scene.

FIGURE 13.9
Transition between scenes and manage shared information.

NOTE
_____

Doesn't each scene need its own view controller subclass? Yes and no. In most applications, you create a view controller for each scene. In this application, we're doing the same thing in each scene so that a single view controller can be used, saving us time and code.

_____

Setting Up the Project

Create a new single-view project called **LetsNavigate**. Before doing anything else, clean up the project so that we only have the things that we need. Start by selecting the ViewController.swift file and pressing the Delete key. When prompted, choose to delete the files (move to trash), not just the references.

NOTE
_____

Simple Names, Happy You

In case you're wondering, yes, we could name this project "Let's Navigate," with an apostrophe and space. Why don't we? To avoid problems down the road. Adding special characters can make source control operations difficult, lead to inconsistencies in your class naming conventions, and generally result in future unpleasantness. The name of your project doesn't have to match the application name that you submit to Apple, so I recommend keeping your project names as simple as you can.

_____

Next, click the Main.storyboard file and then select the View Controller line in the document outline area (Editor, Show Document Outline) and again press Delete. The scene will disappear. We now have the perfect starting point for our app.

Adding the Navigation Controller and Generic View Controller Classes

We need two additional classes added to the project. The first, a subclass of `UINavigationController`, manages our push count variable property and will be named **CountingNavigationController**. The second, a subclass of `UIViewController`, is named **GenericViewController** and handles incrementing the push count as well as displaying the count in each scene.

To add these two additional classes, follow these steps:

1. Click the + button at the bottom-left corner of the project navigator and choose File.

2. Choose the iOS Source category and Cocoa Touch class, and then click Next.

3. Name the new class **CountingNavigationController**, set the subclass to `UINavigationController` (you will have to type in the class name), make sure that iPhone (or iPad) is selected, and set the language to Swift.

4. Click Next.

5. On the last setup screen, make sure that Xcode has chosen the code folder for your project (navigate to it, if not), choose your main project code group from the Group pop-up menu, and then click Create.

Repeat this process to create a new `UIViewController` subclass named **GenericViewController**. Make sure that you choose the right subclass for each of the new classes; otherwise, you'll have difficulty later on.

Adding and Configuring the Navigation Controller

Open Main.storyboard in the IB editor. Display the Object Library (Control-Option-Command-3) and drag a navigation controller into an empty area of the IB editor (or into the document outline area). Your project will now show a navigation controller scene and a root view controller scene. For now, concentrate on the navigation controller scene.

We want to associate this controller with our `CountingNavigationController` class, so select the navigation controller line in the document outline, and then open the Identity Inspector (Option-Command-3). From the class drop-down menu in the Custom Class section, choose `CountingNavigationController`.

Next, we need to make sure that Xcode knows this is the initial view controller to display when the application starts. Make sure that the navigation controller is still selected in the document

outline, and then open the Attributes Inspector (Option-Command-4), and check the Is Initial
View Controller check box within the View Controller section.

Finally, use the Size drop-down within the Simulated Metrics section to set a simulated size, as
we've done previously. This isn't required, of course, but it gives us a consistent interface to
target for the lesson.

Now let's add the additional scenes we need and associate them with the generic view controller
class we created.

Adding Additional Scenes and Associating the View Controller

With the storyboard still open, start by selecting the Root View Controller item (within the Root
View Controller scene) and pressing Delete. This gets rid of the default root view controller for the
navigation controller. We want to associate our own (more flexible) `GenericViewController`
class as the root view controller. To do this, drag a new view controller (`UIViewController`)
from the Object Library into the IB editor. A new scene is created, and your document should
resemble Figure 13.10. This will become your new root view.

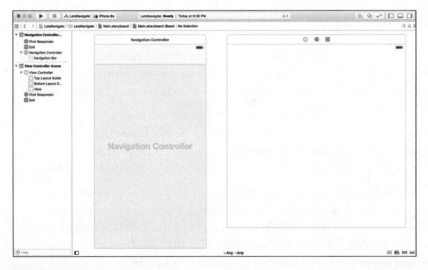

FIGURE 13.10
Add a new view controller to use as a root view controller.

Control-drag from the navigation controller to the new view controller. When finished dragging, release your mouse button. You are prompted for the type of connection to make. Choose
Relationship Segue, Root View Controller. Your storyboard should now look like Figure 13.11.

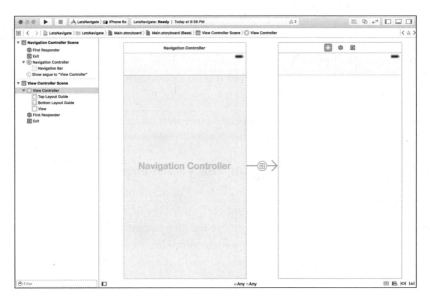

FIGURE 13.11
The new root view controller is in place.

You're ready to add the other two scenes to the storyboard. Drag two more instances of the view controller object from the Object Library into the editor or the document outline. In a few minutes, these will be connected to the root view controller scene to form a series of scenes that are managed by the navigation controller.

After adding the additional scenes, we want to do two things to each of them (including the root view controller scene). First, we need to set the identity of each scene's view controller. Next, it's a good idea to set a label for each view controller so that the scene has a friendlier name.

Start by selecting the view controller connected to the Counting Navigation Controller (the root view controller) and opening the Identity Inspector (Option-Command-3). Within the Custom Class section, use the Class drop-down menu to pick the GenericViewController. Still within the Identity Inspector, set the Label field (within the Document section) to **First**. Move to one of the new scenes you added, select its view controller line, set its class to GenericViewController, and the label to **Second**. Repeat the process for the last scene as well, setting its custom class and a label of **Third**. When finished, your document outline should look like Figure 13.12.

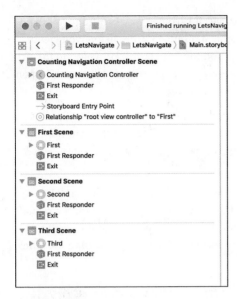

FIGURE 13.12
Your final document outline includes a navigation controller and three scenes (order is not important).

Planning the Variables and Connections

I'm intentionally trying to keep these projects light, so there isn't a great deal of information that needs to be stored or actions that will have to be defined. The CountingNavigationController will have a single variable property (pushCount) that contains the number of times we've pushed a new scene into view using the navigation controller.

The GenericViewController class will also have a single variable property called countLabel that references a label in the UI displaying the current count of pushes. It will also have a private action method named incrementCount that increases the pushCount in the CountingNavigationController by one.

NOTE

The outlet and action in the GenericViewController class will be defined once, but, to be used in each scene, must be connected to the label and button individually in each scene.

Creating the Show Segues

Hey, isn't this the time when we work on the UI? In the past two hours, we created our UI, and then we added the segue. What am I doing by switching things around? Good question. With applications that have only two scenes, it's easy to work on them separately and keep track of what is what. As soon as you start adding additional scenes, it becomes very helpful to lay them out in the storyboard, with segues, so that you can see how it all fits together before you create the interface. In addition, with the navigation controller and tab bar controllers, creating the connection actually adds objects to our scenes that we might want to configure when working on the interface. So, in my opinion, it just makes sense to create the segues first.

To build a segue for the navigation controller, we need something to trigger it. Within the storyboard editor, add a button (UIButton) labeled **Next** to the first and second scenes, but not the third. Why not the third? Because it is the last scene that can be displayed; there's nothing after it to segue to.

Next, Control-drag from the button in the first scene to the second scene's view controller line in the document outline, or target the scene directly in the editor. When prompted for the segue type, choose Show, as shown in Figure 13.13. A new segue line (Show Segue to Second) will be added to the first scene in the document outline, and the second scene will inherit the navigation controller's navigation bar.

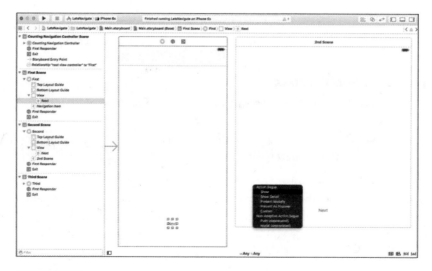

FIGURE 13.13
Create a show segue.

Repeat this process, creating a show segue from the second scene's button to the third scene. Your IB editor should now contain a fully realized navigation controller sequence. Click and drag each scene in the view to arrange it in a way that makes sense to you. Figure 13.14 shows my interconnected views.

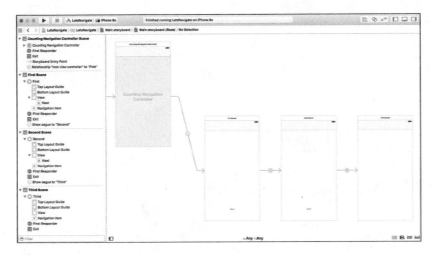

FIGURE 13.14
Connect all of your views via segue.

Designing the Interface

By adding the scenes and buttons, you've really just built most of the interface. The final steps will be adding a navigation item to each scene, customizing the title of the navigation item, and adding an output label to display the push count.

Begin by going through each of the scenes (first, second, and third) and dragging a navigation item into the scene (just drop it anywhere on the view, it doesn't matter). Next, select the navigation item within document outline. Use the Attributes Inspector (Option-Command-4) and the Title field to set each view's title. Title the first view (the root view controller) **1st Scene**, the second **2nd Scene**, and the third... wait for it... **3rd Scene**.

TIP

You can also customize the title of the navigation item by double-clicking in the center of the blank area at the top of each scene. Unfortunately, sometimes it is difficult to hit the right spot, and thus the approach of accessing the Title field through the document outline.

In each scene, add a label (`UILabel`) near the top that reads **Push Count:** and a second label (the output label) with the default text of **0** (and a large, center-aligned font, if you like) to the center of each view.

For my design, I'm setting slightly different backgrounds for each of the three scenes. This can help users identify when they have moved to a different part of the application, but it has no functional bearing on the project. Figure 13.15 shows my final interface design.

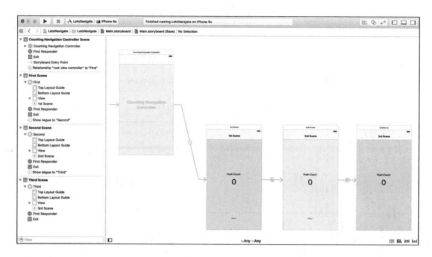

FIGURE 13.15
The final layout of the navigation application.

Creating and Connecting the Outlets and Actions

Only one outlet and one action need to be defined in this project, but they need to be connected several times. The outlet (a connection to the label displaying the push count, `countLabel`) will be connected to each of the three scenes. The action (`incrementCount`) will need to be connected to the button only in the first and second scenes.

Position your display in the IB editor so that the first scene is visible (or just use the document outline), and click its push count label, and then switch to the assistant editor mode. The GenericViewController.swift file should be visible, because we're defining variable properties and methods.

Adding the Outlet

Control-drag from the label in the center of the first scene to just below the `class` line in GenericViewController.swift. When prompted, create a new outlet named **countLabel**.

That created the outlet and the connection from the first scene; now you need to connect it to the other two scenes. Control-drag from the second scene's push count label and target the `count-Label` variable property you just created. The entire line will highlight, as shown in Figure 13.16, showing you are making a connection to an existing outlet. (You can drag from the circle beside the `countLabel` definition in GenericViewController.swift to the label within the scene— essentially the reverse of what you just did—and accomplish the same thing.)

Repeat this for the third scene, connecting its push count label to the same variable property.

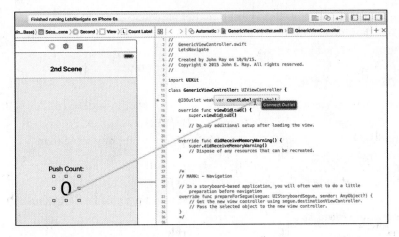

FIGURE 13.16
Create the outlet, and then connect the other scenes' labels.

Adding the Action

Adding and connecting the action works in much the same way. Start by Control-dragging from the first scene's button to just below the variable property definition in GenericViewController. swift. When prompted, create a new action named `incrementCount`.

Switch to the second scene and Control-drag from its button to the existing `incrementCount` action. You've just made all the connections we need.

Implementing the Application Logic

Most of our work is now behind us. To finish the tutorial, we first need to set up the `pushCount` variable property in the `CountingNavigationController` class so that it can keep track of the number of times we've pushed a new scene in the application.

Adding the Push Count Variable Property

Open the CountingNavigationController.swift file and add a variable property definition for an integer named `pushCount` below the `class` line:

```
var pushCount: Int = 0
```

That's all we need to do to implement the custom `CountingNavigationController` class. Because it is a subclass of a `UINavigationController`, it already performs all the navigation controller tasks we need, and now it stores a `pushCount` value.

We're all set to finish our implementation, which is just a matter of adding logic to GenericViewController that increments the counter and makes sure that it is displayed on the screen when a new scene is pushed into view.

Incrementing and Displaying the Counter

To increment the counter in GenericViewController.swift, we use the parentViewController variable property to access the pushCount variable property. The parentViewController, as you've learned, is automatically set to the navigation controller object within any scene managed by the navigation controller.

We need to cast the parentViewController to our custom class of CountingNavigationController, but the full implementation is just a single line. Implement incrementCount, as shown in Listing 13.1.

LISTING 13.1 Implementing the incrementCount Method

```
@IBAction func incrementCount(sender: AnyObject) {
    (parentViewController as! CountingNavigationController).pushCount++
}
```

The final step is to update the display to show the current count. Because pushing the button increments the push count and pushes a new scene into view, the incrementCount action isn't necessarily the best place for this logic to fall. In fact, it won't always be accurate, because the count could be updated in another view, and then the Back button used to "pop" back to the original view, which would now be showing an invalid count.

To get around this, we just add the display logic to the viewWillAppear:animated method (a standard view controller method that we'll need to add). This method is called right before a view is displayed onscreen (regardless of whether it is through a segue or by a user touching the Back button), so it is a perfect place to update the label. Add the code in Listing 13.2 to the GenericViewController.swift file.

LISTING 13.2 Updating the Display in viewWillAppear:animated

```
1: override func viewWillAppear(animated: Bool) {
2:     super.viewWillAppear(animated)
3:     let displayCount=(parentViewController as!
➡CountingNavigationController).pushCount
4:     countLabel.text=String(displayCount)
5: }
```

Line 3 declares a new constant, `displayCount`, and sets it to the `pushCount` variable property of the parent view controller. Line 4 uses the `String()` function to convert this value (an integer) to a string, and sets the `countLabel`'s `text` variable property to the string.

Building the Application

Run the application and test the navigation controller. Use the button to push new scenes on to the navigation controller stack, and then pop them back off with the Back button or the back swipe gesture functionality that we get for free. You can even use the swipe gesture to "peek" at the view underneath a given view. The push count stays in sync through all the different scenes because we now have a central class (`CountingViewController`) managing our shared variable property for us.

Using a Tab Bar Controller

In our second mini-project of the hour, we create an application with a tab bar controller that manages three individual scenes. As in the preceding project, each scene has a button to increment a counter, but these counters are unique for each scene (and visible in each scene's view). We even set the tab bar item's badge to that scene's counter. Again, we demonstrate the use of this custom controller and how scenes can share information through the controller class.

Figure 13.17 shows the result we want.

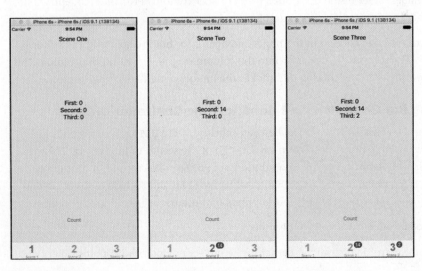

FIGURE 13.17
We will create a tab bar application with centrally stored variable properties.

Implementation Overview

We start with a cleaned-out Single View Application template. In this application, we add a tab bar controller and two custom classes: one a subclass of a tab bar controller to manage the application's variable properties, and the other a subclass of a view controller to manage the display of the other three views.

Each scene will again have a single button that calls a method to increment that scene's counter. Because the project calls for a unique counter for each scene, each button invokes a slightly different action method. This enables us to share all the code that is in common between the views (updating the badge and the count label) but have a slightly different increment action to target the right counter for that scene.

That's it; no segues needed this time around.

Setting Up the Project

Make a new single-view project called **LetsTab**. Clean out the project by removing the `ViewController` class file and the initial scene, just as you did in the previous tutorial. Your starting point should be a project with no view controller and an empty storyboard file.

Adding the Tab Bar Item Images

Each scene that is managed by the tab bar controller needs an icon to represent it in the tab bar UI element. The Images folder inside this hour's project folder contains PNG files (One.png, Two.png, Three.png) that can be used for this example.

Click the Assets.xcassets asset catalog in the project navigator so that it displays in the editor. Drag the Images folder from the OS X Finder into the column on the left within the catalog. This action creates a new folder in the catalog and makes the images available to your project.

Adding the Tab Bar Controller and Generic View Controller Classes

This project requires two custom classes. The first is a subclass of the `UITabBarController` that will hold three variable properties—counters for each of the scenes in the project. This custom controller class will be named `CountingTabBarController`. The second, a subclass of `UI-ViewController`, will be named `GenericViewController` and include a private action to increment a scene-specific count of each button press that occurs.

To create these two custom classes, follow these steps:

1. Click the + button at the bottom-left corner of the project navigator and choose File.

2. Choose the iOS Source category and Cocoa Touch class, and then click Next.

3. Name the new class `CountingTabBarController` and configure the subclass to `UITabBarController`.

4. Set the language to Swift, and then click Next.

5. Be sure to create the class files inside your main project code group, or drag the files there later.

Repeat these steps, creating a new `UIViewController` subclass named **GenericViewController**. We did almost exactly this for the previous example, so if you're experiencing déjà vu, it's okay.

Adding the Tab Bar Controller

Open the project's storyboard, and drag a tab bar controller into an empty area of the IB editor (or into the document outline area). Your project will now show a tab bar controller scene with two scenes.

Associate the tab bar controller with the custom `CountingTabBarController` by selecting the Tab Bar Controller line in the document outline, and then open the Identity Inspector (Option-Command-3). Within the Custom Class section, use the class drop-down menu to choose CountingTabBarController.

Like the last project, we must make sure Xcode knows this is the view controller to display when the application starts. With the tab bar controller still selected in the document outline, open the Attributes Inspector (Option-Command-4) and check the Is Initial View Controller check box. Finally, use the Size drop-down within the Simulated Metrics section to set a simulated size of your choosing.

Adding Additional Scenes and Associating the View Controller

The tab bar controller, by default, includes two scenes in your project. Why two? Because a tab bar controller only makes sense with more than one scene, so Apple chose to include two to start. This project, however, calls for three scenes to be managed by the tab bar controller, so drag an additional instance of the view controller object from the Object Library into the editor or the document outline.

After adding the additional scene, use the Identity Inspector to set each scene's custom class to be the `GenericViewController` and establish a label for easy identification.

Select the Item 1 scene that corresponds to the first tab in the tab bar. Using the Identity Inspector (Option-Command-3), set the Class drop-down menu to `GenericViewController` and the Label field to **First**. Move to the second scene and repeat, but set the label to **Second**. Finally, select the view controller line in the new scene you created. Set its class to `GenericViewController` and the label to **Third**. Note that the third scene isn't yet connected to the tab bar controller; this is perfectly fine.

Planning the Variables and Connections

In this project, we need to track three different counts. The `CountingTabBarController` will have variable properties for each scene's counter: `firstCount`, `secondCount`, and `thirdCount`.

The `GenericViewController` class will have two variable properties. The first, `outputLabel`, references a `UILabel` that contains the current values of the counters for all three scenes. The second variable property, `barItem`, connects to each scene's tab bar item so that we can update its badge value.

Because there are three separate counters, the `GenericViewController` class requires three action methods: `incrementCountFirst`, `incrementCountSecond`, and `incrementCountThird`. A button in each scene invokes the method specific to that scene. Two additional methods (`updateCounts` and `updateBadge`) will also be added so that we can easily update the current count and badge value without having to rewrite the same code in each increment method.

Creating the Tab Bar Relationships

As with the navigation controller, it makes sense to connect the tab bar scenes to the tab bar controller before spending much time on the user interface. The act of making the connection will actually add the tab bar item object to each scene, which is something we need if we want to manipulate the item's badge value.

Control-drag from the Counting Tab Bar Controller line in the document outline to the view controller of the scene you added (labeled Third). When prompted for the segue type, choose Relationship Segue, View Controllers, as shown in Figure 13.18. A new segue line (`Relationship from "view controllers" to Item`) will be added to the counting tab bar controller scene. In addition, the tab bar will become visible in the third scene, and a tab bar item will appear in the third scene's view.

Because all the other scenes are already connected to the tab bar controller, we're done here. Now we can move on to creating the interface.

Designing the Interface

Visually, each scene in this project is identical, with the exception of the tab bar item and a label showing the scene's name.

Begin by adding a label (reading **Scene One**) to the first scene near the top of the view. Add a second label, to be used for output, to the center of the view. The output will span multiple lines, so use the Attributes Inspector (Option-Command-4) to set the number of lines for the label to 5. You can also center the text and adjust its size as desired.

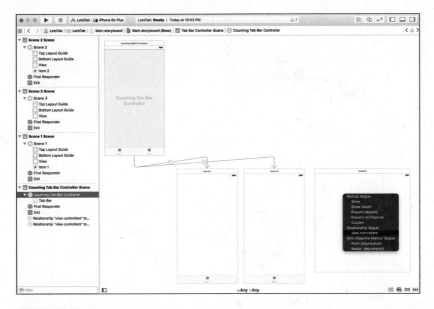

FIGURE 13.18
Create a relationship with the third scene.

Next, add a button labeled **Count** to the bottom center of the view. This will increment the counter for the view.

Now update the tab bar item to set its icon and label. Click the tab bar item at the bottom of the view, and open the Attributes Inspector. Use the Bar Item settings to set the title to **Scene 1** and the image to One, as shown in Figure 13.19.

Repeat these design steps for the other two scenes. The second scene should be labeled **Scene 2** and use the Two image file, and the third **Scene 3** with Three.

As with the previous project, I'm setting a different background color for each of my views. This is purely optional, but can be used as a visual indicator that the user has moved to a different area of the application.

Figure 13.20 shows my completed tab bar application design.

FIGURE 13.19
Configure the tab bar item for each scene.

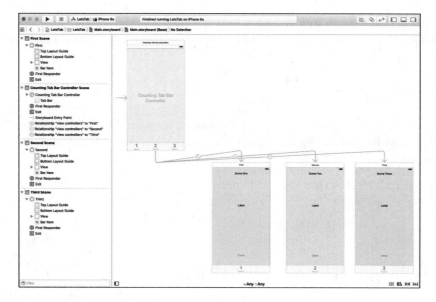

FIGURE 13.20
The final layout of the tab bar application.

Creating and Connecting the Outlets and Actions

Two outlets and three actions need to be defined in this project. The outlets will be connected identically in each scene, but the actions will be unique for each. Let's review these connections now, starting with the outputs:

- ▶ `outputLabel` (`UILabel`): Used for displaying the results of each scene's counter, this label must be connected in each scene.

- ▶ `barItem` (`UITabBarItem`): References the tab bar item that was automatically added to each view by the tab bar controller. This connection must be made in each scene.

And the actions:

- ▶ `incrementCountFirst`: Connected to the Count button in the first scene, this action method updates the first scene's counter.

- ▶ `incrementCountSecond`: Connected to the Count button in the second scene, this action method updates the second scene's counter.

- ▶ `incrementCountThird`: Connected to the Count button in the third scene, this action method updates the third scene's counter.

Make sure that the first scene is visible in IB (or just use the document outline), and then switch to the assistant editor mode.

Adding the Outlets

Control-drag from the label in the center of the first scene to just below the `class` line in GenericViewController.swift. When prompted, create a new private outlet named `outputLabel`.

Next, Control-drag from the tab bar item in the first scene to below the `outputLabel` variable property. Add another new outlet named **barItem**.

After creating the outlets for the first scene, connect them to the other two scenes. Control-drag from the second scene's output label and target the `outputLabel` in GenericViewController. swift. Do the same for the second scene's tab bar item, targeting `barItem`.

Repeat this for the third scene, connecting its label and tab bar item to the defined outlets.

Adding the Actions

The private actions are unique for each scene because each scene has a unique counter that needs to be updated. Start in the first scene and Control-drag from the Count button to below the variable property definitions in GenericViewController.swift. When prompted, create a new action named `incrementCountFirst`.

Move to the second scene and Control-drag from its button to a line below the `incrementCountFirst` action. Name this new action **incrementCountSecond**. Repeat this for the third scene, connecting to a new action named **incrementCountThird**.

Implementing the Application Logic

Only a little bit of development, and we have a fully functional tab bar application. It won't be particularly useful, but making useful content is your job! Switch back to the standard editor now.

We start by establishing the three variable properties to track the Count button presses in each of three scenes. These are going to be added in the `CountingTabBarController` class and will be named `firstCount`, `secondCount`, and `thirdCount`.

Adding the Push Count Variable Property

Open the CountingTabBarController.swift file and add three integer variable property definitions below the `class` line:

```
var firstCount: Int = 0
var secondCount: Int = 0
var thirdCount: Int = 0
```

To complete the implementation, we'll create two methods to update the display within the scenes and then add the actions to increment the counters and call the update methods.

Implementing the Counter Display

Even though the counter differs between scenes, the logic to update the display of all three counter values is entirely the same and is simply an expanded version of the code we used in the previous tutorial. We implement this logic in a new method named `updateCounts`.

Edit the GenericViewController.swift file and add the `updateCounts` method, as shown in Listing 13.3.

LISTING 13.3 Updating the Display Using the Counter Values

```
 1: func updateCounts() {
 2:     let first=(parentViewController as!
 3:         CountingTabBarController).firstCount
 4:     let second=(parentViewController as!
 5:         CountingTabBarController).secondCount
 6:     let third=(parentViewController as!
 7:         CountingTabBarController).thirdCount
 8:     self.outputLabel.text =
 9:         "First: \(first) \nSecond: \(second) \nThird: \(third)"
10: }
```

Lines 2–7 set three constants (first, second, third) to the three variable properties in the parent view controller. Lines 8-9 set the outputLabel to a nicely formatted string using Swift's string interpolation along with the first, second, and third constants.

Incrementing the Tab Bar Item Badge

To increment a scene's tab bar item badge, we read the current value from the badge (badgeValue), convert it to an integer, add 1, convert the new value to a string, and then set the badgeValue to the string. Why is all of that conversion necessary? Because the badgeValue is a string, not an integer, so we need to make sure we have a properly formatted string to change it.

Because we have added a uniform barItem variable property accessible from all the scenes, we only need a single method in the GenericViewController class to handle incrementing the badge value. We'll call this method updateBadge.

Add the code in Listing 13.4 to GenericViewController.swift.

LISTING 13.4   Updating the Tab Bar Item's Badge

```
 1: func updateBadge() {
 2:     var badgeCount: Int
 3:     if (barItem.badgeValue != nil) {
 4:         badgeCount = Int(barItem.badgeValue!)!
 5:         badgeCount++
 6:         barItem.badgeValue=String(badgeCount)
 7:     } else {
 8:         barItem.badgeValue="1"
 9:     }
10: }
```

Line 2 declares a new integer variable, badgeCount, that will ultimately hold the number that will be displayed in the tab bar item's badge.

Line 3 checks to see if the barItem's badgeValue is nil (entirely empty). If it *is*, that means that updateBadge hasn't be called before, and the badge should be set to 1 (line 8).

If the badgeValue is anything other than nil, lines 4–6 are executed. Line 4 sets the badgeCount to Int(barItem.badgeValue!)!. Kinda weird looking, don't you think? Ignore the !'s, and it's a bit easier to understand: We get the badgeValue of barItem, and then use Int() to return it as an integer. The !'s are necessary because badgeValue is an optional variable property and Int()'s return value is optional—meaning that if it can't create an integer, it returns nil.

In Line 5, badgeCount is incremented by 1.

Finally, line 6 sets the barItem.badgeValue to the badgeCount (converted to a string).

Triggering the Counter Updates

The very last step of this project is to implement the `incrementCountFirst`, `increment-CountSecond`, and `incrementCountThird` methods. If that sounds like a lot, don't worry. Because the code to update the display and the badge is in a separate method, each of these methods is a total of three lines of code, and all of that code, with the exception of a single variable property, is the same in all three.

This method must update the appropriate counter in the `CountingTabBarController` class and then call the `updateCounts` and `updateBadge` methods to update the interface appropriately. Listing 13.5 shows an implementation for the `incrementCountFirst` method.

LISTING 13.5   Adding a Method in GenericViewController.swift to Update Each Scene's Counter

```
@IBAction func incrementCountFirst(sender: AnyObject) {
    (parentViewController as! CountingTabBarController).firstCount++
    updateBadge()
    updateCounts()
}
```

Add similar code for each of the other methods: `incrementCountSecond` and `increment-CountThird`. The only difference will be the variable property you increment. Instead of `firstCount`, you use `secondCount` and `thirdCount`.

Building the Application

Run the application and switch between the different scenes. Use each scene's Count button to increment its unique counter. Thanks to the decision to store values in the centrally shared class, `CountingTabBarController`, all three counts can be accessed and displayed by any scene.

The tab bar items should also show and increment their badges when the Count button is used, providing yet another form of visual feedback that you can give to the user.

You should now be comfortable creating projects based around the tab bar and navigation controllers—a dramatic improvement over just a single scene, don't you think? The next hour's lesson finishes up our look at custom view controllers by introducing another interesting UI element and an entirely new application template. Get your fingers ready for more typing!

Further Exploration

By now, you should have a good idea of how to implement multiple views and switch between them either manually or via segue. There was quite a bit of information covered in this past hour, so I recommend reviewing the topics that we covered and spending some time in the Apple documentation reviewing the classes, the variable properties, and their methods. Inspecting the UI elements in IB will give you additional insight into how they can be integrated into your apps.

The navigation controller (UINavigationController) is often combined with other types of views, such as the table view, to enable the viewing of structured information in a logical manner. You learn a bit more about this in the next hour, but a read of the UINavigationController class reference is highly recommended. Unlike many class references, the navigation controller documentation fully describes how navigation controllers can and should be used. You'll want to learn about the UINavigationController view hierarchy, as well as the UINavigationControllerDelegate protocol, which can help you respond to advanced user events within a navigation controller.

The tab bar controller (UITabBarController) also offers additional features beyond what we were able to cover here. If there are too many buttons to be displayed in a single tab bar, for example, the tab bar controller provides its own "more" view in the form of a navigation controller. This enables you to expand the user's options beyond the buttons immediately visible onscreen. The UITabBarControllerDelegate protocol and the UITabBarDelegate can even implement optional methods to enable the user to customize the tab bar within the application. You can see this level of functionality within Apple's Music application.

Apple Tutorials

Tabster (accessible via the Xcode developer documentation): This example demonstrates a complex multiview interface using a tab bar controller.

TheElements (accessible via the Xcode developer documentation): This project shows how to drill down to more detailed information using a navigation controller and the table of elements as its subject matter.

Summary

This hour's lesson introduced two new view controller classes to your iOS toolkit. The first, the navigation controller, displays a sequence of scenes that are displayed one after the other (and are often used to drill down into detailed information about something). Navigation controllers also provide an automatic way to back out of a scene and return to the previous scene. The process of moving to a new scene is called *pushing*, and returning to the previous scene is called *popping*.

The second view controller, the tab bar controller, is used to create applications with a single unifying bar at the bottom that can be used to switch between different scenes. Each scene, according to Apple's guidelines, should perform a unique function. Unlike the navigation controller, all the scenes managed by a tab bar controller are "random access," meaning that users can switch between whatever tabs they like; there is no preset order.

Both of these controllers present an opportunity for sharing information between the different scenes that they manage by implementing variable properties and methods on a custom subclass of the controller.

Finally, and possibly the best thing you learned in this hour's lesson, both of these controllers can be implemented almost entirely visually with the Xcode storyboard tools. This is a significant change from earlier releases where the code required to implement these features made them difficult to discuss.

Q&A

Q. What if I want to share information between objects that don't have a central controller class?

A. The fact that the tab bar controller and navigation controller have a nice place to implement shared variable properties is great, but not necessary. You can always create a custom class in your application and reference it in other classes that need to exchange data.

Q. Can I mix and match scenes and segues?

A. Yes and no. Navigation controllers are required for pushing and popping views, and you can't create a working tab bar application without a tab bar controller. You can, however, implement a navigation controller that is used in conjunction with a tab bar controller, display a segue that transitions to a navigation controller-managed series of scenes, and so forth.

Q. Are tab bar and toolbar objects interchangeable?

A. Absolutely not. A tab bar is for switching between different functional areas of an application. A toolbar is for activating a feature within a single functional area of an app.

Workshop

Quiz

1. A navigation controller will use which segue to connect to other views?

   a. Display

   b. Shove

   c. Push

   d. Show

2. Adding additional scenes to a tab bar control involves establishing a new what?

    a. Relationship

    b. Push

    c. Modal dialog

    d. Link

3. A tab bar icon has what dimensions?

    a. 30×30 points

    b. 30×30 pixels

    c. 60×60 points

    d. 90×90 points

4. To set the badge displayed on a tab bar item, you'll access which variable property?

    a. `badge`

    b. `badgeText`

    c. `badgeValue`

    d. `badgeCircle`

5. To reference the tab bar view controller or the navigation view controller from one of the child controllers, what variable property do you use?

    a. `parent`

    b. `parentViewController`

    c. `superViewController`

    d. `viewControllerTop`

6. The recommended approach for starting a tab bar application uses which template?

    a. Tab Bar Application

    b. Single View Application

    c. Master Detail Application

    d. Empty Application

7. What is used to set the badge value of a tab bar item?

   a. `Integer`

   b. `Float`

   c. `String`

   d. Any object

8. When you connect additional scenes to a navigation controller, what will they inherit?

   a. Navigation title

   b. Navigation bar

   c. Navigation icon

   d. Navigation button

9. How many additional classes were used to manage the content of the scenes (not including the controller) in this hour's exercises?

   a. 1

   b. 2

   c. 3

   d. None

10. Although Xcode automatically adds some new objects to your navigation scenes, you must add which of the following?

   a. `UINavigationButton`

   b. `UINavigationBar`

   c. `UINavigationItem`

   d. `UINavigationList`

Answers

1. D. The Show segue is used to push a new scene onto a navigation controller.

2. A. New scenes are added to a tab bar controller by establishing relationships between new view controllers and the tab bar controller.

3. A. Tab bar icons should be roughly 30×30 points.

4. C. You'll update the `badgeValue` variable property to change the badge displayed on a tab bar item.

5. B. Use the `parentViewController` variable property to grab the navigation or tab bar controller from any of the child controllers.

6. B. I always recommend using the Single View Controller as the starting point for tab bar applications, despite a separate tab bar template being available.

7. C. A `String` is used to set a tab bar item's badge value.

8. B. New scenes added to a navigation controller will automatically inherit the navigation bar.

9. A. A single generic view controller class was used to handle all the additional scenes in both projects.

10. C. The `UINavigationItem` is no longer added automatically to scenes connected to a navigation controller.

Activities

1. Create a simple calculator application using the tab bar controller. Use one view, for example, for calculating the area of common shapes (circles, squares, and so on) and another for calculating volumes of their 3D equivalents (spheres, cubes, and so on). Use the central tab bar controller class to automatically populate dimensions that are entered in one view so that they can be reused in another.

2. Update the navigation controller example so that the navigation branches depending on a user's selection.

Navigating Information Using Table Views and Split View Controllers

---

What You'll Learn in This Hour:

▶ The types of table views

▶ How to implement a simple table view and controller

▶ Ways to add more structure and impact to a table with sections and cell images

▶ The purpose of split view controllers

▶ How to use a Master-Detail Application template

So far, our exploration of iOS development has included typical interface elements that focus on getting information from the user, with little attention paid to output. What's missing is the ability to *present* categorized information in a structured manner. Everywhere you look (websites, books, applications on your computer), you see methods for displaying information in an attractive and orderly manner. iOS has its own conventions for displaying this type of information.

First, the table view. This UI element is essentially a categorized list, like what you see when browsing your iOS contacts. Second, the `SplitViewController` object combines tables, a sliding panel (essentially a popover that slides in from the side), and a detail view into an experience very similar to using Apple's Mail app on the iPad or 5.5"+ iPhone. In this hour, we explore how to implement a table view, and then we take that knowledge and apply it to a universal application that navigates information using a table/navigation controller combination on smaller-screened iPhones and a split view on the iPad and "plus-sized" iPhones.

Understanding Tables

Like the other views you've seen in this book, a table view (`UITable`) holds information. A table view's appearance, however, is slightly counterintuitive. Instead of showing up as a true table (like an Excel worksheet), a table view displays a single list of cells onscreen. Each cell can be structured to contain multiple pieces of information but is still a single unit. In addition, the cells can be broken into sections so that the clusters of information can be communicated visually. You might, for example, list computer models by manufacturer or models of the Macintosh by year.

Table views respond to touch events and enable the user to easily scroll up and down through long lists of information and select individual cells through the help of a table view controller (UITableViewController) and two protocols: UITableViewDataSource and UITableViewDelegate.

NOTE
A table view controller is just a standard view controller that displays only a table view. You can use this if a table view is going to be your entire view. That said, it offers no benefits over using a standard view controller and adding a table view except that its delegate and data source variable properties are set automatically. That's it!

In fact, by using a standard view controller and adding the two protocols, we can create tables that are sized any way we want within our views. We just need to connect the table's delegate and data source outlets to the view controller class.

Because creating our own table view controller from a standard view controller offers the greatest flexibility, that's what we do in this lesson.

Table Appearance

There are two basic styles of table views: plain and grouped, as demonstrated in Figure 14.1. Plain tables lack the clear visual separation of sections of the grouped tables, but are often implemented with a touchable index (like the Contacts list of people). Because of this, they are sometimes called indexed tables. This text continues to refer to them by the names (plain/grouped) designated in Xcode.

Table Cells

Tables are only a container. To display content in a table, you must provide information to the table by configuring table view cells (UITableViewCell). By default, a cell can display a title, a detail label, an image, and an accessory—usually a disclosure indicator that tells the user he can "drill down" to more information through a push segue and a navigation controller. Figure 14.2 shows a sample table cell layout with each of these features active.

In addition to its visual design, each table cell has a unique identifier called the reuse identifier. This is used to refer to the cell layout by name when we're coding and must be set when configuring the table.

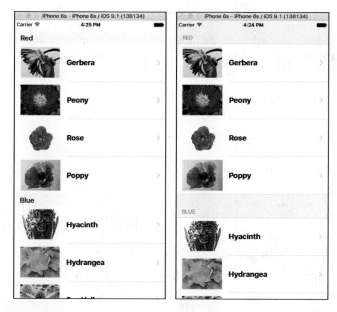

FIGURE 14.1
Plain tables look like simple lists, whereas grouped tables have more distinct divisions.

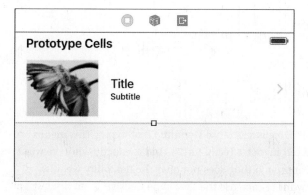

FIGURE 14.2
Table cells make up the content of a table.

Adding a Table View

To add a table to your view, drag the `UITableView` from the Object Library into one of your views. After adding the table, you can resize it to fill the view, or only a portion, if you prefer. If you drag a `UITableViewController` into the editor instead, you'll get a whole new scene in the storyboard with a table filling the entire view.

Setting Table Attributes

After adding the view, you can set its styling by selecting the table view and then opening the Attributes Inspector (Option-Command-4) in the Interface Builder (IB) editor, demonstrated in Figure 14.3.

FIGURE 14.3
Set the attributes of the table.

The first thing you'll see is that the default table is set to use Dynamic Prototypes. This means that we can visually design the table and cell layout directly in IB—and is exactly what we want. The other option, Static Cells, is an older approach that does not offer the flexibility we now have in the latest versions of Xcode. You want to increase the Prototype Cells value to at least 1 (as is visible in Figure 14.3). This setting shows what the cells in the table will look like. You can update Prototype Cells to as many as you need; each one can take on a unique appearance and be accessed in code via its reuse identifier. (Just a minute and you'll see where that's set.)

Use the Style pop-up menu to choose between Plain and Grouped table styles, the Separator to choose the separator appearance between sections, and the Color pop-up to set the color of the lines that separate cells.

The Selection and Editing settings change the behavior of the table when it is touched. We won't be getting into table editing, so the default settings are sufficient (allowing only one row at a time to be touched and highlighting it when it is touched).

Once the setup of the table container is complete, you need to design the cell prototype.

Setting the Prototype Cell Attributes

To control the cells that are displayed in a table, you must configure the prototype cell (or cells) that you want to use in your application. By default, there are no prototype cells made available when adding a table, so make sure you add one; otherwise, you won't have anything to edit.

Begin editing the prototype by expanding the table view item within your view and selecting the table view cell (or just click the cell directly in the editor). Once the cell is highlighted, you can use its selection handle to increase the cell height. Everything else, however, needs the Attributes Inspector, as shown in Figure 14.4.

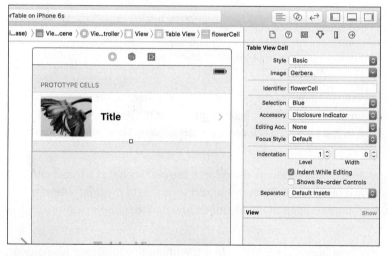

FIGURE 14.4
Configure your prototype cell.

CAUTION

Sizing Consistency Is Crucial!

Increasing the cell height by dragging the selection handle changes the height listed in the Size Inspector for both the cell and its parent table view object. If you select the cell and use the Size Inspector alone to change the height, it will appear to work, but the table view object won't inherit the changes. You must then select the table view separately, open the Size Inspector, and use the Row Height field to set the height to match the cell.

A different (and more consistent) approach is to forego using the selection handles to resize the cell. Instead, simply select the table view and use the Size Inspector to set the Row Height. The height you set on the table will be automatically inherited by the cell.

At the top of the Attributes Inspector is a cell style. Custom cells require you to create a custom subclass for `UITableViewCell`, which is beyond the scope of this book. Thankfully, most tables use one of the standard styles:

▶ **Basic:** Only a cell title is visible.

▶ **Right Detail:** Title and detail labels are shown, detail on the right.

▶ **Left Detail:** Title and detail labels are shown, detail on the left.

▶ **Subtitle:** A detail label is displayed directly below the main cell title.

TIP

After setting a cell style, you can select the title and detail labels by clicking them within the prototype cell or the cell's view hierarchy in the document outline. Once selected, you can use the Attributes Inspector to customize the appearance of the label as desired.

Use the Image drop-down to add an image to the cell. You will, of course, need to have image resources in your project for anything to show up. Bear in mind that the image you set and the title/detail text you stylize in the prototype cell are just placeholders. They'll be replaced by actual data in code.

The selection and accessory drop-downs configure the color of the cell when it is selected and the accessory graphic (usually a disclosure indicator) that can be added to the right side of a cell. The other attributes, with the exception of the identifier, are used to configure editable table cells.

The identifier is probably the most important attribute to set. Without it, you cannot reference a prototype cell and display content in your code. You can use any arbitrary string for the identifier. Apple uses Cell in its sample code, for example. If you add multiple prototype cells with different designs, each must have its own unique identifier.

That covers the visual design of a table. Now, how about the code that makes it work? To populate a table, you use the Connections Inspector for the table view to connect the delegate and data source outlets to the class (probably your view controller) that will implement the `UITableViewDelegate` and `UITableViewDataSource` protocols, respectively.

The Table View Data Source Protocol

The table view data source protocol (UITableViewDataSource) includes methods that describe how much information the table will be displaying, as well as provide the UITableViewCell objects to the application for display. This is a bit of a contrast to what we experienced with picker views, where the data source provided only the amount of information being displayed.

We focus on four of the most useful data source methods:

▶ **numberOfSectionsInTableView:** Returns the number of sections that the table will be divided into.

▶ **tableView:numberOfRowsInSection:** Returns the number of rows of information within a given section. Sections are numbered starting at 0.

▶ **tableView:titleForHeaderInSection:** Returns a string that represents the section number provided to the method.

▶ **tableView:cellForRowAtIndexPath:** Returns a properly configured cell object to display in the table.

For example, suppose that you want to create a table with two sections with the headings One and Two. The first section will have a single row, and the second will have two. This setup is handled by the first three methods, as demonstrated in Listing 14.1.

LISTING 14.1 Configuring the Sections and Row Count for the Table View

```
 1: func numberOfSectionsInTableView(tableView: UITableView) -> Int {
 2:     return 2
 3: }
 4:
 5: func tableView(tableView: UITableView,
 6:     numberOfRowsInSection section: Int) -> Int {
 7:     if section==0 {
 8:         return 1
 9:     } else {
10:         return 2
11:     }
12: }
13:
14: func tableView(tableView: UITableView,
15:     titleForHeaderInSection section: Int) -> String? {
16:     if section==0 {
17:         return "One"
18:     } else {
19:         return "Two"
20:     }
21: }
```

Lines 1–3 implement the `numberOfSectionsInTableView` method, which returns 2; the table will have two sections.

Lines 5–12 handle the `tableView:numberOfRowsInSection` method. When the section number specified by iOS is 0 (the first section), the method returns 1 (line 10). When the section is 1 (the second table section), the method returns 2 (line 12).

Lines 14–21 implement the `tableView:titleForHeaderInSection` method, which is very similar to the previous method, except it returns a string to be used as a section's title. If the section is 0, the method returns `"One"` (line 20); otherwise, it returns `"Two"` (line 22).

These three methods set up the table's layout, but to provide content to a table cell, you must implement the `tableView:cellForRowAtIndexPath`. iOS passes an object called an `NSIndexPath` to the method. This includes a variable property called `section` and one named `row` that identify the specific cell you should return. The method initializes a `UITableViewCell` and sets its `textLabel`, `detailTextLabel`, and `imageView` variable properties to change the information it displays.

Let's walk through a quick implementation of a method that could provide cell objects to a table view. This assumes that the table cell has the identifier `"Cell"`; that it has been configured to show an image, title, and detail label; and that we have an image file named generic.png that we want displayed in every cell. It's not a very realistic real-world example, but we'll save that for the exercises. Listing 14.2 shows a possible implementation of `tableView:cellForRowAtIndexPath`.

LISTING 14.2 A Silly Implementation of `tableView:cellForRowAtIndexPath`

```
 1:  func tableView(tableView: UITableView,
 2:      cellForRowAtIndexPath indexPath: NSIndexPath) -> UITableViewCell {
 3:
 4:      let cell: UITableViewCell =
 5:          tableView.dequeueReusableCellWithIdentifier("Cell")! As
 6:          UITableViewCell
 7:      let cellImage: UIImage = UIImage(named: "generic.png")!
 8:
 9:      if indexPath.section==0 {
10:          cell.textLabel!.text="Section 0, Row 0"
11:          cell.detailTextLabel!.text="Detail goes here."
12:          cell.imageView!.image=cellImage
13:      } else {
14:          if indexPath.row==0 {
15:              cell.textLabel!.text="Section 1, Row 0"
16:              cell.detailTextLabel!.text="Detail goes here."
17:              cell.imageView!.image=cellImage
18:          } else {
```

```
19:                    cell.textLabel!.text="Section 1, Row 1"
20:                    cell.detailTextLabel!.text="Detail goes here."
21:                    cell.imageView!.image=cellImage
22:              }
23:          }
24:
25:      return cell
26:  }
```

The method starts on line 4 by initializing a cell object based on the prototype call with the identifier "Cell". All implementations of this method should start with these lines.

Lines 7 initializes a UIImage (cellImage) from a project resource named generic.png. In a real project, you'll likely want a different image for each cell.

Lines 9–13 configure the cell for the first section (indexPath.section==0). Because there is only a single row, we don't need to worry about which row is being requested.

The cell is populated with data by setting its textLabel, detailTextLabel, and imageView variable properties. These are just instances of UILabel and a UIImageView, so in the case of the labels, we need to assign the text variable property, and for the image view, we set the image variable property.

Lines 14–22 set up the cells for the second section (1). In the second section, however, the row matters (since it has two rows). So the row is checked to see whether it is 0 or 1 (the first two rows), and then the contents of the cell are modified appropriately.

Line 25 returns the properly initialized cell.

That's all it takes to get a table view populated, but to react to a user's touch inside a table row, we need a method from the UITableViewDelegate protocol.

The Table View Delegate Protocol

The table view delegate protocol includes several methods for reacting to a user's interactions with a table—everything from selection rows to touching the disclosure indicator to editing the cells in the rows. For our purposes, we're only interested in when the user touches and highlights a row, so we will use the tableView:didSelectRowAtIndexPath method.

A table selection is provided to the tableView:didSelectRowAtIndexPath method using the NSIndexPath object. This means that you need to react to the section and row that the user touched. Listing 14.3 shows how we can react to a touch in the hypothetical table we've created.

LISTING 14.3 Reacting to a User's Touch

```
func tableView(tableView: UITableView,
    didSelectRowAtIndexPath indexPath: NSIndexPath) {
    if indexPath.section==0 {
        // The user chose the first cell in the first section
    } else {
        if indexPath.row==0 {
            // The user chose the first row in the second section
        } else {
            // The user chose the second row in the second section
        }
    }
}
```

Nothing to it, right? The comparison logic is the same as Listing 14.2, so refer back to it if you're wondering how the method determines which section/row is which.

That's all we need for tables! We'll now take a look at a special type of view controller and application template that pulls together navigation controllers, tables, and a universal iPad/iPhone application. You won't need any new coding knowledge for this, but you will need to call on several things you've learned over the past few hours.

TIP

If you want to make full use of tables in your applications, you should read Apple's documentation on `UITableView` and the `UITableViewDataSource` and `UITableViewDelegate` protocols. There's a great deal of information available that can help you create tables with far more features than we can fit in a single hour's lesson.

Exploring the Split View Controller

The second interface element we look at in this lesson is the split view controller. This controller isn't just a feature that you add to an application; it is a structure that you build entire applications around. It is also unrelated to the "Split View" multitasking feature for iPads introduced in iOS 9 (but it does serve as a nice starting point for Split View multitasking apps).

A split view controller enables you to display two distinct view controller scenes in a single iPad or 5.5"+ iPhone screen. In landscape mode, the left third of the screen is occupied by the "master" view controller's scene, and the right half contains the "detail" view controller scene. In portrait mode, the scene managed by the detail view controller shifts to take up the entire screen. You can use any views and controls you want in either of these areas—tab bar controllers, navigation controllers, and so on. On smaller iPhone screens, a "master" table view slides away to reveal a "detail" screen.

As mentioned earlier, the split view controller pulls together tables, a sliding panel, and a number of views. For users, it works like this: In landscape mode on iPads and large-screened iPhones, a table is displayed on the left so that the user can make a selection. When an element from the table is touched, the detail area shows (guess what?) details about the selection. If the device is rotated to a portrait mode, the table disappears, and the detail fills the screen. To navigate between different items in portrait mode, the user can touch a toolbar button or swipe in from the left side of the screen to display the detail table. Small-screen devices show the same table, wait for a user selection, and then reveal a new screen with detail information. A different user interface, but using the same classes and storyboard.

This application structure is widely used in both Apple and third-party applications. Mail, for example, uses a split interface for showing the list of messages and the body of a selected message. Popular note/file management apps, like Evernote, show a list of entries on the left and the content in the detail view, as shown in Figure 14.5.

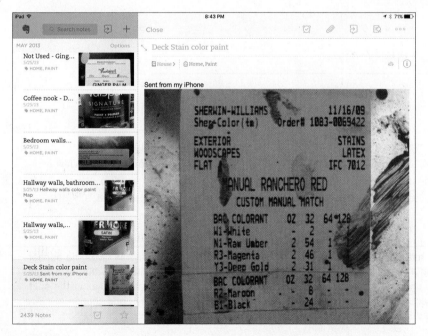

FIGURE 14.5
A table on the left and details on the right.

Implementing the Split View Controller

You can add the split view controller to your project by dragging it from the Object Library to your storyboard. It must be set as the initial scene in the storyboard; you cannot transition to it from any other view. When first added, as shown in Figure 14.6, it automatically includes several default views that are associated with the master and detail view controllers.

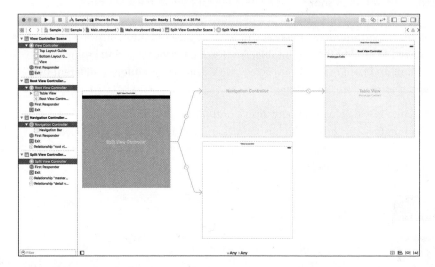

FIGURE 14.6
Adding a split view controller includes a bit of cruft in your application interface.

These can be removed, new scenes added, and then the relationships between the split view controller and the master/detail scenes reestablished by Control-dragging from the split view controller object to the master scene and the detail scene and choosing Relationship, Master View Controller and Relationship, Detail View Controller, respectively, when prompted.

TIP

The split view controller appears in the IB editor in portrait mode by default. This gives the appearance of only having a single scene (the detail scene) contained in it. To switch it to the landscape mode and see the division between the master/detail portions of the display, first select the split view controller object. Next open the Attributes Inspector (Option-Command-4) and change the Size popup menu to iPad Full Screen, and Orientation pop-up menu to Landscape.

This is purely a visual change in the editor; it doesn't change how the application functions at all.

After you've established a split view controller in your application, you build it out as you normally would, but you essentially have two unique "parts" that can work independently of one another (the master scene and the detail scene). To share information between them, each side's view controller can access the other side through the split view controller that manages them.

The master view controller, for example, can return the detail view controller using this:

```
splitViewController!.viewControllers.last
```

And the detail view controller can get ahold of the master view controller with the following:

```
splitViewController!.viewControllers.first
```

The `splitViewController` variable property contains an array called `viewControllers`. Using the `Array` method `last`, we can grab the last item in the view controller array (the detail view). Using the method `first`, we can get the first item in the array (the master view). From there, we're set; both view controllers can exchange information freely.

The Master-Detail Application Template

If it seems like I rushed through that, it's because I did. The split view controller can be whatever you want it to be; however, to be used as Apple intended, it needs a navigation controller and quite a few different views. Doing all the setup necessary to make it work like the iPad Mail app, for example, would take quite a few hours out of this book.

Thankfully, Apple has created an application template called the Master-Detail Application template that makes this easy. In fact, Apple recommends, in its documentation of the split view controller, that you use this template as a starting point instead of starting from scratch.

All the functionality is handled for you automatically. No need to deal with the sliding panel, no need to set up view controllers, no handling the swipe gesture, no manually rearranging the view after a user rotates the device. It just works. Your only job is to supply the content for the table, implemented in the template's `MasterViewController` class (a table) and the detail view, handled by the `DetailViewController` class.

It gets better! The Master-Detail Application template is set up so that you can easily create a universal application that works on any device. The same code works for both iPad and iPhone, so you'll get another taste of universal development in this exercise. Before we get to that, however, first we need to try our hand at creating a table.

A Simple Table View Application

To begin this hour's tutorials, we create a two-section table that lists the names of common red and blue flowers under a heading that describes their colors. Each table cell, in addition to a title, contains an image of the flower and a disclosure indicator. When the user touches an entry in the table, an alert appears showing the chosen flower name and color. The final application will look similar to Figure 14.7.

FIGURE 14.7
In our first application, we create a table that can react to a user's interactions.

Implementation Overview

The skills needed to add table views to your projects are very similar to what you learned when working with pickers. We add a table view to a Single View Application template and then implement the `UITableView` delegate and data source protocols.

We use two arrays to store the data for the table, but no additional outlets or actions are needed; everything is handled by conforming to the appropriate protocols.

Setting Up the Project

Begin by creating a new iOS single-view project named **FlowerColorTable**. We use the standard `ViewController` class to act as our table's view controller because this gives us the greatest flexibility in the implementation.

Adding the Image Resources

The table we create will display images for each flower it lists. To add the flower images, first open the project navigator. Next, click the Assets.xcassets icon to open the project's image assets. Now, drag the Images folder from this hour's Projects folder in the Finder into the left-hand column inside the asset catalog.

Planning the Variables and Connections

In this project, we need two arrays (we'll call them `redFlowers` and `blueFlowers`) that, as their names imply, contain a list of the red flowers and blue flowers that we are going to display. These arrays will be added as constants. The image file for each flower is titled after the flower's name; we'll take advantage of this to simplify the project.

The only connections required are from the data source and delegate outlets of the `UITableView` object back to `ViewController`.

Adding Table Section Constants

Instead of referring to table sections by number, it is helpful to work with them a bit more abstractly. To this end, we can add a few constants to ViewController.swift so that, instead of needing to remember that "section 0" is the red flower, we can refer to it by something a bit friendlier.

Edit ViewController.swift and add these lines so that they follow the `class` line:

```
let kSectionCount:Int = 2
let kRedSection: Int = 0
let kBlueSection: Int = 1
```

The first constant, `kSectionCount`, is the number of sections the table will display; the other two constants, `kRedSection` and `kBlueSection`, are used to refer to the individual sections within the table view.

That's all the setup that's required.

Designing the Interface

Open the Main.storyboard file and use the Attributes Inspector to change the simulated size to something familiar—like a 4.7-inch iPhone.

Next, drag an instance of a table view (`UITableView`) into your application's scene. Resize the table view to fit the entire scene.

CAUTION

Table View, Not Table View Controller

Remember, drag *just* a table view into the editor, not a table view controller. If you drag in a controller, it will add an entirely new scene. If you want to do that, no problem, but you'll need to delete the existing scene and set the table's view controller identity to the `ViewController` class.

Now, select the Table View and open the Attributes Inspector (Option-Command-4). Use the Content pop-up menu to choose Dynamic Prototypes (if it isn't already selected), and then update the Prototype Cells count to 1. Set the table style to Grouped if you want to exactly match my example, as shown in Figure 14.8.

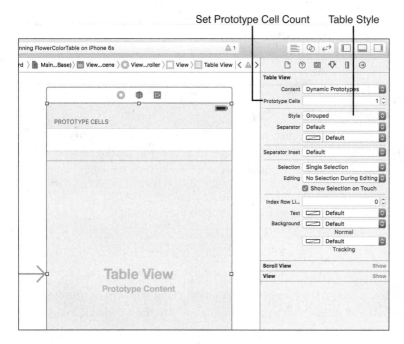

FIGURE 14.8
Set the table view attributes.

Congratulations, you've just completed 99% of the interface design! All that remains is configuring the prototype cell. Select the cell by clicking it in the editor or by expanding the table view object in the document outline and selecting the table cell object. Within the Attributes Inspector, begin by setting the cell identifier to `flowerCell`; if you leave this step out, your application won't work!

Next, set the style to Basic, and use the Image pop-up menu to pick one of the image resources you added earlier. Use the Accessory pop-up to add the Disclosure Indicator accessory to the cell and finish its layout.

At this point, your cell will be ready, but it's probably looking a bit cramped. Click and drag the handle on the bottom of the cell to expand its height until it looks the way you want. Figure 14.9 shows my completed user interface (UI).

FIGURE 14.9
A completed prototype cell.

Connecting the Delegate and Data Source Outlets

Isn't it nice to work on a project that doesn't have a bazillion outlets and actions to define?
I thought so. For our table to show information and react to a user's touch, it needs to know
where it can find its delegate and data source prototype methods. We implement those in the
`ViewController` class, so let's get it connected.

Select the table view object in the scene, and then open the Connections Inspector (Option-
Command-6). In the Connections Inspector, drag from the `delegate` outlet to the
`ViewController` object in the document outline. Do the same for the `dataSource` outlet. The
Connections Inspector should now resemble Figure 14.10.

The UI is done and the connections are in place. All we need now is code.

Implementing the Application Logic

At the start of this hour, you learned about the two protocols that we must implement to
populate a table view (`UITableViewDataSource`) and react to a user's selection of a cell
(`UITableViewDelegate`). The difference between the earlier example and now is that we will
be pulling data from an array. Because the array doesn't yet exist, creating it sounds like a good
first implementation task, don't you think?

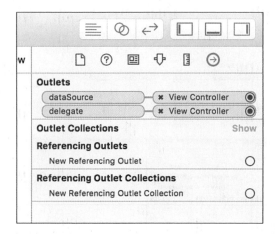

FIGURE 14.10
Connect the data source and delegate to the view controller.

Populating the Flower Arrays

We need two arrays to populate the table: one containing red flowers, and one containing blue. We need to access these throughout our class, so declaring them as variable properties or constants is required. Edit ViewController.swift and add two constants for redFlowers and blueFlowers, after the constants you created earlier:

```
let redFlowers: [String] =
    ["Gerbera","Peony","Rose","Poppy"]
let blueFlowe [String] =
    ["Hyacinth","Hydrangea","Sea Holly","Phlox","Iris"]
```

These two lines both declare and define the array constants with the names of flowers.

We now have all the data we need for the table view data source protocol—constants to determine the layout of the table and flower array constants to provide information.

Implementing the Table View Data Source Protocol

We need to implement a total of four data source methods to provide information to the table in our view: numberOfSectionsInTableView, tableView:numberOfRowsInSection, table View:titleForHeaderInSection, and tableView:cellForRowAtIndexPath. We'll work through each of these, one at a time, but first we need to declare our intention to conform the ViewController class to the UITableViewDataSource protocol. Update the class line in ViewController.swift to read as follows:

```
class ViewController: UIViewController, UITableViewDataSource {
```

Now, we add the methods, starting with `numberOfSectionsInTableView`. This method returns the number of sections the table will display, something we've conveniently stored in `kSectionCount`. Return this constant, and we're done. Implement this method as shown in Listing 14.4.

LISTING 14.4   Returning the Number of Sections in the Table

```
func numberOfSectionsInTableView(tableView: UITableView) -> Int {
    return kSectionCount
}
```

The next method, `tableView:numberOfRowsInSection`, returns the number of rows within a section (that is, the number of red flowers in the red section and the number of blue flowers in the blue section). By checking the provided section parameter against the red and blue section constants and then using the array method `count` to return a count of the items in the array, the implementation becomes trivial, as demonstrated in Listing 14.5.

LISTING 14.5   Returning a Count of the Rows (Array Elements) in Each Section

```
func tableView(tableView: UITableView,
    numberOfRowsInSection section: Int) -> Int {
    switch section {
    case kRedSection:
        return redFlowers.count
    case kBlueSection:
        return blueFlowers.count
    default:
        return 0
    }
}
```

The only thing that might throw you off here is the `switch` statement. This looks at the incoming section parameter, and if it matches the `kRedSection` constant, it returns a count of the `redFlowers` array and does the same for the blue flowers. The default case should be impossible to reach, so returning 0 is fine.

The `tableView:titleForHeaderInSection` method is even easier. It, again, must check the section against the red and blue flower constants, but it only needs to return a string (`"Red"` or `"Blue"`) to title each section. Add the implementation in Listing 14.6 to your project.

LISTING 14.6   Returning a Heading for Each Section

```
func tableView(tableView: UITableView,
    titleForHeaderInSection section: Int) -> String? {
    switch section {
```

```
case kRedSection:
    return "Red"
case kBlueSection:
    return "Blue"
default:
    return "Unknown"
}
}
```

The last data source method is the most complicated and the most important. It provides the cell objects to the table view for display. In this method, we must create a new cell from the `flowerCell` identifier we configured in IB and then populate its `imageView` and `textLabel` attributes with the data we want displayed for each incoming `indexPath` parameter. Create this method in ViewController.swift using Listing 14.7.

LISTING 14.7 Configuring a Cell to Display in the Table View

```
 1: func tableView(tableView: UITableView,
 2:     cellForRowAtIndexPath indexPath: NSIndexPath) -> UITableViewCell {
 3:
 4:     let cell: UITableViewCell =
 5:         tableView.dequeueReusableCellWithIdentifier("flowerCell")!
 6:         as UITableViewCell
 7:     switch (indexPath.section) {
 8:     case kRedSection:
 9:         cell.textLabel!.text=redFlowers[indexPath.row]
10:     case kBlueSection:
11:         cell.textLabel!.text=blueFlowers[indexPath.row]
12:     default:
13:         cell.textLabel!.text="Unknown"
14:     }
15:
16:     let flowerImage: UIImage=UIImage(named: cell.textLabel!.text!)!
17:     cell.imageView!.image=flowerImage
18:     return cell
19: }
```

Lines 4–6 create a new `UITableViewCell` object named `cell` based on the prototype cell we created with the identifier `flowerCell`.

Lines 7–17 handle the majority of the logic. By looking at the `section` variable of the incoming `indexPath` parameter, we can determine whether iOS is looking for something from the red or blue flower arrays. The `indexPath row` variable, however, identifies the row number within the section whose cell we need to configure.

Line 9 uses the row to index into the red flower array, setting the `textLabel` of the cell to the string stored at that position in the array. Line 11 does the same for the blue array.

Lines 12–13 should never be reached.

To get and set the image of the flower, we can implement the logic in one place, rather than separately for red and blue flowers. How? Using the `textLabel` variable property that we've already configured for the cell, remember—the name of the flower is also the name of an image file!

Line 16 declares a new `UIImage` object, `flowerImage`, by using the existing cell object `textLabel.text` string to find an image with the same name.

TIP
_____

iOS will automatically find the right PNG image from just the base name of the file; no extension is required. This is why we can take the shortcut of using the name of the flower (which is identical to the base image name) to retrieve the image file.

_____

Line 17 sets the cell `imageView` object's image variable property to the newly created `flowerImage`.

Finally, the fully configured cell is returned in line 18.

You should now be able to build the application and view a beautiful scrolling list of flowers, but touching a row won't do a thing. To react to a row's touch, we must implement one more method, this time in the `UITableViewDelegate` protocol.

Implementing the Table View Delegate Protocol

The table view delegate protocol handles a user's interactions with a table. To detect that a user has selected a cell in the table, we must implement the delegate method `tableView:didSelect RowAtIndexPath`. This method will automatically be called when the user makes a selection, and the incoming `IndexPath` parameter's `section` and `row` variable properties tell us exactly what the user touched.

Before writing the method, update the `class` line in ViewController.swift one more time to show that we will be also conforming to the `UITableViewDelegate` protocol:

```
class ViewController: UIViewController, UITableViewDataSource, UITableViewDelegate
{
```

How you react to a row selection event is up to you, but for the sake of this example, we're going to use `UIAlertView` to display a message. The implementation, shown in Listing 14.8, should look very familiar by this point. Add this delegate method to the ViewController.swift file.

LISTING 14.8 Handling a Row Selection Event

```
 1: func tableView(tableView: UITableView,
 2:   didSelectRowAtIndexPath indexPath: NSIndexPath) {
 3:
 4:   var flowerMessage: String
 5:
 6:   switch indexPath.section {
 7:   case kRedSection:
 8:       flowerMessage =
 9:           "You chose the red flower - \(redFlowers[indexPath.row])"
10:   case kBlueSection:
11:       flowerMessage =
12:           "You chose the blue flower - \(blueFlowers[indexPath.row])"
13:   default:
14:       flowerMessage = "I have no idea what you chose?!"
15:   }
16:
17:   let alertController = UIAlertController(title: "Flower Selected",
18:       message: flowerMessage,
19:       preferredStyle: UIAlertControllerStyle.Alert)
20:
21:   let defaultAction = UIAlertAction(title: "Ok",
22:       style: UIAlertActionStyle.Cancel,
23:       handler: nil)
24:
25:   alertController.addAction(defaultAction)
26:   presentViewController(alertController, animated: true, completion: nil)
27: }
```

Lines 4 declares `flowerMessage` that will be used for the message string shown to the user.

Lines 6–15 use a `switch` statement with `indexPath.section` to determine which flower array our selection comes from and the `indexPath.row` value to identify the specific element of the array that was chosen. The `flowerMessage` string is formatted to contain the value of the selection.

Lines 17–26 create and display an alert controller instance (`alertController`) containing the message string (`flowerMessage`).

Building the Application

After adding the delegate method to the implementation, build and run the application. You will now be able to scroll up and down through a list of flowers divided into section. Each cell in the table is configured with an image and a title string and shows a disclosure indicator (showing that touching it will do something).

Selecting a row displays an alert that identifies both the section where the touch occurred and the individual item the user selected. Of course, a "real" application would do something a bit more, so we will end this hour by doing something a bit more spectacular: creating a universal app that uses split view controllers, navigation controllers, tables, and web views.

Sounds difficult, but you'll find that the only real code required is what you just wrote while building a table.

Creating a Master-Detail Application

With a basic understanding of table controllers under our belt, we can move on to building an application that takes things to the next level by implementing a split view controller. Not only that, it will run on both the iPad and iPhone. Apple's Master-Detail Application template takes care of the tough stuff; we just need to provide content and handle a few loose ends that Apple left lying around.

This tutorial uses what we know about tables to create a list of flowers, by color, including images and a detail URL for each row. It also enables the user to touch a specific flower and show a detail view. The detail view loads the content of a Wikipedia article for the selected flower. The finished application will resemble Figure 14.11.

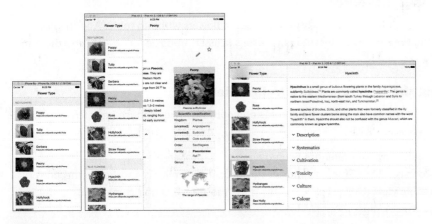

FIGURE 14.11
Our master-detail application will show flowers, including thumbnails, and details on specific flower types.

Implementation Overview

In the preceding example, we created a table view and went through all the steps of adding methods to display content. We need to repeat that process again, but UI is already provided. We will, however, need to make a few changes to the storyboard before things will work as expected.

To manage the data, we use a combination of a dictionary and an array. In Hour 15, "Reading and Writing Application Data," you'll learn about persistent data storage, which will simplify the use of data even more in your future projects.

A big change in this project is that we will be building it as a universal application (for both iPhone and iPad)—from the start. You learn more about universal applications in Hour 23, "Building Universal Applications." For now, however, you need to know just one thing: The project will contain one storyboard that services both platforms. It does this through the iOS miracle of *size classes* (yes, also in Hour 23).

Setting Up the Project

Start Xcode and create a new project using the Master-Detail Application template. Name the project **FlowerDetail**. Be sure, when stepping through the project creation assistant, that you choose Universal from the device family selection and *do not* use Core Data.

The Master-Detail Application template does all the hard work of setting up scenes and view controllers for displaying a table (MasterViewController) and one for showing details (DetailViewController). This is the "heart and soul" of many applications and gives us a great starting point for adding functionality.

Adding the Image Resources

As in the previous tutorial, we want to display images of flowers within a table. Add the flower images by dragging the Images folder into your Assets.xcassets image catalog—exactly the same as the last exercise.

Understanding the Split View Controller Hierarchy

After creating the new project, explore the Main.storyboard file. You'll notice an interesting hierarchy, as shown in Figure 14.12.

Connected to the split view controller are two navigation controllers (UINavigationController). From the master navigation controller is another connection to a scene with a table view (UITableView); this is the master scene and corresponds to the MasterViewController class files.

From the detail navigation controller is a connection to a simple empty scene; this is the detail scene and is handled by the DetailViewController class. The navigation bar at the top of the detail scene includes a button for accessing the master view and making another selection.

We need to make several changes to these files, but we'll get back to that in a few minutes. Let's take a look at the variables and connections we need to power this monster.

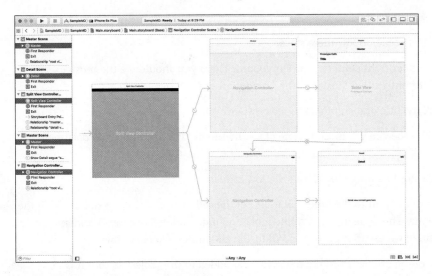

FIGURE 14.12
The storyboard contains a split view controller, which connects to additional view controllers.

Planning the Variables and Connections

Apple already has a number of variables and connections established in the project. You're welcome to review them and trace their function or just assume that Apple knows how to build software and focus on adding additional functionality. I choose the latter.

For our part, we will add two `Array` variable properties to the `MasterViewController`: `flowerData` and `flowerSections`. The first holds objects (dictionaries) that describe each flower, and the second holds the names (strings) of the sections within the table that we are creating. This structure makes it easy to interact with the table view data source and delegate methods.

In the `DetailViewController`, we add one outlet (`detailWebView`) for a `UIWebView` object that will be added to the interface and display details about a selected flower. That's the only additional object that we need to "talk" to.

Tweaking the Interface

In this tutorial, we aren't determining the application interface so much as the template is providing it for us. That said, we still need to make some changes to the storyboard. Select it in the project navigator to begin making edits.

Updating the Master Scene

To update the master scene, follow these steps:

1. Scroll to the upper-right corner of the storyboard. There you should see the master scene's table view, currently titled Master in the navigation bar.

2. Double-click the title and change it to read **Flower Type**.

3. Select the table view in the master scene object hierarchy (it's best to use the document outline for this) and open the Attributes Inspector (Option-Command-4).

4. Use the inspector to change the table style to Grouped.

5. Turning your attention to the table cell itself, set the cell identifier to `flowerCell` and the style to Subtitle. This style includes a title label and a detail label displayed underneath the title (a subtitle); we use that to show a Wikipedia URL unique to each flower.

6. Choose one of the images from the resources you added to the project so that it is previewed in the prototype cell.

7. Set a disclosure indicator using the Accessory pop-up menu, if you want.

8. Finish the design by selecting the subtitle label and changing its font size to 10 (or smaller). Then select the cell and use its handle to expand the cell to a vertical size that is visually appealing. Figure 14.13 shows my finished view.

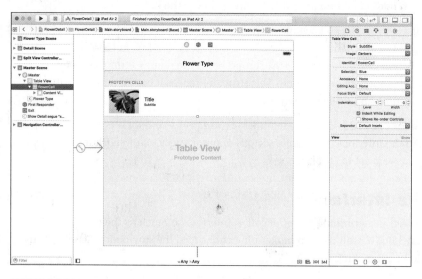

FIGURE 14.13
Tweak the master scene as shown here.

9. Before moving to the Detail scene, scroll to the navigation controller for the table view you just edited. Click in the middle of the scene to select its view controller.

10. Using the Attributes Inspector (Option-Command-4), set the view controller title to **Flower Type**. This isn't necessary for the application to run, but if you don't do this, the application will show Master for the flower list in some orientations.

Updating the Detail Scene

To update the detail scene, follow these steps:

1. Scroll down from the master scene and you should find yourself staring at a big white scene with a label that reads `Detail View Content Goes Here`.

2. Update the label to say **Please Choose a Flower**, because it is the first thing the user will see on the large-screen version of the app.

3. Drag a web view (`UIWebView`) from the Object Library into the scene.

4. Size it to fill the entire view, making sure that it snaps to the sides; this is used to display a Wikipedia page describing the flower the user selected.

5. Select the web view, then choose Editor, Resolve Auto Layout Issues, Add Missing Constraints from the menu bar (within the All Views section)

6. Position the "choose a flower" label on top of the web view by selecting the web view and using the Editor, Arrange, Send to Back menu option or by dragging the web view to the top of the view hierarchy in the document outline.

7. Finish the detail scene by updating its navigation bar title. Double-click the title and change it to read **Flower Detail**.

In step 5, we created constraints—similar to what we did in the universal project in Hour 11, "Implementing Multiple Scenes and Popovers." You'll learn more about this in Hour 16, "Building Responsive User Interfaces," but for now understand that these constraints will keep the web view sized to fill whatever sized screen it is on.

Creating and Connecting the Web View Outlet

Select the web view in the IB editor, and then switch to the assistant editor; it should display the DetailViewController.swift file.

Control-drag from the web view to just below the existing variable declarations (there should be a `detailDescriptionLabel` variable property automatically added), and create a new outlet named `detailWebView`, as shown in Figure 14.14. You've just finished the interface and connections.

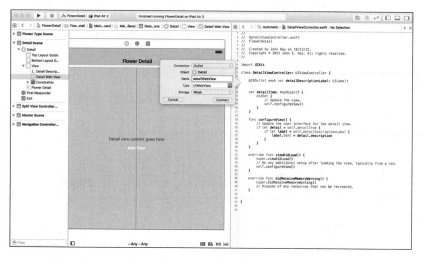

FIGURE 14.14
Connect the new web view to an outlet in the detail view controller.

Implementing the Application Data Source

In the previous table implementation project, we used multiple arrays and `switch` statements to differentiate between the different sections of flowers. This time around, however, we need to track the flower sections, names, image resources, and the detail URL that will be displayed.

Creating the Application Data Structures

What the application needs to store is quite a bit of data for simple arrays. Instead, we make use of an `Array` of `Dictionaries` to hold the specific attributes of each flower and a separate `Array` to hold the names of each section. We'll index into each based on the current section/row being displayed, so no more `switch` statements.

To begin, we will need to update MasterViewController.swift to include variable property declarations for `flowerData` and `flowerSections`. Add these lines following the `class` line in MasterViewController.swift:

```
var flowerData: [AnyObject] = []
var flowerSections: [String] = []
```

The two arrays, referenced through `flowerData` and `flowerSections`, will hold our flower and section information, respectively. We start by initializing the arrays as empty, and will populate them within the `createFlowerData` method.

What's an Object?

You may notice that Apple has a variable property named `objects` defined in the project template. This was Apple's placeholder for storing data to use in the project, but we won't be using it for anything. The `flowerData` and `flowerSections` arrays will store our data.

Next step? Loading the data! Implement the `createFlowerData` method in MasterViewController.swift, as shown in Listing 14.9. It will likely look a bit strange, but we cover the how's and why's in a minute.

LISTING 14.9   Populating the Flower Data Structures

```
 1: func createFlowerData() {
 2:     var redFlowers: [Dictionary<String,String>] = []
 3:     var blueFlowers: [Dictionary<String,String>] = []
 4:
 5:     flowerSections = ["Red Flowers","Blue Flowers"]
 6:
 7:     redFlowers.append(["name":"Poppy","picture":"Poppy.png",
 8:         "url":"https://en.wikipedia.org/wiki/Poppy"])
...
19:     redFlowers.append(["name":"Straw Flower","picture":"Strawflower.png",
20:         "url":"https://en.wikipedia.org/wiki/Peony"])
21:
22:     blueFlowers.append(["name":"Hyacinth","picture":"Hyacinth.png",
23:         "url":"https://en.wikipedia.org/wiki/Hyacinth_(flower)"])
...
34:     blueFlowers.append(["name":"Iris","picture":"Iris.png",
35:         "url":"https://en.wikipedia.org/wiki/Iris_(plant)"])
36:
37:     flowerData=[redFlowers,blueFlowers]
38: }
```

First, let's concentrate on the individual flower data within each section. Lines 2 and 3 define two Arrays: redFlowers and blueFlowers. Both are defined as being a Dictionary where the keys and values are Strings.

The `flowerSections` array is initialized in line 5. The section names are added to the array so that their indexes can be referenced by section number. For example, Red Flowers is added first, so it is accessed by index (and section number) 0. Blue Flowers is added second and will be accessed through index 1. When we want to get the label for a section, we just reference it as `flowerSections[section]`.

The `flowerData` structure is a bit more complicated. As with the `flowerSections` array, we want to be able to access information by section. We also want to be able to store multiple flowers per section, and multiple pieces of data per flower.

So, how can we get this done? By first dealing with the flowers in each section by populating `redFlowers` and `blueFlowers`. Lines 7–35 do just that; the code initializes `Dictionaries` with key/value pairs for the flower's name (`name`), image file (`picture`), and Wikipedia reference (`url`) and inserts it into each of the two arrays.

Wait a second. Doesn't this leave us with two arrays when we wanted to consolidate all the data into one? Yes, but we're not done. Lines 37 creates this final array `flowerData` using the two `redFlowers` and `blueFlowers` arrays. What this means for our application is that we can reference the red flower array as `flowerData[0]` and the blue flowers as `flowerData[1]` (corresponding, as we wanted, to the appropriate table sections).

The end result will be a structure in memory that resembles Table 14.1.

flowerData (Array)				
Index	**Array**			
0	**Red Flowers**			
	Index	**Dictionary**		
	0	**Name**	**Picture**	**URL**
		Poppy	Poppy.png	https://en.wikipedia.org/wiki/Poppy
	1	**Name**	**Picture**	**URL**
		Tulip	Tulip.png	https://en.wikipedia.org/wiki/Tulip
1	**Blue Flowers**			
	Index	**Dictionary**		
	0	**Name**	**Picture**	**URL**
		Hyacinth	Hyacinth.png	https://en.wikipedia.org/wiki/Hyacinth_(flower)
	1	**Name**	**Picture**	**URL**
		Hydrangea	Hydrangea.png	https://en.wikipedia.org/wiki/Hydrangea

TABLE 14.1
The `flowerData` Structure

NOTE

The data that we included in the listing of the `createFlowerData` method is a small subset of what is used in the actual project files. If you would like to use the full dataset in your code, you can copy it from this hour's project files or add it manually to the method using these values.

Populating the Data Structures

The `createFlowerData` method is now ready for use. We can call it from within the MasterViewController's `viewDidLoad` method. Update the method in MasterViewController.swift by adding the following line at the end of its implementation:

```
createFlowerData()
```

CAUTION

Look, But Don't Touch

Unless you're positive of its purpose, be sure not to disturb any of the existing code in the project template files. Changing Apple's template code can render the project inoperable.

Implementing the Master View Controller

We've reached the point where we can build out our table view in the `MasterViewController` class. Very little changes between how we implemented our initial tutorial table controller and how we will be building this one. Once again, we need to satisfy the appropriate data source and delegate protocols to add an interface and event handling to our data.

The biggest change to the implementation is how we access our data. Because we've built a somewhat complex structure of arrays of dictionaries, we need to make absolutely sure that we're referencing the data that we intend to be.

Creating the Table View Data Source Methods

Instead of completely rehashing the implementation details, let's just review how we can return the needed information to the various methods.

As with the previous tutorial, start by implementing the three basic data source methods within MasterViewController.swift. Remember that these methods (`numberOfSectionsInTableView`, `tableView:numberOfRowsInSection`, and `tableView:titleforHeaderInSection`) must return the number of sections, the rows within each section, and the titles for the sections, respectively.

To return the number of sections, we just need to return the count of the elements in the `flowerSections` array:

```
return flowerSections.count
```

Retrieving the number of rows within a given section is only slightly more difficult. Because the `flowerData` array contains an array for each section, we must first access the appropriate array for the section, and then return its count:

```
return flowerData[section].count
```

Finally, provide the label for a given section in the `tableView:titleforHeaderInSect ion` method (you'll need to add this method into MasterViewController.swift). The application should index into the `flowerSections` array by the section value and return the string at that location:

```
return flowerSections[section]
```

Update the appropriate methods in MasterViewController.swift so that they return these values. As you can see, each of these three method implementations is now a single line (hopefully making up for what seemed to be a complicated structure holding the data).

Creating the Table Cell

Now we're left with the most important method of the data source protocol: `tableView:cellForRowAtIndexPath`. Unlike the previous tutorial, we need to dig down into our data structures to retrieve the correct results. Let's review the different pieces of code required in the implementation.

First, we must declare and initialize a new cell object using the `flowerCell` identifier we established in the prototype cell:

```
let cell = tableView.dequeueReusableCellWithIdentifier("flowerCell",
    forIndexPath: indexPath)
```

Nothing new there, but that's where the similarities to what we've seen before end. To set a cell's title label, detail label (subtitle), and image (all of which are optional values), we need code like this:

```
cell.textLabel!.text="Title String"
cell.detailTextLabel!.text="Detail String"
cell.imageView!.image=UIImage(named:"MyPicture")
```

Not too bad, right? We have all the information; we just need to retrieve it. Let's quickly review the three-level hierarchy of our `flowerData` structure:

```
flowerData(Array) → Array → Dictionary
```

The first level, the top `flowerData` array, corresponds to the sections within the table. The second level, another array contained within the `flowerData` array, corresponds to the rows within the section, and, finally, the `Dictionary` provides the individual pieces of information about each row. Refer back to Table 14.1 if you're still having trouble picturing how information is organized.

So, how do we get to the individual pieces of data that are three layers deep? By first using the `indexPath.section` value to return the right array, and then from that, using the `indexPath.row` value to return the right dictionary, and then finally, using a key to return the correct value from the dictionary.

For example, to get the value that corresponds to the `"name"` key for a given section and row and assign it to a cell's main label, we can write the following:

```
cell.textLabel!.text =
    flowerData[indexPath.section][indexPath.row]["name"] as! String!
```

Because the `flowerData` structure is an `Array` of `AnyObject`, we must force it to a String through type casting. We also have to explicitly unwrap the value because the dictionary we ultimately reference could potentially not have a value for a given key. We know it does, so that's okay. Applying the same logic, we can assign a cell object's detail label to the value stored in the `"url"` key for a given section and row with this:

```
cell.detailTextLabel!.text =
    flowerData[indexPath.section][indexPath.row]["url"] as! String!
```

Likewise, we can assign the image with the following:

```
cell.imageView!.image =
    UIImage(named:flowerData[indexPath.section][indexPath.row]["picture"]
        as! String!)!
```

The only other step is to return the fully configured cell. Implement this code in your MasterViewController.swift file now. Remove any additional lines cell-generating method, as we aren't really interested in Apple's sample implementation.

Your master view should now be able to display a table, but we still need to be able to handle the selection of an item in the table and update the detail view accordingly. Before that, however, we should disable a feature we *don't* want: editing.

What Happened to Our Image-Naming Shortcut?

Remember in the last tutorial we used the name of the flower to get a reference to the image file (because the files are named *exactly* the same as the flower names)? Why aren't we doing that here?

Realistically, you can't expect the labels in your cells to be the same as your image asset names. The approach we take here would allow you to use any image filename you'd want. Does the original "shortcut" still work? Of course, but that would be too easy!

Disabling Editing

Apple has been kind enough to include the beginnings of some advanced features in the Master-Detail Application template, including the editing of the table view. This, however, isn't something that we want within our project, and is unfortunately outside the scope of what we can cram into this book. To disable editing within this project, edit the MasterViewController.swift method `tableView:canEditRowAtIndexPath` to return `false`, as shown in Listing 14.10.

LISTING 14.10   Disabling Editing of Table Cells

```
override func tableView(tableView: UITableView,
    canEditRowAtIndexPath indexPath: NSIndexPath) -> Bool {
    // Return false if you do not want the specified item to be editable.
    return false
}
```

Now, comment out (or remove) the lines related to buttons and button bars in the MasterViewController.swift viewDidLoad method. This will keep the user interface from display-ing buttons for editing the table items. The final version of viewDidLoad (including changes you made earlier) should resemble Listing 14.11.

LISTING 14.11   Disabling Editing of the UI

```
override func viewDidLoad() {
    super.viewDidLoad()
    // Do any additional setup after loading the view, typically from a nib.
    createFlowerData()
    if let split = self.splitViewController {
        let controllers = split.viewControllers
        self.detailViewController = (controllers[controllers.count-1] as!
            UINavigationController).topViewController as? DetailViewController
    }
}
```

Our project will now ignore attempts to edit the flower table; it's time to handle the actions we *do* want the user to perform.

Handling Navigation Events from a Segue

In the previous tutorial application, we handled a touch event with the tableView:didSelectRowAtIndexPath UITableViewDelegate protocol method and dis-played an alert to the user. In this example, Apple's template is already set up to begin a segue when a selection is made. The method prepareForSegue (refer to Hour 11 for more details) will be used to pick up the selected table row and pass information to the detailViewController.

We'll be communicating with the detailViewController through one of its Apple-provided variable properties (of type AnyObject) called detailItem. Because detailItem can point to any object, we set it to the Dictionary of the chosen flower; this will give us access to the name, url, and other keys directly within the detail view controller.

Implement prepareForSegue in MasterViewController.swift, as shown in Listing 14.12. Note that you're just adding a *single* line (bolded) and removing a few of Apple's sample implementation code chunks:

LISTING 14.12   Setting the Detail View Controller's `detailItem`

```
override func prepareForSegue(segue: UIStoryboardSegue, sender: AnyObject?) {
    if segue.identifier == "showDetail" {
        if let indexPath = self.tableView.indexPathForSelectedRow {
            let controller =
                (segue.destinationViewController as!
                UINavigationController).topViewController as!
                DetailViewController
            controller.detailItem =
                self.flowerData[indexPath.section][indexPath.row]
            controller.navigationItem.leftBarButtonItem =
                self.splitViewController?.displayModeButtonItem()
            controller.navigationItem.leftItemsSupplementBackButton = true
        }
    }
}
```

When a flower is selected, it is passed to the `detailViewController`'s `detailItem` variable property.

Well now, that seems too easy, doesn't it? There's probably lots of work to be done trapping the event in the detail view controller and updating the view, right? Nope. To implement the detail view controller, we need to update a single method: `configureView`.

Implementing the Detail View Controller

We've already updated the detail view controller interface with a web view, and we know how it should work. When the user picks one of our flowers, the `UIWebView` instance (`detailWebView`) should be instructed to load the web address stored within the `detailItem` variable property. The method where we can implement this logic is `configureView`. It is automatically invoked whenever the detail view should update itself. Both `configureView` and `detailItem` are already in place, so all that we need is a tiny bit of logic.

Displaying the Detail View

While we could use `detailItem` directly, Apple begins its implementation of the `configureView` method with:

```
if let detail = self.detailItem {
```

This sets the `detail` variable to `self.detailItem` if `detailItem` is defined. This is a nicety that protects against `detailItem` not being properly defined. We'll leave it in the code, but it means that we'll be working with the variable `detail`, not `detailItem`.

Because `detail` is a single `Dictionary` for one of our flowers, we need to use the `"url"` key to access the URL string and turn that into a `NSURL` object. This is accomplished quite simply:

```
let detailURL: NSURL = NSURL(string: detail["url"] as! String!)!
```

First we declare the `NSURL` object `detailURL`, and then we initialize it using the URL stored in the dictionary.

You might remember from earlier lessons that loading a web page in a web view is accomplished with the `loadRequest` method. This method takes an `NSURLRequest` object as its input parameter. Because we only have an `NSURL` (`detailURL`), we also need to use the `NSURLRequest` class method `requestWithURL` to return the appropriate object type. One additional line of code takes care of all of this:

```
webview.loadRequest(NSURLRequest(URL: detailURL))
```

Now, remember that navigation item that we changed to read `Flower Detail` in the detail scene? Wouldn't it be nifty to set that to the name of the flower (`detailItem[@"name"]`)? We can! Using the `navigationItem.title`, we can update the title in the navigation bar and set it to whatever we want. The code to set the title in the bar at the top of the detail view becomes the following:

```
navigationItem.title = detail["name"] as! String!
```

Finally, the label that displays the Choose a Flower message should be hidden after an initial selection is made. The variable (already included in the template) for the label is `detailDescriptionLabel`. Setting its `hidden` variable property to `true` hides the label:

```
detailDescriptionLabel.hidden = true
```

Unfortunately, if we put all of this together in `configureView`, it's not going to work, because `configureView` may be called before the web view is even instantiated by the storyboard. To get around an error, we can do exactly what Apple did with `configureView` and wrap the code that displays the web view into the `if` statement that begins with the following:

```
if let webview = detailWebView {
```

Pull all of this together into a single method by updating `configureView` in DetailViewController.swift to read as shown in Listing 14.13.

LISTING 14.13   Configuring the Detail View Using the `detailItem`

```
func configureView() {
    // Update the user interface for the detail item.
    if let detail = self.detailItem {
        let detailURL: NSURL = NSURL(string: detail["url"] as! String!)!
        if let webview = detailWebView {
```

```
        webview.loadRequest(NSURLRequest(URL: detailURL))
        navigationItem.title = detail["name"] as! String!
        detailDescriptionLabel.hidden = true
    }
  }
}
```

How Does Setting the `detailItem` Cause the `configureView` Method to Execute?

When variables are defined, you can also define methods that execute when data is, or will be set (stored) or retrieved. For example, a variable `myObject.coolVariable=<something>` will call a method `didSet` in the variable definition (if it exists) immediately after a value is stored. The `DetailViewController` implementation takes advantage of this and defines its own `didSet` method for `detailItem` that invokes the `configureView` method. This means that any time `detailItem` is set, the custom `didSet` method is called.

Building the Application

Run and test the application on the iOS Simulator using both iPhone and iPad hardware simulation. Try rotating the device on the iPad and the iPhone 6+; the interface should update appropriately (and somewhat dramatically). Smaller devices, however, use the same code to provide the same functionality, but with a very different interface.

I know this is a somewhat unusual tutorial, but it's one that I consider important. The Master-Detail Application template is used very, very often and can jump-start your development of high-quality tablet and handheld applications.

Further Exploration

Although the most "dramatic" part of this hour was implementing the `UISplitViewController`, there is a wealth of additional features to be uncovered in the topic of tables. To continue your experience in working with tables, I suggest focusing on a few important enhancements.

The first is expanding what you can do with table cells. Review the variable property list for `UITableViewCell`. In addition to the `TextLabel` and `ImageView` variable properties, you can make numerous other customizations—including setting backgrounds, detail labels, and much, much more. In fact, if the default table cell options do not provide everything you need, Interface Builder supports visual customization of table cells by creating a completely custom cell prototype.

Once you have a handle on the presentation of the table views, you can increase their functionality by implementing a few additional methods in your table view controller. Read the reference for `UITableViewController`, `UITableViewDataSource`, and `UITableViewDelegate`. You can quickly enable editing functionality for your table by implementing a handful of additional methods. You'll need to spend some time thinking of what editing controls you want to use and what the intended result will be, but the basic functionality of deleting, reordering, and inserting rows (along with the associated graphic controls you're used to seeing in iOS applications) will come along "for free" as you implement the methods.

Apple Tutorials

Table Terminology and Development Basics – Table View Programming Guide (accessible via the Xcode developer documentation): This guide covers nearly everything related to programming tables on iOS (from layout to handling sorting, editing, and other table control topics).

Customizing Table Cells and Views – TableView Fundamentals for iOS (accessible via the Xcode developer documentation): The TableView Fundamentals tutorial is an excellent look at how table views can be customized to suit a particular application.

Summary

This hour introduced two of the most important iOS interface components: the table view and the split view controller. Table views enable users to sort through large amounts of information in an orderly manner. We covered how table cells are populated, including text and images, as well as the mechanism by which cell selection occurs.

We also explored the role of the split view controller in managing a master view and detail view and how it can be easily implemented by way of the Master-Detail Application template.

Coming away from this hour, you should feel comfortable working with tables in your applications and building basic apps using the new project template.

Q&A

Q. What is the most efficient way to provide data to a table?

A. You've almost certainly come to the conclusion that there has got to be a better way to provide data to complex views rather than manually defining all the data within the application itself. Starting in Hour 15, "Reading and Writing Application Data," you learn about persistent data and how it can be used within applications. This will likely become the preferred way of working with large amounts of information as you move forward in your development efforts.

Q. Can a table row have more than a single cell?

A. No, but a customized cell can be defined that presents information in a more flexible manner than the default cell. As described in the "Further Exploration" section, custom cells can be defined in Interface Builder through the `UITableViewCell` class.

Q. Do split view controllers have to be implemented using the Apple Master-Detail Application template?

A. Absolutely not. The template, however, provides all the right methods for many split view applications and is a great starting place for beginners.

Workshop

Quiz

1. Which view controller can create iPad-like applications on the iPhone?

    a. Split view

    b. Dual pane

    c. Single universal

    d. Multimodal

2. Tables are made up of objects of what type?

    a. `UITableViewCell`

    b. `UITableViewRow`

    c. `UITableViewColumn`

    d. `UITableViewContent`

3. Uniquely styled table cells have unique cell _____.

    a. Purposes

    b. Labels

    c. Colors

    d. Identifiers

4. A division within a table is known as a what?

    a. Column

    b. Title

    c. Section

    d. Divider

5. Individual cells within a table are referenced through an object of what type?

   a. NSRowColumn

   b. NSIndexPath

   c. NSCellIndex

   d. NSIndexRow

6. Which of the following methods is called when a variable has been set?

   a. didStore

   b. willSet

   c. didSet

   d. didGet

7. To access the master and detail controllers within a split view controller object, you can use which of the following variable properties?

   a. start, last

   b. first, end

   c. start, end

   d. first, last

8. The methods that provide data to a table are part of which protocol?

   a. UITableViewDataSource

   b. UITableViewDataProvider

   c. UITableViewData

   d. UITableViewDataDelegate

9. Interactions with a table cell are often handled by methods within which protocol?

   a. UITableViewActions

   b. UITableViewMethodDelegate

   c. UITableViewClassAction

   d. UITableViewDelegate

10. Which of the following templates implements a split view controller?

    a. Split Application

    b. Single View

    c. Master-Detail

    d. Tab Bar

Answers

1. A. The split view controller can be used to create iPad-like applications on the larger-screened iPhones.

2. A. The content of a table view is made of up instances of the `UITableViewCell` class.

3. D. Uniquely styled table cells must have unique cell identifiers.

4. C. Tables can be divided into logical groupings called sections.

5. B. The `NSIndexPath` object contains a row and a section that uniquely identify an individual table cell.

6. C. The `didSet` method is called on a variable as soon as its value has been changed.

7. D. The `first` and `last` variable properties can be used to grab the individual view controllers contained within a split view controller.

8. A. The `UITableViewDataSource` protocol defines the methods that provide content to a table.

9. D. The `UITableViewDelegate` protocol can be used to handle interactions between a user and a table cell.

10. C. The Master-Detail template provides a great starting place for implementing split view controllers.

Activities

1. Update the first tutorial to use a more expandable data structure that doesn't rely on constants to define the number of sections or the type of sections. Your finished project should also be able to accommodate image files with arbitrary names.

2. Use IB to create and customize an instance of the `UITableViewCell` class.

HOUR 15

Reading and Writing Application Data

What You'll Learn in This Hour:

▶ Good design principles for using application preferences

▶ How to store application preferences and read them later

▶ How to expose your application's preferences to the Settings application

▶ How to store data from your applications

Most substantial applications, whether on a computer or mobile device, allow users to customize their operation to their own needs and desires. You have probably cursed an application before, only to later find a setting that removes the unholy annoyance, and you probably have a favorite application that you've customized to your exact needs so that it fits like a well-worn glove. In this hour, you learn how your iOS application can use preferences to allow the user to customize its behavior and how, in general, the user can store data on iDevices.

NOTE

Apple uses the term *application preferences*, but you might be more familiar with other terms such as *settings*, *user defaults*, *user preferences*, or *options*. These are all essentially the same concept.

---

iOS Applications and Data Storage

The dominant design aesthetic of iOS applications is for simple single-purpose applications that start fast and do one task quickly and efficiently. Being fun, clever, and beautiful is an expected bonus. How do application preferences fit into this design view?

You want to limit the number of application preferences by creating opinionated software. There might be three valid ways to accomplish a task, but your application should have an opinion on the one best way to accomplish it and then should implement this one approach in such a polished and intuitive fashion that your users instantly agree that it's the best way. Leave the other two approaches for someone else's application. It might seem counterintuitive, but a much bigger market exists for opinionated software than for applications that try to please everyone.

This might seem like odd advice to find in a chapter about application preferences, but I'm not suggesting that you avoid preferences altogether. There are some very important roles for application preferences. Use preferences for the choices your users must make, rather than for all the choices they could possibly make. For example, if you are connecting to the application programming interface (API) of a third-party web application on behalf of your user and the user must provide credentials to access the service, this is something the user must do, not just something users might want to do differently. So, it is a perfect case for storing as an application preference.

Another strong consideration for creating an application preference is when a preference can streamline the use of your application (for example, when users can record their default inputs or interests so that they don't have to make the same selections repeatedly). You want user preferences that reduce the amount of onscreen typing and taps that it takes to achieve the user's goal for using your application.

After you decide a preference is warranted, you have an additional decision to make. How will you expose the preference to the user? One option is to make the preference implicit based on what the user does while using the application. An example of an implicitly set preference is returning to the last state of the application. For example, suppose a user flips a toggle to see details. When the user next uses the application, the same toggle should be flipped and showing details.

Another option is to expose your application's preference in Apple's Settings application, shown in Figure 15.1. The Settings application is built in to iOS. It provides a single place to customize a device's operation. From the Settings application, you can customize everything from the hardware, built-in applications from Apple, and third-party applications.

A settings bundle lets you declare the user preferences of your application so that the Settings application can provide the user interface (UI) for editing those preferences. There is less coding for you to do if you let Settings handle your application's preferences, but less coding is not always the dominant consideration. A preference that is set once and rarely changes, such as the username and password for a web service, is ideal for configuring in Settings. In contrast, an option that the user might change with each use of your application, such as the difficulty level in a game, is not appropriate for Settings.

CAUTION

Simplicity Is Key

Users will be annoyed if they have to repeatedly exit your application, launch Settings to change the preference, and then relaunch your application. Decide whether each preference belongs in the Settings application or within your own application. Sometimes it might even be wise to put them in both places for ease of access.

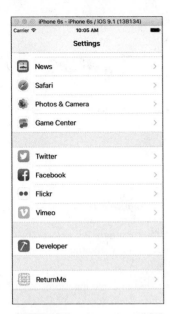

FIGURE 15.1
The Settings application.

Also keep in mind that the UI that Settings can provide for editing your application preferences is limited. If a preference requires a custom interface component or custom validation code, it can't be set in Settings. Instead, you must set it from within your application.

State Preservation and Restoration: Pseudo Preferences

Apple includes a feature in iOS that enables you to (somewhat) easily restore portions of an application's interface to its previous condition when it starts. Your scrolling views would still be scrolled to the right places, your tab bars might still have the proper tabs selected, and so on. You pick and choose what gets restored.

So, how does this differ from implicit preferences that you store yourself?

State preservation can make it appear like your application is picking up where it left off, similar to what happens when you press the Home button and exit and then go back to an application. Unlike a suspended application, it works even if your application has exited (you reboot your phone, for example). State preservation, however, restores the *interface only*, not the state of the *logic*. What's more, if the user uses the task manager to force quit the application, the state preservation is deleted. The short story is that state preservation should *not* be used in place of implicit preferences. It's useful for getting a user back into an application quickly, but you must still save relevant state/preference information on your own, in case the state preservation information is deleted by iOS.

To get started with state preservation, add these two methods to your application delegate (AppDelegate.swift):

```
func application(application: UIApplication,
    shouldRestoreApplicationState coder: NSCoder) -> Bool {
    return true
}

func application(application: UIApplication,
    shouldSaveApplicationState coder: NSCoder) -> Bool {
    return true
}
```

You may then select the object (such as a text view) that you want to automatically restore, open the Identity Inspector (Option-Command-4), and enter a restoration ID (an arbitrary string to identify the object). You should also do the same for the view controller object that contains the UI objects you're restoring. Make sure that your restoration IDs are unique (such as using the same name as the variable property referring to the objects).

That's a quick and dirty way to play with this feature, but if you're interested in exploring more, begin by reading "State Preservation and Restoration" in the *iOS Programming Guide* in Xcode.

Data Storage Approaches

Once you decide that your application needs to store information, your next step is to decide how it is done. There are many, many ways for iOS applications to store information, but we focus on three approaches in this hour:

- **User defaults:** Settings that are stored on a per-application basis, typically without requiring user intervention

- **Settings bundles:** Provide an interface for configuring an application through the iOS settings application

- **Direct file system access:** Enables you to write and read files in your application's portion of the iOS file system

Each approach offers its own pros and cons, and so you have to determine which is appropriate for your own applications. Before we start using them, though, let's review a bit more detail about how they work and what they are usually used for.

User Defaults

Application preferences is Apple's name for the overall preference system by which applications can customize themselves for the user. The application preferences system takes care of the low-level tasks of persisting preferences to the device, keeping each application's preferences separate from other applications' preferences, and backing up application preferences to the computer via iTunes so that users do not lose their preferences if the device needs to be restored. Your interaction with the application preferences system is through an easy-to-use API that consists mainly of the NSUserDefaults singleton class.

The NSUserDefaults class works similarly to a dictionary. The differences are that NSUserDefaults is a singleton and is more limited in the types of objects it can store—and it stores them persistently. All the preferences for your application are stored as key/value pairs in the NSUserDefaults singleton.

NOTE

A singleton is just an instance of the Singleton pattern, and a pattern in programming is just a common way of doing something. The Singleton pattern is fairly common in iOS, and it is a technique used to ensure that there is only one instance (object) of a particular class. Most often, it is used to represent a service provided to your program by the hardware or operating system.

Writing and Reading User Defaults

All access to application preferences begins by getting a reference to your application's NSUserDefaults singleton:

```
let userDefaults: NSUserDefaults = NSUserDefaults.standardUserDefaults()
```

Values can then be written to and read from the defaults database by specifying the type of data being written and a key (an arbitrary string) that will be used to access it later. To specify the type, you use one of six different functions (depending on the type of data you want to store):

> setBool:forKey
>
> setFloat:forKey
>
> setInteger:forKey
>
> setObject:forKey
>
> setDouble:forKey
>
> setURL:forKey

The setObject:forKey function can be used to store strings, arrays, dictionaries, and other common object types.

For example, to store an integer value under the key `"age"` and a string using the key `"name"`, you could use code that looks like this:

```
userDefaults.setInteger(10, forKey: "age")
userDefaults.setObject("John", forKey: "name")
```

When you write data to the defaults database, it isn't necessarily saved immediately. This can lead to issues if you assume that your preferences are stored but iOS hasn't gotten around to it yet. To ensure that all data is written to the user defaults, you use the `synchronize` method:

```
userDefaults.synchronize()
```

To read these values back into the application at a later time, you use a set of functions that read and return the value or object given their key. For example:

```
var myAge: Int = userDefaults.integerForKey("age")
var myName: String = userDefaults.stringForKey("name")!
```

(Note that `stringForKey` has an optional return value, thus the `!`.) Unlike the "set" storage methods, retrieving values requires specific methods for strings, arrays, and so on so that you can easily assign the stored objects to a particular type object when you need to access them. Choose from `arrayForKey`, `boolForKey`, `dataforKey`, `dictionaryForKey`, `floatForKey`, `integerForKey`, `objectForKey`, `stringArrayForKey`, `doubleForKey`, or `URLForKey` to retrieve your data into a usable object.

Settings Bundles

Another option for dealing with application preferences is through the use of settings bundles. Settings bundles use the underlying user defaults system that you just learned about, but they provide a UI that is managed through the iOS Settings application.

What makes settings bundles attractive from the development standpoint is that they are created entirely in Xcode's plist editor. There is no UI design or coding—just defining the data you intend to store and the keys that it is stored under.

By default, applications do not include a settings bundle. You add them to your project by choosing File, New File and then picking Settings Bundle from the iOS Resource section, as shown in Figure 15.2.

The file that controls how an application's settings will appear in the Settings application is the Root.plist file in the settings bundle. Seven different preference types (see Table 15.1) can be read and interpreted by the Settings application to provide the UI to set our application's preferences.

FIGURE 15.2
Settings bundles must be added to projects manually.

TABLE 15.1 Preference Types

Type	Description
Text field	Editable text string
Toggle switch	On/off toggle button
Slider	Slider across a range of values
Multi value	Drop-down value picker
Title	Read-only text string
Group	Title for a logical group of preferences
Child pane	Child preferences page

Creating custom settings bundles is just a matter of creating rows in the Preference Items key within the Root.plist file. You just follow the simple schema in the *Settings Application Schema Reference* in the iOS Reference Library to set all the required properties, and some of the optional properties, of each preference, as shown in Figure 15.3.

When the settings bundle is complete, the user can alter user defaults through the Settings application, and you, the developer, can access the settings through the same techniques described in the section "Writing and Reading User Defaults."

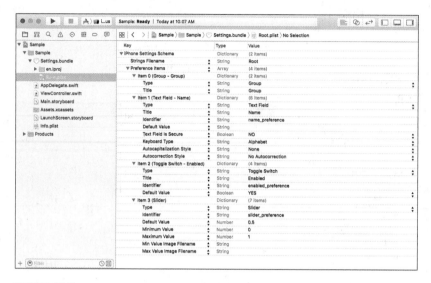

FIGURE 15.3
The settings UI is defined through the Root.plist file.

TIP

The `identifier` attribute of a preference item within the settings bundle is the same as the `key` you use to retrieve a value from the user defaults.

Direct File System Access

The final file access approach that we'll be looking at in this hour is direct file system access (the ability to open files and read or write their contents). This technique can be used to store any data you want—files you download off the Internet, files your app creates, and so on—but not anywhere you want.

In creating the iOS software development kit (SDK), Apple introduced a wide range of restrictions designed to protect users from malicious applications harming their devices. The restrictions are collectively known as the application sandbox. Any application you create with the SDK exists in a sandbox. There is no opting out of the sandbox and no way to get an exemption from the sandbox's restrictions.

Some of these restrictions affect how application data is stored and what data can be accessed. Each application is given a directory on the device's file system, and applications are restricted to reading and writing files in their own directory. This means a poorly behaved application can, at worst, wipe out its own data but not the data of any other application.

It also turns out that this restriction is not terribly limiting. The information from Apple's applications, such as contacts, calendars, and the photo and music libraries, is for the most part already exposed through APIs in the iOS SDK. (For more information, see Hour 19, "Working with Rich Media," and Hour 20, "Interacting with Other iOS Services.")

CAUTION

Play Within the Sandbox

Although Apple makes it clear what you can or can't do in an iOS, many of the restrictions are enforced via policy rather than technical controls. Just because you find a location on the file system where it is possible to read or write files outside the application sandbox doesn't mean you should. Violating the application sandbox is one of the surest ways to get your application rejected from the iTunes Store.

Storage Locations for Application Data

Within an application's directory, four locations are provided specifically for storing the application's data: the Library/Preferences, Library/Caches, Documents, and tmp directories.

NOTE

When you run an application in the iOS Simulator, it is actually installed in a directory on your mac, and its data stored in a file that you can open and review. Take a look at the folder /Users/<your username>/Library/Developer/CoreSimulator/Devices/ on your development machine. Within this directory, you'll see a number of other directories with hexadecimal names—each represents one of the simulators you have installed (iPad simulator, iPhone simulator, for example). There isn't a particularly good way to tell these apart other than looking at the modified date. If you install and run an application, that simulator folder's modified date will change.

After locating the right folder for your simulator, you can find your data by drilling down into data/Containers/Data/Application. Here you'll find another list of strangely named folders—one for each installed application. Again, to find the directory for the application you're working on, look for the modified date. Inside the application directory, you'll find a Documents directory where your data is stored. Take a few minutes now to look through the directory of a couple applications from previous hours.

In modern releases of OS X, the Library directory is hidden by default. You can access it by holding down Option and clicking the Finder's Go menu.

You encountered the Library/Preferences directory earlier in this hour. It's not typical to read and write to the Preferences directory directly. Instead, you use the NSUserDefaults API. The Library/Caches, Documents, and tmp directories are, however, intended for direct file manipulation. The main difference between them is the intended lifetime of the files in each directory.

The Documents directory is the main location for storing application data. It is backed up to the computer when the device is synced with iTunes, so it is important to store in the Documents directory any data users would be upset to lose.

The Library/Caches directory is used to cache data retrieved from the network or from any computationally expensive calculation. Files in Library/Caches persist between launches of the application, and caching data in the Library/Caches directory can be an important technique used to improve the performance of an application.

Any data you want to store outside of the device's limited volatile memory, but that you do not need to persist between launches of the application, belongs in the tmp directory. The tmp directory is a more transient version of Library/Caches; think of it as a scratch pad for the application.

CAUTION

Space Concerns

Applications are responsible for cleaning up all the files they write, even those written to Library/Caches or tmp. Applications are sharing the limited file system space (16GB to 128GB) on the device. The space an application's files take up is not available for music, podcasts, photos, and other applications. Be judicious in what you choose to persistently store, and be sure to clean up any temporary files created during the lifetime of the application.

Getting a File Path

Every file on an iOS device has a path, which is the name of its exact location on the file system. For an application to read or write a file in its sandbox, it needs to specify the full path of the file.

Core Foundation provides a function called `NSSearchPathForDirectoriesInDomains` that returns the path to the application's Documents or Library/Caches directory. Asking for other directories from this function can return multiple directories, so the result of the function call is an array. When this function is used to get the path to the Documents or Library/Caches directory, it returns exactly one string in the array, which is extracted using an index of 0.

`String` objects include a method for joining two path fragments called `stringByAppendingPathComponent`. By putting the result of a call to `NSSearchPathForDirectoriesInDomains` together with a specific filename, it is possible to get a string that represents a full path to a file in the application's Documents or Library/Caches directory.

Suppose, for example, that your next blockbuster iOS application calculates the first 100,000 digits of pi and you want the application to write the digits to a cache file so that they won't need to be calculated again. To get the full path to this file's location, you first need to get the path to the Library/Caches directory and then append the specific filename to it:

```
let paths = NSSearchPathForDirectoriesInDomains(
    NSSearchPathDirectory.CachesDirectory,
    NSSearchPathDomainMask.UserDomainMask, true)
let docDir:String=paths[0]
let piFile:String=(docDir as
    NSString).stringByAppendingPathComponent("American.pi")
```

To get a path to a file in the Documents directory, use the same approach but with `NSSearchPathDirectory.DocumentDirectory` as the first argument to `NSSearchPathForDirectoriesInDomains`:

```
let paths = NSSearchPathForDirectoriesInDomains(
    NSSearchPathDirectory.DocumentDirectory,
    NSSearchPathDomainMask.UserDomainMask, true)
let docDir:String=paths[0] as String
let surveyFile:String=(docDir as

    NSString).stringByAppendingPathComponent("HighScores.txt")
```

Core Foundation provides another function called `NSTemporaryDirectory` that returns the path of the application's tmp directory. As before, you can use this to get a full path to a file:

```
let scratchFile: String = (NSTemporaryDirectory()
    as NSString).stringByAppendingPathComponent("Scratch.data")
```

Constants, Constants, Everywhere

Notice I'm using `let` a lot in this hour? That's because when you're working with paths and file handles and the such, it's pretty unlikely they'd need to be modified again. These statements would work fine with variables (`var`) instead of constants (`let`); but if it's obviously something that would never be modified, we might as well make it a constant.

Reading and Writing Data

After creating a string that represents the path to the file that you want to use, reading and writing is rather straightforward. First, you'll likely want to check to see whether the file even exists. If it doesn't, your application will need to create it; otherwise, you'll need to present an error condition. To check for the presence of a file represented by the string `myPath`, you use the `NSFileManager` method `fileExistsAtPath`:

```
if NSFileManager.defaultManager().fileExistsAtPath(myPath) {
    // File Exists
}
```

Next, you use the `NSFileHandle` convenient class methods `fileHandleForWritingAtPath`, `fileHandleForReadingAtPath`, or `fileHandleForUpdatingAtPath` to grab a reference to the file for the purpose of writing, reading, or updating. Note that because we're in Swift, the `fileHandle` portion of the method name isn't included in the actual method call.

For example, to create a file handle for writing, you could code the following:

```
let fileHandle:NSFileHandle=NSFileHandle(forWritingAtPath:myPath)!
```

To write data to the file referenced by `fileHandle`, use the `NSFileHandle` method `writeData`. To write the string `stringData` to the file, you could use this:

```
fileHandle.writeData(stringData.dataUsingEncoding(NSUTF8StringEncoding)!)
```

The `String` method `dataUsingEncoding` ensures that the data is in a standard Unicode format before it is written to the file. After you've finished writing to the file, you must close it:

```
fileHandle.closeFile()
```

Later, to read the contents of the file into a string, you must perform similar operations, but with read methods rather than write. First get the file handle for reading, then read the entire contents into a new string with the `NSFileHandle` instance method `availableData`, and then close the file:

```
let fileHandle:NSFileHandle=NSFileHandle(forReadingAtPath:surveyFile)!
let myData:String=NSString(data: fileHandle.availableData,
    encoding: NSUTF8StringEncoding)! as String
fileHandle.closeFile()
```

The code here should be pretty obvious, but `fileHandle.availableData` returns an `NSString` that we can't directly use as a `String`. By converting it to an `NSString` with the proper encoding, we can then convert it back and make the assignment to `myData`.

When you need to update the contents of a file, you can use other `NSFileHandle` methods, such as `seekToFileOffset` or `seekToEndOfFile`, to move to a specific location in the file. You use this approach in a tutorial later in this hour.

That concludes this introduction to data storage approaches in iOS. Now let's put them to practice in three short tutorial exercises.

 File Storage in the Playground

It may surprise you to learn that the Playground can be used for file storage to test the various techniques we've just talked about. The only "tricky" part is finding out *where* the Playground is saving files—and that's not even that tricky.

For example, let's assume we want to try using the user defaults system to store some key/value pairs and then find the plist file that the Playground creates. Create a new Playground, and then input the following code:

```
import UIKit

let userDefaults: NSUserDefaults = NSUserDefaults.standardUserDefaults()
userDefaults.setInteger(10, forKey: "age")
userDefaults.setObject("John", forKey: "name")
userDefaults.synchronize()
let Library:String =
NSSearchPathForDirectoriesInDomains(NSSearchPathDirectory.LibraryDirectory,
    NSSearchPathDomainMask.UserDomainMask, true)[0] as String + "/Preferences"
```

Feel free to change the preferences being stored. I doubt your name is John, and you probably aren't 10 years old. If you are, I apologize for doubting you.

The code used here is identical to the example code for preferences. The only addition is the last line, which will generate a string `Library` that contains the location where the Playground has decided to store the plist file.

Click the "eye" icon that appears on the line to the right of the `let Library:String` = declaration. The path should appear, and from there, you should be able to copy it.

Open the OS X Terminal and type **open** followed by a space, and then paste in the path and press Return. In the Finder window that opens, you'll see the plist file that was generated. If you'd like to see what the contents look like, double-click it to open it in Xcode.

As long as you know how to find the Playground files, it can be a great tool for testing your data storage code!

Creating Implicit Preferences

In our first exercise, we create an admittedly ridiculous application. The application has an on/off switch and a slider control for users to set a background color that they like. We use preferences to return the application to the last state the user left it in.

Implementation Overview

This project requires a total of two interface elements:

- A switch to turn the custom background color on and off
- A slider to change the background hue

These are connected to outlets so that they are accessible in the application. The on/off status and hue, upon being changed, will be stored using user defaults. The stored values will automatically be restored when the application is restarted.

Setting Up the Project

Create a new single-view iOS application in Xcode and call it **BackgroundColor**. You're only going to be coding up one method and modifying another, so little setup is work needed.

Planning the Variables and Connections

We need a total of two outlets and one action. The switch connects to an outlet that we call `toggleSwitch`, and the slider to `hueSlider`. When either the slider or switch changes values, it triggers a method, `setBackgroundHueValue`.

NOTE

To control the background color, you will be setting the view's `backgroundColor` variable property to a `UIColor` object. To create the `UIColor` object, you'll use the method `colorWithHue:saturation:brightness:alpha`.

Adding Key Constants

As you learned at the start of this hour's lesson, accessing the user default preferences system requires that you define keys for whatever you want to store. These are strings that you need when storing or accessing any stored data. Because these are used in multiple places and are static values, they're good candidates for constants. We'll define two constants for the project: `kOnOffToggle` for the key that refers to the current on/off state, and `kHueSetting` for the color of our application background.

Add these constants to the top of the ViewController.swift interface file, following the `class` line:

```
let kOnOffToggle="onOff"
let kHueSetting="hue"
```

Now, let's lay out a simple UI.

Designing the Interface

Open the Main.storyboard file in the Interface Builder (IB) editor, select the View Controller within the Document Outline and then use the Attributes Inspector (Option-Command-4) to switch the view to a reasonable simulated size.

Drag a UISwitch from the Object Library (View, Utilities, Show Object Library) onto the bottom left of the view. Drag a UISlider to the bottom right of the view. Size the slider to take up all the horizontal space not used by the switch and set its initial value to 0.

Your view should now look like Figure 15.4. Easiest interface layout ever, don't you think?

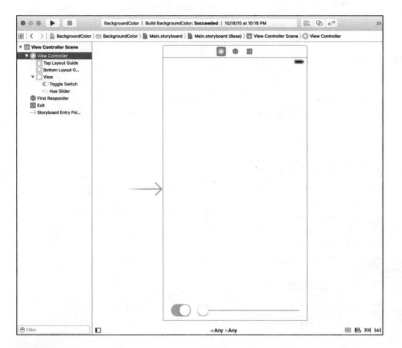

FIGURE 15.4
The BackgroundColor UI.

Creating and Connecting the Outlets and Actions

The code we will write will need access to the switch and slider. We will also trigger the change of the background color based on the Value Changed event from the switch as well as the slider. In summary, you create and connect these outlets:

▶ **The on/off switch (UISwitch):** toggleSwitch

▶ **The Hue (color) slider (UISlider):** hueSlider

And the single action:

▶ **Changing the value of the switch or slider (UISwitch/UISlider):** setBackgroundHueValue

Switch to the assistant editor, hiding the project navigator and utility area if needed.

Adding the Outlets

Control-drag from the switch that you added to the UI to just below the constants you defined in ViewController.swift. When prompted, create a new outlet named **toggleSwitch**. Repeat this for the slider, connecting it to hueSlider.

In addition to being able to access the two controls, our code needs to respond to changes in the toggle state of the switch and changes in the position of the slider.

Adding the Actions

To create the action that, ultimately, both the switch and the slider will use, Control-drag from the slider to below the variable property declarations in ViewController.swift. Define a new action, setBackgroundHueValue, that will be triggered on the Value Changed event, as shown in Figure 15.5.

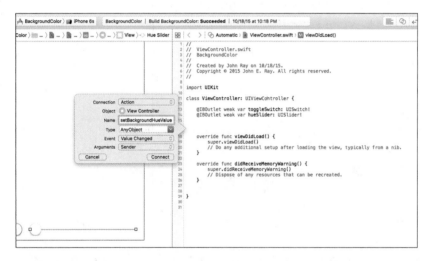

FIGURE 15.5
Connect the switch and slider to the setBackgroundHueValue method.

To connect the switch to the same action, we can use the Connections Inspector (Option-Command-5) to drag from the Value Changed event of the switch to the newly added IBAction line, or we can rely on the fact that Control-dragging from the switch to the IBAction line will automatically select the Value Changed event. Whichever method you are comfortable with, complete it now.

Making sure that both the switch and slider are connected to the action ensures that immediate feedback is provided when the user adjusts the slider value or toggles the switch.

Implementing the Application Logic

What can I say? There's not much logic here!

When the user toggles the custom background on or off and adjusts color, the application responds by adjusting the backgroundColor variable property of the default view. We use the UIColor initialization method colorWithHue:saturation:brightness:alpha to return an appropriate color object. Each argument in this method is a floating-point value between 0.0 and 1.0. The only argument we'll vary is for the hue, based directly on the slider's value. We'll pick a few "middle of the road" values for saturation and brightness, and set the alpha to 1.0, because there's no real point in having a transparent color for the background (there's nothing behind it!).

When the custom background is toggled off, we'll set the background to white, using the UIColor class method whiteColor. Update the setBackgroundHueValue method in ViewController.swift, as shown in Listing 15.1.

LISTING 15.1 Implementing the Initial `setBackgroundHueValue` Method

```
@IBAction func setBackgroundHueValue(sender: AnyObject) {

    if toggleSwitch.on {
        view.backgroundColor=UIColor(hue: CGFloat(hueSlider.value),
            saturation: 0.75, brightness: 0.75, alpha: 1.0)
    } else {
        view.backgroundColor=UIColor.whiteColor()
    }
}
```

This simple method checks the on variable property of the toggleSwitch object, and, if it is true (that is, the switch is on) creates a new UIColor object using the colorWithHue: saturation:brightness:alpha convenience method and assigns it the view's backgroundColor. The arguments to UIColor are of the type CGFLoat.

When creating the color, the hue is set to the value of the slider, while saturation, brightness, and alpha are set to 0.75, 0.75, and 1.0, respectively. Xcode automatically provides conversion if we provide static numbers—but we must use CGFloat() with slider's value.

Is there anything magic about these numbers? Nope. I tried a few and liked these settings. Feel free to try other values between 0 and 1.0 to see the effect. If the toggleSwitch is set to off, the code sets the backgoundColor to white.

This is already enough code to make the application work. You can run the project yourself and see.

Storing the BackgroundColor Preferences

We don't just want the custom color feature to work; we want it to return to its last state when the user uses the application again later. We'll store the on/off state and the hue value as implicit preferences. Recall that we've defined two constants, kOnOffToggle and kHueSetting, to use as the keys for our storage.

Update the setBackgroundHueValue method, adding the lines shown in Listing 15.2.

LISTING 15.2 Implementing the Final **setBackgroundHueValue** Method

```
 1: @IBAction func setBackgroundHueValue(sender: AnyObject?) {
 2:     let userDefaults: NSUserDefaults =
 3:         NSUserDefaults.standardUserDefaults()
 4:     userDefaults.setBool(toggleSwitch.on, forKey: kOnOffToggle)
 5:     userDefaults.setFloat(hueSlider.value, forKey: kHueSetting)
 6:     userDefaults.synchronize()
 7:
 8:     if toggleSwitch.on {
 9:         view.backgroundColor=UIColor(hue: CGFloat(hueSlider.value),
10:             saturation: 0.75, brightness: 0.75, alpha: 1.0)
11:     } else {
12:         view.backgroundColor=UIColor.whiteColor()
13:     }
14: }
```

In lines 2–3, we get the NSUserDefault singleton using the standardUserDefaults method and then use the setBool and setFloat methods to store our preferences in lines 4 and 5. We wrap up in line 6 by using the synchronize method in NSUserDefaults to make sure that our settings are stored immediately.

One final change that we should make is to set the sender variable as an optional AnyObject by adding a question mark in Line 1. This will come in handy for calling this method manually, which we'll be doing in the *next* method.

NOTE

Our code now saves the values for our two keys, but where do they go? The idea here is that we don't *have* to know because we are using the NSUserDefaults API to shield us from this level of detail and to allow Apple to change how defaults are handled in future versions of the iOS.

It can still be useful to know, however, and the answer is that our preferences are stored in a plist file. If you are an experienced OS X user, you may already be familiar with plists, which are used for OS X applications, too. When running on a device, the plist will be local to the device, but when we run our application in the iOS Simulator, the Simulator uses our computer's hard drive for storage, making it easy for us to peek inside the plist.

Run the BackgroundColor application in the iOS Simulator, and then use Finder to navigate to your application within the simulator as described earlier in the chapter. This time, however, instead of drilling down into the `data/Containers/Data/Application` folder, go into `data/Library/Preferences`. Here you should be able to find a `.plist` file that corresponds to your application. Opening the file will open a window in Xcode and show you the preferences you've stored.

Reading the BackgroundColor Preferences

Now our application is writing out the state of the two controls anytime the user changes the settings. So, to complete the desired behavior, we need to read in and use the preferences for the state of the two controls anytime our application launches. For this, we use the `viewDidLoad` method and the `floatForKey` and `boolForKey` methods of `NSUserDefaults`. Edit `viewDidLoad` and get the `NSUserDefaults` singleton in the same way as before, but this time set the value of the controls from the value returned from the preference rather than the other way around.

In the ViewController.swift file, update `viewDidLoad`, as shown in Listing 15.3.

LISTING 15.3   Updating the Settings in `viewDidLoad`

```
1: override func viewDidLoad() {
2:     super.viewDidLoad()
3:     let userDefaults: NSUserDefaults =
4:         NSUserDefaults.standardUserDefaults()
5:     hueSlider.value=userDefaults.floatForKey(kHueSetting)
6:     toggleSwitch.on=userDefaults.boolForKey(kOnOffToggle)
7:
8:     setBackgroundHueValue(nil)
9: }
```

In lines 3-4, we get the `NSUserDefault` singleton and use it to grab and set the hue slider (line 5) and toggle switch (line 6). Since we've just programmatically set the state of the interface objects, we can now just call the `setBackgroundHueValue` method we wrote previously, and it will handle updating the background accordingly. We can pass `nil` to this method because we set its parameter to be optional.

Building the Application

That's all there is to it. Run the application to verify its operation (see Figure 15.6). I assure you that this isn't going to make you millions on the App Store, but it does demonstrate just how easy it is for your applications to read and write preferences.

FIGURE 15.6
BackgroundColor application in action.

TIP

If you're running the application and press the Home button, be aware that your application won't quit; it will be suspended in the background. To fully test the BackgroundColor app, be sure to stop the application using the Xcode Stop button. Then use the iOS task manager to force the application completely closed, and then verify that your settings are restored when it relaunches fresh.

Now that we're through seeing red (or whatever color you've chosen as your background in this fine application), let's look at a new app where the user takes more direct control of the application's preferences.

Implementing System Settings

A second option to consider for providing application preferences is to use the Settings application. You do this by creating and editing a settings bundle for your application in Xcode rather than by writing code and designing a UI, so this is a very fast and easy option (*once you get used to editing settings bundles*). Initially, you might have to take a few cracks at making all the plist changes you need; there is a learning curve for the process.

For our second application of the hour, we create an application that tells someone who finds a lost device how to return it to its owner. The Settings application is used to edit the contact information of the owner and to select a picture to evoke the finder's sympathy.

Implementation Overview

What you'll soon come to appreciate with settings bundles is that a great deal of tedious UI/storage work happens "automagically," without needing to write any code. In this application, you create a settings bundle that defines several values that you can set within the iOS Settings application. These settings are read by the app and used to update the onscreen display when it is running. There will be no user inputs in the application itself, making our logic even simpler than the last tutorial.

Setting Up the Project

As we often do, begin by creating a new single-view iOS application in Xcode called **ReturnMe**.

We want to provide the finder of the lost device with a sympathy-invoking picture and the owner's name, email address, and phone number. Each of these items is configurable as an application preference, so we need outlets (but no actions) for these UI elements.

Planning the Variables and Connections

For the three text values that we want to display, we need to define labels (`UILabel`), which we'll call `name`, `email`, and `phone`. The image that we will be displaying will be contained within a `UIImageView` that will be named `picture`. That's it. We don't need any input controls; instead, all our values will be managed through our settings bundle.

Adding Key Constants

As in the previous project, we are referencing stored user default values using a key. We need a total of four keys to each of the values we're working with. To keep things orderly, let's define constants that we can use to refer to the keys whenever we want. Edit the ViewController.swift file and add the following lines after the existing `class` line:

```
let kName:String = "name"
let kEmail:String = "email"
let kPhone:String = "phone"
let kPicture:String = "picture"
```

These should be self-explanatory; the names and string values are a dead giveaway.

Adding the Image Resources

As part of this project, we display an image that will help goad our Good Samaritan into returning the lost device rather than selling it to Gizmodo. Within the project navigator, click the

Assets.xcassets file to open the project's asset catalog. Then drag the Images folder from the Finder into the column on the left inside the Asset Catalog. You'll see a new Images folder appear.

TIP

Remember, to support Retina-class displays, you need to create images with both two and three times the horizontal and vertical resolution as your standard image resources. Include an @2x and @3x suffix on the respective filenames, and add them to your project. The developer tools and iOS take care of the rest.

I've included @2x and @3x image resources with many of the projects in this book.

Designing the Interface

Now let's lay out the ReturnMe application's UI, as follows:

1. Open the IB editor by clicking the Main.storyboard file.

2. Switch the View Controller to a manageable simulated size using the Attributes Inspector.

3. Open the Object Library so that you can start adding components to the interface.

4. Drag three `UILabels` onto the view.

5. Set the text to a default value of your choosing for the name, email, and phone number.

6. Drag a `UIImageView` to the view.

7. Size the image view to take up the majority of the device's display area.

8. With the image view selected, use the Attributes Inspector to set the mode to be Aspect Fill, and pick one of the animal images you added to the Xcode project from the Image drop-down.

9. Add some additional `UILabels` to explain the purpose of the application and labels that explain each preference value (name, email, and phone number).

As long as you have the three labels and the image view in your UI, as shown in Figure 15.7, you can design the rest as you see fit. Have fun with it.

Sharp Vision? Let's Blur It, iOS Style

In my UI layout, I've chosen to use an iOS blur effect behind my labels, rather than simply a slightly transparent view. If you'd like to do the same, you can do it without any additional work. Because this isn't anything more than a visual effect, it isn't mandatory.

To include the blur effect, follow these steps:

1. Drag a Visual Effects View with Blur from the Object Library to storyboard.

2. The Visual effects view contains a normal View (`UIView`) object. Place your labels within this view and position the view as desired.

3. Select the Effects View and use the Attributes Inspector to choose between one of the available blur settings.

The end result of this simple change is the cool "frosted glass" iOS appearance.

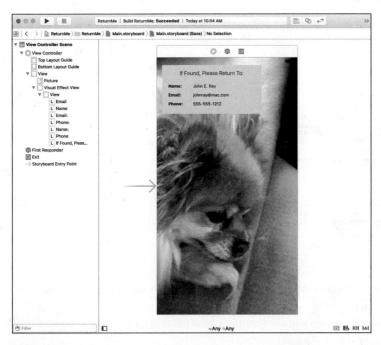

FIGURE 15.7
Create an interface with an image, labels, and anything else you want.

Creating and Connecting the Outlets

After you've finished building the interface, switch to the assistant editor and connect the `UIImageView` and three `UILabels` to corresponding outlets in ViewController.swift: `picture`, `name`, `email`, and `phone`. There aren't any actions to connect, so just Control-drag from each UI element to the ViewController.swift file, providing the appropriate name when prompted.

Now that the interface is built, we create the settings bundle, which will enable us to integrate with the iOS Settings application.

Creating the Settings Bundle

Create a new settings bundle in Xcode by selecting File, New File from the menu bar and select-ing Settings Bundle from the iOS Resource group in the sidebar, as shown in Figure 15.8. To choose where the settings bundle is stored, click Next. When prompted, leave the default location and name unchanged, but make sure the Supporting Files group is selected in the pop-up menu at the bottom of the Save dialog box.

FIGURE 15.8
Settings bundle in Xcode's New File dialog.

The ReturnMe preferences are grouped into three groups: Sympathy Image, Contact Information, and About. The Sympathy Image group will contain a Multi Value preference to pick one of the images, the Contact Information group will contain three text fields, and the About group will link to a child page with three read-only titles.

CAUTION

Read Slowly and Practice

Before you start building your application preferences, be aware that the language of Apple's tools makes it difficult to describe the process without tying one's tongue in knots.

Here are a few important things to keep in mind:

▶ When I refer to a *property*, I am referring to a line within the plist file. Properties are defined by a key, a type, and one or more values.

▶ Properties can contain multiple other properties. I refer to these as being *within* an existing property (or *children* of the original property).

The specific attributes that define a property (key, type, and value) are represented as columns within the plist editor. When possible, I refer to these by name where you need to make a change.

▶ You can accomplish the same thing in *many* different ways. Don't worry if you find a better way that accomplishes the same results.

Expand the Settings.bundle in Xcode and click the Root.plist file. You'll see a table of three columns: Key, Type, and Value. Expand the iPhone Settings Schema property, then Preference Items property within it. You'll see a series of four dictionary properties. Xcode provides these as samples, and each is interpreted by Settings as a preference. You follow the simple schema in the *Settings Application Schema Reference* in the iOS Reference Library to set all the required properties, and some of the optional properties, of each preference.

Expand the first dictionary property under Preference Items called Item 0, and you'll see that it has a Type property with a value of Group. This is the correct type to define a preference group (which groups together a set of related preferences), but we will need to make some changes to reflect the settings we want. Change the Title property's value column to read Sympathy Image by clicking it and typing the new title. This provides a nice group heading in the Settings display.

The second preference item will contain multichoice settings for our Sympathy Image. Look at the value in parentheses to the right of the Item 1. Note that it is currently set to be a Text Field. Our Sympathy Image will be selected as a multivalue, not a text field, so change it to Multi Value by clicking the Key column of the property and picking from the pop-up list that appears. Next, expand the property and edit its child properties. Change the Title to Image Name, the Identifier (what we will use to reference the value in our app) to picture, and the Default Value to Dog.

NOTE

You can change the type for most properties by simply clicking the label in the Key column; doing so opens a drop-down menu showing the available types. Unfortunately, not all types are represented in the menu. To access the full list of types, you need to expand the property and then set the underlying Type child property using the drop-down menu to the right of the Value column.

The choices for a multivalue picker come from two array properties: an array of item names and an array of item values. In our case, the name and value array properties will be the same, but we still must provide both of them. To add another property, click to select one of the existing properties (such as Default Value), and then click the + icon that appears (see Figure 15.9). This adds another property at the same level as the property you selected.

Add a Property

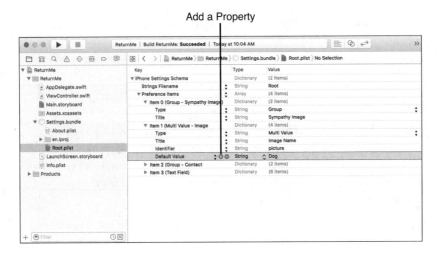

FIGURE 15.9
Add another property in Xcode's property list editor.

Set the name of the new property to Values and set the Type column to Array using the drop-down menus. Each of the three possible image names needs a property under Values. Expand the Values property to see what it contains (initially nothing). *With it expanded*, click the Values property and click the + icon three times to add new string properties as children: Item 0, Item 1, and Item 2, as shown in Figure 15.10.

Add a Property

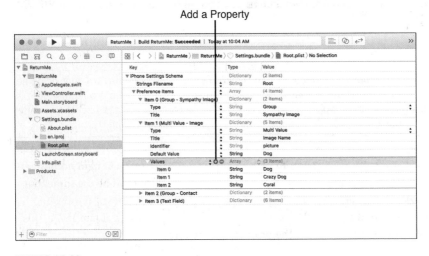

FIGURE 15.10
Add child properties in Xcode's property list editor.

NOTE

The +/− icon we're using to add rows will add a row at the same level as the highlighted property, directly below the highlighted property. This holds true unless the property is a dictionary or array and is *also* expanded. In that case, it adds a new child property within the item.

In some cases, the +/− icons might not be visible (thanks a bunch, Xcode!). If you want to add a row below a property and you don't see these icons, you can right-click a given property on the far-right side of its line and choose Add Row from the menu that appears.

Change the Value column of the three new child properties to **Dog**, **Crazy Dog**, and **Coral**. Repeat what you've done for the Values property to add a new array property at the same level as Values called Titles. Titles should also be an `Array` type with the same three `String` type children properties, as shown in Figure 15.11.

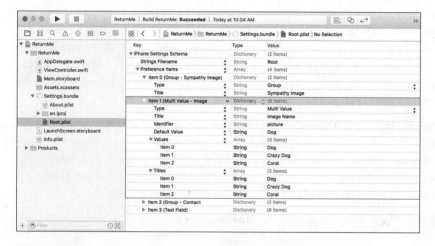

FIGURE 15.11
The completed image selector preference in Xcode's property list editor.

The third property (Item 2) in our Preference Items should be the type `Group` with a title of Contact Information. Click the Key column to change the type; then expand the property and update the `Title` child property and remove all other items. The ultimate effect of this change will be that second group of settings with the title Contact Information appears within the Settings app.

The fourth property (Item 3) is the name preference. Click the Key column and change it to be a text field. Expand the property and configure the children properties as follows: Set the identifier property value to **Name**, and the default value to **Your Name**. The Type column should be set to String for both. Add three more children properties under Item 3. Set the Property keys to Keyboard Type, Autocapitalization Style, and Autocorrection Style; and the values to Alphabet, Words, and No Autocorrection, respectively. The Type column, again, should be set to String for all three child properties. You may have surmised that these are optional parameters that set up the keyboard for text entry.

You can test your settings so far by running the ReturnMe application in the iOS Simulator, exiting the application with the Home button, and then starting the Settings application in the Simulator. You should see a Settings selection for the ReturnMe application and settings for the Sympathy Image and Name.

Add two more Text Field properties as children to the Preference Items property in the plist. The easiest way to do this so that the properties are added below Item 3 is to make sure that Item 3 is collapsed and then right-click on the far right of the Item 3 line and choose Add Row from the pop-up menu that appears. After adding the properties, mirror what you set up for the name preference: one for email and one for phone number. Use the keys of **email** and **phone**, and change the values of child Keyboard Type property to Email Address and Number Pad, respectively. When you add the new properties, you might have more child properties than you were expecting. The Text Field properties you're adding now, for example, include a Title property that can be removed by selecting it and pressing Delete or clicking the – icon. They don't, however, contain the Keyboard Type, Autocapitalization Style, and so on. You can add these by adding a new row and then use the pop-up menus in the Key, Type, and Value columns to configure the missing properties.

The final preference is About, and it opens a child preference pane. We'll add two more items to accomplish this. First, add a new property (Item 6) to the plist. Click the Key column for the property and set it to be a Group. Expand Item 6 and set the Title child property to a value **About ReturnMe** (configured with a Type column of String). As with the previous two groups, this creates a nicely titled division, About ReturnMe, within the Settings display.

Next, add Item 7. It can be any type you want, because the type property it contains needs to be adjusted a bit differently. Expand Item 7 and set the Type child property to Child Pane; unlike other preference types, this property is not available by clicking the property's Key column. Update the Title child property's value to **About**, and add a new child property with the key set to Filename, a type column of String, and a value column of **About**. Your completed Root.plist should resemble Figure 15.12. The child pane element assumes the value of the Filename identifier exists as another plist in the settings bundle. In our case, this is a file called About.plist.

The easiest way to create this second plist file in the settings bundle is by copying the Root.plist file we already have. Select the Root.plist file in the project navigator, right-click, and choose "Show In Finder". Duplicate the Root.plist file in the Finder, and name the copy **About.plist**. It will immediately appear in the Xcode settings bundle.

Select the About.plist file and right-click any property it contains. From the menu that appears, choose Property List Type, iPhone Settings plist. This tells Xcode what we intend to use the plist file for, which in turn gives us property names in plain English.

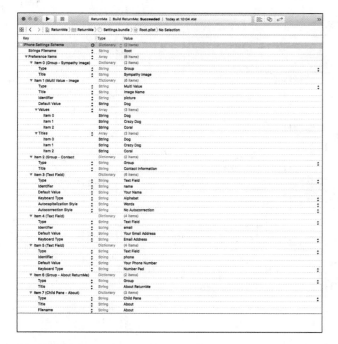

FIGURE 15.12
The completed Root.plist file.

Edit About.plist's Preference Items array to have four child properties. The first is a group property with a Title child property of **About ReturnMe**. The remaining three should be set to Title properties and are used for Version, Copyright, and Website Information. The Title properties contain three children properties by default: Type, Title, Identifier. Type should already be set to **Title**, and the Title property value set to the title strings for the information we want to display: **Version**, **Copyright**, or **Website**. The Identifier value doesn't matter because we won't be setting any of these in our code. Each of these three Title properties also needs a new (fourth) child property with the key Default Value added to them. This will be of the type string, and the value will be set to whatever text information you want displayed in the Settings app for the parent property. Figure 15.13 shows my finished About.plist file.

If you have any difficulties setting up your plist files, run the application, exit it, and then compare your preferences UI to Figure 15.14 and your plists to the plists in the settings bundle in the sample project's source code to see where you might have made a misstep.

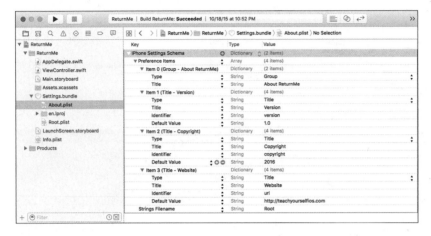

FIGURE 15.13
The About.plist file.

FIGURE 15.14
ReturnMe's settings in the Settings application.

CAUTION

Value and Values, Types and Type Keys, Aarrrrgh!

The plist editor can be confusing to deal with because the UI and the terminology are convoluted. In this exercise, for example, we created a multivalue picker that requires an array named `Values`. The items in the array also have a value, so we have to work with values' `Values`. Fun, huh?

This is exacerbated by our need to add new properties of a certain type. Each property has an underlying data type (`Array`, `Dictionary`, `String`, and so on), but it may also have a child property with the identifier of `Type` that defines what that property (and its child properties) represents (like a text field). The result is a mishmash of terms that will drive you up the wall.

I recommend working through the exercise and changing keys and values to see the effect. It isn't difficult once you get the hang of it, but Apple has made it an absolute bear to describe.

Implementing the Application Logic

We have now bundled up our preferences so that they can be set by the Settings application, but our ReturnMe application also has to be modified to use the preferences. We do this in the ViewController.swift file's `viewDidLoad` event. Here we will call a helper method we write called `setValuesFromPreferences`. Our code to use the preference values with the `NSUserDefaults` API looks no different from the BackgroundColor application. It doesn't matter whether our application wrote the preference values or if the Settings application did; we can simply treat `NSUserDefaults` like a dictionary and ask for objects by their key.

We provided default values in the settings bundle, but it's possible the user just installed ReturnMe and has not run the Settings application. We should provide the same default settings programmatically to cover this case, and we can do that by providing a dictionary of default preference keys and values to the `NSUserDefaults registerDefaults` method.

Implement the method in ViewController.swift. Listing 15.4 shows a completed implementation of `setValuesFromPreferences`.

LISTING 15.4   Implementing the `setValuesFromPreferences` Method

```
 1: func setValuesFromPreferences() {
 2:     let userDefaults:NSUserDefaults=NSUserDefaults.standardUserDefaults()
 3:
 4:     let initialDefaults:[String:String]=[kPicture:"Dog",
 5:         kName:"Your Name",
 6:         kEmail:"you@yours.com",
 7:         kPhone:"(555)555-1212"]
 8:
 9:     userDefaults.registerDefaults(initialDefaults)
10:
11:     let picturePreference:String=userDefaults.stringForKey(kPicture)!
12:
```

```
13:        if picturePreference=="Dog" {
14:            picture.image=UIImage(named: "dog1.png")
15:        } else if picturePreference=="Crazy Dog" {
16:            picture.image=UIImage(named: "dog2.png")
17:        } else {
18:            picture.image=UIImage(named: "coral.png")
19:        }
20:
21:        name.text = userDefaults.stringForKey(kName)
22:        email.text = userDefaults.stringForKey(kEmail)
23:        phone.text = userDefaults.stringForKey(kPhone)
24:
25: }
```

Note that I'm using lots of constants in this implementation because it's unlikely that after making the initial assignments I'd want to change many of the values in the method.

Things kick off in line 2, where we grab a reference to the NSUserDefaults singleton.

Lines 4–7 initialize a dictionary named initialDefaults that contains the default value/key pairs that our application should use if no preferences have been set in the Settings app yet. The pairs are added to the dictionary value first, followed by the key (represented by the constants we added to the project earlier).

In line 9, we use the NSUserDefaults method registerDefaults to register our sample default values. After that, the code should remind you of the previous tutorial. Lines 11–23 simply get the values stored for each of our keys and set the user interface elements accordingly.

We still, however, need to load the preferences when the application starts. Update the viewDidLoad method to call setValuesFromPreferences, as shown in Listing 15.5.

LISTING 15.5   Loading the Settings When the Initial View Loads

```
override func viewDidLoad() {
    super.viewDidLoad()
    setValuesFromPreferences()
}
```

Building the Application

Run the ReturnMe application, wait until it starts in the iOS Simulator, and then click the Xcode Stop button. Using the iOS Simulator's Settings app, change a few items for the ReturnMe application. Next, use the iOS application manager to terminate ReturnMe so that it isn't waiting in the background, and then relaunch it. Your new settings should be represented in the application display.

CAUTION

Use the Xcode Stop Button!

If you do not use the Xcode Stop button to exit your application and then stop and restart it manually in the iOS Simulator, you will get an error in Xcode. The Xcode debugger will be upset because it can't connect to the application anymore. For that reason, when testing the app, be sure to use Xcode's Stop button and then run your tests of ReturnMe.

When we explore backgrounding in Hour 22, "Building Background-Ready Applications," you learn how to programmatically deal with applications that are starting, stopping, and moving to and from the background.

You can see that with very little code on our part, we were able to provide a sophisticated interface to configure our application. The Settings bundle plist schema provides a fairly complete way to describe the preference needs of an application.

Implementing File System Storage

In the final example for this hour, we create a simple survey application. The application collects a person's first name, last name, and email address and then stores them in a CSV file on the iOS device's file system. Touching another button retrieves and displays the contents of the file.

Implementation Overview

The survey application's user interface will be simple: three fields that collect data, a button to store the data, and another button to read all the accumulated results and display them in a scrolling text view. To store the information, we first generate a path to a new file in our application's Documents directory. We then create a file handle to that path and output our survey data as a formatted string. Reading the data back in will be much the same, except we grab the file handle and read the entire contents of the file into a string and then display that in a read-only text view.

Setting Up the Project

Create a new single-view iOS application in Xcode and call it **Survey**. We do have several UI elements that our code will need to interact with, so let's decide what they are and what they'll be called.

Planning the Variables and Connections

Because this is a survey and we'll be collecting information, obviously we need input areas for our data. In this case, these are text fields for collection first and last name and email address. We'll call these `firstName`, `lastName`, and `email`, respectively. To demonstrate that we've properly stored a CSV file, we'll read it in and output it in a text view that we will name `resultsView`.

We also need a total of three actions in this tutorial: two obvious and one less so. First, we need to store the data, so we add a button that triggers an action called `storeSurvey`. Next, we need to read the results and display them, so we have a second button that triggers an action called `showResults`. Unfortunately, there's a third action we want to add—our handy `hideKeyboard` implementation so that the user can touch the background of the view or the Done button on the mini keyboard to hide the onscreen keyboard.

Designing the Interface

To design the interface, follow these steps:

1. Shift into design mode by clicking the Main.storyboard file and then opening the Object Library.

2. Drag three text fields (`UITextField`) into the view and position them near the top of the view. Add three labels beside the fields that read **First Name:**, **Last Name:**, and **Email:**.

3. Using the Attributes Inspector (Option-Command-4), select each field in turn, and then apply an appropriate Keyboard attribute (Email for the email field, for example), Return Key (such as Done), Capitalization, and any other features you think are appropriate. That completes our data entry form.

4. Drag a text view (`UITextView`) into the design and position it below the entry fields; this will display the contents of our survey results CSV file.

5. Add a label above it titled **Results**.

6. Using the Attributes Inspector, set the text view to be read-only, since a user won't be able to use it to edit the survey results being displayed.

7. Add two buttons (`UIButton`) below the text view—one titled **Store Survey** and the other **Show Results**. These trigger our two actions that interact with files.

8. To deal with hiding the keyboard when the background is tapped, add a single `UIButton` sized to cover the entire view. Use the Attributes Inspector to set the button type to Custom; this will make it invisible.

9. Use the Editor, Arrange menu to set the custom button to the back (behind the rest of the UI), or simply drag the custom button to the top of the list of objects in the view using the document outline.

Your final survey UI should resemble Figure 15.15.

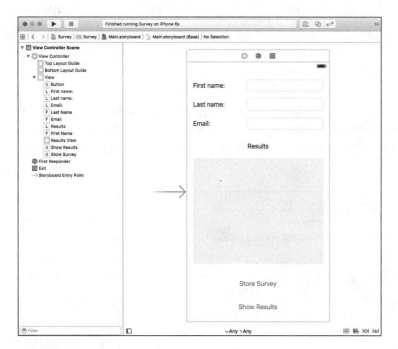

FIGURE 15.15
The Survey application UI.

Creating and Connecting the Outlets and Actions

We need to wire up a number of connections in this project to interact with the user interface. Let's review what we'll be adding, starting with the outlets:

▶ **The first name field (UITextField):** firstName

▶ **The last name field (UITextField):** lastName

▶ **Email address (UITextField):** email

▶ **Text view results area (UITextView):** resultsView

And the actions:

▶ **Touching the Store Survey button (UIButton):** storeSurvey

▶ **Touching the Show Results button (UIButton):** showResults

▶ **Touching the background button (UIButton), or receiving the Did End on Exit event from any of the text fields:** hideKeyboard

Switch to the assistant editor to begin adding outlets and actions. Make sure that the document outline is available so that you can get an easy handle on the invisible custom button.

Adding the Outlets

Add each of the necessary outlets by Control-dragging from their representation in the view to the space following the `class` line in ViewController.swift. Connect the field beside the First Name label to `firstName`, as shown in Figure 15.16. Repeat this for each of the other fields, and for the text view, naming them with the conventions we've decided on. None of the other objects require an outlet.

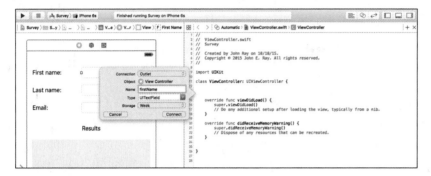

FIGURE 15.16
Connect the fields and text view to their outlets.

Adding the Actions

Once the outlets are in place, begin adding the connections to the actions. Control-drag from the Store Survey button to below the variable property definitions in the ViewController.swift interface file, creating a new action named `storeSurvey`, as shown in Figure 15.17. Do the same for the Show Results button, creating a new action called `showResults`.

As you probably remember, creating and connecting the `hideKeyboard` action isn't quite as straightforward. Begin by creating the action by Control-dragging from the custom button to the ViewController.swift file. It may be easiest to use the Button line in the document outline rather than trying to target the button in the view. Name the new action `hideKeyboard`. That takes care of the user touching the background, but we still need to handle the user touching the onscreen keyboard's Done button.

Select the first of the text fields, and then open the Connections Inspector. You may need to hide the project navigator or document outline to make room in your workspace. From the Connections Inspector, drag from the Did End on Exit connection point to the `hideKeyboard` IBAction line at the top of ViewController.swift. Do the same for the other two fields.

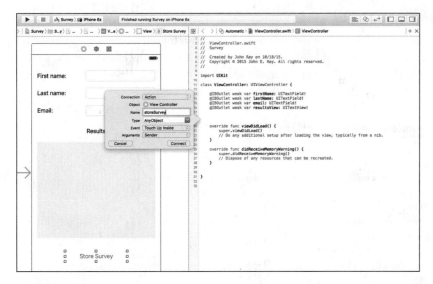

FIGURE 15.17
Connect the buttons to their actions.

We're done with the interface. Switch back to the standard editor and open the ViewController. swift file to finish up the implementation.

Implementing the Application Logic

We need to implement three pieces of code to finish the application. First, we drop in the hideKeyboard code, just to get it out of the way. Next, we add storeSurvey and showResults using the methods you learned at the beginning of this hour's lesson.

Hiding the Keyboard

To hide the keyboard, the object that currently has "control" of the keyboard must resign its first responder status using the method resignFirstResponder. In other words, our three text fields must each do this when hideKeyboard is invoked. Refer to Hour 7, "Working with Text, Keyboards, and Buttons," if you have any questions about how this works, and then implement hideKeyboard, as shown in Listing 15.6.

LISTING 15.6 Hiding the Keyboard When It Isn't Needed

```
@IBAction func hideKeyboard(sender: AnyObject) {
    firstName.resignFirstResponder()
    lastName.resignFirstResponder()
    email.resignFirstResponder()
}
```

Storing the Survey Results

To store the survey fields, we format our incoming data, establish a path for the file that will contain the results, create a new file if needed, store the survey fields at the end of the file, and then close the file and clear out our survey form. Go ahead and enter the storeSurvey implementation in Listing 15.7, and then let's walk through the code.

LISTING 15.7   Implementing the storeSurvey Method

```
 1: @IBAction func storeSurvey(sender: AnyObject) {
 2:     let csvLine:String =
 3:         "\(firstName.text!),\(lastName.text!),\(email.text!)\n"
 4:     let paths = NSSearchPathForDirectoriesInDomains(
 5:             NSSearchPathDirectory.DocumentDirectory,
 6:             NSSearchPathDomainMask.UserDomainMask, true)
 7:     let docDir:String=paths[0]
 8:     let surveyFile:String=(docDir
 9:             as NSString).stringByAppendingPathComponent("surveyresults.csv")
10:
11:     if !NSFileManager.defaultManager().fileExistsAtPath(surveyFile) {
12:             NSFileManager.defaultManager().createFileAtPath(surveyFile,
13:                 contents: nil, attributes: nil)
14:     }
15:
16:     let fileHandle:NSFileHandle=NSFileHandle(forUpdatingAtPath:surveyFile)!
17:     fileHandle.seekToEndOfFile()
18:     fileHandle.writeData(csvLine.dataUsingEncoding(NSUTF8StringEncoding)!)
19:     fileHandle.closeFile()
20:
21:     firstName.text=""
22:     lastName.text=""
23:     email.text=""
24: }
```

The implementation begins by creating a new string (csvLine) in lines 2-3 that is formatted with comma-separated values. The \n at the end of the string adds a newline (usually indicating a new record in a CSV file).

Lines 4–7 return the document directory for our application in the string docDir, which is then used in lines 8–9 to create the full survey path string, surveyPath, by appending the filename surveyresults.csv.

In lines 11–14, we check for the presence of the file represented by the path in surveyPath; if it does not exist, a new empty file with that name is created. After we've established that a file is present, we can write our data.

Lines 16 creates a new file handle that points to our `surveyPath` file. The file handle is created using the method `fileHandleForUpdatingAtPath` because we want to update the existing contents of the file. Line 17 moves to the end of the existing file with `seekToEndOfFile` so that any data we write is written at the very end.

In line 18, our `csvLine` string is written to the file with the method `writeData`, and then the file is closed in line 19.

Lines 21–23 clean up the survey form by clearing the current values in the text fields.

Now that we've written to a file, let's see whether we can get data back out.

Showing the Survey Results

To retrieve and display the survey results, we start by doing exactly what we did when storing them: establishing a path to the file. Next, we check for the existence of the file. If it is there, we have results we can read and display. If not, we don't need to do anything. Assuming there are results, we create a file handle using the `NSFileHandle` class method `fileHandleForReadingAtPath` and then read the contents of the file with the method `availableData`. The last step is just to set the text view's contents to the data we've read.

Implement the `showResults` method, as shown in Listing 15.8.

LISTING 15.8   Implementing the `showResults` Method

```
 1: @IBAction func showResults(sender: AnyObject) {
 2:     let paths = NSSearchPathForDirectoriesInDomains(
 3:         NSSearchPathDirectory.DocumentDirectory,
 4:         NSSearchPathDomainMask.UserDomainMask, true)
 5:     let docDir:String=paths[0] as String
 6:     let surveyFile:String=(docDir
 7:         as NSString).stringByAppendingPathComponent("surveyresults.csv")
 8:
 9:     if NSFileManager.defaultManager().fileExistsAtPath(surveyFile) {
10:         let fileHandle:NSFileHandle =
11:             NSFileHandle(forReadingAtPath:surveyFile)!
12:         let surveyResults:String=NSString(data: fileHandle.availableData,
13:             encoding: NSUTF8StringEncoding)! as String
14:         fileHandle.closeFile()
15:         resultsView.text=surveyResults
16:     }
17: }
```

Lines 2–7 create the `surveyPath` string, which is then used to check for the existence of the file in line 8.

If the file exists, it is opened for reading in lines 10-11, and the `availableData` method is used to retrieve the entire contents, which is stored in the string `surveyResults` (lines 12–13). Remember that `fileHandle.availableData` returns an `NSString` which can't directly be assigned to a `String` (at least not here!). By converting it to an `NSString` with the proper encoding, *then* we can convert it back to a String and make the `surveyResults` assignment.

Finally, the file is closed in line 14, and the results view in the UI is updated with the contents of the `surveyResults` string (line 15).

Run the application and store a few surveys, and then read and display the results, as shown in Figure 15.18. You now have the ability to write and read any data you want in the iOS file system.

FIGURE 15.18
The Survey application stores and reads data.

TIP

I know I've been saying this a lot in this hour, but remember that iOS doesn't "quit" applications when you exit them; it suspends the app and moves it to the background. To verify that data is truly persisting between runs of your app, you can use the iOS task manager to force-quit your programs.

You'll learn more about application backgrounding in Hour 22. For now, be aware that there is a method called `applicationDidEnterBackground` in your application delegate class where you can put any application cleanup code that absolutely must be run before it exits.

Further Exploration

You have been exposed to most of what you need to know about preferences at this point. My main advice is to gain some more experience in working with preferences by going back to previous hours and adding sensible preferences to some of the applications you have already worked on. The application preferences system is well documented by Apple, and you should take some time to read through it.

I also highly recommend that you read Apple's *Archives and Serializations Programming Guide for Cocoa*. This guide provides examples of not just how to save data but also how to store objects in files and read and instantiate them at will. This can be used, for example, to create database applications with rich objects containing images, sound, and so forth. For even more complex data needs, you should begin reviewing the documentation on Core Data.

Core Data is a framework that provides management and persistence for in-memory application object graphs. Core Data attempts to solve many of the challenges that face other, simpler forms of object persistence such as object archiving. Some of the challenging areas Core Data focuses on are multilevel undo management, data validation, data consistency across independent data assessors, efficient (that is, indexed) filtering, sorting and searching of object graphs, and persistence to a variety of data repositories. In layman terms, if you think your application might require a real database engine, you need Core Data.

Apple Tutorials

Preferences and Settings Programming Guide: A tutorial-style guide to the various parts of the application preferences system.

Information Property List Key Reference (in the iOS Reference Library): An indispensable guide to the required and optional properties for the preferences in your plist files that will be edited by the Settings application.

Core Data Core Competencies: An Apple tutorial for learning the basics of Core Data. This is a good place to start for an exploration of Core Data.

Summary

In this hour, you developed three iOS applications, and along the way you learned three different ways of storing the application's data. You captured the user's implicit preferences with the BackgroundColor application, allowed the ReturnMe application to be explicitly configured from the Settings application, and stored the Survey application's data through direct file system access. You also learned some important design principles that should keep you from getting carried away with too many preferences and should guide you in putting preferences in the right location.

This hour covered a lot of ground, and you have explored the topic of application data storage fairly exhaustively. At this point, you should be ready for most storage needs you will encounter while developing your own applications.

Q&A

Q. What about games? How should game preferences be handled?

A. Games are about providing the player with an immersive experience. Leaving that experience to go to the Settings application or to interact with a stodgy table view is not going to keep the player immersed. You want users to set up the game to their liking while still remaining in the game's world, with the music and graphical style of the game as part of the customization experience. For games, feel free to use the `NSUserDefaults` API but provide a custom in-game experience for the UI.

Q. I have more complex data requirements. Is there a database I can use?

A. Although the techniques discussed in this hour's lesson are suitable for most applications, larger apps may want to utilize Core Data. Core Data implements a high-level data model and helps developers manage complex data requirements. Although what happens behind the scenes is hidden from your application, Core Data uses SQLite to do its heavy lifting, so it is a database engine; you just don't need to worry about managing it.

Workshop

Quiz

1. You would use which method to store a string in the user defaults database?

   a. `setChar:forKey`

   b. `setData:forKey`

   c. `setString:forKey`

   d. `setObject:forKey`

2. A file handle coupled with what variable property is used to return all data that is currently in the file?

   a. `readData`

   b. `availableData`

   c. `currentData`

   d. `readyData`

3. To read a string from the user defaults, which of the following methods would you use?

   a. `objectForKey`

   b. `charForKey`

   c. `stringForKey`

   d. `dataForKey`

4. User defaults are stored in what type of file?

   a. Plist

   b. Xlist

   c. Nib

   d. Xib

5. Which method is used to set default properties for a plist file?

   a. `storeDefaults`

   b. `registerDefaults`

   c. `saveDefaults`

   d. `saveInitial`

6. To create application settings that are presented through the Settings bundle, you include what within your application?

   a. Settings bundle

   b. Settings class

   c. Class file

   d. Settings storage

7. When testing an application's behavior, you should stop the application by using which of the following?

   a. The Simulator Home button

   b. The Simulator Process Manager

   c. Quitting Xcode

   d. The Xcode Stop button

8. Global constants are useful for storing which values, used with user defaults?

    a. Arrays

    b. Strings

    c. Keys

    d. Names

9. The default file you will edit within a Settings bundle is named what?

    a. Default.plist

    b. Root.plist

    c. Start.plist

    d. Initial.plist

10. Preferences that are stored based on settings that a user makes while interacting with an application are known as what?

    a. Stored preferences

    b. Usage preferences

    c. Default preferences

    d. Implicit preferences

Answers

1. D. When saving a string, you'll need to use the `setObject:forKey` method.

2. B. The `availableData` property will return all data that is available from a file handle at the time it is accessed.

3. C. The `stringForKey` method is used to read a string that was saved with the `setObject:forKey` method.

4. A. User defaults, in the form of key/value pairs, are stored within a plist file.

5. B. To set the default values within the user defaults database, you'll want to use the `registerDefaults` method in conjunction with a dictionary that contains your defaults.

6. A. A settings bundle is used to create application settings that are displayed within the Settings application.

7. D. *Always* use the Xcode Stop button to stop application when testing it in Xcode.

8. C. Defining a constant for the keys stored in your defaults database can be helpful in keeping track of how you've stored your preferences.

9. B. After creating a settings bundle, you'll edit the root.plist file to define the settings interface.

10. D. Implicit preferences are those that are based on a user's actions within an application, not on explicit "settings" made elsewhere.

Activities

1. Update the BackgroundColor application to include preferences for all of the arguments to `colorWithHue:saturation:brightness:alpha`. Create a settings bundle to also manage these preferences in the iOS Settings app.

2. Return to an earlier application, such as ImageHop, and use implicit preferences to save the state of the program (the hop rate and whether the bunnies are hopping) before it exits. When the user relaunches the application, restore the application to its original state. This is a key part of the iOS user experience and something you should strive for.

HOUR 16
Building Responsive User Interfaces

What You'll Learn in This Hour:

▶ How to make an application "responsive"

▶ Using Auto Layout to enable automatic resizing and orientation changes

▶ Creating UI elements programmatically for the ultimate control

You can use almost every iOS interface widget available, create multiple views and view controllers, add sounds and alerts, write files, and even manage application preferences, but until now, your applications have been missing a very important feature: responsive interfaces. The ability to create interfaces that display correctly regardless of your iDevice's screen size or orientation is one of the key features that users expect in an application—and the key target of responsive interface design.

This hour's lesson explores the Xcode Auto Layout system and a purely programmatic way of adding rotatable and resizable interfaces to your apps.

As you read this hour's lesson, an important fact to keep in mind is that there are *many* different ways to solve the problem of responsive interface design. What works best for you may be entirely different than what I describe here.

Responsive Interfaces

Years ago, when I had my first Windows Mobile smartphone, I longed for an easy way to look at web content in landscape mode. There was a method for triggering a landscape view, but it was glitchy and cumbersome to use. The iPhone introduced the first consumer phone with on-the-fly interface rotation that feels natural and doesn't get in the way of what you're trying to do.

Over the past few years, Apple has gone wild with new device sizes and shapes. Does that mean you need a different storyboard for every single device variation? Nope! The iOS Auto Layout system makes it easy to adapt to different resolution displays and change your interface layout as your device resolution changes.

Although you should definitely plan to accommodate all sizes of the iPhone screen in your iPhone apps, the decision to handle orientation changes is entirely up to you. Consider how the user will be interfacing with the app. Does it make sense to force a portrait-only view? Should the view rotate to accommodate any of the possible orientations the phone may assume? The more flexibility you give users to adapt to their own preferred working style, the happier they'll be. Best of all, enabling multiple orientations is a simple process.

TIP

Apple's user interface guidelines for the iPad strongly encourage the support of any orientation: portrait, left landscape, right landscape, and upside-down.

Will This Hour Teach Me How to Make Universal Applications?

A universal application is one that runs on any type of iDevice—iPhone, iPhone Plus, or iPad (or iPad Pro, if one appears!) and requires nothing more than changing the devices supported by a project. The techniques discussed in this hour will, indeed, make it possible to create interfaces that change to fit your different device screen sizes (in fact, what we build will be Universal). Unfortunately, these interfaces would be identical on all devices—not customized to fit the individual capabilities of each. This is "universal" at the most basic level.

A truly universal application may present one interface on an iPhone, a different interface on an iPhone Plus, and a totally different design on an iPad. Hour 23, "Building Universal Applications," covers the details on how to create these unique user experiences on each device, all managed by a single piece of code.

Enabling Interface Orientation Changes

When an iOS device wants to check to see whether it should rotate your interface, it calls the `supportedInterfaceOrientations` method in your view controller. The implementation of `supportedInterfaceOrientations` just returns a value that describes the supported orientation. To cover more than one orientation, you just return the list of constants you want to use, separated by the | character.

There are seven screen orientation support constants, as listed here:

- ▶ **Portrait:** `UIInterfaceOrientationMask.Portrait`

- ▶ **Portrait Upside-Down:** `UIInterfaceOrientationMask.PortraitUpsideDown`

- ▶ **Landscape Left:** `UIInterfaceOrientationMask.LandscapeLeft`

- ▶ **Landscape Right:** `UIInterfaceOrientationMask.LandscapeRight`

- ▶ **Any Landscape:** `UIInterfaceOrientationMask.Landscape`

▶ **Anything But Upside-Down:** `UIInterfaceOrientationMask.AllButUpsideDown`

▶ **Anything:** `UIInterfaceOrientationMask.All`

For example, to allow your interface to rotate to either the portrait or landscape left orientations, you implement `supportedInterfaceOrientations` in your view controller with the code in Listing 16.1.

LISTING 16.1   **Activating Interface Rotation**

```
override func supportedInterfaceOrientations() -> Int {
    return Int(UIInterfaceOrientationMask.Portrait) |
        Int(UIInterfaceOrientationMask.LandscapeLeft)
}
```

The `return` statement handles everything. It returns the combination of the two constants that describe landscape left and portrait orientations.

NOTE

In addition to adding this method to your view controllers, you must also choose the orientations supported by your app by clicking the Device Orientation check boxes in the application Deployment Info settings. This is described in the section "Setting Supported Device Orientations" in Hour 2, "Introduction to Xcode and the iOS Simulator."

At this point, take a few minutes and go back to some of the earlier hours and modify this method in your view controller code to allow for different orientations. Test the applications in the iOS Simulator or on your device. For iPhone apps, try switching between devices with different horizontal and vertical dimensions displays.

Some of the applications will probably look just fine, but you'll notice that others, well, don't quite "work" in the different screen orientations and sizes, as shown in Figure 16.1 (ImageHop, from Hour 8, "Handling Images, Animation, Sliders, and Steppers").

Everything we've been building has defaulted to a portrait design and, for the most part targeted a very specific screen height and width. So how can we create interfaces that look good regardless of the orientation and size of the screen? We obviously need to make some tweaks.

Designing Rotatable and Resizable Interfaces

In the remainder of this hour, we explore several different techniques for building interfaces that rotate and resize themselves appropriately depending on the device, or when the user changes the device's screen orientation. Before we get started, let's quickly review the different approaches and when you'd want to use them.

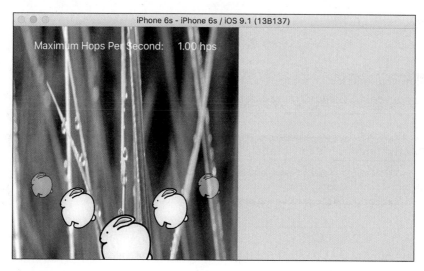

FIGURE 16.1
Enabling an orientation doesn't mean it will look good.

Auto Layout

The Xcode Interface Builder (IB) editor provides tools for describing how your interface should react when it is rotated or when the size of the screen can be variable. It is possible to define a single view in IB that positions and sizes itself appropriately—no matter what the situation— without writing a single line of code. This bit of Apple magic is called *Auto Layout*. It will be your best friend and worst enemy in creating responsive interfaces.

Using Auto Layout should be the starting point for all interfaces. If you can successfully define portrait and landscape modes in a single view in the IB editor, your work is done.

Unfortunately, Auto Layout alone doesn't work well when there are many irregularly positioned interface elements. A single row of buttons? No problem. Half a dozen fields, switches, and images all mixed together? Probably not going to work.

NOTE

You've already used Auto Layout a teensy bit in Hours 10, 11, and 12 to create universal applications that present consistent views on the iPhone and iPad. In this hour, however, you'll learn how the Auto Layout constraints you added actually worked.

Programming Interfaces

As you've learned, each UI element is defined by a rectangular area on the screen: its `frame`. If we programmatically define an application interface, we can make it into anything we want.

Although this might sound challenging, it's actually very simple and very effective for creating interfaces that vary dramatically between different sizes and orientations.

For example, to detect when the interface changes size (such as through a device rotation), we can implement the method `viewWillTransitionToSize:withTransitionCoordinator` in our view controller. This method gives us a variable—`size` of the type `CGSize`—that we can use to check to see how large our interface area is. We can even use this to quickly tell if we are dealing with a landscape or portrait layout, by implementing the code in Listing 16.2 within our view controllers.

LISTING 16.2   React to Changes in Available Screen Space

```
override func viewWillTransitionToSize(size:CGSize,withTransitionCoordinator
    coordinator: UIViewControllerTransitionCoordinator) {
    if size.width > size.height {
        // Landscape view
    } else {
        // Portrait view
    }
    super.viewWillTransitionToSize(size,
        withTransitionCoordinator: coordinator)

}
```

NOTE

Landscape? Portrait? Does It Matter?

Prior to iOS 9, Apple provided a quick means of checking to see if you were in landscape or portrait modes. With slide-in multitasking in iOS 9, the notion of "portrait" or "landscape" became less meaningful. You might hold an iPad in landscape, but be using two apps side-by-side in a portrait orientation. Because of this change, methods have been adjusted to deal mostly with sizes, rather than device orientations. If you really want to know your device's orientation, however, we'll look at a way to precisely detect it in the next hour.

The drawback to doing everything in code is that you are doing *everything* in code. It becomes very difficult to prototype interface changes and visualize what your final interface will look like. In addition, it is harder to adapt to changes in the future.

TIP

Apple has implemented a screen-locking function so that users can lock the screen orientation without it changing if the device rotates. (This can be useful for reading while lying on your side.) When the lock is enabled, your application will not receive notifications about a change in orientation. In other words, to support the orientation lock, you don't need to do a thing.

Swapping Views

A more dramatic approach to changing your view to accommodate different screen orientations is to use entirely different views for landscape and portrait layouts. When the user rotates the device, the current view is replaced by another view that is laid out properly for the orientation.

This means that you can define two views in a single scene that look exactly the way you want, but it also means that you must keep track of separate IBOutlets for each view. Although it is certainly possible for elements in the views to invoke the same IBActions, they cannot share the same outlets, so you'll potentially need to keep track of twice as many UI widgets within a single view controller. I ran out of room in the book with my view-swapping tutorial, but I've included a sample application called Swapper in this hour's Projects folder that demonstrates the approach. The only real code in the project is an implementation of Listing 16.1 that replaces the main view when a size change is detected.

Size Classes

Size classes, covered in Hour 23, give us the best of all worlds. Using the techniques in this hour, we can create interfaces that resize or shift depending on orientation—*but* they aren't focused on a particular device. Size classes enable us to combine the features of Auto Layout with the ability to have independent/unique views—all tied to a specific class of device (that is, the *size class*).

Of course, you're welcome to build your application in whatever manner suits you. I recommend waiting until Hour 23 before starting a complex app that aims to take advantage of all of Apple's unique device screen sizes.

Using Auto Layout

As already mentioned, Auto Layout enables us to build responsive interfaces without writing a line of code. Because of that, our first tutorial is a series of examples that you can follow along with, rather than a project that we build. I've included several sample storyboard files in this hour's Storyboards folder, but you should definitely get yourself into IB and attempt the examples on your own.

NOTE

You'll be making changes to the Empty.storyboard file to test several of the concepts in this hour's lesson. I recommend copying this file and making changes to your copies. This will save you the time of having to create a new storyboard file (or deleting the contents of the current file) each time you want to try something new.

In addition, the examples in this section are all platform-agnostic; you can simulate the results on any iOS device in any orientation.

The Language and Tools of Auto Layout

When I see something with *auto* in the name, I expect that it is going to do things for me: automatically. Auto Layout lives up to this, but not without a reasonably long "getting to know you" phase. To use Auto Layout effectively, you must understand the terminology and know where to look for the tools. We spend the next few minutes getting into details, and then walk through a few examples that should get you started on the way to mastery. (Perhaps of archery or speed skating. Auto Layout if you're lucky.)

Adding Basic Constraints

Auto Layout works by building a series of *constraints* for your onscreen objects. Constraints define placement of objects, distances between objects, and how flexible these relationships are. A vertical constraint for a button, for example, might be along the lines of "keep X many points of space between this object and the top of the screen" or "keep object Y vertically centered in the view." Unfortunately, the language used for positioning can be a bit confusing; you may not be familiar with these terms:

▶ **Leading:** The "front" or left side of an object.

▶ **Trailing:** The "back" or right side of an object.

▶ **Superview:** The view that contains an object. In our examples, this is the "view" that makes up the scene itself.

NOTE

Xcode *must* always have enough constraints defined for an object that it can determine its horizontal and vertical position at any point in time (regardless of the screen orientation/size). If you don't add constraints of your own, Xcode transparently adds them for you when you build your project. This is *very* different from the initial releases of Xcode with Auto Layout support, which always added constraints. Now you can build interfaces without worrying about constraints, and then add them when you're ready.

For example, try adding a button to the window in the Empty.storyboard file; make sure that it is located toward the top-left side of the view and that you've resized the button slightly. In its initial state, your button layout doesn't display any constraints. That doesn't mean that your layout won't use them; it just means that Xcode will automatically add what it feels is appropriate when you build your project.

To add constraints that you can actually work with and adjust, you'll use the Editor, Resolve Auto Layout Issues, Add Missing Constraints menu option (as shown in Figure 16.2). This adds constraints for the currently selected object. To add constraints to *all* objects in a scene, you can choose Add Missing Constraints under the All Views in View Controller heading instead. Go ahead and try either of these options on your scene with the button.

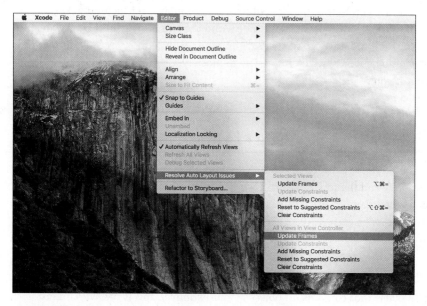

FIGURE 16.2
Use the Add Missing Constraints menu option to add default constraints to your UI objects.

After you've added constraints, you'll notice two visual changes. First, there are blue lines (representing the constraints) attached to your UI objects. In addition, a new Constraints entry appears parallel to the button in the document outline hierarchy, as well as a Constraints item within the button object itself, as shown in Figure 16.3. Let's figure out how to make sense of these new additions to the Document Outline.

TIP
___
If you ever feel like your constraint editing has gotten out of hand, you can use the Clear Constraints and Reset to Suggested Constraints options in the Resolve Auto Layout Issues menu to remove all existing constraints or to reset the object to the default constraints.
___

Navigating the Constraints Objects

Within the view's Constraints object are two constraints: horizontal space and vertical space constraint. The horizontal constraint states that the left side of the button will be a certain number of points from the left edge of the view. This is known as the *leading space* (versus the space between the right side and the edge of the view, which is called the *trailing space*). The vertical constraint is the distance from the top layout guide (essentially the top margin) to the top of the button.

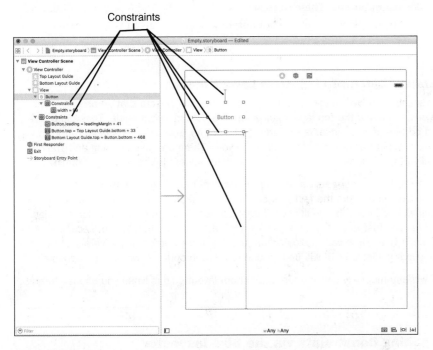

FIGURE 16.3
The constraint elements represent the positioning relationships within a view or size constraints on the UI elements themselves.

What constraints are added depend on where the object is in relation to its containing view. When you use Xcode to automatically add constraints, it does its best to choose what makes the most sense. If you position a button near the bottom of the view and add suggested (or missing) constraints, for example, Xcode will add a constraint for the distance between the bottom of the button and the bottom layout guide.

Constraints, however, are more than just entries that tie an object to the view it is within. They can be flexible, ensuring that an object maintains *at least* or *at most* a certain distance from another object, or even that two objects, when resized, maintain the same distance between one another.

Alignment constraints control the centering of objects, or the alignment of their edges or centers to one another. *Pinning* constraints set a specific size or distance between objects. The flexibility (or inflexibility) of any constraint is managed by configuring a *relationship*.

Notice the second constraint object in the document outline: constraints on the object itself, not on its positioning. When you've resized a user interface (UI) element or set constraints on how the content *within* it is positioned, Xcode will add a pinning constraint object *inside* the UI element entry in the document outline. These constraints determine the width or height of the element (or both). Not surprisingly, when you've got dozens of components in your UI, you'll have *lots* of constraints in your document outline.

Special Constraint Objects: Top/Bottom Layout Guides

When editing your scenes, you've almost certainly come across two objects that sit around in the document outline doing nothing: the top layout guide and the bottom layout guide. These just represent the top and bottom of your visual layout area. You can, for example, pin a label to the top layout guide to have it appear at the top of the screen. (Note: There are also Leading and Trailing Margin guides to align to the sides of a view—but these don't appear in the document outline.)

How does this differ from just *putting* text at the top of the screen and ignoring these "layout guides"? The difference comes from the fact that certain UI elements may "shrink" your screen. A tab bar, for example, can implement multiple different scenes. To ensure that you don't design below the tab bar, you can just align objects to the bottom layout guide. In addition, FaceTime or phone calls might push your "on a call" indicator into the top of the screen. If you've aligned your objects to the top layout guide, your UI will update and resize appropriately when this happens.

By default, Xcode will automatically use the top and bottom layout guides when you choose to add missing constraints.

Viewing and Editing Constraints via the Size Inspector

While sorting through constraints in the document outline can be a pain, you can quickly view *all* the constraints applied to an element (whether located in the Constraints object on the view the element is in, or within the UI element itself) within the Size Inspector (Option-Command-5). For example, if you've added a resized button to the storyboard, and then used Xcode to add the default missing constraints, opening the Size Inspector should look something like Figure 16.4. Here horizontal and vertical positioning for the button are represented as constraints, as well as the width of the button.

TIP

To quickly see which constraint is which, hover your cursor over one of the constraints in the Size inspector. The corresponding constraint highlights in the Interface Builder editor. This is demonstrated with the Bottom Space constraint in Figure 16.4.

Use the Edit button to the right side of each constraint to select and edit it. For example, if you pick a width constraint and click Edit, Xcode shows a popover with simple settings for adjusting it, as shown in Figure 16.5.

Constraints

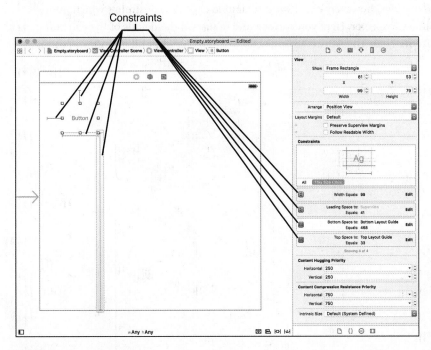

FIGURE 16.4
Use the Size Inspector to view your constraints.

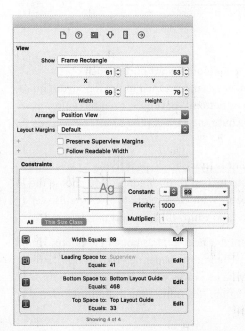

FIGURE 16.5
Click edit to display a popover and quickly edit a constraint.

For full editing capabilities, however, you'll want to double-click the constraint, which jumps you into the Attributes Inspector. Here you can see and adjust all the details of the constraint, as demonstrated in Figure 16.6. The Attributes-Inspector approach is what I'll be showing throughout the hour.

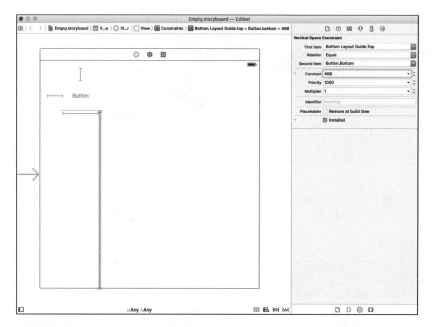

FIGURE 16.6
Use the Attributes Inspector to edit constraints.

The First Item and Second Item drop-downs are used to configure what part of each object involved in a constraint is being considered. A button that is constrained to the top layout guide, for example, might have the constraint set on its top or bottom—or maybe even its center. In general, these aren't something you'll often touch, because the correct pieces parts are chosen for you when you create the constraints.

The Relation drop-down determines what the constraint is trying to do. Is it trying to keep a distance or size equal to a value? Greater than or equal to it? Less than or equal? You choose the relation that gives your interface the flexibility you need. With each relation, you can also set a constant. This is a measurement, in points, that the relationship will be maintaining.

You'll also notice that a Priority value, Multiplier, Identifier field, a Placeholder check box, and a Standard check box (sometimes) appear in the editor. The Priority slider determines how "strong" the constraint relationship is. For example, there may be instances when multiple constraints must be evaluated against one another. The priority setting determines the importance of any given constraint. A value of 1000 is a constraint that is required. If you move the slider, Xcode shows a description of what to expect at a given constraint priority.

The multiplier is exactly what its name suggests—a value that is used for multiplying. Multiplying what? The second item involved in a relationship. Imagine you have two buttons that include a constraint for their widths to be equal. If you'd like the first button's width to be maintained as twice as large as the second, you would add a multiplier of 2, as follows:

```
Button1.width = 2 (the multiplier) x Button2.width
```

The Standard check box (not visible in Figure 16.6) lets Xcode use its internal database of spacing to set the recommended space between two objects. This, in many cases, is preferred because it ensures a consistent interface.

The last two settings are code specific - The Identifier field holds an arbitrary value that can be used to identify and interact with the constraint through your code. The Placeholder check box is used if you plan to resize or move the UI object in your code. If you check this option, you can use Auto Layout tools to set up your UI element, but the constraints will be removed when your application runs.

CAUTION
Installed? What's That?

For now, don't mess with the Installed check box or the very light + buttons you'll see when inspecting constraints. These features are related to size classes, which you'll learn about in Hour 23.

In a few minutes, we'll make use of the editor to configure a few relationships. Trust me, it makes more sense once you get started.

TIP

Constraints can also be edited by selecting them in the design view and opening the Attributes Inspector, double-clicking opens a quick-editing popover.

If you're good at clicking on thin lines, you can do this without going into the Size Inspector. I personally prefer starting by selecting the UI element, viewing the constraints in the Size Inspector, and then jumping into editing from there.

Content Hugging and Content Compression Resistance

When viewing an interface object with constraints in the Size Inspector, you noticed settings for Content Hugging Priority and Content Compression Resistance Priority. These features are related to Auto Layout, but what do they do?

These settings control how closely the sides of an object "hug" the content in the object and how much the content can be compressed or clipped. Imagine a button that you want to expand horizontally, but not vertically. To allow horizontal expansion, you'd set horizontal hugging as a low priority. To keep it from growing vertically, you set vertical hugging to a high priority.

Similarly, the content (the button label) should not be compressed or clipped at all, so the content compression resistance settings for both horizontal and vertical compression should be very high priority.

You will not often need to adjust these settings beyond their defaults, which IB adds for you.

TIP

UI objects like buttons have *intrinsic* constraints that do not appear in the interface. These are the sizes that Xcode determines the object should have in order to display your content (such as a button label or button image). Xcode will automatically try to maintain these constraints unless you override them with your own user constraints and content compression/hugging settings. Other objects, such as switches, cannot resize at all, so there's no tweaking that will cause them to violate their intrinsic constraints. Text views, image views, and other "generic" content holders, however, will happily resize with no difficulty. You'll see this behavior in a few minutes.

Understanding and Correcting Constraint Errors

When I am reading a book, I tend to skip over anything that talks about errors. Why? Because I don't make mistakes… and I'm sure you don't either. Unfortunately, no matter how careful you are with Auto Layout, you're going to see errors—lots of them—and they're going to look *ugly*.

For example, we've been looking at a button in the Empty.storyboard. We added the button, added the constraints, and everything was fine. Now, try dragging the button to a new position in the window and see what happens. As soon as you drag the button, you'll see constraints appear drawn in orange, along with a dotted line where your button was originally located, as shown in Figure 16.7.

The solid lines (and numbers on the lines) show the changes in the original constraints. A +5 on a vertical constraint, for instance, means the object has shifted down 5 points from the original constraint. A –5 on a horizontal constraint indicates a shift to the left. The dotted line shows the frame of the original object.

What's important to understand here is that even though you've moved the object in IB, the original constraints remain—so your object is now considered "misplaced" in Xcode.

In addition to highlighting constraints in another color, Xcode also shows Auto Layout errors in the document outline. When you moved the button an orange indicator appeared by the scene in the object hierarchy; you can see this in Figure 16.7. To get a description of the error, click the indicator icon in the document outline. The display refreshes to show the error, as shown in Figure 16.8.

Original Frame

Error Indicator   Change In Constraint Values

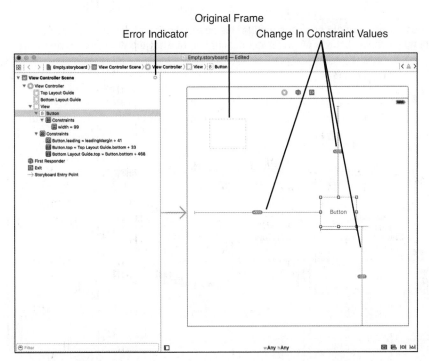

FIGURE 16.7
Constraint errors appear if you do anything that would change the existing constraints.

View Error Description   Fix Errors

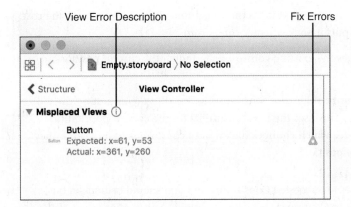

FIGURE 16.8
Looks like we have a Misplaced Views error.

TIP

If you hover your mouse over the main error heading (in this case, Misplaced Views), a small *i* icon will appear. Clicking this icon will show a plain English description of what the error means and ways to correct it.

To fix the error, click the error indicator icon beside the UI object with an error that you want to fix. Xcode displays a list of possible fixes. Try this with the button example. Your display should resemble Figure 16.9.

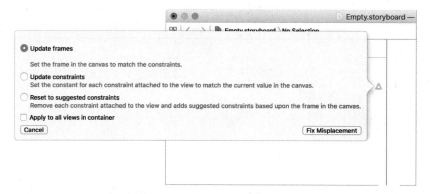

FIGURE 16.9
Choose how you want to fix the detected errors.

You have three options for automatically fixing placement errors:

▶ **Update Frame:** Moves the control so that it fits the constraints that are defined. In the case of the button example, this puts it back where it came from.

▶ **Update Constraints:** Changes the existing constraints to match the current positioning of the object.

▶ **Reset to Suggested Constraints:** Adds new constraints to the object (eliminating the old) to match its current position. This uses the best constraints for the current position (in contrast to Update Constraints, which changes the original constraints to fit, even if they aren't the best choice for the position).

Choose Update Constraints or Reset to Suggested Constraints and you should be back in business. Check the Apply to All Views in Container check box to apply to all similar errors, if desired. Click Fix Misplacement to update the storyboard accordingly.

TIP

From the menu bar, you can find the options for fixing Auto Layout issues under the Editor, Resolve Auto Layout Issues. Within this menu, you'll also find selections for applying a fix to your entire view controller, not just a single control.

Although this scenario (in my opinion) is the most common that you will encounter, other constraint errors are possible. In some cases, you may have multiple conflicting constraints (two constraints pinning the height to different values, for example)—in which case, you'll be prompted to delete one of the conflicts.

On the other end of the spectrum, if you don't have enough constraints to determine an object's position, you will see an error for missing constraints. Clicking through the error indicators will present you with the option to add the missing constraints, as shown in Figure 16.10.

FIGURE 16.10
Find and fix your Auto Layout errors, whatever they may be.

Manually Defining Constraints

So far, we've talked about how to use Xcode to add constraints to our layouts, and then edit the automatically-generated constraints. That's not the only way to add all these magic blue lines to our projects – we can also manually define constraints using two buttons at the bottom of the Interface Builder editor: pin and align.

NOTE

All Aligns Are Not Equal

Apple insists on making revisions of this book as difficult as possible. Previously, align and pin constraint tools were found in the Xcode menus. Now, they've been hidden behind two little buttons. In addition, the Align function in the menu bar is just for visual alignment; it does not create alignment constraints. Grumble.

For example, Figure 16.11 shows the Alignment Constraints popover.

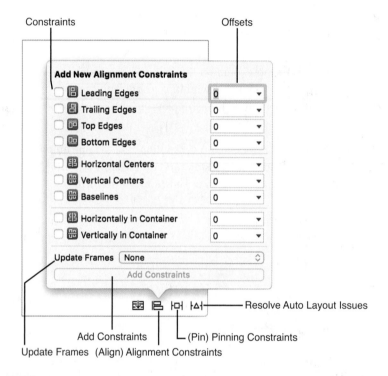

FIGURE 16.11
Use the Align button at the bottom of the editor to add new Alignment constraints.

To use the alignment constraints popover, you select the objects that should be aligned, click the Align button, and then click the check box in front of the type of alignment you want. You can also specify a value for the constraints if you want to apply an offset between objects. Aligning leading edges (left sides) of several objects with a value of 20, for example, aligns all the objects along the left side of the first object selected (plus 20 points), effectively indenting everything after the first object. Clicking Add Constraints adds the new constraints to your design.

CAUTION

Align Your Objects. Create an Error. Neato!

Adding Alignment constraints for your objects adds the necessary constraints as if the objects had moved, but it doesn't move them. The result? Errors. Lots and lots of errors.

The easiest way to deal with alignment is to add missing (default) constraints, select your alignment constraints, and then use the Update Frames popup menu at the bottom of the Alignment popover to choose to update the frames for Items of New Constraints.

For Pinning Constraints, click the Pin button, just to the right of the Align button in the IB editor, as shown in Figure 16.12.

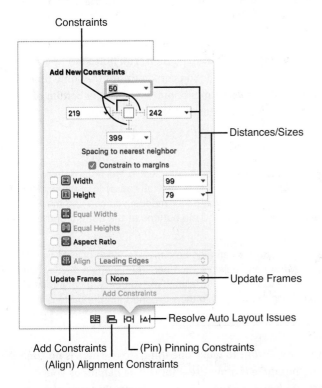

FIGURE 16.12
Use the Pin button at the bottom of the editor to add new Pinning constraints.

Adding constraints via the Pinning popover is a bit different than the Alignment constraints. Recall that these constraints are concerned with distances between objects and object size. At the top of the popover is a white box surrounded on four sides by fields and little dashed red lines. The box represents your object. The red lines represent the top, bottom, left (leading), and right (trailing) constraints, and the fields are the distances that the constraint should maintain. To configure a constraint of 50 points between the top of your object and the nearest object above it, you'd fill in 50 in the top field, and then click the top dashed line so that it turned into a solid line. Finally, you'd click the Add Constraints button at the bottom of the popover. Note that the Constrain to Margins check box should remain checked in most cases. (It ensures that Xcode uses the proper margin spacing between objects.)

Width and height constraints are exactly as they appear. Check the box in front of whichever (or both) you'd like to apply, fill in the size in points in the rights to the right, and click Add

Constraints to create the constraints. Equal heights, widths, and aspect ratio constraints are even easier, not requiring any configuration beyond checking the appropriate box. You can even use the Pinning popover to set alignment constraints—although without the fine-tuning control of applying offset values.

As with the Alignment constraints configuration, if you set a constraint that would alter the size or location of an object, it *won't* actually change the object in the design. You'll need to update the object's frame to make everything look the way it should. You can do this at the same time you're configuring your constraints by using the Update Frames popup menu at the bottom of the Alignment popover to choose to update the frames for Items of New Constraints.

Constraint Tools: Click Your Poison

First of all, the title of this sidebar is a play on "pick your poison." (You should laugh uncontrollably at my humor.) Now that we've cleared that up, let's get to the point: You can access the basic constraint features in the Xcode in many ways. You can use the Editor menus, you can use the Fix options when an Auto Layout error is detected, and you can use the buttons at the bottom of the IB editor.

If clicking and dragging is more up your alley, constraints can also be added between objects by Control-dragging (or right-clicking and dragging) from one object to another. This opens a display (very similar to what you've used to make connections to outlets) that allows you to define a constraint between objects. Personally, I prefer just choosing the objects in the view and then the buttons at the bottom of the editor.

Before we put what we've learned into practice, I want to make one thing clear: There is no "one way" to build interfaces with Auto Layout, but there *is* a mindset that will be helpful as you build your own designs. Specifically, start by identifying the interface elements that you want to anchor somewhere on the screen, regardless of orientation or screen size. From there, begin looking for the relationships between those elements and the other objects that make up your interface. Building relationships between objects, rather than trying to tie each element to specific coordinates within a view, is a good tactic for successful UI design.

Example One: Centering Constraints

Let's look at a very simple example: a button that stays centered regardless of the screen size of your device, including changes between portrait and landscape orientations. To do this, begin by adding and positioning the button:

1. Open a copy of the Empty.storyboard file and add a button to the scene. Resize the button slightly so that it is larger than the default size.

2. First, we'll pin the width and height. Without a width and height set, the object won't know whether it should grow, shrink, or move to center itself during an interface change.

Pinning a width and height makes centering unambiguous. Select the button, and then click the Pin button at the bottom of the editor.

3. Click the check boxes beside Width and Height, and then click the Add Constraints button.

4. To set the Align constraints, select the button, and then click the Align button at the bottom of the editor.

5. Click the check boxes beside Horizontally in Container and Vertically in Container, and then click the Add Constraints button.

6. For the last step, select the button one more time, and then choose Editor, Resolve Auto Layout Issues, Update Frames. Your layout should now be finished and resemble Figure 16.13.

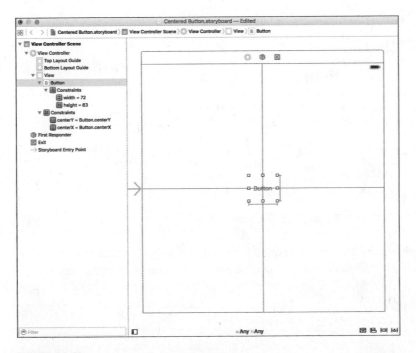

FIGURE 16.13
The final constraints for a nicely centered button.

NOTE

Notice the little preview at the top of the list of constraints in the Size Inspector? This view gives you a quick visual representation of the constraints applied to an object, and allows you to click the lines to immediately select the corresponding constraint and hide all the others.

Switch to the assistant editor (View, Assistant Editor, Show Assistant Editor), and select Preview from the path bar above the editor (click where it initially shows Automatic). Use the control at the bottom of the preview display to rotate the display; use the + button in the lower-left corner of the preview to add additional device previews. Assuming your constraints are correct, the button should also properly center itself regardless of your settings, as demonstrated in Figure 16.14.

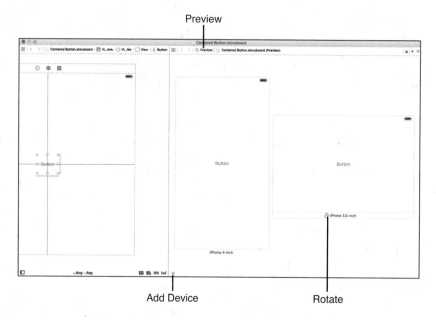

FIGURE 16.14
The button centers itself, regardless of orientation, screen size, and device.

That was pretty simple, wasn't it? Of course, not all your applications will consist of just a single button (only the best ones). For that reason, we cover a few more examples, starting with resizing controls.

TIP
I highly recommend (if your screen space allows) turning on the assistant editor's Preview feature while playing with Auto Layout. You will be able to see the changes you make take effect in real time (which makes debugging constraints a much easier process).

Example Two: Expanding Controls

A common design problem is where you have a series of controls on the screen and they need to expand to fill the size of the screen. As an example, let's create an interface with two text views at the top and a button at the bottom. The button should always remain anchored at the bottom, but should grow horizontally to fill the width of the display. The text views should grow or shrink vertically, and expand horizontally to fill the screen.

Creating the Interface

Starting from a fresh copy of Empty.storyboard, follow these steps:

1. Drag a button to the storyboard, positioning it at the bottom center of the view using the guides that appear while dragging.

2. Resize each side of the button by dragging toward the side of the view, and then release when you see the blue guide appear.

3. Select the button, and then from the menu bar, choose Editor, Resolve Auto Layout Issues, Add Missing Constraints.

By using the guides in steps 1 and 2, Xcode knows that when it adds the missing constraints, it should use the default margins for pinning the button. You should see three constraints that anchor to the side and bottom margins of the view, as shown in Figure 16.15.

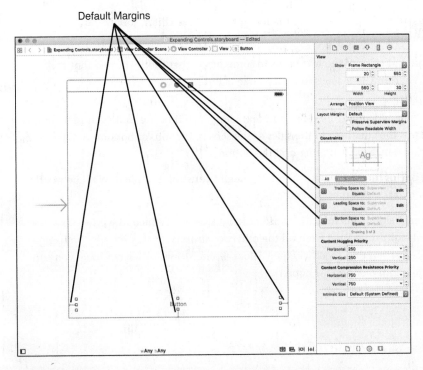

FIGURE 16.15
These three constraints make the button resize and stay anchored at the bottom, regardless of the screen size or orientation.

The constraints that have been created are a good start for the button. These ensure that the sides of the button are always an equal distance from the sides of the view, regardless of the orientation. The same goes for the distance from the bottom of the view to the bottom of the button.

TIP

The Pin menu at the bottom of the IB editor lets you quickly update constraints on whatever object is selected in the editor, or add new constraints. This tool gives you yet another way to add and edit constraints in Xcode.

Next, add two text views to the scene:

1. Drag two text views to the scene, stacking one on top of the other.

2. Resize the text views to fill the scene horizontally, until the blue guides appear at the margins.

3. Size the text views vertically until the guides appear to keep the views from overlapping the button, one another, or the top margin of the scene.

4. Select both text views. And then from the menu bar, choose Editor, Resolve Auto Layout Issues, Add Missing Constraints.

5. Set the background color of the text views to something other than white so that they are easier to see. Your finished view should look like Figure 16.16.

Depending on how you added and sized for your text views, you'll notice that each of them has a variety of constraints that tie them to the sides of the screen, the top (or bottom) of the screen, and maintain spacing between each other and the button.

You'll also see that one of the text views will have a height constraint applied. We'll be working with this constraint in a few minutes, so find it now.

Why is there only one height constraint? Because as long as one is defined, the other text view can have a relative height calculated from all the other constraints. (If this sounds confusing, think of two lengths of string that together equal 1 foot. If one string is 7 inches long, you can calculate the second length of string... I hope.)

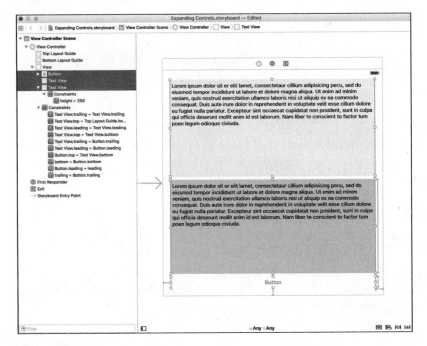

FIGURE 16.16
You've added three UI elements and quite a few constraints.

Setting the Constraints

Try resizing and rotating the display using the assistant editor's Preview feature. What you'll notice is that resizing it vertically (switching between 3.5-inch and 4-inch screens) likely works okay. What definitely doesn't is rotating to landscape. In landscape mode, one of the text views will shrink so much that it isn't even visible. To make the scene work right, you need to set some additional constraints.

Specifically, you need to accomplish these things:

1. Pin the height of the button so that it can't get squished by one of the text views.

2. Choose the text views to be the first to shrink when the size changes. We set this view so that its height is greater than or equal to the smallest size we want it to reach. I will use the top view for this purpose and set its minimum height to 100 points or greater.

3. Set a fixed height on the bottom text view (I'll use ~250 points) so that it doesn't change size. But, we need to set its priority to less than 1000 (the default). This lets the text view change sizes in an extreme situation. That "extreme situation" would otherwise occur in landscape mode where the top view would try to maintain a height of 100 points but the bottom view's fixed height of 250 would force a condition where both can't hold.

Begin by selecting the button. Then, use the Pin button to add a Height constraint. Simple enough!

Next, take a look at which of your text views already has a height constraint. We need to make sure that *both* do. So, select the one that *doesn't* and again use the Pin popover to add a height constraint. You're now ready to add some logic to the constraints.

Select the top text view; then use the Size Inspector to select and edit the height constraint.

Using the Relation drop-down, choose Greater Than or Equal. Set the constant to 100 (the text view must be 100 points in height or greater) and leave the priority alone. Your configuration should look like Figure 16.17.

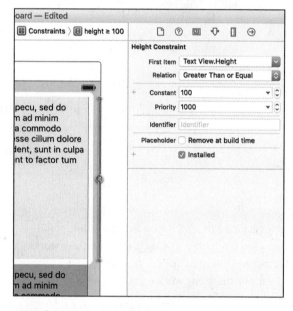

FIGURE 16.17
Set the relation for the height constraint.

Now the top text view will shrink when it needs to, but it can also grow; in fact, until a constraint is set on the bottom text view, it can grow *too large*, pushing the bottom text view until it is too small in any orientation.

Select the bottom text view and again edit its height constraint. (Add one if it isn't already there.) Make sure that the relation is set to Equal with whatever constant Xcode added, as shown in Figure 16.18. This time, however, set the priority down to 999. This makes the constraint turn into a dotted line (visible in Figure 16.17) showing that the constraint will *try* to be maintained, but, if necessary, it can resize to avoid violating other constraints.

Go ahead and try resizing the view between iDevice screen sizes and rotating to landscape mode. Everything should work like a charm, with the top text view resizing when needed and the bottom text view resizing when it absolutely has to.

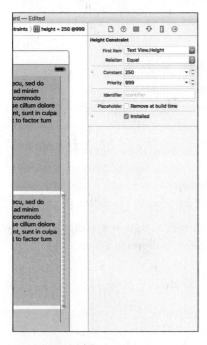

FIGURE 16.18
Set a height constraint with a priority lower than 1000 to enable the text view to change sizes if absolutely necessary.

CAUTION

What If It Doesn't Work?

If something doesn't appear to be working, it's likely because there are extra height constraints. Look for multiple height constraints (or any others that look out of place) and delete any duplicates that may be conflicting.

TIP

Combining multiple constraints with variable relationships, like this, is what you need to do to accommodate complex interfaces. You can also manually add all your constraints using the Pin options—instead of getting the default set with Add Missing Constraints.

Don't be shy about trying different relationships and priorities to see how they interact. This, for example, is a great place to try pinning Equal Heights with both the text views selected. You can even modify this constraint with a multiplier so that one text view is always sized proportionally to the other.

There isn't a "recipe" for making effective Auto Layout designs. Spend a few hours playing with the tools—laying out interfaces in different ways. Hands-on is the only way you'll get the experience you need to be comfortable with Auto Layout.

Example Three: Variable and Matching Sizes

Okay, one more quick exercise to round things out. This time, we add three buttons in a horizontal line, and we add enough constraints to make the buttons all resize equally when we shift to landscape or a different device.

Create a new copy of the Empty.storyboard document, and then drag a new button into the middle of the display. Size the button to be a bit under $1/3^{rd}$ of the screen width (doesn't matter what the simulated size of the display is)—you're going to be placing three in a horizontal row. Next, set a background color for the button's view so you can more easily see the width.

Copy your button to create a total of three, and label them **Button A**, **Button B**, and **Button C**. Use the guides to align them in the vertical center of the display, as shown in Figure 16.19.

FIGURE 16.19
Add three buttons, nothing more.

You now know enough to make one of the buttons resize, but how could we constrain them so that *all* the buttons resize to fill in the screen in landscape mode? These are the steps constraints that I came up with:

1. Start by manually positioning the buttons where you'd like them—using the guides wherever possible.

2. Align all the buttons to the vertical center in the container. This keeps them centered vertically on the screen.

3. Align the middle button to the horizontal center of the container; it should always remain in the middle of the screen.

4. Pin the Leading Space of Button A to the superview (the edge of the view). In other words, you want to pin the left side of Button A. Because there is nothing to the left of it, it will automatically pin to the side of the view that contains it (that is, the superview).

5. Pin the Trailing Space of Button C to the superview.

6. Pin the Horizontal Spacing between Button A and Button B. Do this by adding either a leading constraint to button B, or a trailing constraint to button A.

7. Pin the Horizontal Spacing between Button B and C. (If we stopped here, the center button [Button B] would stretch, while the other buttons would stay the same size.)

8. Pin the buttons so that they all share the same width. (Select all the buttons, and then click the Pin button and choose Equal Widths).

9. Resolve any errors that appear by choosing Editor, Resolve Auto Layout Issues, Add Missing Constraints.

Use the Pin popover to add these constraints to your storyboard; you should know how to do it by now. There is no need to adjust the priority or relationships in this case. Your finished layout will hopefully be similar to Figure 16.20. (One of the = constraints may be on a different button. This is fine.)

Switch to the assistant editor and open a preview. When you view your design in landscape or on varying devices, all the buttons should resize equally and fill in the space across the screen, as shown in Figure 16.21.

Wait, There's More

There is much more to the Auto Layout system than can be described in an hour. Be sure to explore the Pin and Align options to see the different types of constraints that you can put in place.

Review Apple's documentation, starting with Auto Layout Guide, for more information.

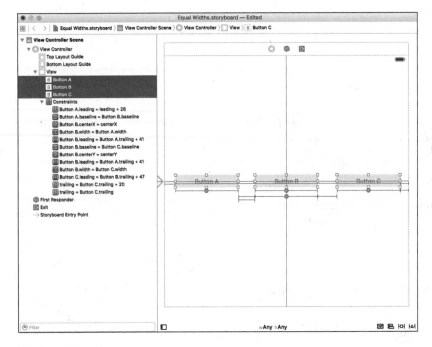

FIGURE 16.20
Your scene should have constraints much like these.

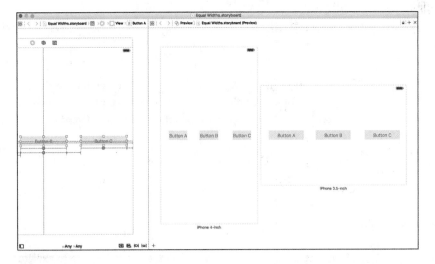

FIGURE 16.21
The buttons' constraints force them to spread out across the screen and match sizes.

Programmatically Defined Interfaces

In the previous example, you learned how the IB editor can help quickly create interface layouts that look as good horizontally as they do vertically and that can resize between the various iDevice displays. Unfortunately, in plenty of situations, IB can't quite accommodate your dream UI. Irregularly spaced controls and tightly packed layouts rarely work out the way you expect. You may also find yourself wanting to tweak the interface to look completely different—positioning objects that were at the top of the view down by the bottom and so on.

In cases like this, consider implementing the UI (or portions of it) completely in code. But, what about the nice and neat drag-and-drop approach? Well, using code isn't as convenient as drawing your interface in IB, but it *isn't* difficult. We're going to move to a project that is the exact opposite of our last few examples—rather than building a responsive interface without code, we're going to *only* use code to create an interface.

Implementation Overview

In this tutorial, we create a very simple application with three UI elements: two buttons (Button A and Button B) and a label. The buttons trigger a method to set the label to the title of the button. Most important, however, is that the interface reacts properly to orientation and size changes.

In the portrait orientation, the buttons are drawn with the label sandwiched between them. In landscape, the buttons move closer to the bottom, and the label repositions above them. The final output will resemble Figure 16.22.

Take note that the positioning of the buttons and the label cannot be handled in Auto Layout (at least not with our current toolset). When you encounter issues that can't be solved in Auto Layout, there's no harm in coding your way out of the forest.

To handle the rotation and resizing of the objects, we will implement the method `viewWillTransitionToSize:withTransitionCoordinator` along with the new screen size that it returns. This gives us the width and height of the display corresponding to whatever orientation or size change is about to take place. We then use these values to position the UI elements on the screen. By basing the positioning on the size of our application's view, the physical size of the screen and orientation are largely irrelevant, as you'll soon see.

Setting Up the Project

Unlike the previous example, we can't rely on pointing and clicking for the interface, so there is a bit of code in the project. Once again, create a new single-view iOS application project, targeting Universal devices, and name it **AllInCode**.

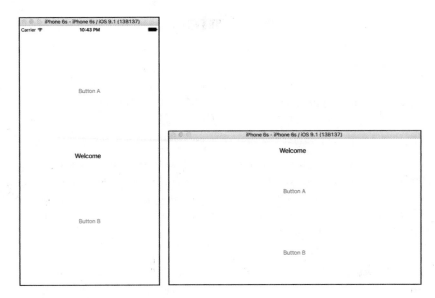

FIGURE 16.22
Buttons resize and reposition appropriately (all handled in code).

Planning the Variables and Connections

In this exercise, you manually resize and reposition three UI elements: two buttons (UIButton) and one label (UILabel). Although we aren't creating these with outlets, we define variable properties for them: buttonA, buttonB, and theLabel should suffice.

We also implement a method: handleButton, which updates the onscreen label to show the title of a button that was tapped. Like the variables, this won't be declared using IB, but we'll be using it just like an IBAction. We also add two additional methods, initInterface and updateLayoutWithScreenWidth:screenHeight, to handle setting up and updating the interface, respectively. The updateLayoutWithScreenWidth:screenWidth method will be triggered by a change in orientation, so our next step is to set up the project to properly handle orientation changes.

Enabling Orientation Changes

For this project, enable support of all orientations. To do this, start by updating the project summary (click the blue project icon at the top of the project navigator) and select all the device orientations within the Deployment Info section. Next, add the supported InterfaceOrientations method to ViewController.swift and have it return the constant UIInterfaceOrientationMask.All, as shown in Listing 16.3.

LISTING 16.3   Supporting All Interface Orientations

```
override func supportedInterfaceOrientations() -> UIInterfaceOrientationMask
{
    return UIInterfaceOrientationMask.All
}
```

Programming the Interface

We've now reached the point in the project where normally I'd say, "Let's design the interface." This time, however, there isn't going to be a visual design, just code. In fact, you've already seen the two screenshots that accompany this project, so if you're just skimming pictures, you'd better flip through a few more pages.

Defining Variables and Methods

We start by defining the objects that the view controller will be using. Recall that we're adding three objects: buttonA, buttonB, and theLabel. Because we can define these at the application start, we can actually add them as constants.

Edit ViewController.swift, adding the constant definitions below the class block, as shown here:

```
let buttonA: UIButton = UIButton(type: UIButtonType.System)
let buttonB: UIButton = UIButton(type: UIButtonType.System)
let theLabel: UILabel = UILabel()
```

Notice that I'm initializing the objects, not just declaring them. The buttons are created with the type UIButtonType.System—the standard type of button we get when adding buttons through Interface Builder.

Initializing the Interface Objects

The next step is to add the initInterface method to ViewController.swift. The purpose of this method is to configure all the interface elements (the two buttons and the label) so that they're added to the view.

This method will also grab the size of the current view, and pass the width and height to update LayoutWithScreenWidth:screenHeight to configure the layout of buttons on the screen. By keeping the layout logic separated from the initialization logic, we can use the update method at any time to change the interface – not just during initialization.

Add the initInterface method from Listing 16.4 to ViewController.swift.

LISTING 16.4   Prepare the Interface (But Don't Display It Yet)

```
 1:  func initInterface() {
 2:      buttonA.addTarget(self, action: "handleButton:",
 3:          forControlEvents: UIControlEvents.TouchUpInside)
 4:      buttonA.setTitle("Button A", forState: UIControlState.Normal)
 5:
 6:      buttonB.addTarget(self, action: "handleButton:",
 7:          forControlEvents: UIControlEvents.TouchUpInside)
 8:      buttonB.setTitle("Button B", forState: UIControlState.Normal)
 9:
10:      theLabel.text="Welcome"
11:
12:      let screenWidth: CGFloat = view.bounds.size.width
13:      let screenHeight: CGFloat = view.bounds.size.height
14:
15:      updateLayoutWithScreenWidth(screenWidth,
16:          screenHeight: screenHeight)
17:
18:      view.addSubview(buttonA)
19:      view.addSubview(buttonB)
20:      view.addSubview(theLabel)
21:  }
```

This might be the first time we've manually created a number of UI elements, but because you've been working with these objects and adjusting their variable properties for hours, this code shouldn't seem completely foreign.

Lines 2–3 set the action for buttonA. The addTarget:action:forControlEvents method configures what will happen when the Touch Up Inside event occurs for the button—in this case, calling the method handleMethod. This is exactly the same as connecting a button to an IBAction in IB.

Line 4 sets the title for the button to Button A.

Lines 6–8 repeat the same process for Button B (buttonB).

Lines 10 initializes the label (theLabel) with the default text Welcome.

Lines 12–13 grab the view's width and height and store them in screenWidth and screenHeight.

Lines 15–16 call updateLayoutWithScreenWidth:screenHeight to calculate the positions of the buttons and label on the screen. In order for the method (which we'll write shortly) to know how to setup the screen, we pass it the screenWidth and screenHeight values.

Lastly, lines 18-20 add the buttons and label to the current view. So, what do we do now? Implementing updateLayoutWithScreenWidth:screenHeight seems like a good next step.

Implementing the Interface Update Method

The `updateLayoutWithScreenWidth:screenHeight` method does the heavy lifting for the application. It checks to see what the current orientation is, and then it draws content based on the view's height and width, as determined by the `initInterface` method, and, shortly, by the size returned during a screen orientation or size change. By basing the drawing on the height and width, we can scale the interface to any screen size at all.

For example, assume we've determined the available screen's width and height and stored them in `screenWidth` and `screenHeight` respectively.

The dimensions and position of UI objects are determined by their `frame`, which is a variable of type `CGRect`. To set the `frame` of a button named `theButton` so that it filled the top half of the screen, I'd write the following:

```
theButton.frame = CGRectMake(0.0,0.0,screenWidth,screenHeight/2)
```

The first two values of `CGRectMake` (which create a `CGRect` data structure) set the origin point at 0,0. The second two parameters determine the width and height of the `CGRect`. Using `screenWidth` sets the button to the same width of the screen, and `screenHeight/2` sets the height of the button to half the height of the screen. In an actual implementation, you want to include some margin around the edges. This is why you'll see +20 and other values tacked onto my coordinates. Speaking of which, go ahead and implement `updateLayoutWithScreen Width:screenHeight`, as shown in Listing 16.5. When you're done, we step through the code.

LISTING 16.5 Implementing `updateLayoutWithScreenWidth:screenHeight`

```
 1:  func updateLayoutWithScreenWidth(screenWidth:CGFloat,
 2:      screenHeight:CGFloat) {
 3:
 4:      if screenWidth>screenHeight {
 5:          buttonA.frame=CGRectMake(20.0,60.0,
 6:              screenWidth-40.0,screenHeight/2-40.0)
 7:          buttonB.frame=CGRectMake(20.0,screenHeight/2+30,
 8:              screenWidth-40.0,screenHeight/2-40.0)
 9:          theLabel.frame=CGRectMake(screenWidth/2-40,20.0,
10:              200.0,20.0)
11:      } else {
12:          buttonA.frame=CGRectMake(20.0,20.0,
13:              screenWidth-40.0,screenHeight/2-40.0)
14:          buttonB.frame=CGRectMake(20.0,
15:              screenHeight/2+20,screenWidth-40.0,screenHeight/2-40.0)
16:          theLabel.frame=CGRectMake(screenWidth/2-40,screenHeight/2-10,
17:              200.0,20.0)
18:      }
19:  }
```

Line 4 checks to see if the `screenWidth` provided to the method is greater than the `screenHeight`, if it is, we can assume the display is in a landscape orientation. If so, lines 5–10 are executed, if not, the display is in a portrait orientation and lines 12–17 are run. These blocks both have the same purpose: defining the `frame` for each of the UI elements (`buttonA`, `buttonB`, and `theLabel`).

Lines 5–10 position the buttons lower on the screen and put the label at the top. Lines 12–17 define positions for the buttons so that there are margins on the edges of the screen and a space in the middle for the label. The margins and spacing I used is completely arbitrary. You can try changing these values around to see what effect they have.

Everything is now in place for the interface, but we need to take care of three small tasks before the project is complete. First, we need to make sure that the interface is drawn when the application first loads. Second, the interface must update when an orientation change occurs. Third, we need to implement `handleButton` to update the label when the buttons are pressed.

NOTE

Orientation Changes That Aren't

Although I refer to "landscape" and "portrait" orientations, it's important to keep in mind that these don't necessarily mean that a device has that physical orientation. A full-screen landscape app on an iPad could suddenly find itself shrunk in half (to support side-by-side multitasking) and would need to adapt to a portrait-style display.

When you read "portrait" or "landscape," think of the available screen area that your app has to work with–not the physical orientation of a device.

Drawing the Interface When the Application Launches

When the application first launches, there isn't an orientation change to trigger the interface to be drawn. To make sure there is something on the screen, we need to call `initInterface` when the application loads. Add this to `viewDidLoad`, as shown in Listing 16.6.

LISTING 16.6   Initializing the Interface When the Application Loads

```
override func viewDidLoad() {
    super.viewDidLoad()
    initInterface()
}
```

We're getting closer. The application will now initialize and display the interface, but it still can't adapt to a change in orientation.

Updating the Interface When Orientation Changes

To handle orientation changes, the application needs to implement `viewWillTransition` `ToSize:withTransitionCoordinator`. This method provides us with the size the screen will be after the orientation change occurs (`size.width`, `size.height`) so we have everything we need to call `updateLayoutWithScreenWidth:screenHeight` and update the display. Note that this method requires that you call `super` (with the same method name/parameters) so that changes are made available to other view controllers.

Add `viewWillTransitionToSize:withTransitionCoordinator` to ViewController.swift, as shown in Listing 16.7.

LISTING 16.7   Handling Rotation in viewWillTransitionToSize: withTransitionCoordinator

```
override func viewWillTransitionToSize(size:CGSize,withTransitionCoordinator
    coordinator: UIViewControllerTransitionCoordinator) {
    super.viewWillTransitionToSize(size,
            withTransitionCoordinator: coordinator)

    updateLayoutWithScreenWidth(size.width, screenHeight: size.height)
}
```

Handling the Button Touches

The last piece of the puzzle is implementing `handleButton` so that it updates the onscreen label with the label of the button being touched. This is just a single line, so add Listing 16.8 to the view controller, and you're done.

LISTING 16.8   Handling Button Touches

```
func handleButton(theButton: UIButton) {
    theLabel.text = theButton.currentTitle
}
```

The one line of the implementation uses the `theButton` parameter (the `UIButton` touched) to grab the title of the button and set the label to the title.

Building the Application

Build and run the application. It should rotate and resize with no problem. What's more, because all of the interface layout was based on the height and width of the view, this same code will work, without changes, on any device you choose to run it on.

I hope this didn't scare you too much. The purpose of this exercise was to show that responsive and flexible interfaces can be accomplished in code without it being too much of a hassle. The biggest challenge is determining how the controls will be laid out and then coming up with the CGRectMake functions to define their locations.

Further Exploration

Although we covered different ways of working with interface rotation, you may want to explore additional features outside of this hour's lesson. Using the Xcode documentation tool, review the UIViewControllerTransitionCoordinator class. This object is created automatically during a view controller transition (such as a size change). You'll see that you can tie into this object's methods for triggering additional animations and code blocks when size changes occur.

Later in the book (Hour 23), we'll look at tools for developing Universal Applications that can completely adapt to different devices and orientations. The foundation for using these advanced tools, however, is a solid understanding of Auto Layout and how user interfaces are built and displayed. It's a good idea to practice the techniques discussed in this hour because they will form the basis for everything you build.

Summary

iDevices are all about the user experience—a touchable display, intuitive controls, and now, rotatable and resizable interfaces. Using the methods described in this hour, you can adapt to almost any type of size or rotation scenario. To handle interface size changes without a line of code, for example, you can take advantage of the Auto Layout. For more complex changes, however, you might want to programmatically define your onscreen elements, giving you absolute control over their size and placement—or even create multiple different views and swap them as the application orientation/size changes.

By implementing orientation and size-aware applications, you give your users the ability to use their devices in the way that feels most comfortable to them.

Q&A

Q. Why don't many iPhone applications implement the upside-down portrait mode?

A. Although there is no problem implementing the upside-down portrait orientation using the approaches described in this hour, it isn't recommended. When the iPhone is upside-down, the Home button and sensors are not in the "normal" location. If a call comes in or the user needs to interact with the phone's controls, the user will need to rotate the phone 180 degrees—a somewhat complicated action to perform with one hand.

Q. How do I get the controls in application XYZ to behave using Auto Layout?

A. This is a difficult question with no clear answer because there may be dozens of ways of implementing constraints that have the desired effect. I have implemented Auto Layout constraints in all my sample projects. You may want to take a look at those to get an idea of how I solved resizing problems. (Landscape, however, is up to you!)

Workshop

Quiz

1. To correct a constraint error after moving a view, you would likely apply which of the following as a fix?

    a. Update Frame

    b. Remove Frame

    c. Clear Frames

    d. Remove Constraints

2. Which method is executed before an interface change has taken place?

    a. `viewWillTransitionToSize:withTransitionCoordinator`

    b. `didMoveFromInterfaceOrientation`

    c. `viewDidTransitionToSize:withTransitionCoordinator`

    d. `changedInterfaceOrientation`

3. We can assume an interface is in a landscape orientation if this is true?

    a. `width>0`

    b. `height>width`

    c. `height==width`

    d. `width>height`

4. Apple's system for creating interfaces that adapt to different-sized displays is called what?

    a. Auto Layout

    b. Springs and Struts

    c. Flow System

    d. Smart Grid

5. You can define a proportional relationship between object sizes using which constraint property?

   a. Value

   b. Constant

   c. Multiplier

   d. Priority

6. The space from the front of one object to the edge of another is called what?

   a. Trailing space

   b. Front space

   c. Preface space

   d. Leading space

7. If you use a constraint to set the width of an object to a specific value, you are doing what to the object?

   a. Setting

   b. Pinning

   c. Forcing

   d. Dimensioning

8. To determine the point in the middle of a screen (X,Y), what logic should you use?

   a. `screen width/2, screen height/2`

   b. `screen width*2, screen height*2`

   c. `screen width-screen height, screen height-screen width`

   d. `screen width-screen height, screen height-screen width`

9. To programmatically set an action for a button, you can use which of the following methods?

   a. `addButton:action:forControlEvents`

   b. `addSelector:forControlEvents`

   c. `addAction:forControlEvents`

   d. `addTarget:action:forControlEvents`

Answers

1. A. Misplaced views are often fixed using Update Frame.

2. A. Immediately before an interface rotation takes place, the method `viewWillTransitionToSize:withTransitionCoordinator` is called.

3. D. If an application's view's width is greater than the height, we can assume it has a landscape orientation.

4. A. The Auto Layout system is used in OS X and iOS to enable developers to create responsive interface designs.

5. C. The Multiplier setting for a constraint can be used to create a proportional relationship between interface elements.

6. D. The leading space is the amount of space from the edge of one object to the front of another.

7. B. The act of setting a dimension or distance constraint is known as pinning.

8. A. Divide the screen's width and height by 2 to locate a point in the exact center of the screen.

9. D. Use the `addTarget:action:forControlEvents` to programmatically configure the actions for a button.

Activities

1. Using what you've learned about programmatically defining an interface, try rebuilding an early exercise all in code—without using Interface Builder at all.

2. Return to an earlier lesson and revise the interface to support multiple different orientations and screen sizes. Use any of the techniques described in this hour's exercises for the implementation.

Using Advanced Touches and Gestures

What You'll Learn in This Hour:

▶ The multitouch gesture-recognition architecture

▶ How to detect taps, swipes, pinches, and rotations

▶ How to use the built-in shake gesture

▶ Simple ways to add 3D Touch to your multiscene applications

Multitouch and 3D Touch enable applications to use a combination of finger gestures and pressures for operations that would otherwise be hidden behind layers of menus, buttons, and text. From the very first time you use a pinch to zoom in and out on a photo, map, or web page, you realize that's exactly the right interface for zooming. Nothing is more human than manipulating the environment with your fingers.

iOS provides advanced gesture-recognition capabilities that you can easily implement within your applications. This hour shows you how.

Multitouch Gesture Recognition

While working through this book's examples, you've gotten used to responding to events, such as Touch Up Inside, for onscreen buttons. Multitouch gesture recognition is a bit different. Consider a "simple" swipe. The swipe has direction, it has velocity, and it has a certain number of touch points (fingers) that are engaged. It is impractical for Apple to implement events for every combination of these variables; at the same time, it is extremely taxing on the system to just detect a "generic" swipe event and force you, the developer, to check the number of fingers, direction, and so on each time the event is triggered.

To make life simple, Apple has created gesture-recognizer classes for almost all the common gestures that you may want to implement in your applications, as follows:

▶ **Tapping (`UITapGestureRecognizer`):** Tapping one or more fingers on the screen

▶ **"Long" pressing (`UILongPressGestureRecognizer`):** Pressing one or more fingers to the screen for a specific period of time

▶ **Pinching (`UIPinchGestureRecognizer`):** Pinching to close or expand something

▶ **Rotating (`UIRotationGestureRecognizer`):** Sliding two fingers in a circular motion

▶ **Swiping (`UISwipeGestureRecognizer`):** Swiping with one or more fingers in a specific direction

▶ **Panning (`UIPanGestureRecognizer`):** Touching and dragging

▶ **Screen-edge panning (`UIScreenEdgePanGestureRecognizer`):** Touching and dragging, but starting from the edge of the screen

▶ **Shaking:** Physically shaking the iOS device

In early versions of iOS, developers had to read and recognize low-level touch events to determine whether, for example, a pinch was happening: Are there two points represented on the screen? Are they moving toward each other?

Today you define what type of recognizer you're looking for, add the recognizer to a view (`UIView`), and you automatically receive any multitouch events that are triggered. You even receive values such as velocity and scale for gestures such as pinch. Let's see what this looks like translated into code.

TIP
_____

Shaking is not a multitouch gesture and requires a slightly different approach. Note that it doesn't have its own recognizer class.
_____

Adding Gesture Recognizers

You can add gesture recognizers to your projects in one of two ways: either through code or visually using the Interface Builder editor. Although using the editor makes life much easier for us, it is still important to understand what is going on behind the scenes. Consider the code fragment in Listing 17.1.

LISTING 17.1   Example of the Tap Gesture Recognizer

```
1: var tapRecognizer: UITapGestureRecognizer
2: tapRecognizer=UITapGestureRecognizer(target: self, action:"foundTap:")
3: tapRecognizer.numberOfTapsRequired=1
4: tapRecognizer.numberOfTouchesRequired=1
5: tapView.addGestureRecognizer(tapRecognizer)
```

This example implements a tap gesture recognizer that will look for a single tap from a single finger within a view called tapView. If the gesture is seen, the method foundTap is called.

Line 1 kicks things off by declaring an instance of the UITapGestureRecognizer object, tapRecognizer. In line 2, tapRecognizer is initialized with initWithTarget:action. (Remember that the initWith part is left out in Swift versions of initialization methods.) Working backward, the action is the method that will be called when the tap occurs. Using the action foundTap:, we tell the recognizer that we want to use a method called foundTap to handle our taps. The target we specify, self, is the object where foundTap lives. In this case, it will be whatever object is implementing this code (probably a view controller).

Lines 3 and 4 set two variable properties of the tap gesture recognizer:

- ▶ **numberOfTapsRequired:** The number of times the object needs to be tapped before the gesture is recognized

- ▶ **numberOfTouchesRequired:** The number of fingers that need to be down on the screen before the gesture is recognized

Finally, line 5 uses the UIView method addGestureRecognizer to add the tapRecognizer to a view called tapView. As soon as this code is executed, the recognizer is active and ready for use, so a good place to implement the recognizer is in a view controller's viewDidLoad method.

Responding to the event is simple: Just implement the foundTap method. An appropriate method stub for the implementation looks like this:

```
func foundTap(sender: AnyObject) {
    outputLabel.text="Tapped"
}
```

What happens when the gesture is found is entirely up to you. One could simply respond to the fact the gesture took place, use the parameter provided to the method to get additional details about where the tap happened on the screen, and so on.

All in all, not too bad, don't you think? What's even better? In most cases, you can do almost all of this setup entirely within Interface Builder, as shown in Figure 17.1. The tutorial in this hour shows how to do exactly that.

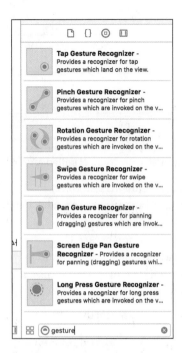

FIGURE 17.1
Gesture recognizers can be added through Interface Builder.

3D Touch Peek and Pop

3D Touch (a.k.a. Force Touch, before Apple Marketing got ahold of it) provides a new way to interact with devices—starting with the iPhone 6s and 6s+. 3D Touch measures the pressure of your finger by watching for minute bending in the glass on your iPhone. Thankfully, rather than just introduce the technology and leave it up to developers to figure out how to implement it, Apple has added three convenient methods of integrating it into your applications: peek and pop gestures and Quick Actions. The latter you'll learn more about in Hour 22, "Building Background-Ready Applications."

Peek and pop refer to actions that applications perform with two levels of pressure. When you want more information about an onscreen object, you push it lightly to "peek" at it without navigating away from where you are. If, while peeking, you decide you want to view the information full screen and interact with it, you push harder, and it "pops" into the foreground. The peek and pop transitions are referred to as the *Preview* and *Commit* segues in Xcode.

I realize that many people may not yet have devices that support this feature, but the first time you try it you'll be delighted at how natural it feels.

BY THE WAY

3D Touch: Is That *Really* a Gesture?

In case you're wondering, Apple really does consider 3D Touch to be a gesture. It may seem odd fitting it in with gestures like swiping and pinching, but if Apple considers it a gesture, and it just-so-happens-to-conveniently-fit-into-this-chapter's-structure-so-that's-where-I-wanted-to-put-it-anyway, then it's a gesture!

Adding 3D Touch Peek and Pop

To implement the 3D Touch peek and pop gestures within code, you'll need to conform to the `UIViewControllerPreviewingDelegate` protocol within the view controller that wants to respond to peek and pop gestures. This requires the implementation of two methods: `previewingContext:viewControllerForLocation` and `previewingContext:commitViewController`. These methods return a view controller for the peek, and then present the view controller for a pop, respectively.

For the application to know *what* you want to peek at, you will also need to register a view as being "3D Touch ready" with the method `registerForPreviewingWithDelegate:sourceView`.

Assume for a moment that you have a button, `myButton`, that you want to use to preview (peek) at content. You'd first register the button using code like this (possibly within your view controller's `viewDidLoad` method):

```
registerForPreviewingWithDelegate(self, sourceView: myButton)
```

Next, you implement the two methods for handing 3D Touch gestures on `myButton`. Listing 17.2 shows a possible implementation that assumes a view controller class named `previewController` has been created, and a scene using has been added to your storyboard with its storyboard ID set to `previewController`. (This configured within the Identity Inspector.)

LISTING 17.2   Add the Methods to Handle Peek and Pop

```
1: func previewingContext(previewingContext: UIViewControllerPreviewing,
2:     viewControllerForLocation location: CGPoint) -> UIViewController? {
3:     let viewController: previewController =
4:         storyboard?
5:             .instantiateViewControllerWithIdentifier("previewController")
6:             as? previewController
7:     return viewController
8: }
9:
```

```
10: func previewingContext(previewingContext: UIViewControllerPreviewing,
11:     commitViewController viewControllerToCommit: UIViewController) {
12:     showViewController(viewControllerToCommit, sender: self)
13: }
```

Looks (of code) can be deceiving. This listing is 13 lines long, but the entire implementation of both methods is just *3* (long) lines!

In method `previewingContext:viewControllerForLocation`, lines 3–6 instantiate `previewController` from the current storyboard using the storyboard ID `previewController`.

The view controller is returned in line 7. To cancel the peek action (if something went wrong, or there isn't anything to preview), you could return `nil` instead. In addition, you can make use of the method's `location` to determine the x and y coordinates where the user touched.

The code for `previewingContext:commitViewController` is a single line (12) that uses the `showViewController` method to transition the display to the new view controller. How does it know what view controller to use? It receives the peek view controller in the variable `viewControllerToCommit`; we just need to display the controller and we're done.

Now that I've shown you how simple doing a peek and pop in code can be, let me blow your mind with Figure 17.2. The Attributes Inspector can be used to configure segues so that they automatically implement peek and pop—no coding needed.

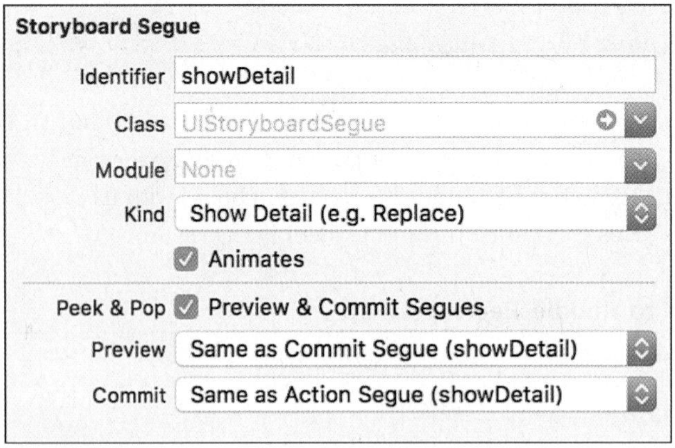

Storyboard Segue	
Identifier	showDetail
Class	UIStoryboardSegue
Module	None
Kind	Show Detail (e.g. Replace)
	☑ Animates
Peek & Pop	☑ Preview & Commit Segues
Preview	Same as Commit Segue (showDetail)
Commit	Same as Action Segue (showDetail)

FIGURE 17.2
Peek and pop can be implemented directly in Interface Builder.

In a few minutes, you'll see how 3D Touch peek and pop gestures can be retrofitted into some of our existing applications with just a click here and there.

CAUTION

3D Out of Touch

Apple, Apple, Apple... You give us a new feature, and no way to test it. Despite the ability to simulate Force Touch in the Apple Watch Simulator, and the availability of Force Touch trackpads for Macs, there is currently no way to test 3D Touch within the iOS Simulator. Hopefully, this will change soon.

Using Gesture Recognizers

As people become more comfortable with touch devices, the use of gestures becomes almost natural—and expected. Applications that perform similar functions are often differentiated by their user experience, and a fully touch-enabled interface can be the deciding factor between a customer downloading your app and passing it by.

Perhaps the most surprising element of adding gestures to applications is just how *easy* it is. I know I say that often throughout the book, but gesture recognizers are one of those rare features that "just works." Follow along and find out what I mean.

Implementation Overview

In this hour's application, which we'll name **Gestures**, you implement five gesture recognizers (tap, swipe, pinch, rotate, and shake), along with the feedback those gestures prompt. Each gesture updates a text label with information about the gesture that has been detected. Pinch, rotate, and shake take things a step further by scaling, rotating, or resetting an image view in response to the gestures.

To provide room for gesture input, the application displays a screen with four embedded views (UIView), each assigned a different gesture recognizer directly within the storyboard scene. When you perform an action within one of the views, it calls a corresponding action method in our view controller to update a label with feedback about the gesture, and depending on the gesture type, updates an onscreen image view (UIImageView), too.

Figure 17.3 shows the final application.

CAUTION

Auto Layout: Our Frenemy

We have to be a bit clever in this application because image views that we add in Interface Builder are subject to Apple's constraint system. Ideally, we want to be able to take advantage of the Auto Layout system to position our image view in a nice default position, regardless of our screen size (exactly what you learned in the preceding hour). Once the application launches, however, we don't want any of the constraints enforced because we want to be able to resize and rotate the image view using our gestures.

You can take care of this in any number of ways, including programmatically finding and removing constraints with the `removeConstraints NSLayoutConstraint` method. The method we take, however, is to add an image view in Interface Builder so that we can position it visually and then replace it with our own constraint-free image view right after the application launches. It's a relatively simple way to take advantage of Auto Layout for the initial interface object layout and then gain the flexibility of working with a constraint-free object as the application executes.

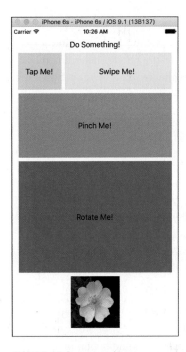

FIGURE 17.3
The application detects and acts upon a variety of gestures.

Setting Up the Project

Start Xcode and create a new single-view iOS application called **Gestures**. This project requires quite a few outlets and actions, so be sure to follow the setup closely. You'll also be making connections directly between objects in Interface Builder. So, even if you're used to the approach we've taken in other projects, you might want to slow down for this one.

Adding the Image Resource

Part of this application's interface is an image that can rotate or scale up and down. We use this to provide visual feedback to users based on their gestures. Included with this hour's project is an

Images folder and a file named flower.png Open the Assets.xcassets asset catalog in your project and drag the Images folder into the column on the left of the catalog.

Planning the Variables and Connections

For each touch gesture that we want to sense, we need a view where it can take place. Often, this would be your main view. For the purpose of demonstration, however, we will add four UIViews to our main view that will each have a different associated gesture recognizer. Surprisingly, none of these require outlets, because we'll connect the recognizers to them directly in Interface Builder.

We do, however, need two outlets, outputLabel and imageView, instances of the classes UILabel and UIImageView, respectively. The label is used to provide text feedback to the user, while the image view shows visual feedback to the pinch and rotate gestures.

When the application senses a gesture within one of the four views, it needs to invoke an action method that can interact with the label and image. We will connect the gesture recognizers to methods called foundTap, foundSwipe, foundPinch, and foundRotation.

NOTE
Notice that we don't mention the shake gesture here? Even though we will eventually add shake recognition to this project, it will be added by implementing a very specific method in our view controller, not through an arbitrary action method that we define upfront.

Adding a Variable Property for the Image View Size

When our gesture recognizers resize or rotate the image view in our user interface (UI), we want to be able to reset it to its default position and size. To make this happen, we need to "know" in our code what the default position for the image was. View positioning and sizing is described using a data structure (not an object) called a CGRect that contains four values: x and y coordinates (origin.x and origin.y), and width and height (size.width and size.height). We will add a variable property to the project that, when the application first launches, stores the size and location of the image view (the CGRect of the view) we added in Interface Builder. We'll name this **originalRect**.

Open your ViewController.swift file and add the following line after the class statement:

```
var originalRect: CGRect!
```

The originalRect variable property is declared and ready to be used in our implementation, but first we need an interface.

Designing the Interface

Open the Main.storyboard file, change to an appropriate simulated device (or use the Auto Layout/Size Class techniques you learned in the preceding hour), and make room in your workspace. It's time to create our UI.

To build the interface, start by dragging four `UIView` instances to the main view. Size the first to a small rectangle in the upper-left portion of the screen; it will capture taps. Make the second a long rectangle beside the first (for detecting swipes). Size the other two views as large rectangles below the first two (for pinches and rotations). Use the Attributes Inspector (Option-Command-4) to set the background color of each view to be something unique.

TIP

The views you are adding are convenient objects that we can attach gestures to. In your own applications, you can attach gesture recognizers to your main application view or the view of any onscreen object.

TIP

Gesture recognizers work based on the starting point of the gesture, not where it ends. In other words, if a user uses a rotation gesture that starts in a view but ends outside the view, it will work fine. The gesture won't "stop" just because it crosses a view's boundary.

For you, the developer, this is a big help for making multitouch applications that work well on a small screen.

Next, drag labels into each of the four views. The first label should read **Tap Me!**. The second should read **Swipe Me!**. The third label should read **Pinch Me!**. The fourth label should read **Rotate Me!**.

Drag a fifth `UILabel` instance to the main view, and center it at the top of the screen. Use the Attributes Inspector to set it to align center. This will be the label we use to provide feedback to the user. Change the label's default text to **Do something!.**

Finally, add a `UIImageView` layout, and then position it in an appropriately attractive location at the bottom center of the scene; use the Auto Layout constraints if you so desire (see Figure 17.4). Remember that we will not actually be using *this* image view to display gesture feedback; we want it solely for positioning. So, there is no need to set a default image for the image view.

With the view finished, in most projects we start connecting our interface to our code through outlets and actions—but not this hour. Before we can create our connections, we need to add the gesture recognizers to the storyboard.

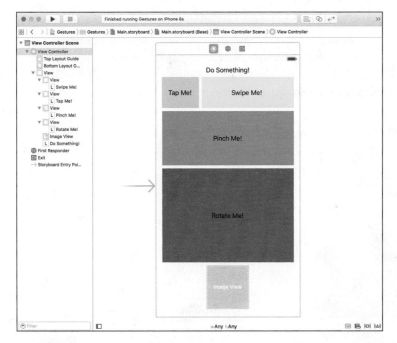

FIGURE 17.4
Size and position the `UIImageView` similar to what is shown here.

TIP

We're about to do a bunch of dragging and dropping of objects onto the `UIViews` that you just created. If you often use the document outline to refer to the objects in your view, you may want to use the `Label` field of the Document group in the Identity Inspector (Option-Command-3) to give them more meaningful names than the default View label they appear with. You can also edit the names directly in the document outline by clicking to select them, then pressing return.

Labels are arbitrary and do not affect the program's operation at all.

Adding Gesture Recognizers to Views

As you learned earlier, one way to add a gesture recognizer is through code. You initialize the recognizer you want to use, configure its parameters, and then add it to a view and provide a method it will invoke if a gesture is detected. Alternatively, you can drag and drop from the Interface Builder Object Library and barely write any code. We're going to do this now.

Make sure that Main.storyboard is open and that the document outline is visible.

The Tap Recognizer

Our first step is to add an instance of the `UITapGestureRecognizer` object to our project. Search the Object Library for the tap gesture recognizer and drag and drop it onto the `UIView` instance in your project that is labeled Tap Me!, as shown in Figure 17.5. The recognizer will appear as an object at the bottom of the document outline, regardless of where you drop it.

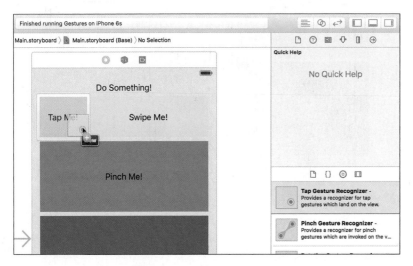

FIGURE 17.5
Drag the recognizer onto the view that will use it.

CAUTION

Everything Is a View

Be careful not to drag the recognizer onto the label within the view. Remember that every onscreen object is a subclass of `UIView`, so you *could* potentially add a gesture recognizer to the label rather than to the intended view. You might find it easier to target the views in the document outline rather than in the visual layout.

Through the simple act of dragging the tap gesture recognizer into the view, you've created a gesture-recognizer object and added it to that view's gesture recognizers. (A view can have as many as you want.)

Next, you need to configure the recognizer so that it knows what type of gesture to look for. Tap gesture recognizers have two attributes to configure:

- ▶ **Taps:** The number of times the object needs to be tapped before the gesture is recognized

- ▶ **Touches:** The number of fingers that need to be down on the screen before the gesture is recognized

In this example, we're defining a *tap* as one finger tapping the screen once, so we define a single tap with a single touch. Select the tap gesture recognizer, and then open the Attributes Inspector (Option-Command-4), as shown in Figure 17.6.

FIGURE 17.6
Use the Attributes Inspector to configure your gesture recognizers.

Set both the Taps and Touches fields to 1 (or just go nuts); this is a perfect time to play with the recognizer. Just like that, the first gesture recognizer is added to the project and configured. We still need to connect it to an action a bit later, but now we need to add the other recognizers.

TIP

If you look at the connections on the `UITapGestureRecognizer` object or the view that you dropped it onto, you'll see that the view references an *outlet collection* called `Gesture Recognizers`. An outlet collection is an array of outlets that make it easy to refer to multiple similar objects simultaneously. If you add more than one gesture recognizer to a view, the recognizer is referenced by the same outlet collection.

The Swipe Recognizer

You implement the swipe gesture recognizer in almost the same manner as the tap recognizer. Instead of being able to choose the number of taps, however, you can determine in which direction the swipes can be made—up, down, left, or right—as well as the number of fingers (touches) that must be down for the swipe to be recognized.

Again, use the Object Library to find the swipe gesture recognizer (`UISwipeGestureRecognizer`) and drag a copy of it in into your view, dropping it on top of the view that contains the Swipe Me! label. Next, select the recognizer and open the Attributes

Inspector to configure it, as shown in Figure 17.7. For this tutorial, I configured the swipe gesture recognizer to look for swipes to the right that are made with a single finger.

NOTE

If you want to recognize and react to different swipe directions, you must implement multiple swipe gesture recognizers. It is possible, in code, to ask a single swipe gesture recognizer to respond to multiple swipe directions, but it cannot differentiate between the directions.

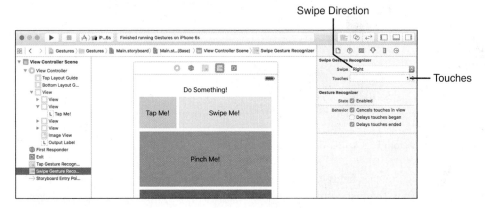

FIGURE 17.7
Configure the swipe direction and the number of touches required.

The Pinch Recognizer

A pinch gesture is triggered when two fingers move closer together or farther apart within a view, and it is often used to make something smaller or larger, respectively. Adding a pinch gesture recognizer requires even less configuration than taps or swipes because the gesture itself is already well defined. The implementation of the action that interprets a pinch, however, will be a bit more difficult because we are also interested in "how much" a user pinched (called the *scale* of the pinch) and how fast (the *velocity*), rather than just wanting to know that it happened. More on that in a few minutes.

Using the Object Library, find the pinch gesture recognizer (`UIPinchGestureRecognizer`) and drag it onto the view that contains the Pinch Me! label. No other configuration is necessary.

TIP

If you look at the Attributes Inspector for a pinch, you'll see that you can set a `scale` attribute that corresponds to a `scale` variable property on the object. The `scale`, by default, starts at `1`. Imagine you move your fingers apart to invoke a pinch gesture recognizer. If you move your fingers twice as far apart as they were, the scale becomes 2 (1 × 2). If you repeat the gesture, moving them twice as far apart again, it becomes 4 (2 × 2). In other words, the scale changes using its previous reading as a starting point.

Usually you want to leave the default scale value to 1, but be aware that you *can* reset the default in the Attributes Inspector if need be.

The Rotation Recognizer

A rotation gesture is triggered when two fingers move opposite one another as if rotating around a circle. Imagine turning a doorknob with two fingers on the top and bottom and you'll get the idea of what iOS considers a valid rotation gesture. As with a pinch, the rotation gesture recognizer requires no configuration; all the work occurs in interpreting the results—the rotation (in radians) and the speed (velocity) of the rotation.

Find the rotation gesture recognizer (UIRotationGestureRecognizer) and drag it onto the view that contains the Rotate Me! label. You've just added the final object to the storyboard.

TIP

Just like the pinch gesture recognizer's scale, the rotation gesture recognizer has a rotation variable property that you can set in the Attributes Inspector. This value, representing the amount of rotation in radians, starts at 0 and changes with each successive rotation gesture. If you want, you can override the initial starting rotation of 0 radians with any value you choose. Subsequent rotation gestures start from the value you provide.

GESTURE OVERLOAD

Be mindful of the built-in iOS gestures when you start using gestures in your own applications. Apple has been increasingly adding gestures throughout iOS, including bottom and side swipes. If your gesture conflicts with those provided by the system, the user experience will likely be poor.

Creating and Connecting the Outlets and Actions

To respond to gestures and access our feedback objects from the main view controller, we need to establish the outlets and actions we defined earlier.

Let's review what we need, starting with the outlets:

▶ **The image view (UIImageView):** imageView

▶ **The label for providing feedback (UILabel):** outputLabel

And the actions:

- ▶ **Respond to a tap gesture:** `foundTap`

- ▶ **Respond to a swipe gesture:** `foundSwipe`

- ▶ **Respond to a pinch gesture:** `foundPinch`

- ▶ **Respond to a rotation gesture:** `foundRotation`

Prepare your workspace for making the connections. Open the Main.storyboard file and switch to the assistant editor mode with ViewController.swift visible. Because you will be dragging from the gesture recognizers in your scene, make sure that the document outline is showing (Editor, Show Document Outline) or that you can tell the difference between them in the object dock below your view.

Adding the Outlets

Control-drag from the Do Something! label to just below the variable property `originalRect` that you added earlier. When prompted, create a new outlet called `outputLabel`, as shown in Figure 17.8. Repeat the process for the image view, naming it **imageView**.

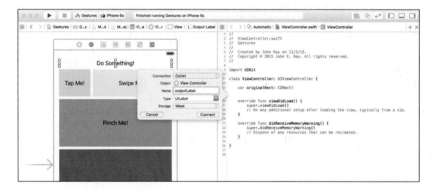

FIGURE 17.8
Connect the label and image view.

Adding the Actions

Connecting the gesture recognizers to the action methods that we've identified works as you probably imagine, but with one difference. Usually when you connect an object to an action, you're connecting a particular event on that object—such as Touch Up Inside, for buttons. In the case of a gesture recognizer, you are actually making a connection from the recognizer's "selector" to a method. Recall in the earlier code example that the selector is just the name of the method that should be invoked if a gesture is recognized.

TIP
Some gesture recognizers (tap, swipe, and long press) can also trigger segues to other storyboard scenes by using the Storyboard Segues section in the Connections Inspector. You learned about multiscene storyboards in Hour 11, "Implementing Multiple Scenes and Popovers."

To connect the gesture recognizer to an action method, just Control-drag from the gesture recognizer entry in the document outline to the ViewController.swift file. Do this now with the tap gesture recognizer, targeting just below the variable properties you defined earlier. When prompted, configure the connection as an action with the name foundTap, as shown in Figure 17.9.

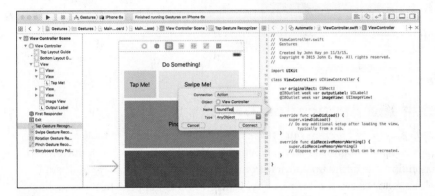

FIGURE 17.9
Connect the gesture recognizer to a new action.

Repeat this process for each of the other gesture recognizers—connecting the swipe recognizer to foundSwipe, the pinch recognizer to foundPinch, and the rotation recognizer to foundRotation. To verify your connections, select one of the recognizers (here, the tap recognizer) and view the Connections Inspector (Option-Command-6). You should see the action defined in Sent Actions and the view that uses the recognizer referenced in the Referencing Outlet Collections section, as shown in Figure 17.10.

TIP
Hover your mouse over a given connection in the Connection Inspector to see that item highlighted in your scene (shown in Figure 17.9). This is a quick way of verifying that your gestures are connected to the right views.

We're done with our interface and done adding gesture recognizers to our project; now let's make them do something.

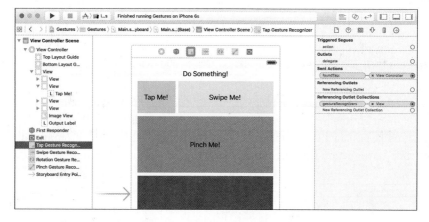

FIGURE 17.10
Confirm your connections in the Connections Inspector.

Implementing the Application Logic

To begin the implementation, we address our image view problem: We need to replace the image view that gets added through Interface Builder with one we create programmatically. We also grab the position and size of the image view from its `frame` variable property (a `CGRect`) and store it in the `originalRect` variable property. Where will this happen? In the view controller method `viewDidLoad`, which is called as soon as the interface loads.

Replacing the Image View

Make sure that the standard editor mode is selected, and then open the ViewController.swift file and update the `viewDidLoad` the method, as shown in Listing 17.3.

LISTING 17.3 Implementing the `viewDidLoad` Method

```
 1: override func viewDidLoad() {
 2:     super.viewDidLoad()
 3:
 4:     originalRect=imageView.frame;
 5:     var tempImageView: UIImageView
 6:     tempImageView=UIImageView(image:UIImage(named: "flower.png"))
 7:     tempImageView.frame=originalRect
 8:     view.addSubview(tempImageView)
 9:     self.imageView=tempImageView
10: }
```

Line 4 grabs the frame from the image view that we added in Interface Builder. This is a data structure of the type CGRect and consists of four floating-point values: origin.x, origin.y, size.width, and size.height. The original values are stored in originalRect.

Lines 5–6 declare and initialize a new UIImageView (tempImageView) using the flower.png image that we added to our project earlier.

In line 7, we set the frame of the new image view to the frame of the original image view, conveniently stored in originalRect. That finishes up the configuration of the constraint-free image view; it is added to the view controller's main view (the scene) with the addSubview method in line 8.

As a final step in swapping the image views, line 9 reassigns the imageView variable property to the new tempImageView. We can now access the new image view through the variable property that originally pointed to the image view added in Interface Builder.

Now, let's move on to the gesture recognizers, beginning with the tap recognizer. What you'll quickly discover is that after you've added one recognizer, the pattern is very, very similar for the others. The only difference is the shake gesture, which is why we're saving that for last.

Responding to the Tap Gesture Recognizer

Responding to the tap gesture recognizer is just a matter of implementing the foundTap method. Update the method stub in the view controller (ViewController.swift) with the implementation shown in Listing 17.4.

LISTING 17.4 Implementing the foundTap Method

```
@IBAction func foundTap(sender: AnyObject) {
    outputLabel.text="Tapped"
}
```

This method doesn't need to process input or do anything other than provide some indication that it has run. Setting the outputLabel's text variable property to "Tapped" should suffice nicely.

Ta da! Your first gesture recognizer is done. We'll repeat this process for the other four, and we'll be finished before you know it.

TIP

If you want to get the coordinate where a tap gesture (or a swipe) takes place, you add code like this to the gesture handler (replacing <the view> with a reference to the recognizer's view):

```
var location: CGPoint = (sender as!
    UITapGestureRecognizer).locationInView(< the view>)
```

This creates a simple structure named `location`, with members `x` and `y`, accessible as `location.x` and `location.y`.

Responding to the Swipe Recognizer

We respond to the swipe recognizer in the same way we did with the tap recognizer, by updating the output label to show that the gesture was recognized. Implement the `foundSwipe` method as shown in Listing 17.5.

LISTING 17.5   Implementing the `foundSwipe` Method

```
@IBAction func foundSwipe(sender: AnyObject) {
    outputLabel.text="Swiped"
}'
```

So far, so good. Next up, the pinch gesture. This requires a bit more work because we're going to use the pinch to interact with our image view.

Responding to the Pinch Recognizer

Taps and swipes are simple gestures; they either happen or they don't. Pinches and rotations are slightly more complex, returning additional values to give you greater control over the user interface. A pinch, for example, includes a `velocity` variable property (how quickly the pinch happened) and `scale` (a fraction that is proportional to change in distance between your fingers). If you move your fingers 50% closer together, the scale is `.5`, for example. If you move them twice as far apart, it is `2`.

You've made it to the most complex piece of code in this hour's lesson. The `foundPinch` method accomplishes several things. It resets the `UIImageView`'s `rotation` (just in case it gets out of whack when we set up the `rotation` gesture), creates a feedback string with the scale and velocity values returned by the recognizer, and actually scales the image view so that the user receives immediate visual feedback.

Implement the `foundPinch` method as shown in Listing 17.6.

LISTING 17.6   Implementing the `foundPinch` Method

```
 1: @IBAction func foundPinch(sender: AnyObject) {
 2:     var recognizer: UIPinchGestureRecognizer
 3:     var feedback: String
 4:     var scale: CGFloat
 5:
 6:     recognizer=sender as! UIPinchGestureRecognizer
 7:     scale=recognizer.scale
 8:     imageView.transform = CGAffineTransformMakeRotation(0.0)
 9:
10:     feedback=String(format: "Pinched, Scale: %1.2f, Velocity: %1.2f",
11:         Float(recognizer.scale),Float(recognizer.velocity))
12:     outputLabel.text=feedback
13:     imageView.frame = CGRectMake(self.originalRect.origin.x,
14:         originalRect.origin.y,
15:         originalRect.size.width*scale,
16:         originalRect.size.height*scale);
17: }
```

Let's walk through this method to make sure that you understand what's going on. Lines 2–4 declare a reference to a pinch gesture recognizer (`recognizer`), a string object (`feedback`), and a `CGFloat` value (`scale`). These are used to interact with our pinch gesture recognizer, store feedback for the user, and hold the scaling value returned by the pinch gesture recognizer, respectively.

Line 6 takes the incoming sender object of the type `AnyObject` and casts it as a `UIPinchGestureRecognizer`, which can then be accessed through the recognizer variable. The reason we do this is simple. When you created the `foundPinch` action by dragging the gesture recognizer into your ViewController.swift file, Xcode wrote the method with a parameter named `sender` of the generic "handles any object" type `AnyObject`. Xcode does this even though the sender will always be, in this case, an object of type `UIPinchGestureRecognizer`. Line 6 just gives us a convenient way of accessing the object as the type it really is.

Line 7 sets `scale` to the recognizer's scale variable property.

Line 8 resets the `imageView` object to a rotation of `0.0` (no rotation at all) by setting its `transform` variable property to the transformation returned by the Core Graphics `CGAffineTransformMakeRotation` function. This function, when passed a value in radians, returns the necessary transformation to rotate a view.

Lines 10–11 initialize the feedback string to show that a pinch has taken place and output the values of the recognizer's scale and velocity variable properties—after converting them from `CGFloat` data structures to floating-point values. Line 12 sets the `outputLabel` in the UI to the feedback string.

For the scaling of the image view itself, lines 13–16 do the work. All that needs to happen is for the `imageView` object's `frame` to be redefined to the new size. To do this, we can use `CGRectMake` to return a new frame rectangle based on a scaled version of the `CGRect` stored in the original image view position: `originalRect`. The top-left coordinates (`origin.x`, `origin.y`) stay the same, but we multiply `size.width` and `size.height` by the `scale` factor to increase or decrease the size of the frame according to the user's pinch.

Building and running the application will now let you enlarge (even beyond the boundaries of the screen) or shrink the image using the pinch gesture within the `pinchView` object, as shown in Figure 17.11.

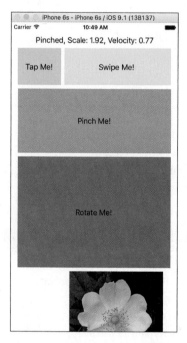

FIGURE 17.11
Enlarge or shrink the image in a pinch (ha ha).

NOTE

If you don't want to downcast the `sender` variable to use it as a gesture recognizer, you can also edit Xcode's method declarations to include the exact type being passed. Just change the method declaration from

```
@IBAction func foundPinch(sender: AnyObject) {
```

to

```
@IBAction func foundPinch(sender: UIPinchGestureRecognizer) {
```

If you do so, you'll be able to access sender directly as an instance of UIPinchGestureRecognizer.

Responding to the Rotation Recognizer

The last multitouch gesture recognizer that we'll add is the rotation gesture recognizer. Like the pinch gesture, rotation returns some useful information that we can apply visually to our onscreen objects, notably velocity and rotation. The rotation returned is the number of radians that the user has rotated his or her fingers, clockwise or counterclockwise.

TIP

Most of us are comfortable talking about rotation in "degrees," but the Cocoa classes usually use radians. Don't worry. It's not a difficult translation to make. If you want, you can calculate degrees from radians using the following formula:

Degrees = Radians × 180 / Pi

There's not really any reason we need this now, but in your own applications, you might want to provide a degree reading to your users.

I'd love to tell you how difficult it is to rotate a view and about all the complex math involved, but I pretty much gave away the trick to rotation in the foundPinch method earlier. A single line of code will set the UIImageView's transform variable property to a rotation transformation and visually rotate the view. Of course, we also need to provide a feedback string to the user, but that's not nearly as exciting, is it?

Add the foundRotation method in Listing 17.7 to your ViewController.swift file.

LISTING 17.7   Adding the foundRotation Method

```
1: @IBAction func foundRotation(sender: AnyObject) {
2:     var recognizer: UIRotationGestureRecognizer
3:     var feedback: String
4:     var rotation: CGFloat
5:
6:     recognizer=sender as! UIRotationGestureRecognizer
7:     rotation=recognizer.rotation
8:
```

```
 9:     feedback=String(format: "Rotated, Radians: %1.2f, Velocity: %1.2f",
10:         Float(recognizer.rotation),Float(recognizer.velocity))
11:     outputLabel.text=feedback
12:     imageView.transform = CGAffineTransformMakeRotation(rotation)
13: }
```

Again, we begin by declaring a reference to a gesture recognizer (recognizer), a string (feedback), and a CGFloat value (rotation), in lines 2–4.

Line 6 takes the incoming sender object of the type AnyObject and casts it as a UIRotationGestureRecognizer, which can then be accessed through the recognizer variable.

Line 7 sets the rotation value to the recognizer's rotation variable property. This is the rotation in radians detected in the user's gesture.

Lines 9–10 create the feedback string showing the radians rotated and the velocity of the rotation, and line 11 sets the output label to the string.

Line 12 handles the rotation itself, creating a rotation transformation and applying it to the imageView object's transform variable property.

NOTE
_____

The foundPinch method can also be implemented by updating the transform variable property for imageView and using the CGAffineTransformMakeScale method. In essence, you could replace lines 13–16 of foundPinch with a single line:imageView.transform = CGAffineTransformMakeScale(scale,scale)

Why did we update the frame of the imageView instead? Two reasons. First, because it gives you experience with two approaches to manipulating a view. Second, because setting a transformation for the image view doesn't really change the view's underlying frame; it changes the appearance instead. If you really want to the view's size and location to change (not just the *appearance* of its size and location), applying a transformation isn't the way to go.
_____

Run and test your application now. You should be able to freely spin the image view using a rotation gesture in the rotate view, as shown in Figure 17.12.

Although it might seem like we've finished, we still need to cover one more gesture: a shake.

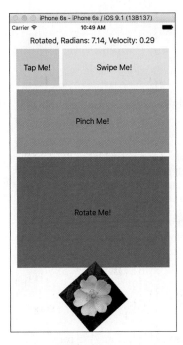

FIGURE 17.12
Spin the image view using the rotation gesture.

TRY IT YOURSELF ▼

Trying Transformations in Xcode Playground

Xcode Playground can be used for many different things—including testing out the transformations you've learned this hour. To transform and display an image in the Playground, first we must create a Playground and add an image resource:

1. Begin by creating a new iOS Playground.

2. With the Playground open, choose View, Navigators, Show Project Navigator from the menu.

3. Drag the flower.png file from the project Images folder in the Finder into the Resources folder in the navigator.

Now, you're ready to work with the flower.png image, just as you would within an application. Unfortunately, there's still *one* difference from a real application, but you'll see it's pretty easy to overcome. Add following code into the playground:

```
import UIKit
var testView: UIView = UIView(frame:CGRectMake(0,0,300,300))
var testImageView: UIImageView =
```

```
    UIImageView(image:UIImage(named: "flower.png"))
testImageView.frame=CGRectMake(50.0,50.0,100.0,100.0)
testImageView.transform = CGAffineTransformMakeRotation(0.8)
testView.addSubview(testImageView)
```

The three lines in the middle should look pretty familiar. The `testImageView` is created from the flower.png file you added. A frame is set to size and position the image view, and, finally, a rotation transformation is applied. (The 0.8 should rotate about 90 degrees to the right.)

Unfortunately, the Playground won't work quite right with these lines alone because the image view needs to be inside another view to work. To that end, the first thing we do in the Playground is create a `UIView` called `testView` sized large enough to hold the image view. After we're done setting up the image view, we add it to the test view with the `addSubView` method.

You should be able to click the "eye" icon to the right of the last line and see the transformed image view within the test view. You can use this same approach to test any transformations you'd like. No fuss, no muss.

Implementing the Shake Recognizer

Dealing with a shake is a bit different from the other gestures covered this hour. We must intercept a `UIEvent` of the type `UIEventTypeMotion`. To do this, our view controller or view must be the first responder in the responder chain and must implement the `motionEnded:withEvent` method.

Let's tackle these requirements one at a time.

Becoming a First Responder

For our view controller to be a first responder, we have to allow it through a method called `can-BecomeFirstResponder` that does nothing but return YES, and then ask for first responder status when the view controller loads its view. Start by adding the new method `canBecomeFirstResponder`, shown in Listing 17.8, to your ViewController.swift implementation file.

LISTING 17.8   **Enabling the Ability to Be a First Responder**

```
override func canBecomeFirstResponder() -> Bool {
    return true
}
```

Next, we need our view controller to become the first responder by sending the message `becomeFirstResponder` as soon as it has displayed its view. Update the ViewController.swift `viewDidLoad` method to do this, as shown in Listing 17.9.

LISTING 17.9 Asking to Become a First Responder

```
override func viewDidLoad() {
    super.viewDidLoad()
    becomeFirstResponder()
    originalRect=imageView.frame;
    var tempImageView: UIImageView
    tempImageView=UIImageView(image:UIImage(named: "flower.png"))
    tempImageView.frame=originalRect
    view.addSubview(tempImageView)
    self.imageView=tempImageView
}
```

Our view controller is now prepared to become the first responder and receive the shake event. All we need to do now is implement `motionEnded:withEvent` to trap and react to the shake gesture itself.

Responding to a Shake Gesture

To react to a shake, implement the `motionEnded:withEvent` method, as shown in Listing 17.10.

LISTING 17.10 Responding to a Shake Gesture

```
1: override func motionEnded(motion: UIEventSubtype,
2:     withEvent event: UIEvent?) {
3:     if motion==UIEventSubtype.MotionShake {
4:         outputLabel.text="Shaking things up!"
5:         imageView.transform=CGAffineTransformIdentity
6:         imageView.frame=originalRect
7:     }
8: }
```

First things first: In line 3, we check to make sure that the motion value we received (an object of type `UIEventSubtype`) is, indeed, a motion event. To do this, we just compare it to the constant `UIEventSubtypeMotionShake`. If they match, the user just finished shaking the device.

Lines 4–6 react to the shake by setting the output label, rotating the image view back to its default orientation, and setting the image view's frame back to the original size and location stored in our `originalRect` variable property. In other words, shaking the device will reset the image to its default state. Pretty nifty, huh?

Building the Application

You can now run the application and use all the multitouch gestures that we implemented this hour. Try scaling the image through a pinch gesture. Shake your device to reset it to the original size. Scale and rotate the image, tap, swipe—everything should work exactly as you'd expect and with a surprisingly minimal amount of coding.

Now that you've mastered multitouch, let's take things to the third dimension with 3D Touch.

Implementing 3D Touch Gestures

You know the drill: For each tutorial, I include an overview, and then describe the different pieces needed to create a project, design the interface, and implement the logic. Not this time, buddy! To implement 3D Touch, you'll spend less time implementing than the amount of time it has taken you to read this paragraph.

Implementation Overview

As of Xcode 7.1, peek and pop gestures can be added to your view-transitioning segues by selecting the existing segue (referred to as the *Action segue*), and then using the Attributes Inspector to check the box beside Peek and Pop, as shown in Figure 17.13. This tells the application that we want to define a Preview segue (peek) and a Commit segue (pop).

By default, the Commit segue (the pop) is the same as the Action segue. Similarly, the Preview segue (peek) is the same as the Commit segue. If this seems confusing, think about it this way: You define segues to take you to a new scene. A peek preview shows you what to expect when you activate a link or press a button (without actually taking you there). Popping the preview, logically, should take you to the same place you'd go to if you didn't preview it in the first place. In other words, the Commit segue and the Action segue should be the same, and, chances are, the preview should be the same as well.

If you want to be clever and break the mold for your peek and pop views, you can set the Preview and Commit segues to the storyboard ID of a view controller of your choice by setting the corresponding pop-up menus to Custom and then completing the additional fields.

After you've configured a segue for peek and pop, you'll see a visual indicator of this change as a dashed circle that appears around the segue icon in the storyboard, as shown in Figure 17.14.

Simple, don't you think? The most expedient way for me to *prove* how simple it can be is to modify two of our existing applications to support these 3D Touch features.

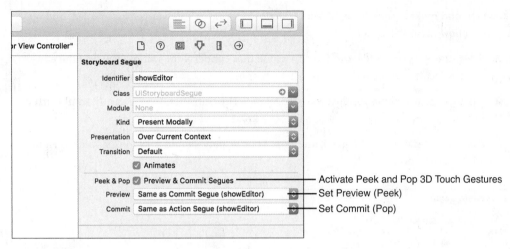

FIGURE 17.13
Check a box, and you've got 3D Touch peek and pop gestures implemented.

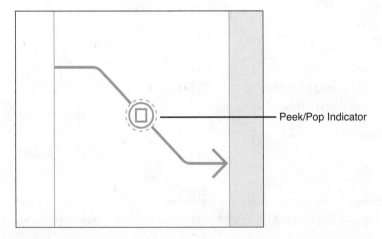

FIGURE 17.14
A dashed circle around the segue icon indicate that peek and pop support has been activated.

Modifying ModalEditor

The first project that we'll modify is the Hour 11 ModalEditor (non-popover version). When the user pushes on the Edit button, they'll see a preview of the edit screen. Push a bit harder, and the editor pops onto the screen. Not very useful, but nifty nonetheless.

Go ahead and make a copy of the Hour 11 ModalEditor (non-popover version) project and open it. Then follow these steps:

1. Select the Storyboard file and find the segue that connects the initial view and the editor view. Select it and open the Attributes Inspector.

2. Change the transition for the segue to Default. The transition type I used (Partial Curl) is not compatible with peek and pop because it uses the full screen.

3. Click the check box beside peek and pop. Your display should now look similar to Figure 17.15. You're done.

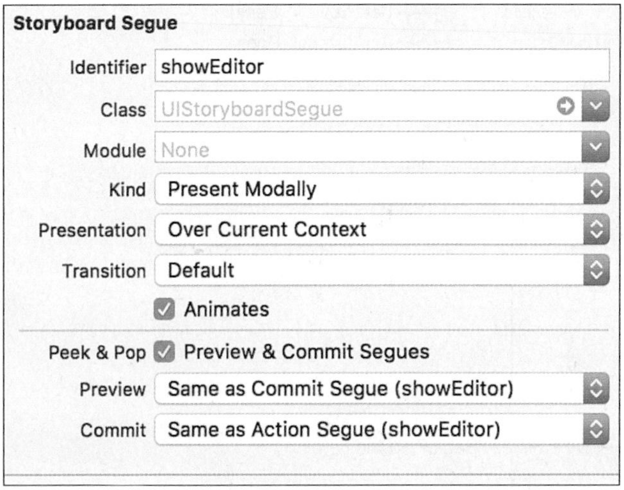

FIGURE 17.15
Activate peek and pop for the segue.

You can now run the application on an iPhone that supports 3D Touch (currently the iPhone 6s and 6s+). Trying pushing firmly on the Edit button. A peek preview of the edit screen appears, as demonstrated in Figure 17.16.

Push a little harder and the editor pops onto the screen. No fuss, no muss, and no code. Let's repeat this process with something a bit more interesting: a table view.

Modifying FlowerDetail

The second project that we'll 3D Touch-enable is Hour 14's FlowerDetail. This time, when the user pushes on one of the flowers in the table, a preview will appear showing the Wikipedia page describing the flower. Push harder, and the Wikipedia page goes full screen, and the user can interact with the web view.

Email Address:

johnray@mac.com

Save

FIGURE 17.16
Peeking at the editor screen

Begin by making copy of the Hour 14 FlowerDetail project and then open it. Follow along once the workspace appears:

1. Select the Storyboard file and find the segue that connects the Master table view (Flower Type) and the Navigation controller (this is set as the Show Detail segue). Select it and open the Attributes Inspector.

2. Click the check box beside Peek and Pop. Your display should look similar to Figure 17.17.

Unfortunately, pushing on a table cell isn't the same as tapping to select it, so Apple's code can't identify what cell you're pushing on. If you attempt to run the application now, the peek and pop gestures will take you to a blank screen.

To fix the problem, open MasterViewController.swift and look at the second line in the method `prepareForSegue`. Change it from this:

```
if let indexPath = self.tableView.indexPathForSelectedRow {
```

To this:

```
if let indexPath = self.tableView.indexPathForCell(sender as! UITableViewCell) {
```

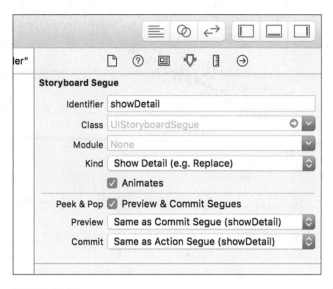

FIGURE 17.17
Activate peek and pop for the Show Detail segue.

This change grabs the appropriate cell by using the `sender` object (whatever the user is pressing on) rather then relying on iOS reporting the cell as being selected.

After making the change, run the application on a 3D Touch-capable device. Pushing firmly on one of the table cells should result in behavior similar to what is shown in Figure 17.18.

This second example is a bit more useful than the first, but again demonstrates how simple it is to support 3D Touch in your applications. I'd be very surprised if Apple didn't modify the Master-Detail application template to handle 3D Touch gestures "out of the box."

Further Exploration

In addition to the multitouch gestures discussed this hour, you should be able to immediately add three other recognizers to your apps: `UILongPressGestureRecognizer`, `UIPanGestureRecognizer`, and `UIScreenEdgePanGestureRecognizer`. The `UIGestureRecognizer` class is the parent to all the gesture recognizers that you've learned about in this lesson and offers additional base functionality for customizing gesture recognition.

You also might want to learn more about the lower-level handling of touches on iOS. See the "Event Handling" section of the Data Management iOS documentation and the `UITouch` class for more information. The `UITouch` class can even let you measure the amount of force of a given "touch" on a 3D Touch-enabled device.

FIGURE 17.18
Peeking at the details of a flower.

We humans do a lot with our fingers, such as draw, write, play music, and more. Each of these possible gestures has been exploited to great effect in third-party applications. Explore the App Store to get a sense of what's been done with the iOS multitouch gestures.

Be sure to look at the SimpleGestureRecognizers tutorial project, found within the Xcode documentation. This project provides many additional examples of implementing gestures on the iOS platform and demonstrates how gestures can be added through code. Although the Interface Builder approach to adding gesture recognizers can cover many common scenarios, it's still a good idea to know how to code them by hand.

Summary

In this hour, we've given the gesture recognizer architecture a good workout. Using the gesture recognizers provided through iOS, you can easily recognize and respond to taps, swipes, pinches, rotations, and more—without any complex math or programming logic.

You also learned how to make your applications respond to shaking: Just make them first responders and implement the `motionEnded:withEvent` method. Your ability to present your users with interactive interfaces just increased dramatically.

Q&A

Q. Why don't the rotation/pinch gestures include configuration options for the number of touches?

A.. The gesture recognizers are meant to recognize common gestures. Although it is possible that you could manually implement a rotation or pinch gesture with multiple fingers, it wouldn't be consistent with how users expect their applications to work and isn't included as an option with these recognizers.

Workshop

Quiz

1. The rotation value of the `UIRotationGestureRecognizer` is returned in what?

    a. Integers

    b. Radians

    c. Degrees

    d. Seconds

2. Which gesture recognizer is often used for enlarging or shrinking content?

    a. `UITabGestureRecognizer`

    b. `UIRotationGestureRecognizer`

    c. `UIPinchGestureRecognizer`

    d. `UIScaleGestureRecognizer`

3. Which of the following attributes can you set for a tap gesture recognizer?

    a. Number of touches

    b. Finger spacing

    c. Finger pressure

    d. Touch length

4. How many recognizers will you need to recognize left, right, and down swipes in a view?

    a. 1

    b. 3

    c. 6

    d. 2

5. Overriding the `motionEnded:withEvent` method is necessary for recognizing what type of gesture?

    a. Panning

    b. Swiping

    c. Tapping

    d. Shaking

6. 3D Touch implements two gestures. What are their names?

    a. Peek and poke

    b. Peek and pop

    c. Preview and pop

    d. Preview and show

7. You can hold an object's `frame` in which data structure?

    a. `AnyObject`

    b. `ObjectRect`

    c. `CGFrame`

    d. `CGRect`

8. To help differentiate between objects in the document outline, you can set which of the following?

    a. Labels

    b. Notes

    c. Classes

    d. Segues

9. To determine how far a user has moved her fingers during a pinch gesture, which variable property do you look at?

    a. `space`

    b. `scale`

    c. `distance`

    d. `location`

10. You can scale or rotate the view without any complex math by using which variable property of a view?

   a. `transform`

   b. `scale`

   c. `rotate`

   d. `scaleandrotate`

Answers

1. B. Rotation is returned in radians, a common unit of measure.

2. C. Use a `UIPinchGestureRecognizer` to implement scaling gestures within an application.

3. A. You can easily set the number of touches that will be required to trigger a tap gesture.

4. B. You need a gesture recognizer for each of the swipe directions that you want to implement; three directions, three recognizers.

5. D. The shake gesture requires an implementation of the `motionEnded:WithEvent` method.

6. B. The 3D Touch gestures are known as peek and pop.

7. D. A `CGRect` data structure can be used to hold an object's frame.

8. A. Labels are a convenient way to provide custom names of the items listed within the Document Outline.

9. B. The scale variable property will help you determine how far a user has moved her fingers relative to her original position.

10. A. The `transform` variable property can be used to apply a nondestructive transformation (such as rotation or scaling) to a view.

Activities

1. Expand the Gestures application to include panning and pressing gestures. These are configured almost identically to the gestures you used in this hour's tutorial.

2. Alter this project to use the image view that you added in Interface Builder rather than the one created programmatically. Practice using the constraints system to see the effect that constraints have on the image view as it changes size and rotates.

3. Improve on the user experience by adding the pinch and rotation gesture recognizers to the `UIImageView` object itself, enabling users to interact directly with the image rather than another view.

HOUR 18
Sensing Orientation and Motion

What You'll Learn in This Hour:

▶ The purpose of Core Motion
▶ How to determine a device's orientation
▶ How to measure tilt and acceleration
▶ How to measure rotation

The Nintendo Wii introduced motion sensing as an effective input technique for mainstream consumer electronics. Apple has applied this technology with great success to the iPhone, iPod touch, iPad, and now Apple TV.

Apple devices are equipped with an accelerometer that provides measurements of the orientation, movement, and tilt of the device. With the accelerometer, a user can control applications by simply adjusting the physical orientation of the device and moving it in space. In addition, Apple has included a gyroscope in all currently shipping iDevices. This enables the device to sense rotation motions that aren't against the force of gravity. In short, if a user moves a gyroscope-enabled device, there are ways that your applications can detect and react to that movement.

The motion-input mechanism is exposed to third-party applications in iOS through a framework called Core Motion. In Hour 17, "Using Advanced Touches and Gestures," you saw how the accelerometer provides the shake gesture. Now you learn how to take direct readings from iOS for determining orientation, acceleration, and rotation. For all the magic that a motion-enabled application appears to exhibit, using these features is surprisingly simple.

Understanding Motion Hardware

All iOS devices, to date, can sense motion through the use of the accelerometer and gyroscope hardware. To get a better sense for what this means to your applications, let's review what information each of these pieces of hardware can provide.

TIP

For most applications in this book, using the iOS Simulator is perfectly acceptable, but the Simulator does not simulate the accelerometer or gyroscope hardware. So for this hour, be sure to have a physical device provisioned for development. To run this hour's applications on your device, follow the steps in Hour 1, "Preparing Your System and iDevice for Development."

Accelerometer

An accelerometer uses a unit of measure called a g, which is short for gravity. 1g is the force pulling down on something resting at sea level on Earth (9.8 meters per second squared). You don't normally notice the feeling of 1g (that is, until you trip and fall, and then 1g hurts pretty bad). You are familiar with g-forces higher and lower than 1g if you've ever ridden on a roller coaster. The pull that pins you to your seat at the bottom of the roller coaster hill is a g-force greater than 1, and the feeling of floating up out of your seat at the top of a hill is negative g-force at work.

NOTE

An accelerometer measures acceleration relative to a free fall—meaning that if you drop your iDevice into a sustained free fall, say off the Empire State Building, its accelerometer will measure 0g on the way down. (Just trust me; don't try this out.) The accelerometer of a device sitting in your lap, however, measures 1g along the axis it is resting on.

The measurement of the 1g pull of Earth's gravity on the device while it's at rest is how the accelerometer can be used to measure the orientation of the device. The accelerometer provides a measurement along three axes, called x, y, and z (see Figure 18.1).

Depending on how your device is resting, the 1g of gravity will be pulling differently on the three possible axes. If it is standing straight up on one of its edges or is flat on its back or on its screen, the entire 1g is measured on one axis. If the device is tilted at an angle, the 1g is spread across multiple axes (see Figure 18.2).

Interpreting iOS accelerometer data depends largely on how it will be used. Acceleration data, for example, provides a measure of the g forces on a device as it is being moved. If the acceleration data returned is greater than 1, it is accelerating in a direction. If it is a negative number, it is decelerating.

When the device is at rest, however, acceleration is 0, but there are still g forces acting on it that can be used to determine how it is positioned. A measurement of the amount of "tilt" of your device around its x, y, and z axis is called its *attitude* and is independent of motion. Attitude values are referred to using the terms *roll*, *pitch*, and *yaw*. For iOS devices, roll is the amount of "tilt" around the y axis, pitch measures tilt around the x axis, and yaw, the z axis. Attitude is sometimes defined relative to a *reference frame*—the "zero" point for tilting. When a game or application asks you to calibrate the tilting of your device, it is setting the reference frame.

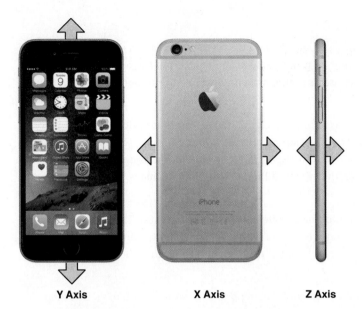

Y Axis   X Axis   Z Axis

FIGURE 18.1
The three measurable axes.

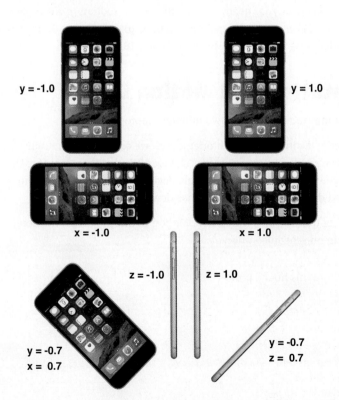

y = -1.0   y = 1.0

x = -1.0   x = 1.0

z = -1.0   z = 1.0

y = -0.7   y = -0.7
x = 0.7   z = 0.7

FIGURE 18.2
The 1g of force on a device at rest.

Gyroscope

Think about what you've just learned about the accelerometer hardware. Is there anything it can't do? It might seem, at first, that by using the measurements from the accelerometer, we can make a good guess as to what the user is doing, no matter what. Unfortunately, that's not quite the case.

The accelerometer measures the force of gravity distributed across your device. Imagine, however, that your iPhone or iPad is lying face up on a table. We can detect this with the accelerometer, but what we *cannot* detect is if you start spinning it around in a rousing game of "spin the bottle... err... iDevice." The accelerometer will still register the same value regardless of how the device is spinning.

The same goes for if the device is standing on one of its edges and rotates. The accelerometer can be used only if the device is changing orientation with respect to gravity; but the gyroscope can determine whether, in any given orientation, the device is also rotating while maintaining the orientation.

When querying a device's gyroscope, the hardware reports back with a rotation value along the x, y, and z axes. The value is a measurement, in radians per second, of the speed of rotation along that axis. If you don't remember your geometry, rotating 2 × pi radians is a complete circle, so a reading of 2 × pi (about 6.3) on any of the gyroscope's three axes indicates that the device is spinning once per second, along that axis, as shown in Figure 18.3.

Accessing Orientation and Motion Data

To access orientation and motion information, we use two different approaches:

▶ First, to determine and react to distinct changes in orientation, we can request that our iOS device send notifications to our code as the orientation changes. We can then compare the messages we receive to constants representing all possible device orientations—including face up and face down—and determine what the user has done.

▶ Second, we take advantage of a framework called Core Motion to directly access the accelerometer and gyroscope data on scheduled intervals.

Let's take a closer look before starting this hour's projects.

FIGURE 18.3
A reading of roughly 6.3 from the gyroscope indicates that the device is rotating (spinning in a complete circle) at a rate of one revolution per second.

Requesting Orientation Notifications Through UIDevice

Although it *is* possible to read the accelerometer hardware directly and use the values it returns to determine a device's orientation, Apple has made the process much simpler for developers. The singleton instance UIDevice (representing our device) includes a method beginGeneratingDeviceOrientationNotifications that will tell iOS to begin sending orientation notifications to the notification center (NSNotificationCenter). Once the notifications start, we can register with an NSNotificationCenter instance to have a method of our choosing automatically be invoked with the device's orientation changes.

Besides just knowing that an orientation event occurred, we need some reading of what the orientation is. We get this via the UIDevice orientation variable property. This property, of type UIDeviceOrientation, can be one of six predefined values:

- ▶ **UIDeviceOrientation.FaceUp:** The device is lying on its back, facing up.

- ▶ **UIDeviceOrientation.FaceDown:** The device is lying on its front, with the back facing up.

- ▶ **UIDeviceOrientation.Portrait:** The device is in the "normal" orientation, with the Home button at the bottom.

- ▶ **UIDeviceOrientation.PortraitUpsideDown:** The device is in portrait orientation with the Home button at the top.

- ▶ **UIDeviceOrientation.LandscapeLeft:** The device is lying on its left side.

- ▶ **UIDeviceOrientation.LandscapeRight:** The device is lying on its right side.

By comparing the variable property to each of these values, we can determine the orientation and react accordingly.

How Does This Differ from Adapting to Interface Rotation Events?

The interface-related events that you learned about in Hour 16, "Building Responsive User Interfaces," are just that: interface related. We first tell the device what orientations our interface supports, and then we can programmatically tell it what to do when the interface needs to change. The method we are using now is for getting instantaneous orientation changes regardless of what the interface supports. The constants `UIDeviceOrientationFaceUp` and `UIDeviceOrientationFaceDown` are also meaningless with regard to creating a user interface.

Reading Acceleration, Rotation, and Attitude with Core Motion

To work directly with motion data (readings from the accelerometer and gyroscope), you need to work with Core Motion. Despite the complex nature of motion sensors, this is one of the easier frameworks to integrate into your applications.

First, you need to include the Core Motion framework to your project. Next, you create an instance of the Core Motion motion manager: `CMMotionManager`. The motion manager should be treated as a singleton—one instance can provide accelerometer and gyroscope motion services for your entire application.

NOTE

Recall that a singleton is a class that is instantiated once in the lifetime of your application. The readings of iOS hardware are often provided as singletons because there is only one accelerometer and gyroscope in the device. Multiple instances of the `CMMotionManager` objects existing in your application wouldn't add any extra value and would have the added complexity of managing them.

Unlike orientation notifications, the Core Motion motion manager enables you to determine how often you receive updates (in seconds) from the motion sensors and allows you to directly define a *closure* that executes each time an update is ready.

TIP

You need to decide how often your application can benefit from receiving motion updates. You should decide this by experimenting with different update values until you come up with an optimal frequency. Receiving more updates than your application can benefit from can have some negative consequences. Your application will use more system resources, which might negatively impact the performance of the other parts of your application and can certainly affect the battery life of the device. Because you'll probably want fairly frequent updates so that your application responds smoothly, you should take some time to optimize the performance of your CMMotionManager-related code.

Setting up your application to use CMMotionManager is a simple three-step process of initializing and allocating the motion manager, setting an updating interval, and then requesting that updates begin and be sent to a handler closure via startDeviceMotionUpdatesTo-Queue:withHandler.

Consider the code snippet in Listing 18.1.

LISTING 18.1   Using the Motion Manager

```
1: var motionManager: CMMotionManager = CMMotionManager()
2: motionManager.deviceMotionUpdateInterval = 0.01
3: motionManager.startDeviceMotionUpdatesToQueue(
4:      NSOperationQueue.currentQueue()!, withHandler: {
5:        (motion: CMDeviceMotion?, error: NSError?) in
6:          // Do something with the motion data here!
7: })
```

In line 1, the motion manager is allocated and initialized.

Lines 3–4 requests that the motion sensors send updates every .01 seconds (or 100 times per second).

Lines 5–7 start the motion updates and define a closure that is called for each update.

The closure can be confusing looking, but in essence, it's like a new method being defined within the startDeviceMotionUpdatesToQueue:withHandler invocation.

The motion handler is passed two parameters: motion, an object of type CMDeviceMotion; and error, of type NSError. The motion object includes variable properties for everything motion-related that you need:

▶ **userAcceleration:** An acceleration variable property of the type `CMAcceleration`. This will be the information we are interested in reading and includes acceleration values, measured in gravities, along the x, y, and z axes.

▶ **rotationRate:** Data of the type `CMRotationRate`. The `rotation` provides rotation rates in radians per second along the x, y, and z axes.

▶ **attitude:** An object that contains information regarding the current tilt of the device. Within the `attitude` object are `roll`, `pitch`, and `yaw` values, measured in radians.

TIP

Unfortunately, the values returned in the motion variables will require conversion before they can be used. You're going to see several uses of `Double()` and a `CGFloat()` or two before we're through.

The basic steps for figuring out when this is necessary are to look at the Xcode documentation to see if the variable types you're using (such as the acceleration, rotation, or attitude) match the method parameters that you're using them in. If they don't, you'll need to wrap them in a conversion method like `CGFloat()`, `Double()`, or `Float()`. Someday, I expect these conversions to be automatic, but for now, there are many type-matching problems that appear with floating point values in Swift.

When you have finished processing motion updates, you can stop receiving them with the `CMMotionManager` method `stopDeviceMotionUpdates`.

Feeling confused? Not to worry; it makes much more sense seeing the pieces come together in code.

NOTE

We've skipped over an explanation of the chunk of code that refers to the `NSOperationQueue`. An operations queue maintains a list of operations that need to be dealt with (such as motion readings). The queue you need to use already exists, and we can access it with the code fragment `NSOperationQueue.currentQueue()`. So long as you follow along, there's no need to worry about managing operation queues manually.

Sensing Orientation

As our first introduction to detecting motion, we create the Orientation application. Orientation won't be wowing users; it's simply going to say which of six possible orientations the device is currently in. The Orientation application will detect these orientations: standing up, upside down, left side, right side, face down, and face up.

Implementation Overview

To create the Orientation application, we build an interface that contains a single label and then code up a method that executes whenever the orientation changes. For this method to be called, we must register with the `NSNotificationCenter` to receive notifications when appropriate.

Remember, this isn't the same as interface rotation and resizing; it doesn't necessitate a change in the interface, and it can handle upside-down and right-side-up orientations as well.

Setting Up the Project

As you've grown accustomed, begin by starting Xcode and creating a new project. We use our old standby, the Single View Application template, and name the new project **Orientation**.

Planning the Variables and Connections

In this project, we need a single label in our main application view that can be updated from code. We name this `orientationLabel` and, as you might guess, set it to a string containing the current device orientation.

Designing the Interface

Orientation's UI is simple (and very stylish); I've used a yellow text label in a field of gray. To create your interface, select the Main.storyboard file to open the Interface Builder (IB) editor. Use the Attributes Inspector with the view controller selected to switch to a standard device size.

Next, open the Object Library (View, Utilities, Show Object Library) and drag a label into the view. Set the label's text to read **Face Up**.

Using the Attributes Inspector (Option-Command-4), set the color of the label, increase its font size, and set its alignment to center. After configuring the attributes of your label, do the same for your view, setting an appropriate background color for the label.

TIP
_____
Now is a good time to put into use the techniques you learned in Hour 16 to keep the text centered onscreen while the device rotates. It isn't necessary for the completion of the project, but it is good practice!
_____

The finished view should look like Figure 18.4.

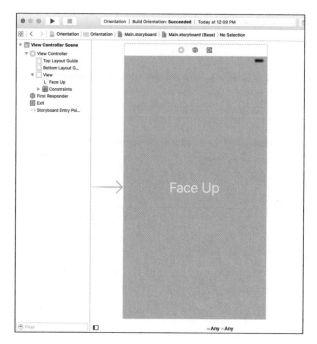

FIGURE 18.4
The Orientation application's UI.

Creating and Connecting the Outlet

Our application will need to be able to change the text of the label when the accelerometer indicates that the orientation of the device has changed. We need to create a connection for the label that we added. With the interface visible, switch to the assistant editor and make sure you are editing the ViewController.swift file.

Control-drag from the label to just below the `class` line in ViewController.swift. Name the new outlet **orientationLabel** when prompted. That's it for the bridge to our code: just a single outlet and no action.

Implementing the Application Logic

Two pieces remain in this puzzle. First, we must tell iOS that we are interested in receiving notifications when the device orientation changes. Second, we must react to those changes. Because this is your first encounter with the notification center, it might seem a bit unusual, but concentrate on the outcome. The code patterns for notifications aren't difficult to understand when you can see what the result is.

Registering for Orientation Updates

When our applications view is shown, we must register a method in our application to receive `UIDeviceOrientationDidChangeNotification` notifications from iOS. We also need to tell the device itself that it should begin generating these notifications so that we can react to them. You can accomplish all of this setup work in the ViewController.swift `viewDidLoad` method. Let's implement that now. Update the `viewDidLoad` method to read as shown in Listing 18.2.

LISTING 18.2 Watching for Orientation Changes

```
 1: override func viewDidLoad() {
 2:     super.viewDidLoad()
 3:
 4:     UIDevice.currentDevice().beginGeneratingDeviceOrientationNotifications()
 5:
 6:     NSNotificationCenter.defaultCenter().addObserver(self,
 7:         selector: "orientationChanged:",
 8:         name: "UIDeviceOrientationDidChangeNotification",
 9:         object: nil)
10: }
```

In line 4, we use the method `UIDevice.currentDevice()` to return an instance of `UIDevice` that refers to the device our application is running on. We then use the `beginGeneratingDeviceOrientationNotifications` method to tell the device that we're interested in hearing about it if the user changes the orientation of his or her device.

Lines 6–9 tell the `NSNotificationCenter` object that we are interested in subscribing to any notifications with the name `UIDeviceOrientationDidChangeNotification` that it may receive. They also set the class that is interested in the notifications to `ViewController` by way of the `addObserver` method's first parameter: `self`. We use the `selector` parameter to say that we will be implementing a method called `orientationChanged`. In fact, coding up `orientationChanged` is the only thing left to do.

Determining Orientation

To determine the orientation of the device, we use the `UIDevice` variable property `orientation`. Unlike other values we've dealt with in the book, the `orientation` is of the type `UIDeviceOrientation` (a simple constant, not an object). Therefore, you can check each possible orientation via a simple `switch` statement and update the `orientationLabel` in the interface as needed.

Implement the `orientationChanged` method as shown in Listing 18.3.

LISTING 18.3 Changing the Label as the Orientation Changes

```
 1: func orientationChanged(notification: NSNotification) {
 2:
 3: let orientation:UIDeviceOrientation=UIDevice.currentDevice().orientation
 4:
 5:     switch (orientation) {
 6:     case UIDeviceOrientation.FaceUp:
 7:         orientationLabel.text="Face Up"
 8:     case UIDeviceOrientation.FaceDown:
 9:         orientationLabel.text="Face Down"
10:     case UIDeviceOrientation.Portrait:
11:         orientationLabel.text="Standing Up"
12:     case UIDeviceOrientation.PortraitUpsideDown:
13:         orientationLabel.text="Upside Down"
14:     case UIDeviceOrientation.LandscapeLeft:
15:         orientationLabel.text="Left Side"
16:     case UIDeviceOrientation.LandscapeRight:
17:         orientationLabel.text="Right Side"
18:     default:
19:         orientationLabel.text="Unknown"
20:     }
21: }
```

The logic is straightforward. This method is called each time we have an update to the device's orientation. The notification is passed as a parameter, but we don't really need it for anything.

In line 3, we declare an `orientation` constant equal to the device's `orientation` variable property (*UIDevice.currentDevice().orientation*).

Lines 5–20 implement a `switch` statement (refer to Hour 3, "Discovering Swift and the iOS Playground," for details on `switch`) that compares each possible orientation constant to the value of the orientation variable. If they match, the `orientationLabel` text variable property is set appropriately.

TIP

Technically, the application is done; but when it runs, you'll notice that the iPhone *interface* doesn't support all orientations. The application runs as expected, but when you turn the phone upside down, the text will also be upside down. You can enable *all* possible orientations for your interface by adding this method to your view controller:

```
override func supportedInterfaceOrientations() ->
    UIInterfaceOrientationMask {
    return UIInterfaceOrientationMask.All
}
```

Adding this is purely optional—it corrects what you might consider a visual flaw, rather than a bug in functionality.

Building the Application

Save your files, and then run the application. Your results should resemble Figure 18.5. If you're running in the iOS Simulator, rotating the virtual hardware (Hardware, Rotate Left/Right) will work, but you won't be able to view the face-up and face-down orientations.

FIGURE 18.5
Orientation in action.

Detecting Acceleration, Tilt, and Rotation

In the Orientation application, we ignored the precise values coming from the accelerometer and instead just allowed iOS to make an all-or-nothing orientation decision. The gradations between these orientations, such as the device being somewhere between its left side and straight up and down, are often interesting to an application.

Imagine you are going to create a car racing game where the device acts as the steering wheel when tilted left and right and the gas and brake pedals when tilted forward and back. It is helpful to know how far the player has turned the wheel and how hard the user is pushing the pedals to know how to make the game respond.

Likewise, consider the possibilities offered by the gyroscope's rotation measurements. Applications can now tell whether the device is rotating, even if there is no change in tilt. Imagine a turn-based game that switches between players just by rotating the iPhone or iPad around while it is lying on a table or sitting in a charging dock.

Implementation Overview

In our next application example, ColorTilt, we use acceleration to set the background color of a view, and rotation or tilt to make it progressively more transparent. The current attitude will be displayed at all times via roll, pitch, and yaw readouts. Three toggle switches (UISwitch) will be added to enable/disable motion updates, and accelerometer/gyroscope reactions.

The application logic is broken down into four methods: one to toggle motion manager updates on and off; and three others to react to attitude readings, device acceleration, and device rotation.

It's not as exciting as a car racing game, but it is something we can accomplish in an hour, and everything learned here will apply when you get down to writing a great iOS motion-enabled application.

Setting Up the Project

Open Xcode and begin by creating a new project based on the Single View Application template. Name this application **ColorTilt**.

Planning the Variables and Connections

Next, we'll identify the variable properties and connections we need. Specifically, we want a view (UIView) that changes colors (colorView) and three UISwitch instances. Two of the switches will let us indicate whether we should watch the accelerometer and gyroscope data (toggleAccelerometer and toggleGyroscope). The third does the heavy lifting of turning on or off the motion monitoring via a method controlHardware. To provide output of attitude values (roll, pitch, and yaw), we will use three UILabels: rollOutput, pitchOutput, and yawOutput.

We also need a constant (or a variable property) for our CMMotionManager object, which we'll call **motionManager**. Because this is not directly related to an object in the storyboard and is part of enabling the functional logic, we add this in the implementation of the view controller logic.

Adding a Radian Conversion Constant

Later in the project, we'll be asking Core Motion to provide us with the attitude of our iOS device. Core Motion supplies this information in radians, but we are mere mortals and tend to think in degrees. Converting radians to degrees requires multiplying by a constant, which we'll add now. Update ViewController.swift to include a kRad2Deg constant after its class line:

```
let kRad2Deg:Double = 57.2957795
```

NOTE

As I write this hour, I struggle not to make a joke each time I type about an iOS device's "attitude." This has been very difficult for me, and I apologize for even thinking about it.

Designing the Interface

Like the Orientation application, the ColorTilt application's interface is not a work of art. It requires a few switches, labels, and a view. Open the interface by selecting the Main.storyboard file. Use the Attributes Inspector with the view controller selected to switch to a standard device size, if desired.

Lay out the user interface by dragging three UISwitch instances from the Object Library to the top-right of the view. Stack them, one under the other. Use the Attributes Inspector (Option-Command-4) to set each switch's default to Off.

Add three labels (UILabel), naming them **Motion Tracking**, **Accelerometer**, and **Gyroscope**, to the view, positioned beside each switch.

Next, add three more labels, positioned horizontally to output roll, pitch, and yaw, setting the default value of each to **0**. Add **Roll:**, **Pitch:**, and **Yaw:** labels in front of each. Yes, that's quite a few labels.

Finally, drag a UIView instance into the view and size it to fit in the view below the switches and labels. Use the Attributes Inspector to change the view's background to green.

Your view should now resemble Figure 18.6. If you want to arrange the controls differently, feel free.

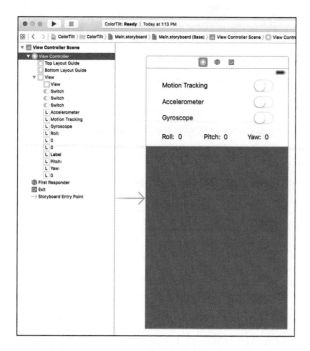

FIGURE 18.6
Create a layout that includes three switches, a boatload of labels, and a color view.

Creating and Connecting the Outlets and Actions

Despite its functional simplicity, quite a few connections are required in this application. Here's what we'll be using, starting with the outlets:

▶ **The view that will change colors (UIView):** colorView

▶ **Toggle switch that activates/deactivates the accelerometer (UISwitch):** toggleAccelerometer

▶ **Toggle switch that activates/deactivates the gyroscope (UISwitch):** toggleGyroscope

▶ **Toggle switch that activates/deactivates motion tracking (UISwitch):** toggleMotion

▶ **Label displaying the attitude value *roll* in degrees (UILabel):** rollOutput

▶ **Label displaying the attitude value *pitch* in degrees (UILabel):** pitchOutput

▶ **How you make a horse move (UILabel):** yawOutput

And the action:

▶ **Toggle motion tracking on and off from the toggleMotion switch:** controlHardware

Select the Main.storyboard file and open the assistant editor, making sure that ViewController. swift is visible on the right side. Clear some room in your workspace if necessary.

Adding the Outlets

Control-drag from the green `UIView` to just below the constant `kRad2Deg` in ViewController. swift. Name the outlet **colorView** when prompted, as shown in Figure 18.7. Repeat the process for the three switches, connecting the switch beside the Motion Tracking label to `toggleMotion`, and the switches beside the Accelerometer and Gyroscope labels to `toggleAccelerometer` and `toggleGyroscope`, respectively.

Complete the outlets by connecting the roll, pitch, and yaw readouts to `rollOutput`, `pitchOutput`, and `yawOutput`.

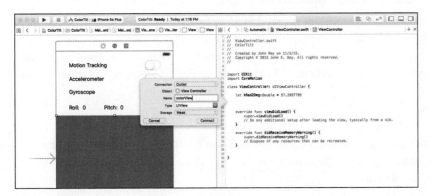

FIGURE 18.7
Connect the objects to the outlets.

Adding the Action

To finish the connections, the `toggleMotion` switch must be configured to call the `controlHardware` method when the `Value Changed` event occurs. Define the action by Control-dragging from the switch to just below the last `@IBOutlet` line in the ViewController. swift file.

When prompted, create a new action named `controlHardware` that responds to the switch's `Value Changed` event.

Implementing the Application Logic

Our ColorTilt application isn't complicated, but will require several different methods to add all the motion features we want. So, we need to cover the following areas:

1. Initialize and configure the Core Motion motion manager (`CMMotionManager`).

2. Manage events to toggle the motion tracking on and off (`controlHardware`), registering a handler closure when the hardware is turned on.

3. React to the accelerometer/gyroscope readings, updating the background color and alpha transparency values appropriately.

4. Prevent the device interface from rotating; the rotation will interfere with displaying feedback to fast events.

Let's work our way through the corresponding pieces of code now.

Initializing the Core Motion Motion Manager

When the ColorTilt application launches, we need to allocate and initialize a Core Motion motion manager (`CMMotionManager`) instance. Before we can do that, however, we need to make sure that our code knows about the Core Motion framework by importing the Core Motion module. Add the following `import` statement to ViewController.swift following the default UIKit import:

```
import CoreMotion
```

Next, we need to declare our motion manager. Create a new constant, `motionManager`, by updating the code at the top of the ViewController.swift file and adding this line following the `@IBOutlets` you added earlier:

```
let motionManager: CMMotionManager = CMMotionManager()
```

Now we have an instance of the Core Motion motion manager already assigned to a constant, `motionManager`. We're ready to start configuring and accessing the motion manager.

Configuring the manager is simple; we only need to set its variable property `deviceMotionUpdateInterval` to match the frequency (in seconds) with which we want to get updates from the hardware. We'll update at 100 times a second, or an update value of .01. This configuration is done in `viewDidLoad` so that we are ready to start monitoring as soon as our interface loads.

Update the `viewDidLoad` method, as shown in Listing 18.4.

LISTING 18.4 Initializing the Motion Manager

```
override func viewDidLoad() {
    super.viewDidLoad()
    // Do any additional setup after loading the view, typically from a nib.
    motionManager.deviceMotionUpdateInterval = 0.01
}
```

The next step is to implement our action, `controlHardware`, so that when one of the `UISwitch` instances is turned on or off, it tells the motion manager to begin or end readings from the accelerometer/gyroscope.

Managing Motion Updates

The `controlHardware` method acts as the "master control" for our application. If the motion tracking switch is toggled on, the `CMMotionManager` instance, `motionManager`, is asked to start monitoring for motion updates. Each update is processed by a handler closure that calls up to three additional methods: `doAttitude` to display attitude values, `doAcceleration` to handle acceleration events, and `doGyroscope` to process data related to rotation.

I say "up to three additional methods" because we don't necessarily want the device trying to react to acceleration changes *and* rotation at the same time, so we take into account the status of the Accelerometer and Gyroscope switches before deciding to call each method.

In the case of the motion tracking switch being toggled off, the `controlHardware` method stops updates from the motion manager.

Update the `controlHardware` method stub, as shown in Listing 18.5.

LISTING 18.5   Implementing the `controlHardware` Method

```
 1: @IBAction func controlHardware(sender: AnyObject) {
 2:     if toggleMotion.on {
 3:         motionManager.startDeviceMotionUpdatesToQueue(
 4:             NSOperationQueue.currentQueue()!,
 5:             withHandler: {
 6:             (motion: CMDeviceMotion?, error: NSError?) in
 7:             self.doAttitude(motion!.attitude)
 8:             if self.toggleAccelerometer.on {
 9:                 self.doAcceleration(motion!.userAcceleration)
10:             }
11:             if self.toggleGyroscope.on {
12:                 self.doRotation(motion!.rotationRate)
13:             }
14:         })
15:     } else {
16:         toggleGyroscope.on=false
17:         toggleAccelerometer.on=false
18:         motionManager.stopDeviceMotionUpdates()
19:     }
20: }
```

Let's step through this method to make sure we're all still on the same page.

Line 2 checks to see whether the motion tracking switch `toggleMotion` is set to On. If it is, lines 3–6 tell the motion manager to start sending updates and define a code block to handle each update.

The code block (lines 7–13) receives all the device's motion data in a `CMDeviceMotion` object named `motion`. In line 7, we send the attitude data from this object (`motion.attitude`) to the method `doAttitude`. Lines 8–10 check to see whether the `toggleAccelerometer` switch is set to On, and, if it is, sends acceleration data (`motion.userAcceleration`) to the method `doAcceleration`. Lines 11–13 do the same for the `toggleGyroscope` switch, sending rotation data (`motion.rotationRate`) to the `doRotation` method. Notice anything weird here? I'm using `self` in front of the methods I call. The reason for this is because the closure acts as a unique chunk of code that is aware of what class it is in, but is also independent of that class. Without the `self` in front of the method names, Swift doesn't know for sure that we mean the methods within the `ViewController` class—and we'd get an error to that effect.

The final lines (15–19) are evaluated if the motion tracking switch is set to Off. If it is, the other toggle switches are also turned off in lines 16–17. This helps keep our display consistent. Line 18 tells the motion manager to stop sending updates.

TIP

If you know you're only going to use the accelerometer or gyroscope in your application—or want to provide different update rates for each—you can request updates for a specific motion monitor using the motion manager methods `startAccelerometerUpdatesToQueue:withHandler` and `startGyroscopeUpdatesToQueue:withHandler`. As the method names suggest, these are specific to the accelerometer and gyroscope and have their own independent update rates defined by the variable properties `accelerometerUpdateInterval` and `gyroscopeUpdateInterval`.

CAUTION

Building Bigger Closures Isn't Better

It is possible to define all of our application's motion logic within the closure supplied by the `startDeviceMotionUpdatesToQueue:withHandler` method, but following that approach can get ugly. Keeping your closures small and using them to invoke other methods results in more manageable and understandable code.

Displaying Attitude Data

The method `doAttitude` has a very simple purpose, and a very simple implementation. This method updates the roll, pitch, and yaw labels to display the corresponding values in degrees. The method also uses the pitch to determine the amount of tilt, forward and back, to set the alpha value of `colorView`. It will only do this, however, when the `toggleGyroscope` switch is off; otherwise, rotation and tilt are competing with one another.

Before we implement this method, it's important to understand what data we will be getting from Core Motion. The method receives an object of the type CMAttitude. Within this, we'll access variable properties roll, pitch, and yaw—each containing *Euler angles* in radians.

TIP

Learn about Euler angles in this excellent Wolfram Mathworld article: http://mathworld.wolfram. com/EulerAngles.html.

Each angle is expressed in radians. To convert between radians and degrees, we multiply by the constant kRad2Deg that was added at the start of the project. The raw radian values for pitch for an iOS device sitting straight up and tipped completely over vary between 1/–1 and 0, so we can use the absolute value of the pitch to set the alpha for colorView. No additional math needed!

Open ViewController.swift and add the implementation of doAttitude shown in Listing 18.6.

LISTING 18.6   Implementing the doAttitude Method

```
1: func doAttitude(attitude: CMAttitude) {
2:     rollOutput.text=String(format:"%.0f",attitude.roll*kRad2Deg)
3:     pitchOutput.text=String(format:"%.0f",attitude.pitch*kRad2Deg)
4:     yawOutput.text=String(format:"%.0f",attitude.yaw*kRad2Deg)
5:     if !toggleGyroscope.on {
6:         colorView.alpha=CGFloat(fabs(attitude.pitch))
7:     }
8: }
```

In line 1, the method receives attitude data from controlHardware and references it in the object attitude. Lines 2–4 set the rollOutput, pitchOutput, and yawOutput labels to attitude's corresponding roll, pitch, and yaw variables (after converting them to degrees). I use a string format of %.0f, which effectively tells the system to output the floating-point value without any decimal points.

Lines 5–7 check whether the toggleGyroscope switch is on. If it *isn't*, the code updates the colorView and sets its alpha value to the absolute value of attitude.pitch. The alpha variable property must be set to a CGFloat, so we use CGFloat() to convert the absolute value to the right type before making the assignment.

Handling Acceleration Data

Next we need to react to the accelerometer data. This method has one purpose: to change the color of colorView if the user moves the device suddenly.

To change colors, we need to sense motion. One way to do this is to look for g-forces greater than 1g along each of our x, y, and z axes. This is good for detecting quick, strong movements. As luck would have it, the `doAcceleration` method will be receiving a `CMAcceleration` structure that contains a measurement of the force of gravity along x, y, and z.

Implement `doAcceleration`, as shown in Listing 18.7.

LISTING 18.7   Implementing the `doAcceleration` Method

```
 1: func doAcceleration(acceleration: CMAcceleration) {
 2:     if (acceleration.x > 1.3) {
 3:         colorView.backgroundColor = UIColor.greenColor()
 4:     } else if (acceleration.x < -1.3) {
 5:         colorView.backgroundColor = UIColor.orangeColor()
 6:     } else if (acceleration.y > 1.3) {
 7:         colorView.backgroundColor = UIColor.redColor()
 8:     } else if (acceleration.y < -1.3) {
 9:         colorView.backgroundColor = UIColor.blueColor()
10:     } else if (acceleration.z > 1.3) {
11:         colorView.backgroundColor = UIColor.yellowColor()
12:     } else if (acceleration.z < -1.3) {
13:         colorView.backgroundColor = UIColor.purpleColor()
14:     }
15: }
```

Lines 2–14 check the acceleration along each of the three axes to see whether it is greater (or less) than 1.3—that is, greater than the force of gravity on the device. If it is, the `colorView` `UIView`'s `backgroundColor` variable property is set to one of six different predefined colors. In other words, if you jerk the device in any direction, the color will change.

TIP

A little experimentation shows that +/−1.3g is a good measure of an abrupt movement. Try it out yourself with a few different values; you might decide another value is better.

Not that bad, right? We finish up by reading device rotation via the gyroscope.

Reacting to Rotation

The goal of the `doRotation` method is to alter the `alpha` value of `colorView` as the user spins the device. Instead of forcing the user to rotate the device in one direction to get the alpha channel to change, we combine the rotation rates along all three axes. Rotation data is supplied to us in the form of another structure (this time, of type `CMRotationRate`). We access the x, y, and z values of this structure to determine the rotation, in radians per second, around each access.

Implement doRotation, as shown in Listing 18.8.

LISTING 18.8   Implementing the doRotation Method

```
1: func doRotation(rotation: CMRotationRate) {
2:      var value: Double =
3:          fabs(rotation.x)+fabs(rotation.y)+fabs(rotation.z)/12.5
4:      if (value > 1.0) { value = 1.0 }
5:      colorView.alpha = CGFloat(value)
6: }
```

In line 1, we receive the rotation rate data in the variable rotation. Lines 2–3 declares value as a double-precision floating-point number (the same as the rotation rates) and sets it to the sum of the absolute values of the three axes' rotation rates (rotation.x, rotation.y, and rotation.z) divided by 12.5.

NOTE

Why are we dividing by 12.5? Because an alpha value of 1.0 is a solid color, and a rotation rate of 1.0 means that the device is rotating at about 1/6 of a rotation a second (1 radian × pi = 3.14; that is, half of a complete rotation). In practice, this is way too slow a rotation rate to get a good effect; barely turning the device at all gives us a solid color.

By dividing by 12.5, the rotation rate would have to be roughly two revolutions a second (2 revolutions × 2 radians × pi = 12.56) for value to reach 1, meaning that it takes much more effort to make the view's background color solid.

In line 4, if value is greater than 1.0, it is set back to 1.0 because that is the maximum that the alpha variable property of colorView can accept. Finally, in line 5, alpha is set to value.

Preventing Interface-Orientation Changes

At this point, you can run the application, but you probably won't get very good visual feedback from the methods we've written. Apple's iOS templates include interface rotation settings that are turned on by default. The animation of the interface rotation will interfere with the quick color changes we need to see in the view.

To fix the problem, we need to disable support for rotation. Do this by selecting the project group in the project navigator, then using the Deployment Info section under the General settings to uncheck all but the Portrait orientation. Alternatively (and possibly easier), add the method in Listing 18.9 to ViewController.swift.

LISTING 18.9   Disabling Interface Rotation

```
override func shouldAutorotate() -> Bool {
    return false
}
```

This turns off interface orientation changes for all possible orientations except Portrait orientation, making our UI static.

Building the Application

You've finished the application. Plug in your iDevice (this won't work right in the Simulator), choose your Device from the Xcode Scheme pop-up menu, and then click Run. Experiment first with simple motion tracking and the attitude readings, as shown in Figure 18.8. Once you have a sense for how the attitude readings vary, try activating the accelerometer to read acceleration data and use sudden motions to change the background color. Your last test should be of the gyroscope. Activate the gyroscope to change the opacity of the background based on rotation speed, rather than tilt.

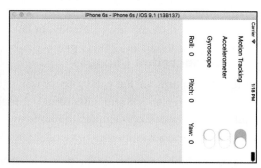

FIGURE 18.8
Tilt the device to change the opacity of the background color.

It's been a bit of a journey, but you can now tie directly into one of the core features of Apple's iOS device family: motion. Even better, you're doing so with one of Apple's latest-and-greatest frameworks: Core Motion.

Further Exploration

The Core Motion framework provides a great set of tools for dealing with all the iOS motion hardware in a similar manner. As a next step, I recommend reviewing the *Core Motion Framework Reference* and the *Event Handling Guide for iOS*, both available through the developer documentation system in Xcode. You also want to review the CMAttitude class documentation, which offers additional methods to establish *reference frames*. These will help you determine device orientation and motion in reference to known frames of reference, such as "north."

If you're lucky enough to be able to target Apple's latest iOS devices, including the iPhone 5s, you will want to look into the CMMotionActivityManager and CMMotionActivity classes. These classes work with the M7 coprocessor to provide access to motion data on an ongoing and historical basis, even when an application isn't running. You can, for example, ask the new APIs to provide the number of steps taken since your app last started, or whether or not your user is using the app while in an automobile. Nifty stuff!

Regardless of how you read motion data or what data you use, the biggest challenge is to use motion readings to implement subtler and more natural interfaces than those in the two applications we created in this hour. A good step toward building effective motion interfaces for your applications is to dust off your old math, physics, and electronics texts and take a quick refresher course.

The simplest and most basic equations from electronics and Newtonian physics are all that is needed to create compelling interfaces. In electronics, a low-pass filter removes abrupt signals over a cutoff value, providing smooth changes in the baseline signal. This is useful for detecting smooth movements and tilts of the device and ignoring bumps and the occasional odd, spiked reading from the accelerometer and gyroscope. A high-pass filter does the opposite and detects only abrupt changes; this can help in removing the effect of gravity and detecting only purposeful movements, even when they occur along the axes that gravity is acting upon.

When you have the right signal interpretation in place, there is one more requirement for your interface to feel natural to your users: It must react like the physical and analog world of mass, force, and momentum, and not like the digital and binary world of 1s and 0s. The key to simulating the physical world in the digital is just some basic seventeenth-century physics.

Wikipedia Entries

Low-pass filter: http://en.wikipedia.org/wiki/Low-pass_filter

High-pass filter: http://en.wikipedia.org/wiki/High-pass_filter

Momentum: http://en.wikipedia.org/wiki/Momentum

Newton's laws of motion: http://en.wikipedia.org/wiki/Newton's_laws_of_motion

Summary

At this point, you know all the mechanics of working with orientation, and with the accelerometer and gyroscope via Core Motion. You understand how to use the Core Motion motion manager (`CMMotionManager`) to take direct readings from the available sensors to interpret orientation, tilt, movement, and rotation of the device. You understand how to create an instance of `CMMotionManager`, how to tell the manager to start sending motion updates, and how to interpret the measurements that are provided.

Q&A

Q. Should I base my game's controls off of gyroscope and accelerometer readings?

A. I recommend that you offer more traditional touchscreen controls in addition to motion-based options. Although many users enjoy using motion controls, they require a certain amount of space and privacy that isn't always available.

Q. Are motion features only good for games?

A. Absolutely not! By combining the different sensor readings from the iPhone or iPad, you can learn a lot about how your users interact with your applications and adjust accordingly. Is your application sensing a face-down orientation? Your user is likely lying down and reading in bed. So, offering to switch to night colors may be appropriate. Are you getting frequent spikes in the accelerometer readings? If yes, your application is likely being used while the user is walking or riding in a vehicle. Allowing more time to react to interface events might be an appropriate adaptation under these circumstances.

Workshop

Quiz

1. An accelerometer measures acceleration relative to what?

   a. Shaking

   b. Free fall

   c. Speed

   d. Thrust

2. Acceleration is measured along how many axes at once?

   a. 0

   b. 1

   c. 2

   d. 3

3. The tilt of a device at a point in time is called what?

   a. Altitute

   b. Acceleration

   c. Rotation

   d. Attitude

4. On iOS, rotation is measured in what?

   a. Degrees/second

   b. Radians/second

   c. Feet/second

   d. Meters/second

5. To set how quickly your device receives motion updates, you should set what variable property?

   a. `deviceMotionUpdateInterval`

   b. `motionUpdateSetting`

   c. `deviceIntervalMotionSetting`

   d. `updateInterval`

6. An independent block of code used with a handler (among other things) is known as a what?

   a. Method

   b. Blockset

   c. Closer

   d. Closure

7. An instance of which class is used to manage motion events?

   a. CMMotionHandle

   b. CMMotionManager

   c. CMMotionMaker

   d. CMMotion

8. Yaw is the measure of tilt around which axis?

   a. y

   b. x

   c. z

   d. x, y, and z

9. When a device is lying facing up, the orientation is set to what constant?

   a. UIDeviceOrientation.FaceUp

   b. UIDeviceOrientation.Up

   c. UIDeviceOrientation.BackDown

   d. UIDeviceOrientation.Face

10. To stop motion readings, you would use which method of the Core Motion motion manager?

   a. cancelDeviceMotionUpdates()

   b. cancelUpdates()

   c. stopUpdates()

   d. stopDeviceMotionUpdates()

Answers

1. B. An accelerometer measures acceleration relative to free-fall. Acceleration is measured in gravities.

2. D. Acceleration is measured along x, y, and z axis simultaneously.

3. D. The measure of tilt of a device at a given moment in time is called its attitude.

4. B. iOS returns rotation rates in radians per second.

5. A. The deviceMotionUpdateInterval is a variable property that sets how quickly motion events are measured.

6. D. A closure is an independent block of code that acts independently of the code around it, without requiring a formal method/function definition.

7. B. To handle motion events, you'll need to use the CMMotionManager singleton.

8. C. Yaw is the measurement of tilt around the z axis.

9. A. When a device is laying face up, its orientation is set to (surprise!) the UIDeviceOrientation.FaceUp.

10. D. Use the stopDeviceMotionUpdates() method to stop the Core Motion motion manager from sending motion updates to your code.

Activities

1. When the Orientation application is in use, the label stays put and the text changes. This means that for three of the six orientations (upside down, left side, and right side), the text itself is also upside down or on its side. Fix this by changing not just the label text but also the orientation of the label so that the text always reads normally for the user looking at the screen. Be sure to adjust the label back to its original orientation when the orientation is standing up, face down, or face up.

2. In the final version of the ColorTilt application, sudden movement is used to change the view's color. You may have noticed that it can sometimes be difficult to get the desired color. This is because the accelerometer provides a reading for the deceleration of the device after your sudden movement. So, what often happens is that ColorTilt switches the color from the force of the deceleration immediately after switching it to the desired color from the force of the acceleration. Add a delay to the ColorTilt application so that the color can be switched at most once every second. This makes switching to the desired color easier because the acceleration will change the color but the deceleration will be ignored.

HOUR 19
Working with Rich Media

What You'll Learn in This Hour:

▶ How to play full-motion video from local or remote (streaming) files
▶ Embedding view controllers with the Container object
▶ Ways of recording and playing back audio files on your iDevice
▶ How to access the built-in music library from within your applications
▶ How to display and access images from the built-in photo library or camera
▶ The use of Core Image filters to easily manipulate images

Each year, new iPads and iPhones come out, and each year I find myself standing in line to snatch them up. Is it the new amazing features? Not so much. In fact, my primary motivation is to keep expanding my storage space to keep up with an ever-growing media library. Sounds, podcasts, movies, TV shows—I keep them all on my iDevices. When the original 8GB iPhone came out, I assumed that I'd never run out of space. Today, my 128GB iPad and iPhone are feeling cramped.

There's no denying that iOS is a compelling platform for rich media playback. To make things even better, Apple provides a dizzying array of Cocoa classes that will help you add media to your own applications—everything from video, to photos, to audio recording. This hour's lesson walks you through a few different features that you may want to consider including in your development efforts.

Exploring Rich Media

Hour 10, "Getting the User's Attention," introduced you to System Sound Services for playing back short (30-second) sound files. This is great for alert sounds and similar applications, but it hardly taps the potential of iOS. This hour takes things a bit further, giving you full playback capabilities, and even audio recording, within your own applications.

In this hour, we use four new frameworks: Media Player, AV Kit, AV Foundation, and Core Image. These frameworks encompass more than a dozen new classes. Although we cannot cover everything in this hour, you will get a good idea of what's possible and how to get started.

In addition to these frameworks, we introduce the `UIImagePickerController` class. You can add this simple object to your applications to allow access to the photo library or camera from within your application.

Media Player Framework

The Media Player framework is used for playing back audio from either local or remote resources. It can be used to call up a modal music player (iPod) interface from your application, select songs, and manage playback. This is the framework that provides integration with many of the built-in media features that your device has to offer. We use four different classes in our tutorial later in this hour:

- ► **MPMediaPickerController:** Presents the user with an interface for choosing media to play. You can filter the files displayed by the media picker or allow selection of any file from the media library.

- ► **MPMediaItem:** A single piece of media, such as a song.

- ► **MPMediaItemCollection:** Represents a collection of media items that will be used for playback. An instance of `MPMediaPickerController` returns an instance of `MPMediaItemCollection` that can be used directly with the next class—the music player controller.

- ► **MPMusicPlayerController:** Handles the playback of media items and media item collections. Unlike the movie player controller, the music player works "behind the scenes"— allowing playback from anywhere in your application, regardless of what is displayed on the screen.

To use any of the media player functionality, your project must include the Media Player framework. Because it is a system framework and can be imported as a module, this is simply the following:

```
import MediaPlayer
```

Let's take a look at a few simple use cases for these media player classes.

Using the Media Picker

When Apple opened iOS for development, it didn't initially provide a method for accessing the iOS music library. This led to applications implementing their own libraries for background music and a less-than-ideal experience for the end user. Thankfully, this restriction is now a thing of the past.

To program a full music-playback function into your application, you need to implement a media picker controller (MPMediaPickerController) for choosing your media, along with a music player controller (MPMusicPlayerController) for playing it back.

The MPMediaPickerController class displays an interface for choosing media files from a user's device. The initWithMediaTypes method initializes the media picker and filters the files that are available to the user in the picker.

Before the media picker is displayed, we can tweak its behavior by setting the prompt variable property to a string that is displayed to the user when choosing media and enable or disable multiple pieces of media from being returned with the allowsPickingMultipleItems variable property.

The object's delegate will also need to be set so that the application can react appropriately when a choice is made—more on that in a minute. Once configured, the media picker is displayed with the presentViewController:animated:completion method. Listing 19.1 displays the setup and display of a typical media picker.

LISTING 19.1 Typical Setup and Display of a Media Picker

```
let mediaPicker: MPMediaPickerController =
    MPMediaPickerController(mediaTypes: MPMediaType.Music)
mediaPicker.prompt = "Choose a few songs to play"
mediaPicker.allowsPickingMultipleItems = true
mediaPicker.delegate = self

presentViewController(mediaPicker, animated: true, completion: nil)
```

Notice in this sample code that the value we provide for initWithMediaTypes is MPMediaType.Music. This is one of several types of filters that you can apply to the media picker, including the following:

▶ **MPMediaType.Music:** The music library

▶ **MPMediaType,Podcast:** Podcasts

▶ **MPMediaType,AudioBook:** Audio books

▶ **MPMediaType,AnyAudio:** Any type of audio file

When the media picker is displayed and songs are chosen (or not), that's where the delegate comes in. By conforming to the MPMediaPickerControllerDelegate protocol and implementing two new methods, we can handle the cases where a user has chosen media or canceled his selection entirely.

The Media Picker Controller Delegate

When a user displays the media picker and makes a selection, we need to do something—what that is, exactly, depends on conforming to the delegate protocol and implementation of two delegate methods. The first, `mediaPickerDidCancel`, is called if the user taps the Cancel button in the middle of choosing his media. The second, `mediaPicker:didPickMediaItems`, is invoked if the user made a valid selection from his media library.

In the case of a cancellation, a proper response is just to dismiss the view. Nothing was chosen, so there's nothing else to do, as shown in Listing 19.2.

LISTING 19.2   Handling the Cancellation of a Media Selection

```
func mediaPickerDidCancel(mediaPicker: MPMediaPickerController) {
    dismissViewControllerAnimated(true, completion: nil)
}
```

When media *is* selected, however, it is returned to the `mediaPicker:didPickMediaItems` delegate method by way of an instance of the class `MPMediaItemCollection`. This object contains a reference to all the chosen media items and can be used to queue up the songs in a music player. We haven't yet seen the music player object, so we'll come back to the handling of the `MPMediaItemCollection` shortly. In addition to providing the media item collection, this method should dismiss the view controller, because the user has finished making his selection. Listing 19.3 shows the beginnings of the method for handling media selection.

LISTING 19.3   Handling the Selection of Media Items

```
func mediaPicker(mediaPicker: MPMediaPickerController,
    didPickMediaItems mediaItemCollection: MPMediaItemCollection) {
    // Do something with the media item collection here
    dismissViewControllerAnimated(true, completion: nil)
}
```

That's it for the delegate methods. We can now configure and display a media picker, handle a user canceling the media selection, and receive a `MPMediaItemCollection` if the user decides to choose something. Now let's explore how to actually do something with that media collection.

Using the Music Player

Using the music player controller class (`MPMusicPlayerController`) is similar to using the movie player—but there are no onscreen controls, nor do you need to allocate or initialize the controller. Instead, you simply declare it, and then you choose whether it should be a controller that integrates with the iPod functionality or if it is localized to the application:

```
let musicPlayer: MPMusicPlayerController =
    MPMusicPlayerController.systemMusicPlayer()
```

Here, I've created a `systemMusicPlayer`, which means that the songs I queue and the playback controls affect the system-level iPod controls. Had I chosen to create an `applicationMusicPlayer`, nothing I might do in my application would have any effect on the iPod playback outside of the program.

Next, to get audio into the player, I can use its method `setQueueWithItemCollection`. This is where the media item collection that was returned by the media picker comes in handy. We can use that collection to queue up the songs in the music player:

```
musicPlayer.setQueueWithItemCollection(mediaItemCollection)
```

After the media is queued in the player, we can control playback by using methods such as `play`, `stop`, `skipToNextItem`, and `skipToPreviousItem`:

```
musicPlayer.play()
```

To verify that the music player is playing audio, we can check its `playbackState` variable property. The `playbackState` indicates what operation the player is currently performing. For example:

- ▶ **MPMusicPlaybackState.Stopped**: Audio playback has been stopped.
- ▶ **MPMusicPlaybackState.Playing**: Audio playback is underway.
- ▶ **MMPMusicPlaybackState.Paused**: Audio playback is paused.

In addition, we may want to access the audio file that is currently playing to provide some feedback to the user; we do this through the `MPMediaItem` class.

Accessing Media Items

A single piece of media in an `MPMediaItemCollection` is an `MPMediaItem`. To get the current `MPMediaItem` being accessed by the player, just reference its `nowPlayingItem` variable property:

```
var currentSong: MPMediaItem = musicPlayer.nowPlayingItem!
```

The `MPMediaItem` can be used to access all the metadata stored for a media file by using the `valueForProperty` method, along with one of several predefined names. For example, to get the title of the current song, you could use the following:

```
var songTitle: String =
currentSong.valueForProperty(MPMediaItemPropertyTitle) as! String!
```

Other properties include the following:

- ▶ **MPMediaItemPropertyArtist:** The artist of the media item

- ▶ **MPMediaItemPropertyGenre:** A string representing the genre of the item

- ▶ **MPMediaItemPropertyLyrics:** The lyrics, if available, for the item

- ▶ **MPMediaItemAlbumTitle:** The name of the album the media item comes from

These are just a few of the pieces of metadata available. You can even access the artwork, beats per minute (BPM), and other data using similar properties that you'll find documented in the MPMediaItem class reference.

The Media Player framework provides much more than we can cover in a single hour, let alone part of an hour; so I encourage you to use this as a starting point.

AV Foundation and AV Kit Frameworks

Although the Media Player framework is great for your music library playback needs, Apple has transitioned video playback to a combination of two frameworks: AV Foundation and AV Kit.

For video playback, we'll make use of these classes:

- ▶ **AVPlayerViewController (AV Kit):** Provides a player interface, with controls for viewing local or streamed media files. Think of this as the "container" that will hold your video files during playback. Each AVPlayerViewController contains a player property of type AVPlayer.

- ▶ **AVPlayer (AV Foundation):** Loads and manages playback of video. The player provided by this class is embedded in an instance of AVPlayerViewController.

- ▶ **AVPlayerItem (AV Foundation):** This class represents a piece of media that will be played in an AVPlayer object. You will frequently initialize AVPlayer with a piece of media when creating the player—eliminating the need to work directly with this class.

Apple also recommends the AV Foundation framework for most audio playback functions that exceed the 30 seconds allowed by System Sound Services. In addition, the AV Foundation framework offers audio recording features, making it possible to record new sound files directly in your application.

You need just two new classes to add audio playback and recording to your apps:

- ▶ **AVAudioRecorder:** Records audio (in a variety of different formats) to memory or a local file on the device. The recording process can even continue while other functions are running in your application.

▶ `AVAudioPlayer`: Plays back audio files of any length. Using this class, you can implement game soundtracks or other complex audio applications. You have complete control over the playback, including the ability to layer multiple sounds on top of one another.

To use the AV Foundation and AV Kit frameworks, you must import the corresponding modules:

```
import AVFoundation
import AVKit
```

Which Formats Are Supported?

iOS supports a wide range of standards for recording and playing audio and video. Be sure to check the iOS developer documentation, as support has changed over time. A partial list is included here:

▶ AAC (16Kbps to 320Kbps)

▶ ALAC (Apple Lossless)

▶ HE-AAC (MPEG-4 High Efficiency AAC)

▶ iLBC (internet Low Bitrate Codec)

▶ IMA4 (IMA/ADPCM)

▶ Linear PCM (uncompressed, linear pulse-code modulation)

▶ MP3 (MPEG-1 audio layer 3)

▶ μ-law and a-law

▶ H.264 video in .m4v, .mp4, and .mov file formats

▶ MPEG-4 video in .m4v, .mp4, and .mov file formats

Using the Video Player

The `AVPlayerViewController` class is used to present a video player for playback of local or streaming video. It can display movies in both full-screen and embedded views—and toggle between them. On its own, `AVPlayerViewController` does nothing; it requires a corresponding `AVPlayer` object to load and manage playback of the movie.

The steps for loading and displaying a movie usually follow these steps:

1. Identify a file for playback either by filename or URL

2. Initialize an instance of the default `AVPlayerViewController` class.

3. Initialize an instance of `AVPlayer`, typically using the `initWithURL` method to provide it with a file or URL where it can find a video.

4. Assign the `player` property of the `AVPlayerViewController` object to the instance of `AVPlayer`.

5. Add the `AVPlayerViewController` to your application's view.

For example, to create a movie player that will play a file named movie.m4v, I could use the following:

```
let movieFile: String =
    NSBundle.mainBundle().pathForResource("movie", ofType: "m4v")!

let playerController: AVPlayerViewController = AVPlayerViewController()
let myPlayer: AVPlayer = AVPlayer(URL: NSURL.fileURLWithPath(movieFile))

playerController.player = myPlayer
```

By default, AirPlay and external device playback (such as the Apple Lightning to HDMI adaptor) is supported without doing anything else. If you want to remove support, it's as simple as setting the video player object's `allowsExternalPlayback` variable property to `false`:

```
playerController.player?.allowsExternalPlayback = false
```

To choose where the video player is added to your screen, you must use the `CGRectMake` function to define a rectangle that it will occupy, and then add the `AVPlayerViewController` object and its view to your main application view. Recall that the `CGRectMake` takes four values: x, y coordinates followed by a width and height in points. For example, to set the display of the video player to a location of 50 points over and 50 points down (x,y) with a width of 100 points and a height of 75 points, I could use the following:

```
playerController.view.frame = CGRectMake(50.0, 50.0, 100.0, 75.0)
addChildViewController(playerController)
view.addSubview(playerController.view)
```

NOTE

I Didn't Know My View Controller Had a Family!

In this example, I'm doing something you really haven't seen before: adding a *child* view controller to an existing view controller. An `AVPlayerViewController` isn't just a view; it is a container that holds a view (the player). Although we haven't done this before, any view can embed another view controller that manages its own UI.

When we get around to building the project, you'll see that (unless you really want to do this in code) you can just drag and drop an embedded view controller into your application design. It's just like adding a new view and view controller with a segue, but it appears *within* your existing view.

To initiate playback, the user can use the default buttons located below the video, or you can use the `play` method of the video player instance:

```
playerController.player?.play()
```

To pause playback, you can use the `pause` method, move to a specific time with the `seekTo-Time` method, or control the volume with the player's `volume` variable property.

TIP

Player Versus Controller

Notice that in these examples, I'm manipulating the `AVPlayer` object, but I'm accessing it through the `AVPlayerViewController` variable property `player`? Because the `AVPlayer` can't function without an `AVPlayerViewController`, *and* the player controller *always* provides a reference back to the player, this approach makes the most sense to me. If you'd prefer to keep a variable property around to reference the `AVPlayer`, that's fine too.

Handling Video Player Completion

When the video player finishes playing a file, it's possible that we will need to do a bit of cleanup, or react in some way. To do this, we use the `NSNotificationCenter` class to register an "observer" that will watch for a specific notification message from the `AVPlayerItem` (the video in our player) and then call a method of our choosing when it receives the notification. For example:

```
NSNotificationCenter.defaultCenter().addObserver(self,
    selector: "playMovieFinished:",
    name: AVPlayerItemDidPlayToEndTimeNotification,
    object: playerController.player?.currentItem)
```

This statement adds an observer that will watch for an event with the name `AVPlayerItemDidPlayToEndTimeNotification`. When it sees that event, it calls the method `playMovieFinished`. The object that is responsible for triggering this event is the currently playing video (`AVPlayerItem`), accessed through the `AVPlayer`'s `currentItem` variable property.

In the implementation of `playMovieFinished`, we must remove the notification observer (because we're done waiting for a notification) and then perform any additional cleanup – such as removing the current player object. Listing 19.4 shows a possible implementation example.

LISTING 19.4   Handling the Notification of Playback Completion

```
func playMovieFinished(notification: NSNotification) {

    let playerController: AVPlayerViewController =
            childViewControllers.last as! AVPlayerViewController
```

```
        NSNotificationCenter.defaultCenter().
            removeObserver(self,
                name: AVPlayerItemDidPlayToEndTimeNotification ,
                object: playerController.player!.currentItem)
    playerController.player = nil
}
```

TIP

Referencing the `AVPlayerViewController`

In this (Listing 19.4) implementation, I get a reference to the `AVPlayerViewController` by asking the current view controller for `childViewControllers.last`. The property `childViewControllers` is an array of all view controllers embedded in the current controller, and `last` returns the last item in the array. This works because I'm assuming there is only one child view controller. If you've embedded multiple controllers, you make need to create variable properties to reference them. This, however, is a convenient trick to get ahold of a single child controller.

Using AV Audio Player

To play back an audio file in AV Audio Player, you follow similar steps as using the video player, but you don't need a separate controller object.

First, you create an `NSURL` instance that references a local or remote file, and then you allocate and initialize the player using the `AVAudioPlayer` method `initWithContentsOfURL`.

For example, to prepare the audio player to play back a sound file named sound.wav stored inside the current application, we write this:

```
let soundFile: String = NSBundle.mainBundle()
    .pathForResource("mysound", ofType: "wav")!
let audioPlayer: AVAudioPlayer! = try? AVAudioPlayer(
    contentsOfURL:NSURL(fileURLWithPath: soundFile))
```

To hear the sound, we ask the player to `play`:

```
audioPlayer.play()
```

Pausing or stopping the playback is just a matter of using `pause` or `stop`. You'll find additional methods in the class reference for adjusting audio and jumping to specific points within the audio file.

Try? Yes! Try? *And* Try!

In the preceding code snippet, you'll see the keyword `try?` before assigning the `audioPlayer` constant. This is required because the `AVAudioPlayer` initialization method will formally throw an error if it fails. When there is the potential for an error to be thrown, it *must* be handled in the code by putting it in a `do-try-catch` block, as described in Hour 3, "Discovering Swift and the iOS Playground."

Rather than writing the whole block, however, we can also just put the keyword `try?` or `try!` in front of an assignment that may throw an error. The `try?` keyword says "if an error occurs, the assignment will equal nil." The alternative, `try!`, states that "no error will occur, and if one does, it's okay to just crash."

In this Hour's code, you'll see `try?` used several times. In a real production application, you should properly react to an error condition if one occurs.

Handling AV Audio Player Completion

If you have a need to react to the condition of your AV Audio Player finishing playing a sound, you can do this by conforming to the `AVAudioPlayerDelegate` protocol and setting the `delegate` for the player to the class that will handle the completion state:

```
audioPlayer.delegate = self
```

Then implement the method `audioPlayerDidFinishPlaying:successfully`, as shown in the method stub in Listing 19.5.

LISTING 19.5   Handling Playback Completion

```
func audioPlayerDidFinishPlaying(player: AVAudioPlayer,
    successfully flag: Bool) {
    // Do something here, if needed.
}
```

No need to add a notification to the notification center (like the video player). Just indicate that you're conforming to the protocol, set the delegate, and implement the method. In many cases, you won't even need to do this; you'll just play the file and walk away, so to speak.

Using AV Audio Recorder

For the most part, recording audio in your application is only marginally more difficult than playing it back. Beginning in iOS 7, you must signal the intent of your application to record before setting up the recording. This amounts to including a single line prior to setting up the recording:

```
try! AVAudioSession.sharedInstance()
    .setCategory(AVAudioSessionCategoryPlayAndRecord)
```

Once again, this method can throw an error, so we prefix it with a `try!` statement. This time, I'm using `try!` rather than `try?`. The reason is that the `setCategory` method doesn't return a value, so if it were to fail and we used `try?`, the resulting `nil` would have nowhere to go. Using `try!` tells the system that we're confident the line will succeed, and that we understand the consequences if something fails (the app crashes).

To prepare the audio recorder, you must identify a file (`NSURL`) where you can store the audio, configure the parameters of the sound file to be created (a `Dictionary`), and then initialize an instance of the `AVAudioRecorder` class with the file and settings.

If you're recording without the intention of keeping the sound file, you can record to the temp directory. Otherwise, you should target the documents directory. See Hour 15, "Reading and Writing Application Data," for more details on accessing the file system. Here, I prepare an `NSURL` that references a file sound.caf in the temp directory:

```
let soundFileURL: NSURL =
    NSURL.fileURLWithPath(NSTemporaryDirectory()+"sound.caf")
```

Next, I need to create a Swift `Dictionary` that contains the settings for my recorded audio:

```
let soundSetting = [
    AVSampleRateKey: 44100.0,
    AVFormatIDKey: NSNumber(unsignedInt:kAudioFormatMPEG4AAC),
    AVNumberOfChannelsKey: 2,
    AVEncoderAudioQualityKey: AVAudioQuality.High.rawValue
]
```

This code creates a `Dictionary` called `soundSetting` with keys and values that should be completely obvious, so I'll just move on. Just kidding. Unless you're familiar with audio recording, many of these might be pretty foreign sounding. Here's the 30-second summary:

- ▸ **AVSampleRateKey:** The number of audio samples the recorder will take per second.

- ▸ **AVFormatIDKey:** The recording format for the audio. This must be converted to an NSNumber; otherwise, it will fail.

- ▸ **AVNumberofChannelsKey:** The number of audio channels in the recording. Stereo audio, for example, has two channels.

- ▸ **AVEncoderAudioQualityKey:** A quality setting for the encoder.

TIP

To learn more about the different settings, what they mean, and what the possible options are, read the *AVAudioRecorder Class Reference* (scroll to the "Constants" section) in the Xcode Developer Documentation utility.

After getting the sound file and settings ready, we can finally prepare an instance of the AV Recorder by allocating it and initializing it with the `initWithURL:settings` method:

```
soundRecorder = try? AVAudioRecorder(URL: soundFileURL,
    settings: soundSetting)
```

We're now ready to record. To record, we use the `record` method; to stop, we use `stop`:

```
soundRecorder.record()
```

When recording is complete, we can play back the new sound file using the AV Audio Player.

The Image Picker

The image picker (`UIImagePickerController`) works like the `MPMediaPickerController`, but instead of presenting a view where songs can be selected, the user's photo library is displayed instead. When the user chooses a photo, the image picker hands us a `UIImage` object based on the user's selection.

Like the `MPMediaPickerController`, the image picker is presented within your application modally. The good news is that both of these objects implement their own view and view controller, so there's very little work that we need to do to get them to display—other than a quick call to `presentViewController:animated:completion`. On the iPad, the image picker is required to be displayed within a popover, so your code will need to change a bit for this; we cover that in the tutorial project a bit later this hour.

Using the Image Picker

To display the image picker, allocate and initialize an instance of `UIImagePickerController`, and then set the `sourceType` to what the user should be allowed to pick from:

▸ **`UIImagePickerControllerSourceType.Camera`**: A picture that will be taken from the device's camera.

▸ **`UIImagePickerControllerSourceType.PhotoLibrary`**: A picture chosen from the device's photo library.

▸ **`UIImagePickerControllerSourceType.SavedPhotosAlbum`**: The device's camera roll.

Next, you want to set the image picker's `delegate`; this is the class that will handle doing something when the user picks a photo (or takes a picture) or taps the Cancel button. Finally, the image picker is displayed using the `presentViewController:animated:completion` method. Listing 19.6 shows a sample setup and display of an image picker that uses the camera as the source.

LISTING 19.6 Setting Up and Displaying the Image Picker

```
let imagePicker: UIImagePickerController = UIImagePickerController()

imagePicker.sourceType = UIImagePickerControllerSourceType.PhotoLibrary
imagePicker.delegate = self
presentViewController(imagePicker, animated: true, completion: nil)
```

NOTE

You might have encountered instances where you can choose an image and apply filters or scale and crop it before using it. This functionality is "baked into" the image picker. To enable it, set the variable property `allowsEditing` to `true` on the `UIImagePickerController` instance.

TIP

If you want to determine exactly what sort of camera devices are available on your system, you can test using the `UIImagePickerController` class method `isCameraDeviceAvailable`, which returns a Boolean value: `UIImagePickerController.isCameraDeviceAvailable(<camera type>)`, where the camera type is `UIImagePickerControllerCameraDevice.Rear` or `UIImagePickerControllerCameraDevice.Front`.

The UI Image Picker Controller Delegate

To handle the actions of when a user either cancels picking an image or picks one, you must conform your class to the `UIImagePickerControllerDelegate` protocol and implement the methods `imagePickerController:didFinishPickingMediaWithInfo` and `imagePickerControllerDidCancel`.

The first, `imagePickerController:didFinishPickingMediaWithInfo`, is called automatically when the user makes a selection in the image picker. The method is passed a `Dictionary` object that can contain several things: the image itself, an edited version of the image (if cropping/scaling is allowed), or information about the image. We must provide the key value to retrieve the value we want. For example, to get back the chosen image, we use the `UIImagePickerControllerOriginalImage` key, a `UIImage`. Listing 19.7 shows a sample implementation that retrieves the selected image and dismisses the image picker.

LISTING 19.7 Handling the Selection of an Image

```
func imagePickerController(picker: UIImagePickerController,
    didFinishPickingMediaWithInfo info: [String : AnyObject]) {
    dismissViewControllerAnimated(true, completion: nil)
    let chosenImage: UIImage =
```

```
        info[UIImagePickerControllerOriginalImage] as! UIImage!
    // Do something with the image here
}
```

TIP

To learn more about the data that can be returned by the image picker, read the *UIImagePickerControllerDelegate Protocol Reference* within the Apple developer documentation.

In the second delegate method, we react to the user canceling the image selection and get rid of the image picker view. Listing 19.8 shows an implementation example.

LISTING 19.8 **Handling the Cancellation of an Image Selection**

```
func imagePickerControllerDidCancel(picker: UIImagePickerController) {
    dismissViewControllerAnimated(true, completion: nil)
}
```

As you can see, there's more than a little similarity to the media picker controller; once you get the hang of one, using the other will be a piece of cake.

CAUTION

Using an Image Picker? Conform to the Navigation Controller Delegate

The navigation controller delegate (`UINavigationControllerDelegate`) is required whenever you use an image picker. The good news is that you won't need to implement any additional methods for it—just a reference in your Swift file.

CAUTION

Popover Enforced on iPad

If you are building your application for the iPad, you'll need to display the media picker via a popover, similar to what you did with alert action sheets in Hour 10, "Getting the User's Attention." If you don't, your application will encounter an error when it attempts to show the picker onscreen.

The Core Image Framework

Core Image provides nondestructive methods for applying filters to images and performing other types of image analysis (including face detection). If you've ever wondered how to add fancy image effects to an application without needing to understand the complex math behind image manipulation, Core Image can be your best friend.

To use Core Image in your application, import the corresponding module:

```
import CoreImage
```

Using Core Image Filters

To get a feel of how Core Image works, let's examine its use to apply a "sepia tone" image filter (`CIFilter`) to an image in your application. Core Image defines a new "nondestructive" image type of `CIImage`, but we've been dealing exclusively with `UIImages` (often within `UIImageViews`) to this point. No worries—converting between these two types is not difficult. For example, assume we have an image view called `myImageView`. To access its underlying `UIImage` and create a new `CIImage` called `imageToFilter` that we can manipulate, we could write the following:

```
let imageToFilter: CIImage = CIImage(image: myImageView.image!)!
```

To apply a filter, we must know the name of a filter and the names of the parameters that it requires. For example, the Core Image sepia tone filter is named `CISepiaTone`, and it takes a parameter called `inputIntensity` that is a number between 1.0 and 0.0. (1.0 is no sepia tone applied.) Armed with that information, we can create a new `CIFilter`, set its default values, perform any additional configuration, and then pass it the input image (`imageToFilter`) and get back the result in a new `CIImage`, as demonstrated in Listing 19.9. This is the process for applying *any* `CIFilter`.

LISTING 19.9   Processing a `CIImage` with a `CIFilter`

```
1: let activeFilter: CIFilter = CIFilter(name: "CISepiaTone")!
2: activeFilter.setDefaults()
3: activeFilter.setValue(0.5, forKey: "inputIntensity")
4: activeFilter.setValue(imageToFilter, forKey: "inputImage")
5: let filteredImage: CIImage =
6:     activeFilter.valueForKey("outputImage") as! CIImage
```

Line 1 declares and returns a new instance of the sepia `CIFilter`, and line 2 sets its defaults. In line 3, the `inputIntensity` parameter is configured to a floating-point value of `0.5`.

Line 4 uses this same method to pass the input image (`imageToFilter`) to the filter. Lines 5–6 return the filtered image in `filteredImage` by accessing the `outputImage` key from the filter.

The `filteredImage` object is a `CIImage`, so chances are, to use it, we need to convert it back to a `UIImage`. The `UIImage` convenience method `initWithCIImage` makes this a breeze:

```
let myNewImage: UIImage = UIImage(CIImage: filteredImage)
```

The new UIImage, myNewImage, contains the final filtered image with sepia tone applied. To display it in a UIImageView, you can just set the UIImageView's image variable property to myNewImage.

TIP
More than a dozen built-in Core Image filters are available for use in your applications. To learn the names of the filters and the parameters they require, be sure to read the developer document *Core Image Filter Reference*.

You've just learned the basics of working with quite a few of the iOS media frameworks; now it's time to put them to use in a media sandbox application.

The Media Playground Application

This hour's exercise is less about creating a real-world application and more about building a sandbox for testing out the rich media classes that we've introduced. The finished application shows embedded or fullscreen video, records and plays audio, browses and displays images from the photo library or camera, applies a filter to the images, and browses and selects music from the device's music library.

Implementation Overview

Because *so* much is going on in this application, be careful that you don't miss any of the connections or variables that we will be defining. We start by creating an application skeleton for all the different functionality, and then we fill them in to implement the features we've been discussing.

The application has five main components, as follows:

▶ A video player that loads an MPEG-4 video file when a button is pressed. After the video is played, it is unloaded from memory.

▶ We create an audio recorder with playback features.

We add a button that shows the photo library or camera and a UIImageView that displays the chosen photo. A toggle switch controls the image source.

▶ After an image is chosen, the user will be able to apply a CIFilter to it.

We enable the user to choose songs from the music library and start or pause playback. The title of the currently playing song is displayed onscreen in a label.

Setting Up the Project

Begin by creating a new single-view iOS application project in Xcode. Name the new project **MediaPlayground**. We need to add more than a few frameworks and define many variable properties, so follow along closely. If you experience any errors while building the application, it's likely that an `import` statement is missing.

Adding the Media Files

For this tutorial, we need to add two media files to our project: movie.m4v and norecording.wav. The first is used to demo the movie player, and the second is used as a default sound to play in our audio recorder if we haven't made a recording yet.

Locate the Media folder included in this hour's project folder, and drag it into your Xcode project code group so that you can access it directly in the application. Be sure to choose to copy the files and choose to create a new group when prompted.

NOTE

Why Don't I Add These to the Asset Catalog?

Asset catalogs currently support arbitrary file types and can deliver them to our application as objects of the type `NSData`. Unfortunately, most of the methods for working with media can't deal with `NSData` without *lots* of workarounds. Maybe in iOS 10.

Adding the Frameworks

This application requires that a total of four additional frameworks be added to accommodate music playback (MediaPlayer.framework), sound/video playback/recording (AVFoundation. framework and AVKit.framework), and image filtering (CoreImage.framework). Let's get these out of the way up front by importing the corresponding modules after the existing `import` line in ViewController.swift:

```
import CoreImage
import AVFoundation
import MediaPlayer
import AVKit
```

Planning the Variables and Connections

There's no way to sugarcoat this: We need a lot of stuff to make this application work. Let's start with the outlets/variables and then move on to the actions. For the movie player (`AVPlayer` and `AVPlayerViewController`), we really won't need any outlets; we'll manage most everything in code.

For the AV Foundation audio recording and playback, we want an outlet for the Record button so that we can toggle its title between record and stop; we'll name this `recordButton`. We also want a variable property declared for both the audio recorder (`AVAudioRecorder`) and the audio player (`AVAudioPlayer`): `audioRecorder` and `audioPlayer`, respectively. These do not need to be exposed as outlets, because there is nothing in the user interface (UI) to connect to them.

To implement music playback, we need a reference to a Play Music button that changes between Play and Pause (`musicPlayButton`) and a label that presents the name of the current track (`displayNowPlaying`). As with the other players/recorder, we also need a variable property for the music player itself: `musicPlayer`.

For the camera, the toggle switch to enable the camera is connected via `toggleCamera`. The image view that displays the chosen image will be accessed via `displayImageView`.

Moving to the actions, we define a total of seven: `loadMovie`, `recordAudio`, `playAudio`, `chooseImage`, `applyFilter`, `chooseMusic`, and `playMusic`. Each is triggered from a similarly named button.

None of this is difficult, but there's a lot to do. Open the Main.storyboard file, switch to a simulated view size that is comfortable (or use your Hour 16 skills to build for *any* interface size) and get started.

Designing the Interface

This application has a total of seven buttons (`UIButton`), one switch (`UISwitch`), two labels (`UILabel`), a `UIImageView`, and an embedded view controller (no worries, we'll get to that in a sec). Developers targeting larger-screened devices will find this exercise much easier than those squeaking by with a 3.5-inch to 4-inch screen; we're really pushing the limits of what can fit in a view.

Figure 19.1 represents a potential design for the application. Use this pattern with your layout, or modify it to suit your fancy - with a few minor exceptions. First, leave a large empty space to hold your video player. Next, be sure to title the button for recording audio **Record Audio** and the button for initiating music library playback as **Play Music**. We'll be changing those titles programmatically, so it's important to have a consistent starting point. Finally, make sure that you add a label with the default text **No Song Playing** at the bottom of the view. This updates with the name of the song the user has chosen to play.

TIP
_____

You might want to consider using the Attributes Inspector (Option-Command-4) to set the `UIImageView` mode to Aspect Fill or Aspect Scale to make sure that your photos look right within the view.
_____

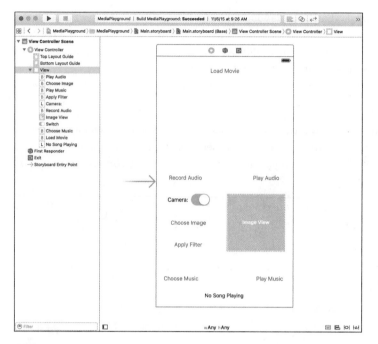

FIGURE 19.1
Create an interface for the different functions we'll be implementing.

Embedding an AVPlayerViewController with a Container View

You've build the majority of the interface for the MediaPlayground application, but there's one big thing missing: the `AVPlayerViewController` instance where movie playback will take place.

This, as the name probably tips you off, is a view controller (like other view controllers that we've used). We need to add on to our project, so make sure that the storyboard is open, and then find the object labeled AVKit Player View Controller in the Object Library. Drag it to an empty place in your storyboard editor (outside of the main application view). An entirely new view (and corresponding scene) will appear.

Right now, you should be scratching your head and thinking, "But I want this to appear *in* my main application view—not be a separate scene!" Not to worry; we're going to make that happen now.

Use the Object Library to locate a container view and drag it into your main application view. It appears as a gray rectangle; size it to fill the area where you want the video to appear. Your storyboard and interface should look similar to Figure 19.2.

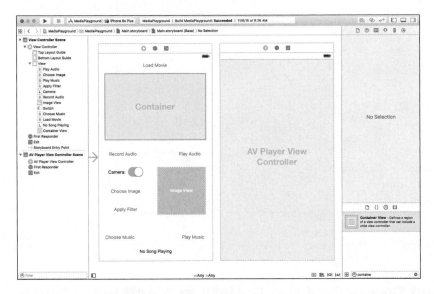

FIGURE 19.2
Add a container view to the main interface.

A container view can hold *any* view controller you want! You can define half a dozen scenes and add them to different controllers in a single view (if you wanted to.) For this exercise, we want to put the AVPlayerViewController scene inside of the container. Unfortunately, Xcode decides to add an empty scene for the container (without us even asking). Select this new scene and press Delete to remove it.

Now, we'll add our own scene.

To do this, we use the same process as the other segues we've used in the book: Control-drag from the container view in your design to the AVPlayerViewController in the Document Outline or the main editor window. When prompted for the type of segue to create, choose Embed.

Your design should now reflect that the AVPlayerViewController is embedded in the container, as demonstrated in Figure 19.3. We can now use it for video playback.

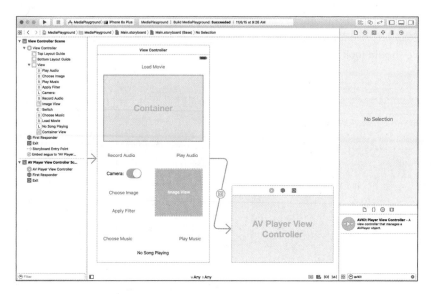

FIGURE 19.3
An embed segue connects the container view to the `AVPlayerViewController`.

Creating and Connecting the Outlets and Actions

When finished creating your view, switch to the assistant editor to get ready to start making connections. For your reference, the following list presents the required outlets, and then the actions, from top to bottom in my version of the interface:

- ▶ The Record Audio button (`UIButton`): `recordButton`

- ▶ The camera toggle switch (`UISwitch`): `toggleCamera`

- ▶ The image view (`UIImageView`): `displayImageView`

- ▶ The Play Music button (`UIButton`): `musicPlayButton`

- ▶ The default No Song Playing feedback label (`UILabel`): `displayNowPlaying`

The actions:

- ▶ The Load Movie button (`UIButton`): `loadMovie`

- ▶ The Record Audio button (`UIButton`): `recordAudio`

- ▶ The Play Audio button (`UIButton`): `playAudio`

- ▶ The Choose Image button (`UIButton`): `chooseImage`

▶ **The Apply Filter button (UIButton):** `applyFilter`

▶ **The Choose Music button (UIButton):** `chooseMusic`

▶ **The Play Music button (UIButton):** `playMusic`

Adding the Outlets

The bad news is that you need to add a bunch of outlets. The good news is that there isn't anything tricky about any of them. With the assistant editor open and the Main.storyboard and ViewController.swift files visible, Control-drag from the Record Audio button to just below the `class` line in ViewController.swift. When prompted, make a connection to `recordButton`, as shown in Figure 19.4.

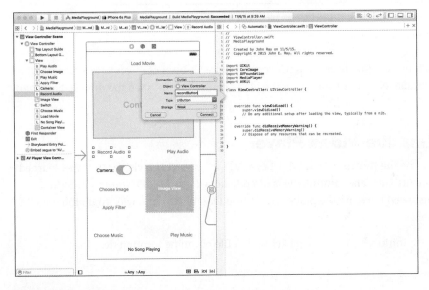

FIGURE 19.4
Work through the outlet list, adding each to ViewController.swift.

Move through the rest of the outlets listed, repeating this process until each outlet has been added to the file. Time for the actions.

Adding the Actions

Once all five outlets are accounted for, move on to the actions. Begin by Control-dragging from the Load Movie button to below the variable property you added. When prompted, create a new action named `loadMovie`, as shown in Figure 19.5.

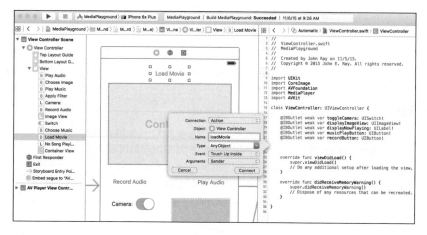

FIGURE 19.5
Connect the buttons to their actions.

Repeat this for each of the other buttons, until you've created a total of seven new actions in the ViewController.swift file. Now pat yourself on the back; you've just finished the most tedious part of the project.

Implementing the Video Player

In this exercise, we use the AVPlayer and AVPlayerViewController classes that you learned about earlier this hour. The view controller was already added graphically through Interface Builder, so we'll just need to create the player object and load it with a movie. To do that, we'll use a single method:

▶ **initWithURL:** Initializes the video picker with a file or online location described in an NSURL object.

We'll need to access two variable properties to fully setup the playback:

▶ **player:** Set on the Player View Controller, this property will be configured with the initialized AV Player.

▶ **currentItem:** Accessed from the player object, the current item (of type AVPlayerItem) references the media file loaded in the player.

The AVPlayerViewController implements a graphical user interface (GUI) for controlling playback, so we don't need to add interface features ourselves. If we wanted to, however, there are many methods that we could call on to control playback.

TIP
Dozens of methods and variable properties are available for the AV Player and AV Player View Controller. You can get pointers to additional resources in the "Further Exploration" section at the end of this hour.

Implementing Movie Playback

For movie playback in the MediaPlayground application to work, we need to actually load a movie file into a player object. We do this by implementing the `loadMovie` method. This is invoked by the Load Movie button we added to the interface earlier. Let's add the method, and then walk through how it works.

Update the `loadMovie` method in the ViewController.swift file, as shown in Listing 19.10.

LISTING 19.10   Loading the Movie and Preparing the Player

```
 1: @IBAction func loadMovie(sender: AnyObject) {
 2:     let movieFilename: String =
 3:     NSBundle.mainBundle().pathForResource("movie", ofType: "m4v")!
 4:     let moviePlayer: AVPlayer =
 5:         AVPlayer(URL: NSURL(fileURLWithPath: movieFilename))
 6:     let playerViewController: AVPlayerViewController =
 7:         childViewControllers.last as! AVPlayerViewController
 8:     playerViewController.player = moviePlayer
 9:
10:     NSNotificationCenter.defaultCenter().addObserver(self,
11:         selector: "playMovieFinished:",
12:         name: AVPlayerItemDidPlayToEndTimeNotification,
13:         object: moviePlayer.currentItem)
14: }
```

Line 2–3 declares a string `movieFile` that will hold the path to the movie file (movie.m4v) we added to our project.

Next, lines 4–5 initialize `moviePlayer` itself using an `NSURL` instance that contains the path from `movieFile`.

Lines 6–7 take advantage of the fact that we have a single embedded `AVPlayerViewController` (a "child" of our main view controller) to grab a reference to the object and store it in `playerViewController`.

Line 8 sets the player property of the `AVPlayerViewController` (`playerViewController`) to the `AVPlayer` that we initialized (`moviePlayer`). This completes the setup for basic movie playback. Once this code is executed, the user can immediately use the controls presented by the

Player View Controller to play the movie. We could also initiate playback programmatically by adding the line `moviePlayer.play()`.

`AVPlayerItem` sends the `AVPlayerItemDidPlayToEndTimeNotification` when it has finished playing. In lines 10–13, we register that notification for the current item loaded in the player and ask the notification center to invoke the `playMovieFinished` method when it receives the notification. Put simply, when the movie player is finished playing the movie the `playMovieFinished` method is called.

Do we really need a `playMovieFinished` method ? No, but it's good practice.

Handling Cleanup

To clean up after the movie playback has finished, we remove the player from the Player View Controller. This isn't necessary, but it will allow iOS to free up memory occupied by the movie and player until the user decides to load it again.

To handle the cleanup, implement the `playMovieFinished` method (triggered by the notification center) to the ViewController.swift file, as shown in Listing 19.11.

LISTING 19.11   Cleaning Up After the Movie Player

```
1: func playMovieFinished(notification: NSNotification) {
2:     let playerViewController: AVPlayerViewController =
3:         childViewControllers.last as! AVPlayerViewController
4:     NSNotificationCenter.defaultCenter().removeObserver(self,
5:         name: AVPlayerItemDidPlayToEndTimeNotification,
6:         object: playerViewController.player!.currentItem)
7:     playerViewController.player = nil
8: }
```

Before we do anything, we grab a reference to the `AVPlayerViewController` so that we can access the player and the media item that the player has loaded (lines 2–3).

Next, we tell the notification center that it can stop looking for the `AVPlayerItemDidPlayToEndTimeNotification` notification (lines 4–6). Because we're done with playback from the AV player object, there's no point in keeping it around until we play the movie again. Line 7 removes the player from the Player View Controller.

Movie playback is now available in the application, as demonstrated in Figure 19.6. Choose Run in the Xcode toolbar, press the Load Movie button, and then press Play. Try going full screen, even try AirPlay. It all works.

FIGURE 19.6
The application will now play the video file when Play Movie is touched.

Implementing Audio Recording and Playback

In the second part of the tutorial, we add audio recording and playback to the application. Unlike the movie player, we use classes within the AV Foundation framework to implement these features.

For the recorder, we use the AVAudioRecorder class and these methods:

- ▶ **initWithURL:settings:** Provided with an NSURL instance pointing to a local file and NSDictionary containing a few settings, this method returns an instance of a recorder, ready to use.

- ▶ **record:** Begins recording.

- ▶ **stop:** Ends the recording session.

Not coincidentally, the playback feature, an instance of AVAudioPlayer, uses some very similar methods:

- ▶ **initWithContentsOfURL:** Creates an audio player object that can be used to play back the contents of the file pointed to by an NSURL object.

- ▶ **play:** Plays back the audio.

NOTE

We do not implement the `AVAudioPlayerDelegate` protocol in this implementation because we don't really need to know when the audio player has finished; it can take as long as it needs.

Implementing Audio Recording

To add audio recording to the project, we need to create the `recordAudio` method. Before we do, though, let's think through this a bit. What happens when we initiate a recording? In this application, recording continues until we press the button again.

To implement this functionality, the "recorder" object itself must persist between calls to the `recordAudio:` method. We make sure that this happens by adding an `audioRecorder` variable property in the ViewController.swift file to hold the `AVAudioRecorder` object. Update ViewController.swift, adding this line after the other variables and outlets:

```
var audioRecorder: AVAudioRecorder!
```

Next, we initialize the controller in the `viewDidLoad` method, making it available anywhere and anytime we need it. Edit ViewController.swift and add the code in Listing 19.12 to `viewDidLoad`.

LISTING 19.12   Creating and Initializing the Audio Recorder

```
 1:  override func viewDidLoad() {
 2:      super.viewDidLoad()
 3:
 4:      try! AVAudioSession.sharedInstance()
 5:          .setCategory(AVAudioSessionCategoryPlayAndRecord)
 6:
 7:      // Setup the audio recorder
 8:      let soundFileURL: NSURL =
 9:          NSURL.fileURLWithPath(NSTemporaryDirectory()+"sound.caf")
10:
11:      let soundSetting = [
12:          AVSampleRateKey: 44100.0,
13:          AVFormatIDKey: NSNumber(unsignedInt:kAudioFormatMPEG4AAC),
14:          AVNumberOfChannelsKey: 2,
15:          AVEncoderAudioQualityKey: AVAudioQuality.High.rawValue
16:      ]
17:
18:      audioRecorder = try? AVAudioRecorder(URL: soundFileURL,
19:          settings: soundSetting)
20:  }
```

The audio recorder implementation begins at line 4.

Starting with the basics, lines 4–5 indicates our intention to produce an application that both plays and records audio.

Lines 8–9 initialize a URL, soundFileURL, which points to the sound file we are going to record. We use the NSTemporaryDirectory() function to grab the temporary directory path where your application can store its sound, and we concatenate on the name of the sound file itself: sound.caf.

Lines 11–16 create an Dictionary that contains keys and values for configuring the format of the sound being recorded. This is identical to the code introduced earlier in this hour.

In lines 18–19, the audio recorder, audioRecorder, is initialized with soundFileURL and the settings stored in the soundSettings dictionary.

Controlling Recording

With audioRecorder initialized, all that we need to do is implement recordAudio so that the record and stop methods are invoked as needed. To make things interesting, we'll update the recordButton title to read Record Audio or Stop Recording when pressed.

Update the recordAudio method stub in ViewController.swift with the code in Listing 19.13.

LISTING 19.13   Updating the Initial recordAudio Method

```
 1:  @IBAction func recordAudio(sender: AnyObject) {
 2:      if recordButton.titleLabel!.text == "Record Audio" {
 3:          audioRecorder.record()
 4:          recordButton.setTitle("Stop Recording",
 5:              forState: UIControlState.Normal)
 6:      } else {
 7:          audioRecorder.stop()
 8:          recordButton.setTitle("Record Audio",
 9:              forState: UIControlState.Normal)
10:      }
11:  }
```

Notice that I said this is in the initial implementation. We'll be modifying this slightly when implementing the audio playback because it serves as a lovely place to load up the audio we've recorded and prepare to play it.

For now, let's check out what this does.

In line 2, the method checks the title of the recordButton variable. If it is set to Record Audio, the method uses audioRecorder.record() to start recording (line 3), and then in lines 4–5, it sets the recordButton title to Stop Recording. If the title *doesn't* read Record Audio, we're already in the process of making a recording. In this case, we use `audioRecorder.stop()` in line 7 to end the recording and set the button title back to Record Audio in lines 7–8.

That's it for recording. Let's implement playback so that we can actually *hear* what we've recorded.

Not So Fast, Mr. Spy!

In recent releases of iOS, applications will prompt users before they can record audio with the microphone. If the user chooses *not* to allow access, the `record` method won't work. If you want to check for this scenario, just check to see whether `record` returns `true`; if it does, you're in good shape. If not, your recording will be empty.

Implementing Audio Playback

To implement the audio player, we create a variable property, `audioPlayer`, that we can use throughout our application. We then initialize it to a default sound in `viewDidLoad` so that there is something to play back even if the user hasn't made a recording.

Begin by adding the new variable in ViewController.swift:

```
var audioPlayer: AVAudioPlayer!
```

Now, initialize the player in the `viewDidLoad` method by adding the code in Listing 19.14.

LISTING 19.14   Preparing the Audio Player with a Default Sound

```
 1:  override func viewDidLoad() {
 2:      super.viewDidLoad()
 3:
 4:      try! AVAudioSession.sharedInstance()
 5:          .setCategory(AVAudioSessionCategoryPlayAndRecord)
 6:
 7:      // Setup the audio recorder
 8:      let soundFileURL: NSURL =
 9:          NSURL.fileURLWithPath(NSTemporaryDirectory()+"sound.caf")
10:
11:      let soundSetting = [
12:          AVSampleRateKey: 44100.0,
13:          AVFormatIDKey: NSNumber(unsignedInt:kAudioFormatMPEG4AAC),
14:          AVNumberOfChannelsKey: 2,
15:          AVEncoderAudioQualityKey: AVAudioQuality.High.rawValue
16:      ]
17:
18:      audioRecorder = try? AVAudioRecorder(URL: soundFileURL,
19:          settings: soundSetting)
20:
```

```
21:        // Setup the audio player
22:        let noSoundFileURL: NSURL =
23:            NSURL.fileURLWithPath(NSBundle.mainBundle()
24:            .pathForResource("norecording", ofType: "wav")!)
25:        audioPlayer = try? AVAudioPlayer(contentsOfURL: noSoundFileURL)
26:    }
```

The setup of the audio player begins in lines 22–24. Here, an NSURL, noSoundFileURL, is created to reference the file norecording.wav that was added to your project when you added the Media folder.

Line 25 initializes the audio player (audioPlayer) with the contents of the noSoundFileURL. The audioPlayer object can now be used to initiate playback of this default sound.

Controlling Playback

To start playing back the audio file that is referenced by audioPlayer, all we need to do is use the method play. Update the playAudio method to do just that. Listing 19.15 shows the full implementation of playAudio.

LISTING 19.15 Implementing playAudio Method

```
@IBAction func playAudio(sender: AnyObject) {
    audioPlayer.play()
}
```

If you run the application now, you should be able to record sounds, but every time you press Play Audio, you'll hear the sound norecording.wav. This is because we never load the sound that has been recorded.

Loading the Recorded Sound

The perfect place to load the recording is after the user has clicked Stop Record in the recordAudio method. Update recordAudio, as shown in Listing 19.16.

LISTING 19.16 Completing the recordAudio Method

```
1:  @IBAction func recordAudio(sender: AnyObject) {
2:      if recordButton.titleLabel!.text == "Record Audio" {
3:          audioRecorder.record()
4:          recordButton.setTitle("Stop Recording",
5:              forState: UIControlState.Normal)
6:      } else {
7:          audioRecorder.stop()
8:          recordButton.setTitle("Record Audio",
```

```
 9:                    forState: UIControlState.Normal)
10:          let soundFileURL: NSURL =
11:              NSURL.fileURLWithPath(NSTemporaryDirectory()+"sound.caf")
12:          audioPlayer = try? AVAudioPlayer(contentsOfURL: soundFileURL)
13:      }
14:  }
```

Lines 10–11 should look familiar because, once again, they grab and store the temporary directory and use it to initialize an `NSURL` object, `soundFileURL`, that points to the sound.caf file we've recorded.

In line 12, the audio player, `audioPlayer`, is initialized with the contents of `soundFileURL`.

Try running the application again and see what happens. Now when you press the Play Audio button, you'll hear the default sound when no recording has been made; or, if the user has recorded audio, the recording will play.

It's time to move on to the next part of this hour's exercise: accessing and displaying photos from the photo library and camera.

Implementing the Photo Library and Camera

iDevices are great for storing pictures and, with the new high-quality camera in the iPhone, great for taking pictures, too. By integrating the photo library with your apps, you can directly access any image stored on the device or take a new picture and use it within your application. In this hour's tutorial, we interact with the library by implementing an instance of the `UIImagePickerController` class. We display the image picker interface using the method `present ViewController:animated:completion` within our main `ViewController` instance.

Preparing the Image Picker

To use the `UIImagePickerController`, we need to state that our class will conform to a few protocols, specifically the `UIImagePickerControllerDelegate` and `UINavigationControllerDelegate` protocols.

Update the `class` line in ViewController.swift to include these new protocols:

```
class ViewController: UIViewController,
    UIImagePickerControllerDelegate, UINavigationControllerDelegate {
```

Now we're set to implement the `UIImagePickerController` using the methods described at the start of this hour. In fact, the code we use is very similar to what you've already seen.

Displaying the Image Picker

When a user touches the Choose Image button, our application triggers the method `chooseImage`. Within this method, we will initialize a `UIImagePickerController`, configure the type of media (camera or library) that it will be browsing, set its delegate, and then display it.

Enter the `chooseImage` method shown in Listing 19.17.

LISTING 19.17   Implementing the `chooseImage` Method

```
 1:  @IBAction func chooseImage(sender: AnyObject) {
 2:      let imagePicker: UIImagePickerController =
 3:          UIImagePickerController()
 4:
 5:      if toggleCamera.on {
 6:          imagePicker.sourceType =
 7:              UIImagePickerControllerSourceType.Camera
 8:      } else {
 9:          imagePicker.sourceType =
10:              UIImagePickerControllerSourceType.PhotoLibrary
11:      }
12:      imagePicker.delegate = self
13:
14:      imagePicker.modalPresentationStyle =
15:          UIModalPresentationStyle.Popover
16:      if (imagePicker.popoverPresentationController != nil) {
17:          imagePicker.popoverPresentationController!.sourceView =
18:              sender as! UIButton
19:          imagePicker.popoverPresentationController!.sourceRect =
20:              (sender as! UIButton).bounds
21:      }
22:
23:      presentViewController(imagePicker, animated: true,
24:          completion: nil)
25:  }
```

In lines 2–3, `imagePicker` is initialized as an instance of `UIImagePickerController`.

Lines 5–11 set the `sourceType` variable property of the image picker to `UIImagePickerControllerSourceType.Camera` if the `toggleCamera` switch is set to on or `UIImagePickerControllerSourceType.PhotoLibrary` if it isn't. In other words, the user can use the toggle switch to choose from photo library images or the camera.

Line 12 sets the image picker delegate to be the `ViewController` class. This means we need to implement some supporting methods to handle when the user is finished choosing a photo.

Lines 14–21 configure the view controller so that it will be presented as a popover. Since presentation styles are adaptive in iOS 9, this will only affect the iPad. Lines 17–20 only execute if a popover presentation controller is present (currently just iPads) and set the location that the popover will originate from. Refer to Hour 10 for more details on setting up popovers in this manner.

Lines 23–24 add the `imagePicker` view controller over the top of our existing view.

Showing the Chosen Image

With what we've written so far, the user can now touch the Pick Image button, but not much is going to happen when the user navigates to an image. To react to an image selection, we implement the delegate method `imagePickerController:didFinishPickingMediaWithInfo`.

Add the `imagePickerController:didFinishPickingMediaWithInfo` delegate method shown in Listings 19.18 to the ViewController.swift file.

LISTING 19.18   Handling the User's Selection of an Image

```
1:  func imagePickerController(picker: UIImagePickerController,
2:      didFinishPickingMediaWithInfo info: [String : AnyObject]) {
3:      dismissViewControllerAnimated(true, completion: nil)
4:      displayImageView.image =
5:          info[UIImagePickerControllerOriginalImage] as! UIImage!
6:  }
```

After the image is chosen, we can dismiss the image picker using `dismissViewControllerAnimated:completion` in line 3.

Lines 4–5 do the remaining work. We access the `UIImage` that the user has chosen by grabbing the object in the `info` dictionary that is referenced by the `UIImagePickerControllerOriginalImage` key. This is assigned to the `image` of `displayImageView`, displaying the image, in all its glory, in the application's view.

Cleaning Up After the Image Picker

There is still a scenario that must be accounted for before we can call the image-picking portion of our MediaPlayground application complete. A user can touch a Done button within the image picker, leaving the picker without choosing anything. The `imagePickerControllerDidCancel` delegate method was made for exactly this situation. Implement this method to dismiss the image picker by calling `dismissViewControllerAnimated:completion`.

Listing 19.19 shows the full implementation of this simple method.

LISTING 19.19   Handling the Cancellation of an Image Selection

```
func imagePickerControllerDidCancel(picker: UIImagePickerController) {
    dismissViewControllerAnimated(true, completion: nil)
}
```

You should now run the application and use the Choose Image button to display photos from the photo library and camera, as shown in Figure 19.7.

CAUTION

Be Careful When Using the Simulator!

If you're using the iOS Simulator, don't try picking an image with the camera active; you'll crash the app because we didn't check for the presence of a camera.

Our next step in this hour's lesson is implementing a Core Image filter. This is applied to the chosen image when the user presses the Apply Filter button.

FIGURE 19.7
Choose (or capture) and display photos in your application.

Implementing a Core Image Filter

In my mind, manipulating an image *should* be one of the more difficult pieces of programming that you encounter. Core Image, however, makes it easy for developers to add advanced image features to their software. In fact, implementing a filter is the easiest thing you're going to do in this hour.

Preparing and Applying a Filter

Remember that applying a filter requires that we work with an instance of a `CIImage`, but all we have is a `UIImageView`. We have to do a bit of conversion to apply the filter and then to display the result. Because we covered this earlier, the code shouldn't be a surprise. Implement the `applyFilter` method, as shown in Listing 19.20.

LISTING 19.20   Applying a Filter to the Image in the `UIImageView`

```
 1:  @IBAction func applyFilter(sender: AnyObject) {
 2:      let imageToFilter: CIImage =
 3:          CIImage(image: self.displayImageView.image!)!
 4:
 5:      let activeFilter: CIFilter = CIFilter(name: "CISepiaTone")!
 6:      activeFilter.setDefaults()
 7:      activeFilter.setValue(0.75, forKey: "inputIntensity")
 8:      activeFilter.setValue(imageToFilter, forKey: "inputImage")
 9:
10:      let filteredImage: CIImage =
11:          activeFilter.valueForKey("outputImage") as! CIImage
12:
13:      let myNewImage: UIImage = UIImage(CIImage: filteredImage)
14:      displayImageView.image = myNewImage
15:  }
```

Lines 2–3 declares a new `CIImage` called `imageToFilter` and then initializes it with the `UIImage` contained within the `displayImageView` object (a `UIImageView`).

Line 5 declares and initializes a new Core Image filter: `"CISepiaTone"`.

Line 6 sets the filter's defaults. You want to do this for any filter that you use.

Line 7 configures the filter's `"InputIntensity"` key, setting its value to a floating-point value of `0.75`. Remember, these are documented in the Core Image Filter Reference in the Xcode documentation.

Line 8 uses the filter's `"inputImage"` key to set the image that the filter will work on (`imageToFilter`), while lines 10–11 grab the filtered result in a new `CIImage` (`filteredImage`).

Finally, line 13 converts the filtered image to a new UIImage (myNewImage) using the UIImage class method imageWithCIImage. The filtered image is displayed (line 14) by assigning the displayImageView's image variable property to myNewImage.

Run the application, choose a photo, and then click the Apply Filter button. The sepia filter should remove most of the saturation from the original photo and make it look all "old timey," as shown in Figure 19.8.

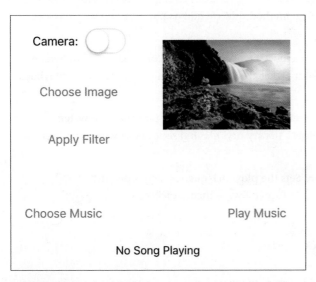

FIGURE 19.8
Apply a filter to your photos.

Our final step in this hour's lesson is accessing the music library and playing content. You'll notice quite a few similarities to using the photo library in this implementation.

Accessing and Playing the Music Library

To finish off this hour's project, we implement access to the iDevice music library—both selecting sound files and playing them. First, you use the MPMediaPickerController class to choose the music to play. We call only a single method from this class:

▶ **initWithMediaTypes:** Initializes the media picker and filters the files that are available in the picker.

We'll configure its behavior with a handful of variable properties that can be set on the object:

- ▶ `prompt`: A string that is displayed to the user when choosing songs.

- ▶ `allowsPickingMultipleItems`: Configures whether the user can choose one or more sound files.

We need to conform to the `MPMediaPickerControllerDelegate` protocol so that we can react when the user chooses a playlist. The method that we add as part of the protocol is `media Picker:didPickMediaItems`.

To play back the audio, we take advantage of the `MPMusicPlayerController` class, which can use the playlist returned by the media picker. To control starting and pausing the playback, we use four methods:

- ▶ `systemMusicPlayer`: This class method initializes the music player as the system music player, capable of accessing the music library and playing songs even when your app isn't running.

- ▶ `setQueueWithItemCollection`: Sets the playback queue using a playlist (`MPMediaItemCollection`) object returned by the media picker.

- ▶ `play`: Starts playing music.

- ▶ `pause`: Pauses the music playback.

As you can see, when you get the hang of one of the media classes, the others start to seem very familiar, using similar initialization and playback control methods.

Preparing to Use the Media Picker

Because the media picker uses the same Media Player framework as the movie player, we're already halfway done with our preparation; there's no need to import any additional files. What we do need to do, however, is state that we will be conforming to the MPMediaPickerControllerDelegate, because this enables us to react to a user's selections. Update the ViewController.swift file to include the new protocol in the class line:

```
class ViewController: UIViewController, MPMediaPickerControllerDelegate,
    UIImagePickerControllerDelegate, UINavigationControllerDelegate {
```

Preparing the Music Player

To react in a meaningful way to a selection in the media picker, we need to have a way of playing back music files. Like the movie player, audio recorder, and audio player, we want to create a new music player object that we can access from anywhere in the application.

Add a final variable property, musicPlayer, which will hold an instance of the MPMusicPlayerController class at the top of your ViewController.swift file:

```
var musicPlayer: MPMusicPlayerController!
```

That sets up the variable to refer to the music player, but we still need to create an instance of it. As we did with the audio player and recorder, we'll initialize the music player in the viewDidLoad method. Update viewDidLoad one last time, using the MPMusicPlayerController class method systemMusicPlayer to return a new instance of the music player, as demonstrated in Listing 19.21.

LISTING 19.21 The Final viewDidLoad Implementation

```
 1:   override func viewDidLoad() {
 2:       super.viewDidLoad()
 3:
 4:       try! AVAudioSession.sharedInstance()
 5:           .setCategory(AVAudioSessionCategoryPlayAndRecord)
 6:
 7:       // Setup the audio recorder
 8:       let soundFileURL: NSURL =
 9:           NSURL.fileURLWithPath(NSTemporaryDirectory()+"sound.caf")
10:
11:       let soundSetting = [
12:           AVSampleRateKey: 44100.0,
13:           AVFormatIDKey: NSNumber(unsignedInt:kAudioFormatMPEG4AAC),
14:           AVNumberOfChannelsKey: 2,
15:           AVEncoderAudioQualityKey: AVAudioQuality.High.rawValue
16:       ]
17:
18:       audioRecorder = try? AVAudioRecorder(URL: soundFileURL,
19:           settings: soundSetting)
20:
21:       // Setup the audio player
22:       let noSoundFileURL: NSURL =
23:           NSURL.fileURLWithPath(NSBundle.mainBundle()
24:           .pathForResource("norecording", ofType: "wav")!)
25:       audioPlayer = try? AVAudioPlayer(contentsOfURL: noSoundFileURL)
26:
27:       //Setup the music player
28:       musicPlayer = MPMusicPlayerController.systemMusicPlayer()
29:   }
```

The only new code is line 28, where the musicPlayer instance is assigned. We now have everything we need to display the media picker and handle playing any music files that a user may select.

Displaying the Media Picker

The display of the media picker in our application is triggered by the user touching the Choose Music button, which, in turn, starts the action `chooseMusic`.

To use a media picker, we follow steps similar to the image picker: Initialize and configure the behavior of the picker, and then show the picker's view controller. When the user is done with the picker, we add the playlist it returns to the music player and dismiss the picker view controller. If users decide they don't want to pick anything, we can dismiss the picker and move on.

Update the `ViewController.swift` file with the `chooseMusic` method in Listing 19.22.

LISTING 19.22   **Displaying the Media Picker**

```
 1:  @IBAction func chooseMusic(sender: AnyObject) {
 2:      musicPlayer.stop()
 3:      displayNowPlaying.text = "No Song Playing"
 4:      musicPlayButton.setTitle("Play Music",
 5:          forState: UIControlState.Normal)
 6:
 7:      let musicPicker: MPMediaPickerController =
 8:      MPMediaPickerController(mediaTypes: MPMediaType.Music)
 9:      musicPicker.prompt = "Choose Songs to Play"
10:      musicPicker.allowsPickingMultipleItems = true
11:      musicPicker.delegate = self
12:
13:      musicPicker.modalPresentationStyle =
14:          UIModalPresentationStyle.Popover
15:      if (musicPicker.popoverPresentationController != nil) {
16:          musicPicker.popoverPresentationController!.sourceView =
17:              sender as! UIButton
18:          musicPicker.popoverPresentationController!.sourceRect =
19:              (sender as! UIButton).bounds
20:      }
21:
22:      presentViewController(musicPicker, animated: true,
23:          completion: nil)
24:  }
```

Lines 2–5 make sure that when the picker is called the music player will stop playing its current song, the `nowPlaying` label in the interface is set to the default string `"No Song Playing"`, and the playback button is set to read Play Music. These lines aren't necessary, but they keep our interface from being out of sync with what is actually going on in the application.

Lines 7–8 initialize the media picker controller instance. It is initialized with a constant, `MPMediaType.Music`, that defines the type of files (music) the user will be allowed to choose with the picker. Line 9 sets a message that will display at the top of the music picker.

In line 10, we set the `allowsPickingMultipleItems` variable property to a Boolean value (`true` or `false`) to configure whether the user can select one or more media files.

Line 11 sets the delegate music picker's delegate. In other words, it tells the `musicPicker` object to look in the `ViewController` for the `MPMediaPickerControllerDelegate` protocol methods.

Lines 13–20 configure media picker to be displayed as a popover, just like the image picker. Again, these lines run on any iOS device, but only have an effect (currently) on the iPad.

Lines 22–23 present the music library over the top of our application's view.

Handling a User's Selection

To get the playlist that is returned by media picker (an object called `MPMediaItemCollection`) and clean up after ourselves, we add the `mediaPicker:didPickMediaItems` protocol delegate method from Listing 19.23 to our growing implementation.

LISTING 19.23   Handling a User's Music Selection

```
func mediaPicker(mediaPicker: MPMediaPickerController,
        didPickMediaItems mediaItemCollection: MPMediaItemCollection) {
    musicPlayer.setQueueWithItemCollection(mediaItemCollection)
    dismissViewControllerAnimated(true, completion: nil)
}
```

When the user finishes picking songs in the media picker, this method is called and passed the chosen items in an `MPMediaItemCollection` object, `mediaItemCollection`. For all intents and purposes, you can consider the `mediaItemCollection` object to be the equivalent of a media file playlist.

In the first line of this implementation, the music player instance, `musicPlayer`, is configured with the playlist via the `setQueueWithItemCollection:` method.

To clean things up, the view is dismissed in the second line.

Handling an Empty Selection

We've got one more situation to account for before we can wrap up the media picker: the possibility of a user exiting the media picker without choosing anything (touching Done without picking any tracks). To cover this event, we add the delegate protocol method `mediaPickerDidCancel`. As with the image picker, we just need to dismiss view controller. Add this method to the ViewController.swift file, as demonstrated in Listing 19.24.

LISTING 19.24 Handling Empty Selections in the Media Picker

```
func mediaPickerDidCancel(mediaPicker: MPMediaPickerController) {
    dismissViewControllerAnimated(true, completion: nil)
}
```

Congratulations! You're almost finished. The media picker feature is now implemented, so our only remaining task is to add the music player and make sure that the corresponding song titles are displayed.

Playing Music

Because the musicPlayer object was created in the viewDidLoad method of the view controller (see the start of "Implementing the Media Picker") and the music player's playlist was set in mediaPicker:didPickMediaItems:, the only real work that the playMusic method must handle is starting and pausing playback.

To spice things up a bit, we'll try to be a bit clever—toggling the musicPlayButton title between Play Music (the default) and Pause Music as needed. As a final touch, we access a variable property of the musicPlayer MPMusicPlayerController object called nowPlayingItem. This is an object of type MPMediaItem, which, in turn, contains a string variable called MPMediaItemPropertyTitle set to the name of the currently playing media file (if one is available).

Putting this all together, we get the implementation of playMusic in Listing 19.25.

LISTING 19.25 Implementing the playMusic Method

```
 1:  @IBAction func playMusic(sender: AnyObject) {
 2:      if musicPlayButton.titleLabel!.text == "Play Music" {
 3:          musicPlayer.play()
 4:          musicPlayButton.setTitle("Pause Music",
 5:              forState: UIControlState.Normal)
 6:
 7:          let currentSong: MPMediaItem = musicPlayer.nowPlayingItem!
 8:          displayNowPlaying.text = currentSong
 9:              .valueForProperty(MPMediaItemPropertyTitle) as! String!
10:      } else {
11:          musicPlayer.pause()
12:          musicPlayButton.setTitle("Play Music",
13:              forState: UIControlState.Normal)
14:          displayNowPlaying.text = "No Song Playing"
15:      }
16:  }
```

Line 2 checks to see whether the `musicPlayButton` title is set to Play Music. If it is, line 3 starts playback, lines 4–5 reset the button to read Pause Music, and lines 7–9 set the `displayNowPlaying` label to the title of the current audio track.

If the `musicPlayButton` title is *not* Play Music (line 10), the music is paused, the button title is reset to Play Music, and the onscreen label is changed to display No Song Playing.

After completing the method implementation, run the application on your iDevice to test it. Pressing the Choose Music button opens a media picker, as shown in Figure 19.9.

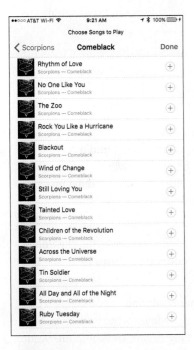

FIGURE 19.9
The media picker enables browsing the device's music library.

After you've created a playlist, press the Done button in the media picker, and then touch Play Music to begin playing the songs you've chosen. The title of the current track is displayed at the bottom of the interface.

CAUTION

The Music Library Is Not Accessible on the iOS Simulator

If you're trying to test the music playback features on the Simulator, they *will not* work. You need to use a real device for this portion of the tutorial.

This hour's lesson covered quite a bit, but consider the capabilities you've uncovered. Your projects can now tie into the same media capabilities that Apple uses in its own apps—delivering rich multimedia to your users with a relatively minimal amount of coding.

Further Exploration

We touched on only a few of the configuration options available for the MPMusicPlayerController, AVPlayer, AVPlayerViewController, AVAudioPlayer, UIImagePickerController, and MPMediaPickerController classes—but much more customization is possible if you dig through the documentation.

The AVPlayerViewController class, for example, offers the ability to set custom playback controls, and display picture in picture playback on the iPad. You can use the AVPlayer class to programmatically "scrub" through the movie by setting the playback point with the seekToTime method. As mentioned (but not demonstrated) in this lesson, this class can even play back a media file hosted on a remote URL (including streaming media).

Custom settings on AVAudioPlayer can help you create background sounds and music with variable properties such as numberOfLoops to set looping of the audio playback and volume for controlling volume dynamically. You can also enable and control advanced audio metering, monitoring the audio power in decibels for a given sound channel.

On the image side of things, the UIImagePickerController offers variables such as allowsEditing to enable the user to trim video clips or edit images directly within the image picker. Check out the capability of this class to further control a device's cameras (rear and front) and record video.

Core Image opens up new possibilities for image editing and manipulation in your apps that would have required an extensive amount of development previously. The *Core Image Programming Guide* is a great starting point for learning about Core Image, including filters, face detection, and more.

For those interested in going a step further, you may also want to review the documents *OpenGL ES Programming Guide for iOS*, *Core Animation Programming Guide*, and *Core Audio Overview*. These Apple tutorials introduce you to the 3D, animation, and advanced audio capabilities available in iOS.

As always, the Apple Xcode documentation utility provides an excellent place for exploring classes and finding associated sample code.

Apple Tutorials

AddMusic (accessible through the Xcode documentation): Demonstrates the use of the `MPMediaPickerController` and the `MPMediaPickerControllerDelegate` protocol and playback via the `MPMusicPlayerController` class.

Summary

It's hard to believe, but in the span of an hour, you've learned about ten new media classes, three protocols, and a handful of class methods and variables. These provide much of the functionality you need to create applications that handle rich media. The AV Foundation and AV Kit frameworks gives us a simple method for recording and playing back high-quality audio and video streams. The Media Player framework handles streaming audio and can even tap into the existing resources stored in the music library. The easy-to-use `UIImagePickerController` class gives us surprisingly straightforward access to visual media and cameras on the device, while Core Image allows us to manipulate our images with ease.

Because many more methods are available in the Media Player and Core Image frameworks, I recommend spending additional time reviewing the Xcode documentation if you are at all interested in building multimedia applications using these technologies.

Q&A

Q. How do I make the decision between using `MPMusicPlayerController` **versus** `AVAudioPlayer` **for sound playback in my applications?**

A. Use the `AVAudioPlayer` for audio that you include in your application bundle. Use the `MPMusicPlayerController` for playing files from the music library. Although the `MPMusicPlayerController` is capable of playing back local files, its primary purpose is integrating with the existing music library media.

Q. **I want to specifically control what camera a device is using to take a picture. How can I do this?**

A. You'll want to take a look at the `cameraDevice` variable property of the `UIImagePickerController` class. Setting this to `UIImagePickerControllerCamera.Front` will use the iPhone/iPad's front-facing camera, for example.

Workshop

Quiz

1. To apply effects to an image within an iOS application, you would likely use which framework?

   a. Core Filters

   b. Image Compositing

   c. Core Effects

   d. Core Image

2. To provide integration with the iOS Music Library, you would need to create an instance of which class?

   a. `UIAudioPlayerController`

   b. `MPMusicPlayerController`

   c. `MPMusicController`

   d. `MPMusicMediaController`

3. To configure where a `UIImagePickerController` gets its images, you would set which variable property?

   a. `sourceType`

   b. `sourceLoc`

   c. `sourceCamera`

   d. `sourceLibrary`

4. A single piece of media (such as a song in a playlist) is represented by which of the following classes?

   a. `MPAudioItem`

   b. `MPMedia`

   c. `MPItem`

   d. `MPMediaItem`

5. What method creates a music player that functions outside of the currently active application?

  a. `staticMusicPlayer`

  b. `appMusicPlayer`

  c. `systemMusicPlayer`

  d. `iOSMusicPlayer`

6. To configure an audio recorder, you must provide it with what data structure, populated with audio-specific settings?

  a. `Array`

  b. `Dictionary`

  c. `Object`

  d. `String`

7. To get rid of a media or image picker when the user cancels or chooses an item, which of the following methods should you use?

  a. `removeFromSuperView`

  b. `destroyViewControllerAnimated`

  c. `dismissViewControllerAnimated`

  d. `removeFromSubview`

8. Core Image Filters work with _____ objects, whereas we tend to use _____ within our basic application UIs.

  a. `UIImage, CIImage`

  b. `UIImage, UIImageView`

  c. `UIImageView, CIImage`

  d. `CIImage, UIImage`

9. An `AVAudioRecorder` is started using which method?

  a. `record()`

  b. `begin()`

  c. `start()`

  d. `save()`

10. To handle what happens when a user chooses a piece of media from the media picker, you should implement which protocol?

    a. `MPMediaPickerChoice`

    b. `MPMediaPickerControllerDelegate`

    c. `MPMediaPickerDelegate`

    d. `MPMediaDelegate`

Answers

1. D. The Core Image framework provides a wide range of image-manipulation features, including filters.

2. B. The `MPMusicPlayerController` provides integration with the existing iOS music library and playlists.

3. A. Use the `sourceType` variable property to choose where an image picker will get its images.

4. D. The `MPMediaItem` class represents a single piece of media and contains all the metadata for that item.

5. C. The `systemMusicPlayer` object operates across all applications, not just the current app.

6. B. Configuring a sound recorder requires creating a `Dictionary` with a number of audio-related key/value pairs.

7. C. Use the `dismissViewControllerAnimated` method to remove the "picker" views from your application interface after your user has made a selection.

8. D. The Core Image filters work with `CIImage` data, but most of the images we use are of the type `UIImage`.

9. A. To start an `AVAudioRecorder` object recording, just use the `record()` method.

10. B. To act upon a user's media choice, you should implement the `MPMediaPickerControllerDelegate` protocol to handle both selections and cancellations.

Activities

1. Return to an earlier application, adding an instance of AVAudioPlayer that plays a loop-ing background soundtrack. You need to use the same classes and methods described in this hour's lesson, as well as the numberOfLoops variable property.

2. Implement image editing with the UIImagePickerController object. To do this, you need to set the allowsImageEditing variable property and use the UIImagePickerControllerEditedImage key to access the edited image when it is returned by the UIImagePickerControllerDelegate protocol.

3. Experiment with implementing additional Core Image filters in the MediaPlayground application. Provide a user interface for configuring the filter's parameters.

Interacting with Other iOS Services

What You'll Learn in This Hour:

▶ How to compose and post updates to social networking sites
▶ Ways to create and send email with the Mail application
▶ How to access contacts
▶ Methods of displaying and manipulating map views
▶ How to forward and reverse geocode
▶ How to open URLs in Safari view controllers

In previous hours, you learned how your applications can interact with various parts of an iDevice's hardware and software. In the preceding hour, for example, you accessed the music library. In Hour 18, "Sensing Orientation and Motion," you used the accelerometer and gyroscope. It is typical of a full-featured application to leverage these unique capabilities of a device's hardware and software that Apple has made accessible through iOS. Beyond what you have learned already, the iOS applications you develop can take advantage of some additional built-in services.

Extending iOS Service Integration

In the previous hours, you've learned how to display photos that are stored on your device, take camera pictures, play iPod music, and even add web views (essentially mini Safari windows) to your apps. In this hour, you take your apps to the next level of integration by adding access to contacts, email, social networking sites Twitter and Facebook, Safari, and mapping capabilities.

Contacts

Contacts are a contained shared database of contact information that is available to any iOS application. Having a common, shared set of contact information provides a better experience for the user than if every application manages its own separate list of contacts. With shared contacts, there is no need to add contacts multiple times for different applications, and updating an individual in one application makes the update available instantly in all the other applications.

iOS provides comprehensive access to the Contacts database through two frameworks: the Contacts and the Contacts UI frameworks.

The Contacts UI Framework

The Contacts UI framework is a set of user interface classes that wrap around the Contacts framework and provide a standard way for users to work with their contacts, as shown in Figure 20.1.

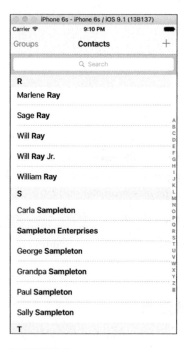

FIGURE 20.1
Access contact details from any application.

You can use the Contacts UI framework's interfaces to allow users to browse, search, and select contacts, display and edit a selected contact's information, and create new contacts. On the iPhone, the Contacts interface is displayed over top of your existing views in a modal view. You can choose to do the same on the iPad, or you can code it into a popover if you want.

To use the Contacts UI framework, you add it to your project by way of a module `import`:

```
import ContactsUI
```

To display the UI for choosing a person from the Contacts database, we must declare, initialize, and allocate an instance of the class CNContactPickerViewController. This class gives us a new view controller that displays our Contacts UI and enables us to "pick people." We must also set a delegate that will handle dealing with the person who is returned (if any).

From our main application's view controller, we display the people picker with presentViewController:animated:completion, like this:

```
let picker: CNContactPickerViewController =
    CNContactPickerViewController()
picker.delegate = self
presentViewController(picker, animated: true, completion: nil)
```

Once the people picker is displayed, our application simply waits until the user does something. The people picker handles the UI and user interactions within the Contacts interface on its own. When the user does choose something, however, we must deal with it by way of the CN contact picker delegate.

CN Contact Picker Delegate

The contact picker delegate determines what happens when a user selects a person from the displayed contacts by implementing up to three methods. The class that is implementing these methods (such as your application's view controller class) must conform to the CNContactPickerDelegate protocol.

The first delegate method that you *can* implement (but may not need) is contactPickerDidCancel. This is called if the user cancels his interactions with the people picker, and is shown in Listing 20.1. If you don't care what happens when the user cancels, you can leave this method out—no worries.

LISTING 20.1   Handling a Cancel Action in the People Picker

```
func contactPickerDidCancel(picker:
        CNContactPickerViewController) {
        // The user didn't pick anyone. Uh oh!

}
```

We can implement two other methods as part of the picker delegate, but we only have to choose one. The first, contactPicker:didSelectContact, provides us with a reference to the contact that the user touched. We can then use the Contacts framework (remember, this is all in the Contacts *UI* framework) to work with the contact information.

For example, consider Listing 20.2.

LISTING 20.2   Handling the Selection of a Person in the Contacts Database

```
func contactPicker(picker: CNContactPickerViewController,
    didSelectContact contact: CNContact) {
    // The user picked a contact. We should do something with it!
}
```

So, this seems straightforward enough, right? What could we possibly need another people picker controller delegate method for?

For when we don't want our users selecting people, of course! If you've used other applications that let you select individuals from your contacts, you'll notice that sometimes they let you drill down to choose a contact's phone number, address, email, and so on. In these cases, they're not just choosing a person, they're choosing properties that describe a person. For cases where you want this level of granularity, you *don't* implement `contactPicker:didSelectContact`, instead, you implement `contactPicker:didSelectContactProperty`, as shown in Listing 20.3.

LISTING 20.3   Handling Drilling Down to Individual Properties

```
func contactPicker(picker: CNContactPickerViewController,
    didSelectContactProperty contactProperty: CNContactProperty) {
    // Let's work with a person, and a specific property
    // within their contact details.
}
```

These methods provide the basis for interacting with the Contacts UI, but it provides no facility for working with the actual data that is returned. To do that, we must turn to the Contacts framework.

The Contacts Framework

With the Contacts framework, your application can access the Contacts database to retrieve and update contact data and create new contacts. You'll need it (obviously) to manage the data returned by the Contacts UI framework. Both of these frameworks are new, as of iOS 9, and replace older Address Book frameworks that were difficult to work with and required far more code to extract information from a contact's record.

To use the Contacts framework, `import` the corresponding module:

```
import Contacts
```

Imagine that we're implementing the `contactPicker:didSelectContact` method and have just received a variable, `contact` (of the type `CNContact`), from the method. From this reference, we can access all of the contact's data just by using the variable properties (read-only) defined within the `CNContact` class. There are *many*, so we're not going to cover all of them here; that's what documentation is for.

For example, to get the contact's first name from the variable property `givenName`, the code would look like the following:

```
let firstname: String = contact.givenName
```

Some properties might contact multiple values—such as email addresses. (I have dozens.) These are returned as an Array of `CNLabeledValue` objects. These are nothing more than a value property and a label property associated with it. My email address for day job might have the label "work," for example.

To work with `CNLabeledValue` arrays, we first index into the array to get the particular entry we want (or loop through the array to work with all of them), and then cast the value of that entry as whatever type of data we are expecting. For example, an email address is a String, whereas postal addresses are yet another object type called `CNPostalAddress`.

Let's see what some real world code might look like for checking how many email addresses a contact object has:

```
let emailCount: Int = contact.emailAddresses.count
```

The `emailAddresses` variable property gives us an Array of `CNLabeledValues` containing email strings and labels for them. Accessing the `count` property on any Array provides us with the total number of elements in that array (in this case, the total number of email addresses).

To grab the first (index 0) email address listed for the contact, we can either index into the array (`emailAddresses[0]`) or use the `first` property of the Array which acts as a shortcut for accessing index 0:

```
let emailAddress: String? =
    contact.emailAddresses.first!.value as? String
```

You get quite a bit of practice interacting with contacts in the tutorial in this hour. For a full list of all the properties that can be stored for a person (including whether they are multivalue properties), review the `CNContact` reference for iOS in the developer documentation. You may also wish to review the class reference for `CNPostalAddress` to understand how contact mailing addresses are stored.

TIP

?!?!??!!!!!????

If you've made it this far in the book and you're still wondering what requires ! versus ?, you're not alone. As mentioned early in the book, Swift is still being developed. Some values that were optional in the last edition are now required, and vice versa. Xcode does an excellent job of telling you when you should be unwrapping, when forced downcasts are required, and so on—without having to read every single piece of API docs.

In a production application, you should be checking to see whether key optional values are nil rather than just assuming they hold something. For our purposes (demonstrating core concepts), we unwrap and use the values as needed.

Email Messages

In the preceding hour, you learned how to enable a user to use Apple's image picker interfaces to select a photo for your application. Showing a system-supplied view controller is a common pattern in iOS, and the same approach is used in the Message UI framework to provide an interface for sending email, as demonstrated in Figure 20.2.

FIGURE 20.2
Present an email composition view to your users.

Your application provides the initial values for the email and then acts as a delegate while temporarily stepping out of the way and letting the user interact with the system-supplied interface for sending email. This is the same interface users use in the Mail application to send email, so they will find it familiar.

NOTE
_____

Similar to how the previous hour's app did not include any of the details of working with the iOS database of photos or music, you do not need to include any of the details about the email server your user is using or how to interact with it to send an email. iOS takes care of the details of sending email at the expense of some lower-level control of the process. The trade-off makes it very easy to send email from your application.

_____

To use the Message UI framework, `import` the MessageUI module:

```
import MessageUI
```

To display a Mail compose window, you must create a `MFMailComposeViewController` object. This handles the display of the email message. Next, you need to create an array of email addresses that will be used as recipients and use the `setToRecipients` method to configure the Mail compose view controller with the addresses. Finally, a delegate for handling completion of sending the message is assigned, and the compose view controller is presented with `present ViewController:animated:completion`. Listing 20.4 shows a simple implementation of this process.

LISTING 20.4   Preparing and Showing the Compose Dialog

```
1: let mailComposer:MFMailComposeViewController =
2:        MFMailComposeViewController()
3: let emailAddresses:[String]=["johnray@mac.com"]
4:
5: mailComposer.mailComposeDelegate=self
6: mailComposer.setToRecipients(emailAddresses)
7:
8: presentViewController(mailComposer, animated: true, completion: nil)
```

In lines 1–2, the Mail compose view controller is initialized.

Line 3 initializes the array of addresses with a single address: `"johnray@mac.com"`.

Line 5 sets the delegate for the Mail compose view controller. The delegate is responsible for handling any tasks that need to happen after the message is sent or canceled.

Line 6 assigns the recipients to the Mail compose view controller, and line 8 displays the compose window.

The Mail Compose View Controller Delegate

Like the Contacts people picker, the Mail compose view controller requires that we conform to a protocol (MFMailComposeViewControllerDelegate) that implements a cleanup method that is called when the user finishes using the compose window. This method is mailComposeController:didFinishWithResult:error. In most cases, this method needs only to dismiss the Mail Compose view controller, as shown in Listing 20.5.

LISTING 20.5   **Handling the Composition Completion**

```
func mailComposeController(controller: MFMailComposeViewController,
    didFinishWithResult result: MFMailComposeResult, error: NSError?) {
        dismissViewControllerAnimated(true, completion: nil)
}
```

If you're interested in what happened that resulted in the message composition view going away, however, you can look at the MFMailComposeResult result value, which may be one of these (self-explanatory) constants: MFMailComposeResultCancelled, MFMailComposeResultSaved, MFMailComposeResultSent, MFMailComposeResultFailed. If an error occurred when trying to display the composition window (maybe a mail account hasn't been configured?), it will be returned in the error object. We'll look a bit at some similar error-handling cases in the next hour.

Posting to Social Networking Sites

Very similar to preparing email messages with iOS is the process of posting to social networking sites. Just include the Social framework, create a compose view controller for the service you want to use, and then display it modally. Figure 20.3 shows the iOS tweet compose view in action.

Unlike Mail, however, after you've presented the compose view, you don't need to deal with any cleanup. You simply display the view and you're done. Let's take a quick look at what this might look like in code.

Like all the other frameworks, you use the Social framework by importing its module:

```
import Social
```

After that, you must create an instance of the SLComposeViewController using the class method composeViewControllerForServiceType. This specialized view controller provides the user interface and can currently target three social networking websites: Twitter, Facebook, and Sina Weibo/Tencent Weibo (Chinese) using the constants SLServiceTypeTwitter, SLServiceTypeFacebook, SLServiceTypeSinaWeibo, and SLServiceTypeTencentWeibo, respectively.

FIGURE 20.3
Provide social networking integration in your applications.

Before composing a post, it is important to use the `SLComposeViewController` class method `isAvailableForServiceType` to ensure that users have an active account configured for the service they're trying to use. Then, we can set the default text for the post, an image, and even a URL with the class methods `setInitialText`, `addImage`, and `addURL`. Finally, the controller is presented onscreen. Listing 20.6 shows an implementation example for Facebook.

LISTING 20.6   Preparing to Post to Facebook

```
let messageComposer: SLComposeViewController =
    SLComposeViewController(forServiceType: SLServiceTypeFacebook)
if SLComposeViewController.isAvailableForServiceType(SLServiceTypeFacebook) {
    messageComposer.setInitialText("Hello Facebook frenemies!")
    presentViewController(messageComposer, animated: true, completion: nil)
}
```

After presenting the view controller, there's nothing else to do. The user can use the interface to change the initial text, add personal images/locations/URLs, and, of course, post the message.

NOTE

This is just a simple example. Other methods are available to add additional functionality with multiple Twitter accounts, locations, and so on. You can also add a callback function if you want to be notified when the user is done posting. If you need more advanced social networking features, start with the Social Framework Reference in the Xcode documentation.

Accessing the Safari Web Browser

Early in the book, we used web views to display HTML content from remote websites. I even gave you a few ideas on how you *could* build your own web browser using `UIWebView`.

I'd like to apologize for that. With the new `SFSafariViewController` in iOS 9, you'd be silly to write your own browser.

iOS has, for many years, had the ability to launch other applications, including Safari, by using the `UIApplication` class's `openURL` method:

```
let webURL = NSURL(string: "https://www.apple.com")!
UIApplication.sharedApplication().openURL(webURL)
```

Unfortunately, `openURL` takes the user out of the current application and drops them into Safari. With the new `SFSafariViewController`, you can embed Safari directly in your application, and keep your users at the URL you define. Best of all, it's crazy easy to do.

To use the `SFSafariViewController`, first import the SafariServices framework:

```
import SafariServices
```

Then, initialize and present the controller:

```
let safariController = SFSafariViewController(URL:NSURL(string:
    "https://www.apple.com")!)
    self.presentViewController(safariController, animated: true, completion: nil)
```

The result is a modal Safari browser window, with access to plug-ins and share extensions, that appears directly in your app, as demonstrated in Figure 20.4.

Mapping

The iOS implementation of Apple Maps puts a responsive and fun-to-use mapping application in your palm. Yes, the original launch brought some controversy with the switch away from Google Maps, but Apple has been making rapid updates, and there is no denying that the new maps are *beautiful.* You can bring the Apple Maps experience to your apps using Map Kit.

FIGURE 20.4
The Safari View Controller provides a simple way of adding Safari's capabilities to your application.

Map Kit enables you to embed a map into a view and provides logic needed to display the map. It handles the scrolling, zooming, and loading of new map data as needed. Applications can use Map Kit to annotate locations on the map. Map Kit can also do reverse geocoding, which means getting place information (country, state, city, address) from coordinates.

You can start using Map Kit with no code at all, just by adding the Map Kit framework to your project and an `MKMapView` instance to one of your views in Interface Builder (IB). After adding a map view, you can set several properties within the Attributes Inspector to further customize the view (see Figure 20.5). You can select between map, satellite, and hybrid modes, you can determine whether the map should use Core Location (which you learn more about in the next hour) to center on the user's location, and you can control whether the user should be allowed to interact with the map through swipes and pinches for scrolling and zooming.

If you want to control your map object (`MKMapView`) programmatically, you can do so through a variety of methods. Moving and sizing the map, for example, are common activities that you may want to do programmatically. First, however, you must import the Map Kit framework module:

```
import MapKit
```

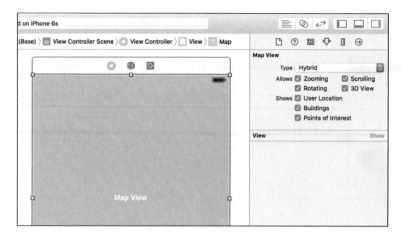

FIGURE 20.5
A map view in the Attributes Inspector.

In most cases where you manipulate a map, you also need to include the Core Location framework:

```
import CoreLocation
```

We manage our map's view by defining a map "region" and then using the setRegion:animated method. A region is a simple structure (not an object) called a MKCoordinateRegion. It has members called center, which is another structure called a CLLocationCoordinate2D (coming from Core Location and containing latitude and longitude); and span (an MKCoordinateSpan structure), which denotes how many degrees to the east, west, north, and south of the center are displayed. A degree of latitude is 69 miles. A degree of longitude, at the equator, is 69 miles. By choosing small values for the span within the region (like 0.5), we narrow our display down to just a few miles around the center point. For example, if we want to define a region centered at 60.0 degrees latitude and 60.0 degrees longitude with a span of 0.5 degrees in each direction, we can write the following:

```
let centerRegion: CLLocationCoordinate2D =

    CLLocationCoordinate2D(latitude: 60.0, longitude: 60.0)
let spanRegion:MKCoordinateSpan =
    MKCoordinateSpan(latitudeDelta: 0.5, longitudeDelta: 0.5)
let mapRegion: MKCoordinateRegion =

    MKCoordinateRegion(center: centerRegion, span: spanRegion)
```

To center and zoom in on this region in a map object called map, we use the following:

```
map.setRegion(mapRegion, animated: true)
```

Another common map activity is the addition of annotations. Annotations enable us to display important points on top of the map.

Annotations

You can add annotations to maps within your applications—just like they can in online mapping services. Using annotations usually involves implementing a new subclass of MKAnnotationView that describes how the annotation should appear and what information should be displayed.

For each annotation that we add to a map, we first need a "place mark" object, MKPlaceMark, that describes its location. For the tutorial in this hour, we need just one—to show a chosen address.

To understand how these objects come together, let's work through a quick example. To add an annotation to a map called map, we must initialize and position an MKPlacemark object. Initializing the place mark requires an address dictionary and a structure called CLLocationCoordinate2D that contains the latitude and longitude where the marker should be placed. Once initialized, the place mark is added to the map with the MKMapView method addAnnotation, as shown in the code fragment in Listing 20.7.

LISTING 20.7   Placing an Annotation

```
1: let myCoordinate: CLLocationCoordinate2D =
2:     CLLocationCoordinate2D (latitude: 20.0, longitude: 20.0)
3: let myMarker: MKPlacemark =
4:     MKPlacemark(coordinate: myCoordinate, addressDictionary: fullAddress)
5: map.addAnnotation(myMarker)
```

In this example, lines 1–2 initialize a CLLocationCoordinate2D structure (myCoordinate) that holds a latitude of 20.0 and a longitude of 20.0.

Lines 3–4 initialize a new MKPlacemark (myMarker) using myCoordinate and fullAddress, which we must create by hand using the definition of an Address structure in the ABPerson reference documentation.

Finally, line 5 adds the annotation to the map.

CAUTION

Catch Up, MapKit Engineers!

Address dictionaries are a remnant of deprecated iOS contact management frameworks called Address Book and Address Book UI. Hopefully, MapKit will be updated in the near future to be easier to work with when using the modern Contacts and Contacts UI frameworks.

TIP

To remove an existing annotation from a map view, just use `removeAnnotation` in place of `addAnnotation`; the parameters are the same.

When we add the annotation, iOS is (behind the scenes) being nice. Apple provides a subclass of the `MKAnnotationView` called `MKPinAnnotationView`. When you call `addAnnotation` on the map view object, iOS is automatically creating an instance of the `MKPinAnnotationView` for you (a pin that is placed on the map). In many cases, this is all we need. To customize the pin drop, however, we must implement the map view's delegate method `mapView:viewForAnnotation`.

Annotations and the Map View Delegate Protocol

To customize an annotation view further, we must implement the `mapView:viewForAnnotation` delegate method, and state that we are conforming the map view delegate protocol. Let's start with the easy part first. To state that we're conforming to the protocol, we will add `MKMapViewDelegate` to the `class` line of the class implementing the annotation view method, and then set the map object's `delegate` variable property to that same class. If we're implementing this in our view controller, we'll probably just be adding the line:

```
map.delegate = self
```

This can also be handled by control-dragging from the map's delegate connection to the appropriate class in Interface Builder.

After we've finished that setup, we can implement `mapView:viewForAnnotation` to return a customized marker for the map. For example, consider this implementation (see Listing 20.8), which initializes a custom instance of `MKPinAnnotationView`.

LISTING 20.8 Customizing the Annotation View

```
1: func mapView(aMapView: MKMapView,
2:   viewForAnnotation annotation: MKAnnotation) -> MKAnnotationView? {
3:   let pinDrop:MKPinAnnotationView =
4:     MKPinAnnotationView(annotation: annotation, reuseIdentifier: "myspot")
5:   pinDrop.animatesDrop=true
6:   pinDrop.canShowCallout=true
7:   pinDrop.pinTintColor=UIColor.blueColor()
8:   return pinDrop
9: }
```

Line 3–4 declares and initializes an instance of `MKPinAnnotationView` using the annotation parameter that iOS sends to the `mapView:viewForAnnotation` method (we don't touch this), along with a `reuseIdentifier` string. This `reuse` identifier is a unique identifying string that allows an allocated annotation to be reused in other places. For our purposes, this could be any string you want.

The new pin annotation view, `pinDrop`, is configured through three variable properties in lines 5–8. The `animatesDrop` Boolean variable property, when true, animates the pin dropping onto the map. The `canShowCallout` variable property sets the pin so that it displays additional information in a callout when touched, and `pinTintColor` sets the color of the onscreen pin graphic.

Once properly configured, the new pin annotation view is returned to the map view in line 8.

Adding this method (and the proper delegate/protocol lines) into your code creates purple pins with callouts that are animated when added to a map. Your applications, however, can create entirely new annotation view types that don't necessary look like pins. We're just reusing Apple's `MKPinAnnotationView` and adjusting the attributes only slightly beyond what we would get if this method were not included at all.

Geocoding

A cool feature of iOS—often used in conjunction with maps—is geocoding. Geocoding works in two "directions": forward and reverse. Forward geocoding takes an address and turns it into latitude and longitude. Reverse geocoding returns a location name for a given latitude and longitude. To geocode in iOS, you make use of the `CLGeocoder` and `CLPlacemark` classes. The `CLGeocoder` class does the hard work of translating coordinates and addresses, and the `CLPlacemark` stores the results—latitude, longitude, address, locality, and so on. What's more, you can easily turn a `CLPlacement` into an `MKPlacemark`.

So, what does all of that mean?

It means that by using a `CLGeocoder` object, you can use *just* an address to set a placemark on a map. iOS automatically takes care of looking up where the address actually is! For example, consider Listing 20.9.

LISTING 20.9   Forward Geocoding

```
1: let geocoder: CLGeocoder = CLGeocoder()
2: geocoder.geocodeAddressString(addressString, completionHandler:
3:     {(placemarks: [CLPlacemark]?, error: NSError?) -> Void in
4:     let firstPlacemark:CLPlacemark = placemarks!.first!
5:     let mapPlacemark: MKPlacemark = MKPlacemark(placemark: firstPlacemark)
6:     self.map.addAnnotation(mapPlacemark)
7: })
```

Lines 1 sets up a new instance of a CLGeocoder object. Lines 3–7 define a handler closure that is executed after the geocodeAddressString:completionHandler method is executed.

This method takes an address string and returns an array of CLPlacemark objects for each match it finds by forward geocoding the address. Because we're really only interested in *one* address, line 4 stores a reference to that CLPlacemark object in firstPlacemark.

Line 5 uses an MKPlacemark method, initWithPlacemark, to convert the CLPlacemark firstPlacemark object into an MKPlacemark named mapPlacemark.

Finally, Line 6 adds mapPlacemark to the map.

Geocoding uses your network connection to operate, so lines 3–7 *might* take a second or two to execute. Subsequent code (lines 8+) may execute *before* the code in the closure finishes, so plan accordingly. If an error occurs, the object error will be defined—so you'll want to implement error checking if getting a result is critical to your application.

Reverse geocoding works similarly to forward geocoding. The difference is that instead of providing an address to a method, you provide a CLLocation object, which contains a latitude and longitude. What you get back is another CLPlacemark, but one that is populated with address information automatically.

For example, take a look at Listing 20.10.

LISTING 20.10 Reverse Geocoding

```
1: let geocoder: CLGeocoder = CLGeocoder()
2: let theLocation: CLLocation = CLLocation(latitude: 37.7833,
3:      longitude: 122.4167)
4: geocoder.reverseGeocodeLocation(theLocation, completionHandler:
5:      {(placemarks: [CLPlacemark]?, error: NSError?) -> Void in
6:
7:          let myPlacemark: CLPlacemark = placemarks!.first!
8:          // Do something useful with the placemark data!
9: })
```

Line 1 again creates a CLGeocoder object named geocoder. Lines 2-3 creates a new CLLocation (theLocation) using the CLLocation method initWithLatitude:longitude. (I'm using the latitude and longitude for San Francisco here, for no reason in particular.)

Lines 4–9 define the reverse geocoding closure using the GLGeocoder method reverseGeocodeLocation:completionHandler. The closure is passed the theLocation parameter, and returns a list of matching placemarks in the array placemark. Again, I'm really only interested in one of the placemarks, so I assign myPlacemark to placemarks!.first! for easy referencing in my code.

Line 8 (and subsequent lines in the closure) would do something meaningful with myPlacemark. To give you an idea of what that might look like, here are a few of the variable properties that will be available in myPlacemark after the reverse geocoding takes place:

locality—The city name of the location

ocean—The name of the ocean (if the location is in an ocean!)

postalCode—The ZIP code of the location

thoroughfare—The street name of the location

country—The country that contains the location

areasOfInterest—An array of the names of points of interest in the immediate vicinity

addressDictionary—A Dictionary containing all the address information

As you can see, that's quite a bit of data that we get for "free" just by providing a latitude and longitude. We'll implement some very simple geocoding with our maps in this hour's project.

NOTE

In the next hour, we take a closer look at Core Location in Hour 21, "Implementing Location Services." Core Location gives you direct access to the GPS and compass capabilities of your device.

TRY IT YOURSELF ▼

Geocoding in the Playground

With a small bit of effort, we can turn the iOS Playground into a great place to work with geocoding. You might even call it a *playground* for geocoding.

For example, create a new iOS playground, and then enter the following code:

```
import UIKit
import CoreLocation
import XCPlayground
XCPlaygroundPage.currentPage.needsIndefiniteExecution = true
let geocoder: CLGeocoder = CLGeocoder()
let myAddress: String="Wakeman, OH"
geocoder.geocodeAddressString(myAddress, completionHandler:
    {(placemarks: [CLPlacemark]?, error: NSError?) -> Void in
        let myCoordinates:CLPlacemark=placemarks!.first!
        myCoordinates.location!.coordinate.latitude
        myCoordinates.location!.coordinate.longitude
})
```

The `import XCPlayground` line adds the module necessary to deal with code that executes over time—such as the asynchronous closure within a geocoding method. Setting the variable property `XCPlaygroundPage.currentPage.needsIndefiniteExecution = true` ensures that the code in the closure actually gets to execute.

The closure itself gets the first location returned by the forward geocoding and then displays the latitude and longitude.

After a few seconds, the column beside your code will update to show the latitude and longitude of Wakeman, Ohio.

For fun, try displaying other variable properties of the `CLPlacemark` class—and try some different addresses in `myAddress`. You can, for example, put in a string like `"Starbucks"` to find all the Starbucks in your vicinity (presumably 30 or 40).

Maps, Locations, and Permissions

In earlier editions of the book, I often mentioned during the hour's project a teensy tweak that would be needed when working with a map view—no biggie. Starting in iOS 8, Apple has umm... "refined" things enough that I need a few more words to get my point across. Previously, when you wanted to use a `MKMapView` and show a user's location, you'd check a box in Interface Builder. That's it. No code required. Now, two additional steps are needed before using location data.

You must make sure that your code creates a `CLLocationManager` object and calls either `requestWhenInUseAuthorization` or `requestAlwaysAuthorization` before attempting to use the location—*even if the location is just the built-in "blip" on a map view.* The former authorizes your app to use the location only when it is in the foreground and active, and the latter asks for location information to be available all the time.

In many projects (such as this hour's example), this comes down to creating a location manager constant in the class handling the map:

```
let locMan:CLLocationManager=CLLocationManager()
```

And a line of code in ViewDidLoad (or a method of your choice) that looks like this:

```
locMan.requestWhenInUseAuthorization()
```

Once these lines are in place, you *still* aren't good to go. You must also add one of two keys to your application's Info.plist file (in the "Supporting Files" group): `NSLocationWhenInUseUsageDescription` or `NSLocationAlwaysUsageDescription`. These keys should be set with a string value with a message you'd like displayed to the user when asking for permission to use their location, as demonstrated in Figure 20.6.

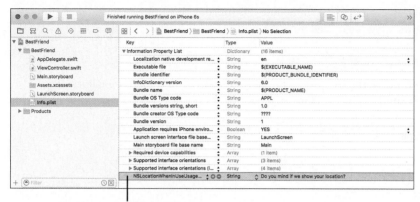

Location authorization prompt

FIGURE 20.6
Want to use the location? You'd better update your plist file.

What happens if you *don't* complete these steps? The answer is absolutely nothing. The location will not be returned, and the user will never be prompted.

Using Contacts, Email, Social Networking, Safari, and Maps

In this hour's example, we enable users to pick a contact as their best friend from their Contacts. After they have picked their best friend, we retrieve information from the Contacts database about that friend and display it nicely on the screen—including their name, photo, email address, and website. We enable users to show their friend's address in an interactive map, send that friend an email, post a tweet, or open the friend's website (all within a single app screen).

Implementation Overview

This project covers quite a bit of area, but you don't have to enter an extensive amount of code. We start by creating the interface, and then add Contacts, map, email, Twitter, and finally Safari features. Each of these requires frameworks to be included in our view controller's interface file. In other words, if something doesn't seem to be working, make sure that you didn't skip any steps on importing the framework modules.

Setting Up the Project

Start Xcode and create a new single-view iOS application called BestFriend. This tutorial has a high level of functionality, but most of the action happens in methods behind the scenes. We need to add several frameworks to accommodate this functionality, and we must add a handful of connections that we know we'll need from the start.

Adding the Frameworks

Start by adding the frameworks, by modifying ViewController.swift so that these lines are included after the existing `import` statement:

```
import MapKit
import CoreLocation
import MessageUI
import Social
import Contacts
import ContactsUI
import SafariServices
```

Planning the Variables and Connections

Within our application, we allow users to select a contact, and we display a name, email address, photo, and website for the person they choose. We show the name and email strings through two labels (`UILabel`) named name and email, and the image by way of a `UIImageView` named photo. For the website, we use a button named web and modify its title to show the URL. This, incidentally, gives us a convenient way of opening a Safari view when the URL is touched.

Finally, we have an onscreen map (`MKMapView`) referenced through an outlet we name map, and an instance of the Core Location Location Manager (`CLLocationManager`) to ask our users to use location services. We'll call this `locMan`.

The application also implements four actions: newBFF, which is called to enable the user to choose a new friend from Contacts; sendEmail, to send an email to your buddy; sendTweet, to post a tweet to your Twitter timeline; and openWeb to open the friend's website.

Designing the Interface

Now, open the Main.storyboard interface file, switch to a manageable simulated screen size, and build the application UI. The BestFriend app is a sandbox of features. Instead of me trying to describe where everything goes, take a look at Figure 20.7 to see my approach to an interface.

Drag a new instance of a map view (`MKMapView`) into the interface. This is the map view that ultimately displays your location and the city your buddy is in. Use the Attributes Inspector (Option-Command-4) to set the map to show the user location. This adds an animated annotation that shows the user's location.

I've sized my map to cover a little over half of the screen with the idea that my friend's photo and details will be superimposed over top of the map.

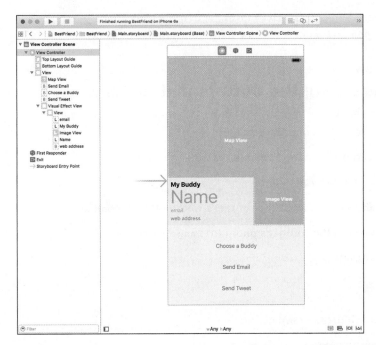

FIGURE 20.7
Create the application interface to resemble this (or use your own design).

Add three labels (`UILabel`): one (bold) that acts as a title (`My Buddy`), another for your friend's name, and the third for his or her email address. Below the labels, add a UIButton and set the Control alignment to left justified and the font size to match the font of the labels (System 14.0). We'll use the button like a label, but it will also be able to respond to touch.

Add an image view (`UIImageView`) that will hold your buddy's photograph from the Contacts. Use the Attributes Inspector to change the image scaling to Aspect Fit. I've positioned mine to the right of the labels and button.

In my UI, I've placed all of these elements inside a `UIVisualEffectView`, but you can use a `UIView` with a translucent white background or whatever you want. This view is positioned overlapping the bottom 25% or so of the map.

Finally, add three buttons (`UIButton`): one to choose a buddy (titled `Choose a Buddy`), another to email your buddy (titled `Send Email`), and the last to post a tweet (`Send Tweet`) to your Twitter account.

Configuring the Map View

After adding the map view, select it and open the Attributes Inspector (Option-Command-4). Use the Type drop-down menu to pick which type of map to display (satellite, hybrid, or standard), and then activate all the interaction options. This makes the map show the user's current location and enables the user to pan and zoom within the map view (just like in the iOS Maps application).

Creating and Connecting the Outlets and Actions

You've done this a thousand times (okay, maybe a few dozen), so this should be pretty familiar. You need to define a total of five outlets and three actions:

▶ **The label that will contain the contact's name (`UILabel`):** name

▶ **The email address label (`UILabel`):** email

▶ **The button that will show and launch the contact's website (`UIButton`):** web

▶ **The image view for showing the contact's photo (`UIImageView`):** photo

▶ **The map view (`MKMapView`):** map

And four actions:

▶ **The Choose Buddy button (`UIButton`):** newBFF

▶ **The Send Email button (`UIButton`):** sendEmail

▶ **The Send Tweet button (`UIButton`):** sendTweet

▶ **The Web Address button (`UIButton`):** openWeb

Switch to the assistant editor with Main.storyboard and the ViewController.swift file open to begin making connections.

Adding the Outlets

Control-drag from the label that will display our chosen contact's name to just below the `class` line at the top of ViewController.swift. When prompted, name the new outlet name. Repeat this for the email address label, connecting it to an outlet named `email` and the web address button, connecting it to (guess what) `web`. Do the same for the image view, connecting to an outlet named `photo`. Finally, Control-drag from the map view to ViewController.swift, creating a new outlet named `map`.

Adding the Actions

Next, create the new actions. Control-drag from the Choose Buddy button to below the variable properties you've just created. When prompted, create a new action called `newBFF`. Following the same process, connect the Send Email button to an action named `sendEmail`, and the Send

Tweet button to `sendTweet`. Lastly, connect the web address button to a new action named `openWeb`.

As mentioned earlier, our map view implementation can include a delegate method (`mapView:viewForAnnotation`) for customizing the display of annotations. To set the map view's delegate to our view controller, we can write `map.delegate=self` in code, or we can connect the map view's delegate outlet to the view controller line in our IB document outline.

Select the map view and open the Connections Inspector (Option-Command-6). Drag from the delegate outlet to the view controller line in the document outline area, as shown in Figure 20.8.

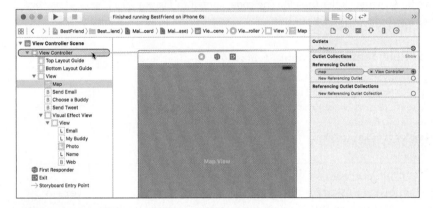

FIGURE 20.8
Set the delegate for the map view.

With those connections, you're done with the interface and its connections. Even though we will be presenting interfaces for email, Twitter, Safari and Contacts, these elements are going to be generated entirely in code.

Implementing the Contacts Logic

There are two parts to accessing the Contacts database: displaying a view that allows the user to choose a contact (an instance of the class `ABPeoplePickerNavigationController`) and reading the data that corresponds to that contact. Two steps... two frameworks that we need to use.

Conforming to the People Picker Delegate Protocol

Before we access either the Contacts UI or the internal data, we must indicate that we intend to implement the `CNContactPickerViewController` protocol.

Modify the ViewController.swift file and update the class line, adding CNContactPickerDelegate to show that we are conforming to the Contact Picker Delegate protocol:

```
class ViewController: UIViewController, CNContactPickerDelegate {
```

Displaying the Contacts Picker View

When the user presses the button to choose a buddy, we want to show the Contacts picker view controller, which will provide the user with the familiar interface from the Contacts application.

Update the `newBFF` method in ViewController.swift to initialize and present a picker, setting the picker's delegate to the view controller (`self`). The code, shown in Listing 20.11, should be very similar to what you saw earlier in this hour.

LISTING 20.11   Implementing the `newBFF` Method

```
1: @IBAction func newBFF(sender: AnyObject) {
2:     let picker: CNContactPickerViewController =
3:         CNContactPickerViewController()
4:     picker.delegate = self
5:     presentViewController(picker, animated: true, completion: nil)
6: }
```

In lines 2–3, we declare `picker` as an instance of `CNContactPickerViewController`—a graphical user interface (GUI) object that displays the system's Contacts database. Line 4 sets its delegate to our `ViewController` (`self`).

Line 5 displays the people picker as a view over top of our existing user interface.

Choosing, Accessing, and Displaying Contact Information

For the BestFriend application, we want to know only the friend the user has selected; we don't want the user to go on and select or edit the contact's properties. This means we should implement the `contactPicker:didSelectContact` delegate method; this will be our workhorse for the project. We don't really care if the user cancels while selecting a user, so no other delegate methods are required.

The `contactPicker:didSelectContact` delegate method is called automatically when a user touches a contact's name, and with it we are passed the selected person as an CNContact (part of the Contacts framework that we imported earlier).

For this example, we read five things: the person's name, picture, email address, web address, and postal address. We also check whether the `contact` record has a picture before attempting to read it.

Unfortunately, we need to manipulate a bit of the `contact` data before we can display it. For example, with the contact image, we only have access to the image data, so we'll need the `imageWithData` initialization method of `UIImage`.

For the email address, web address, and postal address, we must deal with the possibility of multiple values being returned in an Array. For these pieces of data, we access the first value that we find, convert them to Strings or, in the case of postal address, an object of the type `CNPostalAddress`.

Sounds complicated? It's not the prettiest code, but it's not difficult to understand. Add the delegate method `contactPicker:didSelectContact` to the ViewController.swift file, as shown in Listing 20.12.

LISTING 20.12   Handling the Selection of a Contact

```
 1: func contactPicker(picker: CNContactPickerViewController,
 2:     didSelectContact contact: CNContact) {
 3:     name.text = "\(contact.givenName) \(contact.familyName)"
 4:     email.text = contact.emailAddresses.first!.value as? String
 5:     web.setTitle(contact.urlAddresses.first!.value as? String,
 6:         forState: UIControlState.Normal)
 7:     if contact.imageDataAvailable {
 8:         photo.image = UIImage(data: contact.imageData!)
 9:     }
10:     showAddress(contact.postalAddresses.first!.value
11:         as! CNPostalAddress)
12: }
```

Let's walk through the logic we've implemented here. First, note that when the method is called, it is passed a `contact` variable of the type `CNContact`. This is a reference to the person who was chosen and is used throughout the method.

Line 3 sets the `name` label to the contact's first and last names (`givenName` and `familyName`, respectively) using String interpolation.

Line 4 grabs the first email address stored for the contact (`emailAddresses.first`), casts it as a String and set the `email` label to the result.

Lines 5–6 use get the first web address stored for the contact (`urlAddresses.first`), casts it as a String, and sets the title of the web button to the result.

Line 6 checks the property `imageDataAvailable`. If it is `true`, line 8 is executed, loading the photo `imageview` with the image stored for the contact (`imageData`).

Lines 10–11 pass the first address for the contact (`postAddresses.first`) to a method `showAddress` that we'll write next. This method will display the address on a map. Addresses are managed using objects of the type `CNPostalAddress`, so that is what we pass to the method.

Implementing the Map Logic

Earlier in the hour, we added two frameworks to the project: Core Location, which deals with locations; and Map Kit, which displays the embedded Apple Maps. We're going to do three things with the map:

► First, we'll show our current location.

► Second, we're going to center and zoom it around the address the user has chosen.

► Third, we'll add an annotation (a pushpin marker) at the address, making it easy to pick out.

Requesting Permission to Use the User's Location

Even though we check a little box on the map settings to show a user's location, it isn't going to work unless we explicitly ask for permissions. To do this, we need to create an instance of the `CLLocationManager` object, and then use the `requestWhenInUseAuthorization`. We'll also need to add a new key to the project's plist file. Hooray.

Add a new constant, `locMan`, to the end of list of `IBOutlets` that you've defined at the top of the ViewController.swift file:

```
let locMan:CLLocationManager=CLLocationManager()
```

Next, update the `viewDidLoad` method to include a call to the authorization method, as shown in Listing 20.13.

LISTING 20.13   Update the `viewDidLoad` Method to Ask for Location Authorization

```
override func viewDidLoad() {
    super.viewDidLoad()
    locMan.requestWhenInUseAuthorization()
}
```

Finish off the authorization process by updating the project's plist file. Use the Project Navigator to open the Supporting Files group and click the Info.plist file.

Expand the Information Property List entry, and position your cursor over its name. A plus button appears to the right of the name. Click that button. Within the Key field, type `NSLocationWhenInUseUsageDescription`. Make sure that the Type column is set to string, and then type a message in the Value field, such as `Do you mind if we show your loca-tion?`. Figure 20.9 shows the setting within my version of the project.

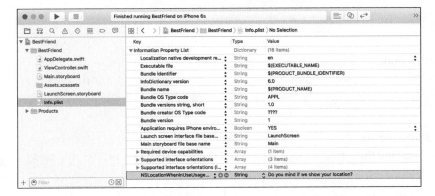

FIGURE 20.9
Add a message to display when the application prompts for location data.

Controlling the Map Display

We've got the display of the map and the user's current location with the `MKMapView`, so the only other map tasks we need to handle are geocoding and annotation. To keep things nice and neat in our application, we implement all this functionality in a new method called `showAddress`. `showAddress` takes one input: a `CNPostalAddress` (the address object pulled from Contacts). The `CLGeocoder` class does all the heavy lifting of looking up the address and finding its latitude and longitude, but is written to work with an older style of address structures—not `CNPostalAddress` objects. For that reason, we'll need to take the components of the address (street, state, and so on) and put them into a string for processing.

Open ViewController.swift and enter the new `showAddress` method shown in Listing 20.14.

LISTING 20.14 Centering the Map and Adding an Annotation

```
 1: func showAddress(f:CNPostalAddress) {
 2:     let addressString: String =
 3:         "\(f.street),\(f.city),\(f.state),\(f.postalCode)"
 4:     let geocoder: CLGeocoder = CLGeocoder()
 5:     geocoder.geocodeAddressString(addressString, completionHandler:
 6:         {(placemarks: [CLPlacemark]?, error: NSError?) -> Void in
 7:             let friendPlacemark:CLPlacemark = placemarks!.first!
 8:             let mapRegion:MKCoordinateRegion =
 9:                 MKCoordinateRegion(
10:                 center: friendPlacemark.location!.coordinate,
11:                 span: MKCoordinateSpanMake(0.2, 0.2))
12:             self.map.setRegion(mapRegion, animated: true)
```

```
13:                let mapPlacemark: MKPlacemark =
14:                    MKPlacemark(placemark: friendPlacemark)
15:                self.map.addAnnotation(mapPlacemark)
16:        })
17: }
```

Let's explore how this works. The `CNPostalAddress` is passed into the method in the variable `f`. Why did I use `f`? Because the original name, `fullAddress`, caused the subsequent lines to wrap without there being *anywhere* I could break the line and still have it be valid code. Thanks Swift!

I digress. Lines 2–3 take the variable properties of the address object (`street`, `city`, `state`, `postalCode`) and combine them into a single string (`addressString`) that will be processed by the geocoder.

Line 4 by declares a new instance of a Core Location geocoder object: `geocoder`. As you may recall from earlier in this hour's lesson, the geocoder function `geocoder.geocodeAddressString` method takes an address string and creates a `CLPlacemark` object with its location, which can then be accessed by a closure. This is precisely what happens in lines 5–17.

Line 5 performs forward geocoding on the `addressString`. When the geocoding completes, lines 7–15 are executed.

Line 7 stores the first `CLPlacemark` returned by the geocoding in the object `friendPlacemark`. This object contains a variable property, `location`, which, in turn, contains another variable, `coordinate` that holds latitude and longitude values. We can use this `coordinate` value directly when creating out map region.

Lines 8–11 use the `coordinate` value and a calculated span to define the region of the map to display and then use `setRegion:animated` (line 12) to redraw the map accordingly. This is identical to the map-centering approach we explored earlier this hour. Review the earlier code if you have any concerns about the logic.

Finally, lines 13–14 handle the annotation. In lines 13–14, we create a new map place-mark (`MKPlacemark`), `mapPlacemark`, using the Core Location placemark (`CLPlacemark`) `friendPlacemark`.

With the `friendPlacemark` defined, we can add it to the map using the `addAnnotation` method in line 15.

Customizing the Pin Annotation View

Earlier in the hour, you learned that if you want to customize your annotation view, you can conform to `MKMapViewDelegate` protocol and implement the `mapView:viewForAnnotation` map view delegate method. Update the ViewController.swift file now to include the MKMapViewDelegate protocol:

```
class ViewController: UIViewController,
    CNContactPickerDelegate, MKMapViewDelegate {
```

To implement the custom annotation view, we'll use exactly the same code as in Listing 20.8. The code is included again here (Listing 20.15) for your reference.

LISTING 20.15 Customizing the Annotation View

```
 1: func mapView(aMapView: MKMapView,
 2:     viewForAnnotation annotation: MKAnnotation) -> MKAnnotationView? {
 3:         let pinDrop:MKPinAnnotationView =
 4:             MKPinAnnotationView(annotation: annotation,
 5:                 reuseIdentifier: "myspot")
 6:         pinDrop.animatesDrop=true
 7:         pinDrop.canShowCallout=true
 8:         pinDrop.pinTintColor=UIColor.blueColor()
 9:         return pinDrop
10: }
```

Implementing the Email Logic

In this example of using the Message UI framework, we want to allow users to email a buddy by pressing the Send Mail button. We populate the To field of the email with the address that we located in the Contacts database. The user can then use the interface provided by the MFMailCompose ViewController to edit the email and send it.

Conforming to the Mail Compose Delegate Protocol

The class implementing the Message UI framework (in this case, ViewController) must also conform to the MFMailComposeViewControllerDelegate, which includes a method mailComposeController:didFinishWithResult that is called after the user is finished sending a message. Update the class line in ViewController.swift to include this protocol:

```
class ViewController: UIViewController,
    CNContactPickerDelegate, MKMapViewDelegate,
    MFMailComposeViewControllerDelegate {
```

Displaying the Mail Compose View

To compose a message, we need to initialize an instance of MFMailComposeViewController. The recipients are configured with the MFMailComposeViewController method setToRecipients. One item of interest is that the method expects an array, so we need to take the email address for our buddy and create an array with a single element in it so that we can use the method. Once configured, the message composition view is displayed with presentViewController:animated:completion.

Speaking of the email address, where will we access it? Glad you asked. Earlier we set the email UILabel to the address, so we just use email.text to get the address of our buddy.

Create the sendEmail method using Listing 20.16 as your guide.

LISTING 20.16   Configuring and Displaying the Mail Compose View

```
1: @IBAction func sendEmail(sender: AnyObject) {
2:     let emailAddresses:[String]=[self.email.text!]
3:     let mailComposer:MFMailComposeViewController =
4:         MFMailComposeViewController()
5:     mailComposer.mailComposeDelegate=self;
6:     mailComposer.setToRecipients(emailAddresses)
7:     presentViewController(mailComposer, animated: true, completion: nil)
8: }
```

There are few surprises here. Line 2 defines an array, emailAddresses, that contains a single element grabbed from the email UILabel.

Lines 3–4 declare mailComposer as an instance of the MFMailComposeViewController—the object that displays and handles message composition. Lines 5–6 configure the MFMailCompose ViewController object, setting its delegate to self (ViewController) and the recipient list to the emailAddresses array. Line 7 presents the Mail compose window onscreen.

Do More for Your Users!

Be sure to read the MFMailComposeViewController documentation to see what other methods can help you customize the mail composer content before it is displayed. For example, the setSubject method will set a subject, while setMessageBody:isHTML sets the content of the message itself. You can use these (and other methods) to populate the mail composer view so that when it appears, your user may just need to tap Send without having to type any additional information.

Handling Mail Completion

When a user is finished composing/sending a message, the composition window should be dismissed. To do this, we need to implement the mailComposeController:didFinishWith Result method defined in the MFMailComposeViewControllerDelegate protocol—exactly as demonstrated in Listing 20.5, re-created here for your reference (see Listing 20.17).

Add this to your ViewController.swift file. Note that Apple says that this method is *expected* but *optional*. If you leave it out, the application works, but if it's expected, we'd better include it!

LISTING 20.17   Dismissing the Mail Compose View

```
func mailComposeController(controller: MFMailComposeViewController,
    didFinishWithResult result: MFMailComposeResult, error: NSError?) {
        dismissViewControllerAnimated(true, completion: nil)
}
```

A single line to dismiss the view controller, and we're good to go.

Implementing the Social Networking Logic

The next piece of the BestFriend application is adding the logic behind the `sendTweet` method. When a user presses the Send Tweet button, we want to display a tweet compose window with the default text "Hello all - I'm currently in <somewhere>!". Huh? Where's <somewhere>? Well, it's going to depend on where you're standing. We're going to have our tweet automatically filled in with the *reverse* geocoded name of our current location.

Using the basic social networking features doesn't require any delegate methods or protocols to be added, so `importing` the framework, as we did at the start of the project, is all we need to start tweeting.

Displaying the Compose View

To display a tweet compose window, we complete four tasks:

1. Declare, allocate, and initialize an instance of the `SLComposeViewController`.

2. Use the compose view controller class method `isAvailableForServiceType` to verify that we're even allowed to use Twitter.

3. Create a default message to be displayed by calling the compose view controller instance method `setInitialText`. Obviously, if you don't want to create a default message, this is optional.

4. Display the view with our old standby, `presentViewController:animated: completion`.

So, where is the reverse geocoding going to fit in this process? The geocoding closure is going to wrap around it. We'll use our `map` object to access `map.userLocation.location`—a structure containing the user's latitude and longitude. This will be passed to the geocoder, which will figure out where we are. After it has made the determination, and *then* we complete the four steps required to display a tweet composition window with a default tweet.

Open ViewController.swift and implement our last method, `sendTweet`, as shown in Listing 20.18.

LISTING 20.18   Implementing a Simple Tweet Compose View

```
 1: @IBAction func sendTweet(sender: AnyObject) {
 2:     let geocoder: CLGeocoder = CLGeocoder()
 3:     geocoder.reverseGeocodeLocation(map.userLocation.location!,
 4:         completionHandler:
 5:         {(placemarks: [CLPlacemark]?, error: NSError?) -> Void in
 6:             let myPlacemark:CLPlacemark = placemarks!.first!
 7:             let tweetText:String =
 8:                 "Hello all - I'm currently in \(myPlacemark.locality!)!"
 9:
10:             let tweetComposer: SLComposeViewController =
11:             SLComposeViewController(forServiceType: SLServiceTypeTwitter)
12:
13:             if SLComposeViewController.isAvailableForServiceType(
14:                 SLServiceTypeTwitter) {
15:                 tweetComposer.setInitialText(tweetText)
16:                 self.presentViewController(tweetComposer,
17:                     animated: true, completion: nil)
18:             }
19:     })
20: }
```

Line 2 initializes a new Core Location geocoder object (`CLGeocoder`): geocode. Lines 3–5 begin the closure that is executed when geocoding is completed. Here we use `reverseGeocodeLocation:completionHandler`, with `map.userLocation.location` as the argument. This takes the current location of the user—as provided by our map object—and figures out where the person is (city, address, and so on).

Line 6 grabs the first location returned by the geocoder and stores it in a Core Location placemark (`CLPlacemark`) named `myPlacemark`. This object contains all the information returned by the geocoder.

In lines 7–8, we use `myPlacemark.locality` (the name of the user's city) to create a string, `tweetText`, that will be displayed as a default tweet in the tweet composition window.

Lines 10–11 declare `tweetComposer`, an instance of the social networking compose view controller of the type `SLServiceTypeTwitter`. Lines 13-14 check to make sure we are allowed to send tweets for that same service type. If we can, Line 15 sets the initial tweet to `tweetText`, and Lines 16-17 display `tweetComposer`.

One more little method and we're all done.

Implementing the Safari View Controller

The final piece of our application is implementing the method `openWeb`. Recall that this action is called when the user touches the button whose title is set to the friend's web address. It should open a Safari view controller containing the website.

Implement `openWeb` as shown in Listing 20.19

LISTING 20.19 Open a URL Using Safari Web Views

```
@IBAction func openWeb(sender: AnyObject) {
    let safariController = SFSafariViewController(URL: NSURL(string:
        web.titleForState(UIControlState.Normal)!)!)
    presentViewController(safariController, animated: true, completion: nil)
}
```

Only two lines of code in this method (broken across three lines, but still...). The first initializes the Safari View Controller (`safariController`) using the title of the web button as the URL.

The second line presents `safariController` onscreen.

Find a mirror, look around nervously, and now take a bow. You've finished the BestFriend app.

Setting the Status Bar to White (Optional)

Depending on how you positioned the map in your interface, you might want to switch the iOS status bar to a light color, rather than the default black. To lighten the status bar, add the method in Listing 20.20 to your ViewController.swift file

LISTING 20.20 Setting the Status Bar Appearance in `preferredStatusBarStyle`

```
override func preferredStatusBarStyle() -> UIStatusBarStyle {
    return UIStatusBarStyle.LightContent
}
```

Building the Application

Use Run to test the application. I highly recommend using an actual device, because as of this writing, the Simulator is not handling email properly. (Trying to enter anything in the email fields will crash the app.)

Select a contact (choose one that includes *all* the attributes that we access) and watch as the map finds your friend's home location, zooms in, and then sets an annotation. Use the Email button to compose and send an email. Try tweeting. Touch the web address. Fun and excitement for all.

In this project, shown in Figure 20.10, we've combined mapping, email, Twitter, Safari, and Contact features in a single integrated application. You should now have some ideas about what is possible when you integrate existing iOS services into your software.

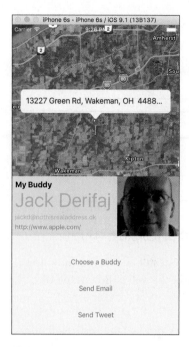

FIGURE 20.10
Mapping, email, Twitter, Safari, and Contact integration—all in one app.

Further Exploration

Over the past few hours, you've learned much of what there is to know about accessing images, music, and sending email, but we haven't even scratched the surface of the Contact and Contact UI frameworks. In fact, the Contact UI framework contains three additional modal view controllers. You can use the framework to create new contacts, set properties, and edit and delete contacts. Anything the Contacts application can do, you can do with the framework. For more detailed information about the use of these APIs, refer to the excellent framework guides in the iOS Help. Beware of a guide called the *Address Book Programming Guide for iOS* – this is still included in the documentation, but refers to an *old* method for working with contact data. It's ugly.

In addition, review the Apple guide for Map Kit and complete the Core Location exercises in the next hour. Using these two frameworks, you can create complex map annotation views (MKAnnotationView) well beyond the simple pushpin annotations presented here. You can deploy these features in nearly any application that works with addresses or locations.

If your application presents a social networking opportunity, implementing Twitter and Facebook support is both fast and straightforward. What is shown here, however, only scratches the surface of what the Social framework can do. Refer to Apple's Social framework reference for more examples of this exciting new tool.

Once you've mastered these integration topics, check out the *Calendar and Reminders Programming Guide*, which introduces you to Event Kit and Event Kit UI frameworks. Similar in design and function to the Contacts frameworks, these provide access to the iOS Calendar and Reminder information, including the ability to create new events and reminders directly in your application.

Summary

In this hour, you learned how to allow the user to interact with contacts from the Contact database, how to send email messages, open Safari views, tweet, and how to interact with the Map Kit and Core Location frameworks. Although there are some challenges to working with Contact data (lots of embedded data structures), after you've established the patterns to follow, it becomes much easier. The same goes for the Map Kit and Core Location features. The more you experiment with the coordinates and mapping functions, the more intuitive it will be to integrate them into your own applications. As for email and Safari, there's not much to say: They're easy to implement *anywhere*.

Q&A

Q. Can I use the `MKMapView` when my device is offline?

A. No, the map view requires an Internet connection to fetch its data.

Q. Is there a way to differentiate between address (mailing or email) types in the Contact data?

A. Yes. Although we did not use these features in our code, you can identify specific types (home, work, and so on) of addresses when reading Contact data by examining the `label` properties (we only used the `value`).

Workshop

Quiz

1. An onscreen map is an instance of what class?

    a. `UIMapView`

    b. `MKMapView`

    c. `MapView`

    d. `CLMapView`

2. The framework responsible for providing social networking interaction is known simply as what?

    a. Core Data

    b. Social

    c. SNetworking

    d. Twitbook

3. The CNContactPickerDelegate protocol requires that a minimum of how many methods be implemented?

    a. 1

    b. 2

    c. 3

    d. 4

4. The people picker, mail interface, safari view, and twitter composer views are all displayed using which method?

    a. `displayViewController:animated:completion`

    b. `presentViewController:completion`

    c. `displayViewController:completion`

    d. `presentViewController:animated:completion`

5. Forward geocoding takes which of the following as input?

    a. Latitude and longitude

    b. An address

    c. An address book

    d. A person

6. Accessing data for an individual contact requires us to use what class?

    a. `ABContact`

    b. `ABContactData`

    c. `CNContactData`

    d. `CNContact`

7. Contact addresses are returned as an Array of this object?

    a. `ABPostalAddress`

    b. `CNPostalAddress`

    c. `ABAddressList`

    d. `CNAddressList`

8. To zoom in on a portion of a map, which of the following methods should you use?

    a. `setRegion:animated`

    b. `setRegion`

    c. `getRegion:animated`

    d. `zoomRegion:animated`

9. Geocoding will only work in the iOS Playground if you set the playground to do what?

    a. Run in the iOS Simulator

    b. Show invisibles

    c. Run outside of the iOS Simulator

    d. Run in the foreground

10. A location on a map is known as a what?

    a. Pin

    b. Location mark

    c. Placemark

    d. Mark

Answers

1. B. Maps are displayed via the `MKMapView` object.

2. B. The Social framework provides all the social networking features in iOS.

3. A. The `CNContactPickerDelegate` protocol requires just a single method be implemented in order to function.

4. D. The views within this hour's exercises make heavy use of the `presentView Controller:animated:completion` method.

5. B. An address is all that forward geocoding requires as input.

6. D. We use the `CNContact` object to access attributes of an individual contact.

7. B. The Contacts framework gives us access to an individual's addresses as an Array of `CNPostalAddress` objects.

8. A. To zoom in on a portion of an `MKMapView`, you should use the `setRegion:animated` method.

9. A. Geocoding in the iOS Playground will result in an error unless you've set it to run in the iOS Simulator.

10. C. A location on a map (in iOS land) is known as a place mark.

Activities

1. Apply what you learned in Hour 15, "Reading and Writing Application Data," and make the BestFriend application persist the name and photo of the selected friend so that the user doesn't need to repeat the selection each time the application is run.

2. Enhance the BestFriend application to include, by default, your current location (city and street) in the email message composition window.

3. Update the iPad version of the project so that the Person Picker is displayed in a popover rather than taking over the entire screen.

4. Add error checking throughout the application so that picking a contact that *doesn't* include all the accessed attributes does not crash the application.

Implementing Location Services

What You'll Learn in This Hour:

▶ The available iOS location-sensing hardware
▶ How to read and display location information
▶ Detecting orientation with the compass

In the preceding hour's lesson, we looked briefly at the use of Map Kit to display map information in an application. In this lesson, we take the GPS capabilities of our devices a step further: We tie into the hardware capabilities of the iDevice lineup to accurately read location data and compass information.

In this hour, we work with Core Location and the electromagnetic compass. With location-enabled apps enhancing the user experience in areas such as Internet searches, gaming, and even productivity, you can add value and interest to your own offerings with these tools.

Understanding Core Location

Core Location is a framework in the iOS SDK that provides the location of the device. Depending on the device and its current state (within cell service, inside a building, and so forth), any of three technologies can be used: GPS, cellular, or WiFi. GPS is the most accurate of these technologies and will be used first by Core Location if GPS hardware is present. If the device does not have GPS hardware (WiFi iPads, for example), or if obtaining the current location with GPS fails, Core Location falls back to cellular and then to WiFi.

Getting Locations

Core Location is simple to understand and to use despite the powerful array of technologies behind it. (Some of it had to be launched into space on rockets.) Most of the functionality of Core Location is available from the location manager, which is an instance of the `CLLocationManager` class. You use the location manager to specify the frequency and accuracy of the location updates you are looking for and to turn on and off receiving those updates.

To use a location manager, you must first import the Core Location framework to your project. This can be done with a single statement:

```
import CoreLocation
```

Next, you initialize an instance of the location manager, specify a delegate that will receive location updates, ask the user for permission to use her location (more on that in a second), and then start the updating, like this:

```
let locMan: CLLocationManager = CLLocationManager()
locMan.delegate = self
locMan.requestWhenInUseAuthorization()
locMan.startUpdatingLocation()
```

When the application has finished receiving updates (a single update is often sufficient), stop location updates with location manager's `stopUpdatingLocation` method.

Requesting Authorization and the Plist File

As you learned in the preceding hour, previous versions of iOS (before 8) automatically asked for permission to use a user's location. In iOS 9, this (as you can seen in the previous code snippet) is now an explicit action. You must make sure your code calls either `requestWhenInUseAu-thorization` or `requestAlwaysAuthorization` before attempting to use the location. The former authorizes your app to use the location only when it is in the foreground and active, whereas the latter asks for location information to be available all the time. Apple advises against using `requestAlwaysAuthorization` unless you have a really good reason to track location in the background.

In addition to making the request for permission, you must also add one of two keys to your application's Info.plist file (in the Supporting Files group): `NSLocationWhenInUseUsageDescription` or `NSLocationAlwaysUsageDescription`. These keys should be set with a string value with a message you'd like displayed to the user when asking for permission to use their location.

If you leave these methods or plist keys out of your project, it will likely sit there and do absolutely nothing. This is a big change over earlier versions of the system, so don't rush your code!

Location Manager Delegate

The location manager delegate protocol defines the methods for receiving location updates. Whatever class we've designated as our delegate for receiving location updates must conform to the `CLLocationManagerDelegate` protocol.

Two methods in the delegate relate to location: `locationManager:didUpdateLocations` and `locationManager:didFailWithError`.

The `locationManager:didUpdateToLocations` method's argument are the location manager object and an array `CLLocation` objects. (Multiple locations may be returned depending on how quickly you're moving.) A `CLLocation` instance provides a coordinate variable property that is a structure containing `longitude` and `latitude` expressed in `CLLocationDegrees`. `CLLocationDegrees` is just an alias for a floating-point number of type `double`.

As already mentioned, different approaches to geolocating have different inherit accuracies, and each approach may be more or less accurate depending on the number of points (satellites, cell towers, WiFi hot spots) it has available to use in its calculations. `CLLocation` passes this confidence measure along in the `horizontalAccuracy` variable property.

The location's accuracy is provided as a circle, and the true location could lie anywhere within that circle. The circle is defined by the `coordinate` variable property as the center of the circle and the `horizontalAccuracy` as the radius of the circle in meters. The larger the `horizontalAccuracy`, the larger the circle defined by it will be, so the less confidence there is in the accuracy of the location. A negative `horizontalAccuracy` indicates that the `coordinate` is completely invalid and should be ignored.

In addition to longitude and latitude, each `CLLocation` provides altitude (in meters) above or below sea level. The `altitude` property is a `CLLocationDistance`, which is, again, just a floating-point number. A positive number is an altitude above sea level, and a negative number is below sea level. Another confidence factor, this one called `verticalAccuracy`, indicates how accurate the altitude is. A positive `verticalAccuracy` indicates that the altitude could be off, plus or minus, by that many meters. A negative `verticalAccuracy` means the `altitude` is invalid.

Listing 21.1 shows an implementation of the location manager delegate's `locationManager:didUpdateToLocations` method that logs the longitude, latitude, and altitude.

LISTING 21.1   Implementing Location Updates

```
 1: func locationManager(manager: CLLocationManager,
 2:         didUpdateLocations locations: [CLLocation]) {
 3:     let newLocation: CLLocatlion=locations[0]
 4:
 5:     var coordinateDesc:String = "Not Available"
 6:     var altitudeDesc:String = "Not Available"
 7:
 8:     if newLocation.horizontalAccuracy >= 0 {
 9:       coordinateDesc =
10:         "\(newLocation.coordinate.latitude), \(newLocation.coordinate.longitude)"
11:       coordinateDesc = coordinateDesc +
12:           " +/- \(newLocation.horizontalAccuracy) meters"
```

```
13:      }
14:
15:      if newLocation.verticalAccuracy >= 0 {
16:          altitudeDesc = "\(newLocation.altitude)"
17:          altitudeDesc = altitudeDesc +
18:              " +/- \(newLocation.verticalAccuracy) meters"
19:      }
20:
21:      NSLog("Lat/Long: \(coordinateDesc)   Altitude: \(altitudeDesc)")
22: }
```

The key statements to pay attention to in this implementation are the references to the accuracy measurements in lines 8 and 15, and accessing the `latitude`, `longitude`, and `altitude` in lines 9–12, and 16–18. These are just variable properties, something you've grown accustomed to working with over the past 20 hours.

One element in this example that you might not be familiar with is line 21's `NSLog` function. `NSLog`, which you learn to use in Hour 24, "Application Tracing, Monitoring, and Debugging," provides a convenient way to output information (often debugging information) without having to design a view.

The resulting output looks like this:

```
Lat/Long: 35.904392, -79.055735 +/- 76.356886 meters
Altitude: 28.000000 +/- 113.175757 meters
```

CAUTION

Watch Your Speed

`CLLocation` also provides a variable property `speed`, which is based on comparing the current location with the prior location and comparing the time and distance variance between them. Given the rate at which Core Location updates, `speed` is not very accurate unless the rate of travel is fairly constant.

Handling Location Errors

As I wrote earlier, before using a user's location, you must prompt for permission (this only occurs once, if the user accepts), as shown in Figure 21.1.

FIGURE 21.1
Core Location asks permission to provide an application with location data.

If the user chooses to disallow location services, iOS does not prevent your application from running, but instead generates errors from the location manager.

When an error occurs, the location manager delegate's `locationManager:didFailWith Error` method is called, letting you know the device cannot return location updates. A distinction is made as to the cause of the failure. If the user denies permission to the application, the error argument is `CLError.Denied`; if Core Location tries but cannot determine the location, the error is `CLError.LocationUnknown`; and if no source of trying to retrieve the location is available, the error is `CLError.Network`. Usually Core Location continues to try to determine the location after an error. After a user denial, however, it doesn't, and it is good form to stop the location manager with location manager's `stopUpdatingLocation` method. Listing 21.2 shows a simple implementation of `locationManager:didFailWithError`.

LISTING 21.2   Reacting to Core Location Errors

```
1: func locationManager(manager: CLLocationManager,
2:         didFailWithError error: NSError) {
3:      if error.code == CLError.Denied.rawValue {
4:         NSLog("Permission to retrieve location is denied.")
5:         locMan.stopUpdatingLocation()
6:      } else if error.code==CLError.Network.rawValue {
```

```
 7:              NSLog("Network used to retrieve location is unavailable.")
 8:          } else if error.code==CLError.LocationUnknown.rawValue {
 9:              NSLog("Currently unable to retrieve location.")
10:          }
11: }
```

As with the previous example implementation of handling location manager updates, in the error handler we also work solely with the objects the method receives. In lines 3, 6, and 8, we check the incoming NSError object's code variable property against the possible error conditions and react accordingly. Note that in order to make the comparison, we must add rawValue to the end of each core location error constant.

CAUTION

Please Wait While I Get My Bearings

Keep in mind that the location manager delegate will not immediately receive a location. It usually takes a number of seconds for the device to pinpoint the location, and the first time it is used by an application, Core Location first asks the user's permission. You should have a design in place for what the application will do while waiting for an initial location and what to do if location information is unavailable because the user didn't grant permission or the geolocation process failed. A common strategy that works for many applications is to fall back to a user-entered ZIP code.

Location Accuracy and Update Filter

It is possible to tailor the accuracy of the location to the needs of the application. An application that needs only the user's country, for example, does not need 10-meter accuracy from Core Location and will get a much faster answer by asking for a more approximate location. You do this by setting the location manager's desiredAccuracy variable property, before you start the location updates. desiredAccuracy is an enumerated type, CLLocationAccuracy. Six constants are available with varying levels of precision (with current consumer technology, the first two are the same): kCLLocationAccuracyBest, kCLLocationAccuracyNearestTenMeters, kCLLocationAccuracyBestForNavigation, kCLLocationAccuracyNearestHundred Meters, kCLLocationAccuracyKilometer, and kCLLocationAccuracyThreeKilometers.

After updates on a location manager are started, updates continue to come into the location manager delegate until they are stopped. You cannot control the frequency of these updates directly, but you can control it indirectly with location manager's distanceFilter variable property. distanceFilter is set before starting updates and specifies the distance in meters the device must travel (horizontally, not vertically) before another update is sent to the delegate.

For example, starting the location manager with settings suitable for following a walker's progress on a long hike might look like this:

```
let locMan: CLLocationManager = CLLocationManager()
locMan.delegate = self
locMan.desiredAccuracy = kCLLocationAccuracyHundredMeters
locMan.distanceFilter = 200
locMan.requestWhenInUseAuthorization()
locMan.startUpdatingLocation()
```

CAUTION

Location Comes with a Cost

Each of the three methods of locating the device (GPS, cellular, and WiFi) can put a serious drain on the device's battery. The more accurate an application asks the device to be in determining location, and the shorter the distance filter, the more battery the application will use. Be aware of the device's battery life and only request as accurate and as frequent location updates as the application needs. Stop location manager updates whenever possible to preserve the battery life of the device.

Getting Headings

The location manager includes a `headingAvailable` variable property that indicates whether the device is equipped with a magnetic compass. If the value is `YES`, you can use Core Location to retrieve heading information. Receiving heading events works similarly to receiving location update events. To start receiving heading events, assign a location manager delegate, assign the `headingFilter` variable property for how often you want to receive updates (measured in degrees of change in heading), and call the `startUpdatingHeading` method on the location manager object:

```
locMan.delegate=self
locMan.headingFilter=10
locMan.startUpdatingHeading()
```

CAUTION

North Isn't Just "Up"

There isn't one true north. Geographic north is fixed at the North Pole, and magnetic north is located hundreds of miles away and moves every day. A magnetic compass always points to magnetic north; but some electronic compasses, like the one in the iPhone and iPad, can be programmed to point to geographic north instead. Usually, when we deal with maps and compasses together, geographic north is more useful. Make sure that you understand the difference between geographic and magnetic north and know which one you need for your application. If you are going to use the heading relative to geographic north (the `trueHeading` variable property), request location updates as well as heading updates from the location manager; otherwise, the `trueHeading` won't be properly set.

The location manager delegate protocol defines the methods for receiving heading updates. Two methods in the delegate relate to headings: `locationManager:didUpdateHeading` and `locationManagerShouldDisplayHeadingCalibration`.

The `locationManager:didUpdateHeading` method's argument is a `CLHeading` object. The `CLHeading` object makes the heading reading available with a set of variable properties: the `magneticHeading` and the `trueHeading`. (See the relevant Caution.) These values are in degrees, and are of type `CLLocationDirection`, which is a floating-point number. In plain English, this means that

▶ If the heading is 0.0, we're going north.

▶ When the heading reads 90.0, we're headed due east.

▶ If the heading is 180.0, we're going south.

▶ Finally, if the heading reads 270.0, we're going west.

The `CLHeading` object also contains a `headingAccuracy` confidence measure, a `timestamp` of when the reading occurred, and an English language description that is more suitable for logging than showing to a user. Listing 21.3 shows an implementation example of the `location Manager:didUpdateHeading` method.

LISTING 21.3   **Handling Heading Updates**

```
 1:  func locationManager(manager: CLLocationManager,
 2:          didUpdateHeading newHeading: CLHeading) {
 3:      var headingDesc: String = "Not Available."
 4:      if newHeading.headingAccuracy >= 0 {
 5:          let trueHeading: CLLocationDirection =
 6:              newHeading.trueHeading
 7:          let magneticHeading: CLLocationDirection  =
 8:              newHeading.magneticHeading
 9:          headingDesc =
10:  "\(trueHeading) degrees (true), \(magneticHeading) degrees (magnetic)"
11:      }
12:      NSLog(headingDesc)
13:  }
```

This implementation looks very similar to handling location updates. We check to make sure there is valid data (line 4), and then we grab the true and magnetic headings from the `true-Heading` and `magneticHeading` variable properties passed to us in the `CLHeading` object (lines 5–8). The output generated looks a bit like this:

```
180.9564392 degrees (true), 182.684822 degrees (magnetic)
```

The other delegate method, `locationManager:ShouldDisplayHeadingCalibration`, literally consists of a line returning `true` or `false`. This indicates whether the location manager can display a calibration prompt to the user. The prompt asks the user to step away from any source of interference and to rotate the device 360 degrees. The compass is always self-calibrating, and this prompt is just to help that process along after the compass receives wildly fluctuating readings. It is reasonable to implement this method to return `false` if the calibration prompt would be annoying or distracting to the user at that point in the application (in the middle of data entry or game play, for example).

NOTE
_____
The iOS Simulator reports that headings are available, and it provides just one heading update.
_____

Creating a Location-Aware Application

Many iOS and Mac users have a, shall we say, "heightened" interest in Apple Computer; visiting Apple's campus in Cupertino, California, can be a life-changing experience. For these special users, we're going to create a Core Location-powered application that keeps you informed of just how far away you are.

Implementation Overview

The application is created in two parts: The first introduces Core Location and displays the number of miles from the current location to Cupertino. In the second section, we use the device's compass to display an arrow that points users in the right direction, should they get off track.

In this first installment, we create an instance of a location manager and then use its methods to calculate the distance between our current location and Cupertino, California. While the distance is being determined, we display a Please Wait message. In cases where we happen to be *in* Cupertino, we congratulate the user. Otherwise, a display of the distance, in miles, is shown.

Setting Up the Project

For the rest of this hour, we work on a new application that uses the Core Location framework. Create a new single-view iOS application in Xcode and call it **Cupertino**.

Adding Background Image Resources

To ensure that the user remembers where we're going, we have a nice picture of an apple as the application's background image. Click the main Assets.xcassets asset catalog to open the project's image assets. Now, within the Finder, drag the project's Images folder into the left column of the asset catalog in Xcode. The new addition to the asset catalog contains apple.png, our background image, along with several other images we'll be using later.

Planning the Variables and Connections

The view controller serves as the location manager delegate, receiving location updates and updating the user interface to reflect the new locations. Within the view controller, we need a constant or variable property for an instance of the location manager. We will name this **locMan**.

Within the interface itself, we need a label with the distance to Cupertino (`distanceLabel`) and two subviews (`distanceView` and `waitView`). The `distanceView` contains the `distanceLabel` and is shown only after we've collected our location data and completed our calculations. The `waitView` is shown while our iDevice gets its bearings.

Adding Location Constants

To calculate the distance to Cupertino, we obviously need a location in Cupertino that we can compare to the user's current location. According to http://gpsvisualizer.com/geocode using Google Maps as the source, the center of Cupertino, California, is at 37.3229978 latitude, –122.0321823 longitude. Add two constants for these values (`kCupertinoLatitude` and `kCupertinoLongitude`) after the `class` line in the ViewController.swift file:

```
let kCupertinoLatitude: CLLocationDegrees = 37.3229978
let kCupertinoLongitude: CLLocationDegrees = -122.0321823
```

You can ignore the errors that appear regarding the unknown type `CLLocationDegrees`. This is a data type that will be defined for us in a few minutes when we include the Core Location framework.

Designing the View

The user interface for this hour's lesson is simple: We can't perform any actions to change our location (teleportation isn't yet possible), so all we need to do is update the screen to show information about where we are.

Open the Main.storyboard file and use the Attributes Inspector to switch to a "normal" simulated screen size. Next, open the Object Library (View, Utilities, Show Object Library), and commence design:

1. Start by adding an image view (`UIImageView`) onto the view and position it so that it covers the entire view. This serves as the background image for the application.

2. With the image view selected, open the Attributes Inspector (Option-Command-4). Select apple from the Image drop-down menu.

3. Drag a new view (`UIView`) on top of the image view. Size it to fit in the bottom of the view; it serves as our primary information readout, so it needs to be sized to hold about two lines of text.

4. Use the Attributes Inspector to set the background to black. Change the Alpha to 0.75, and check the Hidden check box.

5. Add a label (`UILabel`) to the information view. Size the label up to all four edge guidelines and change the text to read **Lots of miles to the Mothership**. Use the Attributes Inspector to change the text color to white, aligned center, and sized as you want. Figure 21.2 shows my view.

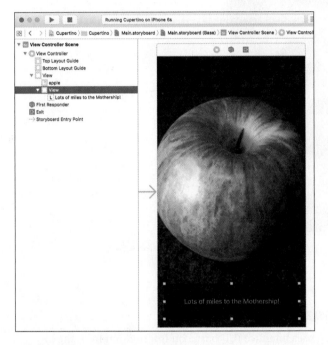

FIGURE 21.2
The beginnings of the Cupertino Locator UI.

6. Create a second semitransparent view with the same attributes as the first, but *not* hidden, and with a height of about an inch.

7. Drag the second view to vertically center it on the background. This view will contain the Please Wait message while the device is finding our location.

8. Add a new label to the view that reads **Checking the Distance**. Resize the label so that it takes up approximately the right two-thirds of the view.

9. Drag an activity indicator (`UIActivityIndicatorView`) to the new view and align it to the left side of the label. The indicator shows a "spinner" graphic to go along with our Checking the Distance label. Use the Attributes Inspector to set the Animated attribute; it makes the spinner spin.

The final view should resemble Figure 21.3.

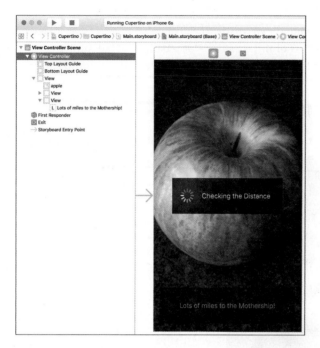

FIGURE 21.3
The final Cupertino Locator UI.

Creating and Connecting the Outlets

In this exercise, all we do is update the user interface (UI) based on information from the location manager. In other words, there are no actions to connect (hurray). We need connections from the two views we added as well as the label for displaying the distance to Cupertino.

Switch to the assistant editor. Control-drag from the Lots of Miles label to below the `class` line in ViewController.swift. Create a new outlet named **distanceLabel** when prompted. Do the same for the two views, connecting the view with the activity indicator to a `waitView` outlet and the view that contains the distance estimate to a `distanceView` outlet.

Implementing the Application Logic

Based on the interface we just laid out, the application starts up with a message and a spinner that let the user know that we are waiting on the initial location reading from Core Location. We'll request this reading as soon as the view loads in the view controller's `viewDidLoad` method. When the location manager delegate gets a reading, we calculate the distance to Cupertino, update the label, hide the activity indicator view, and unhide the distance view.

Preparing the Location Manager

To use Core Location and create a location manager, we need to make a few changes to our setup to accommodate the framework. First, update ViewController.swift by importing the Core Location module, and then add the CLLocationManagerDelegate protocol to the class line. The top of ViewController.swift file should now look at bit like this:

```
import UIKit
import CoreLocation
class ViewController: UIViewController, CLLocationManagerDelegate {
```

Our project is now prepared to use the location manager, but we still need to add and initialize a constant to use it (locMan).

Update the code at the top of your ViewController.swift file one last time, so that it reads as follows:

```
import UIKit
import CoreLocation

class ViewController: UIViewController, CLLocationManagerDelegate {

    @IBOutlet weak var waitView: UIView!
    @IBOutlet weak var distanceView: UIView!
    @IBOutlet weak var distanceLabel: UILabel!

    let locMan: CLLocationManager = CLLocationManager()

    let kCupertinoLatitude: CLLocationDegrees = 37.3229978
    let kCupertinoLongitude: CLLocationDegrees = -122.0321823
```

It's time to configure the location manager and distance calculation code.

Configuring the Location Manager Instance

To use the location manager, we must first configure it. Update the viewDidLoad method in ViewController.swift, and set self as the delegate, a desiredAccuracy of kCLLocationAccuracyThreeKilometers, and a distanceFilter of 1,609 meters (1 mile). Request permission to use the location with requestWhenInUseAuthorization, and then start the updates with the startUpdatingLocation method. The implementation should resemble Listing 21.4.

LISTING 21.4   Creating the Location Manager Instance

```
override func viewDidLoad() {
    super.viewDidLoad()
    locMan.delegate = self
    locMan.desiredAccuracy = kCLLocationAccuracyThreeKilometers
    locMan.distanceFilter = 1609; // a mile
```

```
locMan.requestWhenInUseAuthorization()
locMan.startUpdatingLocation()
}
```

If you have any questions about this code, refer to the introduction to location manager at the start of this hour's lesson. This code mirrors the examples from earlier, with some slightly changed numbers.

Implementing the Location Manager Delegate

Now we need to implement the two methods of the location manager delegate protocol. We start with the error condition: `locationManager:didFailWithError`. In the case of an error getting the current location, we already have a default message in place in the `distanceLabel`, so we just remove the `waitView` with the activity monitor and show the `distanceView`. If the user denied access to Core Location updates, we also shut down location manager updates. Implement `locationManager:didFailWithError` in ViewController.swift, as shown in Listing 21.5.

LISTING 21.5 Handling Location Manager Errors

```
1:  func locationManager(manager: CLLocationManager,
2:          didFailWithError error: NSError) {
3:     if error.code == CLError.Denied.rawValue {
4:         locMan.stopUpdatingLocation()
5:     } else {
6:         waitView.hidden = true
7:         distanceView.hidden = false
8:     }
9:  }
```

In this error handler, we're only worried about the case of the location manager not being able to provide us with any data. In line 3, we check the error code to make sure access wasn't denied. If it was, the location manager is stopped (line 4).

In line 6, the wait view is hidden and the distance view, with the default text of Lots of miles to the Mothership, is shown (line 7).

NOTE

In this example, I use `locMan` to access the location manager. I could have used the `manager` variable provided to the method; there really wouldn't have been a difference in the outcome. Because we have the variable property, however, using it consistently makes sense from the perspective of code readability.

Our next method (`locationManager:didUpdateLocations`) does the dirty work of calculating the distance to Cupertino. This brings us to one more hidden gem in `CLLocation`. We don't
need to write our own longitude/latitude distance calculations because we can compare two
`CLLocation` instances with the `distanceFromLocation` method. In our implementation of
`locationManager:didUpdateLocations`, we create a `CLLocation` instance for Cupertino
and compare it to the instance we get from Core Location to get the distance in meters. We
then convert the distance to miles, and if it's more than 3 miles, we show the distance with an
`NSNumberFormatter` used to add a comma if more than 1,000 miles. If the distance is less than
3 miles, we stop updating the location and congratulate the user on reaching "the Mothership."
Listing 21.6 provides the complete implementation of `locationManager:didUpdate`
`Locations`.

LISTING 21.6   Calculating the Distance When the Location Updates

```
 1: func locationManager(manager: CLLocationManager,
 2:         didUpdateLocations locations: [CLLocation]) {
 3:     let newLocation: CLLocation=locations[0]
 4:     if newLocation.horizontalAccuracy >= 0 {
 5:         let Cupertino:CLLocation = CLLocation(
 6:             latitude: kCupertinoLatitude,
 7:             longitude: kCupertinoLongitude)
 8:         let delta:CLLocationDistance =
 9:             Cupertino.distanceFromLocation(newLocation)
10:         let miles: Double = (delta * 0.000621371) + 0.5 // to miles
11:         if miles < 3 {
12:             // Stop updating the location
13:             locMan.stopUpdatingLocation()
14:             // Congratulate the user
15:             distanceLabel.text = "Enjoy the\nMothership!"
16:         } else {
17:             let commaDelimited: NSNumberFormatter =
18:                 NSNumberFormatter()
19:             commaDelimited.numberStyle =
20:                 NSNumberFormatterStyle.DecimalStyle
21:             distanceLabel.text=commaDelimited
22:                 .stringFromNumber(miles)!+" miles to the\nMothership"
23:         }
24:         waitView.hidden = true
25:         distanceView.hidden = false
26:     }
27: }
```

The method starts off in line 3 by grabbing the first location returned in the `locations` array and storing it in `newLocation`.

Line 4 checks the new location to see whether it is useful information (an accuracy greater than zero). If it is, the rest of the method is executed; otherwise, we're done.

Lines 5–7 create a `CLLocation` object (`Cupertino`) with the latitude and longitude of Cupertino.

Lines 8–9 create a `CLLocationDistance` variable named `delta`. Remember that `CLLocationDistance` isn't an object; it is a double-precision floating-point number, which makes using it quite straightforward. The number is the distance between the `CLLocation` (`Cupertino`) object we just made and `newLocation`.

In line 10, the conversion of the distance from meters to miles is calculated and stored in miles.

Lines 11–16 check to see whether the distance calculated is less than 3 miles. If it is, the location manager is stopped, and the message `Enjoy the Mothership` is added to the distance label.

If the distance is greater than or equal to 3 miles, we initialize a number formatter object called `commaDelimited` in lines 17–18. Lines 19–20 set the style for the formatter.

TIP

Number formatters work by first setting a style for the object with the `setNumberStyle` method (in this case, `NSNumberFormatterDecimalStyle`). The `NSNumberFormatterDecimalStyle` setting defines decimal numbers with properly placed commas (for example, 1,500).

Once configured, the formatter can use the method `stringFromNumber` to output a nicely formatted number as a string.

Lines 21–22 set the distance label to show the number of miles (as a nicely formatted number).

Lines 24 and 25 hide the "wait" view and show the distance view, respectively.

Setting the Status Bar to White

One final method and we're done with code. Like some of the other projects in this book, Cupertino has a dark background that obscures the iOS status bar. To lighten it up, add the method in Listing 21.7 to your ViewController.swift file.

LISTING 21.7 Setting the Status Bar Appearance in `preferredStatusBarStyle`

```
override func preferredStatusBarStyle() -> UIStatusBarStyle {
    return UIStatusBarStyle.LightContent
}
```

Updating the Project's Plist file

Before the application can run, there's one more piece of work we need to complete: adding the location prompt string to the application's plist file. Using the Project Navigator, find and click the Info.plist file.

Expand the Information Property List entry, and then position your cursor over its name. A plus button appears to the right of the name. Click that button. Within the Key field, type **NSLocationWhenInUseUsageDescription**. Make sure the Type column is set to string, and then type a friendly message in the Value field, such as **Let's find Cupertino!**. Figure 21.4 shows the setting within my version of the project.

Location Prompt

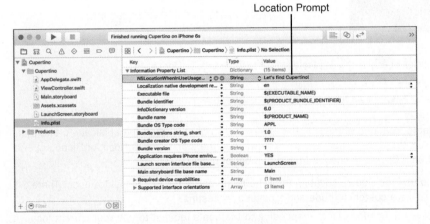

FIGURE 21.4
Add a message to display when the application prompts for location data.

Building the Application

Choose Run and take a look at the result. Your application should, after determining your location, display the distance to Cupertino, California, as shown in Figure 21.5.

FIGURE 21.5
The Cupertino application in action showing the distance to Cupertino, California.

TIP

You can set simulated locations when your app is running. To do this, start the application, and then look at the bottom-center of the Xcode window. You will see the standard iOS "location" icon appear (among other controls). Click it to choose from a number of preset locations.

Another option is to use the Debug, Location from the menu bar in the iOS Simulator itself. There, you can easily configure a custom latitude and longitude for testing.

Note that you must set a location before responding to the app's request to use your current location; otherwise, it assumes that no locations are available as soon as you click OK. If you make this mistake, stop the application's execution in Xcode, uninstall the app from the iOS Simulator, and then run it again. This forces it to prompt for location information again.

Adding the iOS Blur

In a few places in the book, I've mentioned how the iOS blur effect can be added to your interface; this is another one of those places. In this hour's projects, for example, you have several UIViews (waitView and distanceView) that are slightly transparent.

If you've followed along with my other blurry examples, adding the blur effect here should be no problem:

1. Remove the existing `waitView` and `distanceView` and their outlets. Add two Visual Effects Views with Blur to the design. These will become your new `waitView` and `distanceView` objects.

2. Add the appropriate labels and objects to the UIViews contained within effects views.

3. Add new outlets for the two effects views—naming them `waitView` and `distanceView` (the same as the old UIViews) respectively.

4. Because the effects views are named the same as the original UIViews, nothing else needs to change. The effects views (and their content) are hidden and shown appropriately.

That should do the trick. Anytime you want to use the blur effect, just replace your UIViews with visual effects views and you'll have users squinting in no time.

Using the Magnetic Compass

The iPhone 3GS was the first iOS device to include a magnetic compass. Since its introduction, the compass has been added to the iPad. It is used in Apple's Compass application and in the Maps application (to orient the map to the direction you are facing). The compass can also be accessed programmatically within iOS, which is what we look at now.

Implementation Overview

As an example of using the compass, we are going to enhance the Cupertino application and provide the users with a left, right, or straight-ahead arrow to get them pointed toward Cupertino. As with the distance indicator, this is a limited look at the potential applications for the digital compass. As you work through these steps, keep in mind that the compass provides information much more accurate than what we're indicating with three arrows.

Setting Up the Project

Depending on your comfort level with the project steps we've already completed this hour, you can continue building this directly off the existing Cupertino application or create a copy. You'll find a copy of Cupertino Compass, which includes the additional compass functionality for comparison, in this hour's projects folder.

Open the Cupertino application project, and let's begin by making some additions to support the use of the compass.

Adding the Direction Image Resources

The Images folder that you added to the asset catalog in the Cupertino project contains three arrow images: arrow_up.png, arrow_right.png, and arrow_left.png. If you removed these extra images from your first project (thought you were being clever, didn't you?), add them back in now.

Planning the Variables and Outlets

To implement our new visual direction indicator, the view controller requires an outlet to an image view (UIImageView) to show the appropriate arrow. We'll name this **directionArrow**.

We also need the *last* location that we were at, so we create another variable property called **recentLocation**. We need to store this because we'll be doing a calculation on each heading update that uses the current location. We implement this calculation in a new method called **headingToLocation:current**.

Adding Radian/Degree Conversion Constants

Calculating a relative direction requires some rather complicated math. The good news is that someone has already written the formulas we need. To use them, however, we need to be able to convert between radians and degrees.

Add two constants to ViewController.swift, following the latitude and longitude for Cupertino. Multiplying by these constants allows us to easily perform our conversions:

```
let kDeg2Rad: Double = 0.0174532925
let kRad2Deg: Double = 57.2957795
```

Updating the User Interface

To update our application for the compass, we need to add a new image view to the interface, as follows:

1. Open the Main.storyboard file and the Object Library.

2. Drag an image view (UIImageView) onto the interface, positioning it above the waiting view.

3. Using the Attributes Inspector (Option-Command-4), set the image for the view to up_arrow.

4. We'll be setting this dynamically in code, but choosing a default image helps with designing the view.

5. Use the Attributes Inspector to configure the image view as hidden; you can find this in the Drawing settings of the View section of the attributes. We don't want to show a direction until we've calculated one.

6. Using the Size Inspector (Option-Command-5), set the width and height of the image view to be 150 points × 150 points.

7. Adjust the view so that it is centered nicely on the screen and not overlapping the "waiting" view. Feel free to shift things around as you see fit.

My final UI resembles Figure 21.6.

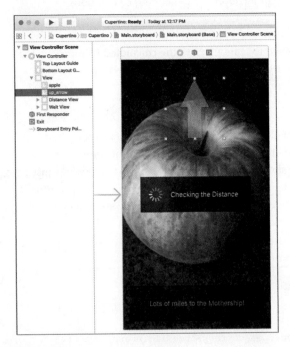

FIGURE 21.6
The updated Cupertino application UI.

Creating and Connecting the Outlet

When finished with your interface, switch to the assistant editor and make sure that ViewController.swift is showing on the right. We need to make a single connection for the image view we just added. Control-drag from the image view to just below the last @IBOutlet line. When prompted, create a new outlet named **directionArrow**.

We can now wrap up our app by implementing heading updates. Switch back to the standard editor and open the ViewController.swift file.

Updating the Application Logic

To finish the project, we must do four things:

1. We need to ask our location manager instance to start updating us whenever it receives a change in heading.

2. We need to store the current location whenever we get an updated location from Core Location so that we can use the most recent location in the heading calculations.

3. We must implement logic to get a heading between our current location and Cupertino.

4. When we have a heading update, we need to compare it to the calculated heading toward Cupertino and change the arrow in the UI if any course adjustments need to be made.

Starting Heading Updates

Before asking for heading updates, we should check with the location manager to see whether heading updates are available via the class method `headingAvailable`. If heading updates aren't available, the arrow images are never shown, and the Cupertino application works just as before. If `headingAvailable` returns `true`, set the heading filter to 10 degrees of precision and start the updates with `startUpdatingHeading`. Update the `viewDidLoad` method of the ViewController.swift file, as shown in Listing 21.8.

LISTING 21.8 **Requesting Heading Updates**

```
 1:  override func viewDidLoad() {
 2:      super.viewDidLoad()
 3:      // Do any additional setup after loading the view
 4:      locMan.delegate = self
 5:      locMan.desiredAccuracy = kCLLocationAccuracyThreeKilometers
 6:      locMan.distanceFilter = 1609; // a mile
 7:      locMan.requestWhenInUseAuthorization()
 8:      locMan.startUpdatingLocation()
 9:
10:      if CLLocationManager.headingAvailable() {
11:          locMan.headingFilter = 10 // 10 degrees
12:          locMan.startUpdatingHeading()
13:      }
14:  }
```

The squeaky-clean new code just takes up four lines. In line 10, we check to see whether a heading is available. If one is, we ask to be updated only if a change in heading is 10 degrees or more (line 11). In line 12, the location manager instance is asked to start updating us when there are heading changes. If you're wondering why we didn't just set a delegate, it's because the location manager already has one set from our earlier code in line 4. This means that our class must handle both location updates and heading updates.

Storing the Recent Location

To store the recent location, we need to declare a new variable property that we can use in our methods; this, like the location manager, should be declared after the `class` line in

ViewController.swift. Unlike the location manager, however, the recent location needs to be a variable property—not a constant—because it is going to be updated over time.

Locations are managed as objects of type CLLocation; we'll name ours **recentLocation**. Update the code at the top of ViewController.swift to include this new variable. The block should now read as follows:

```
import UIKit
import CoreLocation

class ViewController: UIViewController, CLLocationManagerDelegate {

    @IBOutlet weak var waitView: UIView!
    @IBOutlet weak var distanceView: UIView!
    @IBOutlet weak var distanceLabel: UILabel!
    @IBOutlet weak var directionArrow: UIImageView!

    let locMan: CLLocationManager = CLLocationManager()
    var recentLocation: CLLocation!
```

Next, we need to add a line to set recentLocation to the value of newLocation in the loc ationManager:didUpdateLocations method. We should also stop updating the heading if we are within 3 miles of the destination, just as we stopped updating the location. Listing 21.9 shows these two changes to the method.

LISTING 21.9   Storing the Recently Received Location for Later Use

```
 1:  func locationManager(manager: CLLocationManager,
 2:          didUpdateLocations locations: [CLLocation]) {
 3:      let newLocation: CLLocation=locations[0]
 4:      if newLocation.horizontalAccuracy >= 0 {
 5:          recentLocation=newLocation
 6:          let cupertino:CLLocation = CLLocation(
 7:              latitude: kCupertinoLatitude,
 8:              longitude: kCupertinoLongitude)
 9:          let delta:CLLocationDistance =
10:              cupertino.distanceFromLocation(newLocation)
11:          let miles: Double = (delta * 0.000621371) + 0.5 // to miles
12:          if miles < 3 {
13:              // Stop updating the location and heading
14:              locMan.stopUpdatingLocation()
15:              locMan.stopUpdatingHeading()
16:              // Congratulate the user
17:              distanceLabel.text = "Enjoy the\nMothership!"
18:          } else {
19:              let commaDelimited: NSNumberFormatter =
20:                  NSNumberFormatter()
```

```
21:                    commaDelimited.numberStyle =
22:                        NSNumberFormatterStyle.DecimalStyle
23:                    distanceLabel.text=commaDelimited
24:                        .stringFromNumber(miles)!+" miles to the\nMothership"
25:                }
26:            waitView.hidden = true
27:            distanceView.hidden = false
28:        }
29:    }
```

The only changes from the previous tutorial are the addition of line 5, which stores the incoming location in recentLocation, and line 15, which stops heading updates if we are sitting in Cupertino.

Calculating the Heading to Cupertino

In the previous two sections, we avoided doing calculations with latitude and longitude. This time, it requires just a bit of computation on our part to get a heading to Cupertino and then to decide whether that heading is straight ahead or requires the user to spin to the right or to the left.

Given two locations such as the user's current location and the location of Cupertino, it is possible to use some basic geometry of the sphere to calculate the initial heading the user would need to use to reach Cupertino. A search of the Internet quickly finds the formula in JavaScript (copied here in the comment), and from that we can easily implement the algorithm in Objective-C and provide the heading. We add this as a new method, headingToLocation:current, that takes two locations and returns a heading that can be used to reach the destination from the current location.

Add the headingToLocation:current method to the ViewController.swift file, as in Listing 21.10.

LISTING 21.10   Calculating a Heading to a Destination

```
/*
 * According to Movable Type Scripts
 * http://mathforum.org/library/drmath/view/55417.html
 *
 *   Javascript:
 *
 * var y = Math.sin(dLon) * Math.cos(lat2);
 * var x = Math.cos(lat1)*Math.sin(lat2) -
 * Math.sin(lat1)*Math.cos(lat2)*Math.cos(dLon);
 * var brng = Math.atan2(y, x).toDeg();
 */
```

```
 1:  func headingToLocation(desired: CLLocationCoordinate2D,
 2:      current: CLLocationCoordinate2D) -> Double {
 3:      // Gather the variables needed by the heading algorithm
 4:      let lat1:Double = current.latitude*kDeg2Rad
 5:      let lat2: Double = desired.latitude*kDeg2Rad
 6:      let lon1: Double  = current.longitude
 7:      let lon2: Double = desired.longitude
 8:      let dlon: Double = (lon2-lon1)*kDeg2Rad
 9:
10:      let y: Double = sin(dlon)*cos(lat2)
11:      let x: Double =
12:          cos(lat1)*sin(lat2) - sin(lat1)*cos(lat2)*cos(dlon)
13:
14:      var heading:Double = atan2(y,x)
15:      heading=heading*kRad2Deg
16:      heading=heading+360.0
17:      heading=fmod(heading,360.0)
18:      return heading
19:  }
```

Don't worry about the math here. I didn't make it up, and there's no reason you need to understand it. What you do need to know is that, given two locations—one current and one desired (the destination)—this method returns a floating-point number in degrees. If the returned value is 0, we need to head north to get where we're going. If it's 180, we need to go south (and so on).

If you're interested in the history of the process and how it works, look up "great circle navigation" on your search engine of choice.

Handling Heading Updates

The last piece of our implementation is handling heading updates. The ViewController class implements the CLLocationManagerDelegate protocol, and as you learned earlier, one of the optional methods of this protocol, locationManager:didUpdateHeading, provides heading updates anytime the heading changes by more degrees than the headingFilter amount.

For each heading update our delegate receives, we should use the user's current location to calculate the heading to Cupertino, compare the desired heading to the user's current heading, and then display the correct arrow image: left, right, or straight ahead.

For these heading calculations to be meaningful, we need to have the current location and some confidence in the accuracy of the reading of the user's current heading. We check these two conditions in an if statement before performing the heading calculations. If this sanity check does not pass, we hide the directionArrow.

Because this heading feature is more of a novelty than a true source of directions (unless you happen to be a bird or in an airplane), there is no need to be overly precise. Using +/–10 degrees from the true heading to Cupertino as close enough to display the straight-ahead arrow. If the difference is greater than 10 degrees, we display the left or right arrow based on whichever way would result in a shorter turn to get to the desired heading. Implement the `locationManager:didUpdateHeading` method in the ViewController.swift file, as shown in Listing 21.11.

LISTING 21.11 **Handling the Heading Updates**

```
1:  func locationManager(manager: CLLocationManager,
2:      didUpdateHeading newHeading: CLHeading) {
3:      if (recentLocation != nil && newHeading.headingAccuracy >= 0) {
4:          let cupertino:CLLocation = CLLocation(
5:              latitude: kCupertinoLatitude,
6:              longitude: kCupertinoLongitude)
7:          let course: Double = headingToLocation(
8:              cupertino.coordinate,
9:              current:recentLocation.coordinate)
10:         let delta: Double = newHeading.trueHeading - course
11:         if (abs(delta) <= 10) {
12:             directionArrow.image = UIImage(named: "up_arrow.png")
13:         } else {
14:             if (delta > 180) {
15:                 directionArrow.image = UIImage(named: "right_arrow.png")
16:             }
17:             else if (delta > 0) {
18:                 directionArrow.image = UIImage(named: "left_arrow.png")
19:             }
20:             else if (delta > -180) {
21:                 directionArrow.image = UIImage(named: "right_arrow.png")
22:             }
23:             else {
24:                 directionArrow.image = UIImage(named: "left_arrow.png")
25:             }
26:         }
27:         directionArrow.hidden = false
28:     } else {
29:         directionArrow.hidden = true
30:     }
31: }
```

We begin in line 3 by checking to see whether we have valid information stored for `recentLocation` and a meaningful heading accuracy. If these conditions aren't true, the method hides the `directionArrow` image view in line 29.

Lines 4–6 create a new `CLLocation` object that contains the location for Cupertino. We use this for getting a heading from our current location (stored in `recentLocation`) in lines 7–9. The heading that would get us to our destination is stored as a floating-point value in `course`.

Line 10 is a simple subtraction, but it is the magic of the entire method. Here we subtract the course heading we calculated from the one we've received from core location (`newHeading.trueHeading`). This is stored as a floating-point number in the variable `delta`.

Let's think this through for a second. If the course we should be going in is north (heading 0) and the heading we're actually going in is also north (heading 0), the delta is 0, meaning that we do not need to make a course correction. However, if the course we want to take is east (a heading of 90), and the direction we are going in is north (a heading of 0), the delta value is –90. Need to be headed west but are traveling east? The delta is –270, and we should turn toward the left. By looking at the different conditions, we can come up with ranges of delta values that apply to the different directions. This is exactly what happens in lines 14–25. You can try the math yourself if you need convincing. Line 11 differs a bit; it checks the absolute value of delta to see whether we're off by more than 10 degrees. If we aren't, the arrow keeps pointing forward.

NOTE

We don't have a backward-pointing arrow here, so any course correction needs to be made by turning left or right. Understanding this can be helpful in seeing why we compare the `delta` value to greater than 180 and greater than –180 rather than greater than or equal to. 180/–180 is *exactly* in the opposite direction we're going, so left or right is ambiguous. Up until we reach 180/–180, however, we can provide a turn direction. At exactly 180, the `else` clause in line 23 kicks in and we turn left. Just because.

Building the Application

Run the project. If you have a device equipped with an electromagnetic compass, you can now spin around in your office chair and see the arrow images change to show you the heading to Cupertino (see Figure 21.7). If you run the updated Cupertino application in the iOS Simulator, you might not see the arrow; heading updates seem to be hit or miss in the Simulator.

Usually miss.

FIGURE 21.7
The completed Cupertino application with compass.

Further Exploration

In the span of an hour, you covered a great deal of what Core Location has to offer. I recommend that you spend time reviewing the *Core Location Framework Reference* as well as the *Location Awareness Programming Guide*, both of which are accessible through the Xcode documentation.

In addition, I greatly recommend reviewing Movable Type Scripts documentation on latitude and longitude functions (http://www.movable-type.co.uk/scripts/latlong.html). Although Core Location provides a great deal of functionality, there are some things (such as calculate a heading/bearing) that it just currently cannot do. The Movable Type Scripts library should give you the base equations for many common location-related activities.

Apple Tutorials

LocateMe (accessible through the Xcode documentation interface): A simple Xcode project to demonstrate the primary functions of Core Location.

Summary

In this hour, you worked with the powerful Core Location toolkit. As you saw in the application example, this framework can provide detailed information from an iDevice's GPS and magnetic compass systems. Many modern applications use this information to provide data about the world around the user or to store information about where the user was physically located when an event took place.

You can combine these techniques with the Map Kit from the previous hour to create detailed mapping and touring applications.

Q&A

Q. Should I start receiving heading and location updates as soon as my application launches?

A. You can, as we did in the tutorial, but be mindful that the hardware's GPS features consume quite a bit of battery power. After you establish your location, turn off the location/ heading updates.

Q. Why do I need that ugly equation to calculate a heading? It seems overly complicated.

A. If you imagine two locations as two points on a flat grid, the math is easier. Unfortunately, the Earth is not flat but a sphere. Because of this difference, you must calculate distances and headings using the great circle (that is, the shortest distance between two points on a curved surface).

Q. Can I use Core Location and Map Kit to provide turn-by-turn directions in my application?

A. Yes and no. You can use Core Location and Map Kit as part of a solution for turn-by-turn directions, and some developers do this, but they are not sufficiently functional on their own. In short, you have to license some additional data to provide this type of capability.

Workshop

Quiz

1. To work with location data, you must create an instance of which of the following?

    a. `CLLocationManager`

    b. `CILocationManager`

    c. `CLManager`

    d. `CoreData`

2. The framework responsible for providing location services in iOS is known as what?

    a. Core Data

    b. Location manager

    c. Core Location

    d. Location data manager

3. A traditional mechanical compass points to where?

    a. True north

    b. True south

    c. Magnetic south

    d. Magnetic north

4. Before using the iOS location data in an application, what must you request?

    a. Memory

    b. Authorization

    c. Network resources

    d. Data storage

5. iOS represents a location using which class?

    a. `CLLocationData`

    b. `CLPlace`

    c. `CLLocation`

    d. `CLLocationManager`

6. To begin receiving location updates, you must use what location manager method?

    a. `getLocation`

    b. `beginUpdatingLocation`

    c. `startUpdatingLocation`

    d. `getLocationUpdates`

7. A class that should receive location updates will need to implement which protocol?

    a. `CLLocationManagerDelegate`

    b. `CLLocationManagerUtility`

    c. `LocationDelegate`

    d. `CLLocationDelegate`

8. To prevent an overwhelming number of heading updates, you can set a what?

   a. Heading stop

   b. Heading filter

   c. Heading slowdown

   d. Heading limit

9. To request that an application always have access to the location, you should use what method?

   a. `requestConstantAuthorization`

   b. `requestPermanentAuthorization`

   c. `requestPerpetualAuthorization`

   d. `requestAlwaysAuthorization`

10. The accuracy of location updates is managed using which location manager variable property?

    a. `requiredAccuracy`

    b. `desiredAccuracy`

    c. `reportAccuracy`

    d. `setAccuracy`

Answers

1. A. An instance of the Core Location location manager (`CLLocationManager`) class is needed to begin working with locations.

2. C. The Core Location framework provides location services for iOS applications.

3. D. A traditional compass points to magnetic north, versus geographic north.

4. B. You must request authorization from the user before attempting to use location services.

5. C. Instances of the `CLLocation` class represent geographic locations within iOS.

6. C. Use the `startUpdatingLocation` method to begin receiving location updates.

7. A. A class must implement the `CLLocationManagerDelegate` protocol in order to handle location information.

8. B. Implementing a heading filter can keep your application from being overwhelmed by insignificant changes to a device's orientation.

9. D. Although not recommended by Apple, the `requestAlwaysAuthorization` method can be used to give an application access to location information regardless of its state.

10. B. The `desiredAccuracy` variable property can be set to a variety of constants that generate location events that will be accurate for walking, driving, and so on.

Activities

1. Adopt the Cupertino application to be a guide for your favorite spot in the world. Add a map to the view that displays your current location.

2. Identify opportunities to use the location features of core location. How can you enhance games, utilities, or other applications with location-aware features?

Building Background-Ready Applications

What You'll Learn in This Hour:

▶ How iOS supports background tasks

▶ What types of background operations are supported

▶ How to disable backgrounding

▶ Ways to execute code in the background

▶ How to add 3D Touch Quick Actions

"Real multitasking" claims the commercial for a competitor's tablet. "Unlike Apple, you can run multiple things at once," chides another ad. As a developer and a fan of iOS, I've found these threads amusing in their naiveté and somewhat confusing. iDevices have always run multiple applications simultaneously in the background, but they were limited to Apple's applications. This restriction has been to preserve the user experience of the device instead of letting it bog down to the point of being unusable. Rather than an "anything goes" approach, Apple has taken steps to ensure that iOS devices remain responsive at all times.

In recent years, Apple has dramatically opened up background processing with many new capabilities. Unlike the competitors, however, Apple has been cautious in its backgrounding approach—preventing a single process from completely taking over the operating system. In this hour's lesson, you learn several of the multitasking techniques that you can implement in your applications.

Understanding iOS Backgrounding

As you've built the tutorials in this book, you might have noticed that when you quit the applications on your device or in the iOS Simulator, they still show up in the iOS task manager, and unless you manually stop them, they tend to pick up right where they left off. The reason for this is that projects are background ready as soon as you click the Run button. That doesn't mean that they will run in the background, just that they're aware of the background features and will take advantage with a little bit of help.

Before we examine how to enable backgrounding (also called multitasking) in our projects, let's first identify exactly what it means to be a background-aware application, starting with the types of backgrounding supported and then the application life cycle methods you can tie into.

Split-Screen Multitasking Is Free

We're going to be talking about all sorts of ways that your application can interact with iOS to perform actions or present options *without being open on your screen*. Split-screen multitasking, introduced in iOS 9 and available on Apple's current shipping iPad line, doesn't require special programming to function. This type of multitasking requires that you implement an application using Size Classes and Auto Layout. If your application can properly resize to different screen sizes, it can split-screen multitask. In fact, you must explicitly add the Boolean key `UIRequiresFullScreen` with a value of `true` to your project's Info.plist file if you want to opt out of split-screen multitasking.

Assuming you *do* want your app to be used in a split-screen mode, you must also be aware that it won't have full control over the device's resources. In other words, if you follow good programming practices and use memory and device resources efficiently, your app will work wonderfully in Apple's new split-screen environment.

Types of Backgrounding

We explore six types of background operations in iOS: application suspension, local notifications, task-specific background processing, task completion, background fetches, and 3D Touch Quick Actions.

Suspension

When an application is suspended, it ceases executing code but is preserved exactly as the user left it. When the user returns to the application, it appears to have been running the whole time. In reality, all tasks are stopped, keeping the app from using up your device's resources. Any application that you compile will, by default, support background suspension. You should still handle cleanup in the application if it is about to be suspended (see the "Background-Aware Application Life Cycle Methods" section, later in this hour), but beyond that, it "just works."

In addition to performing cleanup as an application is being suspended, it is your responsibility to recover from a background suspended state and update anything in the application that should have changed while it was suspended (time/date changes and so on).

Local Notifications

The second type of background processing is the scheduling of local notifications (`UILocalNotification`). If you've ever experienced a push notification, local notifications are the same but are generated by the applications that you write. An application, while running, can schedule notifications, with sounds and app icon badges to appear at a point in time in the future.

Before this can happen, however, you must request permission, using the `UIApplication` method `registerUserNotificationSettings`. For example, to request that my app be able to generate notifications that include sound, icon badges numbers, and alert boxes, I would add the following code to my `application:didFinishLaunchingWithOptions` method in AppDelegate.swift:

```
let notificationTypes:UIUserNotificationType =
    [UIUserNotificationType.Sound,
     UIUserNotificationType.Badge,
     UIUserNotificationType.Alert]

let notificationSettings =
    UIUserNotificationSettings(forTypes: notificationTypes,
        categories: nil)

UIApplication.sharedApplication()
    .registerUserNotificationSettings(notificationSettings)
```

Once permission has been requested, you can generate a notification. The following code initializes a notification (`UILocationNotification`), configures it to appear in 5 minutes (300 seconds from "now"), and then uses the application's `scheduleLocalNotification` method to complete the scheduling:

```
let scheduledAlert: UILocalNotification = UILocalNotification()
scheduledAlert.fireDate=NSDate(timeIntervalSinceNow: 300)
scheduledAlert.timeZone=NSTimeZone.defaultTimeZone()
scheduledAlert.alertBody="Hey, remember me?"
```

These notifications, when invoked by iOS, can show a message, play a sound, and even update your application's notification badge. They cannot, however, execute arbitrary application code. In fact, it is likely that you will simply allow iOS to suspend your application after registering your local notifications. A user who receives a notification can click the View button in the notification window to return to your application.

NOTE

iOS allows remote notifications to be sent to a device to trigger applications to activate and begin processing. This can be useful for asking an application to retrieve new information when it becomes available (having it instantly appear when the user next opens the app). Using remote notifications requires you to have a server infrastructure set up to track and communicate with your user's iOS devices (which, unfortunately, is beyond the scope of this book). Learn more by reading the document *Local and Push Notification Programming Guide* found in the Xcode help system.

Task-Specific Background Processing

Before Apple decided to implement background processing, it did some research on how users worked with their devices. Apple found that people needed specific types of background processing. First, they needed audio to continue playing in the background; this is necessary for applications like Pandora. Next, location-aware software needed to update itself in the background so that users continued to receive navigation feedback. Finally, Voice over IP (VoIP) applications like Skype needed to operate in the background to handle incoming calls.

These three types of tasks are handled uniquely and elegantly in iOS. By declaring that your application requires one of these types of background processing, you can, in many cases, enable your application to continue running with little alteration. To declare your application capable of supporting any (or all) of these tasks, you will add the Required Background Modes (UIBackgroundModes) key to the project's plist file and then add features (background audio, picture-in-picture support, and so on) that you'll be supporting. Xcode even lets you do this in a cool point-and-click way, so you can avoid the manually editing Info.plist. Don't worry; you still have plenty of opportunities to experience the nightmare of plist editing elsewhere this hour.

Task Completion for Long-Running Tasks

The fourth type of backgrounding that we'll use is task completion. Using task-completion methods, you can "mark" the tasks in your application that will need to finish before the application can be safely suspended (file upload/downloads, massive calculations, and so on).

For example, to mark the beginning of a long-running task, first declare an identifier for the specific task:

```
var myLongTask: UIBackgroundTaskIdentifier!
```

Then use the application's beginBackgroundTaskWithExpirationHandler method to tell iOS that you're starting a piece of code that can continue to run in the background:

```
myLongTask =
    UIApplication.sharedApplication()
        .beginBackgroundTaskWithExpirationHandler({ () -> Void in
        // If you're worried about exceeding 10 minutes, handle it here
    })
```

And finally, mark the end of the long-running task with the application endBackgroundTask method:

```
UIApplication.sharedApplication().endBackgroundTask(myLongTask)
```

Each task you mark will have roughly 10 minutes (total) to complete its actions, which is plenty of time for most uses. After the time completes, the application is suspended and treated like any other suspended application.

Background Fetches

The fifth and final multitasking feature we review this hour is background fetches. Using the background fetch feature, your application can periodically launch and execute a method that retrieves and processes update data. Scheduling of the updates happens automatically based on a user's usage. If a user starts an app and uses it each morning, iOS will make sure that a background fetch occurs *before* the time the user is typically using it. In addition, iOS prevents multiple applications from attempting background fetches at the same time, thus keeping the device responsive even if background processing is taking place.

As a developer, you need to do just two things to implement background updates. First, you must edit the `application:didFinishLaunchingWithOptions` method in the application delegate (AppDelegate.swift) to set the *minimum* amount of time between fetches. This consists of a single line (broken here for readability):

```
UIApplication.sharedApplication().setMinimumBackgroundFetchInterval(
    UIApplicationBackgroundFetchIntervalMinimum)
```

The constant `UIApplicationBackgroundFetchIntervalMinimum` tells the application that you want updates to happen as often as they can. If you have a specific interval in mind, you can provide a number in seconds instead. You aren't guaranteed an interval by iOS; it is intended to be scheduled around a user's activities.

The second step is to implement the background fetch itself. To do this, you add the following method to the application delegate:

```
func application(application: UIApplication,
    performFetchWithCompletionHandler completionHandler:
    (UIBackgroundFetchResult) -> Void) {

    // Do something useful here

    //Indicate completion
    completionHandler(UIBackgroundFetchResult.NewData)

}
```

This method has 30 seconds to execute and perform the background fetch. When completed, it should call `completionHandler(UIBackgroundFetchResult.NewData)` to indicate success.

3D Touch Quick Actions

What do you do when you launch an application? Chances are, you perform a series of actions each time it starts up—choose to open a new document, switch to a new mode, and so on. With 3D Touch-enabled devices, you can enable your users to configure your application, before it ever appears onscreen, by firmly pressing the app icon, as shown in Figure 22.1.

FIGURE 22.1
3D Touch Quick Actions give users access to application functionality before the application launches, or when it is in the background.

3D Touch Quick Actions themselves do not execute code in the background, but instead they present a limited interface to your application while it isn't running.

There are two parts to implementing Quick Actions. The first is to define the actions (and associated icons, if desired) in the project's Info.plist, and the second is to check for those actions in an AppDelegate.swift method: `application:performActionForShortcutItem`.

To add the Quick Actions to the Info.plist file, edit the file and add a new property with the key `UIApplicationShortcutItems` of the type Array. Within this array, you add items for each Quick Action that you want to display. Each item must be of the type Dictionary and typically contains up to four keys, all of the type String:

> **UIApplicationShortcutItemTitle:** The title that should be displayed to the user.
>
> **UIApplicationShortcutItemSubtitle:** An optional subtitle that can be displayed below the title.
>
> **UIApplicationShortcutItemType:** A unique string that your application will receive when the user chooses that action.
>
> **UIApplicationShortcutItemIconFile:** The name of an image within the Assets.xcassets library that will be displayed alongside the title. This is optional, but highly recommended.

NOTE
Additional 3D Touch Quick Actions settings are available for further fine-tuning your menus. Learn more by reading the document **Adopting 3D Touch on iPhone: 3D Touch APIs** found in the Xcode Documentation.

After the quick actions have been defined in info.plist, they'll be displayed automatically when the app icon is pressed on a 3D Touch-enabled device. To react to an action being chosen, you'll implement application:performActionForShortcutItem in AppDelegate.swift.

For example, to react to a Quick Action with a UIApplicationShortcutItemType defined as doStuff, you might use something like this:

```
func application(application: UIApplication,
    performActionForShortcutItem shortcutItem: UIApplicationShortcutItem,
    completionHandler: (Bool) -> Void) {
    var success: Bool = false
    if shortcutItem.type == "doStuff" {
        // The "doStuff" action was chosen
        success = true
    } else {
        // Something went wrong
        success = false
    }
    completionHandler(success)
}
```

The method checks shortcutItem.type to see whether it matches one of the defined Quick Actions. If it does, your custom code is executed. As a final step, you must call completion Handler with a Bool (Boolean) value to indicate success or failure of the action.

TIP
Want Pretty Quick Action Icons? Use a Template
Quick Action icons should be transparent line drawings, similar to those used with tab bar items. To get you started on the right path, Apple has published templates for creating your own icons. You can download these downloaded from https://developer.apple.com/design/downloads/Quick-Action-Guides.zip

Background-Aware Application Life Cycle Methods

In Hour 4, "Inside Cocoa Touch," you started learning about the application life cycle, shown in Figure 22.2. You learned that applications should clean up after themselves in the applicationDidEnterBackground delegate method. This replaces applicationWillTerminate in earlier versions of the OS, or as you'll learn shortly, in applications that you've specifically marked as not capable (or necessary) to run in the background.

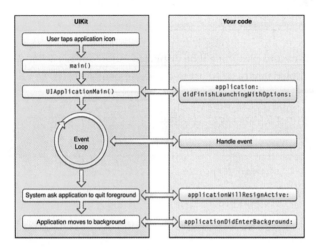

FIGURE 22.2
The iOS application life cycle.

In addition to applicationDidEnterBackground, you should implement several other methods to be a proper background-aware iOS citizen. For many small applications, you do not need to do anything with these other than leave them as is in the application delegate. As your projects increase in complexity, however, make sure that your apps move cleanly from the foreground to background (and vice versa), avoiding potential data corruption and creating a seamless user experience.

CAUTION

Your Application Can Terminate at Any Time

It is important to understand that iOS can terminate your applications, even if they're backgrounded, if it decides that the device is running low on resources. You can expect that your applications will be fine, but plan for a scenario where they are forced to quit unexpectedly.

NOTE

If you're interested in implementing background fetching, you can take advantage of the methods we discuss here, but they aren't necessary. You're only required to set the minimum fetch time and then to define a method for handling the data fetching itself. We'll implement some simple background fetching later this hour.

Apple expects to see the following methods in your background-aware apps:

- ▶ **application:didFinishLaunchingWithOptions**: Called when your application first launches. If your application is terminated while suspended or purged from memory, it needs to restore its previous state manually. (You did save it to your user's preferences, right?)

- ▶ **applicationDidBecomeActive**: Called when an application launches or returns to the foreground from the background. This method can be used to restart processes and update the user interface, if needed.

- ▶ **applicationWillResignActive**: Invoked when the application is requested to move to the background or to quit. This method should be used to prepare the application for moving into a background state, if needed.

- ▶ **applicationDidEnterBackground**: Called when the application has become a background application. This largely replaces applicationWillTerminate, which was used when an application quit. You should handle all final cleanup work in this method. You may also use it to start long-running tasks and use task-completion backgrounding to finish them.

- ▶ **applicationWillEnterForeground**: Called when an application returns to an active state after being backgrounded.

- ▶ **applicationWillTerminate**: Invoked when an application on a nonmultitasking version of iOS is asked to quit or when iOS determines that it needs to shut down an actively running background application.

Method stubs for all of these exist in your application delegate file. If your application needs additional setup or teardown work, just add the code to the existing methods. As you'll see shortly, many applications, such as the majority of those in this book, require few changes.

Now that understand the background-related methods and types of background processing available to you, let's look at how you can implement them. To do this, we reuse tutorials that we've built throughout the book (with two exceptions). We do not cover how these tutorials were built, so be sure to refer to the earlier hours if you have questions on the core functionality of the applications.

Disabling Backgrounding

We start with the exact opposite of enabling backgrounding: disabling it. If you think about it, many different "diversion" apps don't need to support background suspension or processing. These are apps that you use and then quit. They don't need to hang around in your task manager afterward.

For example, consider the HelloNoun application in Hour 6, "Model-View-Controller Application Design." There's no reason that the user experience would be negatively affected if the application were to start from scratch each time you ran it. To implement this change in the project, follow these steps:

1. Open the project in which you want to disable backgrounding (such as HelloNoun).

2. Choose the main project group and click the HelloNoun target, and then expand the Custom iOS Target Properties under the Info tab. Or open the project's plist file (Info.plist).

3. Add an additional row to the displayed property list (right-click the list, choose Add Row), selecting Application Does Not Run in Background (UIApplicationExitsOnSuspend) from the Key pop-up menu.

4. Choose Yes from the pop-up menu at the right side of the Value column, as shown in Figure 22.3.

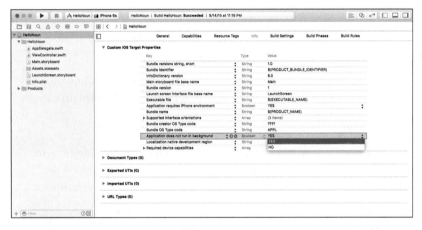

FIGURE 22.3
Add the Application Does Not Run in Background (UIApplicationExitsOnSuspend) key to the project.

NOTE

By default, the plist editor shows the "developer friendly" names for plist entries. To see the underlying keys/values, right-click on the list and choose Show Raw Keys/Values from the menu.

Run the application on your device or in the iOS Simulator. When you exit the application with the Home button, it will not be suspended, and it will restart fresh when you launch it the next time.

Handling Background Suspension

In the second tutorial, we handle background suspension. As previously noted, you don't have to do anything to support this other than build your project with the iOS development tools. That said, we use this example as an opportunity to prompt users when they return to the application after it was backgrounded.

For this example, we update the ImageHop application from Hour 8, "Handling Images, Animation, Sliders, and Steppers." It is conceivable (work with me here, folks) that a user will want to start the bunny hopping, exit the application, and then return to exactly where it was at some time in the future.

To alert the user when the application returns from suspension, we edit the application delegate method `applicationWillEnterForeground`. Recall that this method is invoked only when an application is returning from a backgrounded state. Open AppDelegate.swift and implement the method, as shown in Listing 22.1.

LISTING 22.1   Implementing the `applicationWillEnterForeground` **Method**

```
 1: func applicationWillEnterForeground(application: UIApplication) {
 2:     let alertController = UIAlertController(title: "Yawn!",
 3:         message: "Was I asleep?",
 4:         preferredStyle: UIAlertControllerStyle.Alert)
 5:
 6:     let defaultAction = UIAlertAction(title: "Welcome Back",
 7:         style: UIAlertActionStyle.Cancel,
 8:         handler: nil)
 9:
10:     alertController.addAction(defaultAction)
11:     self.window!.rootViewController!
12:         .presentViewController(alertController, animated: true,
13:             completion: nil)
14: }
```

Within the method, we declare, configure, and show an alert controller, exactly as we did in the Getting Attention tutorial in Hour 10, "Getting the User's Attention." After updating the code, run the application. Start the ImageHop animation, and then use the Home button to background the app.

After waiting a few seconds (just for good measure), open ImageHop again using the task manager or its application icon (*not* with Xcode's Run). When the application returns to the foreground, it should pick up exactly where it left off and present you with the alert shown in Figure 22.4.

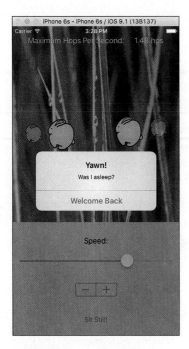

FIGURE 22.4
The `applicationWillEnterForeground` method is used to display an alert upon returning from the background.

Implementing Local Notifications

Earlier in this lesson, you saw a short snippet of the code necessary to generate a local notification (`UILocalNotification`). As it turns out, there's not much more you need beyond those few lines. To demonstrate the use of local notifications, we update Hour 10's `doAlert` method. Instead of just displaying an alert, it also shows a notification 5 minutes later and then schedules local notifications to occur every day thereafter.

Requesting Authorization for Notifications

Before displaying a notification, your application must request authorization. Without proper permission, notifications will fail silently (that is, your code will run, but nothing will be displayed).

Open the GettingAttention application and edit AppDelegate.swift file, updating the `application:didFinishLaunchingWithOptions` method, as shown in Listing 22.2.

LISTING 22.2   Requesting Notification Authorization

```
 1: func application(application:UIApplication,didFinishLaunchingWithOptions
 2:     launchOptions: [NSObject: AnyObject]?) -> Bool {
 3:
 4:     let notificationTypes:UIUserNotificationType =
 5:         [UIUserNotificationType.Sound,
 6:         UIUserNotificationType.Badge,
 7:         UIUserNotificationType.Alert]
 8:
 9:     let notificationSettings =
10:         UIUserNotificationSettings(forTypes: notificationTypes,
11:             categories: nil)
12:
13:     UIApplication.sharedApplication()
14:         .registerUserNotificationSettings(notificationSettings)
15:
16:     return true
17: }
```

To request authorization to use notifications, you must first define the types of notifications
(`UIUserNotificationType`) you want to display (lines 4–7). In this example, we're requesting the ability to use *any* type of notification (sounds, alerts, and badges)—so all the bases are
covered. Next, you must create a `UIUserNotificationSettings` object that includes the types
(lines 9–11). Finally, the settings are registered with the application (lines 13–14), which generates an alert and prompts the user for permission.

What's the takeaway here? Use this code block and you'll properly request the ability to use any
local notifications. Let's move on to the notifications themselves.

Common Notification Properties

You want to configure several properties when creating notifications. A few of the more interesting of these include the following:

▶ **applicationIconBadgeNumber:** An integer that is displayed on the application icon
when the notification is triggered.

▶ **fireDate:** An `NSDate` object that provides a time in the future for the notification to be
triggered.

▶ **timeZone:** The time zone to use for scheduling the notification.

▶ **repeatInterval:** How frequently, if ever, the notification should be repeated.

▶ **soundName:** A string (`NSString`) containing the name of a sound resource to play when
the notification is triggered.

▶ **alertBody:** A string (`NSString`) containing the message to be displayed to the user.

Creating and Scheduling a Notification

Open the GettingAttention application and edit the doAlert method so that it resembles Listing 22.3. (Bolded lines are additions to the existing method.) Once the code is in place, we walk through it together.

LISTING 22.3 Updating doAlert to Register a Local Notification

```
 1: @IBAction func doAlert(sender: AnyObject) {
 2:     let scheduledAlert: UILocalNotification = UILocalNotification()
 3:
 4:     UIApplication.sharedApplication().cancelAllLocalNotifications()
 5:     scheduledAlert.applicationIconBadgeNumber=1
 6:     scheduledAlert.fireDate=NSDate(timeIntervalSinceNow: 300)
 7:     scheduledAlert.timeZone=NSTimeZone.defaultTimeZone()
 8:     scheduledAlert.repeatInterval=NSCalendarUnit.Day
 9:     scheduledAlert.soundName="soundeffect.wav"
10:     scheduledAlert.alertBody="I'd like to get your attention again!"
11:     UIApplication.sharedApplication()
12:         .scheduleLocalNotification(scheduledAlert)
13:
14:     let alertController =
15:         UIAlertController(title: "Alert Me Button Selected",
16:         message: "I need your attention NOW!",
17:         preferredStyle: UIAlertControllerStyle.Alert)
18:
19:     let defaultAction = UIAlertAction(title: "Ok",
20:         style: UIAlertActionStyle.Cancel,
21:         handler: nil)
22:
23:     alertController.addAction(defaultAction)
24:     presentViewController(alertController,
25:         animated: true, completion: nil)
26: }
```

First, in line 2, we create scheduledAlert as an object of type UILocalNotification. This local notification object is what we set up with our desired message, sound, and so on and then pass off to the application to display sometime in the future.

In line 4, we use UIApplication.sharedApplication() to grab our application object and then call the UIApplication method cancelAllLocalNotifications. This cancels any previously scheduled notifications that this application may have made, giving us a clean slate.

In line 5, we configure the notification's applicationIconBadgeNumber variable property so that when the notification is triggered, the application's badge number is set to 1 to show that a notification has occurred.

Line 6 uses the `fireDate` along with the `NSDate` class method `DateWithTimeIntervalSinceNow` to set the notification to be triggered 300 seconds in the future.

Line 7 sets the `timeZone` for the notification. This should almost always be set to the local time zone, as returned by `NSTimeZone.defaultTimeZone()`.

Line 8 sets the `repeatInterval` variable property for the notification. This can be chosen from a variety of constants, such as `NSCalendarUnit.CalendarUnitDay` (daily), `NSCalendarUnit.CalendarUnitHour` (hourly), and `NSCalendarUnit.CalendarUnitMinute` (every minute). You can find the full list in the `NSCalendar` class reference in the Xcode developer documentation.

In line 9, we set a sound to be played along with the notification. The `soundName` variable property is configured with a string with the name of a sound resource. Because we already have soundeffect.wav available in the project, we can use that without further additions.

Line 10 finishes the notification configuration by setting the `alertBody` of the notification to the message we want the user to see.

When the notification object is fully configured, we schedule it using the `UIApplication` method `scheduleLocalNotification` (lines 11–12). This finishes the implementation.

Choose Run to compile and start the application on your device or in the iOS Simulator. After GettingAttention is up and running, click the Alert Me! button. After the initial alert is displayed, click the Home button to exit the application. Go get a drink, and come back in about 4 minutes and 59 seconds. Exactly 5 minutes later, you'll receive a local notification, as shown in Figure 22.5.

FIGURE 22.5
Local notifications are displayed onscreen even when the application isn't running.

Using Task-Specific Background Processing

So far, we haven't actually done any real background processing. We've suspended an application and generated local notifications, but in each of these cases, the application hasn't been doing any processing. Let's change that. In our final two examples, we execute *real* code behind the scenes while the application is in the background. Although it is well beyond the scope of this book to generate a VoIP application, we can use our Cupertino application from the preceding hour's lesson, with some minor modifications, to show background processing of location and audio.

Preparing the Cupertino Application for Audio

When we finished off the Cupertino application in the preceding hour, it told us how far away Cupertino was and presented straight, left, and right arrows on the screen to indicate the direction the user should be traveling to reach the mothership. We can update the application to audio using `SystemSoundServices`, just as we did in Hour 10's GettingAttention application.

The only tricky thing about our changes is that we won't want to hear a sound repeated if it was the same as the last sound we heard. To handle this requirement, we define a variable, `lastSound`, which is set to the last sound that has been played. We can then use this as a point of comparison to make sure that what we're about to play isn't the same thing we did just play.

Adding the AudioToolbox Framework

To use System Sound Services, we need to first add the AudioToolbox framework. Make a copy of the Cupertino compass application and name the folder **Cupertino Audio Compass**. Then open the Cupertino project in Xcode. Select the ViewController.swift file and add an `import` line for `AudioToolbox` after the existing import of the Core Location framework:

```
import AudioToolbox
```

Adding the Audio Files

Within the project folder included with this hour's lesson, you'll find an Audio folder containing simple direction sounds: straight.wav, right.wav, and left.wav. Drag the audio folder to the main project code group within the Xcode project. Choose to copy the files and create groups when prompted.

Adding System Sound ID Variables

Next, we need to update the code following the `class` line in ViewController.swift to declare four new variable properties for three `SystemSoundIDs` referencing our sound files (`soundStraight`, `soundLeft`, and `soundRight`) and a fourth (`lastSound`) to hold the last `SystemSoundID` we played. Remember that sound IDs aren't objects, they're just integers; so, we'll initialize all four sound IDs to 0, giving us a clean starting point:

```
var soundStraight: SystemSoundID = 0
var soundRight: SystemSoundID = 0
var soundLeft: SystemSoundID = 0

var lastSound: SystemSoundID = 0
```

The setup is complete. We're now ready to implement the code to generate the audio directions for the application.

Implementing the Cupertino Audio Directions

To add sound playback to the Cupertino application, we need to modify two of our existing ViewController methods. The viewDidLoad method will give us a good place to load all three of our sound files and set the soundStraight, soundRight, and soundLeft references appropriately.

Edit ViewController.swift and update the second half of viewDidLoad to match Listing 22.4.

LISTING 22.4   Initializing the Sound File References in `viewDidLoad`

```
 1: override func viewDidLoad() {
 2:     super.viewDidLoad()
 3:     locMan.delegate = self
 4:     locMan.desiredAccuracy =
 5:         kCLLocationAccuracyThreeKilometers
 6:     locMan.distanceFilter = 1609; // a mile
 7:     locMan.requestWhenInUseAuthorization()
 8:     locMan.startUpdatingLocation()
 9:
10:     if CLLocationManager.headingAvailable() {
11:         locMan.headingFilter = 10 // 10 degrees
12:         locMan.startUpdatingHeading()
13:     }
14:
15:     var soundFile:String!
16:
17:     soundFile = NSBundle.mainBundle()
18:         .pathForResource("straight", ofType: "wav")!
19:     AudioServicesCreateSystemSoundID(
20:         NSURL(fileURLWithPath: soundFile),&soundStraight)
21:
22:     soundFile = NSBundle.mainBundle()
23:         .pathForResource("right", ofType: "wav")!
24:     AudioServicesCreateSystemSoundID(
```

```
25:              NSURL(fileURLWithPath: soundFile),&soundRight)
26:
27:      soundFile = NSBundle.mainBundle()
28:              .pathForResource("left", ofType: "wav")!
29:      AudioServicesCreateSystemSoundID(
30:              NSURL(fileURLWithPath: soundFile),&soundLeft)
31: }
```

TIP

If you are having difficulties understanding the sound playback process, refer back to the Hour 10 tutorial.

The final logic that we need to implement is to play each sound when there is a heading update. The ViewController.swift method that implements this is `locationManager:didUpdateHead ing`. Each time the arrow graphic is updated in this method, we prepare to play the corresponding sound with the `AudioServicesPlaySystemSound` function. Before we do that, however, we check to make sure that it isn't the same sound as `lastSound`; this helps prevent a Max Headroom stuttering effect as one sound file is played repeatedly over top of itself. If `lastSound` doesn't match the current sound, we play it and update `lastSound` with a new value. For the left arrow, for example, we might use this code fragment to play the sound and set the `last-Sound` variable property:

```
if lastSound != soundLeft {
    AudioServicesPlaySystemSound(soundLeft)
    lastSound=soundLeft
}
```

Edit the `locationManager:didUpdateHeading` method as described. Your final result should look similar to Listing 22.5.

LISTING 22.5 Adding Audio Feedback When the Heading Updates

```
 1: func locationManager(manager: CLLocationManager,
 2:      didUpdateHeading newHeading: CLHeading) {
 3:      if (recentLocation != nil && newHeading.headingAccuracy >= 0) {
 4:          let cupertino:CLLocation =
 5:              CLLocation(latitude: kCupertinoLatitude,
 6:                  longitude: kCupertinoLongitude)
 7:          let course: Double =
 8:              headingToLocation(cupertino.coordinate,
 9:                  current:recentLocation.coordinate)
10:          let delta: Double = newHeading.trueHeading - course
```

```
11:          if (abs(delta) <= 10) {
12:              directionArrow.image =
13:                  UIImage(named: "up_arrow.png")
14:              if lastSound != soundStraight {
15:                  AudioServicesPlaySystemSound(soundStraight)
16:                  lastSound=soundStraight
17:              }
18:          } else {
19:              if (delta > 180) {
20:                  directionArrow.image =
21:                      UIImage(named: "right_arrow.png")
22:                  if lastSound != soundRight {
23:                      AudioServicesPlaySystemSound(soundRight)
24:                      lastSound=soundRight
25:                  }
26:              }
27:              else if (delta > 0) {
28:                  directionArrow.image =
29:                      UIImage(named: "left_arrow.png")
30:                  if lastSound != soundLeft {
31:                      AudioServicesPlaySystemSound(soundLeft)
32:                      lastSound=soundLeft
33:                  }
34:              }
35:              else if (delta > -180) {
36:                  directionArrow.image =
37:                      UIImage(named: "right_arrow.png")
38:                  if lastSound != soundRight {
39:                      AudioServicesPlaySystemSound(soundRight)
40:                      lastSound=soundRight
41:                  }
42:              }
43:              else {
44:                  directionArrow.image =
45:                      UIImage(named: "left_arrow.png")
46:                  if lastSound != soundLeft {
47:                      AudioServicesPlaySystemSound(soundLeft)
48:                      lastSound=soundLeft
49:                  }
50:              }
51:          }
52:          directionArrow.hidden = false
53:      } else {
54:          directionArrow.hidden = true
55:      }
56: }
```

The application is now ready for testing. Click Run to install the updated Cupertino application on your device, and then try moving around. As you move, it will speak "right," "left," and "straight" to correspond to the onscreen arrows. Try exiting the applications and see what happens. Surprise. It won't work. That's because we haven't yet updated the project to allow background processing.

TIP

If you're testing the application and it still seems a bit "chatty" (playing the sounds too often), you might want to update `locMan.headingFilter` to a larger value (like 15 or 20) in the `viewDidLoad` method. This will help cut down on the number of heading updates.

Adding the Background Modes

Our application performs two tasks that should remain active when in a background state. First, it tracks our location. Second, it plays audio to give us a general heading. We need to add both audio and location background mode capabilities to the application for it to work properly. Update the Cupertino project by following these steps:

1. Choose the main project group and click the Cupertino target, and then expand the Background Modes section under the Capabilities tab.

2. Click the switch to turn on Background Modes.

3. Check both the "Audio, Airplay and Picture in Picture" and the "Location Updates" check boxes, as shown in Figure 22.6.

After updating the capabilities, install the updated application on your device and try again. This time, when you exit the application, it will continue to run. As you move around, you'll hear spoken directions as Cupertino continues to track your position behind the scenes.

By declaring the location and audio background modes, your application is able to use the full services of Location Manager and iOS's many audio playback mechanisms when it is in the background.

FIGURE 22.6
Add the background modes required by your application.

TIP

iPad Picture in Picture

Notice that when you add the mode for playing audio in the background, you're also adding Picture in Picture capabilities? Yes, this actually *does* work. To see what I mean, go back to the MediaPlayground project in Hour 19, "Working with Rich Media," and turn on the same background mode. Start the project, and then load and play the video. As it is playing, press the home button on your device. The application exits, and the video detaches into a small window on your iPad that continues to play!

For more information about interacting with Picture in Picture features, read the *Picture in Picture Quick Start* found in the Xcode documentation.

Completing a Long-Running Background Task

In our next tutorial of the hour, we need to create a project from scratch. Our book isn't about building applications that require a great deal of background processing, so we need to be creative to demonstrate this feature. Sure, we could add code to an existing project that *would* allow a method to run in the background, but we don't have any long-running methods that *could* make use of it.

Implementation Overview

To demonstrate how we can tell iOS to allow something to run in the background, we create a new application, SlowCount, that does nothing but count to 1,000—slowly. We use the task-completion method of background to make sure that, even when the application is in the background, it continues to count until it reaches 1,000 (as shown in Figure 22.7).

FIGURE 22.7
To simulate a long-running task, our application will count slowly.

Setting Up the Project

Create a new single-view application named **SlowCount**. We move through development fairly quickly because, as you can imagine, this application is pretty simple.

Planning the Variables and Connections

The application has a single outlet, a `UILabel` named `theCount`, which we use to present the counter onscreen. In addition, it needs several variable properties: an integer to use as a counter (`count`), an `NSTimer` object that triggers the counting at a steady interval (`theTimer`), and a `UIBackgroundTaskIdentifier` variable (not an object) that we use to reference the task we have running in the background (`counterTask`).

NOTE

Every task that you want to enable for background task completion needs its own
`UIBackgroundTaskIdentifier`. This is used along with the `UIApplication` method `end-`
`BackgroundTask` to identify which background task has just ended.

Designing the Interface

It's a bit of a stretch to claim that this application has a user interface (UI), but we still need to
prepare Main.storyboard to show the `theCount` label on the screen.

Open the initial scene, and drag a label (`UILabel`) into the center of the view. Set the label's
text to read 0. With the label selected, use the Attributes Inspector (Option-Command-4) to set
the label alignment to center and the font size to something a bit bigger. Finally, align the right
and left sides of the label with the right and left sizing guides. You've just created a UI masterpiece, as shown in Figure 22.8.

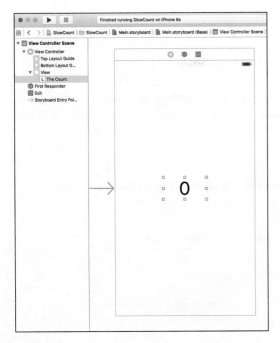

FIGURE 22.8
Add a `UILabel` to the view to hold the current count.

Creating and Connecting the Outlet

We've got one UI object to connect to a single outlet. Switch to the assistant editor, and then Control-drag from the label to below the `class` line in ViewController.swift. Name the outlet `theCount` when prompted to make the connection.

Implementing the Application Logic

To finish our application's core functionality (counting), we need to declare and deal with the additional variable properties: the counter (`count`), the `NSTimer` object to give us a nice delay while counting (`theTimer`), and a `UIBackgroundTaskIdentifier` to track the task (`counterTask`). In addition, we implement a method that does the counting (and nothing else) called `countUp`.

Update the ViewController.swift file after the existing `@IBOutlet` to declare the variable properties:

```
var count: Int = 0
var counterTask: UIBackgroundTaskIdentifier!
var theTimer: NSTimer!
```

With most of the prep work done, we have two more things left to complete. First, we need to initialize the `NSTimer` to fire at a regular interval. Second, when the timer fires, we ask it to invoke a second method, `countUp`. In the `countUp` method, we check to see whether `count` is `1000`. If it is, we turn off the timer and we're done; if not, we update `count` and display it in our `UILabel theCount`.

Initializing the Timer and Counter

Let's start with initializing the timer. What better place to do this than in the `viewDidLoad` method? Implement `viewDidLoad`, as shown in Listing 22.6.

LISTING 22.6 Scheduling a Timer When the Application Starts

```
1: override func viewDidLoad() {
2:     super.viewDidLoad()
3:
4:     theTimer = NSTimer.scheduledTimerWithTimeInterval(0.1, target: self,
5:         selector: "countUp", userInfo: nil, repeats: true)
6: }
```

Lines 4–5 initialize the `theTimer` `NSTimer` object with an interval of `0.1` seconds. The selector is set to use the method `countUp`, which we write next. The timer is set to keep repeating with `repeats:true`.

All that remains is to implement countUp so that it increments the counter and displays the result.

Updating the Counter and Display

Add the countUp method, as shown in Listing 22.7, in ViewController.swift. This should be quite straightforward: If the count equals 1000, we're done and it's time to clean up (we can disable the timer); otherwise, we count.

LISTING 22.7 Updating the Counter

```
1: func countUp() {
2:     if count==1000 {
3:         theTimer.invalidate()
4:     } else {
5:         count++
6:         theCount.text="\(count)"
7:     }
8: }
```

Lines 2–4 handle the case where we've reached the limit of our counting (count==1000). When that occurs, we use the timer's invalidate method to stop it because it isn't needed anymore (line 3).

Lines 4–7 handle the actual counting and display. Line 5 updates the count variable property. Line 6 updates our theCount label with the contents of count.

Run the application. It should do exactly what you expect: count slowly until it reaches 1,000. Unfortunately, if you background the application, it will suspend. The counting will cease until the application returns to the foreground.

Enabling the Background Task Processing

To enable the counter to run in the background, we need to mark it as a background task. We use this code snippet to mark the beginning of the code we want to execute in the background:

```
counterTask =
    UIApplication.sharedApplication()
    .beginBackgroundTaskWithExpirationHandler({ () -> Void in
    // If you're worried about exceeding 10 minutes, handle it here
    })
```

And we use this code snippet to mark the end:

```
UIApplication.sharedApplication().endBackgroundTask(counterTask)
```

NOTE

If you are worried about the application not finishing the background task before it is forced to end (roughly 10 minutes), you could implement the optional code in the beginBackgroundTaskWith-ExpirationHandler closure. You can always check to see how much time is remaining by checking the UIApplication variable property backgroundTimeRemaining.

Let's update our viewDidLoad and countUp methods to include these code additions.

In viewDidLoad, we start the background task right before we initialize the counter. In countUp, we end the background task after count==1000 and the timer is invalidated.

Update viewDidLoad, as shown in Listing 22.8 (lines 4–8).

LISTING 22.8   Setting the Start of Background Processing

```
 1: override func viewDidLoad() {
 2:     super.viewDidLoad()
 3:
 4:     counterTask =
 5:         UIApplication.sharedApplication()
 6:             .beginBackgroundTaskWithExpirationHandler({ () -> Void in
 7:                 // If you're worried about exceeding 10 min, handle it here
 8:             })
 9:
10:     theTimer = NSTimer.scheduledTimerWithTimeInterval(0.1, target: self,
11:         selector: "countUp", userInfo: nil, repeats: true)
12: }
```

Then make the corresponding additions to countUp (line 4), as demonstrated in Listing 22.9.

LISTING 22.9   Setting the End of Background Processing

```
1: func countUp() {
2:     if count==1000 {
3:         theTimer.invalidate()
4:         UIApplication.sharedApplication().endBackgroundTask(counterTask)
5:     } else {
6:         count++
```

```
7:          theCount.text="\(count)"
8:      }
9: }
```

That's all it takes. Your project should now be able to run in the background.

For This to Work, Don't I Need to Enable Background Modes?

No. Background modes are used only for task-specific background multitasking. The code for handling long-running tasks doesn't require any special capabilities to be defined.

Building the Application

Run the application on your device or in the Simulator. After the counter starts counting, press the Home button to move the application to the background. Wait a minute or so, and then reopen the application through the task manager or the application icon. The counter will have continued to run in the background.

Obviously, this isn't a very compelling project itself, but the implications for what can be achieved in real-world apps is definitely exciting.

Performing a Background Fetch

Our next tutorial is, in your author's opinion, one of the most interesting: implementing a background fetch. If you recall from the introduction, this is the ability of an application to periodically activate and retrieve information without the user needing to do a thing. We'll make this happen in the final project (and with just a surprisingly small amount of code).

Implementation Overview

The purpose of our new application, BackgroundDownload, is to download and display a new background image using a background fetch. Depending on how often a user uses the application, he'll see a new image each time it starts (without having to wait for it to download). There isn't a UI to speak of, beyond the UIImageView used as the background, as shown in Figure 22.9.

FIGURE 22.9
The background fetch will periodically download a new image, even when the application isn't running.

Setting Up the Project

As always, create a new single-view application named **BackgroundDownload**. This application is even simpler than the last, so we'll be finished before you know it.

And we're done.

Not really.

Planning the Variables and Connections

BackgroundDownload will have a single outlet, a `UIImageView` named `backgroundImage`, which will contain the background image.

Designing the Interface

Open the Main.Storyboard file and drag a `UIImageView` into the initial scene's view. Size it to cover the entire view, and then open the Attributes Inspector and set the image view's View mode to Aspect Fill, as shown in Figure 22.10.

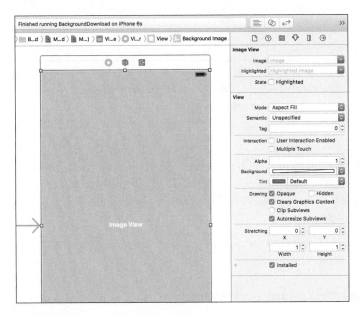

FIGURE 22.10
Configure the image view to be Aspect Fill.

Creating and Connecting the Outlet

Like the last project, there's a single UI element (the `UIImageView`) that we need to connect to an outlet (`backgroundImage`). Switch to the assistant editor, and be sure to select the ViewController.swift file on the right.

Control-drag from the `UIImageView` to below the `class` line in ViewController.swift. Name the outlet `backgroundImage` when prompted to make the connection.

Implementing the Application Logic

To add the background fetching functionality, we will be making some edits in the `AppDelegate` class. First, we'll define the minimum frequency with which the application requests background fetches. This consists of a single line within `application:didFinishLau nchingWithOptions`. Open AppDelegate.swift and edit the method, as shown in Listing 22.10.

LISTING 22.10 Defining the Minimum Background Fetch Interval

```
func application(application: UIApplication, didFinishLaunchingWithOptions
    launchOptions: [NSObject: AnyObject]?) -> Bool {
    // Override point for customization after application launch.
    UIApplication.sharedApplication().setMinimumBackgroundFetchInterval(
```

```
         UIApplicationBackgroundFetchIntervalMinimum)
      return true
}
```

The method setMinimumBackgroundFetchInterval defines the *minimum* amount of time between fetches. Rather than setting an exact time, we use the constant UIApplicationBackgroundFetchIntervalMinimum to tell iOS that we want the fetch to occur as often as possible.

Now that the application knows we want to perform background updates, we must implement the method application:performFetchWithCompletionHandler. The method will retrieve an image from a website, then use it to set the image variable property of the background Image ViewController variable property.

Implement the application:performFetchWithCompletionHandler using Listing 22.11 as your guide. We'll go through the details afterward.

LISTING 22.11   Finishing the Background Fetch by Implementing application: performFetchWithCompletionHandler

```
 1: func application(application: UIApplication,
 2:     performFetchWithCompletionHandler completionHandler:
 3:     (UIBackgroundFetchResult) -> Void) {
 4:
 5:     let url: NSURL = NSURL(string:
 6:         "https://teachyourselfios.info/?hour=22")!
 7:     let data: NSData = NSData(contentsOfURL: url)!
 8:     let imageData: UIImage = UIImage(data: data)!
 9:     let myViewController: ViewController =
10:         self.window!.rootViewController! as! ViewController
11:     myViewController.backgroundImage.image = imageData
12:
13:     //Indicate completion
14:     completionHandler(UIBackgroundFetchResult.NewData)
15: }
```

Lines 5–6 allocates an NSURL object with a web address that will return a random image from teachyourselfios.info. Line 7 reads the data returned by the URL into an NSData object named data. At this point, we've performed the background fetch; now we just need to do something with the image we've downloaded.

In Line 8, that data is transformed into a UIImage using the UIImage convenience method imageWithData. In lines 9–10, we take advantage of the fact that the window object defined in the application delegate has a reference to the active view controller through the variable property rootViewController. This is cast as an instance of our ViewController class and stored in myViewController so that it's easier to access.

Line 11 accesses the `backgroundImage` variable property of `ViewController` and sets `image` to the image we downloaded.

Line 14 is a required function call to `completionHandler` tell iOS that we've successfully completed a background fetch operation. Depending on the outcome, we might also pass the constant `UIBackgroundFetchResult.Failed` (to indicate a failure) or `UIBackgroundFetchResult.NoData` (if nothing has changed).

Adding the Background Fetch Mode

Only one thing remains before we can give this a try: setting the Background Fetch background mode. Update the BackgroundDownload project by completing these steps:

1. Choose the main project group and click the BackgroundDownload target, and then expand the Background Modes section under the Capabilities tab.

2. Click the switch to turn on Background Modes.

3. Check the Background Fetch check box, as shown in Figure 22.11.

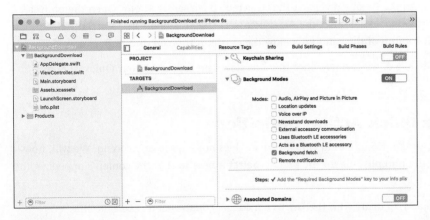

FIGURE 22.11
Add the Background Fetch mode to your application.

Building the Application

Go ahead and run the finished BackgroundDownload application in the iOS Simulator. You'll notice that it does *absolutely nothing!* The reason you won't see a background image is because we've only implemented fetching of an image when the application is in the background. You can either move the app to the background and wait, or you can choose Debug, Simulate Background Fetch from the Debug menu in Xcode. This automatically exits the app and forces it to perform a fetch. The next time you start it, the background image will be set.

Adding 3D Touch Quick Actions

In the final exercise of the hour, we'll be updating the ImageHop application (yes, again) to support 3D Touch Quick Actions. Quick Actions enables your users (assuming they have a 3D Touch-capable device) to access common application functions directly from the application icon—before the app even launches.

In the case of ImageHop, we'll add the option of having the user launch the application to a slow hopping bunny, or a fast hopping bunny (without them needing to configure a speed or touch the Hop! button). This requires surprisingly little code, but we will need a few more resources added to the application.

Adding the Quick Action Icons

Quick Actions often have an icon associated with them to give the user a more visual experience. I've included two new icons (slow and fast) in the folder BunnyIcons included in this hour's project folder. Let's load them now.

Begin by creating a new copy of the ImageHop application. Use the original project as the starting point, rather than the modified version that we created earlier this hour. Open the project and use the project navigator to select the Assets.xcassets asset catalog. Drag the BunnyIcons folder into the left column of the catalog—below the existing AppIcon and Images entries.

Once the icons are added, we can reference them as slow and fast within our Quick Action configuration.

Adding the Quick Action Definitions

Unlike many features in iOS, defining Quick Actions does not require any coding. We will, however, need to edit the Info.plist file for the project. Select it now so that the contents appear in the Xcode editor.

The first step is to add an array with the key `UIApplicationShortcutItems` to the Information property list:

1. Right-click anywhere in the existing list and choose Add Row.

2. When the row appears, type **UIApplicationShortcutItems** as the key.

3. Click the Type column to the right of the key and choose Array.

For each Quick Action you want to add, you must add a dictionary (with several keys and values) to the shortcut items array. We have two Quick Actions we're adding in this exercise. We'll start with the Slow Hop action:

1. Make sure that the disclosure arrow is expanded (pointing down) in front of the `UIApplicationShortcutItems` entry in the plist.

2. With your cursor hovering over the `UIApplicationShortcutItems` keyword, you'll see a + and – button appear to the right. Click +.

3. A new item will appear within the array. Click the Type column for the item and change it to Dictionary.

4. Much as you did for the parent Array, expand the disclosure arrow for Dictionary item.

5. Click the + button beside the Dictionary item *three* times to add three new entries within the dictionary. These will appear as String items.

6. Set the Key of one of the new String items to `UIApplicationShortcutItemTitle` with a value of. This is the Quick Action title displayed to the user.

7. Set the Key of another String item to `UIApplicationShortcutItemType` and a value of `startSlowHop`. This is the value our application will receive when the Quick Action is executed.

8. Set the third String item to a Key of `UIApplicationShortcutItemIconFile` and a value of `slow`. This is the name of the icon image to be displayed in the Quick Action.

9. You've just configured a 3D Touch Quick Action! Our application has two actions, so repeat steps 2–8, but supplying the values of `Start Fast Hop`, `startFastHop`, and `fast`.

Figure 22.12 shows the completed 3D Touch Quick Action configuration.

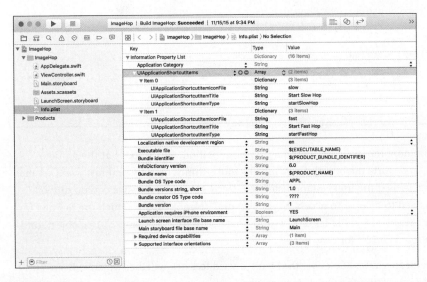

FIGURE 22.12
Configure your Quick Actions within the project's Info.plist file.

Implementing the Quick Action Logic

If you test the application on a 3D Touch-enabled device, the Quick Actions should appear when you press firmly on the application's icon. Unfortunately, at the time of this writing, there is no way to test this in the iOS Simulator.

Regardless, even the actions, while present, don't actually do anything yet. We still need to implement the method application:performActionForShortcutItem to process the chosen action. Open the AppDelegate.swift file and add Listing 22.12 to the file.

LISTING 22.12   Reacting to Quick Action events

```
 1:  func application(application: UIApplication,
 2:    performActionForShortcutItem shortcutItem:UIApplicationShortcutItem,
 3:    completionHandler: (Bool) -> Void) {
 4:
 5:    let myViewController: ViewController =
 6:        self.window!.rootViewController! as! ViewController
 7:
 8:    var success: Bool = false
 9:
10:    if shortcutItem.type == "startSlowHop" {
11:        myViewController.speedSlider.value = 0.25
12:        myViewController.setSpeed(nil)
13:        success = true
14:    } else if shortcutItem.type == "startFastHop" {
15:        myViewController.speedSlider.value = 1.75
16:        myViewController.setSpeed(nil)
17:        success = true
18:    } else {
19:        success = false
20:    }
21:
22:    completionHandler(success)
23:  }
```

To start the bunnies hopping, we can use the setSpeed method, which looks at the value of the speedSlider and starts the bunnies moving. To make things go slow and fast, we'll set the speedSlider.value as if the user had adjusted the speed himself. Before we can do any of that, however, we need to be able to access setSpeed and speedSlider, which are defined in the ViewController.swift class. Lines 5–6 grab a reference to ViewController object, and store it in myViewController for easy access.

Line 8 defines a Boolean value, success, that will be used to track whether we have been successful (or failed) in processing the Quick Actions.

Lines 10, 14, and 18 examine `shortcutItem.type` to see which Quick Action was executed. If `shortcutItem.type` is equal to `startSlowHop` (line 10), the user picked the Start Slow Hop action. If it is equal to `startFastHop` (line 14), the Start Fast Hop action was selected. If neither is true (line 18), something has gone wrong.

Lines 11–12 and 15–16 set the speed and start the bunnies hopping at the desired rate.

Line 22 finishes up by calling the `completionHandler` method with true or false, depending on whether we could properly react to the Quick Action. This, incidentally, is required by iOS, not something I added just to take up space.

Building the Application

You can now launch the application on a 3D Touch-enabled iOS device (currently the iPhone 6s/6s+). When you firmly press on the application icon, you'll see the Quick Action menu appear, as shown in Figure 22.13.

FIGURE 22.13
A firm press reveals the 3D Touch Quick Actions.

Choosing an action immediately launches ImageHop (or moves it to the foreground), configures the speed slider to an appropriate value, and then starts the bunnies happily hopping.

Further Exploration

When I sat down to write this lesson, I was torn. Background tasks/multitasking is definitely the "must have" feature of iOS, but it's a challenge to demonstrate anything meaningful in the span of a dozen or two pages. What I hope we've achieved is a better understanding of how iOS multitasking works and how you might implement it in your own applications. Keep in mind that this is not a comprehensive guide to background processing; there are many more features available and many ways that you can optimize your background-enabled apps to maximize battery life and speed.

As a next step, you should read the sections "App States and Multitasking" and "Background Execution and Multitasking" in Apple's *iOS Application Programming Guide* (available through the Xcode documentation).

As you review Apple's documentation, pay close attention to the tasks that your application should be completing as it works in the background. There are implications for games and graphic-intensive applications that are well beyond the scope of what we can discuss here. How well you adhere to these guidelines will determine whether Apple accepts your application or kicks it back to you for optimization.

Summary

Background applications on iOS devices are not the same as background applications on your Macintosh. There are well-defined rules that background-enabled applications must follow to be considered "good citizens" of iOS. In this hour's lesson, you learned about the different types of backgrounding available and the methods available to support background tasks. Over the course of seven tutorial applications, you put these techniques to the test, creating everything from notifications triggered when an application isn't running, to a navigation app with background voice prompting, an application that automatically updates its content when it isn't actively running, and Quick Actions that display outside of an application's main interface.

You should now be well prepared to create your own background-capable apps and take full advantage of the powerful hardware in your iPhone, iPad, or iPod.

Q&A

Q. Why can't I run any code I want in the background?

A. Someday I suspect you will, but for now the platform is constrained to the specific types of background processing we discussed. The security and performance implications of running anything and everything on a device that is always connected to the Internet are enormous. Apple intends to ensure that your device remains operational in any conditions, unlike the competitors, where anything goes.

Q. **If my application handles background operations, do I need to worry about iOS forcing my app to quit?**

A. Absolutely. The currently executing application (in the foreground) always has priority. Your application should be prepared to exit at any time if resources are constrained.

Workshop

Quiz

1. To start a long running task, which of the following methods would you use?

    a. `backgroundTaskWithExpirationHandler`

    b. `startBackgroundTaskWithExpirationHandler`

    c. `beginBackgroundTaskWithExpirationHandler`

    d. `begin]TaskWithExpirationHandler`

2. To clear any pending local notifications for your app, you should use which method?

    a. `cancelNotifications`

    b. `disableAllLocalNotifications`

    c. `removeAllLocalNotifications`

    d. `cancelAllLocalNotifications`

3. Playing audio is an example of what type of backgrounding?

    a. Task-specific

    b. Forbidden

    c. Automatic

    d. Time-limited

4. Before scheduling a local notification, you must first ask for what?

    a. Memory

    b. Authorization

    c. Network resources

    d. Data storage

5. A background fetch has how many seconds to complete?

    a. 30

    b. 10

    c. 60

    d. 120

6. Which method enables you to stop an `NSTimer` when you are finished with it?

    a. `close`

    b. `finish`

    c. `delete`

    d. `invalidate`

7. To enable background processing of GPS data, you use which capability check box?

    a. Location Services

    b. Location Updates

    c. GPS Updates

    d. User Data Updates

8. A 3D Touch Quick Action's title is defined by which plist key?

    a. `UIApplicationQuickItemTitle`

    b. `UIApplicationQuickActionTitle`

    c. `UIApplicationShortcutItemTitle`

    d. `UIApplicationLaunchItemTitle`

9. To request the frequency of background fetches, you must use which method?

    a. `setMinimumBackgroundFetchInterval`

    b. `setMaximumBackgroundFetchInterval`

    c. `setMinimumInterval`

    d. `setMaximumInterval`

10. To set the message displayed in a local notification, you can use which variable property?

    a. `alertText`

    b. `alertInfo`

    c. `alertBody`

    d. `alertDisplay`

Answers

1. C. Long-running tasks are started by including a call to the `beginBackgroundTaskWith-ExpirationHandler` method.

2. D. Use the `cancelAllLocalNotifications` to clear any existing notifications that your application may have generated.

3. A. Background audio is an example of task-specific backgrounding.

4. B. You must request authorization from the user before attempting to use local notifications.

5. A. Background fetches must complete within 30 seconds; otherwise, iOS will terminate them automatically.

6. D. The `invalidate` method is used to stop an `NSTimer` when you are finished using it.

7. B. The Location Updates check box must be checked in order for your application to receive and process changes in the user's location while in the background.

8. C. Quick Action titles are configured using the property list key of `UIApplicationShortcutItemTitle`.

9. A. You can only set the minimum amount of time between background fetches; this is managed through the `setMinimumBackgroundFetchInterval` variable property.

10. C. The `alertBody` is used to set the message contents for a local notification.

Activities

1. Return to a project in an earlier hour and properly enable it for background processing or 3D Touch Quick Actions.

2. Test to see what happens when an application with background processing attempts to run longer than 10 minutes. Is it suspended? Terminated? How do you recover from this if your application does not finish its task?

HOUR 23
Universal Applications and Size Classes

What You'll Learn in This Hour:

▶ What makes a universal application *universal*

▶ How to configure universal applications

▶ The use of size classes in application design

The iPhone represented Apple's first entry into touch-based computing. It was a single device with a single screen size. Man oh man, how times have changed! We now live in a world with the iPhone, the iPhone Plus, iPad, iPad Pro, and—who knows how many more are the pipeline? Throughout this book, we've been targeting one platform or another. But you know what's even better? Targeting *all of them*. We've already built a few universal applications, but we have always had an interface that looks the same on the iPad and iPhone. The applications have also been effectively unaware of what platform they are running on. In this hour's lesson, you will learn how your apps can be created to be universal, but also have distinct user interfaces on the iPhone and iPad.

Universal Application Development

A *universal* application is one that contains the necessary resources to run on the iPhone and the iPad. Although the iPad already supports running iPhone applications, they don't look so great being all stretched out. Unlike other platforms that try to reformat a small screen to a large display, Apple recognizes that these are unique user experiences. To build a true iPad application, you may need different scenes, images, and maybe even completely different classes. Your code might even need to make decisions on-the-fly about the type of device it is running on.

NOTE

Keep in mind that not all capabilities (vibration support, for example) are shared across your development platforms (iPhone/iPad/iPod touch). Be sure that you plan your universal apps appropriately.

Not all developers have decided that a universal application is the best approach for their projects. Many have created separate HD versions of their apps that are sold at a slightly higher price than an iPhone version. If your application is going to be substantially different on the two platforms, this might be the route you want to take, too.

Configuring a Project as Universal

To create a universal application project, you have two possible approaches. First, you can use the Devices drop-down menu during project setup to choose Universal, as shown in Figure 23.1.

FIGURE 23.1
Set the Devices to Universal.

Alternatively, if you've already created the project for a single device, follow these steps to update it to be universal:

1. Select the Project group in the project navigator.

2. Make sure that the first target is selected.

3. Click to select the General button at the top of the editor area.

4. Within the Deployment Info section, change the Devices drop-down menu to Universal, as shown in Figure 23.2.

There's really nothing special or complicated about making an application universal. There are a few additional resources, however, required by applications that run on both iPhone and iPads.

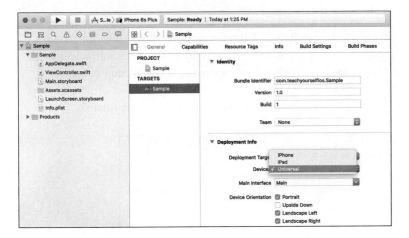

FIGURE 23.2
Update an existing project to be universal.

App Icons

Using a universal application's asset catalog, you can set app icons for both iPhone and iPad. Select the Assets.xcassets asset catalog in the project navigator, and then choose the AppIcon category. Xcode displays image wells for each device and icon type. To calculate the size of icon that is required, look at the measurement beneath each well. The size is given in points, so you'll need to multiple by the scaling factor (1x, 2x, or 3x) to get the dimensions in pixels.

If you don't see spots for both iPhone or iPad image files, open the Attributes Inspector. Here you can activate both iPhone and iPad icons, as shown in Figure 23.3.

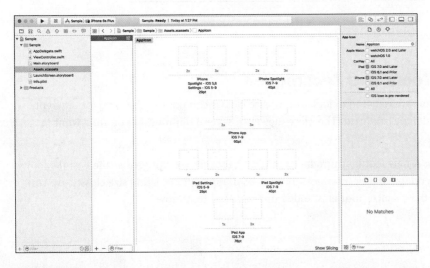

FIGURE 23.3
Add icon files for iPhone and iPad in the asset catalog.

Launch Screen

Each Xcode 7 application template now includes a LaunchScreen.storyboard file that contains a single scene, shown in Figure 23.4. You can use this scene (and all the Interface Builder tools, including Auto Layout) to create the screen that is shown when your application launches. In earlier versions of the development tools, launch screens were actually images—requiring *many* different versions of a single image to cover all possible device sizes and orientations.

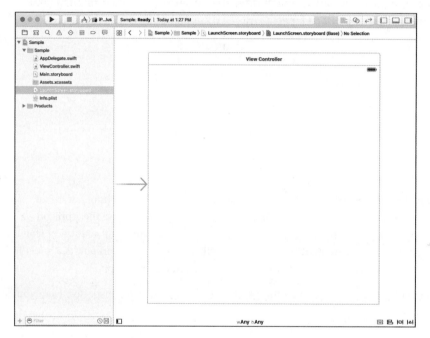

FIGURE 23.4
Build your custom launch screen.

Universal Tools and Techniques

In this hour's lesson, we're going to look at how size classes can address the need for different interfaces on the iPhone and iPad. There are, however, several approaches you may want to investigate:

▶ **Size classes:** A new feature (introduced in iOS 8), size classes will give us the best flexibility for defining adaptive user interfaces for universal applications. Using size classes, we can develop for the iDevices that exist today and *will* exist tomorrow.

▶ **Multiple storyboards:** The classic approach for iPad and iPhone interfaces is to use a different storyboard for each. By keeping the user interfaces separate, we can focus on creating the best possible UI for each device. You can set separate storyboards for iPhones and iPads by adding the keys "Main storyboard file base name (iPhone)" and "Main storyboard file base name (iPad)" to your project's Info.plist file along with the names of two independent storyboard files.

▶ **Device models:** Apple lets us quietly query what kind of device our code is running on. By performing a model or "interface idiom" query, we can programmatically make decisions about how to behave on different devices. This comparison, for example:

```
UIDevice.currentDevice().userInterfaceIdiom ==
    UIUserInterfaceIdiom.Pad
```

Returns `true` if the code is executing on an iPad.

Unless your project is highly dependent on device type or orientation, you should always use size classes to create the most device-agnostic application possible.

Size Classes

You've learned about adaptive segues, storyboards, and, starting now, size classes. Size classes are the final piece of Apple's adaptive technologies that will enable us to create a single storyboard that targets different device types (sort of, but more on that in a second).

The way it works is this: For any given size class, you can define a set of objects and object constraints that apply within that class. Want a button that only appears on a landscape iPhone? Set up the button for that size class, but no others. Want a label that orients in an entirely different position for an iPhone in portrait versus an iPad? Create one set of constraints for the iPhone's size class and another for the iPad.

So, what is a size class? It isn't exactly a device type, but a generic semantic representation of a particular type of device/orientation. What we will refer to as a size class is actually made up of two elements: a horizontal size class and a vertical size class. The horizontal class describes the width of the device, and the vertical class describes the height.

NOTE

The documentation on size classes isn't always consistent. A horizontal and vertical size class are together called a *trait*, but are more often just referred to as the more general *size class*. As you develop, you probably won't find many instances where you'll be referring to a size class as anything other than the combination of horizontal and vertical size classes (and vice versa).

For example, a size class of Compact Width, Regular Height describes any iPhone in portrait view. A size class of Regular Width, Compact Height is an iPhone Plus in landscape. A horizontal or vertical class can also be replaced with Any, meaning that it matches *any* possible values within that class. By default, when you create a universal application, you are designing for a size class of Any, Any; this combination applies to every device that Apple makes. All objects and constraints defined in the Any, Any size class apply to all devices, and are inherited by the more-specific size class.

All of this will make sense if you look at the different devices and orientations and the size classes that target them. Table 23.1 shows all of the current size class definitions and the devices they represent.

TABLE 23.1   **Size Classes and the Devices/Orientations They Represent**

Device/Orientation	Horizontal Size Class (Width)	Vertical Size Class (Height)
Any iPhone Portrait	Compact	Regular
iPhone Landscape	Compact	Compact
iPhone Plus Landscape	Regular	Compact
iPad Portrait	Regular	Regular
iPad Landscape	Regular	Regular

There are a couple things to consider right off the bat. First, these definitions aren't very granular. It's easy to imagine that a Compact width and Regular height describes an iPhone in portrait orientation. But how does Compact width and Compact height describe any iPhone in landscape mode? Apple currently believes that only the iPhone "Plus" models in landscape deserve to be called out separately with the Regular, Compact size class. Don't think about it too much - the goal is to pick the size class closest to what you need (and as generic as possible), and if Apple comes out with devices in that class in the future, your app will be ready for them.

The second thing to notice is that an iPad in a portrait orientation has the exact same size class as an iPad in landscape. No, that doesn't mean that there's some magical way a single size class can do double duty. It means exactly what you think it does: A size class cannot be used to differentiate between an iPad in portrait mode versus one in landscape. For that, you need to turn to the techniques we covered in Hour 16, "Building Responsive User Interfaces." Apple's opinion is that an iPad interface should be roughly consistent between landscape and portrait (so they cannot be targeted independently).

Why is Apple so mean? The answer lies in iOS 9. If you follow iOS development, you know that iOS 9 supports side-by-side multitasking on the iPad in iOS 9. To support iOS 9, your application needs to support Auto Layout along with size classes. Orientation becomes irrelevant when your screen is shared between two applications. In short, you must be able to adapt from Regular (W), Regular (H) layouts to Compact (W), Regular (H) layouts. In multitasking mode, the available iPad screen space is always taller than it is wide; the height is always Regular, whereas the width varies between one-third and two-thirds of the available screen width. In other words, it is Compact.

TIP

iPad Multitasking by Doing Nothing

If you want to support iPad multitasking in your application on iOS 9, you really don't need to do a thing. If you support Auto Layout and size classes, your application will automatically work with split-screen multitasking in iOS 9.

CAUTION

Watch This Space

Size classes are still quite new. Over the next few years, who knows how they'll evolve? Apple may add additional classes for new devices. Of course, if you use Any, Any, the storyboard will function anywhere in any size and orientation.

Using the Size Class Tools

Using size classes is much simpler than many tutorials and the Apple documentation would lead you to believe. In fact, it's as easy as creating your interface—something that you've been doing for hours. When you create a new project and open the storyboard, you're immediately dropped into a design using a size class of Any, Any, as shown in Figure 23.5. This literally means any horizontal class and any vertical class. (That is, every single device in every single orientation will use the objects and constraints you define in this configuration.)

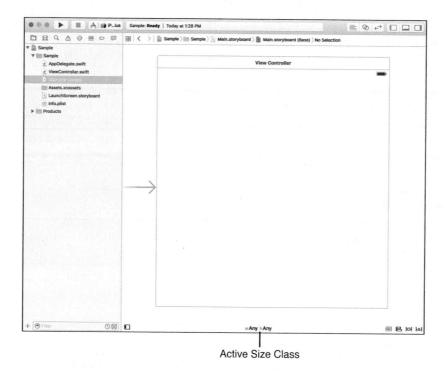

FIGURE 23.5
The default design is set to a size class of Any, Any.

If you have a simple application interface, this makes sense, and you absolutely *should* try to use this "generic" class. If, however, you think you may want to create custom layouts for other size classes in the future, this could lead to trouble. The problem with using one of the Any class designations is that everything you define within that class is inherited by other size class definitions. If you design within Any, Regular, for example, you're effectively designing for Compact, Regular and Regular, Regular.

Setting the Active Size Class

To set which size class you are working with in your storyboard, click the label in the bottom center of the editor. A pop-up selector appears, as shown in Figure 23.6.

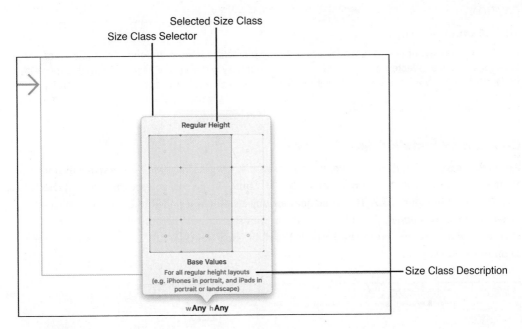

Selected Size Class

Size Class Selector

Regular Height

Base Values

For all regular height layouts
(e.g. iPhones in portrait, and iPads in
portrait or landscape)

Size Class Description

w **Any** h **Any**

FIGURE 23.6
Choose which size class you want to target by clicking, then hovering your cursor over the grid.

When I started working with the size class selector, I thought it was confusing. I still do. What you're doing in this tool is positioning your cursor so that the selected area best represents the size (visually) that you want to target. That said, the visual representation isn't close enough to "reality" for me to know what I'm looking at. Instead, I pay attention to the size class description, and I recommend you do as well. The description shows exactly what device and orientation the selected size class will target.

NOTE

As you move your cursor around the size class selector, you'll see little green dots appear in the grid. Those dots highlight the other size classes that will inherit any settings you make in the one that is currently selected.

After selecting a size class, what do you do? You design. You add objects, constraints, and have yourself a merry old time. In fact, you don't need to know anything else to design for a size class; you just work as you normally would. Of course, there's more to the story than that, but not too much more. After designing for one size class, you use the selector to choose another—and the process begins again, with one exception: You can inherit the constraints and objects from your other size class.

CAUTION

The "Assumed" Any

In the initial release of size classes in Xcode 6, Apple displayed Any at the top of the size class selector when you selected a class that matched either Any width or Any height. This has gone away in Xcode 7. Now, when the width or height is Any, it is simply left out of the selector's label. For example, if the selector says Regular Width at the top, it really means Regular width, Any height.

Configuring Installed Size Classes

An object or constraint that is active in a size class is known as *installed*. You may recall from Hour 16 that when you view constraints in the Attributes Inspector, you see an Installed check box, as shown in Figure 23.7. The same goes for objects that you added to a specific size class. When that box is checked, the object is active in that size class. When the check box isn't checked, the item is ignored. A check box is listed for each size class that could potentially apply to an object/constraint.

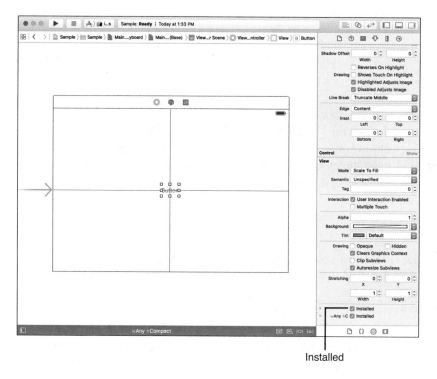

Installed

FIGURE 23.7
Installed objects and constraints are those that are active within the currently selected size class.

Constraints and objects that are being ignored in your currently selected size class are shown grayed out, as shown in Figure 23.8. You can still select them, but they won't become active and until you check their Installed check box.

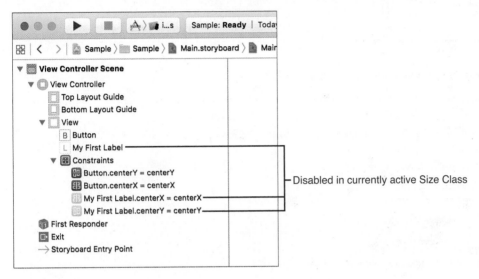

FIGURE 23.8
Grayed-out objects and constraints are not installed for the currently selected size class.

Manually Setting Size Classes

The easiest way to work with size classes is to create your designs in one class, switch to another size class, install the objects/constraints that you want active in that class, and you're done. Apple has also made it possible to add settings for any size class at any time, directly within the Attributes Inspector. Suppose, for instance, that you've installed a label in the Compact, Compact size class and you know you want it in the Regular, Regular class as well. You can select the label and view the Attributes Inspector, then scroll down to the Installed check boxes and click the tiny + button, shown in Figure 23.9.

Add Size Class Setting

FIGURE 23.9
Click the + to add a new size class setting.

A menu appears, as shown in Figure 23.10. Use the menu to choose a new size class that you want to install, such as Regular, Regular.

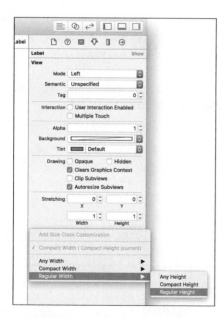

FIGURE 23.10
Choose the new size class to add.

After making your selection, the new size class will be visible in the list of check boxes and can be managed just like any other size class. Personally, I'd rather use the size class selector to switch to the desired class and edit the Installed check box there, but that's just me. There is, however, one very specific instance where using this + button is fast and simple: setting size class-controlled fonts.

Controlling Fonts with Size Classes

When setting the font for a label or control, you'll notice that the Attributes Inspector includes a small + button beside the Font field. You can use this to set custom fonts and sizes for any size class. Clicking the + button opens the same size class selection menu that you saw in Figure 23.10. Choose the size class you want to configure, and you'll see a new font selection field appear for just that size class, as shown in Figure 23.11.

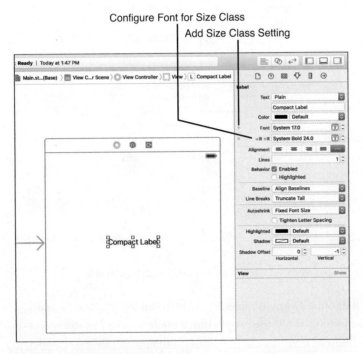

FIGURE 23.11
Set different fonts for different size classes.

You can configure the fonts however you'd like, and they will only be visible when the appropriate Size Class device/orientation is in effect.

Controlling Images with Size Classes

One last piece of Xcode functionality can be modified by size classes: images in asset catalogs. As you've learned, images can come in 1x, 2x, and 3x scaling factors, but you can also define images for different horizontal and vertical size classes, as well as size classes specific to the iPhone and iPad. To see how this works, open any asset catalog and add an image. Next, open the Attributes Inspector with the image name selected in the Asset Catalog list, as shown in Figure 23.12. Use the Width and Height drop-downs to choose a size class, and the Devices drop-down to choose what hardware you're supporting. You can even use the Memory check boxes to enable different image options depending on the amount of memory in the devices you are targeting.

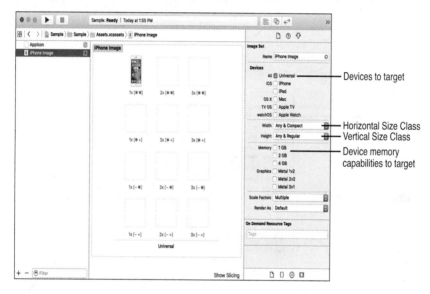

FIGURE 23.12
Customize image sets to include device-specific options as well as size class-based selections.

Within the grid of image wells that appear, Any is represented by an asterisk (*), Regular is a +, and – is Compact. Obviously, you should try to use images that work in as many places as possible, but this feature lets you customize your apps so that different images are shown on different devices/orientations without writing any code at all.

Creating a Storyboard with Size Classes

The problem (in my opinion) with size classes is that they're a heck of a lot easier to use than they are to talk about. For the project this hour, we're going to build out a storyboard that demonstrates how targeting two different size classes can create two unique interface scenarios. We'll be setting *many* constraints during this process, so it's important that you're comfortable with the Auto Layout tools before starting.

Implementation Overview

If you've ever played a game in landscape mode versus portrait mode on an iPhone, you know that the controls are rarely laid out the same. For this project, I'm imagining a hypothetical driving game with two control areas—one to turn right, and one to turn left—and, of course, a content area.

When the game is played in portrait mode (or any orientation on the iPad), I want the controls at the bottom of the display so that they are easily reached without obscuring the screen. When the game is shifted to landscape, however, I'd like the right and left controls to shift to the sides of the screen with the content in the middle. Figure 23.13 shows the layout that I'm imagining. The blue and red areas represent the controls; the beige/yellow is the content.

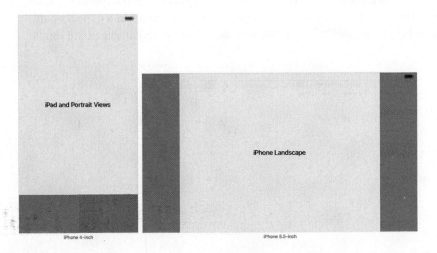

FIGURE 23.13
The controls will reposition entirely based on orientation.

To create the interface, we'll be using simple `UIView`s with colored backgrounds. This should give us clear visual indicators that things are working (or not working) the way that we want.

If you've been reading closely, you know that we'll want to target a size class of Any Width, Compact Height for the landscape layout, and Any Width, Regular Height for portrait modes. Remember, Any includes all possible options for that portion of the size class:

```
Any Width, Compact Height = Compact Width, Compact Height and Regular Width,
                            Compact Height
Any Width, Regular Height = Compact Width, Regular Height and Regular Width,
                            Regular Height
```

You can refer back to Table 23.1 to verify that this does, indeed, include all the devices and orientations that we're concerned about.

We'll begin by implementing the portrait view, and then change size classes and create the landscape design.

Setting Up the Any Width, Regular Height Size Class

Open up the Empty.storyboard file included with this hour's project. I've included a completed version of this example in the file SizeClasses.storyboard—but don't peek unless you get stuck.

Start by clicking the bottom of the editor and setting the size class to Any(w), Regular(h); this will show as Regular Height in the selector. The bar should turn blue to show that we're working in a specific size class.

Next, add three views to the design. Set the background of one to red to represent the right control, one to blue for left, then the other to something else. (I chose a nice Band-Aid color.) Click each view's label in the document outline and change it, too, so that you can tell them apart. I've labeled them as Left, Right, and Content. You now should be looking at something similar to Figure 23.14.

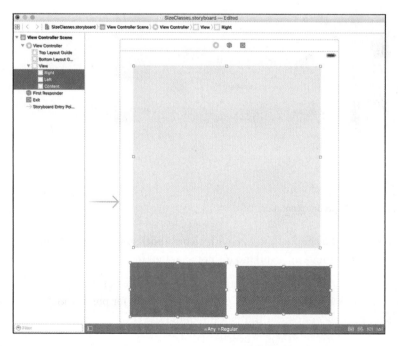

FIGURE 23.14
Add three views to the design, style, and name them to tell them apart.

To save time, I recommend selecting each view and then using the size inspector to position them using these coordinates. You're welcome to drag them into position if you prefer.

Content: X: 0, Y: 0, Width: 600, Height: 700

Left: X: 0, Y: 700, Width: 300, Height: 100

Right: X: 300, Y: 700, Width: 300, Height: 100

These coordinates, of course, are just placeholders. We need Auto Layout constraints added so that the content will shrink and expand as expected and stay where we want it to. Before adding any constraints, add one more object—a label. Drag a `UILabel` from the Object Library into the center of the Content view. Center the label and set it to read **iPad and Portrait Views**.

Your display should now resemble Figure 23.15.

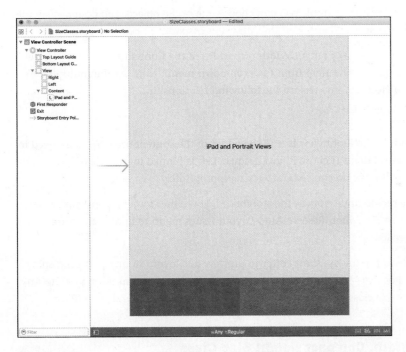

FIGURE 23.15
The laid-out interface for portrait views should look like this.

Now, we add the constraints. I'm providing the instructions for the constraints *I* used, but you're welcome to try your own:

1. Select the Content view and pin the Leading, Trailing, Top, and Bottom spaces to the superview.

2. Select the Right view and pin the Trailing and Bottom spaces to the superview. Pin the height as well.

3. Select the Left view and pin the Trailing space to 0.

4. Select the Left view only and pin the Leading and Bottom spaces to the superview. Pin the height as well.

5. Choose the Label and use the Align constraints to align horizontally and vertically in the container.

One more constraint to add, and this one's ugly. To make sure that the controls at the bottom are exactly 50% of the width of the content, we need to create a proportional constraint. To do this, select the Content view and the Right view and Pin Equal Widths. We don't actually want them to be equal, so select this constraint (you can choose one of the objects and double-click the constraint within the Size Inspector) and open the Attributes Inspector to edit it.

If the First Item field does not show Content.Width (the width of the Content view), click the field and choose Reverse First and Second Item from the drop-down menu. Now, set the multiplier to 2. If you remember from Hour 16, this sets up the following relationship:

```
Content.width = 2 × Right.width
```

In other words, the width of the Right view is half the width of the content area. We only need to do this on one of the control areas (I chose Right) because Left is pinned to the side of Right and to the superview—so it will have no choice but to resize appropriately.

At this point, if you are seeing any errors in the storyboard, you either forgot a constraint or something got shifted. Use the Editor, Resolve Auto Layout Issues menu to update the frames in the view controller if needed.

You should now be able to use the assistant editor to preview this layout in any portrait display mode on any simulated device—but that's not what we're going for. We want to update the Any Width, Compact Height size class to make the design entirely different for landscape iPhone layouts.

Adding the Any Width, Compact Height Size Class

Use the size class selector at the bottom of the editor to change to the Any(w), Compact(h) class—shown simply as Compact Height in the selector. As soon as you do, you're going to notice that everything gets ugly; in fact, objects may vanish altogether. If you are missing any of the views, select them in the document outline, and use the Attributes Inspector to click the Installed check box, as shown in Figure 23.16.

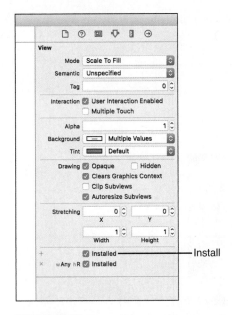

FIGURE 23.16
Click this check box to install the objects for the current size class.

Don't bother installing the label; we'll add an entirely *new* label to the project for this layout. Next, adjust the positioning of each view so that it appears the way you want. Again, I recommend just selecting each view and using the Size Inspector to adjust the coordinates, as shown here:

> **Content:** X: 100, Y: 0, Width: 400, Height: 400
>
> **Left:** X: 0, Y: 0, Width: 100, Height: 400
>
> **Right:** X: 500, Y: 0, Width: 100, Height: 400

CAUTION

Why Not Drag and Drop?

A bit of honesty: Not only am I trying to save you time with moving the objects via the Size Inspector, but I'm also trying to save you from some annoying Interface Builder bugs. When working with size classes, sometimes objects will reposition themselves, suddenly change their dimensions to 0 width and 0 height, and all sorts of fun stuff. It usually happens when I'm dragging things around, so I'm trying to avoid that in this tutorial.

Once everything is where it needs to be, again drag a `UILabel` into the Content view. Center the label and set it to read **iPhone Landscape**. This new label isn't installed in the other size class, and the other class's label isn't installed here, so these will be unique to each layout. The final design will look a lot like Figure 23.17.

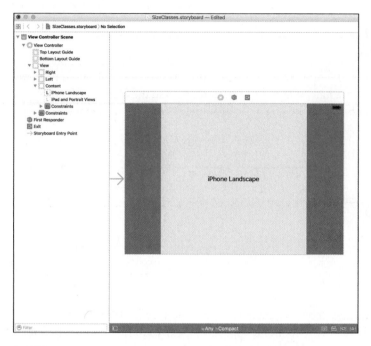

FIGURE 23.17
The iPhone landscape design has a dramatically different layout.

Now, setting the constraints. None of the constraints from the previous layout really make sense here, so we won't be installing any of them. Instead, we'll add new constraints:

1. Select the Content view and pin the Top and Bottom spaces to the superview.

2. Select the Content view and pin the Trailing spacing to 0.

3. Select the Left view and pin the Trailing spacing to 0.

4. Select the Right view and pin the Trailing, Top, and Bottom spaces to the Superview. Pin the Width as well.

5. Select the Left view and pin the Leading, Top, and Bottom spaces to the superview. Again, pin the Width.

6. Choose the Label and use the Align constraints to align horizontally and vertically in the container.

If you noticed any changes to the size of the objects as you added constraints (Interface Builder can go a bit wonky when working with size classes), use the Size Inspector to fix the objects. Once everything is in place, use the Resolve Auto Layout Issues options to resolve any remaining Auto Layout issues. You've just completed the project.

Previewing the Results

Open the Assistant Editor (View, Assistant Editor, Show Assistant Editor) and switch to a preview. Take a look at the interface on the iPhone in various orientations and the iPad. The design should expand and collapse thanks to Auto Layout, and entirely change in the iPhone landscape view courtesy of size classes.

I Switched My Size Class to Any, Any... Yikes!

If you switch your storyboard to the Any, Any size class, it's going to look ugly. That's because we designed with specific devices and orientations in mind, instead of trying to create something that works the same in all situations. Could we have added the Left, Right, and Content views in the Any, Any size class and installed/removed constraints for the other size classes so that they worked out? Yes, we could have, but there's no real point in putting ourselves through that. Taking the approach we did, we still cover all available size classes, and we do not have to tear our hair out installing and uninstalling constraints.

Further Exploration

The best way to learn more about universal applications is to start building them. Apple's developer documentation *iOS Human Interface Guidelines* will help you understand how your application's interface can be presented on each device.

These documents are also important because what is "acceptable" on one platform (according to Apple) might not be acceptable on the other. Classes such as the UIPickerView, for example, cannot be displayed directly within a view on the iPad. These features require the use of a popover (UIPopoverPresentationController) to meet Apple's guidelines. iOS introduce adaptive segues that make universal development much easier, but you should still be cognizant of what *isn't* the same between devices.

Summary

This hour's lesson covered the process of building universal applications on the iPhone and iPad. Using universal iOS application templates and size classes, you can quickly create an application that is customized to the device that it is running on. Size classes are the future of iOS cross-device development. They can quickly turn a project targeting one platform into one that runs on all of Apple's devices. I highly recommend spending time revisiting your development efforts and implementing size classes anywhere you can.

Q&A

Q. Why isn't everyone building universal applications?

A. Surprisingly, many people are *still* creating different versions of apps for different devices. In my opinion, this is being driven by two things. First, many applications, when expanded for the iPad, are "different" enough that a separate application is warranted. Second, I think that many developers see the potential for higher profits by selling multiple copies of their apps.

Q. I want to share code, but my views are too different to share a controller. What do I do?

A. Look for opportunities to create other shared classes. View controllers aren't the only opportunity for shared code. Any application logic that is shared between the iPhone and iPad could potentially be placed in its own class.

Workshop

Quiz

1. A size class cannot differentiate between which two devices/orientations?

    a. Landscape/Portrait iPads

    b. Landscape iPhones/Landscape iPhone Plus

    c. Portrait iPhones/Portrait iPads

    d. Landscape iPhone Plus/Landscape iPad

2. A size class set to Any, Any matches which of the following?

    a. All horizontal and vertical size classes

    b. Regular horizontal and vertical size classes

    c. Compact horizontal and vertical size classes

    d. None. This disables size classes entirely.

3. Size classes can be implemented without which of the following?

    a. Installed objects

    b. Auto Layout constraints

    c. Code

    d. Xcode 6

4. Universal applications, by default, use how many storyboards?

    a. 0

    b. 1

    c. 2

    d. 3

5. An object or constraint that is active within a size class is considered what?

    a. Active

    b. Ready

    c. Installed

    d. Used

Answers

1. A. Size classes cannot differentiate between the different orientations of an iPad.

2. A. Designing in a size class of Any, Any means that your design will be inherited by *all* horizontal and vertical size classes.

3. C. Size classes can be implemented entirely in Interface Builder, without writing any code.

4. B. By default, a universal application uses a single adaptive storyboard.

5. C. An object or constraint that is active in a size class is said to be *installed* in that size class.

Activities

1. Review the App Store to see the current trends in universal versus individual iPhone/iPad apps. What are the pricing differences between the approaches?

2. Return to a project in an earlier hour and create a universal version using size classes.

HOUR 24

Application Tracing, Monitoring, and Debugging

What You'll Learn in This Hour:

▶ Using the NSLog function
▶ Navigating the Xcode debugger
▶ Setting breakpoints and watchpoints
▶ Modifying variable values on-the-fly
▶ Tracing iOS app execution
▶ Monitoring memory and CPU usage

Despite our best efforts, no application is ever bug-free. As we end our 24-hour exploration of iOS development, we look at techniques for finding and fixing issues in our applications. The ability to find and eliminate bugs quickly is an essential skill.

Xcode brings together the five basic tools of the software developer's trade into a single application: the text editor, interface builder, compiler, debugger, and reference documentation. Xcode has debugging tools integrated within it, so all your debugging activities can take place from within the now-familiar interface of Xcode.

This hour covers the debugging and tracing tools included in Xcode. You learn how to use the NSLog function to output debugging information to the Xcode console. You also use Xcode's debugger to find and correct errors. This will give you a good start toward finding and solving problems that might otherwise lead to hours of head scratching, tears, and extreme frustration.

With the term *debugging*, it is assumed your project builds with no errors but then encounters an error or otherwise fails to work as designed when it's executed. If there is an error in your code that prevents it from building, you are still coding, not debugging. The tools in this hour are for improving applications that build but then have logic errors during execution.

Instant Feedback with NSLog

As you've developed applications throughout this book, one that has likely become clear is that producing output in an iOS application is more than just saying "print 'Hello World.'" We must deal with view controllers, scenes, storyboards, labels, outlets, connections, and so on, just to get a bit of text on the screen. This makes the traditional approach of debugging (outputting internal values and messages as a program executes) quite cumbersome. Even if we want to jump through all the hoops of building code and connections to output debugging information, we still have to make sure that none of it appears or interferes with our final production-ready app.

Thankfully, we can quickly generate output from a running application that doesn't interfere with our interface or application logic. To do so, just enter the humble NSLog function, which you briefly saw in Hour 1, "Preparing Your System and iDevice for Development." Many a gnarly bug has been slain with just this function alone. At any point in your application, you can use a call to NSLog to confirm the flow of your application into and out of methods or to check the current value of a variable. Any statement you log with NSLog is echoed to Xcode's debug console.

Why Not print?

Swift also includes the function print, which can be used just like NSLog. So why should we continue to use NSLog, which has been around forever? NSLog automatically adds a timestamp to every line it outputs, which makes it ideal for debugging. In addition, the Swift print statement, while being faster, isn't thread-safe. This means that if you have multiple methods executing at once, each with its own print functions, the output from one may be mixed in with the output of another, making the whole thing difficult to read.

In many cases, print will work just fine, but NSLog is still the king of printing out text for debugging.

Using NSLog

The NSLog function takes a String argument that can optionally contain string format specifiers. You've used these throughout the book to create formatted NSString objects and can get the full list of string format specifiers from the "String Format Specifier" section of the *String Programming Guide* in Xcode's Help.

The three string format specifiers you'll likely need while debugging are %d for integers (often used to debug loop counters and array indices), %f for floating-point numbers, and %@ for any object. Of course, you can also do things "the Swift" way by using string interpolation to substitute your values into an NSLog statement.

Consider the code fragment in Listing 24.1.

LISTING 24.1   Calling the NSLog Function

```
NSLog("Entering method")
var foo: Int = 42
var bar: Float = 99.9
NSLog("Value of foo: %d, Value of bar: %f", foo, bar)

var name: String = "Klaus";
var date: NSDate = NSDate.distantFuture() as NSDate
NSLog("Value of name: %@, Value of date: %@", name, date)
```

In this example, the NSLog function is used to output a string, integer, floating-point value, and two objects (a string and a date). The output looks like this:

```
2015-10-23 10:22:58.133 MyPlayground[2820:308688] Entering method
2015-10-23 10:22:58.146 MyPlayground[2820:308688] Value of foo: 42, Value of bar:
99.900002
2015-10-23 10:22:58.150 MyPlayground[2820:308688] Value of name: Klaus, Value of
date: 4001-01-01 00:00:00 +0000
2015-10-23 10:22:58.151 MyPlayground[2820:308688] foo: 42 bar: 99.9 name: Klaus
date: 4001-01-01 00:00:00 +0000
```

So, where does this output appear? If it isn't on the iOS device screen, where can you see the results of using NSLog? The answer is the Xcode debugger console, but rather than just telling you where, let's see this in action.

NOTE

When an object is output using either string interpolation or the %@ format specifier, the object's description method is called; this can provide additional information about the object within the debugging output. Many of Apple's classes include an implementation of description that is useful for debugging. If you need to debug your own objects with NSLog, you can implement description, which returns a String value.

Viewing NSLog Output

Open the project Counting in this hour's projects folder. Click Run to start running the application in the iOS Simulator. You'll see... nothing... just a blank screen with some static text (nothing at all changing on the screen). Behind the scenes, however, the application ran a counter in the view controller's viewDidLoad method and output the count using NSLog.

If you shift your attention to Xcode, you should be able to see the output in the debug area, as shown in Figure 24.1. If it wasn't shown automatically, choose View, Debug Area, Activate Console (or press Shift-Command-C). The debug area is usually divided in half—one side for viewing variables, the other (the right side) for showing output. This portion is called the *console*.

You can drag the middle divider to create more room for the console, or you can use the buttons in the lower-right of the debug area to hide or show the left and right columns.

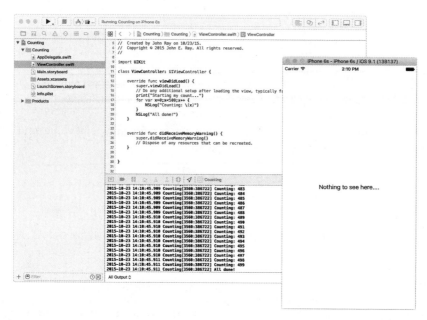

FIGURE 24.1
View the output of NSLog in the console area.

TIP

To quickly access the console area, use the middle button in the Xcode toolbar's view controls, choose an option from the View, Debug Area menu, or click the hide/show icon (an arrow in a box) at the left side of the debug area.

As you build more projects, NSLog will become a powerful tool in determining that your applications are executing as you expect. It isn't, however, the most powerful method of debugging an app. For instances where the size or complexity of the application doesn't lend itself to using NSLog, you'll want to turn to the Xcode debugging tools, which enable you to view your application as it executes without having to change your code.

TIP

Overwhelmed by output in the debugger console? Click the trash can icon in the lower-right corner to discard any output currently in the debugger console.

CAUTION

Don't Go NSLog **Crazy**

As its name implies, the NSLog function is actually intended for logging, not debugging. In addition to printing the statements to Xcode's console, the statements are written out to a file on the file system. Logging to the file system is not what you're intending; it's just a side effect of using NSLog for debugging. It's easy to accidentally leave old NSLog statements in your code after you've finished debugging, which means your application is taking time to write out statements to the file system and is wasting space on the user's device. Search through your project and remove or comment old NSLog statements in your application before you build a release to distribute. If you absolutely must leave output active in your code, print will have less of a negative impact on performance in production.

Using the Xcode Debugger

NSLog is a good quick-and-dirty approach to debugging, but it is not the best tool for debugging more complex issues. It's often more productive to use a debugger, which is a tool that lets you examine a running program and inspect its state. It's been said that what separates true software development professionals from weekend hackers is the ability to proficiently use a debugger. If this statement is true, you are in luck, because using Xcode's debugger is not hard.

Normally an application executes at computer speeds, which on an iDevice is millions of instructions per second. A debugger acts like the developer's brake, slowing down the progress of the application to human speeds and letting the developer control the progress of the program from one instruction to the next. At each step in the program, the developer can use the debugger to examine the values of the variables in the program to help determine what's gone wrong.

Debuggers work on the machine instructions that are compiled from an application's source code. With a source-level debugger, however, the compiler provides data to the debugger about which lines of source code generated which instructions. Using this data, the source-level debugger insulates the developer from the machine instructions generated by the compiler and lets the developer work with the source code he has written.

Xcode's iOS debugger, called lldb, is a source-level debugger. The compiler doesn't always generate the data needed for source-level debugging. It can amount to a lot of data, and it provides no benefit to an application's users, so the data is not generated in a release build configuration. Before you can benefit from source-level debugging, you need to build your application in a debug build configuration that will generate the debug symbols.

By default, a new Xcode project comes with two build configurations: Debug and Release. The Debug build configuration includes debug symbols, whereas the Release build configuration does not. Whenever you are working on developing your application, you use the Debug configuration so that you can drop into the debugger whenever you need to. Because Debug is usually the build configuration you want to work with, it's the default configuration, too. To switch to a release configuration, you must build for an iOS device instead of the Simulator, and you must use the Product, Scheme, Edit Scheme menu to switch to a Release configuration. In Figure 24.2, for example, I've set my Scheme so that when I run my app, I will be running it on an iOS device in a Release configuration.

NOTE

Make sure that you remember to use the Release build configuration when you create a version of your application for distribution.

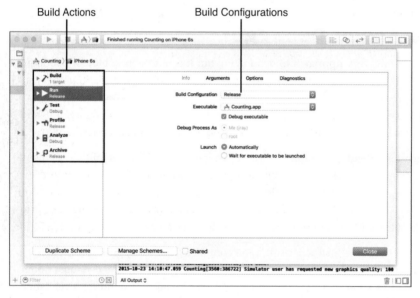

FIGURE 24.2
Set the configuration using the Product, Edit Scheme menu.

Setting Breakpoints and Stepping Through Code

To use the debugger, you must have something to debug. For the rest of this hour, we work through a few simple debugging tests, starting with a very simple counting application.

Create a new Xcode project with the Single View iOS Application template and call it **DebuggerPractice**. There is no user interface (UI); therefore, no outlets and actions are required in this exercise.

TIP

The debugger often references source code line numbers, and it is helpful to have these displayed in the gutter. If your Xcode installation isn't displaying numbers, turn them on by opening the Xcode preferences and activating the Line Numbers option under the Text Editing settings.

Open the ViewController.swift file and begin by adding a new method to the file. This method, describeInteger, returns a string with the word *even* if an integer passed to it is divisible by 2 or the word *odd* if it isn't. Listing 24.2 contains my implementation of this method.

LISTING 24.2   Implementing the `describeInteger` Method

```
func describeInteger(i: Int) -> String {
    if i % 2 == 0 {
        return "even"
    } else {
        return "odd"
    }
}
```

Next, edit the viewDidLoad method. Add a for loop that uses NSLog to display the numbers between 1 and 10 in Xcode's debugger console. For each iteration of the loop, the method should call describeInteger with the loop's index. This provides activity that we can monitor in the debugger. Your method should resemble Listing 24.3.

LISTING 24.3   Editing the `viewDidLoad` Method

```
override func viewDidLoad() {
    super.viewDidLoad()
    // Do any additional setup after loading the view, typically from a nib.
    var description: String
    NSLog("Start")
    for var i=1;i<=10;i++ {
        description=describeInteger(i)
        NSLog("Variables i = \(i) and description = \(description)")
        NSLog("-----")
    }
    NSLog("Done")
}
```

After entering the code, take a moment to look at the editor. Notice the light-gray area (essentially a margin) located to the left of your code. This is called the *gutter* and is where you configure many of Xcode's debugging features. Figure 24.3 shows the gutter.

Show the debug area, and click the Breakpoints button on the toolbar above the debug area; this enables debugging. Alternatively, you can choose Debug, Activate Breakpoints (Command-Y) from the menu bar. Now start your app. The program starts up and brings us to our application's empty view.

The Gutter

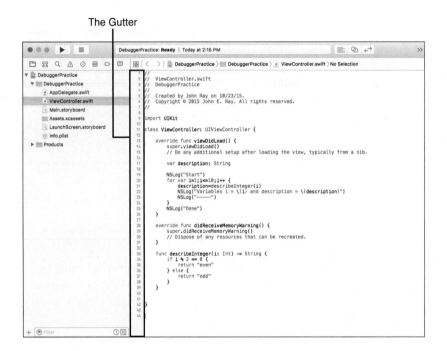

FIGURE 24.3
Xcode's gutter is used for debugging.

The output from our NSLog statements is in the debugger console, but nothing else is, as demonstrated in Figure 24.4.

The lldb debugger is running; we just haven't told it that we want it to do anything. The most common way to start interacting with the debugger is to set a breakpoint in your application's source code.

Setting a Breakpoint

A breakpoint is an instruction to the debugger letting it know you want the program execution to pause at that point. To set a breakpoint, click once in the gutter next to the line where you want the application to pause. A breakpoint will appear as a blue arrow, as demonstrated in Figure 24.5. Click the arrow to toggle the breakpoint off and on. When the breakpoint is on, it is displayed as a solid blue color. When it is off, it is light transparent blue, and the debugger ignores it. To remove a breakpoint, simply drag it out of the Xcode gutter and it will disappear. While a program is executing, a green arrow in the gutter indicates the current line of source that is active.

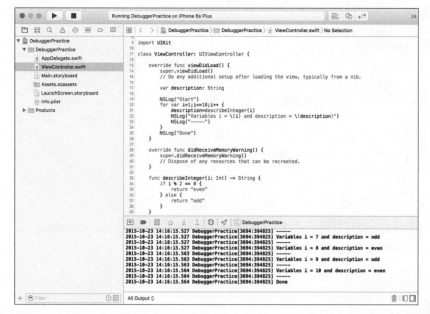

FIGURE 24.4
The debugger is running but not doing anything.

Active Breakpoint

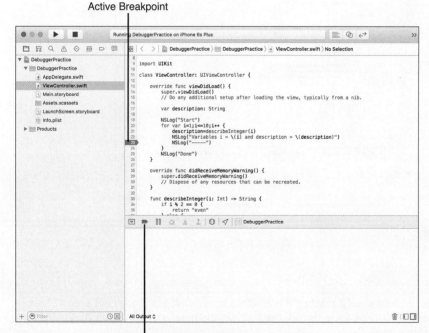

FIGURE 24.5
Set a breakpoint by clicking in the gutter.

Enable/Disable All Breakpoints

Let's create and use a breakpoint. Quit the execution of the application by clicking the Xcode Stop button, and then click the gutter to set a breakpoint next to this line in the `viewDidLoad` method of ViewController.swift:

```
NSLog("-----")
```

Make sure that the breakpoints icon is highlighted in the toolbar (this enables/disables debugging breakpoints), and then click the Run button. Notice that the application stops after printing just one of the inner loop statements to the debugger console:

```
2015-10-23 11:25:31.625 DebuggerPractice[3034:319559] Start
2015-10-23 11:25:31.629 DebuggerPractice[3034:319559] Variables i = 1 and
description = odd
(lldb)
```

The debugger has paused the execution of the application at our breakpoint and is awaiting further direction, as shown in Figure 24.6.

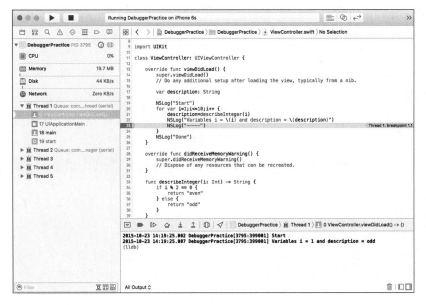

FIGURE 24.6
The debugger pauses at breakpoints.

NOTE

The Xcode debugger pauses when it reaches a line with a breakpoint, but it does not execute that line. You must manually continue execution for the line with the breakpoint to be run. You'll see how this works shortly.

Examining and Changing Variable States

Now that the execution of the program is paused in the debugger, we can inspect the value of any variables that are in scope. One of the easiest ways Xcode provides to examine variables is the debugger *datatip*. Just hover over a variable in the source code of the paused method and Xcode will display a popover, visible in Figure 24.7. For simple variable types, you'll just see the value of the variable. Objects, however, can display more information, including the class type, and a Quick Look icon for displaying details about the object.

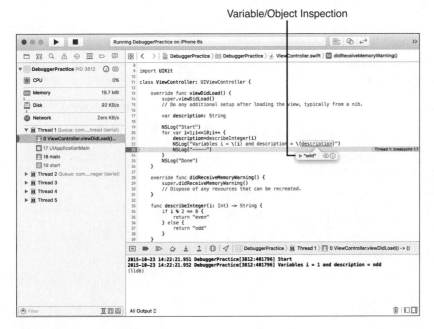

FIGURE 24.7
You can display the datatip by hovering over the variables.

Hover over the i loop counter in the for statement and then the description variable. Notice that the datatip for i is just one level, but the datatip for the more complex String object has multiple levels. Click the disclosure arrows to see the additional levels.

Datatips can also be used to change the value of a variable. Again, hover over the i variable in the for loop statement and click the value in the datatip. It is currently 1, but you can change it to 4 by clicking the current value, typing **4**, and pressing Enter. The value in the running program is immediately changed, so the next trip through the loop logs to the console with a value of 5, and there won't be a logged statement with a value of 2, 3, or 4. To confirm that the program does execute as if the i variable has a value of 4, we need to continue the execution of the program.

Stepping Through Code

By far, the most common debugging activity is watching the flow of your application and following what it does while it's running. To do this, you need to be able to control the flow of execution, pausing at the interesting parts and skipping over the mundane.

The debugger provides five icons for controlling program execution (see Figure 24.8):

▶ **Toggle Breakpoints:** Toggles breakpoints on and off for the entire application.

▶ **Continue:** Resumes execution of the paused program, pausing again at the next error or active breakpoint.

▶ **Step Over:** Steps to the next line of code in the same method.

▶ **Step Into:** Steps into the method that is being called. If a method isn't being called on the current line of code, it acts like Step Over.

▶ **Step Out:** Steps out of the current method back to the caller of the current method.

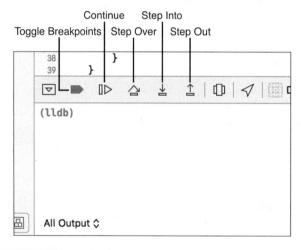

FIGURE 24.8
Program execution control icons.

NOTE

You'll notice a sixth and seventh icon beside the Step Out control. The sixth is for debugging application view hierarchies (we'll see this in a minute). The seventh, a GPS indicator icon, is used to set a simulated location for location services. These features do not affect day-to-day debugging.

Whereas the global breakpoint control is obvious (and *useful*), the other options might not be so clear. Let's take a look at how each of these works to control the flow of our application. First click the Continue icon a couple of times. Control returns back to the same breakpoint each time you continue, but if you hover over the i and description variables, you'll see that i is incrementing and description is switching between even and odd.

Add a breakpoint to this line of code by clicking the gutter:

```
description=describeInteger(i)
```

Click the Continue icon again, and this time you'll see the program stops at the new breakpoint because it's the next breakpoint the program encounters. This breakpoint is on a line of source where we are calling the describeInteger method. If we want to see what's going on inside that method, we need to step into it. Click the Step Into icon, and the program stops on the first line of the describeInteger method, as demonstrated in Figure 24.9.

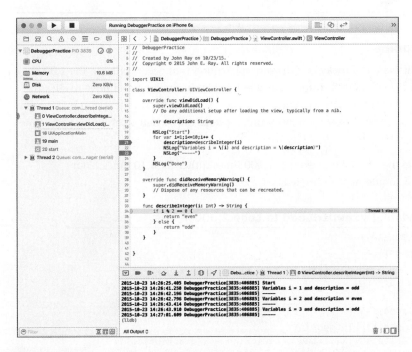

FIGURE 24.9
Program execution after stepping into the describeInteger method.

To step line by line through a method without entering any of the methods that might be called, use the Step Over task. Click the Step Over icon several times to step through the describeInteger method and return to the viewDidLoad method.

Click the Continue icon until you return to the breakpoint on the `describeInteger` method, and click the Step Into icon to step into the method a second time. This time, instead of stepping all the way through `describeInteger`, click the Step Out icon and you'll be stopped back at the line where the `describeInteger` method was called. The rest of the `describeInteger` method still executed; you just didn't watch each step of it. You are stopped where the program flow has just exited the `describeInteger` method.

Continue to Nowhere

As of the time of this writing, an important feature is missing from Xcode and Swift: Continue to Here. When running an Objective-C project (and hopefully someday Swift), you can right-click in gutter when the application is stopped at a breakpoint and choose Continue to Here. This automatically continues the program's execution until it reaches the chosen line.

You can currently see this option when working on Swift projects, but it is grayed out and not selectable.

Setting a Watchpoint

Let's suppose now that there is a tricky bug in your application that occurs only on the 1,000th time through the loop. You wouldn't want to put a breakpoint in the loop and have to click the continue icon 1,000 times. That's where a watchpoint comes in handy. A watchpoint is a conditional breakpoint; it doesn't stop execution every time, it stops only when a condition you define is true.

To test this out, update the `for` loop to execute 2,000 times rather than 10 times. Your `viewDidLoad` method should now resemble Listing 24.4.

LISTING 24.4   Updating `viewDidLoad` to Loop 2,000 Times

```
override func viewDidLoad() {
    super.viewDidLoad()
    // Do any additional setup after loading the view, typically from a nib.
    var description: String
    NSLog("Start")
    for var i=1;i<=2000;i++ {
        description=describeInteger(i)
        NSLog("Variables i = \(i) and description = \(description)")
        NSLog("-----")
    }
    NSLog("Done")
}
```

Now let's set a watchpoint that stops execution when the loop counter equals 1,000. First, remove the existing breakpoints by dragging them out of the gutter. Next, add a normal breakpoint by clicking in the gutter next to this line:

```
NSLog("Start")
```

Add a second breakpoint here:

```
NSLog("Variables i = \(i) and description = \(description)")
```

Then right-click the second breakpoint and choose Edit Breakpoint from the contextual menu. The Breakpoints dialog then opens, as shown in Figure 24.10. Here you can use the Condition field to specify when the breakpoint becomes active. Set the condition to i == 1000.

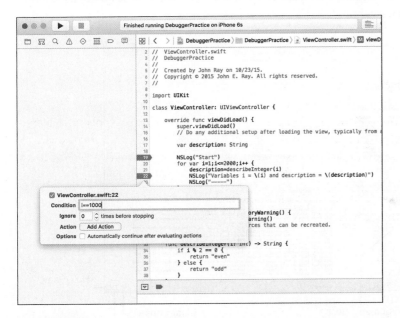

FIGURE 24.10
Program execution stops on the 1,000th iteration.

Click the Run button to execute the application. The program stops at the first breakpoint. Click the Continue icon, and the application will go through the loop 999 times before stopping on the watchpoint on the 1,000th trip through the loop when the loop counter i is equal to 1,000. You can confirm this by looking at the 999 log messages in the debugger console or by hovering over the i variable in the source and looking at its value in the datatip.

Accessing the Variable List

If, at any time, you want to access a list of all variables that are active in your current method, you can do so by viewing the left half of the debugger area. The buttons in the lower-right corner of the debugger toggle the Variable List (left side) and Console (right side). To this point, we've been focusing solely on the Console view.

Make sure that the Variable List is visible, and you'll see that both the i and description variables (and their values) that we've been inspecting with datatips are shown prefixed with an L icon, as shown in Figure 24.11. This means these variables are declared locally in the method that is currently executing. You'll also see A icons for Arguments scope variables that have been passed into the current method as arguments. A pop-up menu at the lower-left corner of the Variable List enables you to show All variables, Local variables only, or Auto—to let Xcode choose what it thinks is relevant.

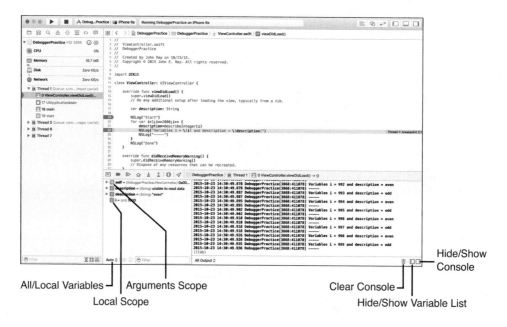

FIGURE 24.11
Use the Variable List to inspect the value of active variables in your application.

TIP

Expanding a variable line in the Variable List, then right-clicking the value and choosing Edit Value enables you to change it, just as you could through the data.

Using the Debugger Navigators

We first looked at the debugger by examining console output, and since then we've focused on debugging in that area alone. There are also two navigator area displays—the debug navigator and the breakpoint navigator—that have some helpful benefits. You may have noticed these appearing on the left side of the Xcode workspace while working with the debugger. You can jump to either at any time by selecting them from the View, Navigators menu.

The Breakpoint Navigator

Large projects with hundreds of breakpoints can get out of hand quickly. Where are all the breakpoints? How do you selectively enable/disable/edit/remove them? The breakpoint navigator, shown in Figure 24.12, is your one-stop shop for managing breakpoints in your project.

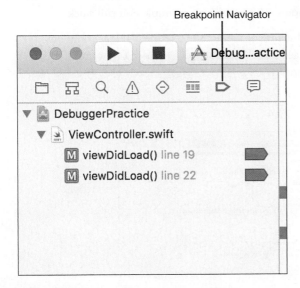

FIGURE 24.12
Use the breakpoint navigator to manage your breakpoints.

All breakpoints are listed by the file where they are located. You can click any breakpoint to jump to that spot in your code or right-click any listed breakpoint to manage it (including setting conditions, disabling it, and so on).

The Debug Navigator

The debug navigator displays the application's call stack listed by thread. A call stack is the list of all the subroutines (methods and functions) currently being executed. Each method in the call stack has been called by the method below it. To better understand this, it is best to see it in action.

Remove the existing breakpoints from your code, and then add a new breakpoint at the start of
`describeInteger` by clicking in front of this line:

```
if i % 2 == 0 {
```

Now, execute your code and let the breakpoint take effect. After execution has halted, open the
debug navigator by choosing View, Navigators, Show Debug Navigator or by clicking the navigator area toolbar icon (two solid lines with dashed lines in the middle).

Notice that the `describeInteger` method of our view controller is at the top of the stack and
was called by the `viewDidLoad` method, exactly as we'd expect. The call stack entries listed with
a blue icon are code that we have implemented in our project; clicking one of these entries shows
a green cursor where the program execution is currently "waiting." The `describeInteger`
method is waiting on our breakpoint, while the `viewDidLoad` method waits on the
`describeInteger` method (and so on). Figure 24.13 shows an example of a call stack.

The rows in the call stack that are not in blue are for methods where the debugger only has
assembly language available. Click one to see some Assembly code. (Doesn't that make you
thankful that we have a source-level debugger?)

Debug Navigator

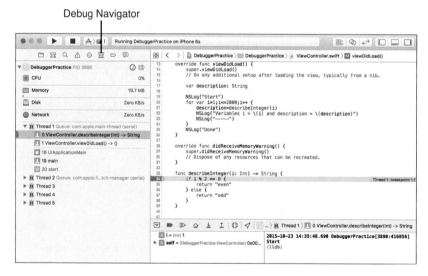

FIGURE 24.13
View the call stack in the debug navigator.

Monitoring CPU and Memory Usage

The Xcode debug navigator has a few other cool tricks up its sleeve. In addition to showing a
stack trace, it also shows the CPU and memory usage of your application over time. This can

show you whether your application is leaking memory or trying to ask the processor to do too much (eating battery life and leading to poor performance).

To show you how this works, I've included a project called CountToDisaster in the Hour 24 Projects folder. This application creates a string, then, every second, sets the string to itself appended with itself (doubling the previous memory usage every second). In a very short time, the application runs out of memory and crashes. As this happens, you can watch the memory usage and CPU usage go up in the debug navigator.

Open the project, switch to the debug navigator, and then click the Run button. Within the Debug Navigator column, you'll see tiny graphs showing memory and CPU usage as the application runs. Clicking one of these graphs, however, expands to show a detailed dashboard with the actual memory (or CPU) usage and how it compares to the other iOS processes running, as shown in Figure 24.14.

The CountToDisaster app will eventually crash, and, with more than a gigabyte of memory used when it does, we can definitely surmise that it is a poorly written app! You'll want to use these tools to verify that your application is a well-behaved iOS citizen, especially if you are using background processing.

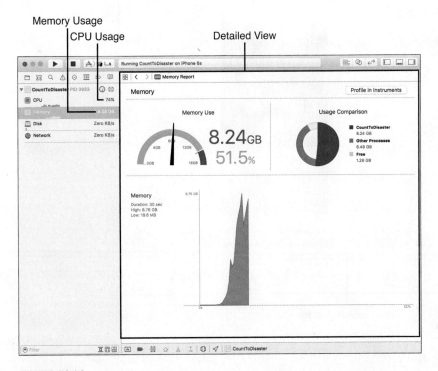

FIGURE 24.14
View your memory and CPU usage in real time.

Checking Your View Hierarchy

As you build applications with increasingly complex interfaces, it can be difficult to see "what is where." Is my label not showing because it's behind something? Is this graphic being cut off by some other object?

These are just a few of the questions that you can answer using the Xcode 6 Debug View Hierarchy feature. This shows an exploded view of the application's user interface, making it easy to see what elements are coming together to create the interface and how they lay on top of one another.

Because this is a visual tool, the best way to understand it is to try using it. Let's do that.

Begin by opening the ImageHop application that we built for the iPhone in Hour 8, "Handling Images, Animation, Sliders, and Steppers." (I've included a copy in your Hour 24 projects folder for easy access.) Click Run to start the application, wait until the main field of bunnies is displayed, and then click Debug View Hierarchy in the debug toolbar at the bottom of the Xcode window (see Figure 24.15).

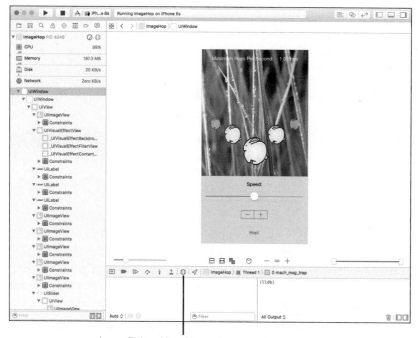

Debug View Hierarchy

FIGURE 24.15
View your... views.

At first glance, you might think you're just looking at a normal rendering of your application interface. To see why this isn't the case, click and drag to rotate the view in three dimensions. You can drag to view the hierarchy from the front, side, back—whatever you want.

Figure 24.16 shows a rotated version of the ImageHop interface.

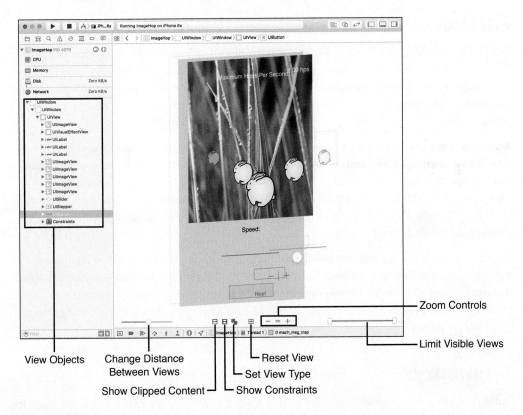

FIGURE 24.16
Explore how your views are laid out onscreen.

Using the view hierarchy in the debug navigator, you can highlight individual elements making up the view. The controls underneath the view itself can be used to increase the spacing between elements, limit what is visible, or manipulate how the views are rendered for debugging.

I highly recommend testing this feature out, because it will give you a true sense for how your interface layout is actually being rendered and why you may be experiencing visual glitches in your design.

You've done enough now to start getting the hang of using the Xcode debugger system. With just these tools for controlling program flow and inspecting and changing program state, you can debug many of the issues that you may encounter as you step into the exciting world of iOS development.

Further Exploration

Invest some time into becoming proficient with Xcode debugging. When you're approaching the launch date for your application, you'll want to check and double-check your code. In these cases, time is short and the stress level is high, so it's not the ideal circumstances to be learning application debugging for the first time. Become comfortable with these tools now, and they'll provide a significant productivity boost when you need it the most.

Xcode offers many other tools for testing and optimizing your applications, but each could take a book in its own right. The Instruments system, for example, allows you to stress-test your application under a number of conditions and identify potential problems. To get a complete overview of the testing/debugging options available within Xcode and its associated tools (including some nifty UI recording and playback features), be sure to read *Testing with Xcode*, available through the Xcode documentation.

As you've learned throughout this book, Xcode is a large, *large* product. You'll be discovering new features for a long time to come. Don't be concerned if your application development workflow varies from what we've covered over the past 24 hours; development is as much a creative process as it is technical. Each developer is unique, and Xcode aims to make each of us empowered and productive.

Summary

In this last hour, you learned how to use NSLog for quick debugging and the Xcode debugger for examining the inner workings of your code. Using a debugger takes much longer than an hour to understand everything it can do for you, but the goal has been to give you enough exposure that you recognize when you need the benefits of the tools.

With that, you've reached the end of this book. I sincerely hope that you've enjoyed yourself and are ready to write some apps. Remember to visit the support website http://teachyourselfios.com for additional materials and corrections.

Q&A

Q. Why is using a debugger easier or better than just using NSLog?

A. NSLog is a great place for beginning developers to start. It gives a degree of insight into what is going on in the code, without having to change the development process. Using the full-blown Xcode debugger, however, will enable you to view and modify values in your code as it is running. In addition, it doesn't require any changes directly to your code, so there isn't a need to remove debugger statements when the code is clean. Using a debugger takes awhile to get used to, but for large projects, it is a must.

Workshop

Quiz

1. NSLog is beneficial for debugging because it includes which of the following?

    a. A timestamp

    b. Syntax highlighting

    c. Object rendering

    d. Graphic output

2. A location within your code at which application execution is halted for the purpose of debugging is called a what?

    a. Halt spot

    b. Breakpoint

    c. Stop point

    d. Pause place

3. What is the debugger you will use in Xcode called?

    a. ggdb

    b. gdb

    c. ldb

    d. lldb

4. Breakpoints are set by clicking within what in the Xcode?

    a. Column

    b. Margin

    c. Gutter

    d. Divider

5. NSLog statements should not be included when doing what with applications?

  a. Developing

  b. Shipping

  c. Debugging

  d. Testing

6. You should use which configuration when preparing an application for submission to the App Store?

  a. Release

  b. Debug

  c. Test

  d. Production

7. You can use lldb to inspect your application on a line-by-line basis because it is what type of debugger?

  a. Source-level debugger

  b. Code-level debugger

  c. Statement-level debugger

  d. Edit-enabled debugger

8. To figure out where your application has been set to halt for debugging, you can use which of the following?

  a. Breakpoint navigator

  b. Debug navigator

  c. Stack trace

  d. Instruments console

9. To view your application's UI split into a 3D view of layers, you may take advantage of which feature?

  a. lldb

  b. Debug console

  c. Debug View Hierarchy

  d. View Layer Inspector

10. The debug feature that enables you to skip a method is called what?

    a. Breakpoint inspection

    b. Continue

    c. Step into

    d. Step over

Answers

1. A. The NSLog function includes a timestamp in all output, making it a handy tool for debugging.

2. B. Breakpoints are the spots in your code where execution should be halted for the purposes of debugging.

3. D. Xcode's debugger is named lldb.

4. C. Click within the Xcode gutter to set a breakpoint.

5. B. Shipping applications should not include NSLog statements because they log to the file system and slow down application execution.

6. A. A Release configuration should be used with applications that are going to be submitted to Apple for listing in the App Store.

7. A. The lldb debugger is a source-level debugger, making it possible to inspect your application code in Swift (not machine language!) as it executes.

8. A. The Breakpoint Navigator shows all the breakpoints that have been configured in your application, across all the files.

9. C. Use the Debug View Hierarchy feature in Xcode 6+ to view a 3D diagram of your application's user interface.

10. D. The Step Over function enables you to skip the execution of individual methods during debugging.

Activities

1. Try breaking applications by using the debugger to set values outside their bounds—text in numeric fields, loops that extend beyond their endpoint, and so on. How does Xcode react?

2. Use the debugging tools to monitor the inner workings of the applications you built earlier in this book. Then take a break, eat a sandwich, and take a walk outside.

Index

REGISTER YOUR PRODUCT at informit.com/register
Access Additional Benefits and SAVE 35% on Your Next Purchase

- Download available product updates.

- Access bonus material when applicable.

- Receive exclusive offers on new editions and related products.
  (Just check the box to hear from us when setting up your account.)

- Get a coupon for 35% for your next purchase, valid for 30 days. Your code will be available in your InformIT cart. (You will also find it in the Manage Codes section of your account page.)

Registration benefits vary by product. Benefits will be listed on your account page under Registered Products.

InformIT.com–The Trusted Technology Learning Source

InformIT is the online home of information technology brands at Pearson, the world's foremost education company. At InformIT.com you can
- Shop our books, eBooks, software, and video training.
- Take advantage of our special offers and promotions (informit.com/promotions).
- Sign up for special offers and content newsletters (informit.com/newsletters).
- Read free articles and blogs by information technology experts.
- Access thousands of free chapters and video lessons.

Connect with InformIT–Visit informit.com/community
Learn about InformIT community events and programs.

informIT.com
the trusted technology learning source

Addison-Wesley · Cisco Press · IBM Press · Microsoft Press · Pearson IT Certification · Prentice Hall · Que · Sams · VMware Press

31901059247868

ALWAYS LEARNING   PEARSON